Thomas F. McManus and the American Fishing Schooners

AMERICAN MARITIME LIBRARY: VOLUME XIV

Thomas F. McManus and the American Fishing Schooners

An Irish-American Success Story

By W.M.P. Dunne

Thomas Francis McManus (1856-1938),
photographed by Frederick William Wallace, 1922.
(Courtesy Maritime Museum of the Atlantic, Halifax, Nova Scotia)

MYSTIC SEAPORT MUSEUM, INC.

MYSTIC, CONNECTICUT

1994

First Edition

Dunne, W. M. P. (William Matthew Patrick), 1934-
    Thomas F. McManus and the American fishing schooners : an
Irish-American success story / by W. M. P. Dunne. — 1st ed. —
Mystic, Conn. : Mystic Seaport Museum, 1994.
        p. : ill., 2 maps, plans ;   cm. — (American maritime
library ; v. 14)
    Includes bibliographical references and index.

    1. McManus, Thomas Francis, 1856-1938. 2. Naval
architects - U.S. - Biography.   3. Schooners. 4. Fishing boats.
5. Naval architecture - History.   I. Title.

VM140.M32D86

ISBN 0-913372-69-2

Designed by Trish Sinsigalli LaPointe

Typeset in Goudy

For

John Rybovich

Who not only taught me the profession, but also made me understand that naval architecture

is neither a science nor an art. It can be a scientific art or an artful science, but never one or the other.

Captain Edward L. Beach, Jr.

Who made me believe in my own research and writing skills and then went on to tell the world about them.

Professor William R. Taylor

Who refused to allow a middle-aged, ocean-oriented graduate student to get his woolies wet,

but insisted on his learning the land view.

Dr. Stuart Quan

Whose skillful hands, thoughtful intellect, and uplifting personality made it possible to complete this work.

Carol Denaro Dunne

Who suffered the M.A. and Ph.D. years, and discovered her own research talents.

Catherine Scanlon and Dermot P. Dunne

My parents, who, sadly did not live long enough.

Louise McManus Will, granddaughter of Tom, and
Edwin Charles McManus, grandson of Charley

For five years of unstinting interest, cooperation, and support.

Contents

Foreword by Erik A.R. Ronnberg, Jr.   ix

1   The McManuses of Skerries   1

2   Boston Beginnings   15

3   The *Black Hawk*   25

4   The *Joseph Henry, Sylph,* and *Vesper*   45

5   The *Actress* and *Em'ly*   65

6   The *Sarah H. Prior* and *Gertie S. Winsor*   81

7   The *John H. McManus* and *Puritan*   105

8   The *Mayflower, Carrie E. Phillips,* and *Nellie Dixon*   127

9   The *James S. Steele*   157

10   The *America, Juniata,* and *Benjamin W. Latham*   185

11   The *Helen B. Thomas, Mooween,* and *Eclipse*   211

12   The *Pontiac, Oriole,* and *Arethusa*   237

13   The *Elsie, Bay State, Catherine,* and *Elizabeth Howard*   261

14   The *Ajax, Surprise* and *Esperanto*   293

15   The *Blanche Ring* and *Henry Ford*   313

16   The *Alabamian* and *Sirod*   341

Appendix 1 *Schooners Possibly Designed By Thomas F. McManus   357
    Including Those Known or Claimed to be Built "Off" His Plans*

Appendix 2 *A Guide to Fishing Schooner Designs by Several   380
    Naval Architects*

Appendix 3 *A Summary of the American and International   389
    Fishermen's Races*

Maps of Boston and the Fishing Grounds   393

Index   395

Foreword

To any admirer of the Gloucester fishing schooner, the name of Thomas F. McManus is immediately associated with the highest development of the type. More avid students know well of his efforts to improve their speed and safety by the development of new designs such as the Indian Headers, the knockabouts, and the semi-knockabouts. Impressive as these accomplishments were, they were but a few parts of a wonderful social and professional mosaic which linked Tom's life to his many family members and friends who shaped, assisted, or brought to fruition his aspirations.

Very atypically of Irish immigrants, Tom's grandfather, Charles McManus of Skerries, brought highly developed skills as a sailmaker to Boston, Massachusetts, where a ready market was waiting. Hard work won a loyal clientele, steady acquisition of property, and a more agreeable domestic setting in which to nurture a growing family. Charles's son, John H. McManus, rose to the pinnacle of esteem as a sailmaker, with the prominent yachtsmen as well as fishermen for customers. When John fathered a second generation of McManuses (which included Tom), the family was as well connected to Boston's business community as to its fishing industry. Marriage to members of the latter were frequently precursors to, or the results of, shared ownership of fishing schooners. As the vessels grew in number, so grew their owners' concerns for hull design and safety afloat.

When John, Tom, and their business partners could afford to build new schooners, they at once sought to improve on the sea-keeping abilities of the then-fashionable "clipper model" hulls, whose tendencies to capsize took a huge toll of lives every year since their inception. An early association with designer-shipwright Dennison J. Lawlor led to the first deep-draft schooners in the New England fishing fleet and the beginning of a trend to make the type safer. Through John's sailmaking work for General Paine's campaigns to defend the America's Cup, the McManuses first participated in the meteoric design career of Edward Burgess. Eventually, they engaged him to design the *Carrie E. Phillips* and the *Nellie Dixon* (the *Fredonia*'s forgotten predecessor, though from the same design), which became landmarks in the evolution of the fishing schooner. By the time Tom was ready for his own ventures into the field of naval architecture, he and his kin could claim virtually sole sponsorship of the major improvements to fishing schooner design from 1860 to the late 1880s, when other vessel owners belatedly caught onto the trend.

When Tom McManus decided to get some formal training in ship design, that artful science as practiced in this country was at a crossroads. Traditionally, it was learned through a master-apprentice system with no opportunity for classroom study except under auspices of the U.S. Navy. In 1872 the city of Boston changed all that by instituting courses in ship design and marine drafting in one of its evening schools. The pioneering nature of this course is better appreciated when one considers that the first courses in naval architecture and marine engineering at the Massachusetts Institute of Technology were not offered until 1886. A major in that subject was not offered at M.I.T. until 1893, while Webb Institute of Naval Architecture, founded in 1889, did not enroll its first class until 1894. By the late 1880s, when Tom was a student, the Boston evening school had already graduated many boatbuilders, shipwrights, and mariners who went on to profit greatly from their training.

From that time, the McManus saga was to become part of the dawning of a new age in American marine technology—a process brought on by industrial expansion and the need for waterborne commerce to satisfy ever-growing demands for trade goods and for food from the sea.

Tom's efforts admirably served the fishing fleet in its golden age of sail. Thus, with the coming of the steam trawlers, he might have been expected to retire from the field to dote on his family; but if his body slowed with age, his mind did not. In 1921 he produced the design for a small wooden-hulled diesel-powered dragger as revolutionary in concept as his most daring schooner designs, and thus launched the modern era of otter trawling. The following year saw the building of the *Henry Ford*, whose grace and speed were intended for the international fishermen's races, only to be undone by myopic legalisms and pettifoggery among the rule-makers. A fitting capstone to a brilliant career instead became the crowning disappointment.

The chapter titles to this book are mostly the names of McManus-owned or McManus-designed vessels—a litany of legendary schooners that mirrored the family's success, Tom's in particular. Author Bill Dunne has chosen these titles astutely and with ample justification, but his story is no mere recitation of the histories of these renowned craft. He writes as well of some very human sides of the McManuses, who in many ways were like other Irish immigrant families: rejoicing in life, walking bravely with death, bound strongly by church and family ties, and as doggedly persistent in the face of adversity as in their aspirations. The theme of family is as central to this story as that of Tom's career in ship design, and it is no more possible to omit the two preceding generations of McManuses than it is to leave out discussion of Tom's favorite knockabout schooners.

In Howard I. Chapelle's standard work, *The American Fishing Schooners*, we have learned of the development of the fishing schooner in purely technical terms, with progressive changes described from logical, analytical, yet detached viewpoints. Bill Dunne has taken an important segment of the chronology and fleshed it out with accounts of the people and their endeavors — and occasional failings. The result is a probing but sympathetic look at a hitherto poorly known aspect of New England's fishing industry and the long shadows it cast on other maritime activities of that region.

The McManuses justly deserve credit for making great improvements to the fishing fleet and to the lot of the fishermen who sailed in it. Historians and lay readers alike are now greatly indebted to Bill Dunne for giving this extraordinary family the attention it has long required.

Erik A.R. Ronnberg, Jr.

Thomas F. McManus and the American Fishing Schooners

CHAPTER ONE

The McManuses of Skerries

Red Island, paradoxically, is neither red nor an island. Crowned by one of the many Martello Towers that dot the Irish coastline, built during the Napoleonic era to defend against a French invasion, it is as green as any other grassy expanse of the Emerald Isle. The bogus island is firmly attached to a half-mile long, gradually curving peninsula that fashions a graceful northeasterly arc. A slender finger, once no more than a *dorn*,[1] this lovely neck of land divides at its seaward end, where a stone quay extends to the northwest, while Red Island lies in the opposite direction, looking toward Ireland's Eye and the Hill of Howth. The quay protects the harbor at Skerries, a picturesque Irish Sea fishing port.

---

[1] A *dorn* is a stretch of land that is submerged at high tide.

Thomas Francis McManus's forebears, although originally from land-locked County Fermanagh, had developed and practiced the family's sailmaking trade in the town of Skerries for generations. Among their artisanal skills, they numbered a common technique to lengthen a sail's service life and improve its ability to retain a desired shape. After cutting and stitching, they typically dipped their handiwork into a large cauldron containing boiling "cutch," a reddish-orange colored astringent manufactured in Dublin from the imported bark of East Indian trees.[2] The artisans then loaded the treated sails onto carts and hauled them from the bark yard, which lay between Quay Street and the beach, along the peninsula to the pseudo island where they stretched the still-dripping russet-colored flax out to dry.[3] A long-standing Skerries tradition has it that the name Red Island originated from this McManus curing process.

Documentary evidence of the McManuses' Skerries roots begins on 26 May 1776, when Father Patrick M. Hoey, the parish priest, noted that he had "Bap'd John McManus Son of Charles and Elizabeth Reilly (a Protestant)."[4] Unlike their relatives and business colleagues, the Herberts, Sweetmans, Knights, Rickards, and Leonards, whose family branches spread widely through the towns of Fingal,[5] the McManuses remained a narrow entity in the parish for seventy years and disappeared entirely when Charles, the son of Charles, emigrated.[6]

The McManus-Reilly marriage brought at least four children into the world, John, Margaret, Charles, and Elizabeth.[7] There is no further trace of the two

---

[2] Interview, Hugh Fitzgerald Ryan, 7 January 1990. Mr. Ryan is a writer and a teacher at Skerries, Ireland, and is the author of *The Kybe* (Dublin: Wolfhound Press, 1983), and *Reprisal* (Dublin: Wolfhound Press, 1989), stories of the Fingal area.

[3] During the first half of the nineteenth century the layout of Skerries, in terms of street names, was quite different from the present. What is known today as Quay Street, was North Strand Street. At the time Quay Street was the lower, narrow section of South Strand Street as it presently exists. Quay Street lay perpendicular to North Strand Street. The Cross was known as Strand Street (Letter, Hugh F. Ryan to the author, 16 April 1990).

[4] Canon Liam Shanahan, Pastor, St. Patrick's Church, Skerries, County Dublin, Ireland, *Baptismal Register for the Parish of Hollom Patrick Skerries 1752 to 1781*, 154.

[5] The County Dublin coastline lying to the north of Dublin Bay is known as the Fingal Coast. The term Fingal derives from a Gaelic term that translates as "the racial territory of foreigners," and refers to most of North County Dublin. The Gaelic word "fionn," meaning white or fair-haired person, is often confused with "fine," resulting in the popular belief that Fingal means fair-haired foreigner (Letter, Dr. Maighréad Mi Mhurchdna, 12 July 1990).

[6] The fact that the elder Charles married a Protestant creates a roadblock to tracing the family further into antiquity. Roman Catholic custom at the time dictated that a mixed marriage take place in the confines of the sacristy of a church, not only outside the home parish of the participants, but also outside their diocese. Locating the record of the McManus-Reilly nuptials would present the daunting task of first deducing the ceremonial locale, then determining whether or not the sacramental registers of that parish still exist, and, finally, whether the parish priest would have officially noted the "distasteful" event at all, or whether McManus himself would have allowed the entry, given a justifiable fear of British reprisals against him as an identifiable Catholic.

[7] *Baptismal Register for the Parish of Hollom Patrick Skerries 1752 to 1781*, 154, John (no further trace of this child was found in the parish registers, but he reappears in civil records); 31, Margaret; corrected page 25, Charles; and corrected page 48, Elizabeth.

daughters in the parish records of Holmpatrick,[8] but both boys became sailmakers and part-time fishermen, and carried on the family business after their father's death. It appears that John remained a bachelor and eventually emigrated. There is also a family tradition that the Royal Navy impressed either John or Charles into service during the War of 1812 between Britain and the United States.[9]

The fishermen of Skerries enjoyed prosperous times in the decades between the 1760s and the turn of the century, especially during the eighteen-year reign of Ireland's "Grattan Parliament," which the Act of Union terminated. In 1764 the Irish legislators awarded bounties to encourage all forms of deep-sea fishing. These ship bounties amounted to £1 per register ton and led to the construction of a great number of vessels, especially in Skerries.[10] Added to the proceeds from the catch of cod, ling, or herring, the bounty frequently made the difference between break-even and profit for the fishing industry.

Skerries, as it looked ca. 1820, with the fishing fleet moored along the quay that extends out to Red Island. Engraving by W. Deeb from a drawing by George Petrie from *Excursions through Ireland* (1820). (Courtesy National Library of Ireland)

---

[8] This lack of presence in the sacramental registers suggests either spinsterhood, or early death. Irish Catholic marriages traditionally took place in the bride's parish.

[9] Letter, Edwin Charles McManus, 10 April 1989. Mr. McManus is the great-great-grandson of Charles McManus.

[10] Joseph Shiels, B.A., "The Fishermen of Skerries, Part I, Before 1800," 3, *Paper No. 31*, Skerries Historical Society, Skerries, Ireland.

Ranging up to sixty feet in length, the Skerries wherry was a small, deep-draft, schooner-rigged vessel well suited to fishing along the rugged Irish coast and throughout the Irish Sea. Lithograph by Samuel Watson, printed by J. Berry and published in Wallop Brabazon's *The deep sea and coast fisheries of Ireland* (1848). (Courtesy Ulster Folk & Transport Museum, L1689/7)

Tonnage incentives enticed the investment capital that underwrote this extensive new construction. The fishery returns for 1771-73 included more than fifty vessels from thirty to fifty tons that belonged to the port of Skerries. By 1789 the fishermen of Skerries were described as "the most important fishing group in Ireland."[11] In fact, as early as 1784, the Skerries fishing fleet was unquestionably the leading one in the land. Fifty-four smacks and wherries ranging from twenty to sixty register tons collected total bounties of £1,843-1-6 that year.[12] "A Skerries wherry of forty-six tons has cost £500, and the nets and sails £100,"[13] thus the annual bounties often amounted to 10 percent of the vessel's cost or 50 percent of the expense of its nets and sails. They later helped mitigate a large portion of the losses caused by the mysterious disappearance of the herring schools from Irish waters.

Through bounty support the Fingal fishermen were also able to construct the larger vessels necessary to pursue their elusive quarry to distant shores.

11 Shiels, "The Fishermen of Skerries, Part I," 3.

12 Trinity College Library, Dublin, Ireland, *The Journals of the House of Commons of the Kingdom of Ireland from the Nineteenth day of January, 1786, inclusive, to the Eighteenth day of April, 1786, inclusive, in the Reign of His Majesty George the Third* (Dublin: George Grierson, 1797), Appendix ccxli-ccli.

13 Shiels, "The Fishermen of Skerries, Part I," 19.

The resultant Skerries wherries, or Skerries hookers,[14] as they were also known, were clinker-or carvel-planked, twin pole-masted, schooner-rigged craft whose deep draft provided a stable platform for the fishermen, even in the rolling troughs of a beam sea. Three to four times larger, and with considerably better offshore capabilities than their smaller cutter-rigged cousins, the ubiquitous Galway or Kinsale hookers, the Skerries wherries became a familiar sight on the fishing grounds of the Irish Sea, on the Atlantic Ocean off Ireland's western and southern coasts, as well as on Scottish, Welsh, and Cornish waters. The Skerries wherrymen not only fished for their own account during their long voyages, but also purchased the catch of hookermen in distant ports for eventual resale to Scotland, England, and the Isle of Man.

For their livelihood the McManus family's artisans largely depended upon the needs of the sail-powered fleets harboring along the Fingal Coast of the Irish Sea, particularly that stretch of a dozen miles between Rush and Balbriggan with Skerries at its center. Fishing vessels, along with a smattering of coasters, comprised local vessel populations. The McManuses' traditional trade revolved around requirements for replacement sails, a need more than enough to fully occupy their skills. The burst of construction prompted by the tonnage bonuses nearly overwhelmed their production capabilities, as sailmaking was very much a cottage industry.[15]

Despite the prosperity Irish fishermen enjoyed during the last three decades of the eighteenth century, their affairs began a slow decline after the failure of the 1798 rebellion of the Society of United Irishmen, and the Act of Union which joined the kingdoms in 1800. The Act also led to a weakening of industrial, and a strengthening of agricultural, occupations in Ireland. The period also saw a loss of a significant portion of Ireland's developing middle class through emigration. The fiscal reversal contributed to increased arrivals of Irish artisans and businessmen in the United States early in the nineteenth century.[16] The failure of the imperial Parliament to renew the bounties after the union tempered new construction, but

---

[14] The name should not be, but is often, confused with the Dutch *hoeker* or *hueker*. Hooker, in any language is a generic term describing the purpose of this design, *i.e.*, long-line, rather than trawl-net fishing. Tonnage of the Skerries hookers ranged from 30 to 60 register tons, while the Galway and Kinsale hookers, single-masted smacks, ranged from 8 to 14 register tons. Richard J. Scott's definitive work, *The Galway Hookers: Working Sailboats of Galway Bay*, 2nd ed. (1983; Swords, Ireland: Ward River Press, 1985), refutes Howard I. Chapelle's claim in *American Small Sailing Craft* (New York: W.W. Norton, 1951), that the Irish west coast hookers descended from English cutters.

[15] Eighteenth-, and early nineteenth-century sails were made from home-woven flax, which had a very loose weave, and was not a notably durable material. Although cotton duck sails appeared early in the nineteenth century, the Royal Navy, the largest consumer of sails in the world, used flaxen sails throughout the Napoleonic Wars, a good indicator that merchantmen and fishing vessels would have continued the practice to an even later date, a propensity that would assure a constant need for replacement units.

[16] Robert E. Kennedy, *The Irish* (Berkeley: California: University of California Press, 1973), 33.

Skerries maintained its prominent position among Irish fishing ports. Two decades later, the fishermen experienced an economic resurgence when Westminster finally reinstated the bounties in 1819.

It was in this economic environment that Father Thomas McMahon married Charles McManus the younger to Ann Herbert on 23 March 1818, in the presence of Pat and Ned Herbert. The McManus-Herbert nuptials produced at least six children, Elizabeth, Margaret, John, Charles, Catherine, and Patrick.[17] Margaret may later have been confirmed as Margaret Mary, for she became known as Mary in Massachusetts. There is no further trace of Elizabeth or Charles in Skerries or Boston, but John, Catherine, Patrick, and Margaret Mary would all remove across the Atlantic.

The British government withdrew the bounties again in 1830, and the Irish fishing industry entered a steady downward spiral. Parliamentary prejudice at Westminster brought about their repeal through the influence of the powerful Scottish fishing lobby, which encouraged legislators to discriminate against the Irish fisheries.[18] The shore-based problems these fishermen faced centered not only upon the inconsistency of supportive legislation for the national fishing fleet,[19] but also on the typically impoverished state of the native fishermen, which precluded them from capital expenditure without outside investment. This resulted in their inability to compete with foreign fishermen, even in lucrative Irish home waters. One quantitative analysis of the country's nineteenth-century economy identified fishing's lowly position among all pre-famine trades, concluding that the paucity of operating capital led to the "backwardness" of the Irish fishing industry.[20] Despite Ireland's surrounding fish-rich seas, ironically, the ancient island nation became an importer of fish and fish products.

After a formal hearing at Balbriggan, County Dublin, on 7 December 1835, examining the Fingal ports, the Commissioners of Inquiry into the State of the Irish Fisheries, reported: "in 1820, in Skerries, Balbriggan and Rush, 667 men were employed. At present the number is 414, being a decrease of 253. The survivors of those excluded from employment as fishermen, have gone on to other avocations,

---

[17] *Hollom Patrick Baptisms 1814-1853*, 21, Elizabeth; 31, Margaret; 40, John; 58, Charles; 69, Catherine; and 81, Patrick.

[18] Brian Jenkins, *Era of Emancipation: British Government of Ireland, 1812-1830* (Toronto: McGill-Queen's University Press, 1988), 25.

[19] John de Courcy Ireland, *Ireland's Sea Fisheries: a History* (Dun Laoghaire, Ireland: Glendale Press, 1981). Parliament legislated the three national fishing fleets, Irish, English, and Scottish, as distinct entities, rather than treating the British fishing industry as a whole. The powerful Scottish lobby at Westminster usually captured the most favorable mandates.

[20] Joel Mokyr, *Why Ireland Starved: A Quantitative and Analytical History of the Irish Economy, 1800-1850*, rev. ed., (1983; London: George Allen & Unwin Ltd., 1985), 172-73.

principally to agricultural labour."[21] Thus, in the period 1820-35, the ranks of the Fingal fishermen were reduced by 38 percent. The greatest part of this reduction, however, occurred between 1831 and 1835.[22]

In the first half of the nineteenth century the population of Skerries peaked in 1831, during the height of the beneficial effect of the bounties. The town comprised 81 acres supporting 578 families in 518 houses. The total included "2,565 males & females," up from 2,273 in 1821.[23] Table 1, centered chronologically on the repeal of the fishing bounties, illustrates the population's rise and fall:

THE McMANUSES
OF SKERRIES

Census	Population	% Change
1821	2,273	N.A.
1831	2,565	+12.9
1841	2,417	-05.8
1851	2,327	-03.7

TABLE 1 - POPULATION TRENDS, SKERRIES, IRELAND[24]

A negative population swing approaching 20 percent occurred with the final loss of the fishing bounties. Yet this table also indicates that the famine years, 1845-49, failed to deepen the local population decline, which actually slowed during those dolorous days. An 1854 commercial directory described Skerries as being chiefly occupied by fishermen and their families, remarking that a coasting trade was

---

[21] National Library of Ireland, Dublin, Ireland, I.R. 639, i4, "First [Second] Report of the Commissioners of Inquiry into the State of the Irish Fisheries, Minutes of Evidence, County Dublin - North of the Bay, Balbriggan - 7th December 1835."

[22] "From the abandonment of a system of government bounties in 1830 until direct government intervention in the economy of the west of Ireland in the 1890s, the Irish fisheries were perceived as a rich national resource for food and employment, which was neglected and under-developed especially by government. Decline was reflected in the falling national figures for numbers of men and boats engaged in the sea fisheries" (Michael McCaughan, "Dandys, Luggers, Herring and Mackerel: a local study in the context of the Irish Sea fisheries in the nineteenth century," in Michael McCaughan and John Appleby, eds., *The Irish Sea: aspects of maritime history* (Belfast: The Institute of Irish Studies, Queen's University of Belfast, and the Ulster Folk and Transport Museum, 1989), 122).

[23] *The Dublin Almanac and General Register of Ireland For the Year of Our Lord 1845 Being the Eighth Year of the Reign of Her Present Majesty Victoria* (Dublin: Pettigrew and Oulton, 1845), 205.

[24] Census Returns 1831, British Parliamentary Papers, Volume 39, Sessional Section 254, Leinster, 24-25; *The Dublin Almanac and General Register of Ireland For the Year of Our Lord 1845* . . . (Dublin: Pettigrew and Oulton, 1845), 205; *The Dublin Almanac and General Register of Ireland For the Year of Our Lord 1854* . . . (Dublin: Alexander Thom & Sons, 1854), 312, commonly referred to as the "Thom's Directories."

Skerries as viewed from inland, ca. 1844, shortly before the McManuses left. Red Island and its Martello Tower lie just to the left of the righthand windmill. Engraved by J.E. Jones and E. Radclyffe for J. D'Alton's *History of Drogheda* (1844). (Courtesy National Library of Ireland)

carried on in potatoes, limestone, and coal, and that prior to the withdrawal of the fishing bounties the trade of Skerries was considerable.[25]

The Irish economy reached its nineteenth-century nadir when the famine struck in the 1840s, a tragedy exacerbated by the repeal of the "Corn Laws" in 1846.[26] France, Belgium, Holland, Germany, and Russia all suffered a potato blight in 1846 and 1847, but, unlike British-ruled Ireland, they halted all food exports to compensate for the loss.[27] Beginning in mid-1846, the specter of the famine sent emigrant waves fleeing from Ireland, especially from the potato-dependent south and west. Then the pestilence diminished somewhat, and in late 1847 and early 1848 the pace of departures fell off, but the total harvest failure that summer

---

25 *Thom's Directory*, 1854, 312. An 1850s' labor survey of Irish ports mentions that in addition to fishing, "upwards of 1,300 females engaged in figuring and embroidering light cotton and muslin." In light of the official census figures, if this statistic is correct, then every lady in Skerries must have been an embroiderer, regardless of rank, station, or age.

26 For years the "Corn Law" legislation provided a guaranteed English market for Irish agricultural products. The loss of this privilege came at a tragic time for Irish tenant farmers and landowners alike.

27 Thomas Gallagher, *Paddy's Lament: Ireland, 1846-1847* (New York: Harcourt Brace Jovanovich, 1982), 87-88.

produced a tidal wave of panic-stricken emigrants that would drain Ireland's population for decades to come.[28]

With the great hunger starving the nation, the elder McManus hardened his decision to leave home, and faced the Irishman's classic choice of three destinations: North America, the United Kingdom, or Australia. The siren call of the United States, the much-publicized land of plenty, succeeded in enticing the sixty-two-year-old sailmaker away from his ancestral roots,[29] and he was among the first to depart from Skerries during the famine era. McManus and his oldest son, John H.,[30] then in his mid-twenties, joined an emigrant body of Fingal fishermen and peripheral waterfront tradesmen that eventually included the Leonard, Herbert, Sweetman, McGinnis, O'Hara, Byrnes, and Kelly families, among others. But, while ultimately driven from Ireland by the economic depression in the wake of the famine, the underlying motivation for their exodus was the industrial downturn caused by the vicissitudes of the British government's uneven subsidy policies. It was the waning Irish fishing economy, its death knell sounded by the final loss of the bounties in 1830, not nature's spoliation, that drove the McManuses from the Coast of Fingal, where the absence of potatoes would have had little effect on the area's normal protein-rich diet of seafood and home-grown vegetables.

For Charles McManus, the grandfather of Thomas Francis, the decision to leave his homeland was an emotional one. Until the famine, the Irish turned to emigration with great reluctance.[31] Speaking in 1845, before the potato crop began to fail, Lord Edward Geoffrey Stanley, a large Irish landholder, later the 14th Earl of Derby, addressed the issue of Irish emigration in Britain's House of Lords: "the warm attachment of the Irish peasant to the locality where he was born and brought up, will always make the best and most carefully conducted scheme of emigration a matter of painful sacrifice for the emigrant."[32]

Through the first half of the century, given the unwelcome acceptance of resettlement, the departure of emigrating family members often prompted an "American wake." People of some substance would hire the local funeral

---

[28] Kerby A. Miller, *Emigrants and Exiles, Ireland and the Irish Exodus to North America* (New York: Oxford University Press, 1985), chapter 7. There was a third, but lesser, potato blight and famine in Ireland during 1863.

[29] The initial genealogical information from the parish of Holmpatrick, Skerries, County Dublin, Ireland, was obtained by John McManus, the great-great-great grandson of Charles McManus, through Bernadette Marks of the Fingal Heritage Project, 10 North Street, Swords, County Dublin.

[30] Born John Patrick, John adopted his mother's family name, Herbert, as his middle name in the United States.

[31] Cecil Woodham-Smith, *The Great Hunger: Ireland, 1815-1849* (1962; New York: E.P. Dutton, 1980), 206.

[32] Woodham-Smith, *The Great Hunger*, 206, citing Lord Stanley's speech of 9 June 1845, *Parliamentary Debates, 1821-1890* (London: Hansard Society for Parliamentary Government), 81:212.

accompanist to solemnify the melancholy episode. In the pre-dawn hours, after a maudlin night of rueful reminiscing, drenched in tears and soaked in good Irish whiskey, porter, or stout, this virtuoso would begin keening over the "dead" person, the emigrant, to climax the sorrowful parting.[33] At Skerries, with heavyhearted resolve, McManus gave up the tenancy of his comfortable home at 3 Quay Street,[34] added himself and his family to the swell of Irish inundating America's Atlantic coast cities, and selected the capital of Massachusetts as the place to revitalize his fortunes.

In Boston, largely as a result of the Irish immigrant invasion, the urban population exploded from 85,475 in 1840 to 133,563 twenty years later.[35] Indeed, even before the enormous Irish influx, overcrowding had already become a way of life in the populous but constricted northeastern entrepôt. One contemporary British visitor described the city as, "a peninsula, extremely limited in extent, about a mile and a half in breadth, three miles in length, and ovally shaped . . . connected to the mainland by a very narrow neck of land."[36] A mere fifteen years after the Irish flood began, the section of the 1860 census encompassing Boston's dormitories, Middlesex, Norfolk, and Suffolk counties, tallied a foreign-born populace of 143,756. Fully 73 percent of these outsiders were Irish, and the bulk of them were crammed into the fetid tenements lining Boston's waterfront.[37] Most of the émigrés were penniless, agrarian workers from the farmlands of Ireland, devoid of urban skills and viewed by Boston's native Anglo-Saxon population as a race apart—a homogeneous, but near-subhuman species.

But Boston bystanders who scrutinized the incoming Irish hordes missed the solvent few among them, whose uniformly bedraggled appearance after the trying transatlantic crossing shrouded their social status. And, while the moneyed minority may have passed unnoticed into America, in Ireland its departure was deplored: the newspapers lamented the country's loss of the "better class of our

---

33 Gallagher, *Paddy's Lament*, 132-33.

34 Charles McManus's address appears in Richard Griffith, Commissioner of Valuation, *General Valuation of Rateable Property in Ireland. Valuation of the Several Tenements Comprised in the Barony of Balrothery, East, in the Union of Balrothery and County of Dublin* (Dublin: Alexander Thom, 25 September 1852), and R.S. Duff, F.R.S.A.I., "The Only Official List of Householders of the Town of Skerries for the Year of 1845, December 16th, 1845," *Paper No. 32*, Skerries Historical Society, Skerries, Ireland.

35 The Back Bay landfill project was not begun until the mid-1850s and required three decades to complete.

36 Henry Marcus Schreiber, "The Working People in the Middle of the Nineteenth Century" (Ph.D. diss., Boston University, 1950), citing James S. Buckingham, *America-Historical, Statistical, Descriptive*, 3 vols., (London: Fisher, Son and Company, 1841), 2:329-30.

37 Oscar Handlin, *Boston's Immigrants, A Study in Acculturation*, rev. ed. (1941; Cambridge, Massachusetts: Belknap Press of Harvard University, 1979), tables 2 and 8. The Irish accounted for 20 percent of the combined total of immigrant and indigenous inhabitants at this time.

population." "Unfortunately for us," a Quaker relief worker wrote, "it is the industrious and enterprising who leave us."[38] Boston's Irish famine immigrants were neither socially nor culturally uniform. The McManuses were anything but stereotypical newcomers. According to family legend at least one servant accompanied them to the New World.[39] They had responded to a more general sense of deterioration. For them, as for many artisans and farmers, the famine was final proof, after three decades of depression, that Ireland was irredeemable.[40]

Bleak prospects awaited those who arrived in Boston without capital or professional capabilities, for the city was a highly developed economic system of skilled trades that offered few economic opportunities for the destitute famine victims who possessed nothing but their gaunt, sapped bodies.[41] For the immigrants the heartbreak of a seldom-fulfilled ambition in America compounded the debilitating effect of unemployment. The majority, those from provincial farming stock, looked upon Boston solely as a staging point to gather the wherewithal for a wishful continuation of their journey toward the agrarian American midlands. But, sadly, their poverty deprived them of the means, and despondence of the desire; therefore, the penniless newcomer landed with no alternative but to stay where he was, thus adding to the immigrants' miseries by thrusting a rural people into the squalor of an urban ghetto.[42] For the McManuses and their kith and kin from the Fingalian fishing industry, however, Boston suited them perfectly. The local waters were bounteous fishing grounds, and this band of immigrants never wasted a westward glance.

---

[38] Miller, *Emigrants and Exiles*, 293-94.

[39] Interview, Mrs. D. Forbes Will née Louise McManus, and Mrs. Dustin Pevear née Priscilla Pierce, granddaughters of Thomas F. McManus, 12 September 1988.

[40] Miller, *Emigrants and Exiles*, 294.

[41] Dennis P. Ryan, *Beyond the Ballot Box, A Social History of the Boston Irish, 1845-1917* (East Brunswick, New Jersey: Fairleigh Dickinson University Press, 1983), 21; Thomas H. O'Connor, *Fitzpatrick's Boston, 1846-1866, John Bernard Fitzpatrick, Third Bishop of Boston* (Boston: Northeastern University Press, 1984), 83.

[42] Handlin, *Boston's Immigrants*, 37, 49.

CHAPTER TWO

Boston Beginnings

Histry has not recorded whether the McManuses crossed the ocean together, as they are not included in the sparse surviving records of Boston's passenger arrivals.[1] The sheer magnitude of the early famine emigration probably shrouded their entry into the United States. Beginning in the spring of 1846, a small number of "'respectable,' 'comfortable'" people like the McManuses, who had been considering emigration, decided to do so during the season of favorable weather.[2]

---

[1] Passengers Lists, 1848-1891, Boston, Microcopy No. JV6461-179, U.S. National Archives and Records Administration, Washington, D.C., hereafter cited as NARA.

[2] Thomas H. O'Connor, *Fitzpatrick's Boston 1846-1866, John Bernard Fitzpatrick, Third Bishop of Boston* (Boston: Northeastern University Press, 1984), 81, citing Cecil Woodham-Smith, *The Great Hunger: Ireland, 1815-1849* (1962; New York: E.P. Dutton, 1980), 211-12; and Edwin C. Guillet, *The Great Migration* (Toronto: 1963), 96-97.

The first firm data supporting a McManus presence in Boston are daughter Mary's 1847 wedding to New York "mariner" Bill Montross, and the 1849 Boston Directory's listing of Charles's rented flat at No. 6 Battery, a cobblestoned passage that connected Hanover and Commercial Streets in the city's North End.[3] Ironically, the landlord of the McManuses' incommodious tenement was the self-righteous Reverend Otis A. Skinner, evidently a failed practitioner of his own preaching.[4] The dark, dank confines of this overcrowded building undoubtedly provided a culture shock to the Skerries family, which had so recently left its cozy Quay Street cottage overlooking the Irish Sea.

It is most likely that Charles McManus brought his family ashore during the 1846 sailing season. Once in Boston, he and his son John H., both journeyman sailmakers, clearly counted on their professional expertise to lift the clan out of its depressing new surroundings as quickly as possible. But just two years after the McManuses arrived the economic environment took a downward turn. The 1848 recession began a four-year decline in the cotton industry. But with the recovery in 1852 many of the American workers failed to regain their jobs when the mill owners replaced them with Irish immigrants, from a belief that the Irish possessed more physical endurance, would be less demanding, and would accept lower wages.[5] This replacement of American workingmen by foreigners fueled the rancor of American nativists against all immigrants. More specific to the McManuses, however, the cutback in cotton production not only limited the availability of raw material for Boston's huge, textile-hungry, ready-made garment trade, but also crippled the city's sizable sailcloth industry, a crisis that directly threatened the success of the family's move to America.

Cotton duck, a lightweight form of canvas with a coarse linen weave, had become the fabric of choice for American sailmaking early in the nineteenth century. Seth Bemis, the owner of a Watertown, Massachusetts, textile mill, began

---

[3] St. Mary's Sacramental Records, Archives of the Archdiocese of Boston, Brighton, Massachusetts, Marriages, vol. 10, page 23; *The Boston Directory Containing the City Record, A General Directory of the Citizens, A Special Directory of Trades, Professions, &c. An Almanac, from July, 1849, to July, 1850, with a Variety of Miscellaneous Matter* (Boston: George Adams, 1 July 1849). Although the McManuses initially settled on Battery Street, their subsequent moves read like a road map of the North End's narrow passageways: 508 Commercial, 1854; 452 Hanover, 1855; 18 Thacher, 1856; 490 Commercial, 1857-58; 435 Commercial, 1859-61; 438 Commercial, 1862-68; 15 Margaret, 1869-92. *The Boston Directory Embracing the City Record, A General Directory of the Citizens, and Business Directory* (Boston: George Adams, 1856-60); *The Boston Directory Embracing the City Record, A General Directory of the Citizens, and Business Directory* (Boston: Adams, Sampson & Company, 1861-67); *The Boston Directory Embracing the City Record, A General Directory of the Citizens, and Business Directory* (Boston: Sampson, Davenport & Company, 1868-93); *Boston Business Directory and Metropolitan Directory of Boston and Vicinity with a new map engraved expressly for this work* (Boston: Dean Dudley & Company, 1870), hereafter cited as *City Directory*, year.

[4] City of Boston, Tax Assessor's Records, Ward 1, 1849, Boston Public Library.

[5] John Raymond Mulkern, *The Know-Nothing Party in Massachusetts: the Rise and Fall of a People's Movement* (Boston: Northeastern University Press, 1990), 28.

the manufacture of pure cotton duck sails in 1809. Prior to this, flax was the principal material for sail manufacture here, just as in Europe. A Philadelphia sailmaker had experimented with the combination of flax and cotton, and this material was produced for a time in Kentucky; but it was no more than an intermediate step from homespun flax to pure machine-woven duck. Even hand-woven cotton duck, with a weave considerably tighter than flax, could not compete with sailcloth manufactured on power looms, which was more closely woven, harder, of greater durability, and of far more uniform texture.[6] This tight, closely woven cotton had proven itself over flax during the War of 1812, when American privateers and blockade-runners using this cotton canvas were able to sail much closer to the wind than those using flax.[7] The use of patented manufacturing methods perfected this cloth, and it became standard in American sailmaking between 1815 and 1831.

Massachusetts sailmakers would be no strangers to labor strife. In the Port of Boston the normally strong demand for sails dramatically increased during early 1852 after the merchant marine and fishing fleets suffered heavy losses during the infamous "Minot's Light Gale" of October 1851. Eleven months later, as cotton manufacturers began to emerge from their four-year depression, sailmakers were among the first tradesmen sufficiently organized to strike for better wages in a rising market, a vehicle they exploited again ten years later in search of further wage adjustments, as well as in protest against the rising number of female workers entering the industry.[8] Those who struck were not from the artisan class of sailmakers, but were employees of the cotton duck manufactories at Boston, Salem, and Newport, Rhode Island.[9]

Overshadowing the social and economic aspects of life for foreigners in Boston was a third environmental element. Death stalked the newcomers in the

---

[6] J. Leander Bishop, *A History of American Manufactures from 1608 to 1860*, 2 vols., (Philadelphia: E. Young & Company, 1864), 2:139-40, 232, 272, 274.

[7] Howard I. Chapelle, *The Search For Speed Under Sail* (New York: W.W. Norton, 1967), 210-11.

[8] Henry Marcus Schreiber, "The Working People in the Middle of the Nineteenth Century" (Ph.D. diss., Boston University, 1950), Table of Strikes, 1842-68, xiii, 226, citing reports in the *Commonwealth* and the *Bee*, 14 September 1852. Factories did not produce sails. They manufactured sailcloth, and sailmakers actually cut and shaped the final product.

[9] "In 1788 or '89, a large manufactory of sail duck was established on Frog Lane, in Boston, where a building one hundred and eighty feet long and two stories high was erected for the purpose. The company was incorporated by the General Court, and encouraged by a bounty upon its manufacture. . . . A sail-cloth manufactory was also commenced at Haverhill, Mass., in 1789 which several years after was in a promising condition, but did not finally succeed. Factories of the same kind were likewise established at Salem and Nantucket, and at Exeter, N.H., and Newport, R.I. Those at Salem and Newport became flourishing concerns" (Bishop, *History of American Manufactures*, 1:419-20).

Viewed from the wharves and shipyards of East Boston, Boston Harbor was alive with ships in 1848. From the navy yard below the Bunker Hill Monument in Charlestown (*right*) to the flats off South Boston and Dorchester (*left*), wharves and shipyards lined the waterfront. The McManuses settled among other Irish immigrants in the North End (*right center*), close to Boston's commercial heart. Lithograph by F. Whitefield. (Courtesy The Mariners' Museum, Newport News, Virginia)

guise of the infamous "Four Horsemen of the Apocalypse": poverty, pestilence, famine, and death. Rampaging through the congested byways and germ-ridden tenements of the city during the decades immediately following the arrival of the famine exiles, the dreaded "horsemen" decimated the immigrant population. In its earlier glory days, the North End sheltered a share of the city's elite, but by the 1850s it had disintegrated into what was arguably the nation's most destitute and pestilent ghetto. Just three years after the McManuses settled into this plagued slum they suffered through a cholera epidemic.

By the time the United States census-takers began their enumerations in July 1850, the elder McManuses, Charley and Annie, with sons John H. and Pat, daughter Mary and son-in-law Bill Montross, had moved around the corner from Battery Street to a brimming tenement building that rose over the lively confines of Commercial Street.[10] Although noisome, this major thoroughfare was broader and lighter than the North End's other twisting alleyways. The busy boulevard bordered the conflicting sights and scents of Boston's semicircular waterfront, where bales of cotton, bags of coffee, barrels of flour, chests of tea, quintals of salted fish, and boxes of ripening fruit piled up on the crowded wharves;[11] but, among this legion of odors, the overpowering one came from the dung-paved streets and byways over which thousands of horses passed each day.

---

10 7th Census of the United States (1850), Suffolk County, Massachusetts (Wards 1-3), Microfilm Publication 432, roll 334, page 96, 651/926, NARA. Catherine McManus is not included in the listing and may well have found work as a servant or a seamstress, occupations that occasionally provided living accommodation.

11 O'Connor, *Fitzpatrick's Boston*, 34.

Life in the promised land of plenty proved less than idyllic for the Fingal migrants, as it did for most of Boston's famine arrivals, moneyed or otherwise. The late-1840s economic recession in Massachusetts discouragingly resembled the depression they had fled from at home, and the bitter nativist backlash to the immigrant invasion supplanted the familiar tyranny of their former British overlords. The basic style of their lives changed dramatically for the worse. No longer did they breathe the clean air of the Fingal coast, or live in their own townhomes or cottages. The miasmic vapors of the North End, with its disease, crammed tenements, and unfamiliar diet, became the new norm.

Mary McManus was the first of her siblings to marry, but obtaining the essential approval of her parents was no easy task—the prospective groom, William W. Montross, was not a Catholic. But she pursued her objective with typical McManus doggedness and determination and eventually succeeded in her quest, perhaps because her father, Charley McManus, remembered that his own mother had been a Protestant. Mary cleared the final hurdle when Montross, a fishing vessel captain who had moved to Boston from New York, agreed to convert to Catholicism. In an early demonstration of the close-knit family unity enjoyed by the McManuses in Boston, the bride's brother John H. agreed to stand as the groom's best man. The couple proudly paraded down the aisle of St. John the Baptist's Church on 9 June 1847.[12] Father George Foxcroft Haskins,[13] the young, Harvard-educated, convert-pastor cheerfully accepted their $3.00 marriage offering after conducting the dual sacramental rites, first baptizing Montross into the Catholic faith, and then consecrating him with Mary in matrimony.[14]

---

[12] The story behind the building the St. John's congregation worshipped in is a unique one. The locale, a former hotbed of Protestantism, was once the home of Cotton Mather, brother of Increase Mather, who received the first degree of D.D. conferred in America. The house stood on the east side of Moon Street at the corner of Moon Street Court, and was pulled down in 1832 to make room for a tobacco warehouse. Bishop Fenwick bought the eleven-year-old structure for $8,000 in 1843 to meet the needs of his parishioners, most of whom resided in the wretched tenements of the Ann Street vicinity, in close proximity to the fishing slips along Commercial, Long, and T Wharves. The bishop ordered the warehouse transformed into the "Free Church of St. John the Baptist," so called because no pew rent was charged to the impoverished congregation. Three years after its consecration, Haskins became the pastor (A Friend of the House of the Angel Guardian [William Kelly], *The Life of Father Haskins* (Boston: Angel Guardian Press, 1899), 68-82; O'Connor, *Fitzpatrick's Boston*, 105).

[13] Father Haskins was one of several diocesan priests who gained prominence during those years of invigorating enlargement by the North American provinces of the Roman Catholic Church. An ordained Episcopal minister before his conversion to Catholicism, Haskins, like his bishop, John Bernard Fitzpatrick, was a native Bostonian. His outstanding achievement was the establishment of the House of the Angel Guardian in 1851, which became a flourishing and successful home for wayward boys. Haskins was well prepared for the new enterprise; as a Protestant minister, he had been the chaplain of South Boston's House of Industry, the city's poorhouse, and the House of Reformation, a reform school for juvenile offenders. Initially, Haskins even financed some of the operating expenses of the House of the Angel Guardian from his own pocket to overcome resistance by the city authorities to the project (Kelly, *Father Haskins*, 68-82; O'Connor, *Fitzpatrick's Boston*, 105).

[14] St. John the Baptist/St. Stephen's Sacramental Records, Archives of the Archdiocese of Boston, Brighton, Massachusetts, Marriages 1836-1915, Volume 10, 1836-1861, roll 4, page 23. John H. McManus's first four sons, Charles A., Thomas F., George A., and Louis, were all baptized at St. John's church.

The 1850 census tabulated patriarch Charley McManus, cousin Tom Herbert, and Chris Leonard, a neighbor in both Ireland and America, with their offspring and in-laws.[15] This growing coterie of Fingal fishing families began the 1850s decade with a profusion of christening and nuptial festivities. Mary Montross led the trend by giving birth to a son in the flat she and her husband shared with her parents and brothers at 434 Commercial Street on 2 November 1850. She named him for her father,[16] and this child, Charles Loveless Montross, became the first of the McManus bloodline born in the United States.

Chris Leonard, the oldest son of a family that associated with the McManuses for generations, including at least two past ones in Ireland and three to come in America, married Julia Sweetman in St. Maur's Church at Rush, County Dublin, on 27 April 1845. They were one of the few Fingal-Irish couples to wed before they emigrated.[17] Sometime after their marriage, possibly in company with the McManuses, they came to Boston where Julia Leonard presented Christopher with their first surviving child in 1848, whom they named Nicholas for his paternal grandfather.[18] Dick Leonard, third and youngest of the emigrating Leonard brothers, with his fiancée, Kate McManus, another of Charley McManus's daughters, sponsored baby Nicholas's baptism at St. John the Baptist's.[19]

About this time Chris Leonard moved from the damply crowded confines of 54 Commercial Street to an equally crowded, but drier tenement house at No. 502,[20] where he began a typical grocery-groggery business. It was a hard life, purveying groceries during the day and dispensing liquor and beer till late at night,

---

[15] 7th Census of the United States (1850), Suffolk County, Massachusetts (Wards 1-3), M432, roll 334, NARA, page 96, 651/926, for Charles McManus; page 96, 579/817 for Christopher Leonard; page 116, 682/975 for Thomas Herbert. The date of census taking varies from Ward 9, begun 1 August, 1850, to Ward 11, begun on 30 September. Ward 8 was completed on 28 September, and Wards 6 and 7 were completed on 11 October. The census information dated 1 June 1850 was thus collected between 1 August and 11 October (Peter R. Knights, *The Plain People of Boston, 1830-1860* (New York: Oxford University Press, 1971), 19-20.

[16] Vital Records 1841-1895, Massachusetts State Archives, Columbia Point, Dorchester, Boston, Massachusetts, *Births*, 1851, vol. 53, page 98, line 4449.

[17] Father Thomas Randles, Pastor, Sacramental Registers, St. Maur's R.C. Church, Rush, Ireland, Marriage Register 1785 to 1856. One of the common threads to the tightly-woven relationship between the McManuses, Wards, Leonards, Herberts, Sweetmans, Kellys, and O'Briens, can be found in the sacramental records of the various North End churches. The same category of records from the Fingal Coast parishes in Ireland yields another, while the ownership documents of Boston's swelling fleet of Irish fishing smacks, the growing Irish presence in the tax assessor's records, and lesser sources such as newspaper accounts and city directories, provide the others necessary to unravel and examine the construction of the underlying fabric of this segment of Boston's Irish immigrant society.

[18] Documentation for the birth of Nicholas Leonard has not been found in the Archives of the Archdiocese of Boston, or the Massachusetts State Archives. Evidence for the Boston birth of Nicholas Leonard is provided by the 1855 and 1865 Massachusetts States Censuses, as well as the Federal Census of 1860. Julia delivered a second son, called Tom after his Uncle Tom Leonard, on 16 November 1850.

[19] *Births*, 1850, vol. 44, page 104, line 4650; St. John the Baptist/St. Stephen's, Baptisms, vol. 2 (1846-1853), page 189.

[20] City of Boston, Tax Assessor's Records, Ward 2, 1850, page 101, for 54 Commercial Street address.

but it was a common route to prosperity for an Irish immigrant entrepreneur, although the competition, particularly on the groggery side, was intense.[21] By the early 1850s hundreds of Irishmen earned their living by purveying spirits to their neighbors. With little capital or overhead, a man could open up one of these saloon stores either within, or in the immediate vicinity of, his own tenement house.[22] Leonard, as well as running his new business, also worked as a hand on fishing vessels, and found other occasional employment as a common laborer. The credit reports of R.G. Dun & Company, the predecessor to Dun & Bradstreet, were quite laudatory concerning him. By 1872 Leonard's dossier noted that he "has been over twenty five years in bus. always paid his debts and is considered worth $30000,"[23] a considerable fortune in that era.

After a cautious courtship that lasted several years, Kate McManus initiated another festive occasion when she married Dick Leonard on May Day 1853.[24] The groom, like his brothers, had been born in the Fingal port of Rush,[25] and was already a respected fishing captain. In the off-seasons, spring and autumn, he found odd jobs along the waterfront as a rigger and a customhouse ballast inspector, an appointment that may have been arranged by an Irish grocer, Matthew Keany, who was beginning to gain prominence as the Irish moved into Democratic party politics.

After their wedding the Leonards joined the rest of the family at No. 434. This tenement remained the clan's stronghold for several years: the resting place where they shared the trials and tribulations of life in America, and reminisced about the "good old days" at home in County Dublin. The address already housed Charley and Ann McManus with their youngest son, Pat, and Bill and Mary Montross with their two children, Charley and Mary, when the Leonards moved in. This building typified the densely-packed, North End lodgings: red-brick or clapboard buildings that averaged three or four stories in height and housed anywhere from three to twelve families. It was not unusual to find twelve to sixteen

---

[21] Oscar Handlin, *Boston's Immigrants, A Study in Acculturation*, rev. ed. (1941; Cambridge, Massachusetts: Belknap Press of Harvard University, 1979), 65, table 13.

[22] Dennis P. Ryan, *Beyond the Ballot Box, A Social History of the Boston Irish, 1845-1917* (East Brunswick, New Jersey: Fairleigh Dickinson University Press, 1983), 83.

[23] R.G. Dun & Company Collection, Baker Library, Harvard University Graduate School of Business Administration, Massachusetts vol. 75.

[24] Vital Records 1841-1895, Massachusetts State Archives, *Marriages*, 1853, vol. 71, page 57, line 960. A distinct possibility exists that Kate arrived in America after the other McManus family members. She first appears in American archives as a baptismal sponsor for Thomas Leonard on 10 June 1850, but does not appear at her father's address in the 1850 U.S. Census, taken on 1 August 1850. She may have been in the U.S., but residing elsewhere, either through employment, or with a relative, perhaps her Uncle John McManus.

[25] Bernadette Marks, Fingal Heritage Project, Swords, Ireland, Baptismal Register, Rush R.C., Reference No. 1198.

people belonging to two or three families inhabiting a single floor within those buildings owned by greedier landlords.[26] Overcrowding became a way of life.

The central event of 1853 from the immediate perspective of the McManus family occurred on 26 May with the marriage of John H. McManus and Margaret Harriet Sweetman at St. Mary's of the Sacred Heart Church on the corner of Endicott and Thacher Streets. Another Rush émigré, Miss Sweetman arrived in Boston during 1852, several years after her sister, Julia Leonard.[27] Father Peter Kroes, a parish curate since the church had been turned over to the Jesuits by Bishop Fitzpatrick six years earlier, conducted the ceremony, with the newly-married Kate Leonard as Meg's maid-of-honor, while her brother-in-law, Chris Leonard, the grocer-fisherman-laborer-liquor dealer stood as best man.[28] The latest newlyweds moved in with the others at 434 Commercial.

Jobs grew scarcer than ever by the time famine immigration began to peak. Whenever the demands for his professional talents slowed, John H., like his Leonard brothers-in-law, often served on board one of the increasingly numerous Irish fishing boats.[29] Pat, John H.'s younger brother, now twenty-two, had been working with his father and brother since shortly after their arrival in America. Like John H., he too risked life and limb to sail with the fishermen at different times throughout the year. For the brothers, these risky excursions had a twofold purpose: the income from their share of the catch was essential to maintaining a share of the family's expenses, and the fishing trips offered the opportunity to put their theoretical knowledge and conclusions about sail forms to the test under actual working conditions at sea. This was of inestimable value to their expanding experience and growing professional reputation.

Underneath the threatening political thunderclouds generated by the increasingly powerful nativist movement, the Fingal families continued to proliferate. The union of Dick Leonard and Kate McManus began to bear fruit when their first child, Nicholas, was born on 2 July 1854.[30] Then, during a winter whose deep chill exceeded even the infamous 1850 season—and which turned out

---

[26] City of Boston, Tax Assessor's Records, 1855.

[27] Rush R.C., Baptisms, Ref. No. 1045; Passengers Lists, 1848-1891, Boston, Microcopy No. JV6461-179, NARA.

[28] St. Mary's Sacramental Records, Archives of the Archdiocese of Boston, Brighton, Massachusetts, Marriages 1836-1915, May 1853; Vital Records, *Marriages*, 1853, vol. 71, page 70, line 1177, gives date as 23 May 1853; Robert H. Lord; John E. Sexton; and Edward T. Harrington, *History of the Archdiocese of Boston*, 3 vols., (New York: Sheed & Ward, 1944), 2:474-75. The following year Father Kroes was appointed pastor of St. Peter's Church at Southbridge, Massachusetts. He had been assigned to St. Mary's to forestall an acrimonious popularity struggle between its previous co-pastors.

[29] Thomas F. McManus, "Autobiographical Essay No. 3." McManus drafted a series of seven autobiographical essays which appear to have been written between 1920 and 1938. They are in the possession of his granddaughter, Mrs. Dustin Pevear.

[30] St. John the Baptist's/St. Stephen's, Baptisms, vol. 3 (1854-62), page 30.

to be the coldest in Boston since official records were first kept in 1821[31]—Meg McManus brought her father-in-law's namesake, Charles, into their waterfront world on Sunday, 3 December 1854. He was the first of John H. McManus's five children, all boys, to survive infancy.[32]

Despite a setback to their political ambitions by the nativists in the 1854 elections, the Irishmen began to exercise their hard-earned monetary muscle to expand their business horizons. Using the profits from his tenement grocery store Christopher Leonard purchased the twenty-five-year-old, forty-seven-foot fishing sloop *Two Brothers* in June 1854 and sent her out to work the market fishery in search of a fare.[33] In September Tom Herbert, one of the family's first emigrants, invested the savings from his career as a mariner to buy the relatively new fishing schooner *Moby Dick*.[34]

Despite the vicissitudes of their first decade in America, the McManuses were firmly entrenched in Boston by 1856. The family leadership gradually passed from the plucky but physically weakening Charles McManus, now in his early seventies, to his eldest son. At this time, John H. moved his family from the riotous environs of Commercial Street to the more placid North End backwaters of Thacher Street. Their new home, a two-story, red-brick dwelling, stood just around the corner from St. Mary's, although the family continued to worship at St. John the Baptist Church. This house was the birthplace of Tom McManus.

---

[31] David M. Ludlum, *The Early American Winters II, 1821-1870* (Boston: American Meteorological Society, 1968), 50-51.

[32] St. John the Baptist's/St. Stephen's, Baptisms, vol. 3 (1854-1862), page 52. A month after Charles was born, Chris Leonard became a father again when Julia delivered their fourth child, and second daughter, Emily, at 502 Commercial.

[33] Enrolment No. 145, Boston and Charlestown, 6 June 1854, U.S. Consolidated Enrolment and Licenses, Bureau of Navigation, Record Group 41, Records of the Department of Commerce, NARA.

[34] Enrolment No. 261, Boston and Charlestown, 21 September 1854.

CHAPTER THREE

The *Black Hawk*

With typically ferocious mid-nineteenth-century New England weather, 1856 arrived in a blinding blizzard and continued with a long deep frost. While the season did not reach the extremes of the previous year, January surpassed its predecessors for continuous cold by maintaining the most frigid median temperature for any month since Boston authorities had begun recording weather thirty-five years earlier. The lowering clouds of the new year's first storm dropped a hefty snowfall on the local landscape over the night of the ninth and tenth, and the next afternoon a thermometer in the city center registered -5.5°F., heralding winter's coldest day. A picturesque white blanket covered the area for more than eight weeks and provided an authentic old-fashioned winter with uninterrupted sleighing.[1] But the constant snow brought no joy to the burgeoning fleet of Irish

---

[1] David M. Ludlum, *Early American Hurricanes, 1492-1870* (Boston: American Meteorological Society, 1963), 51, hereafter cited as Ludlum, *Early Hurricanes*. The thermometer belonged to Jonathan Hall, whom Ludlum cites as Boston: 1821-56, Jonathan Hall, Register of Weather, *Mem. Amer. Acad*. Ns. 6-2 (1857), 229-308, and Boston: 1857-65, Jonathan Hall, Ms. temp. record (American Acad., Harvard).

fishermen whose livelihood sent them out to the wintry waters of Massachusetts Bay in search of fares of cod and haddock during the peak inshore season for those species. In that bitterly cold environment a fishing vessel's sails often froze solid, gravely minimizing its ability to withstand sudden squalls, or even to maneuver safely to variations in the wind's direction and force.

Another contributor to the fishermen's midwinter peril and discomfort came in the form of a heavy build-up of rime ice alow and aloft. For their own safety the men constantly had to chip away at the icy incrustation on the masts, spars, standing rigging, and deck furnishings to prevent the extra, unwanted weight from destroying the stability of their vessel. To make matters worse, saltwater slush carpeted the heaving decks underfoot, heightening the ever-present possibility of the men slipping overboard. A fall into the sea meant freezing to death within minutes.

As that severe winter came to a close, John H. moved Meg and baby Charles to the house at 18 Thacher Street near the Boston end of the Charlestown bridge.[2] After a decade in the city, McManus's professional expertise had gained broad recognition along the waterfront, and justifiably so, for he was no ordinary sailmaker. His talents far outstripped the requisite ability to shape, cut, sew, and stitch, for he understood the relationship between wind and sails, an unusual accomplishment for an artisan with merely empirical knowledge, untutored in the science of naval architecture. As a result, several boatbuilders and designers began to seek his guidance in drafting their sail plans. One of them, the Canadian-Irish naval architect Dennison J. Lawlor, whose mid-1840s arrival in Boston had coincided with that of the Fingal immigrants,[3] began a relationship with the McManus family that survived for half a century.

Spring 1856 brought welcome relief to the cold-stunned New England region and, as summer's warmth finally approached, Chris Leonard became one of the first Irishmen to acquire two fishing schooners when he purchased the *Resolve* and hired Pat Fallon, another Fingal fisherman, as her master.[4] Leonard's brothers,

---

2 *City Directory*, 1856.

3 Lawlor was born at St. John, New Brunswick, in 1822, the son of James Lawlor, a New Brunswick native, and Annie Lawlor who had been born in Ireland (Vital Records 1841-1895, Massachusetts State Archives, *Deaths*, 1892, vol. 429, page 493, line 2). He trained as an apprentice shipwright at St. John before emigrating to Boston.

4 Enrolment No. 49, Boston and Charlestown, 2 May 1856, U.S. Consolidated Enrolment and Licenses, Bureau of Navigation, Record Group 41, Records of the Department of Commerce, NARA.

Tom and Dick, operated his other smack, *Two Brothers*, while he tended to his lucrative liquor business.[5]

One day at the end of that summer, Meg McManus suffered several tortuous hours of labor on the sweat-soaked sheets of her bed before the weary neighborhood midwife delivered a wrinkled but healthy baby boy. After slapping his bottom and setting off an ample pair of lungs for the first time, she shoved the squalling infant, the subject of this biography, into John H.'s arms. Pinning down the exact day this scene took place is a matter of some conjecture, inasmuch as living McManus family members, the archives of the Roman Catholic church, and the State of Massachusetts's vital records are in total disagreement with each other.

The baby's birth date appears in state archives as 11 September,[6] and in those of Boston's Archdiocese as the twenty-seventh.[7] There can be no doubt, however, about the date the family and the man himself adopted: throughout his life he worried about his "unlucky" birthday, 13 September,[8] and, in the matter of births, family traditions are more reliable than those of either church or state.

On the first Sunday in October, with more than a hint of autumn in the Moon Street air, Father Claude M. Losserand, a visiting priest from Orleans, France, whom Father James A. Healy once characterized as "a good, but simple-minded ecclesiastic," answered a knock and found several people clustered about the door of St. John's, a converted tobacco warehouse.[9] The Frenchman, who spoke minimal English, and that with a heavy Gallic accent, responded with a gruff "oui?" The baby's godparents, Bill Gregory, an English-born North End clothier, and Peggy Ward, the daughter of an Irish tailor, stepped forward and gestured to the swaddling-clothed bundle cushioned in Meg McManus's arms, then announced their sponsorship of the baby, and voiced a desire that he be baptized into the Roman Catholic faith. Losserand swung the door open and led the baptismal party to the font, where he christened the infant Thomas Francis McManus, thereby saving his soul from an eternity in Limbo.[10] Afterward the cheerful group meandered along Prince Street past the grocery emporium where Matt Keany offered them his congratulations, up Leverett to Margin Street, and, finally, along

---

[5] Dick Leonard's wife, Kate McManus, gave birth to a son, Joseph Henry, on 17 May, and Father Henry O'Neill baptized him on the twenty-ninth at St. John's with John H. and his sister-in-law Julia Leonard as sponsors (St. John the Baptist's/St. Stephen's, Baptisms, vol. 3 (1854-62), page 131).

[6] Vital Records 1841-1895, Massachusetts State Archives, *Births*, 1856, vol. 98, page 119.

[7] St. John the Baptist/St. Stephen's, Baptisms, vol. 3 (1854-1862), page 152.

[8] Thomas F. McManus, "Autobiographical Essay No. 2."

[9] St. John the Baptist/St. Stephen's, *Baptisms*, vol. 3 (1854-1862), page 152.

[10] As of 8 December 1989, it appears that McManus was named after his father's friend, Thomas F. Ward, who may have preceded the McManuses to Boston from Ireland, as well as guiding their fortunes and housing them afterwards.

Thacher to the McManuses' new home, where they celebrated the occasion with their relatives and in-laws.

But in the immigrant ghettoes the specter of death loomed constantly and joyous occasions were short-lived. Tragedy struck the family just six days later when Nicholas, the oldest son of Dick Leonard and Kate McManus, died of scarlet fever three months short of his third birthday, leaving baby Joseph Henry as their only surviving child.[11]

As Christmas approached, Chris Leonard decided to concentrate more fully on the liquor and grocery business. He sold the *Two Brothers* to Tom and Dick and, for the first time in a quarter-century, the ownership of the ancient fishing schooner once again lived up to her name.[12] But, as the *Two Brothers* went to sea for a winter fare, almost certainly with John H. and Pat McManus on board as crewmen, she sailed into another unusually intense winter along the New England coastline. Fortunately, both of the McManus infants proved robust. Charles Aloyisius, a year and nine months old, and Thomas Francis only three months, unlike many of their peers, were hardy enough to survive the stormy spasms of January 1857. During that riotous weather month Boston suffered its first zero degree day since 1812. Beginning on the twenty-third, the *Evening Traveller*'s prominent downtown thermometer remained below zero for about thirty-six hours. That infamous Thursday dawned with a temperature of -14° at sunrise, rose to -4° at 2 P.M. and peaked at 0° at six in the evening. Five days before, a "winter hurricane," the precursor of the vicious cold spell, had struck the city. Not since the establishment of railroads had there been such an interruption of travel or hindrance to the mails.[13] January's savage weather fronts, with their freezing temperatures and heavy snowfalls, paralyzed transportation, wrecked ships off the coast, and, ultimately, froze the city's fishing fleet at its moorings. Building and property damage was such that New England folklore refers to this icy period as "The Great Cold of 1857."[14]

Emily Leonard, Charley and Tom's cousin, proved less hardy than the boys, succumbing to scarlet fever, the same disease that had killed her cousin Nicholas the previous October.[15] But the Leonards were resilient. A month later Chris and Julia conceived a new daughter. Born on 8 January 1858, and named Emily Frances

---

11 Vital Records 1841-1895, Massachusetts State Archives, *Deaths*, 1856, vol. 104, page 75, line 3257.

12 Enrolment No. 208, Boston and Charlestown, 22 December 1856. Nineteenth-century vessel owners considered it bad luck to change the name of a vessel when she was sold. The *Two Brothers* first owners were Cyrus and Joseph F. Baker (Enrolment No. 87, Boston and Charlestown, 13 May 1853).

13 David M. Ludlum, *The Early American Winters II, 1821-1870* (Boston: American Meteorological Society, 1968), 54, hereafter cited as Ludlum, *Early Winters*.

14 Ludlum, *Early Winters*, 53-55.

15 Vital Records, *Deaths*, 1857, vol. 113, page 23, line 972.

to memorialize the little girl they had lost, she proved a tiny but sturdy survivor.[16] Nicknamed Little Em'ly because of her petite size and the trouble she later had pronouncing the "i" of her name, Em'ly and her brothers were constant childhood companions of the McManus boys during their youthful romps through the alleys, passageways, and wharves of the North End.

Throughout the political ascendancy of the American nativist movement the McManuses, like most of their class of Irish immigrants, ignored the hostile anti-Irish sentiment in much the same attitude and manner as they adjusted to the Yankee structure of Catholicism in Boston. They simply went about their business, maintaining their concern for the function rather than the form of politics and religion. Old Charley, John H., and Pat plied their trade along the waterfront, cutting, stitching, and shaping the cotton duck sails used by both the "Boston Hookers" of the Gaelic Irish inshore fishermen, and the larger offshore schooners of the market fishery now nearly monopolized by the Fingalians. Both fleets were growing apace and their demands occupied the McManuses' sailmaking energies to the exclusion of ethnic strife.

That summer, twelve years after he brought the family to Boston, Charley McManus recognized that his life was close to running its course, and helped to finance his sons into a sail-loft partnership. When the brothers first opened for business at 11 Commercial Wharf, the old man often lent his long-practiced hand at the loft despite his growing infirmities.[17] But perversely, as the business grew quickly in strength and size, Charley's physique weakened and shrivelled with alarming rapidity.

October 1858 turned out to be a dizzying month for the Fingalians. Meg bore a third son, George, on the fourth.[18] Later, Kate McManus brought another Charles into the family on the twenty-first, bringing to three the total of her father's namesake grandchildren: Charles Montross, Charles McManus, and now, Charles Leonard. Then on the twenty-fourth in an all-too-familiar pattern, joy turned to grief for the Fingal families when the elder McManus's hard-used, seventy-four-year-old frame succumbed to one of the most insidious of the tenement plagues, dysentery.[19] It was a difficult death, preceded by excruciating diarrhetic convulsions. Yet, despite the painful nature of his passing,

---

[16] St. John the Baptist's/St. Stephen's, *Baptisms*, vol. 3 (1854-1862), page 221. Father John W. Donahoe performed several of the family baptisms, including Emily Frances Leonard, Willy Cokely, George and Louis McManus, and Charles and Christopher Leonard.

[17] *City Directory*, 1858.

[18] St. John the Baptist/St. Stephen's, *Baptisms*, vol. 3 (1854-1862), page 266; *Births*, 1858, vol. 116, page 100, line 462.

[19] 24 October 1858, Vital Records, *Deaths*, 1858, vol. 122, page 72, line 24.

Charles McManus was one of the rare men who possessed the satisfaction of dying with his life's mission accomplished. A true patriarch to his children and grandchildren, he had lived to see his family's roots firmly and fruitfully transplanted from Ireland to America.[20]

A different type of loss for the McManuses occurred when Lucy Shannon and her parents coaxed brother Pat away from the sailmaking company and into the retail food and drink trade in 1860. He opened one of the ubiquitous tenement grocery-groggeries at 450 Commercial. Soon after Pat forsook the sailmaker's bench for the cash-box, John H. moved his sail loft for the first of several times during its history.[21] With each successive relocation he expanded his manufacturing capabilities, but always kept Commercial Wharf as his center of operations. Although the early success of John H. McManus & Co. arose from the steady demand for replacement sails created by the wear and tear of arduous fishing trips, the company benefitted from the spate of new construction in the Irish fleets that began in 1859 and continued for several years.

Among New England's immigrants, those from Ireland's rural seaside areas were the principal operators of the growing "Boston hooker" fleet. If the people of the Fingal coast had been relatively unaffected by the famine, these Gaelic-Irish farmer-fishermen from the south and west saw their marginal lifestyle perish with the diseased tubers of the potato blight. Those among them who survived nature's spoliation to emigrate arrived in Boston hungry, penniless, and devoid of urban skills. They typified the twentieth-century perception of Boston's Irish famine immigrants.[22] At home, they had habitually harvested the earth and the ocean, and they followed their waterborne pursuits in Massachusetts by getting to sea in anything from broken-down rowing dories to the derelict sailing craft of all descriptions they found abandoned on the shores of the harbor and patched up to

---

[20] Charley McManus's oldest daughter, Mary, had suffered a pair of miscarriages during the six-year period after the birth of her daughter Mary in February 1853. As a reward for her losses she bore a son, George Warren, on 5 June 1859 (Vital Records, *Births*, 1859, vol. 125, page 53, line 23480), and Bill Montross proudly carried his new child down to St. John's on the twenty-sixth for his baptism by Father Jack Donahoe (St. John the Baptist/St. Stephen's, Baptisms, vol. 2 (1846-1853), page 304). On the fraternal side of the family, eleven months after his father died Pat McManus won the hand of Lucy Ann Shannon, the daughter of a North End garment seller, and sister of Maria Gregory. Father Norbert Steinbacher married the couple at St. Mary's on 26 September (25 September 1859, St. Mary's, *Marriages 1836-1915*, September 1859, page 246; Vital Records 1841-1895, Massachusetts State Archives, *Marriages*, 1859, vol. 128, page 92, line 1636). After the ceremonies the couple moved into 433 Commercial Street, next door to John H. and Meg, where Pat's two sisters, Kate Leonard and Mary Montross, then resided (*City Directory*, 1859-60). Pat and Lucy had no sooner settled into the building than, just four days after their wedding, the terrible anguish of a lost child swept through the family. Baby George Warren Montross succumbed to smallpox. The loss of her son, coupled to her two previous miscarriages drove Mary McManus into a period of deep melancholia.

[21] During its formative years the business occupied, in chronological order, Nos. 39, 23, 33, and 34 Commercial Wharf.

[22] Oscar Handlin, *Boston's Immigrants, A Study in Acculturation*, rev. ed., (1941; Cambridge, Massachusetts: Belknap Press of Harvard University, 1979).

their own peril. Within a decade, however, these inshore fishermen prospered sufficiently to build new boats, which they modelled after the small, cutter-rigged Galway and Kinsale hookers of Ireland,[23] whose design ancestry was uniquely Irish.[24] Clusters of these rugged little inshore craft fished the coastal waters of the Emerald Isle from Malin Head in the north, along the west coast to the southwestern peninsulas, and around them to Mine Head in the south.

In Boston the transplanted hookermen trawled along nearby shores and sold their catch to the dealers on Lewis and Commercial Wharves, or more directly to the North End ghetto-dwellers via the ubiquitous neighborhood peddlers. One of these entrepreneurs was Thomas Fitzgerald, the father of John F. "Honey Fitz" Fitzgerald. A traditional Irish tin horn accompanied the trade and signaled the arrival of peddlers and their wares ". . . fresh cod and mackerel, haddock to fry, arrived this morning."[25] As part of his daily routine Fitzgerald walked to Lewis Wharf each morning to meet the boats and fill his basket with fish. Afterward, he would parade up and down the North End hills until he sold them, usually in time for a repeat performance in the afternoon. Although this was "backbreaking and soul-destroying work,"[26] within five years Fitzgerald amassed sufficient savings from his meager profits to open a grocery at 310 North Street, joining ranks with the likes of Pat McManus (450 Commercial), Matt Keany (238 North), and Chris Leonard (502 Commercial).

George Brown Goode, the nineteenth-century ichthyologist and assistant secretary of the Smithsonian Institution, described the inshore fishing area the Boston hookermen favored: "The larger part of [Massachusetts] bay, inside of Stellwagen's Bank, has a muddy bottom, on which large quantities of fish are rarely taken. Farther in, however, on the shore soundings, especially between the entrance to Boston Harbor and Plymouth, exist numerous rocky ledges, which are favorite feeding grounds for cod in fall and winter. This region is frequented by the Swampscott fleet and by other vessels supplying the Boston market."[27]

---

[23] The hookers usually registered between fifteen and twenty-five tons according to the pre-1864 U.S. Congressional formula for tonnage measurement.

[24] Richard J. Scott, *The Galway Hookers: Working Sailboats of Galway Bay*, 2nd ed., (1983; Swords, Ireland: Ward River Press, 1985), 41. "The Galway hooker model had no close counterpart elsewhere in the nineteenth century, discounting the Boston Irish hooker, which was introduced there anyhow by Galway emigrants in the 1850s."

[25] John Henry Cutler, *"Honey Fitz" Three Steps to the White House, The Life and Times of John F. (Honey Fitz) Fitzgerald* (Indianapolis: Bobbs-Merrill Company, 1962), 38.

[26] Doris K. Goodwin, *The Fitzgeralds and the Kennedys* (New York: Simon and Schuster, 1987), 13, citing Irving Howe, *World of Our Fathers* (New York: Harcourt Brace Jovanovich, 1976), 78.

[27] George Brown Goode, ed., *The Fisheries and Fishery Industries of the United States*, 5 vols., (Washington, D.C.: Government Printing Office, 1887), sect. 3, "The Fishing Grounds of North America," 39, emphasis added.

A Boston hooker, the distinctive Irish-immigrant fishing boat developed at Boston late in the 1850s. As seaworthy as their antecedent Galway and Kinsale hookers of Ireland, the Boston hookers were used by Boston Irish inshore fishermen through the end of the nineteenth century. (Courtesy Francis E. Bowker)

During the off season the Boston-Irish part-time fishermen worked as longshoremen,[28] warehousemen, or at other dockside tasks, to earn their daily bread. As a social circle they congregated along the waterfront stubbornly clinging to the Gaelic language and customs. The 1880 U.S. Census study characterized them: "The Irishmen of Boston, with their sloop-cutters and primitive fishing tackle, are west-coast Irishmen still. All retain the peculiar mental characteristics of the districts in which they were trained, though all are more or less broadened and

28 Patrick Kidney, whose daughter Agnes married John H. McManus's son Charles, founded one of the largest stevedoring firms in Boston, after working his way up from a common laborer. His company manhandled all the iron rails exported through Boston to California for the construction of the Union Pacific railroad (Letter, Edwin Charles McManus, 15 February 1990).

developed by the greater freedom which they find in the United States. A large percentage, probably more than a half, of the number of those enumerated in this report as fishermen are actually engaged in the fisheries only a few months in the year, and at other times are occupied in farming or any other pursuits on shore."[29]

But this investigation plainly addressed only the Irish immigrant shore fishery. At this time, New England pursued five distinct fisheries:

Shore Fishery: Mostly small craft, about five to fifty tons (and many rowing craft of far less than five tons), working waters adjacent to the shore and catching species of bottom-dwelling ground fish, which were sold either fresh or salted;

Market Fishery: Vessels of medium or large size, which fished the nearby banks (Georges, Browns, etc.). Like the shore fishery the catch consisted mostly of cod, haddock, pollock, hake, and halibut, and was landed in fresh condition;

Halibut Fishery: Vessels making special trips to the banks for that species and landing their fares in a fresh condition, or fletched and salted;

Mackerel Fishery: All vessels taking the common mackerel, with seines, hooks, or gill nets;

Cod Fishery: Large vessels making prolonged trips as far east as the Grand Bank of Newfoundland, catching codfish and preserving the catch with salt. At this time, cod fishing predominated in Gloucester, Marblehead, and Provincetown in Massachusetts, and most of the Maine ports.[30]

These Irish shore fishermen used an American version of the Galway or Kinsale hooker,[31] an imported fishing boat design that fascinated Captain Joseph W. Collins, a prominent nineteenth-century fisheries expert,[32] and strongly influenced his voluminous writings. Locally known as "Boston hookers," or, more pejoratively,

---

[29] Goode and Captain Joseph William Collins, "The Fishermen of the United States," in Goode, *The Fisheries*, sect. 4, 54.

[30] Captain J.W. Collins and Hugh M. Smith, "Fisheries of the New England States," *Bulletin of the United State Fish Commission*, 10 (1890) (Washington: Government Printing Office, 1892), 73-176).

[31] Howard I. Chapelle, *American Small Sailing Craft* (New York: Kennedy Brothers Incorporated, 1936), 277-

82. Although he quotes from the U.S. Commissioner of Fish & Fisheries, *Report of the Commissioner for 1886* (Washington, D.C.: Government Printing Office, 1889), 107, he does not cite this source.

[32] Howard I. Chapelle discovered this Irish immigrant shore fishery in the 1950s from research into the annual reports and monthly industrial bulletins of the United States Fish Commission, as well as the massive congressional study of the fishing industry edited by Goode. In addition to the broad exposure the Gaelic-Irish received in this contemporary, government-sponsored literature, a model of a Boston-built hooker Chapelle turned up at the United States National Museum attracted his attention to them (Collins donated a fully-rigged model of a Boston Hooker to the United States National Museum, accession no. USNM-57131). From these sources Chapelle concluded that: "the intense concentration of Irish at Boston soon led to a self-contained small-boat fishery there, wholly independent of Yankee influence or economic control" (Chapelle, *Small Sailing Craft*, 278).

"Paddy Boats,"[33] these distinctive vessels were remarkably able craft, but they were not large or seaworthy enough to withstand the rigors of New England's offshore winter cod and market fisheries. This limited working range should have provided a definitive line of demarcation between two different, and rapidly multiplying Irish fleets at Boston. The seasonally employed, traditional day-fishermen of the hookers constituted but one segment of the New England fishing industry in which the Irish immigrants achieved prompt material success. Historians have failed to differentiate the other, which was beginning to dominate the market fishery.

Part of the success of these immigrant fishermen was their familiarity with the form of fishing that would revolutionize the New England fishing industry. Although their Yankee competitors still adhered to the traditional handline method of fishing , wherein each man dangled his line from the vessel's rail, both Boston Irish fishing fleets engaged in trawl-line or "long-line" fishing. Their trawl baskets eventually evolved into a standard tool of the New England fisheries. By that time, the woven basket had been replaced by the pot or tub that is obtained by simply sawing a barrel in half. Each tub is then rigged out with a long line made up in the following manner: "Ground-line 300 fathoms [1,800 feet], 300 No. 14 cod-hooks, 300 gangings, each three feet long and six feet apart (one end of the ganging is bent on the ground line, and the hook is made fast to the other end); two buoys, two buoy-lines and two 16-pound anchors (one at each end) to hold the trawl fast when it is set on the bottom."[34]

With individual fishermen now handling hundreds of hooks rather than just a few, trawl-line fishing produced a dramatic increase in productivity.

By the time of the "Great Hunger," Gaelic fishermen had practiced varieties of trawl fishing for over a hundred years. Americans, despite their familiarity with the methods of the European fishermen they encountered on the fish-rich banks lying between Montauk Point, New York, and Cape Race, Newfoundland, had made only cursory attempts to employ trawling techniques. This diffidence eventually cost them control of Boston's shore and market fisheries. In a joint effort, Goode and Collins described the early history of trawling in America: "As early as 1843 Captain [Nathaniel E.] Atwood set trawls for halibut in Massachusetts Bay. . . . About 1845 the schooner *Oneco*, Charles Aspey, a Welshman, master, went to the Grand Bank fitted out for trawling like the French vessels. She made

---

33 Captain Joseph W. Collins claimed the hookers were known among the Boston-Irish fishermen as "Dungarvan Boats," but no other contemporary reference to this name has been found ("The Sea Fisheries of Eastern North America," U.S. Commissioner of Fish & Fisheries, *Report of the Commissioner for 1886*, 107).

34 Wesley G. Pierce, *Goin' Fishin'* (Salem, Massachusetts: Marine Research Society, 1934), 63.

Immigrant Irish fishermen helped introduce the trawl line to the New England fisheries in the 1850s. As refined in New England, the trawl line for codfish had a stout ground line with three-foot gangings spaced at six-foot intervals to hold the hooks. Use of the flat-bottom, flaring-sided dory like the ones pictured here allowed fishermen to take this form of fishing offshore, revolutionizing the New England fisheries for bottom-dwelling species around the time of the Civil War. This method prevailed through the 1920s.

These views depict offshore dorymen setting a trawl using a heaving stick; inshore fishermen hauling a trawl laden with fish; and offshore dorymen pitching their catch on board the schooner. Drawn by Milton J. Burns. (*Harper's Weekly*, 31 October 1885; *Scribner's Magazine*, April 1902)

only about 5,000 fish, 150 quintals. When he had made a miss it stilled the Provincetown fishermen on the subject of trawling."[35]

These trials were considered failures, and trawl-line fishing spent a few more years in an American limbo, until the advent of the Irish famine immigration. Presumably the lack of competitive pressure in the Boston marketplace prior to the arrival of the Irish contributed to this Yankee aversion to trawling.

Captain Nathaniel E. Atwood eventually left the deck of his fishing boat to become a state legislator. His memoirs, written in the folksy style that propagates myths, outlined the next step toward the American adoption of trawling and the short-lived rivalry of the 1850s between Swampscott's fishermen, the traditional monopolists of Boston's market fishery, and the Gaelic newcomers, who unseated them:[36] "About 1851 or 1852 an old Irishman down at Swampscott bought an old dory and went to work rigging a trawl as he had been accustomed to do in the old country. The Swampscott fishermen laughed at him and the idea that he could catch any fish with his clumsy trawl; but when he went out they soon changed their tune, for he could catch two fish to their one."[37]

The Swampscotters began to adopt the use of trawl-lines themselves but, according to Atwood, it was a case of too little too late. "An entirely new class of fishermen, mostly Irish, were called in and [the local] monopoly of the Boston market was destroyed. A great many Irishmen began trawling, and they soon began to build little vessels, such as they had on their own coast. The first one they got out was called the *Moby Dick*, and they made money like shells."[38]

By 1859, trawls had come into general use, and their efficiency drove the value of haddock from $1.25 to a low of 37.5 cents per hundredweight.[39] The Gaelic-Irish of the shore fishery, nonetheless, happily ensconced in their scorned "Paddy Boats," were able to make money at those levels. Through their native ingenuity and experience, their use of the weatherly hooker as the vehicle, the willing acceptance of a poorer living standard than their competitors would tolerate, and through sheer numbers, these impoverished famine immigrants snatched an important segment of the New England fishing industry during their

---

35 Goode, *The Fisheries*, sect. 5, "History and Methods of the Fisheries," 1:158.

36 Goode and Collins, "The Winter Haddock Fishing of New England," *Bulletin of the United States Fish Commission* (Washington, D.C.: Government Printing Office, 1887), 1:228; Goode and Collins, "The Bank Trawl-line Cod Fishery," in Goode, *The Fisheries*, sect. 5, "History and Methods of the Fisheries," 1:158-59.

37 Goode and Collins, "Trawl-line Cod Fishery," 158-59.

38 Ibid.

39 Captain Nathaniel E. Atwood, in Goode, *The Fisheries*, sect. 5, 1:158-59.

first decade in America. The Boston hookermen, Atwood's "entirely new class of fishermen," profitably worked on the waters of Massachusetts Bay into the early twentieth century; but he confused them with, and Goode's study did not differentiate them from, the second, simultaneously developing Irish fleet–owned and operated, to a large extent, by the men from the Fingal Coast of the Irish Sea— that captured Boston's offshore market fishery.

The men from north County Dublin were culturally and professionally different from their countrymen of the south and west. As descendants of the Norse and the Anglo-Irish, the principal language for the men of Skerries, Balbriggan, and Rush was English, not Gaelic. Indeed, Gaelic had not been spoken along the Fingal Coast for over two centuries at the time of the mid-nineteenth-century famine emigrations. Secondly, they were schoonermen by tradition dating back to the evolution of the Skerries wherry during the eighteenth century, and were inveterate deep-sea fishermen and fish traders.[40]

In America, as in Ireland, their schooner-rigged craft were larger and more seaworthy than the smaller cutter-rigged hookers. Moreover, in direct contrast to the excerpt from the 1887 Congressional study, this breed of Anglo-Irish immigrants swiftly assimilated American ways. Inescapably, the Boston-Irish immigrants from the Fingal Coast, the captors of the market fishery, typified the "better class" of immigrant,[41] rather than the oft-described famine survivors, who suffered so severely in Boston's brutalizing urban environment. Underwritten in part by émigré families such as the McManuses, Leonards, Herberts, Murphys, Quinns, Regans, Cadigans, and O'Haras, who came to America with working capital, these industrious entrepreneurs, for the reasons outlined by Atwood, were soon outcatching their Swampscott-based rivals in Boston's lucrative market fishery. Atwood also stated that the Irishmen's "little boats" quickly increased in number and, before long, "they had the *St. Patrick* and the *St. Mary*, and the *Daniel O'Connell* and the *Maid of Erin*; and in 1857 there were seventy-five Irish boats tending the Boston market,"[42] a verifiable statistic.[43] But the 1852-built *Moby Dick* owned by the McManuses' cousin, Tom Herbert, or William Murray's 1859 *Maid of Erin*, and *St. Mary* and *O'Connell*, launched in 1860 for Dominick Connolly and

---

[40] The hull form of the Skerries wherries differed distinctly from the clipper-schooner hull shape commonly favored in America during the 1850s, although there was little difference in the rig of the two schooner types. The Fingal fisherman, when fishing on the west coast or other distant grounds, habitually purchased fish from the local hookers, to fill the large holds of their Skerries wherries.

[41] Kerby A. Miller, *Emigrants and Exiles, Ireland and the Irish Exodus to North America* (New York: Oxford University Press, 1985), 293-94.

[42] Goode and Collins, "Trawl-line Cod Fishery," 158-59.

[43] Consolidated Enrolment and Licenses, 1850-1892, Record Group 41, Records of the Department of Commerce, Bureau of Navigation, NARA.

Patrick Sullivan, were anything but "little boats." Additionally, given the launching dates of the latter three vessels, they could not have been part of the 1857 Irish fleet Captain Atwood recalled.[44]

Speaking from an aging memory, Atwood had commingled the hookermen, who, among their other peculiarities, could be distinguished from the schoonermen of the market fishery by the Gaelic names they bestowed on their boats, in contrast to the anglicized-Irish ones favored by their eastern brethren. Historians, although occasionally recognizing that the New England small-boat, shore fishery became an Irish province during the 1850s and 1860s, have not identified the concurrent Irish seizure of the market fishery. Accounting for the earlier oversight by Goode and Collins is not difficult, given the Anglicized ethnic characteristics of the Fingalians, particularly their use of the English language, and the ease with which they assimilated American ways, as well as the improbably short time span between their arrival and the acceptance of them as a workaday element on the fishing wharves. They had been an integral part of Boston's waterfront for three decades by the time of the 1887 study.

The actual statistics behind this undiscovered phenomenon are astonishing. Although there was but one distinguishable Irish-owned fishing boat among the sixty-odd smacks that sailed in the market fishery during the 1850 and 1851 seasons, within four years the Irish came to dominate this valuable sector of the New England fisheries.[45] Francis McKann was the only Irish fishing master who worked during those first two years.[46] Twelve of McKann's countrymen, sharing the ownership of nine smacks,[47] joined the fleet in 1852, but the largest increase for a single year in the entire 1850s' decade occurred in 1853, when Irish ownership surged to thirty-three vessels, more than half the number then engaged in Boston's market fishery.

Attention to the effect of the legal process for obtaining citizenship papers, within the framework of famine immigration dates, is essential when evaluating this accelerating rate of increase. The maritime laws of the United States required the owners and masters of merchant vessels sailing under the Stars and Stripes to have American citizenship, and commercial fishing vessels fell into this category. Immigrants, even those with the necessary resources, could not hold title to an

---

44 Atwood, "Autobiography of Capt. Nathaniel E. Atwood, of Provincetown, Mass.," in Goode, *The Fisheries*, 4:149-68. In quoting Atwood's memoirs Goode initiated the historical confusion surrounding these Irishmen that misled Chapelle and his followers, and precipitated their failure to discover Boston's Fingal fleet.

45 Goode, *The Fisheries*, sect. 5, "History and Methods of the Fisheries," 1:158-59.

46 In the 1830, 52-foot Maine-built *Norah K.* during 1850, and the 1836, 53 foot Essex-built *Mediator* in 1851.

47 See Appendix I.

American bottom before becoming citizens. The stiffest requirement of the federal naturalization statutes confronting Irishmen who had reached their majority and were thus qualified as "free, white, and over twenty-one," was proof of five-years residence in the United States.[48] Aliens could petition for citizenship in any state court of common law.

In appearance the archetypal smack acquired by Fingal-Irish after they became citizens was most likely schooner-rigged, averaged fifty-four feet in length, and measured forty-eight tons, or more than twice the size of the largest hookers. She was likely, however, to be thirty-two years old, a decrepit age for a wooden workboat forced to battle the pernicious weather of Massachusetts Bay, the South Channel east of Nantucket, Georges and Middle Banks, and Jeffrey's Ledge northeast of Cape Ann. The advanced age of these boats with their worn-out canvas, was a business boon for the McManuses, the leading purveyors of sails to the Irish fleets.

When Congress passed the enabling legislation for the new Anglo-American Reciprocity Treaty on 3 August 1854,[49] American and Canadian fishermen gained permission to work inside the three-mile limit of each country's coastal boundary, beginning with the winter fishing season of 1854-55. This legislation initiated a robust period of growth for the New England fishing industry by allowing American vessels access to Canadian bays that teemed with fish, and permitting the free import of Newfoundland herring, an essential bait fish for the New Englanders. On the negative side, the treaty allowed cheap Canadian fish into American retail markets in direct competition with the produce of the American fishermen;[50] nevertheless, the treaty worked to the benefit of both parties, until post-Civil War inflation in the United States upset the economic balance between them. At the time the treaty went into effect, the expansion of Irish ownership in the market fleet was exponential. Fifty-one additional Irish-held hulls entered it during 1854-58. Over this span their average length crept up to fifty-five feet and the tonnage to fifty-six tons. The greatest change, however, was in the age of the

---

[48] Until the latter part of the nineteenth century, the naturalization laws of the United States were written with slave-holding and black citizenship in mind. The Act of 3 March 1813, established basic residence requirements and was modified by further acts of 1813, 1816, 1824, 1828, 1848, 1850, 1855, 1862, 1866, 1867, 1868, 1870, 1887, and 1888. The most valuable works illuminating the naturalization process are Frank George Franklin, *The Legislative History of Naturalization in the United States* (1906; reprint, New York: Arno Press and The New York Times, 1969); and James H. Kettner, *Development of American Citizenship, 1608-1870* (Chapel Hill: University of North Carolina Press, 1978).

[49] This treaty succeeded the earlier ones with Great Britain: the Treaty of Paris of 1783, after the American Revolution, and the Convention of 20 October 1818, a codicil to the Treaty of Ghent of 1815, following the War of 1812. The convention of 1818 was considerably more restrictive to American fishing interests than the earlier treaty (Raymond McFarland, *A History of the New England Fisheries* (New York: D. Appleton and Company, 1911), 321-26).

[50] Samuel Eliot Morison, *Maritime History of Massachusetts, 1783-1860* (1921; reprint Boston: Northeastern University Press, 1979), 312.

latest additions, which dropped more than ten years. Nevertheless, as late as 1858 the median age for their vessels was nineteen years, still too long-in-the-tooth to face the rigors of New England's coastal climate with a reliable degree of safety, although this did not deter the Irishmen.

Natives of the tempestuous eastern Atlantic, the Irish were no strangers to wild weather systems, but the equinoctial gales that ravaged the American coast as each winter and summer came to a close flabbergasted them. Coinciding with the Irish move into the New England fisheries, but from an unrelated cause, the losses of fishermen and their craft to these tempests rose dramatically. At that time, the fast clipper-type schooner reached the peak of popularity it would retain for three decades. For architectural reasons covered in greater detail later, these unstable vessels were susceptible to the sudden wind shifts and squalls that typified the equinoxes.[51] Samuel Eliot Morison listed some of the losses that occurred in two of the great storms, during the time of the famine immigration: "eleven vessels from Marblehead, with sixty-seven men and boys, went down in the September gale of 1846;[52] and the 'Minot's Light' gale of October, 1851, took a fearful toll from every fishing village in New England."[53] The Boston-Irish fleets suffered their first serious losses due to weather from the tropical storm system that swept over Massachusetts Bay on 16 September 1858. Coupled to the series of record-breaking winters, it was a stern warning of ill winds to come.[54]

The phase of rapid modernization during the final years preceding the Civil War brought twenty newly-constructed smacks into the Boston market fleet. To meet the prevailing conditions, including the turbulent weather fronts of the Western Atlantic, the Irish fishermen arrived at an optimum size and type of smack. Except for one sloop, all of the new vessels were schooner rigged, fell between forty-five and fifty feet in length, and had a median tonnage of thirty-eight tons. Built to specifications worked out by the Irish, these fishing vessels were considerably smaller than the previous fleet norms, although still double the size of a hooker, and required a smaller crew to work them. In 1859 the average age of the new boats was twelve years, a strong trend toward youth, but in 1860 the mean of the fleet's newcomers, including fifteen built that year, dropped to a remarkably young five years; just seven years earlier they had averaged a weary thirty-two years old. Their expropriation of Boston's shore and market fisheries preceded the Irish ascendancy

---

[51] Robert G. Albion, William A. Baker, and Benjamin W. Labaree, *New England and The Sea* (Mystic: Mystic Seaport Museum, 1972), 138-39, emphasis original.

[52] This was the northern edge of the Hatteras Inlet hurricane of 9 September 1846 (Ludlum, *Early Hurricanes*, 193).

[53] Morison, *Maritime History*, 311.

[54] Ludlum, *Early Hurricanes*, 100-101.

to political hegemony, a socio-economic process that had yet to begin when the McManuses disembarked in 1846, the same year that iced fresh fish began to arrive in Boston from Gloucester via the new railroad.

Intolerance of the Irish far outlived the nativist era, and resistance to the Irish became an element of Massachusetts Republicanism.[55] Despite the resiliency of nativism, the financial rewards accruing from the Irish domination of the fishing trades underwrote the initial stages of the Irish political ascendancy in the city. As the Irish voters' share of the electorate reached meaningful proportions, the Democratic Party began to court them, fashioning a mutual romance that would blossom fully after the Civil War. John H. McManus became an early supporter and frequent business partner of the Irish grocer turned capitalist and-politician, Matthew Keany, the prototypic political boss of Boston's Ward Six,[56] whose wartime rise to power will be discussed in the next chapter. In the burgeoning years of the 1850s, even the Roman Catholic Church lent its rapidly multiplying strength to the support of secular success. The editorial pages of *The Pilot* encouraged that the Irish Catholics "ought to show that the immigrant can build up his worldly house without destroying that habitation that was made for him in a better world."[57]

With the two Boston-based Irish fleets multiplying in direct proportion to the massive Irish immigration, John H. McManus invested a portion of the family earnings in fishing vessels to broaden his business horizons. In January 1858 he and brother-in-law Dick Leonard bought the first of several vessels whose title they would share: the *Black Hawk*, a five-year-old, forty-foot, Duxbury-built schooner, in January 1858.[58] One of the *Black Hawk*'s sellers was Bailey D. Winsor, and his involvement in the transaction marked the start of a fifty-year-long business relationship between the Winsors, an old-line Duxbury family, and the rapidly assimilating McManuses of Boston.

The Irish had gained a monopoly in the Boston market fleet with remarkable swiftness. The incredibly short period in which the Irishmen from

---

[55] John Raymond Mulkern, *The Know-Nothing Party in Massachusetts: the Rise and Fall of a People's Movement* (Boston: Northeastern University Press, 1990), 3-4.

[56] The flexibility of Boston's ward structure during the second half of the nineteenth century can be confusing for both readers and researchers. The North End comprised Wards 1 and 2 (divided by Hanover Street), 1850-54. It became Ward 1, 1854-66, while East Boston comprised Ward 2. From 1867 through 1875 the North End was Ward 2. The North End became Ward 6 in 1876, while East Boston was Ward 1, Chelsea became Ward 2, and Charlestown comprised Wards 3, 4, and 5. There were later revisions, but the ward/neighborhood relationship remained constant.

[57] Donna Merwick, *Boston Priests, 1848-1910, A Study in Social and Intellectual Change* (Cambridge, Massachusetts: Harvard University Press, 1973), 25, citing *The Pilot*, 11 May 1850.

[58] Enrolment No. 2, Boston and Charlestown, 2 January 1858, property change Winsor, *et. al..* to John H. McManus and Richard Leonard.

Kinsale and Galway took over the Boston inshore fishery, and their brethren from the Fingal Coast of County Dublin captured the offshore market fishery, is surely one of the outstanding nineteenth-century success stories for an immigrant worker class. The Irish fishing tradesmen not only monopolized an industry by displacing the Yankee forerunners, but they gleaned better profits by operating in a more efficient manner. Underlying this efficiency was their uniform use of trawl lines, the fishing method that captured the shore and market fisheries for them, and secured their tenure in control.

The first generation of American Irish multiplied in leaps and bounds as the ominous new decade, one that would render the Union asunder, approached. But, as much as the Fingal families concentrated on their own advancement, it proved impossible to avoid the issues that were staggering the city, state, and nation. The pressure of events would force the pro-slavery Irish immigrants of Boston to choose sides in the coming cataclysm. A classic "Hobson's Choice" that many supposed could only lead to Union Irishmen being ordered to slaughter their compatriots clad in Confederate gray.

CHAPTER FOUR

The *Joseph Henry*, *Sylph*, and *Vesper*

By 1860 the Irish had established a wide industrial network at Boston. The fishermen formed a nucleus at the center of a cluster of schooner owners and wholesale and retail fish dealers. An outer ring of service industries radiated from this inner core: auctioneers, brokers, fish peddlers, draymen, hostlers, icemen, handcartmen, grocers, shipbuilders, joiners, carpenters, caulkers, chandlers, sailmakers, foundrymen, ropewalkmen, surveyors, insurers, and bankers, as well as the merchants who purveyed the diverse wants of this corps of traders and craftsmen, and the cafes and saloons that nurtured and soused them. The McManuses, through their sailmaking skills, the beginnings

---

The steep seas that arose on the relatively shallow banks could mean death for a clipper-style fishing schooner. A vessel "tripped" by a wave astern might drive its bow under and roll—like the one illustrated here—and the wide, shallow hull did not have enough resistance to counterbalance the weight of the rig and bring the vessel upright again. Drawn by H.W. Elliott and Joseph W. Collins. (Goode, *Fisheries and Fishery Industries of the U.S.* (1887), sect. 5, plate 13)

of the family vessel-outfitting business, and, most consequentially, the ownership of fishing schooners, played a key role in the early stages of this developing socio-economic phenomenon. The story of the Fingal families as a whole became one of an Irish "niche" in Boston society, reaching well beyond its own community, not that of a tight, inward-facing Irish enclave.

The pale gold sunshine of 8 February 1860, a surprisingly mild midwinter day, provided fitting ambience for an event that illuminated the growing prosperity of the immigrants from County Dublin. From his yard on Darton's Wharf at the foot of Lexington Street in East Boston, Wilbur Laskey took advantage of the spring-like conditions to launch the forty-seven-foot *Mary Frances* for co-owners Captain Jim Herbert and Dick Leonard.[1] With a name honoring her skipper's daughter, she was the newest schooner to join the Irish market fleet.

As the Fingalians' preferred builder, Laskey constructed eleven of the twenty new fishing vessels delivered to that fishery in the seventeen months between June 1859 and October 1860 (detailed in Table 2), a prodigious production for a small shipbuilding firm. Through the late 1860s, notwithstanding that the Civil War halted new fishing vessel construction, between them Laskey,[2] his brother Charles A. Laskey,[3] and their master carpenter John A. McPhail,[4] built more than a score of schooners for the Irishmen. The yard's next launch, a fifty-one-footer that slid into the waters of Boston Harbor several weeks later, was a smack with a difference. John H. McManus had recognized that the shallow draft of the clipper hull contributed heavily to its high loss rate. He concluded that Irish schooners, the familiar Skerries wherries of his youth and early sailmaking career, were safer platforms for fishermen than contemporary clippers. Drawing on their familiarity with the Irish model, he and his partner in the *Black Hawk*, brother-in-law Dick Leonard, initiated a trend to deeper draft as soon as they began to fund their own construction. Their schooner *Joseph Henry*, named for the Leonards' four-year-old son,[5] was the first new vessel of more than fifty feet to enter the fleet. At forty-two tons she was the largest of the prewar new construction, principally because of her increased depth of six feet two inches. A clipper schooner of the

---

[1] Enrolment No. 7, Boston and Charlestown, 10 February 1860, U.S. Consolidated Enrolment and Licenses, Bureau of Navigation, Record Group 41, Records of the Department of Commerce, NARA.

[2] Wilbur Laskey, born in Lubec, Maine, died on 18 March 1889, at his 257 Princeton Street, East Boston residence, when he was two weeks short of his seventy-fifth birthday. His active shipbuilding practice spanned four decades, 1855-85.

[3] Charles A. Laskey had tried his boatbuilding fortunes in Maryland before joining his brother in Boston during the late 1850s. A third brother, Stephen, worked with the firm but disappeared from the East Boston waterfront in the mid-1860s.

[4] McPhail, a former Boston harbor pilot, also joined forces with Wilbur Laskey in the late 1850s. He moved into the Boston waterfront and became a partner in the firm of Jordan & McPhail in the 1870s.

[5] Enrolment No. 45, Boston and Charlestown, 20 April 1860.

same length typically had a depth of five feet or less. The following month McManus and Leonard sold the *Black Hawk* to brother-in-law Bill Montross.[6] Dick also sold the *Two Brothers* to Tim Mahoney.[7] The Leonard-McManus combination thereby added two more crews to the Irish fleet about to enter the summer market fishery. In July another East Boston builder, Amos Cutter, delivered the third of the family's 1860-built schooners, the *T. Herbert*, to Tom Herbert in time for the peak of the season.[8] Tom also retained ownership of the *Moby Dick* and sent her out under the command of Peter Rickard, a fellow Fingalian from Rush.

their households. When the tallymen climbed the steps of the tenement at 435 Commercial Street they found nine occupants: John H. and Meg McManus, with their sons, Charley, Tom, and baby George, John H.'s widowed mother, Annie, two journeymen sailmakers who worked in the McManus loft, and an Irish maid from Galway. Their worksheet noted that John H. admitted to assets of an unmistakably fixed nature. He claimed his net worth was only $60 and, with the tabulation taking place just three months after his half-share of the *Joseph Henry* had been paid to Wilbur Laskey, his estimated cash on hand might not have been far off,[9] although the canny McManus was never one to expose his mounting personal wealth to officialdom.

Next door, at No. 433, Dick Leonard, the other half-owner of the *Joseph Henry*, and half of the *Mary Frances*, shared personal assets of $500 with his wife, Kate McManus, who was pregnant again.[10] Their surviving sons, Joe and Charley, and Dick's eighteen-year-old sister Ellen, who kept house for Kate, resided with them.

In the next block, at No. 502, the census takers found Chris Leonard hard at work in his thriving saloon, which functioned as the neighborhood men's club. Leonard had succeeded in the face of overwhelming odds: by this time the Boston metropolitan area had a liquor dealer for every eighty men, women, and children.[11] The enumerator valued his real estate at $2,000, most notably including the building housing his family and business, and his personal assets at $3,000, most of which he was about to invest in the purchase of the building next door at No. 500. His wife Julia, with sons Nick and Tom, and daughters Mary and Em'ly, lived in handsome style for the North End; they were the tenement's sole occupants, and a nanny looked after the children while Julia ran the grocery and Chris served up ale and spirits in the groggery.[12] Soon after the tabulators departed, Julia took a few days off during the humid heat of July to give birth to a son whom they named after Chris.[13]

The census takers further reported that Tom Herbert owned a home around the corner from the others at 19 Tileston Street, and acknowledged $500 in personal assets. He and his wife, Elizabeth McGinnis, shared the house with their

---

[9] 1860 U.S. Census, Suffolk County, Massachusetts (Ward 1), M653, roll 520, page 418, 1664/3269, NARA.

[10] Kate McManus bore a daughter, Ellen, on 4 March 1861 at 433 Commercial Street (Vital Records 1841-1895, Massachusetts State Archives, *Births*, 1861, vol. 143, page 12, line 513).

[11] Roger Lane, *Policing the City: Boston, 1822-1885* (Cambridge, Massachusetts: Harvard University Press, 1967), 111. 2,220 liquor dispensers served Boston's 177,902 inhabitants.

[12] 1860 Census, roll 520, page 263.

daughter Peggy, two sons, Johnny and Jimmy, and a young Dubliner named Johnny O'Brien, who would become famous along the Boston waterfront in the 1880s as the skipper of the race-winning schooner *John H. McManus*.[14]

Then, five days before Christmas, a tremor foreboding the coming cataclysm shook the nation: South Carolina seceded from the Union. In the northeast the war years began with unfamiliar weather for Bostonians, a quixotic system in direct contrast to the steady, pervasive cold of the 1850s' record-breaking winters. A fickle 1861 front wrenched the mercury in local thermometers as never before: The *Traveller's* thermometer climbed to +46°F. at 1:00 P.M. on 7 February, but by the next morning it had plunged 60 degrees to -14°F. at sunrise, the lowest point reached in this thermometer's history since its acquisition in 1824. The rapid drop almost matched the subsequent climb of 74° during the following 79 hours to 60°F. at 2:00 P.M. on the eleventh.[15] But neither the vicissitudes of the climate, the Republicans' political ascendancy, nor the advent of the Civil War, halted the climbing fortunes of the Fingal fishermen.

A month after the war began, Louis, John H.'s fourth son, arrived in that male-dominated household on May seventh. Father Donahoe baptized him at St. John's, when his Uncle Pat and Aunt Kate presented their new nephew for the sacramental rite on the twenty-sixth.[16] His parents earmarked Louis for the Catholic priesthood inasmuch as, even at this early stage of their lives, it was clear that fishing schooners rather than sacred relics fascinated seven-year-old Charley, and Tom, now five and a half.

Well before they reached school age, John H. had begun taking the boys on his weekly jaunts to the shipbuilding sites scattered about the shores of Boston Harbor. On Sundays they traveled on either the East Boston or People's Ferry to visit the yards of East Boston and Chelsea, or to Wood Island Park to sail their hand-carved schooner models.[17] In adulthood, Tom recalled a typical Sabbath with his father: "he took great pleasure in taking my brothers and I around to the different ship yards, which were numerous in those days and he would explain to us the interesting points in the construction of the many vessels of various designs and plans." Through the war years John H. McManus formed a preference for Dennison J. Lawlor's establishment at Chelsea. Born of a Canadian father and an Irish mother

---

[13] Vital Records, *Births*, 1860, vol. 134, page 63, line 2831.

[14] 1860 U.S. Census, Suffolk County, Massachusetts (Ward 1), M653, roll 520, page 223, 894/1734.

[15] David M. Ludlum, *The Early American Winters II, 1821-1870* (Boston: American Meteorological Society, 1968), 67.

[16] St. John the Baptist/St. Stephen's, *Baptisms*, vol. 3 (1854-1862), page 402; *Births*, 1861, vol. 143, page 12, line 514.

[17] Charlton L. Smith, draft version of an 10 April 1922, Boston *Evening Transcript* article, enclosed in a letter from Smith to McManus, 11 April 1922, hereafter "Smith, draft article." Wood Island Park now lies under the runways of Logan International Airport.

at Saint John, New Brunswick, in 1822,[18] Lawlor emigrated to Boston at age twenty-one. A temperamental and exacting genius, Lawlor designed some of the finest pilot boats and fishermen ever to sail New England waters.[19] When he married Caroline E. Littlefield at Cambridge in 1847,[20] the Reverend S. Streeter referred to him as Dennis Joseph Lawlor, a mistake that stoked the naval architect's high-strung temper and caused him to shout: "My name is *Dennison* J. Lawlor."[21] The Canadian migrant's Buck's Wharf shipyard became the kindergarten of schooner technology for the McManus boys.

Throughout their youth, literally from the time they started to walk and talk, John H. saw to it that his sons gained every opportunity to master the arts of hull form and sail shape, whether on shipyard trips, during their waterfront carousing, or on those memorable occasions when he allowed them to sail on a day trip with the fishermen. Both lads had already begun to display the same uncanny sense of the interaction between sails, hull, wind, and water that their father possessed.

Eighteen sixty-three brought good fortune to the Bill Montrosses. Mary had not only recovered her normally happy mien, but also announced to Bill that she was pregnant again. With the accumulated profits from three years of fishing on board the *Black Hawk*, he purchased a second smack, the *Cygnet*,[22] an eighteen-year-old, twenty-eight-tonner. When Mary gave birth to a healthy little girl in July, he felt that they had shaken off the bad luck that had dogged their sixteen-year marriage. They named the baby Catherine after Mary's sister, Kate Leonard, but thereafter always called her Kitty.

Many of the fishermen served in the Union Navy, and several failed to return. The ownership documents of their vessels often bear a notation similar to the one that appears on the papers of the venerable schooner *Elizabeth*, which had first joined the fleet in 1853: "Cornelius Cadigan–now absent [and never to return]."[23] The Irish inhabitants of the North End and Fort Hill districts, no strangers to disaster and death, stoically accepted their losses.

---

[18] Vital Records 1841-1895, Massachusetts State Archives, *Deaths*, 1892, vol. 429, page 493, line 2.

[19] Howard I. Chapelle, *American Sailing Craft* (New York: Kennedy Brothers, 1936), 222.

[20] Vital Records 1841-1895, Massachusetts State Archives, *Marriages*, 1846-1847, vol. 25, page 11.

[21] W.P. Stephens, *Traditions and Memories of American Yachting* (1939-46; rev. ed., Brooklin, Maine: WoodenBoat Publications, Inc., 1989), 196.

[22] Enrolment No. 122, Boston and Charlestown, 9 May 1863.

[23] Edward Quinn and Rudolph G. Fogg (a Yankee shipmaster who ran a shipping office at 120 Commercial Street and invested in schooner ownership [City of Boston, Tax Assessor's Records, Ward 2, May 1850]) purchased the 1835 Essex-built *Elizabeth* in 1853 (Enrolment No. 123, Boston and Charlestown, 5 July 1853); Daniel Mahoney bought out Quinn four months later (Enrolment No. 187, Boston and Charlestown, 7 September 1853); over a year Timothy Santry bought out

In the McManus household, as their second son passed the age of reason, John H.'s Sunday tutorials had already launched his son's professional education, introducing him to the man who was to have a lifelong influence on his creative thinking. Tom later recalled his youthful awe: "many times we had in our Company the late D.J. Lawlor one of the greatest Naval Designers in this part of the Country." Young McManus listened carefully during those Sabbath sessions, for he "liked to hear them discuss the different shapes of hulls and the construction of same." It would be Lawlor's combination of creative genius and mechanical skill that shaped the keel into which the framework of Tom's future career as a naval architect was rabbeted. Beginning in the mid-1860s, John H.'s arrangement with Lawlor became more formal, and the architect began tutoring Tom on school holidays and weekends. Charley, his own spark of brilliance being carefully nurtured, underwent a similar regimen as an apprentice to his father at the McManus sail loft. At the time of an 1864 incident, Tom had been visiting the shipyards for at least four years: "When I was eight years old I was with my father when he was discussing with Mr. Lawlor on a wooden model of a boat that he was about to build for him her name was the schooner *Sylph* and at the same time he built the famous Pilot Boat *Edwin Forrest* their lines were extremely hollow and both boats were very fast in those days, after school hours many a time I visited Lawlor's yard, and watched him get out many of his designs a privilege he granted to very few."[24]

Surprisingly, at that early age Tom understood the difference between an artisan and architect, even if they were embodied in the same person: "Lawlor was a scientific mechanic as well as a designer, every joint would have to be a cabinet one, otherwise he would condemn it." Young McManus demonstrated an awareness of adult personality traits when he realized that Lawlor "would have to have great confidence in you before he would express himself."[25]

Mahoney (Enrolment No. 315, Boston and Charlestown, 7 December 1854); Fogg finally gave up his interest to John Hickey in 1857 (Enrolment No. 36, Boston and Charlestown, 8 April 1857); but three days later Santry sold his interest to Timothy Driscoll (Enrolment No. 40, Boston and Charlestown, 11 April 1857); then, six months later, Hickey sold his share to Patrick O'Donnell (Enrolment No. 228, Boston and Charlestown, 27 November 1857); just two months later Cornelius Cadigan bought the entire vessel (Enrolment No. 17, Boston and Charlestown, 8 February 1858); then, sadly, ownership accrued to his brother, Patrick Cadigan, when Cornelius died in the Union service (Enrolment No. 155, Boston and Charlestown, 10 May 1865). The much-traveled *Elizabeth* is a typical example of the multiplicity of ownership transfers that built the Irish market fleet at Boston.

[24] Thomas F. McManus, "Autobiographical Essay No. 1." Lawlor also started the *Mary Y. Yates* about this time for Pat Connor and Pat O'Connor; *Hibernia* for the triumvirate of Peter Scofield, John Flaherty, and Lawrence Mullen; and the *Thomas E. Evans* for John Evans, who hired Tom McLaughlin as his skipper. For *Sylph* see Enrolment No. 173, Boston and Charlestown, 24 May 1865; for *Mary Y. Yates* see No. 407, 25 November 1865; for *Hibernia* see No. 3, 2 January 1866; for *Thomas E. Evans* see No. 69, 14 April 1866.

[25] McManus, "Essay No. 1."

Tom and Charley habitually played their childhood games around the North End waterfront and, on many days after school hours, ran errands along the wharves for the family sailmaking company. The fishermen, exhibiting the Irishman's remarkably inexhaustible patience with the young, openheartedly adopted them and delighted in "teaching them the ropes," while willingly answering their interminable questions. Always attentive youngsters, the boys never wore out their welcome on the wharves. Both became keen observers of all the vessels in the harbor, although Charley tended to devote his attention to the sails, masts, and spars, while the myriad hull shapes to be seen captured Tom's interest, marking the beginning of his lifelong fascination with their form. Something of a child prodigy, at an early age he was able to match his father's widely acknowledged ability as a whittler.[26] This eye-to-hand coordination, which allowed him to recreate the hull shapes he had observed in scale models, is an essential talent for a naval architect. Charley, to his parents disappointment, displayed no interest in formal education. Other than sail shapes and fishing techniques, he was little given to studying; as a result, John H. and Meg let him to go to sea with the fishing fleet in his early teens, but resolved that their other sons would complete their education. Tom, after two years of primary school, began classes at Eliot Grammar School on North Bennet Street in September 1864.

Spring and summer that year were eventful for the immigrants as many of the Fingal families neared their second decade in the United States. Meg McManus delivered Joseph, John H.'s fifth son, in a new flat across the street at 438 Commercial on April thirteenth.[27] Spurred by his increasing financial strength, Chris Leonard purchased the little 1859-built fishing smack *Eclipse* for daughter Mary Ellen,[28] thereby providing his twelve-year-old with a remarkable dowry.

Although the fishermen suffered losses as a direct result of the war, in a broader picture the passing years as the McManus boys grew to adulthood, 1855-85, were unmatched in terms of catastrophic casualties suffered by New England fleets for quite another reason. By the 1830s the double-ended, schooner-rigged pinky, a very seaworthy craft, had become the predominant vessel type working the fisheries. Ports in Maine, Massachusetts, and Nova Scotia built scores of these popular fishermen.[29] Then, during the 1840s, the sharpshooter–a hull with a long, straight run of keel, and a schooner rig without jibboom or fore-topmast–gradually replaced the pinkies. In the next decade, as the sharpshooter evolved into the swift

---

[26] Captain Charlton L. Smith, "The First Fishermen's Race," *Yachting* (January 1939), 64.

[27] *Births*, 1864, vol. 170, page 23, line 969.

[28] Enrolment No. 175, Boston and Charlestown, 18 June 1864.

[29] Howard I. Chapelle, *The American Fishing Schooners 1825-1925* (New York: W.W. Norton, 1973), 45-57.

clipper, its hull shape grew in length and beam, but without a corresponding increase in draft, and the fleet's mortality figures began their steep climb through the second half of the nineteenth-century. Although inappropriate design led the way to Davy Jones locker, there were several other significant factors contributing to losses of ships and men. Winter fishing on the banks became a way of life–and of death. The 1855-65 changeover from hand-lining on deck to dorymen fishing with trawl-lines provided an abundance of new ways for fishermen to meet their Maker. The attendant increase in winter fishing, too, put fishermen at sea in the most extreme conditions.

Concurrently, by mid-century the nation's technological advances led to a significantly increased marketplace,[30] and the search for sailing speed became paramount to an industry facing the pleasing prospect of a steadily increasing demand for seafood. The wide-ranging expansion of the fisheries, particularly at the port of Gloucester, led to larger and faster vessels, which also raised the capital investment stakes. The resultant breed of clipper schooners were rakish, carried immense sail plans, and possessed great speed, an important quality in vessels racing fish products to market.

At the end of the Civil War, with the transition from sharpshooter to full-blown clipper reaching completion, the Essex-model schooner became the pattern for the fleet: full-bilged, flat-floored, shallow draft, with a deep forefoot below a short full clipper bow, and with negligible, if any, drag in the keel. "Drag" is the difference in depth between the forward end of the keel at the stem and its other extreme at the sternpost. Drag facilitates helm response and is a controlling factor in the ability of a sail-powered vessel to tack, *i.e.*, shift the bow across the wind to alter course. A clipper's long, horizontal keel helped it sail fast and straight, but limited its maneuverability. In the Skerries wherries, as well as American pilot schooners, and other vessels (including the Irish market schooners), the keel sloped to its deepest point at the sternpost, increasing stability through depth and

---

30 Congress passed the enabling legislation for the new Anglo-American Reciprocity Treaty on 3 August 1854. This treaty succeeded the earlier ones with Great Britain: the Treaty of Paris of 1783, after the American Revolution, and the Convention of 20 October 1818, a codicil to the Treaty of Ghent of 1815, following the War of 1812. The convention of 1818 was considerably more restrictive to American fishing interests than the earlier treaty, permitting American and Canadian fishermen to work inside the three-mile limit of each country's coastal boundary (Raymond McFarland, *A History of the New England Fisheries* (New York: D. Appleton and Company, 1911), 321-326). This legislation initiated a robust period of growth for the New England fishing industry by allowing American vessels access to Canadian bays that teemed with fish, and permitting the free import of Newfoundland herring, an essential bait fish for the New Englanders. On the negative side, the treaty allowed cheap Canadian fish into American retailers in direct competition with the domestic catch (Samuel Eliot Morison, *Maritime History of Massachusetts, 1783-1860* (1921; reprint Boston: Northeastern University Press, 1979), 312); nevertheless, it worked well until post-Civil War inflation in the United States eventually upset the international economic balance. The technological advances of machine-made ice, and the growing national railway network abetted the treaty in feeding the growth of the American industry.

increasing maneuverability through relative decrease of lateral resistance at the bow. The clipper shape, with its long straight run of keel and exaggerated top hamper, had reasonable stability, up to a critical point–but was dangerously top-heavy in squally winds and rough seas, and highly susceptible to icing–thus tending to capsize suddenly, or swamp in stormy conditions. These shortcomings, when combined with the winter fishing season's harsh North Atlantic weather, amounted to a recipe for disaster. The swift clipper hulls, with towering masts driven to the breaking point by immense spreads of canvas, but lacking the stability offered by the counterbalance of a deeper draft, simply were not equal to the conditions they now had to face.

From his earliest comprehension of naval architecture, Tom McManus believed that the clipper's design failings caused the loss of many of his boyhood heroes–the Irish fishermen of the North End wharves who had schooled him on board their vessels. He once described the dangers of working along the bowsprit:

> I was in the fish business and knew all the captains. My father was a sailmaker. Because I knew all these people, I was observant about different parts of the boats and noticed where improvements were needed.
>
> I often looked at the footrope [slung under the bowsprit]–the rope the men stand on to take in the jib–and sometimes in rough weather, the rope was covered with thick ice. The men, bundled in their awkward oilskins, often lost their footing and were swept into the sea.[31]

Those human losses provided the determination that grew within McManus to find a way to entirely eliminate that dangerous spar.

Contemporary observers and twentieth-century historians have contended that as a result of the craving for speed, there was little safety advance in naval architectural convention during the deadly decades that the clipper schooner dominated the New England fishing fleet. No less a figure than the crusading Captain Joseph W. Collins, wrote, "the attempted improvements after 1855 can scarcely be considered advantageous, for the tendency was to increase the size of the

---

31 Boston *Evening Transcript*, 14 March 1936.

vessel chiefly by making them longer and wider, while little was added to their depth."[32]

And no one has translated the stability factor of a sail-powered vessel into lay terms better than Joseph E. Garland, a respected chronicler of the Gloucester fishing fleet, who stated simply: "if one adheres to common sense, the more she tips, the more she wants to right herself."[33] The fashionable shallow-draft hulls diametrically opposed Garland's corollary: the more they rolled, the more they wanted to roll over, and their over-sparred and over-canvassed sail plans magnified this instability, leading to the era's horrendous loss of life.

That the clipper-model schooner dominated the fleet, there can be no doubt, but it did not do so without a significant development pattern, or competing hull shapes. In the inventive field of naval architecture there is nothing to equal the search for speed to fertilize the evolution of design.[34] Contrary to Collins's contention of a singular trend to ever-shallower length/depth ratios, those tragic years did witness the development of a few schooners with deeper hulls.

John H. McManus and his Fingal cohort were early proponents of the architectural changes that eventually led to safer schooners. The family leader manifested a deep concern for the lives of his relatives, neighbors, and clients, a quality he bred into his sons. The performance of the experimentally deeper-draft *Joseph Henry*, built with the Skerries wherry in mind, had proved highly satisfactory. Financed by the profits from the sale of the *Black Hawk*, he and Dick Leonard decided to introduce an even safer and more innovative hull model into the New England fisheries. To design and build the new schooner, not surprisingly, they tapped the genius of Dennison J. Lawlor.

The partners also planned a quiet introduction of European beam-trawl technology into the local fleet. Beam trawling–dragging a net bag, held open with a beam across the mouth, along the sea floor to sweep up fish–had become the principal bottom fishing method in the British Isles by 1860, but Americans had been slow to adopt the method. Leonard made a clandestine trip to Ireland in search of the specialized trawling equipment near the close of 1864. The naval war in the North Atlantic had been winding down for some time, and he safely crossed

---

[32] Captain Joseph William Collins, "Evolution of the American Fishing Schooner," *New England Magazine* (May 1898): 346-47. According to Dr. Dean Allard, the biographer of Spencer F. Baird, the driving force behind the formation of the U.S. Fish Commission, and its first Commissioner, Collins was Baird's right-hand man in the area of aid to the fishing industry. The Commissions efforts were directed into three areas: science, fish culture, and industry support (Dean Conrad Allard, Jr., *Spencer Fullerton Baird and the U.S. Fish Commission, a Study in the History of American Science* [Washington, D.C.: George Washington University, 1967]).

[33] Joseph E. Garland, *Down to the Sea, The Fishing Schooners of Gloucester* (Boston: David R. Godine, 1983), 18.

[34] Chapelle argued this point convincingly in *Fishing Schooners*, 76-152, and *Speed Under Sail*.

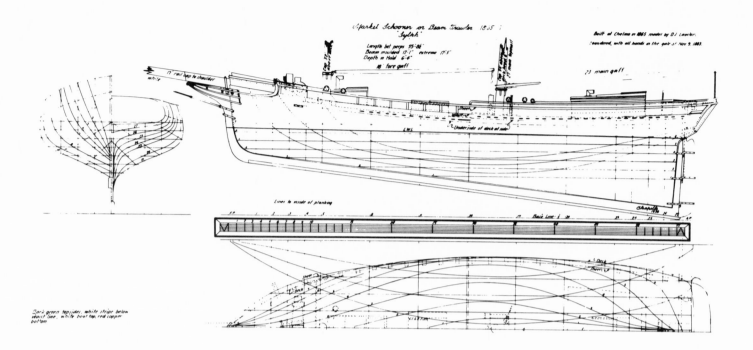

The 30-ton schooner *Sylph* (55.8 x 17.5 x 6.4 feet), designed by D.J. Lawlor with marked drag to her keel, was a distinct contrast to the prevailing clipper schooner design, which had the keel approximately parallel to the waterline. Lines drawn by Howard I. Chapelle, 1938, from the builder's half model. (Plan AFS 36, Smithsonian Institution)

the ocean to Dublin, where he purchased three large trawling rigs, including one with an enormous fifty-foot beam, for transportation back to Boston.[35] During this time John H. worked closely with Lawlor on the design of the new schooner, and then superintended her construction at his Buck's Wharf yard.

In the world beyond Boston's waterfront, General Robert E. Lee handed his sword to General Ulysses S. Grant at Appomattox Court House in Virginia on Sunday, April ninth, surrendered the Confederate Army of Northern Virginia, ensuring the end of the Civil War. The Union forces had achieved victory, and the country began a frenzy of rejoicing over the termination of the bloodiest conflict in its history. A mere five days later, at 10:00 P.M. on the fourteenth, that joy turned to nationwide despondency when John Wilkes Booth shot President Abraham Lincoln at Ford's Theater in Washington, D.C. Although the president's assassination shocked the entire United States, nowhere was the loss more poignantly felt than in abolitionist Massachusetts. In its aftermath, with thoroughly mixed emotions, the New England fishermen set about rebuilding their war-decimated fleet.

---

[35] Captain Joseph W. Collins, "Attempts to Use the Beam-Trawl in the Fisheries of the United States," *Bulletin of the United States Fish Commission* 7 (Washington, D.C.: Government Printing Office, 1887): 400-401.

Five weeks after Lincoln's death, Meg McManus and Kate Leonard christened their husbands' new schooner *Sylph* at Chelsea.[36] On the day of the launch no one was more caught up in Lawlor's expert technique than young Tom McManus, who stood on Bucks Wharf throughout the tricky evolution. The designer-builder faced the task of propelling the nearly eighteen-feet-wide *Sylph* sideways into his granite-lined fitting-out slip, which was not quite a foot wider than the schooner herself. Tom recounted Lawlor's masterful performance: "as a boy I remember hearing different men saying she would crush in her sides as she had to be launched on her side." But as he recalled in old age, "it was as pretty a launching as I ever saw," and by then he had seen quite a number: "He put her in such an angle to the water, she made a cushion of it and did not touch either side." The builder's belief in his own craftsmanship made its mark. Tom recognized that, "he knew what he could do and did it."[37] It was a profound lesson for an eight-year-old. Throughout his career, Tom McManus exuded the confidence born from trusting in his own capabilities.

The *Sylph* was the fourth new postwar schooner to enter the Irish fleet.[38] She was 55.8 feet between perpendiculars (about 60 feet overall), with a beam of 17.5 feet, a hold depth of 6.4 feet–but an almost-10-foot draft right aft–and under the new tonnage law passed by Congress in 1864 she measured 30.24 tons. Lawlor complied with John H.'s wishes and modeled the schooner without the traditional heavy figurehead, a practice that became a McManus custom.

On the *Sylph*'s maiden voyage with Dick Leonard at the helm, John H. deployed the trawl rig with the fifty-foot beam in ten to twenty fathoms of water off Cape Cod.[39] Under his guidance the men set the trawl five times, but the principal catch was flounder, a fish with little market value in those days. In an interview by Captain Collins twenty years later, he succinctly explained why the plan was thrown over: "the crew of the *Sylph*, being all poor men . . . could not afford to continue the trials."[40] Although McManus and Leonard thought that the foot-line they used to hold the mouth of the net on the bottom might not have been heavy enough, they concluded that the rig could not be used to good advantage north of

---

[36] Dennison J. Lawlor donated his lift and fully-rigged models of the *Sylph* to the Smithsonian Institution, USNM Nos. 76036 and 76241 (Howard I. Chapelle, *The National Watercraft Collection* (Washington, D.C.: Government Printing Office, 1960), 201-202).

[37] McManus, "Essay No. 1."

[38] Enrolment No. 173, Boston and Charlestown, 24 May 1865. The first postwar schooners were the *Willie Erdix*, owned by Bill Hooton and operated by Bartholomew "Bat" Whalen (5 May); *Fenian*, jointly owned by Bill Hooton and Joe Everdean (6 May); and *Young America*, jointly owned by Jack Quinn and Andy Manning (12 May).

[39] *Sylph* was the first American beam-trawler, not the ketch-rigged *Resolute* of 1891.

[40] Collins, "Attempts to Use the Beam-Trawl in the Fisheries of the United States," 400-401.

Cape Cod, and sold their beam-trawl outfits to a group in Virginia. Although she failed as a beam trawler, the *Sylph* was a most successful schooner. Her innovative hull lines included a marked increase in deadrise and a keel with a distinct amount of drag,[41] notably reminiscent of a Skerries wherry. But, unlike the bluff bows of her Irish ancestor, the *Sylph*'s entry was Lawlor's own concept–as in his pilot boats, it

This period model of the *Sylph* shows her rigged for market fishing. She has a big rig—notice her long, overhanging main boom—but a removable bonnet on the foot of the jib, and two bands of reef points on the fore- and mainsail, allow her to "shorten down" for winter gales at sea. (Neg. 31221, Smithsonian Institution)

---

[41] "Deadrise" is a term indicative of the included angle between the sloping bottom of the hull from the keel to the turn of the bilge, and a horizontal plane along the vessel's centerline. A modern "deep-vee" bottom configuration has a deadrise in excess of twenty degrees.

was hollow.[42] In a misinterpretation of nature's design technology, as evinced by the duck, he built the *Sylph* with a concave entry. Lawlor's "duck theory" was hotly disputed by the McManuses but, as Tom remarked in a masterpiece of understatement in 1904, the designer "was a very positive man." Lawlor held that if "the duck wanted to make speed it stretched its neck in the water," contending that "when it extended its neck, the neck hollowed on both sides."

John H. disagreed vehemently, maintaining "that there were no such curves, but that, on the contrary, the neck swelled, bringing the point of resistance nearer to the head." According to Tom the argument lasted for years, until Lawlor's son went to England where "he visited a large aquarium in which there were a number of ducks in a glass tank, so that their movements could be observed from below." Young Lawlor watched in astonishment when the ducks were startled into motion. As they stretched out to gain speed, their necks did not curve inward, but bulged outward. Dismayed, but possessed of honest gumption, he immediately wrote to his father, stating: "McManus is right!"[43]

Years later, in 1897, Tom McManus authenticated the accuracy of his father's empirical thesis when his new pilot boat design, *America*, *sans* hollow bows, replaced Lawlor's hallowed, but hollowed, *Hesper* as the Massachusetts Bay trial horse.[44]

Fishing Vessel	Commissioned	Length in ft.	Tonnage (new measure)
Willie Erdix	May 5, 1865	55.1	35.27
Fenian	May 6, 1865	57.9	34.38
Young America	May 12, 1865	58.0	31.97
Sylph	May 24, 1865	57.1	30.24
Flying Eagle	October 26, 1865	49.6	23.87
Mary Y. Yates	November 25, 1865	50.9	25.26
Saint Michael	November 28, 1865	53.9	28.24
Eva G.	December 2, 1865	50.8	21.82
Saint Peter	December 14, 1865	50.0	23.61
Hibernia	January 2, 1866	50.3	24.76
Charles A. Laskey	January 11, 1866	51.0	21.21
Abbie J.	February 5, 1866	55.5	33.70
Margaret A. Jones	April 13, 1866	52.4	24.83
Thomas E. Evans	April 14, 1866	56.5	29.39
Morning Star	September 8, 1866	52.6	22.54

TABLE 3 - IRISH MARKET SCHOONERS BUILT 1865-66

---

[42] During his career Lawlor designed and built several noted pilot boats including the *Dancing Feather*, *Edwin Forrest*, *Florence*, *Phantom*, *Lillie*, and *Hesper*.

[43] "Designer of Flying Fishermen," *The Boston Herald*, 1904.

[44] Chapelle, *American Sailing Craft*, 231.

After her late-summer beam-trawl experiment, Leonard and McManus sent the *Sylph* out as a market boat in company with their *Joseph Henry* for the winter fishery. The schooner excelled in this calling due to her remarkable speed and maneuverability. Table 3 demonstrates that the *Sylph*, in fact, was larger than two-thirds of the new fishing vessels delivered to the Irish market fleet during 1865 and 1866. These data indicate the optimum size the market fishermen decided upon, and confirm that the Fingal immigrants continued in the market fishery at this time. Although the new vessels of 1865-66 averaged five feet longer than the 1859-60 lot, the Irish had yet to embark upon the acquisition of the larger vessels necessary for fishing on the distant Grand Banks.

The first postwar winter season in the market fishery found the family members well-prepared. The *Cygnet*, which Bill Montross had purchased three years earlier, joined the *Sylph* and *Joseph Henry*. Chris Leonard fitted out daughter Mary Ellen's forty-five-foot *Eclipse*. Tom Herbert successfully negotiated the purchase of the thirty-year-old, forty-nine-foot *Ellen*, and outfitted her to join his *T. Herbert* and the others for the season. Despite their buoyant fishing prosperity, the Irish schooner owners, including Tom Herbert, Bill Montross, and Dick Leonard, who spent most of their time at sea, still engaged in other occupations. The time drew near, however, when Herbert, Montross, and Leonard would give up the sea and join John H. McManus and Chris Leonard as shore-based entrepreneurs.

Along the waterfront, the postwar boom experienced by the American fishing industry was not without its industrial depressions. For the Fingal Irish immigrants in particular, a familiar Old World specter came back to haunt them during July 1866, when Congress repealed the codfishing bounty that had been in effect since 1819. The codfishermen were granted the right of duty-free purchase of salt in its place, an inequitable exchange. The old act had required that the smacks sail in the codfishery at least four months each year, and also established the traditional manner in which the individual fishermen earned their wages:

Compensation to fishermen for their service must be by division of fish, or share in the proceeds of the sale of fish; *no person except the cook could receive wages.* The master and three-fourths of the crew must be citizens of the United States. Fishing vessels had to be examined by an inspector as to their seaworthiness, their equipment, and the number and nationality of the crew before sailing on a voyage on which allowances were to be paid. A regular log-book had to be kept on board day by day, setting forth the principal events of the voyage, which later was submitted to the collector of the home port.

The [bounty] allowance to any one vessel during the season, regardless of her tonnage, should not exceed three hundred and sixty dollars.[45]

Following the loss of the bounties, an event of even greater consequence to the New England fishermen occurred when the Anglo-American Reciprocity Treaty of 1854, which had allowed Americans to fish within the three-mile limit of Canadian waters, expired. Regulation of fishing rights in Canadian waters returned to the narrow provisions of the Convention of 1818, which restricted American fishing to a few designated coasts, to land on some uninhabited shores to dry nets and cure fish, and to call at Canadian ports only to obtain shelter, wood, and water, or to make repairs.[46] For several years to come Americans working on Canadian fishing grounds would generate diplomatic friction between Great Britain and the United States, despite the complaisant policy taken up by the provincial authorities of granting inshore licenses to the New Englanders, after the expiration of the treaty.

Yet, despite the loss of the bounties, and of access to the valuable Canadian inshore fisheries, the years from 1866 to 1885 witnessed widespread prosperity for the Americans who harvested the Atlantic Ocean's three most valuable species: cod, herring, and mackerel. The only marked difference to the previous decades, 1845-65, was a decline in the total vessel tonnage of the New England fisheries, a trend that would continue into the twentieth century.

John H. McManus, who came to the United States in 1846 and died here forty-five years later, lived out his American years during those prosperous times. At the middle of life in his adopted land, July 1866, the prosperous sailmaker started taking Meg and the boys to a little port on Boston's south shore for summertime vacations. To anyone who has seen both Scituate, Massachusetts, and Skerries, County Dublin, their similarity is striking. The local shore of Massachusetts Bay is a near mirror image of the Irish sea coast north of Dublin Bay. John H. inaugurated a seven-decade family tradition that summer, which Tom carried on throughout his

---

[45] McFarland, *New England Fisheries*, 162-63, citing Lorenzo Sabine, *Report on the Principal Fisheries of the American Seas* (Washington, D.C.: Government Printing Office, 1852, vol. III, no. 23, 32nd Congress, 2nd Session), 166-69, emphasis added.

[46] Allard, *Spencer Fullerton Baird*, 182. The licenses initially allowed any American fisherman who paid a fee of fifty cents per ton of his vessel to continue to enjoy the provisions of the Reciprocity Treaty: "the fee was nominal, intended only to show that there was a privilege which had to be purchased and not a right to be demanded" (Lester Burrell Shippee, *Canadian-American Relations, 1849-1874* (New Haven: Connecticut: Yale University Press, 1939), 263). After 1 July 1867, the license fee went up to a dollar, but the leeway created by allowing an American vessel caught fishing in restricted Canadian waters without a license to receive three warnings before seizure rendered enforcement ineffectual. In 1868 the fee was raised to two dollars per ton and the warnings concession reduced to a single instance of poaching. The situation intensified through to January 1870, when Canadian authorities ultimately refused to renew the licenses.

own married life.[47] The following year the family reached a consequential landmark in Boston when John H. purchased the first home of their own at 15 Margaret Street on the far side of Snow Hill from the hustle and bustle of Commercial Street. To help pay for it, he rented rooms to George W. Sanborn, a policeman, and Neil Faulkner, a laborer, while Meg saw to their board.[48]

As his reputation grew and his interests broadened, John H. took advantage of the spacious premises of the McManus sail loft to begin sewing sails for Lawlor's racing yachts. The experience he and his son Charley gained through these efforts had a telling effect on the reputation of the family firm, and provided the oldest McManus boy with the opportunity to display his own innate understanding of sail shape. As much as Charley loved his days at sea with the fishermen, his ambitions lay in the sail loft. After the war, yachting became John H.'s personal avocation as he achieved financial security in life. Although Boston Bay could claim four yacht clubs during 1866-70,[49] the plethora of clubs in the Boston area did not arrive until the 1880s. Small-craft yachting in the early 1860s remained very much a family sporting enterprise.[50]

The next vessel that John H. McManus had Lawlor design and build after the *Sylph* was the yacht *Vesper*. She was a keel-sloop with a twenty-one-foot waterline, and she went into the water in time for the 1866 summer sailing season. Lawlor, in addition to his pilot boats, tugs, coasters, fishing schooners, and steamboats, designed and built many yachts. In terms of design theory, he was always at odds with the American shallow-draft, broad-beam, "skimming-dish" school of yacht design. He espoused the deep-draft, narrow, sloops and English cutters championed by the "cutter crank" faction of the yachting fraternity.[51] Tom described an important modification his father made to Lawlor's design for the *Vesper*: "sometime after [the launch of the *Sylph*, Lawlor] got out a small yacht for my father called the *Vesper* and after sailing her one season my father had her hauled out and had a cast iron Keel made, and I believe she was the first boat to have her weight put

[47] Thomas F. McManus eventually purchased a large house at Jericho Beach in Thomas W. Lawson's famous "Dreamwold" section of Scituate. His children and grandchildren always laconically referred to this large structure as "the cottage."

[48] City of Boston, Tax Assessor's Records, Ward 2, Part 1, 48, May 1868: John H. McManus, owner, sailmaker, 15 Margaret Street. 935 feet of land valued at $1,500. House valued at $2,500.

[49] The Boston Yacht Club (1866), the South Boston Yacht Club (1868), the Bunker Hill Yacht Club (1869), and the Dorchester Yacht Club (1870). The first local regatta occurred on 4 July 1866(*The Log of Mystic Seaport* 34:1 (Spring 1982): 31).

[50] Until the founding of the Boston Yacht Club on 21 November 1866, there were no yacht clubs in coastal New England. The prestigious Eastern Yacht Club did not come into being until 1870.

[51]Chapelle, *Fishing Schooners*, 120.

The 70-ton Gloucester schooner *Hattie S. Clark* (73x21x7 feet), built at Essex, Massachusetts, in 1866, represents the shift from sharpshooter to clipper model in the Massachusetts fisheries. Although she was 18 feet longer and 3 1/2 feet wider than the *Sylph*, her hold was only half a foot deeper and her draft was probably less than that of the notably deep *Sylph*. Edward W. Smith photographed her at Newport, Rhode Island, ca. 1890. (M.S.M. 69.822.98)

on outside, and she was better for it, and many races were won by her."[52] If Tom's claim is valid, his father conceived the first use of outside ballast, yet another McManus contribution to improving the art of shipbuilding.[53] The modified *Vesper* became one of the faster keel sloops around Boston Bay, and, as late as the mid-1880s, continued to place well in local regattas.[54] It was not until the 1870s that outside ballast caught on among American yachtsmen in general.

---

[52] McManus, "Essay No. 2."

[53] Previously, it has been believed that Bill McCormack's *Gael, ca.* 1877, whose name indicates her owners origin, was the first yacht with outside ballast in the United States. This technique reappeared in 1897 in Tom's first pilot boat, *America*, Boston's Pilot Boat No. 1, which replaced Lawlor's redoubtable *Hesper* as Massachusetts Bay's trial horse, in 1898 on the first of Tom's ubiquitous Indian Headers, *Juniata*, and also in her sister schooner, *Massasoit*.

[54] R.M. Binney raced *Vesper* to fifth place in the "Fourth Class Keels" category of the Hull Yacht Club's open regatta on 16 August 1884 (*Forest and Stream & Rod and Gun: The American Sportsman's Journal* 23 (August 1884-January 1885), 75; R. Bonner raced *Vesper* to sixth place in the "Third Class Keels" category of the Dorchester Yacht Club's open regatta on 17 June 1885 (*Forest and Stream* 24 (February 1885-July 1885), 438.

CHAPTER FIVE

The *Actress* and *Em'ly*

T he weather during the second half of the 1860s varied as quixotically as the first. On 17 January 1867, a snowstorm of 1850s proportions hit Boston: "[one weather expert] estimated a fall of 14 inches, and others in the suburbs put it at 18 inches,"[1] without doubt the heaviest fall since the Great Cold of 1857. The winter fishermen suffered severely, and many an Irish hearth lost its cheer when the man of the house failed to return from the sea.

The Lawlor-designed *Em'ly* (25x11x5.6 feet) served the McManus family as a racing sloop from 1876 to 1886. She is depicted sailing down Boston Harbor in this oil painting by an unidentified artist. (Courtesy Edwin C. McManus)

---

[1] David M. Ludlum, *The Early American Winters II, 1821-1870* (Boston: American Meteorological Society, 1968), 74, citing "Paine's meteorological column and the regular news column of the *Evening Traveller* gave full documentation in the issue of 19 January."

During the frigid February that followed, in a measure hinting at premonition, Dick Leonard retired from the sea, transferred his half-ownership of the *Sylph* into Kate's name, and hired Michael Saul to operate the schooner.[2] At the same time he moved Kate and the baby, with his unmarried sister Ellen, who still kept house for them, and the three other surviving children: Charles, eight; Ellen, six; and Thomas Joseph, three, from the old Fingal stronghold on Commercial to a house at 57 Salem Street, a change of address that brought them within a short walk of the new McManus home on Margaret Street.

Leonard also invested in another house a few doors down the block at No. 71 and rented it to his in-laws, the Montrosses. The frequent absences at sea of Bill and his son Charley often left Mary at home alone, and it became a matter of concern for the family. Old Annie McManus, who had been spending her widowhood with John H. and Meg, moved into No. 71 to keep her daughter company. Distraught over her own lost children, Mary had again begun to suffer fits of depression and withdrew from the company of family and friends. Her North End neighbors missed her cheerful presence and the sage counseling she had provided for the frightened young women who still arrived from Ireland on a nearly daily basis. A measure of their respect can be found in the number of children for whom she had become a godmother, most of them outside the scope of this biography.

On a more cheerful note, in addition to his activities in the fishing fleet, Chris Leonard's spiraling success in the North End liquor trade soon attracted the attention of the agents of R.G. Dun & Co. His newly-opened credit dossier observed that his personal worth was between $5,000 and $6,000 and his credit was fair for moderate amounts; paradoxically, it also recorded that he "asks No Credit."[3] Nicholas, Julia and Chris's nineteen-year-old son, who had been working as a clerk for his parents, took over Julia's place in the family business, then he and Chris gradually shut down the grocery in order to concentrate on the liquor trade.

It is worthy of mention that either these early credit investigators were slow to recognize the true worth of the close-fisted Irishmen, or Leonard and other North End businessmen such as Patrick Kidney, William Gregory, Patrick

---

[2] Enrolment No. 14, Boston and Charlestown, 19 February 1867; Enrolment No. 16, Boston and Charlestown, 21 February 1867, U.S. Consolidated Enrolment and Licenses, Bureau of Navigation, Record Group 41, Records of the Department of Commerce, NARA. Dick's personal property valuation of $2,000 in May 1867 was identified as the "schr. *Joseph Henry*" (City of Boston, Tax Assessor's Records, Ward 2, Part 2, 161, [May] 1868). Two weeks before the snow came, on the ninth anniversary of the *Black Hawk*'s purchase, Kate McManus bore Dick Leonard another son, Richard Francis (Vital Records, *Births*, 1867, vol. 198, page 9, line 391, 2 January 1867). Mary McManus, making one of her increasingly rare public appearances, presented the baby to Father Tom Sheahan for christening at St. Stephen's on 6 May 1867 (St. John the Baptist/St. Stephen's, *Baptisms*, vol. 5 (1862-1870), page 233).

[3] R.G. Dun & Co. Collection, Baker Library, Harvard University, School of Business Administration, Suffolk County, 1 July 1867, hereafter cited as R.G. Dun & Co. Collection.

McManus, and Matthew Keany got rich overnight. Just four years later, Leonard's updated R.G. Dun & Co. credit report showed a five-fold increase in his worth: "now entirely in Liquor bus[iness] & has been in bus[iness] over 25 years has always paid and is considered worth 30-000."[4] A concurrent example of Irish political manipulation concerns John H. McManus and Boston's property tax records. In May 1868 he was listed as the owner of the 15 Margaret Street property with a normally assessed value; but, although his sail loft did a thriving trade, the tax man identified the location, the third and fourth floors at 33 Commercial Wharf, as solely "for storage."[5] Possibly this reflects the friendship and pervasive influence of Matt Keany, the son of a Leonard, a North End grocer, and the district's undisputed ward boss.

Sometime between early 1868 and May 1869, Dick Leonard mysteriously disappeared from Boston.[6] A dynamic force in the Fingal emigration, tragically, he failed to reach his forty-first birthday. The absence of either an official obituary or mentions in the state's vital records throws up the possibility that he may have perished at sea, possibly in foreign waters. On the other hand, the two-year-long asset shift to Kate suggests an awareness on Leonard's part that death lay in his path. At the time of his demise only the schooner *Golden City*, a late purchase in December 1867,[7] remained in his estate. The houses at 57 and 71 Salem Street, and his shares in the *Sylph* and the *Joseph Henry* had all been safely transferred into his wife's name.[8] As Kate McManus's husband, Chris's brother, and John H.'s brother-in-law and longtime business partner, Dick Leonard–the Irish fishing skipper, American civil servant, Boston schooner owner, and property investor–had been a vital strand in the intricately woven family pattern of the Fingal fishing phalanx that had so quickly assimilated into local society.

For young Tom McManus, a rising star of the Fingalians' first American-Irish generation, the 1869-70 academic year, which would culminate in his

---

[4] R.G. Dun & Co. Collection, Suffolk County, 25 April 1872.

[5] Tax Assessor's Records, May 1868, Ward 2, Part 1, 48, Boston Public Library.

[6] The only official notice of Richard Leonard's death appears in the City of Boston, Tax Assessor's Records, Ward 2, Part 2, 223, May 1869, where the entry for "Richard Leonard, fisherman, includes the property at 57 Salem Street, and a personal property valuation $2000, identified as the "schr. *Golden City*." The ledger entry, written in black ink, has a red ink notation, "dead."

[7] Enrolment No. 276, Boston and Charlestown, 7 December 1867.

[8] City of Boston, Tax Assessor's Records, May 1869, Ward 2, Part 2, 223: Richard Leonard [marked "dead"], fisherman, 57 Salem Street. Personal property valuation $2000 (identified in record as "schr. *Golden City*"). Catherine Leonard owned the property at 57 Salem Street identified as 1125 feet of land valued at $2000, and building at $2000. John H. McManus and his sister, Kate Leonard, sold the *Joseph Henry* to "Peter Rickard, 1/4; William Farrell, 1/2; and John O'Hare, 1/4; Peter Rickard, Master," on 21 January 1870 (Enrolment No. 4, Boston and Charlestown, 22 January 1870).

graduation from Eliot Grammar School, began with yet another New England weather frenzy. The Tuesday of his second week back in the classroom, September eighth, dawned warm and humid with light winds and rain. At two o'clock that afternoon the temperature peaked at 85°, and a thickly overcast frontal system, accompanied by easterly squalls and heavy downpours, passed overhead. At 6:00 P.M., just after Tom arrived home for supper, a treacherous hurricane with a small, intense center smashed into Boston. Fortunately for the fishermen, the storm hit four hours after the flood tide, which greatly reduced potential destruction along the waterfront. The Hanover Street Methodist Church suffered the worst damage in the North End, the loss of its spire, although the storm totally destroyed the large Coliseum downtown.[9]

Later in that storm-launched semester Tom received a commendation certificate that read: "ELIOT SCHOOL, Saturday Dec. 30. 1869., Thos. F.J. McManus is entitled to receive a public expression of approbation for industry, good conduct, and punctual attendance during the past week. Samuel W. Mason, Master."[10] As his Eliot School days came to a close, his professional tutor, Dennison J. Lawlor, widened Tom's architectural education by introducing him to the skills necessary to extrapolate from half model to full-size ship timbers.

In the process of "molding" or "lofting" a vessel, the designer carved a half model out of a multi-layered sandwich of softwood planks. When the model represented his concept for the vessel exactly, he marked it with "stations," equidistant vertical lines representing select ribs or frames. On the broad expanse of the mould-loft floor, he then scaled up the dimensions of these stations to full size and scribed out the shapes of the frames. From these shapes on the floor, he made molds to take into the shipyard to mark the proper shape of the frames as they were assembled. McManus succinctly recalled the experience: "I visited Lawlor's mould loft often and helped him to pin the battens on the lines, laying on the floor and got a lot of knowledge."[11] Thus, through the continuing efforts of his father and Lawlor, Tom acquired an elemental knowledge of the art of hull design and sail shape, as well as in the crafts of shipbuilding, rigging, sail-cutting, and lofting, by his early teenage years.

The vigorous postwar growth in the seafood marketplace continued apace. The transformation of America, from its prewar agrarian economy to the postwar

---

9 David M. Ludlum, *Early American Hurricanes, 1492-1870* (Boston: American Meteorological Society, 1963), 106-107.

10 Thomas F. McManus always cherished his Eliot School years. Among the other prized mementos in the possession of his grandchildren, there is a flyer for the Annual Meeting and Dinner of the Eliot School Association, fifty-eight years later. Tom, by then a sprightly seventy-one-year-old, following his annual custom, travelled up to Boston to partake in the affair, which was organized by John B. Sheridan of 138 North Street, Boston.

11 Thomas F. McManus, "Autobiographical Essay No. 1."

industrialized nation, created an unprecedented demand for affordable food. The
addition of manufacturing to traditional city service industries was an underlying
cause. The demand for unskilled labor stirred urban immigration, both from within
and without the nation. Labor-starved metropolitan factories, in addition to
absorbing the immigrating masses from foreign lands, also drained the population of
the rural United States. Municipalities grew at a previously unseen rate.[12] Cheap
fresh or salted fish soon became a diet staple in overcrowded cities whose
population majority now consisted of European immigrants, many of them
accustomed to a diet of fish.

There is abundant evidence regarding the urban distribution of fish
products shipped by Boston's dealers: "about half . . . were consumed in New
England, about one-fifth in New York State, and the remaining three-tenths in
Philadelphia, Baltimore, Washington, and points south and west."[13] Technological
advances had begun to accelerate this geographically spreading marketplace even
before the Civil War. The facility of a readily available and ever-expanding national
railroad system, as well as progress in preservation from salting to icing to canning,
and eventually to freezing, were key elements. The appearance of manufactured ice
and the cold storage facilities furthered the industrialization of schooner-based
commercial fishing, and these developments began to revamp the traditional
methods of the fisheries.

In 1860 William H. Oakes and Seth Stockbridge of Gloucester, at the
urging of Boston fish brokers, had shipped fresh fish by rail from Gloucester to
Boston and New York packed with ice in old sugar boxes. The experiment was,
literally, an "overnight" success and, before long, a large portion of the Irishmen's
inshore haddock catch, and the fresh halibut brought in by their Georges Bank
vessels, began to reach inland cities.[14] The railroads also brought salted fish, a
relatively inexpensive commodity, to new markets. Thus seafood products reached
out to the hinterlands with salted fish, while iced fish replaced the salted version in
older markets from 1865 onwards. Ultimately, at Gloucester in the 1920s, Clarence
Birdseye would develop this idea into what is now the frozen-food industry. As the
movement of fresh and salted fish by rail increased, several of the Irish families, led
by Tom Herbert, who had also been the first among them to own a schooner,
entered the fish-brokering trade.

---

[12] For a straightforward discussion of this phenomenon see Diane Lindstrom's, "Economic Structure, Demographic Change, and Income Inequality in Antebellum New York," in John Hull Mollenkopf, ed., *Power, Culture, and Place, Essays of New York City* (New York: Russell Sage Foundation, 1988).

[13] George Brown Goode, ed., *The Fisheries and Fishery Industries of the United States*, 5 vols., (Washington, D.C.: Government Printing Office, 1887), Section 2, "A Geographical Review of the Fisheries Industries and Fishing Communities for the Year 1880," 197.

[14] Goode, ed., *The Fisheries*, sect. 2:147.

Yet another of the frequent family-shattering tragedies that visited the McManuses and Leonards ushered in the 1870s. After her husband Dick's death or disappearance, Kate McManus Leonard moved to 71 Salem Street to be with her aging mother and ailing sister, a cheerless home sheltering two widows and a recluse. On 25 April 1870, Mary, one of the very first emigrants from County Dublin, succumbed to "melaena."[15] There is a sense that worrying over the loss of her three children eventually caused the ulcers that led to her early demise. Only forty-three years old, Mary was the oldest daughter of Charley and Annie McManus, and the sister of John H., Kate, and Pat. Her 1847 wedding to Bill Montross had been the first of the family nuptials to take place in America. Her husband and son Charles (now in his nineteenth year and the senior member of old Charley McManus's brood of grandchildren), survived Mary.

The coming of summer brought an unprecedented heat wave and near drought conditions to Boston. In early August another deadly cholera epidemic struck, killing more than eighty children in twelve days. The decennial arrival of the federal census-takers in the North End coincided with the outbreak of the fever. Their 1870 tabulation of the McManus household included: John H., 50, sailmaker, personal property value $5,000, real property $500 (quite a step up from his $60 worth of assets in 1860); Margaret, fifty-one, housewife; Charley, sixteen, fisherman; Thomas, fourteen; George, twelve; and Louis, ten; all students.[16] Charley worked full-time in the market fleet, while Louis's unusually pious demeanor reflected his parents ambitions for a career in the priesthood. George displayed an emerging artistic talent and was happy to tag along with whichever of his older brothers would welcome his affable presence.

Tom divided the summer between his father's sail loft on Commercial Wharf and Lawlor's shipyard in Chelsea. He also studied for and managed to struggle through the rigorous entrance examinations for English High School. When he entered that Bedford Street institution in September 1870, less than 4 percent of the children between fourteen and seventeen regularly attended Boston's secondary schools. The English Classical School had opened in 1821 to educate boys twelve and over. Candidates for admission had to pass "suitable examinations" and, if successful, entered a three-year curriculum. The name later changed to English High School, but the curriculum remained unchanged from the 1870s. The

---

[15] Vital Records 1841-1895, Massachusetts State Archives, *Deaths*, 1870, vol. 231, page 66, line 1770, April 25, 1870. "Melaena, literally means black stools, usually due to stomach bleeding, as in, *e.g.*, peptic ulcers or gastric cancer, but most likely ulcers" (Letter, J. Worth Estes, M.D., Professor of Pharmacology, Boston University School of Medicine, 5 April 1990). Dr. Estes kindly, and most objectively, reviewed the causes of death for twenty-four of the personages in this work, translating nineteenth-century diagnoses into twentieth-century lay terms, and his efforts are greatly appreciated.

[16] 8th U.S. Census (1860), Suffolk County, Massachusetts (Ward 2), M593, roll 641, page 68, line 6664, NARA.

Third Class–sophomore year, in today's terminology–all the boys studied English language and literature, ancient history, algebra, bookkeeping, botany, music, drawing, and their choice of French, German, or Latin.[17]

Another future architect (although of the land-based variety), Louis Sullivan, began the Third Form with McManus, and they spent a year in each other's company. But Tom's brief career at English High, lasting just that one year, demonstrated no evidence of genius. He stood thirty-third out of thirty-eight students in the Fourth Division. Tom's tutor, Mr. Norris, who was responsible for all the instruction his charges received, rather generously identified his "Character" as "Improving."[18] McManus's total score for recitations, composition, declension, penmanship, drawing, and deportment was a lackluster 465, compared to 634 for Charles Keach, the highest, and Joseph Carew's lowest, 401. His grade of 38 out of a possible 60 in drawing gives an early acknowledgement of his distaste for the drafting board. Throughout his architectural career, Tom much preferred to whittle a block of wood into the shape he desired, rather than draft it on paper. He became a great proponent of half or lift models for the development of hull form.

Early in 1871 John H. moved his sail loft farther out on Commercial Wharf. He sublet the fourth floor and the attic loft of No. 57 from Coleman, Son & Co., the fish dealers, for the company's permanent quarters.[19] In dealing with his coterie of clients in those days, he did not trouble to hide his disappointment that the remarkable performance of the *Sylph* and her sisters, the *Thomas E. Evans*,[20] *Mary Y. Yates*, and *Hibernia*, had failed to arrest the rapid spread of the shallow-draft, clipper-model schooners in the offshore fleet. The underlying explanation may simply be lack of contact. Although the Irish built safe, handy fishermen, these vessels worked in the Boston market fleet and seldom intermingled with the Gloucester-based banksmen, who sustained the brunt of the appalling losses of life and vessels.

During Tom's fifteenth year his father commissioned Lawlor to design the sixty-two-foot *Actress* with the objective of making her an even faster sailer than the fifty-seven-foot *Sylph*. Realizing from hard experience that Lawlor was no financial wizard, McManus let the building contract to Malcolm Campbell of Campbell & Brooks, Shipbuilders, of East Boston.[21] The *Actress* was a success from

---

[17] Robert Twombly, *Louis Sullivan, His Life and Work* (New York: Viking, 1986), 23-24.

[18] Kathryn Corcoran, Archivist, English High School, 144 McBride Street, Jamaica Plain, Massachusetts.

[19] Tax Assessor's Records, May 1871, Ward 2, Part 1, 147.

[20] Dennison J. Lawlor donated his lift model of the *Thomas E. Evans* to the Smithsonian Institution, USNM No. 74041 (Howard I. Chapelle, *The National Watercraft Collection* (Washington, D.C.: Government Printing Office, 1960), 203).

[21] Campbell & Brooks became Campbell, Brooks, & Taylor, Inc., and by the latter part of the nineteenth century was known as J.M. Brooks & Son at 334 Border Street in East Boston.

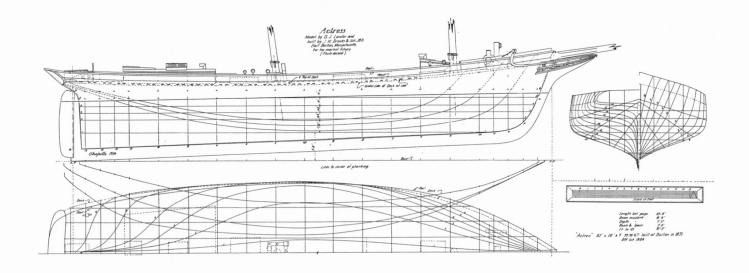

The 39-ton schooner *Actress* (62x20x7 feet), designed by Dennison J. Lawlor to the specifications of John H. McManus in 1871. Although she had a relatively shallow-draft hull, the drag in her keel provided increased stability. She remained a speedy member of Boston's market fleet for thirty years. Lines drawn by Howard I. Chapelle, 1939. (Plan AFS 43, Smithsonian Institution)

the moment she splashed into Boston Harbor at her launching.[22] Tom succinctly explicated his father's objective, and its accomplishment: "The *Actress* was planned and built to beat the *Sylph* which she did."[23] Intended as a market fisherman from the start, Lawlor designed her with very fine lines. But, at first glance, he appears to have sacrificed a measure of safety to gain speed, by reducing her draft as compared to the *Sylph*'s. She was once described as "not a very safe vessel," but her critic failed to credit Lawlor's skill. To counterbalance the *Actress*'s shallowness, Lawlor maintained a substantial amount of drag in the keel, and hardened the turn of the bilges to achieve increased stability. The *Actress* quickly earned a reputation as a speedster, which speaks to the success of her designer's theories. He also gave the *Actress* a sharpshooter rig, without jibboom or foretopmast, thereby making her less hazardous to handle in difficult sea conditions.[24] Following the McManus style, the schooner had a scrollwork billet, rather than a figurehead. To replace the capital that would have ordinarily been provided by Dick Leonard to finance the *Actress*, John H. entered into partnership with his political pal, Matt Keany.[25]

The older members of the Fingalian's first American-Irish generation now began to reach their majority. On 21 March 1872, John H., in keeping with a

---

[22] Enrolment No. 438, Boston and Charlestown, 30 December 1871. The *Actress*'s Master Carpenter's Certificate, issued on 29 December 1871, by Malcolm Campbell described her as having a straight head and elliptic stern.

[23] McManus, "Essay No. 2."

[24] McManus, "Essay Nos. 2 and 4."

[25] Enrolment No. 438, Boston and Charlestown, 30 December 1871. Thomas McLaughlin was her master, marking the beginning of his long relationship with the McManus family. "In Keany's ward, the ties that bound his people to him were unusually tight, as he had become for them over the years not only a friend and a protector but an oracle whose advice was genuinely sought before any significant decision was made" (Doris K. Goodwin, *The Fitzgeralds and the Kennedys* (New York: Simon and Schuster, 1987), 70).

twenty-first birthday promise to his nephew Charley Montross, formally transferred his half-interest in the *Sylph* to him. Montross shared the ownership of the *Sylph* with his Aunt Kate, and became the vessel's master.[26] In April, Chris Leonard made his son Nicholas a full partner in the family liquor business, changed the name of the firm to C. Leonard and Son Co.,[27] and gradually moved it into a totally wholesale operation. Gone were the saloon and the grocery store. Despite the success of his stevedoring company, Patrick Kidney (Charley McManus's future father-in-law) encouraged his son John Augustine Kidney, who had political ambitions, to pursue a career in accounting that would ultimately lead him to the city auditor's office. Several others followed their forebears into the fishing industry, including three of Old Charley McManus's namesake grandchildren. The eldest, Charley Montross ran the *Sylph*; Charley McManus, the next, had been a working fisherman for four years; and Charley Leonard worked as a clerk in a fish market. Charles T. McManus, the son of John H.'s grocer brother Pat, eschewed a fish-related career for one in haberdashery (probably reflecting the same Shannon family thinking that enticed Pat McManus away from the McManus sail loft and into the grocery business).

An event took place during the autumn of 1872 that would have long-lasting effects on the future career of Tom McManus: in October the Boston City School Commission established a school of yacht designing under the direction of John L. Frisbee at East Boston.[28] But 1872 will be best remembered as "the year of the hurricanes." In August and September no less than three of these cyclonic tempests struck the Grand Banks. The hurricane season then paused for a breather before launching a shifty storm that passed inland at the North Carolina coast, swung north, improbably maintained its strength over the continental land mass, and left a swath of destruction across Massachusetts from west to east on 26 October.[29] And there would be no rest from this unmatched season of calamities. One of the greatest disasters in Boston's history, the Great Fire of November 1872, overshadowed even the hurricane season, raging over sixty acres in the southern part of the city, destroying 776 buildings, and leaving 20,000 homeless.[30] Boston's Irish tenement population of more than 60,000, one-fifth of the metropolitan

---

[26] Enrolment No. 35, Boston and Charlestown, 21 March 1872.

[27] R.G. Dun & Co. Collection, Suffolk County, 25 April 1872.

[28] *Forest and Stream & Rod and Gun: The American Sportsman's Journal*, 28 January 1886, 17.

[29] *Tropical Cyclones of the North Atlantic Ocean, 1871-1986*, 3rd ed., (Asheville, North Carolina: National Oceanic and Atmospheric Administration, 1987), 40.

[30] Twombly, *Louis Sullivan*, 33.

total,[31] escaped when the smoldering tendrils of the catastrophic blaze failed to reach into the North End.

In keeping with the stormy surroundings, the partnership of Chris Leonard and his son Nicholas came adrift. For unknown reasons occurring between April and July, they agreed to split up as winter approached. Nicholas then became a partner in the firm of Brennan & Leonard, a wine and liquor dealership at 415 Hanover Street,[32] a shaky venture, as Nicholas "had no means of his own."[33]

The following year brought a different style of problem for the New England fishermen. The Treaty of Washington, which allowed reciprocal free entry of fish between American and Canadian ports, went into effect during July of 1873. It seriously reduced the economic viability of the offshore fleets by allowing cheap Canadian fish to flood the American marketplace. Men who had worked in the fisheries all their lives were forced ashore to seek new types of employment. Within a dozen years only slightly more than half of the workers in the Massachusetts fisheries would be United States citizens.

On May Day 1874, the last survivor of the eighteenth century, Ann Herbert McManus, Old Charley's widow, died of pneumonia and "old age" in Kate's house at 71 Salem Street.[34] The autumn after Annie McManus's death another rogue hurricane passed inland over the North Carolina coast and duplicated the feat of the 1872 storm by maintaining its strength and sweeping across Massachusetts from west to east. In its wake the Fingal immigrants reached the conclusion of their third decade in the United States. The recent years had witnessed the deaths of four key members of the emigration, Charley and Ann McManus, their daughter Mary Montross, and son-in-law, Dick Leonard. With the old guard withering, the time had arrived for the new one, the first American-Irish generation of the Fingalians, to make its mark.

To the delight of the North End, the Democratic Party won the governor's office for the first time in a generation with the November 1874 election of William O. Gaston. Another result of the polling, in which "both prohibition and the means of enforcing it were toppled at last,"[35] was also good news for Irish liquormen the likes of Pat McManus and Chris Leonard, and prompted young

[31] Goodwin, *Fitzgeralds and Kennedys*, 52.

[32] *City Directory*, 1872.

[33] R.G. Dun & Co. Collection, Suffolk County, 15 October 1872.

[34] Vital Records, *Deaths*, 1874, vol. 267, page 89, line 1470. The family matriarch's death certificate listed her age as eighty years, eight months and fifteen days, on 1 May 1874, which computes to a birthday of 16 August 1793, belying her baptism on 21 March 1790. Irish women were famous for disguising their true age.

[35] Roger Lane, *Policing the City: Boston, 1822-1885* (Cambridge, Massachusetts: Harvard University Press, 1967), 163.

Charley Montross to leave the fishing fleet (although he retained his half interest in the *Sylph*), and enter the liquor trade. Another member of Charley's generation, Ned Gregory, the son of clothier Bill Gregory, left Boston for the glitter of New York City, although the charming guile of "Li'l Em'ly" Leonard would see that he was not gone for long.

After his mercifully short-lived career at English High School, Tom McManus entered a school of business administration. In a selection of draft autobiographical essays he wrote many decades later, McManus distinguished his personal educational priorities by dedicating a full third of the essays' content to his architectural tutelage under Dennison J. Lawlor, while synopsizing his entire academic and business education with the single terse phrase: "attended the old Eliot School, English High School and a commercial college."[36] The latter institution was Comer's Commercial College at 666 Washington Street in Boston, a business and stenography school operated by Charles E. Comer.[37] It is not clear from the available evidence when Tom matriculated, but it probably took place after the nationwide depression of 1873.

The time had come for Tom McManus to begin making his own way in the world. After graduating from Comer's College he took a job as a clerk in an Atlantic Avenue fish store.[38] He continued to live with his parents and brothers at 15 Margaret Street; but to denote his new commercial status, he began paying for his room and board.

When John H. converted his keel-configured sloop yacht from inside to outside ballast during her second sailing season back in 1867, he gained a noteworthy ascendancy in racing against his peers.[39] The McManus boys, Charley, Tom, George, and even pious little Louie, were regularly scheduled into the *Vesper*'s crew, a practice that imbued them with a sense of the effect of cut, trim, and set on the handling of sails at sea. Charley, with his deep interest in sailmaking technology, and as the senior son, became the alternate skipper and by far the family's most avid yachtsman. Tom, as with his religious convictions, was never a very convincing advocate of yacht clubs or yacht racing. Unlike Charley's,

---

[36] McManus, "Essay No. 2."

[37] Social Science Division of Boston Public Library, and *Who's Who in the East* (Washington, D.C.: Mayflower Publishing Company, ca. 1920), entry for Thomas Francis McManus of 551 Eliot Street, Milton, Massachusetts.

[38] *City Directory*, 1878.

[39] McManus, "Essay No. 2."

[40] Thomas F. McManus is listed as a member of the Dorchester Yacht Club in 1907.

his name does not turn up on the membership rolls of any yacht club until the twentieth century.[40]

During the era when organized yacht clubs first bloomed around Boston Bay–including the trail-blazing Boston, 1866; the plebeian South Boston, 1868; the aristocratic Eastern, or the more assimilated Dorchester, 1870[41]–the McManuses, with a decade of yachting behind them in the *Vesper*, found a formal outlet for their racing energies when thirty sailors joined together and formed the East Boston Yacht Club on 5 May 1874.[42] Many other local clubs came into existence during the 1870s and 1880s, but it was the East Boston that provided a gateway to the world of yachting for the family, whose place as immigrant Irishmen and middle-class artisans was not socially acceptable for membership in the Boston, South Boston, Eastern, or Dorchester clubs.

In late 1875, four years after the launch of the *Actress*, John H. and Charley, who was about to celebrate his majority, following the sequence set by the fishing schooner *Sylph* and the yacht *Vesper*, commissioned Lawlor to design a powerfully sparred racing sloop. A Boston Bay correspondent for *Forest and Stream*, the national sporting weekly, writing under the pseudonym "Observer," reported: "Mr. D.J. Lawlor has just modeled a very seaworthy sloop for a Mr. McManus, of the East Boston. She is to be 28 feet over all; 11 feet beam; 5 feet 6 inches in draft. Her friends predict a brilliant record for her."[43] Daughterless John H. named the new racer for his favorite niece, "Li'l Em'ly" Leonard. She was now a charming, vivacious, petite young woman of seventeen, but the absent Ned Gregory captured her attention from New York, more than yacht racing in Boston did.

Typically, Lawlor designed the sloop as a keel boat, rather than one of the locally popular centerboard types. As with the *Actress*, the McManuses did not entrust the designer with the building contract, but chose the Wood Brothers' yard at Jeffries Point in East Boston as the builders. Under the guidance of "Mil" Wood, the yard launched the *Em'ly* in time for the 1876 yachting season. As built, the yacht was of above average size for her era–thirty feet overall from the transom to a plumb-stem bow, with an exaggerated bowsprit beyond, a waterline length of twenty-five feet with a five-foot aft overhang, a beam of eleven feet, and a draft of five and a half feet.[44]

---

[41] Albert Langtry, *Metropolitan Boston: A Modern History*, 5 vols. (New York: Lewis Historical Publishing Company, 1929), 1,025; Paul E. Shanabrook, *The Boston (A History of the Boston Yacht Club), 1866-1978* (Boston: Boston Yacht Club, 1978); Joseph E. Garland, *The Eastern Yacht Club, A History from 1870 to 1985* (Camden, Maine: Down East Books, 1989).

[42] *Forest and Stream*, 17 April 1879, 214.

[43] *Forest and Stream*, 264.

[44] *Regattas, List of Members and Yachts of the Hull Yacht Club . . . 1884* (Boston: Kiley, 1884), "List of Cutters enrolled in the Hull Yacht Club, 1884."

An extant painting of the *Em'ly* depicts a mast half again as tall as the hull is long, and an immense spread of sail, which comes as no surprise on a professional sailmaker's yacht. The person who took the most advantage from the *Em'ly's* great spread of Plymouth duck and swift sailing was Tom's older brother. Charley made his reputation as a racing skipper in the sturdy McManus sloop. Tom's turns at the tiller of both the *Vesper* and *Em'ly* continued the development of his early familiarity with hull characteristics, sail handling, and their relationship to helm response. His carefree days on the waters of the bay put his theoretical concepts to the test. He once wrote in his usual terse style: "the yacht *Em'ly*, a great little boat I went yachting on a number of years, on which I learned quite a lot."[45]

A bark lies at Commercial Wharf, perhaps receiving a new suit of sails, ca. 1873. The McManus sail loft at 57 Commercial Wharf is on the granite block building's fourth floor and in the attic behind the fifth dormer from the right. In the foreground, along the new Atlantic Avenue, lie several small Boston Irish market schooners. (Courtesy The Society for the Preservation of New England Antiquities, Boston, Massachusetts)

Those among the waterfront Irish families with an interest in yacht racing continued to find an outlet for their avocation in the unruly membership of the East Boston Yacht Club. Another *Forest and Stream* correspondent, writing under the pseudonym "Kedge," reported that on 4 May 1877 (only the club's third birthday), during the regular meeting held at the Border Street clubhouse, "it was decided to weed out all the useless members and commence anew." The rebelling members proposed "to procure a charter, and have the club act this year as an incorporated body." They wasted no time. Ten days later "Kedge" filed a follow-up story: "at a Special Committee meeting of the East Boston Yacht Club . . . the regular documents were signed for procuring a charter. According to requirements a new election of officers will be held, as there is some dissatisfaction expressed at the present management of the club, and the active members look forward to better times."[46] At the end of the month, in the 1877 season's first open regatta held at the

---

[45] McManus, "Essay No 2."

[46] *Forest and Stream*, 24 May 1877, 232.

South Boston Yacht Club, the McManus boys finished well. With Charley at the helm, the *Em'ly* came in sixth overall, and second in keel boats, behind Bill McCormack's *Gael* in the "First Class" (over twenty-five-foot waterline) category.[47]

On the international front, during the previous summer the Halifax Commission (authorized since 1871), finally met to determine what compensation, if any, the United States owed for the inshore fishing rights granted by Canada and Newfoundland under the Treaty of Washington. The Commission handed down an adverse verdict late in 1877. Spencer F. Baird raised the possibility that "the United States lost the arbitration for the most simple of all reasons: the failure to present a sound case." The United States diplomats had been outwitted throughout the entire affair. The backlash would come later. The Hayes administration grudgingly paid the $5,500,000 compensation, but there was little question that the United States would refuse to renew the fishery and reciprocity clauses of the Washington Treaty when these expired in 1885.[48]

Despite this setback in the international fisheries, an area of budding interest to them, and the lingering effects of the Panic of 1873, the fortunes of Boston's Irish fishermen continued to flourish. The Irish tide began to flood in Boston politics during the closely fought 1876 presidential election. The city's population overwhelmingly supported the narrowly unsuccessful bid of Democratic New York Governor Samuel J. Tilden. The rhetoric aimed by the local Democratic Party's platform during the autumn campaign targeted the rising discontent in many areas of the city over the prohibition reform movement, and, particularly, the licensing policies of the entrenched Republican liquor commissioners. The Democratic mayoralty candidate for the metropolitan area, "the courtly, Harvard-educated Frederick Octavius Prince,"[49] who also held the office of national secretary for the party, incensed the local press with his blatantly "partisan" campaign. Prince, mainly concerned with national problems, left the continuing liquor issue to his local organization, which was more than equal to the task.

The turning point in the city's political hegemony arrived with an unprecedented Democratic sweep of the local elections.[50] Prince won 26,000 votes, and carried three-quarters of the aldermen's seats on his coat-tails, including one for

---

[47] *Forest and Stream*, 7 June 1877, 290. McCormack modeled the *Gael* himself along the modified lines of a "Boston Hooker" in 1874 (W.P. Stephens, *Traditions and Memories of American Yachting* (1939-46; rev. ed., Brooklin, Maine: Woodenboat Publications, Inc., 1989), 198).

[48] Dean Conrad Allard, Jr., *Spencer Fullerton Baird and the U.S. Fish Commission, a Study in the History of American Science* (Washington, D.C.: George Washington University, 1967), 219, 224, 235.

[49] Lane, *Policing*, 165.

[50] Ibid., 165-66.

the future Irish mayor, Hugh O'Brien, who won re-election to his third term as alderman.[51] The incoming Common Council abounded with names from the Emerald Isle including Burke, Doherty, Duggan, Fagan, Flynn, Loughlin, McCluskey, Kelley, McDonald, McGaragle, Nugent, Mullane, O'Connor, and O'Donnell. Another, Pat Kidney's eldest boy John Augustine, a native-born son of the North End and future brother-in-law of Charley McManus, would represent Matt Keany's Ward Six on the council from 1877 through 1880.[52]

But, of even greater significance than the Irish victory itself was the evolution it underlined. The joining of the Irish Democrats to liberal Protestant leaders such as Governor William O. Gaston, ex-mayor Solomon C. Cobb, and Prince marked the political acceptance of the Irish. The Anglo-Saxon and Irish communities had learned to tolerate each other and to coexist, even if at arm's length.[53] Indeed, although the Fingal Irish originated from a solid middle-class background–albeit in a tightly-structured British social order–and solidly re-established their social position in Boston, they soon lent truth to the words of George Brown Goode, "[the Irish] are more or less broadened and developed by the greater freedom which they find in the United States."[54]

By the time that first Irish-American immigrant generation passed the reins to its own American-Irish progeny, the Fingalians' children, armed with the social acumen and other assets engendered by American customs and education, exercised the upward social mobility available in America by setting their sights on social levels that would have been unattainable in Skerries, Rush, and Balbriggan. The swift assimilation achieved by this unique range of Irish famine immigrants was remarkable. Professionally, the Fingalians had arrived in America as fishing boat operators, but within a decade had become fishing boat owners. Politically, the Boston Irish grocery and liquor tradesmen, with the birth of John Francis Fitzgerald and Patrick Joseph Kennedy, would eventually number an American president among their descendants.

---

[51] *A Catalogue of the City Councils of Boston 1822-1908, Roxbury 1846-1867, Charlestown 1847-1873, and of The Selectmen of Boston, 1634-1822 also of Various Other Town and Municipal Officers* (Boston: City of Boston, 1909), 122, 265, 266, 267, 269, 270, 271, 273, 275, 278.

[52] Ibid., 126.

[53] Oscar Handlin, *Boston's Immigrants, A Study in Acculturation*, rev. ed., (1941; Cambridge, Massachusetts: Belknap Press of Harvard University, 1979), 225.

[54] Goode and Collins, "The Fishermen of the United States," in Goode, *The Fisheries*, sect. 4, 54.

CHAPTER SIX

The *Sarah H. Prior* and *Gertie S. Winsor*

During the winter of 1876-77 Tom McManus went into business with a waterfront acquaintance, Charley Lampee, and opened a wholesale and retail fish brokerage at No. 13 Commercial Wharf. That ancient pier, the long-established base for Boston's fishing fleet, had housed the McManus sail loft from the very first day that old Charley, John H., and Pat gave up their journeyman trade to open the business back in 1858. The leased premises of the new firm, Lampee, McManus & Co., consisted of a store built on pilings jutting out over the water at the pierhead with an entrance off Atlantic Avenue. In the street-front windows Tom's hand-carved schooner models competed for

In this view of the Boston waterfront, ca. 1873, the full length of Commercial Wharf fills the background. A small sign identifies the McManus sail loft under the fifth dormer from the outer end of the granite block building. McManus & Lampee opened their fish business in the two-story white building at the inner end of the wharf. At right, the F. Snow & Co. fish store marks the inner end of T Wharf. Between T and Commercial Wharves, a mixture of fishing and coasting schooners fills the dock. (Courtesy Peabody & Essex Museum, Salem, Massachusetts)

space with neatly arranged rows of freshly caught fish lying on beds of crushed ice. The young men had timed and placed their venture well. In addition to its recent political success, the immigrant infrastructure, after three decades in America, had established a strong presence at all levels of the seafood industry. For the fledgling fish dealers, the strength of the Irish market fleet and their shop's close proximity to its catch, were guarantors of success.

Before he joined forces with Tom, Charles W. Lampee, who was by several years the older partner and the son of harbor pilot Bill Lampee, had worked around the city as an itinerant salesman and agent. Like Tom, he lived at his father's home during his bachelor days.[1] McManus himself had reached physical maturity by this time. His stocky, muscular frame surpassed six feet in height, and he sauntered about the waterfront with the erect bearing that singled him out in crowds throughout his life. Customarily attired in a three-piece suit topped off by a fedora or a panama, as the season dictated, he became a man of remarkably imposing presence, even to sporting a natty outfit of starched collar, bow tie, and vest under his fishmonger's apron to maintain a proper "business" appearance, as he doled out various cuts of cod, haddock, and mackerel.

---

1 *Boston City Directory*, 1872-1876.

New businessman or not, Tom did not allow the business to interfere with his part in the family's yacht racing. In the City of Boston's 1878 Union Regatta, held off Strawberry Hill, on Saturday, 20 July, the first prize for keel boats in the second class went to boatbuilder R.M. "Mil" Wood's *Lottie*, which was followed home by Bill McCormack's *Gael*. In the third class, *Nettie* took the first prize ahead of R.G. Hunt's *Posey*, with *Em'ly*, skippered by Charley and crewed by Tom, George, and Louie, next across the line.[2]

But more than business and sport occupied Tom's energies during the summer of 1878. Love had first beguiled him during the mid-1870s when Kate Cokely, a maturing childhood companion, captured his affections. She was the daughter of a Yankee mariner, Charles William Cokely of Wicasset, Maine. Her father was descended from a down-east minister who tended the spiritual needs of an Episcopal congregation at Damariscotta. As a boy, Charley Cokely evinced none of the devoutness required of his pious parent's calling, and chose instead to go to sea. When love bloomed for him at his home port of Boston, he took instruction and converted to the Catholic faith. Then, on 4 September 1853, he wed Letitia Marie Bradley,[3] the daughter of Irish immigrants and a close friend of Mary Dolan, the girl Matt Keany married. The Cokelys became fellow parishioners with the Fingal families at St. John the Baptist Church, and their two daughters were baptized within the precincts of the former tobacco warehouse. Kate, the younger, was born on 10 June 1856, and named for her maternal grandmother.[4]

The relationship between Tom McManus and his American-Irish hybrid sweetheart presents an enigma–the impossible task of unravelling the very private and personal events of 1878. The story begs to be told in retrospect from the day of Kate's 1936 death, when she left Tom an unhappy widower, alone after fifty-eight years of marriage. From the time they began "keeping company," through the moment of her passing, to Tom's own demise two years afterward, neither of them ever had an eye for anyone else. Taking this into consideration in light of the McManuses' idiosyncratically faithful, yet lifetime adherence to the tenets of the Catholic church, the strength of their determination to marry in the face of their moral dilemma emerges. When marriage became the chosen course, their upbringing would brook none other than a Catholic ritual. Clearly the couple did their best to observe the rites of their religion, but equally, they considered their

---

[2] *Forest and Stream & Rod and Gun: The American Sportsman's Journal*, 1 August 1878, 505.

[3] Vital Records 1841-1895, Massachusetts State Archives, *Marriages*, 1853, vol. 70, page 78, line 230.

[4] St. John the Baptist's/St. Stephen's, *Baptisms*, vol. 3 (1854-1862), page 134. Kate Cokely was one of the last children baptized at St. John's by Father Henry O'Neill, the Irish priest who had administered that sacrament to so many of that seagoing flock including Kate's sister Annie, Bill Gregory, Nick Leonard, Charley McManus, Mary Ann Kidney, Johnny Herbert, and Joe Leonard.

own future before confronting church doctrine. In retrospect, as Catholics, the McManuses might have made better Deists, given the extant evidence of their pragmatic attitude toward God and religion. On the other hand, nineteenth-century church custom had its own effect on the couple's circumstances. The separation of canon law and moral theology was less distinct than is the case in the present century and would have presented an awe-inspiring impediment for the young lovers of 1878. Additionally, the church was extremely conscious of scandal, not only of the possibility of exposing it to the community at large, but also of the need to shield the faithful observers of the commandments from it.

Tom married Kate in the presence of two witnesses and a priest on a Tuesday, 10 September 1878. Diocesan practice required that couples be wed in the bride's parish. Generally, only the immediate family and close friends gathered for a nuptial service. Long engagements were unusual: the prospective husband proposed, the lady consulted her family, the covenant was established, and the banns were posted. The proceedings seldom spanned longer than a month and a half. Weekday marriages were quite common, as the church listed a considerable number of days on which weddings could not be performed, thereby limiting the days when they could.

A couple that, in the eyes of the church, came to the altar wrapped in the wages of sin–and, at the time of their secluded sacrament, Kate's wedding dress loosely draped an abdomen that was fully six months pregnant–also dictated a rectory wedding to reduce the opportunity for scandalizing less passionate parishioners. The unanswerable question is why Tom and Kate took so long over their decision to marry. Awaiting confirmation of her condition accounts for part of the delay, but even in those days of medical ignorance on the part of lay people, six months is unlikely; on the other hand, it is conceivable that Kate's buxom frame could have disguised her pregnancy for that long. Regardless of the reason for their delayed decision, once their minds were made up, and there was little choice open to Boston's Irish Catholics considering then contemporary mores, both religious and secular, Kate and Tom took matters into their own hands in a fashion that typified them throughout their lives. They rented an apartment at 85 Warren Avenue in Charlestown, the suburb they would call home for a score of years. With living quarters secured, the couple turned to the youthful curate, Richard J. Neagle,[5] later a notably strict diocesan chancellor, for guidance in their marriage preparations.

[5] Richard J. Neagle, born in Bradford, Massachusetts, on 19 July 1854, graduated from Holy Cross College at nineteen, and went to St. Joseph's Seminary in Troy, New York, where he was ordained in May 1877. As a young man, he became one of Bishop Williams's prized Yankee priests and, in 1886, became Chancellor of the diocese, a post he filled for a decade. Williams rewarded those services with the pastorate of the thriving congregation of the Immaculate Conception in Malden, where Neagle served for nearly half a century, until his death in 1943.

On 10 September 1878, three days before his twenty-second birthday, Tom nervously waited in the confines of St. Mary's rectory (located just off Richmond Street) with his cousin and best man, Jimmy Herbert,[6] for his bride to arrive. Minutes later Kate, assisted by her sister Helena, stepped to the altar and Father Neagle quietly joined Tom and Kate in matrimony.[7]

The records are silent on the attitudes of John H. and Meg McManus, or the widowed Letitia Cokely, toward the nuptials of their errant offspring, but any parental displeasure the deferred wedding may have provoked disappeared three months later when Kate gave birth to their first grandchild on December twelfth,[8] and named the baby Margaret to honor Tom's mother. To the family, of course, the stigma of Margaret's birthday was no secret and, as she grew up, to Margaret herself it presented no stigma at all. She took pride in her status as a "love-child," and lorded it over her sisters throughout their adolescent years.[9]

This generation of Fingalians would be no more immune to tragedy than their immigrating forebears. The unexpected death of his brother Louie, on the twenty-first of the following April,[10] shattered Tom's parental euphoria. The boy, who had been progressing steadily toward his goal of entering the seminary, succumbed to rheumatic fever. He first exhibited symptoms of the disease about the time of Tom's wedding, but apparently recovered. Then a winter cold came on, worsened, stirred up the fever, and he died shortly afterward. The family's inconsolable grief was all the more intense because of Louie's age. Just two weeks shy of his eighteenth birthday, he had survived all the dangers of urban childhood, and was fully prepared to take up his holy calling. With his usually cooperative spirit, the youngest of the surviving McManus brothers had been working as a janitor to help underwrite the cost of his priestly studies.

His parents, suddenly bereft of the second of their five sons, could only take consolation from their remaining offspring: Charley the multifaceted genius of the

---

[6] Jimmy Herbert was the son of Captain Tom Herbert. At the time of the wedding, he worked as a clerk at Lampee & McManus. Richmond Street in Charlestown later became Rutherford Avenue.

[7] Vital Records, *Marriages*, Corrected Volume 8, page 546. Curiously, there remains doubt among her grandchildren that the austere Grandma Catherine they lovingly remember was ever called Kate. She spoke to the issue herself, however, in the 1880 U.S. Census by signing as Kate McManus (1880 U.S. Census, Suffolk County, Massachusetts [Boston ED613], National Archives Microfilm Publication T754, reel 42, page 29, line 27, NARA).

[8] Vital Records 1841-1895, Massachusetts State Archives, *Births*, vol. 297, page 29.

[9] In adulthood, Margaret married Francis J. Quinlan and they had a daughter, Frances Janet, known to the family as "Frankie." Margaret's status was so important to her that she instilled its value in Frankie, who as a teenager bragged to her visiting cousin, Edwin McManus, about her mother's unique family footing–the "love-child" (Letter, Edwin Charles McManus, 27 April 1990).

[10] Vital Records 1841-1895, Massachusetts State Archives, *Deaths*, 1879, vol. 312, page 93, line 2365.

family; Tom the fishmonger *cum* designer; and happy-go-lucky George, now in his majority and practicing his artistic talents as a draftsman in the sail loft. Thankfully none of them displayed any signs of impending weakness. Charlton Smith, one of Tom's oldest friends, once described the maturation process of the three older McManus brothers, starting from the Sunday excursions to what became Wood Island Park with John H. to try out their hand-carved sailboat models:

> But George and Charley outgrew models. They took to the pencil and both entered the father's loft, where they did the office

STATEMENT.

To Mc·MANUS & Co. Dr.

Wholesale & Retail Dealers in

FRESH FISH

OF ALL KINDS.
13 COMMERCIAL WHARF, cor. ATLANTIC AVE.
FISH PACKED WITH CARE AND SHIPPED TO ALL PARTS OF THE COUNTRY.

Lynam-B.Brooks, 103 Milk St. Boston.

Boston, _____ 188__

M. Capt. J. F. Brown 15 *State St N.Y.*

After taking over the fish business in 1879, McManus remained a fish dealer for another twenty years. This billhead dates from the 1880s.(Courtesy Louise V. Will)

work–the bookkeeping and the drawing of sail plans. Tom, grown up, carried on a fish business at Commercial Wharf, where he had ample chance to study vessels. His leisure time was spent either in the family sloop *Em'ly* or at his old hobby of whittling at wood. Nor was the pencil forgotten. It couldn't be. *All three brothers were natural born artists* and Tom, as he sat at the cashier's window of his office used up many and many a block of paper as he gave his ideas shape.[11]

Because Tom lived such a long life, and gained early prominence within the boating community, while both brothers died at relatively young ages, their talents

---

[11] Smith, draft article.

and contributions to the family fortunes tended to be overshadowed and have been unjustly lost to posterity.

The Lampee & McManus partnership was short-lived, ending when Charley Lampee deserted to the hide trade to broker imported California cowskins to busy Massachusetts shoe manufacturers. With his partner's 1879 departure, Tom changed the company from Lampee, McManus & Co. to simply McManus & Co. and soldiered on. But, when Lampee left, Tom, with a new baby at home and another on the way, did not have sufficient personal financial strength to maintain the business. His brother Charley came to the rescue by buying out Lampee's share of the firm. The older McManus had probably saved the money he invested in Tom's company from a moonlighting job he held as a lamplighter.[12] The position, which he picked up in 1875, was an undoubted sinecure with the familiar scent of the pork-barrel politics practiced by Matt Keany's Ward Six Democratic machine, a favor given for favors received. In time, the Atlantic Avenue fish store became a Boston waterfront fixture, remaining at that same location until Tom closed its doors forever during its silver anniversary year.

In George Brown Goode's study, *The Fisheries and Fishery Industries of the United States*, A. Howard Clark provided a quantitative analysis of the industry at Boston as the 1870s came to a close. The Boston market fleet in 1879 numbered seventy-six vessels and 868 fishermen, Clark wrote, adding that "a typical Boston food-fishing vessel" measured slightly over forty-six tons. Actually, the fishery had changed little since the Irish takeover in the 1850s: "sixty vessels engaged in catching food-fish made trips lasting only a few days, fishing near home, and usually returning with fares of fresh fish."

Clark then compared Boston as a fish market to its importance as a fish producing center and found that the annual value of fish and fish products landed annually and distributed by the fish dealers was over $5,000,000, exclusive of $700,000 worth of oysters. The Boston-based fishermen brought in a catch worth about $1,000,000, "therefore only 20 percent of the fish sold in Boston originate from Boston vessels." He next examined the makeup of the ocean produce landed: "About one hundred Boston vessels and large boats, and an equal number belonging to other New England ports, landed fares of fresh fish in Boston during 1879. The Boston vessels landed 1,599 fares or 15,588,000 pounds of cod, haddock, hake, cusk, flounders, and swordfish; 30 fares or 1,749,693 fresh mackerel in number, and 120 fares or 1,998,062 herring in number."

---

[12] City of Boston, Tax Assessor's Records, Ward 2, Part 1, 67, 1875.

Although men of all nationalities manned Boston-based vessels, "those of Irish birth or descent appear to be the largest element in the market fishery."[13] Clark went on to point out that no Boston vessels engaged in the Georges, Grand, or Western Banks salt-cod fisheries, and that the catch from these banks sold in Boston's markets came from other New England ports or the Maritime Provinces of Canada. But, thanks to the Irish immigrants and their descendants, that deficiency would be made up.

During the first summer yachting season of the new decade the lively new Hull Yacht Club came into being.[14] In its first union regatta held during late August, the McManuses brought *Em'ly* home fifth in "Second Class Keels" (up to twenty-six feet); behind *Fairy*, Charles A. Perkins, another "Mil" Wood design; *Lena*, F.F. Creighton; *Wilful*, Paul Butler; and *Empress*, F.H. Blane.[15]

After a year on Warren Avenue, Tom moved his pregnant wife and baby girl to larger rooms at 14 Rutherford Avenue, where Kate delivered a second daughter, Grace Agnes, on 17 November 1880.[16] Six days later, Charley followed his brother into wedlock.[17] In contrast to Tom's five-person gathering in Charlestown two years before, this wedding was an unusually full-blown affair, orchestrated in a style deemed appropriate for the oldest son and heir to a waterfront figure the caliber of John H. McManus. On Tuesday, 23 November 1880, the groom stood next to Father Jerry Millerick on the splendid altar at St. Stephen's and proudly watched his beloved Agnes glide down the long center aisle to join him in matrimony. Clasping the arm of her beaming father, Patrick Kidney, the bride-to-be passed pew after pew filled with the original Fingal immigrants. The magnificent Bulfinch-designed church overflowed that weekday morning. Three generations were in the front row on the groom's side of the church: John H. McManus and Meg Sweetman, his widowed sister Kate Leonard, and brother Pat with his wife Lucy Ann Shannon, represented the original Fingal-born group, while Tom and Kate, babies Margaret and Grace Agnes, and their Uncle George represented the first two

Left: Looking in from T Wharf, Commercial Wharf is at right. Several Boston Irish market schooners lie outboard of a coasting schooner beside the Fresh Fish Depot shed on Commercial Wharf. (M.S.M. 85.82.8)

---

[13] A. Howard Clark, "The Fisheries of Massachusetts," in George Brown Goode, ed., *The Fisheries and Fishing Industries of the United States*, 5 vols., (Washington, D.C.: Government Printing Office, 1887), Section 2, "A Geographical Review of the Fisheries Industries and Fishing Communities for the Year 1880," 193-94.

[14] The club was founded on 25 June 1880, later amalgamated with the Massachusetts Bay Yacht Club, and, finally, in 1903, with the Boston Yacht Club (*Regattas, List of Members and Yachts of the Hull Yacht Club . . . 1884* [Boston: Kiley, 1884]).

[15] *Forest and Stream*, 2 September 1880, 95.

[16] Vital Records, *Births*, vol. 315, page 70. The year ran its sacramental course with the baptism of little Grace Agnes by Father Neagle at St. Mary's on November twenty-third. Her Uncle Charley and an Annie Stephens sponsored the rite (St Mary's, Charlestown, *Baptisms*, vol. 3, page 323).

[17] Vital Records, *Marriages*, 1880, vol. 318, page 168, line 3012. Father Millerick later served as a pastor at East Weymouth (1882-87), at St. Joseph's of Wakefield (1887-1902), and St. Joseph's in Boston's West End (1902-12).

American-born generations. After the beaming Pat Kidney led Agnes to the altar, he slid between his wife, Mary Ann Storrs, and their oldest son John A. Kidney (by now a veteran of Boston's political in-fighting), and the rest of their children and grandchildren. Behind the parents the rows were filled with Leonards, Herberts, Montrosses, Gregorys, and Shannons. Quietly slipping into pews at the back of the church, the fishermen came to pay their respects to the family whose sails powered their profession. They were joined there by Pat Kidney's longshoremen.

During 1881 the five-year-old *Em'ly* had her busiest sailing season yet, beginning with the Boston Yacht Club's union regatta on June sixteenth, where Charley placed the twenty-five-foot sloop fourth behind *Viking*, S.P. Freeman (thirty-six feet); *Gem*, Frank Lincoln (twenty-five feet); and *Hero*, Dr. Charles G. Weld (thirty-seven feet) in "Second Class Keel Sloops."[18] *Gem*, a Mil Wood design built at the Wood Brothers' yard the previous year, had a hull shape quite similar to Nathaniel Herreshoff's invincible *Shadow*, and became one of the most successful boats around the Bay.

The next day a family friend, John F. Towle of the Boston Yacht Club, took the helm at the Marblehead Yacht Club's union regatta and placed *Em'ly* second in

The McManus family kept an active racing schedule with the sloop *Em'ly* through 1886. Although she was not entered in this 1885 Boston City Regatta, these other keel sloops in her class reflect the highly competitive atmosphere. Photograph by Nathaniel L. Stebbins, 4 July 1885. (Courtesy The Society for the Preservation of New England Antiquities, Boston, Massachusetts)

---

18 *Forest and Stream*, 30 June 1881, 32.

"Third Class Keel Sloops," behind club-mate Frank Lincoln's *Gem*.[19] Next, on the Saturday of the same weekend with Charley back at the helm for the Dorchester club's union regatta, *Em'ly* came in a strong second among the "Third Class Sloops and Cat-Boats"; behind *Thisbe*, Sibley A. Freeman (twenty-two feet), but ahead of *Venus*, N.F. and J. Brown (twenty-five feet); *Expert*, E.G. Souther (twenty-five feet); *David Crockett II*, John C. Putnam (twenty-four feet); and *Raven*, "Elwell & Friend" (twenty-four feet).[20] A week later at the Nautilus Yacht Club regatta in Salem harbor on the 23rd, Charley placed third behind *Venus* and *Expert* in the "First Class–22 ft. and over."[21]

The annual City of Boston Fourth of July Regatta came along the following weekend, and Charley steered *Em'ly* into fourth place, behind *Lillie*, Dillingham & Bond (thirty-six feet), *Hero*, and *Gem* in the "Second Class Keels" (up to twenty-six feet) category.[22] On Saturday, August thirteenth, at Hull's open regatta, Jack Towle placed *Em'ly* second in the "Third Class Keels" (up to twenty-six feet), behind Lincoln's apparently uncatchable *Gem*; but ahead of *Banneret*, William K. Prior, twenty-three feet; *Fairy*, and *Raven*.[23]

The busy yachting season continued apace with the McManuses competing against the cream of Boston society. Each of the local yacht clubs, however, established its own idea of what composed a class, with the perplexing result that competitors often raced against vessels that outclassed them or, conversely, yachts that they outclassed. The second weekend in September saw the Hull club's union regatta, where the McManuses brought *Em'ly* in fifth among the "Third Class Keels" behind *Gem*; *Raven*; *Banneret*, sailed this weekend by her new owner, F.A. Daniels; and *Fairy*; but ahead of *Sunbeam*, Winfield S. Nickerson (twenty-four feet); *Volante*, J.C. Davis (twenty-two feet); *Grace*, M.D.C. Musgrave (twenty-five feet); and *Cycia*, Thomas Aspinwall (twenty-four feet).[24]

The next weekend, nuptials replaced yachting on the family social calendar when, at a far less ostentatious wedding than her nephew Charley's a year earlier, Dick Leonard's widow, Kate McManus, now forty, remarried. The groom was an Irish-born Commercial Wharf fish trader, Patrick Grimes, aged thirty-nine. The ceremony took place in the five-year-old Romanesque church of St. Mary's on Thacher Street in the North End, where the Jesuit pastor, Father William H.

---

19 Ibid.

20 Ibid., 33. 21 Ibid., 7 July 1881, 217.

22 Ibid., 14 July 1881, 480.

23 Ibid., 18 August 1881, 56.

24 Ibid., 15 September 1881, 136.

Duncan, performed the service.[25] Afterward the couple moved into 11 Sheafe Street, one of Kate's nearby houses. She now owned several pieces of North End real estate.

The newest Kate in the family, Tom's wife, delivered their third daughter in the spring of 1882. Born on 4 April,[26] Alice was the last of their children to arrive in the Rutherford Avenue flat.

With summer's approach, it did not take long for yachting to regain center stage. At the end of the following month, on Wednesday, 31 May, the new season opened with the Dorchester Yacht Club's Decoration Day open regatta. The McManuses achieved their first interclub victory when they placed *Em'ly* first in "Second Class Keels" (up to twenty-six feet), ahead of *Zulu*, Arthur L. Jackson (twenty-seven feet); F.A. Daniels in *Banneret*; and *Kitty*, Nathaniel N. Thayer (twenty-three feet).[27]

By the time baby Alice came into the world, Tom and his two brothers had gained considerable stature within the fishing and yachting communities, although it would be a long while before they eclipsed the lofty shadow of their father's still mounting reputation. In late 1881, John H., determined as ever to lift the design of fishing schooners, again turned to Lawlor to model a new vessel, one that would lay the path to the Grand Banks for the Fingal fishermen and their descendants. As his first new construction commission in over a decade, her overwhelming success provides a measure of the senior McManus's heretofore unrecognized influence on New England vessels. A large percentage of the New England fishing fleet–estimates vary from 65 percent to 90 percent of the total–called Gloucester's relatively shallow harbor home. As late as 1887, landings at Boston totaled 18,514,086 pounds of fish, a mere 18 percent of Gloucester's 101,511,113 pounds.[28] Therefore, as the New England fishing fleet's principal headquarters, the Cape Ann harbor figured prominently in the calculations of any naval architect exploring design improvements.

The sparse attention paid to the fleets sailing from the port of Boston by historians of the New England fisheries has caused the influence of its vessels on

---

[25] Vital Records, *Marriages*, 1881, vol. 327, page 140.

[26] Vital Records, *Births*, 1882, vol. 333, page 110. Two twenty-four-year-old relatives–Willy Cokely, Kate's brother; and Em'ly Leonard, Tom's cousin–sponsored Alice's christening at St. Mary's. Father Neagle, who remained a close friend and spiritual advisor to the Charlestown McManuses, performed the sacrament (St Mary's, Charlestown, Baptisms, vol. 3, page 371).

[27] *Forest and Stream*, 8 June 1882, 376.

[28] Andrew W. German, *Down on T Wharf: The Boston Fisheries as Seen Through the Photographs of Henry D. Fisher* (Mystic, Connecticut: Mystic Seaport Museum, 1982), 4, citing, Massachusetts Bureau of Statistics of Labor, *The Census of Massachusetts: 1885*, vol. 2, *Manufactures, the Fisheries and Commerce* (Boston: Wright & Potter, 1888), 1411, 1430-31; and the U.S. Commission of Fish and Fisheries, *Report of the Commissioner for 1888* (Washington, D.C.: Government Printing Office, 1892), 304.

the architecture of American fishing schooners to be overlooked. Although such Fingal-Irish trendsetters as the *Sylph*, *Thomas E. Evans*, and *Actress* are occasionally mentioned, the position of the *Sarah H. Prior*, undoubtedly the trendiest fishing schooner built in Boston between 1871 and 1885, has never been clearly established. Arguably, the *Prior* was the most innovative vessel to join the banksmen since the advent of the clippers. Not only did she advance design technology, but also she began the transition to a new class of schooners, and signalled the coming Irish offshore invasion.

John H. McManus's new commission represented a broadening, as well as an extension of, his fishing interests. His usual concerns for safety surfaced strongly in this schooner, but his principal intention was to lead the Irish beyond the market fishery to the fish-rich offshore banks. Tom McManus remembered, "In the year of 1883 [*sic*, 1882], (my father and brother, who constituted the firm of John Herbert McManus & Son), the celebrated sail makers and outfitters,

The 102-ton schooner *Sarah H. Prior* (86.1x23.9x9 feet) was the first large Boston Irish schooner intended to fish on the distant banks. A deep-draft clipper designed for John H. McManus by D.J. Lawlor and launched in 1882, she was such a nimble schooner that her captain exclaimed in admiration, "what a vessel!" Photograph by Nathaniel L. Stebbins, 5 April 1888. (Courtesy The Society for the Preservation of New England Antiquities, Boston, Massachusetts)

commissioned the well known Naval Architect D.J. Lawlor, builder of yachts, pilot-boats and fishermen, to design the schooner *Sarah H. Prior* (for one of the successful fishermen [Captain Tom McLaughlin])."[29] Lawlor went to work on the design of the *Prior* shortly after Alice McManus's birth. When the architect completed the drafts and offset tables, John H., just as he had done with the *Actress* a dozen years earlier, turned them over to Malcolm Campbell, but added a new wrinkle by setting up his son Charley as her construction supervisor at the Taylor, Campbell, and Brooks shipyard in East Boston. The young man had developed the necessary skills, both technical and diplomatic, to handle this demanding assignment while running the family's newest undertaking, a fishing vessel outfitting service. With Charley and Tom deeply involved in the *Prior* venture, and George competently handling the drafting of sail plans in the loft, the years of training John H. had invested in his sons began to pay dividends.

During the lively conceptual discussions for the new schooner between Lawlor, Campbell, and the McManuses another aspect of the old "duck theory" arose. Some contemporary designers, particularly those who advocated the "skimming dish" school of architecture, observed that the birds sat lightly on the water, and used this fact to support their shallow draft design concepts. Tom, however, immediately spotted the weakness in the argument: "The fact that the duck is propelled from below while the sailing vessel is propelled from above was not considered by those who took this view . . . my father and brother believed [and Lawlor definitely agreed] that depth as well as length added to speed, so we got out the Sch. *Sarah Prior* with more depth and greater draft which was superior to the older class [of clipper schooners]."[30]

In addition to changing these design parameters, Lawlor gave the eighty-six-foot schooner much finer lines than then in vogue, topped off by the well-established McManus billethead. Tom later commented to a journalist friend: "she proved to be very speedy, and beat everything she met."[31] The *Sarah H. Prior* gained the encomium "Queen of the Fleet" among the banksmen after just a year at sea–no mean feat for the McManuses' first effort with a large offshore schooner. But she was more than an architectural success and a delightful sailer; she ably earned her keep. Under Captain Tom McLaughlin, the *Sarah H. Prior* took the Irish to the

---

[29] Thomas F. McManus, "Autobiographical Essay No. 3." The fisherman was Captain Tom McLaughlin, who skippered the *Anna Maria* for Winifred Condon (1860), *Thomas E. Evans* for John Evans (1866), *Jane* for William Farrell (1867), *Mary Tracy* for James Tracy (1870), and *Hibernia* for Peter Scofield and Lawrence Mullen (1871), before finally coming into the employ of John H. McManus and Matt Keany on board the *Actress* for the 1872 season. He first worked for the Priors on board the *Mary Amanda* in 1880.

[30] McManus, "Essay No. 2."

[31] "Designer of Flying Fishermen," *The Boston Herald*, 1904.

Grand Banks for the first time. Closer to home, she also fished Georges Bank, occasionally returning with as much as 100,000 pounds of fresh haddock and cod, caught in two or three days.[32] Without doubt, the Boston Irish had taken the first step toward becoming a presence in the banks fisheries.

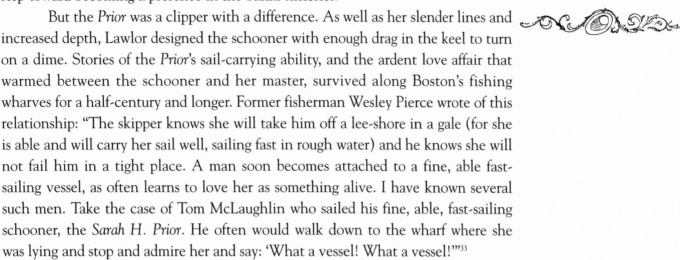

But the *Prior* was a clipper with a difference. As well as her slender lines and increased depth, Lawlor designed the schooner with enough drag in the keel to turn on a dime. Stories of the *Prior*'s sail-carrying ability, and the ardent love affair that warmed between the schooner and her master, survived along Boston's fishing wharves for a half-century and longer. Former fisherman Wesley Pierce wrote of this relationship: "The skipper knows she will take him off a lee-shore in a gale (for she is able and will carry her sail well, sailing fast in rough water) and he knows she will not fail him in a tight place. A man soon becomes attached to a fine, able fast-sailing vessel, as often learns to love her as something alive. I have known several such men. Take the case of Tom McLaughlin who sailed his fine, able, fast-sailing schooner, the *Sarah H. Prior*. He often would walk down to the wharf where she was lying and stop and admire her and say: 'What a vessel! What a vessel!'"[33]

And the *Prior* embodied a socio-economic accomplishment that exceeded even her outstanding performance afloat. While she was under construction, John H. syndicated the schooner. Still a relatively rare form of ownership, syndication had existed in the banks fleet from the late 1850s and, although the vehicle may not have been new, its component parts were. The combination of waterfront merchants such as Parron H. and William K. Prior Jr., George H. Parker, Augustus and Henry Winsor, A.F. Rich, Francis A. Johnson, and John S. Wright with relative North End newcomers the like of the McManuses and Matt Keany, as shareholders in the *Sarah H. Prior*, marked a further immigrant assimilation into Boston society. The Irish now represented more than a burgeoning electorate ripe for courting; by entering the ranks of the commercial classes, they became an integral part of the economic vitality of the city.

While Charley was in the midst of organizing the *Sarah H. Prior* project, Agnes delivered his first son. In keeping with the family tradition of the first born of the first born honoring the grandfather, they named the baby John Herbert McManus. Baptized on 16 July 1882, at St. Mary's of the Sacred Heart Church in the North End,[34] the baby had first seen the light of day a week earlier at 15 Margaret Street. John H., the elder, celebrated the arrival of his first grandson by making Charley a full partner in the sail loft. Thus, by mid-1883, Tom's brother

---

[32] Wesley G. Pierce, *Goin' Fishin'* (Salem, Massachusetts: Marine Research Society, 1934), 152.

[33] Ibid., 87.

[34] St. Mary's, Baptisms 1869-1908, roll 3, page 129.

owned half of the sailmaking company, half of the fish brokerage, and all of the family's outfitting business.

From Tom's point of view as a budding designer, the *Prior* "proved very satisfactory (My father and brother went on various trips in the winter on the *Prior*, one of the improvements that they developed was doing away with the big jib with bonnet attachments)."[35] He went on to describe the hazards inherent to the men who had to douse this extra canvas out on the plunging bowsprit in the face of rising winds, mountainous seas, and freezing weather: "It was pitiful to see the precarious duties that fishermen had to perform in heavy seas and blizzards, crawling over the Knight heads with heavy raw-hide sea-boots with leather soles, and heavy woolen mittens, over icy ropes and with icy sails, to take the bonnet off the jib–one hand holding the rope stops on the bow sprit for protection and working as best they could with the other hand. I have heard of a number of losses occasioned by this performance."[36]

In the *Prior*, as always crew safety figured prominently in any of the McManuses' conjectures. At age twenty-seven, Tom felt a strong commitment, even more than his father if that were possible, to a campaign for safer working conditions on board the fishermen plying the dangerous banks. He once outlined this concern: "and as each year a number of fishing vessels never came back from the banks after some of the terrific storms which they encountered, we thought to improve on the shape of the vessels then in use and we got out the Sch. *Sarah Prior* with more depth and greater draft which was superior to the older class."[37]

Later, in his own early designs Tom zeroed in on "the widow-maker" (the sinister nickname the fishermen gave the bowsprit) as an immediate area for improved safety. Typically, several weeks into a voyage, the footropes slung under this spar often frayed. If they parted, the men working along the spar were doomed. Yet, the bowsprit was the linchpin of a sailing vessel's standing rigging. The staying of the masts depended on the geometric leverage it provided. To eliminate the hazard, he would have to find an alternative method of providing the same mechanical advantage to the spar plan.

---

[35] A "bonnet" was an additional strip of canvas laced to the foot of the jib to increase the sail area exposed to the wind. Removing it was dangerous work for the men on footropes under the bowsprit in heavy wind and sea conditions.

[36] McManus, "Essay No. 4." The "knightheads" were two large timbers, one on each side of the stem, which rose above the deck and supported the heel of the bowsprit between them.

[37] McManus, "Essay No. 2."

Year	Vessels	Valuation	Lives
1830	3	$5,600	7
1831	0	N/A	0
1832	1	1,000	0
1833	1	1,000	0
1834	1	1,500	0
1835	0	N/A	0
1836	1	1,000	4
1837	5	10,100	21
1838	4	7,100	4
1839	2	3,800	4
1840	2	3,800	6
1841	2	2,725	8
1842	3	2,000	0
1843	3	6,000	10
1844	3	4,800	7

Year	Vessels	Valuation	Lives
1845	4	$4,500	8
1846	3	4,900	15
1847	3	6,200	0
1848	0	N/A	0
1849	2	3,500	10
1850	2	12,500	31
1851	9	25,300	32
1852	13	41,200	40
1853	3	10,000	0
1854	4	14,600	26
1855	7	20,900	21
1856	6	14,400	2
1857	5	11,500	9
1858	7	18,700	42
1859	6	21,900	36

TABLE 4 - LOSSES OF SCHOONERS AND FISHERMEN, 1830-1859[38]

Year	Vessels	Value	Lives
1860	7	$26,350	74
1861	15	54,250	44
1862	19	66,500	162
1863	10	40,700	6
1864	13	98,900	84
1865	8	40,300	11
1866	15	114,250	26
1867	11	82,675	66
1868	4	35,000	39
1869	16	83,450	65
1870	13	75,590	97
1871	20	90,560	140
1872	12	55,400	63
1873	31	118,700	174
1874	10	49,100	68
1875	16	96,000	123
1876	27	150,000	212
1877	13	22,936	39
1878	8	59,039	56
1879	29	111,056	249

Year	Vessels	Value	Lives
1880	7	$21,000	52
1881	8	31,000	56
1882	12	79,700	115
1883	17	94,400	209
1884	16	87,100	131
1885	12	67,700	34
1886	26	152,300	136
1887	13	62,900	85
1888	14	63,000	63
1889	14	57,200	70
1890	18	111,455	86
1891	17	91,600	78
1892	12	46,000	46
1893	12	54,700	72
1894	30	175,000	137
1895	11	70,000	94
1896	14	71,500	88
1897	11	75,759	63
1898	20	97,500	62
1899	17	75,600	68

TABLE 5 - LOSSES OF SCHOONERS AND FISHERMEN, 1860-1899[39]

---

[38] *Fishermen of the Atlantic* (Boston: Fishing Masters' Association, 1915), 58.

[39] Ibid., 58-59.

Even to the most hardened fan of speed afloat on Gloucester's waterfront, by the 1880s it had become clear from the mortality rate (a trend that would continue for another decade) that something was fundamentally wrong with schooner design. As fast as the streamlined clipper schooners might be, their lofty press of sail made them unstable and prone to capsizing or otherwise falling prey to winter winds and seas.[40]

The thirty-year era of the pinky and sharpshooter illustrated by Table 4 saw New England fleet losses average eleven fishermen and four schooners with a total value of $8,684, each year. Table 5 below, weighed against an average working fleet of 300 schooners, defines the dramatically increased costs in lives and property that accrued as the clipper schooner came to dominate the fleet. At least two other factors, however, contributed to higher mortality: The advent of dory fishing, with the adoption of the trawl line in the 1850s, led to a new risk, the possibility of the fishermen being tossed from their dories and drowning. Secondly, advancing design technology had long before offered shipwrights the ability to build larger vessels in response to the market opportunities offered by an increasing population, largely of European immigrants, and a vastly improved nationwide distribution infrastructure. Dory fishing provided part of the answer. Fishing schooners, which typically carried crews of ten to fifteen men before the war, carried twenty or more to the banks afterward. And, as the century wound down, schooners grew in size in order to carry more dories, and, therefore, even larger crews.

In direct comparison to the previous decades, annual losses during the clipper era amounted to eighty-nine fishermen in fifteen schooners valued at $76,404. The mean cost, whether totalled in fishermen's lives, vessel losses, or capital, is at once tragic and staggering.

The figures speak to the profitability of an industry in which lives cost nothing when calculating the return on investment, and the era remains unmatched in terms of fishing fleet casualties. And what was the effect of vessel losses? In the tragic year of 1894, although the thirty schooners that went down totalled 2,423 tons and carried a value of $175,000, insurance covered $157,626 of the loss, thereby greatly mitigating the cost to the fleet owners.[41]

But there is an added dimension to the lost schooners: in their rush to condemn the owners, writers of both fact and fiction have habitually ignored or recast the role of the fabled schooner captains, who must share the guilt for the monumental losses suffered by the fleet. Authors including Joseph Rudyard Kipling,

---

[40] Robert G. Albion, William A. Baker, and Benjamin W. Labaree, *New England and The Sea* (Mystic: Mystic Seaport Museum, 1972), 138-39.

[41] Ibid., 59.

Charles Boardman Hawes, James Brendan Connolly, Gordon Thomas, and Joseph E. Garland, among others, have launched scathing attacks on fleet-owners (whose guilt is surely not as uniform as the authors' texts suggest), but either ignored or romanticized the captains' culpability. In an era when hard-bitten masters of clipper ships drove their crews unmercifully to achieve record ocean crossings, fishing skippers, who were no less desirous of fast passages between the fishing grounds and the fish pier, strained their vessel and human resources to achieve a similar goal. They did so regardless of the widely-recognized shortcomings in the design of the clipper schooners, and should have been indicted long before this–the master indubitably knew the weaknesses of his command, certainly more so than the owners.[42]

Even the safest designs could not survive a pernicious combination of adverse weather conditions on the banks. Although the havoc wreaked by the loss of both safe and unsafe schooner designs affected one and all, the disappearance of Captain Tom McKinley's *Sylph* struck home with greater poignancy than most for the McManus family. The long-serving schooner foundered, possibly after colliding with another schooner, during a gale on 9 November 1883, with the loss of all on board. The *Sylph* was the original trendsetter that John H. McManus and Dick Leonard had underwritten eighteen years earlier. In November 1882, Kate McManus had sold her interest to McKinley in time to sail in the 1882-83 winter fishery, and he was beginning his second winter season on board when the *Sylph* went down.

Over the winter of 1882-83 Charley turned his own hand to syndication. Under the sponsorship of Augustus Winsor, he arranged for Malcolm Campbell to build the *Gertie Winsor*. When this eighty-foot schooner was launched in June 1883,[43] he brought her into Commercial Wharf, and outfitted her for a season on the banks. The syndicate he organized took possession in August, when she was ready for sea. With the exception of the shares owned by John H. and Charley through McManus & Co., the owners came from Boston merchant families including the Winsors, Parkers, Riches, Wrights, Priors, Cobbs, Emersons, Nasons, Phillipses, Browns, Freemans, and Wetherells.[44] Tom recalled another aspect of the

---

[42] Only Dean Allard has previously drawn attention to the invidious role of the schooner skippers: "Even the most skilled fishing captains all too often made the tragic mistake of driving their vessels too hard" (Dean Conrad Allard, Jr., *Spencer Fullerton Baird and the U.S. Fish Commission, a Study in the History of American Science* (Washington, D.C.: George Washington University, 1967), 310).

[43] Enrolment No. 279, Boston and Charlestown, 22 June 1883, U.S. Consolidated Enrolment and Licenses, Bureau of Navigation, Record Group 41, Records of the Department of Commerce, NARA; McManus, "Essay No. 3."

[44] Enrolment No. 36, Boston and Charlestown, August 14, 1884.

Winsor's story—the way his brother furthered the career of one of their favorite crewmen, Maurice Powers: "called by Capt. McLaughlin 'the laddie,' and . . . a man in line for promotion, my brother formed a syndicate and they built a schooner called the *Gertie Winsor* of which he was made captain." Proudly underlining Charley's perspicuity, Tom added, "Powers proved to be one of the best skippers from the port of Boston."[45]

Life for the elder McManus was not without it minor nuisances. The spring of 1883 brought an antagonistic assessor to the front door of 15 Margaret Street. He proceeded to rate the land as 935 feet valued at $1,600, and the house at $2,000, no change from before, but the extent of John H.'s personal property attracted the official's intense scrutiny. Reaching a decision to increase its rateable valuation to $1,000, the efficient but petulant civil servant scrawled into the ledger with self-righteous indignation, "not nearly half enough!"[46] At the time McManus was renting to his sons, Charley, with his wife Agnes who was seven months pregnant, and bachelor George. In his report the city employee listed George and John H. as sailmakers, but continued to designate Charley's occupation as "lamplighter." John H., however, was not without a friend at court. Apparently the issue of the revised assessment arose in conversations with Matt Keany and, in a move not only smacking of political cronyism, but demonstrative of the inordinate political power of Boston's ward bosses, the matter was readjusted, as illustrated by the assessor's records for 1884: "John H. McManus, owner, sailmaker, 15 Margaret Street. Tenants Charles A. McManus, sailmaker; George A. McManus, sailmaker. 935 sq. ft. of land valued at $1,600. House valued at $2,000. *Personal property value reduced to no value.*"[47] Is it any wonder that the busy confines of the McManus sail loft had escaped assessment for over a quarter-century, due to its declared use "for storage"?

August 1883 dealt another of those appalling blows to the close-knit Fingal families of Boston. On the fourth, fifty-eight-year-old Julia Leonard suddenly died from a heart attack.[48] Ironically, Chris had just retired so they could spend more time enjoying their four broods of grandchildren. To that end they had recently moved into their retirement home at 184 Salem Street, finally rid of the hustle and bustle of Commercial Street, after thirty-five years of life in the tenement at No. 502. Rather than sell the liquor business, Chris had simply shut it down, and planned to raze the buildings at Nos. 500 and 502, to develop the property. Julia's

---

[45] McManus, "Essay No. 4."

[46] City of Boston, Tax Assessor's Records, Ward 6, Part 1, 103, 1883

[47] City of Boston, Tax Assessor's Records, Ward 6, Part 1, 103, 1884, emphasis added. The Ward Six Tax Assessor's Records now comprise three books, Parts 1, 2, and 3.

[48] *Deaths*, 1883, vol. 348, page 216, line 5806.

survivors, in addition to Chris, included her sons, Nicholas, the thirty-five-year-old liquor dealer, and Thomas, thirty-three, who continued the family's fishing tradition; as well as her daughters, Mary, thirty-one, and Li'l Em'ly, now twenty-five (who had finally managed to elicit a proposal of marriage from Ned Gregory, the jeweler son of Bill Gregory and Maria Shannon). Through either blood, marriage, or friendship, her passing penetrated the homes of the Leonards, McManuses, Herberts, Montrosses, Gregorys, Kings, Knights, Sweeneys, Cassins, and McGinnises. The older sister of Meg McManus, to the McManus boys she was their beloved "Auntie Jewels." The death of this popular Irishwoman not only grieved the entire family, but reverberated widely through the Irish community. From her old grocery clients, many of whom she had nurtured with surreptitious credit, to the fishermen who had brought in her produce, all shared in the grief of her loss.[49]

Both family tragedies and business affairs disrupted the 1883 yachting season for the McManuses. Other than the local races put on by the East Boston Yacht Club, the boys entered only a single open regatta, the one staged by the thriving Hull Yacht Club on 25 August, where they placed a forgettable eighth. The most important event of the season was their abandonment of the fractious East Boston club in favor of the Hull, when Charley switched the membership on 22 October.[50]

Tom had been the first McManus to abandon the North End when he relocated to Kate's Charlestown parish in 1878, the fourth year after that suburb had been incorporated into Boston along with West Roxbury and Brighton. Late in 1883 he deepened his roots by purchasing a house at 39 Mount Vernon Avenue. Along with Kate and the three girls–Margaret, Grace, and Alice–Tom moved up

---

[49] If the loss of Julia Leonard had appalled the Irish fishing families, the sudden death of her younger sister, Meg McManus, on 2 February, stunned them (Vital Records, *Deaths*, 1884, vol. 357, page 30, line 803). The reigning matriarch of the McManuses succumbed to a midwinter attack of typhoid fever and pneumonia at just fifty-five years of age. Grieved beyond measure, the McManus men, John H. and sons Charley, Tom, and George and their families, barely knew where to turn. Widespread mourning cast a melancholy shadow over the North End, and Meg McManus's funeral procession to Calvary Cemetery may have been the most ethnically mixed affair to occur in Boston during the 1880s. But life will go on. Four months later Agnes McManus gave birth to their second child, Mary Ann Storrs "Minnie" McManus, named for Agnes's mother, at 15 Margaret Street on 8 June. Minnie received the baptismal rites on the tenth at St. Mary's on Endicott Street, where her Uncle George McManus and Aunt Winnie Kidney were her sponsors (St. Mary's, Baptisms 1869-1908, roll 3, page 154, 10 June 1884). A week after her birth, Minnie McManus gained a new cousin, when Kate delivered Tom's fourth daughter, Letitia, at 39 Mount Vernon Street (Vital Records, *Births*, 1884, vol. 351, page 37). In what had now become another family tradition, Father Neagle baptized her, with Tom Herbert's oldest son, John T., and his wife, the former Mary J.E. Wilson, as sponsors (St Mary's, Charlestown, Baptisms, vol. 3, page 444).

[50] *Regattas, List of Members and Yachts of the Hull Yacht Club . . . 1884*, 16. At the end of the summer season the sloop's namesake, Em'ly Leonard, married Ned Gregory, who had recently returned home from New York City to take up the jewelry trade in Boston. The wedding must have pressured the consanguinity restrictions of the Catholic Church, for the priest, the bride, and the groom were all cousins by either blood or marriage. Ned Gregory's mother was Maria Shannon, a native of County Clare, Ireland, and the priest was her brother, Father Thomas F. Shannon of the Philadelphia diocese, who traveled up to Boston to perform the ceremony. Additionally, Ned and Em'ly were nephew and niece to John H. McManus, and he delightfully agreed to perform the office of best man at the wedding, with Em'ly's cousin Ellen as the maid-of-honor.

the hill from Rutherford Avenue to the house that would be their home for the next sixteen years.

With the passing of 1883, a major change occurred along the fishing wharves. Thirty dealers achieved an ambition to centralize their trade when they moved into a freshly constructed two-story wooden block of stores on T Wharf in early 1884. The location had one important inconvenience–dock space–for only a thirty-foot-wide section on the north side of the wharf was included in the lease for the wharf, so the association paid $5,000 a year to the Commercial Wharf Corporation to make it possible for fishing vessels to lie abreast of each other on the north side of T Wharf.[51]

On the sporting front, the pace of yacht racing picked up during the 1884 season. The City of Boston's Fourth of July Regatta, run by the Common Council, attracted over a hundred starters. Charley talked his friend Ned Boynton out of his own boat into the *Em'ly*'s crew (with Tom and George), and came home ninth in the heavily subscribed "Third Class Keels," behind *Banneret*, now sailed by N.F. Brown; *Fancy*, E. Herbert Ingalls; *Cricket*, W.H. Buckley; *Kitty*, E.H. Larbell and Charles F. Adams; *Judith*, E.T. Pigeon; *Echo*, John C. Putnam and W. Hudson; *Ibex*, G.G. Williams and L.D. Knowlton; and *Gem*, J.A. Osgood & H.W. Savage.[52] A week later he took third place in the Hull Yacht Club's members' only regatta, coming in after *Transit*, E. Herbert Ingalls, and *Banneret*, J. Brown, in "Second Class Keels."[53]

Some time after little John Herbert was born, Charley moved out of his father's Margaret Street house and headed south. Although Tom had chosen to migrate across the Charles River bridge, Charley was the first of the family to follow the Irish trend of abandoning the crowded confines of the North End to capitalize on the horsecar lines leading to the southern suburbs. With Agnes and the two babies, he settled at 243 Commercial Avenue in Dorchester. Not long after the move, Charley developed a nagging cough, but with the onset of winter Agnes attributed the malaise to the season and thought little more about it.

With the onset of the Irish out-migration typified by Charley's family, Matt Keany moved to insure his Ward Six power base among the "old guard." Sending his ward heelers out to court the Italian and Russian Jewish newcomers, Keany

---

[51] German, *Down on T Wharf*, 3-4. For anecdotal histories of the wharf see, Z. William Hauk, *T Wharf, Notes and Sketches Collected During a Quarter Century of Living on Boston's Waterfront* (Boston: Alden-Hauk, 1952); and Art Hansen's, "Memories of a T-Wharfer," *WoodenBoat* 87 (March-April 1989): 56-65. At this time the Boston fishing fleet numbered 51 schooners, a mere 13 percent of Gloucester's 388, and 876 fishermen compared to Gloucester's 5,778.

[52] *Forest and Stream*, 10 July 1884, 475.

[53] *Forest and Stream*, 17 July 1884, 496.

himself made sure that as each Irishman departed from the dear old North End, he fully understood that his name would remain on the voting lists forever. Loyalty would demand a return trip to the polls on future election days.[54]

Along the waterfront, as schooners grew larger, and the costs of owning and operating them rose, syndication gained in popularity as a form of proprietorship. The McManuses participated in the syndicates that owned the *Edith Emery* (1883); *Cora Dee, Carrier Dove, Emily P. Wright*, and *Loring B. Haskell* (1884); *Belle J. Neal, Carrie and Annie*, and *Hattie I. Phillips* (1885); as well as the *Sarah H. Prior* and *Gertie S. Winsor*.

On the design front, the days of the shallow-draft clipper schooners had finally become numbered. Thanks to the influence and success of the *Sarah H. Prior*, a new class of deep-draft, plumb-stem schooners waited just over the horizon.

---

[54] Doris K. Goodwin, *The Fitzgeralds and the Kennedys* (New York: Simon and Schuster, 1987), 94.

CHAPTER SEVEN

The John H. McManus and *Puritan*

The strategy behind Captain Joseph W. Collins's relentless crusade to displace the shallow-draft type of clipper schooner from New England's offshore fishing fleets began to unfold as early as the spring of 1882, when he wrote a series of letters to a Gloucester newspaper maligning those unstable and unresponsive vessels. Although accepting the need for speed in both market fishermen and banksmen, he believed that this criterion was being used as a license to build unsafe vessels.

Captain Joseph W. Collins (1839-
1904). Massachusetts Fish and Game
Commission, *Annual Report*, 1904.
(Courtesy Boston Public Library)

Collins was well-qualified for his evangelical mission. Born at Isleboro, Maine, to David Collins and his wife, Eliza Sawyer, on 8 August 1839, he followed the pattern of many outport boys when he gave up his schooling at age ten to sign on board a local fishing schooner. By 1860 Collins had settled in Gloucester, where he continued his self-education at sea and at home. He gained his first command at twenty-three and went on to earn a reputation as a successful mackerel fisherman, an occupation that was, at best, chancy. Despite his provincial upbringing, Collins was far more cosmopolitan than his fellow fishing captains. He also gained an early interest in naval architecture. In his own words, "Having had the undesirable experience of seeing my vessel sprawled out on her beam ends twice in one day during a gale," provided the spark for his interest in revamping schooner design. He was also old enough to remember more seaworthy fishing vessels, having been on board a pinky that was able, even with a damaged bowsprit, to claw its way off the lee shore of Prince Edward Island in an 1857 gale.[1]

During the latter part of the 1870s Collins began to act as a consultant to the U.S. Fish Commission. He was a major contributor to the 1880 U.S. Census survey of the fisheries edited by George Brown Goode as *The Fisheries and Fishery Industries of the U.S.*, and joined the Commission's staff on a full-time basis in 1882 as a "fisheries expert."[2] Working from within the Commission, Collins was in an excellent position to advance his aims of improving the New England fishing industry.[3] Despite his limited formal education, he wrote a prodigious amount during his government career to further that cause.

In its second decade of work, the Fish Commission sought to continue scientific study of the nation's marine species and the propagation of commercially important species while actively promoting improvements in fishing vessels, fishing technology, and fish preservation. Collins had the opportunity to examine European fishing vessel models at the Berlin Fishery Exposition in 1880. The British fishing cutters, which he considered "unsurpassed by anything that floats of their size" as seaboats, especially impressed him. With their deep hulls and finely balanced rigs, they could sail to windward in a gale, and even when hove to they

1 Joseph W. Collins, "When Will the Slaughter Cease?," *Cape Ann Weekly Advertiser*, 3 March 1882; "Have We Reached Perfection in Modeling Our Fishing Vessels?," *Cape Ann Weekly Advertiser*, 14 April 1882.

2 *Twentieth Century Biographical Dictionary of Notable Americans* (Boston: The Biographical Society, 1904).

3 Collins spent the next decade in that office and, by 1888, had been placed in charge of the Division of Fishery Statistics. After leaving the commission in 1892, Collins traveled in international fisheries circles for the next several years, culminating with his appointment as U.S. Commissioner to the International Fisheries Exhibition at Bergen, Norway, in 1898. Upon returning to Boston from his Norwegian *tour de force*, he personally delivered several diplomas to Tom McManus which the latter's architectural models had earned for "design excellence." The following year, Collins became Chairman of the Massachusetts Fish and Game Commission, a post he held until his death in 1904.

The 92-ton clipper schooner *Stowell Sherman* (83x23x8.2 feet), coming into Newport, Rhode Island, during a mackerel seining voyage in the 1890s, shows off the all too powerful rig of the clipper schooners. She was built at Essex, Massachusetts, in 1876. Photo by Edward W. Smith. (M.S.M. 69.822.78)

would "jog" to windward rather than drifting leeward, "going sideways like a crab," as shallow New England clipper schooners did.[4] When the Commission decided it needed a schooner with a wet well to transport live fish to its new research station at Woods Hole, Massachusetts, Commissioner Baird asked Collins to design such a vessel that also would serve as a model for more seaworthy New England fishing schooners.[5]

Collins took his anti-clipper message to the newspapers through George F. Proctor, long-time owner and editor of the *Cape Ann Weekly Advertiser*. Over the pseudonym "Skipper," Collins demanded, "When Will the Slaughter Cease?" in the 3 March 1882 issue. He compared the clippers unfavorably to the pinkies and British cutters pointing out that "enough lives have been sacrificed for the sake of attaining a high rate of speed and 'big deck room.'" Proctor, the compiler of industry mortality statistics (for his *Fishermen's Own Book*) and the author of almost weekly articles about fishermen or vessels lost at sea, recognized that "the fishing business as at present conducted, all the year 'round, is liable to greater hardships and perils than any other calling of which we have any knowledge." In support of Collins's efforts, Proctor called for "guarantees of safety which labor has the right to demand of the capital which it creates."[6]

---

[4] J.W. Collins, "Have We Reached Perfection in Modeling Our Fishing Vessels?"

[5] *Report of the Commissioner of Fish and Fisheries for 1883* (Washington, D.C.: Government Printing Office, 1885), xx-xxi, xxxv.

Skipper specifically demonstrated the unseaworthiness of the clippers in the 14 April *Advertiser*. Employing the "skimming dish" *vs.* "cutter crank" controversy from the world of yacht racing to clarify his argument, he came down strongly in favor of the deep-draft cutter school. Proctor published several responses elicited by the rising controversy from opponents as well as advocates. The first adversarial reply came in a letter signed by "Sea Horse" in the 21 April edition, which weakly challenged Collins's claim that the North Sea cutters were more seaworthy than Gloucester's clippers. But Sea Horse's argument rested on shifting sands. The grounds to oppose the move to a deeper design were few: the shallowness of Gloucester's inner harbor until completion of the breakwater, the suspicion that a deeper vessel would be slower, plus the expectation that a deeper vessel would be more expensive to build.

An unexpected result of Sea Horse's letter was its "call to arms" effect on Dennison J. Lawlor, who by this time had been consorting with Boston Irish fishermen for most of his forty-year naval architecture practice. Lawlor leaped into the epistolary fray under the alias "Vidas." Over the next ten months Proctor printed several of the respected designer-builder's letters, all masterpieces of basic architectural theory expounded in understandable lay terms.[7] Meanwhile, Collins continued his onslaught in the editions of 12 and 19 May; but, with the appearance of a proponent of Vidas's stature, he would soon surrender the field to Lawlor's redoubtable prose and professional expertise. Vidas's letters outlined a litany of hull design deficiencies, punctiliously weighing them against the horrendous loss of human lives that resulted. In the end, although Collins raised the question of seaworthiness in clipper schooners, it is apparent that Vidas–Lawlor–actually laid down the design characteristics necessary for an improved type.

Vidas's second letter outlined the problem: "We have adopted for seagoing vessels too nearly the proportions of length, breadth and depth suitable for river boats, sloops and coasters, . . . Beyond this, we have gone on sharpening the bows on the wale line till they are about the shape of a flatiron on deck, and when one of them falls off into the trough of a sea, and is struck by a heavy wave under the unnecessarily full, round quarter, having but little support under the lee bow, and the heavy masts and top hamper lurching to leeward, it ought not to surprise us that she is pitched over on her broadside to sink with all the precious lives aboard."[8] The third of Lawlor's series of six letters is a catechism of the design features he had come to believe in since he first began to practice at Boston in 1846:

---

6 *Cape Ann Weekly Advertiser*, 24 March 1882.

7 *Cape Ann Weekly Advertiser*, 28 April, 5 May 1882, and 25 January, and 1, 8, and 15 February 1883.

8 Vidas, "Models for Fishing Vessels, No. 2," *Cape Ann Weekly Advertiser*, 5 May 1882.

I assume that a vessel of from 100 to 110 carpenters or old measure is sufficiently large for profit in the business, and as safe as a larger one would be. I would have such a vessel say 70 ft. long, 20 feet wide, and 9 feet deep in the hold. That would make her about 110 carpenters' measure. As the depth increases the tonnage very fast, the carpenters could afford to build such a vessel at a cheaper rate than a wide and longer vessel, but I am sure they would not be overpaid if they had the same price per ton that they are getting for the present model. It should be borne in mind that a deep vessel has greater strength than a shoal one on account of her form, and will not bend and hog so easily. The floor should have so much dead rise that when the vessel is careened over all that she should be in a wholesail breeze, it may be level with the water, the bilge [?] lower than the garboard; and the dead rise increasing towards the stern; not like many of our vessels so dug out in the run that the floor in that part is nearly on a dead level, so that when the vessel is careened over there is a hollow for the water to run along in, and as any vessel sailing on the wind must make more or less leeway, the passage of the water under the bilge into this hollow is anything but smooth and easy, and is doubtless hurtful to her sailing qualities. The two ends of the vessel should be formed as much alike as they can be and preserve the square stern, and the lines may be very much alike below the waterline at ballast trim. The quarter should be thin, and the line from the end of the transom to the water should be hollow instead of bulging, thus avoiding the heavy, clumsy looking and dangerous quarters that many of our fishing schooners now have, and allowing the water to pass smoothly around the sternpost and rudder. Such a vessel should have a drag of a foot to eighteen inches, which would give her a better hold on the water where she needs it, and make it easier to form the lines around the stern. The stern should have no more overhang than is necessary to have a good room for the rudder-post, thus, for a given length of deck, giving greater length of hold and making a stronger stern. I know that when owners have to pay for length only as far as the after part of the stern-post, it may seem clear gain to have two or three feet of deck room added abaft that point without additional expense; but somebody has to pay the cost, and the vessel is not benefitted. A vessel always looks homely under the stern when her rudder is wholly covered with water, and a considerable length of

THE JOHN H. MCMANUS
AND THE PURITAN

stern projects beyond it. The vessel should preserve her width well up to her fore chains, and also toward her stern, and would then be as wide, for purposes of stability, as many that are now built of a foot or foot and a half greater breadth amidships. Such a vessel would be likely to be a better sailer, except in very light weather, than the shallow clippers now employed in the fishing business. I would have the floor straight from the keel to a quarter floor, or a little more, so that when the vessel careened over under sail she would put a large broadside under water on the lee side and lift a like one out of the water on the weather side, thus giving her great stability. The vessel should have a good sheer, so that when she is loaded there will be a large reserve lifting capacity forward and aft, to keep her above water in a heavy storm, and to help right her should she be thrown on her beam ends.[9]

Although Lawlor was in full song when he wrote this tract, before Collins put his pen aside he also had a go at Sea Horse: "All evidence goes to prove that, in the open ocean, especially where strong winds and rough seas are to be encountered, deep-bodied vessels are much more rapid than shallow ones. Nor does this depend so much on the vessel's carrying a great amount of sail, as it does on her ability to keep her course and make headway under short canvas, when one of less depth, though of broader beam, must heave to and drift to leeward. Our yachtsmen are waking up to this fact, and heavy draft yachts are being substituted for shallow ones by those who do not care to dodge from harbor to harbor, knowing they will fare hard if caught out in a gale."[10]

When Collins did desist, he refused to become merely an interested bystander, but continued to pursue the architectural changes that brought about the new schooner types. Coupling his political and industrial clout to Lawlor's design mastery, Collins conducted the drive toward a new model. The vessel would have to be a proverbial paragon to convince profit-hungry owners, hard-driving masters, and the decimated fishermen, reluctantly conscious of their own mortality, that a new type of schooner was essential, economically viable, perhaps inevitable.

Historians have too often inflated Collins, who, admittedly, was his own best public-relations man, while only hesitantly identifying Lawlor. Of even

---

[9] "Vidas," "Models for Fishing Vessels, No. 3," *Cape Ann Weekly Advertiser*, 19 May 1882.

[10] Collins, "Some Facts About the North Sea: A Reply to 'Sea Horse,'" *Cape Ann Weekly Advertiser*, 19 May 1882.

more historical significance, they have completely ignored Collins's superior, Spencer F. Baird, the U.S. Fish Commissioner, and his right-hand man, George Brown Goode. Also beginning in 1882, Baird pushed efforts to build a new research vessel for the Fish Commission, a schooner to be designed on the advanced deep-draught model:[11]

> Another important point for consideration is that of improvement in the pattern of fishing vessels. There is annually a terrible mortality in the fishing crews of New England, especially those belonging to the port of Gloucester, to say nothing of the total loss and wreck of the fishing vessels and their contents. There has gradually developed in connection with the mackerel and cod fisheries of New England a pattern of vessel which, while admirable for speed and beauty of lines and of rig, is less safe under certain emergencies than the more substantial and deeper vessel used abroad, especially in England and Scotland.
>
> The study of the best form of fishing vessel has been intrusted to Captain Collins, of the Commission, himself a most experienced fisherman, and, after a careful study of the boats of all nations, he has prepared a model which is believed to combine the excellencies of both English and American vessels.
>
> An appropriation will be asked from Congress for means to construct an experimental vessel and test it qualities; *but until a successful experiment has been made, it will be difficult to induce the fishermen to change their present form of construction.*[12]

In the question of hierarchy, if Collins was the field leader of the schooner safety crusade, Baird commanded it, with Goode as his adjutant. But Baird was clearly first and most of all a realist.

The culmination of Lawlor's collaboration with Collins appeared in the form of a model presented at the 1883 London Fishery Exposition, which "was highly approved by those who were competent to criticize and judge," Baird reported, while pragmatically recognizing the coming political and budgetary problems: "It is hoped that Congress may at an early date furnish the means for

---

[11] Dean Conrad Allard, Jr., *Spencer Fullerton Baird and the U.S. Fish Commission, a Study in the History of American Science* (Washington, D.C.: George Washington University, 1967), 309.

[12] Baird, *Report of the Commissioner . . . 1882*, xx, emphasis added. Baird repeated this entry in his 1883 report, published during 1885.

The collaboration of J.W. Collins and D.J. Lawlor produced the 83-ton schooner *Grampus* (81x22.9x10 feet), launched at Noank, Connecticut, in 1886. *Annual Report of the U.S. Commissioner of Fish and Fisheries, 1886.* (Photo by Claire White-Peterson)

building such a vessel, and not only aid the Commission in carrying out its work, but also in supplying a pattern for imitation by the fishermen."[13]

Predictably, Congressional bureaucracy delayed the necessary authorization to build a schooner to the Lawlor-Collins specifications until, on 23 March 1886, the deep-draft, plumb-stem schooner *Grampus* finally went down the ways at Noank, Connecticut. Afterward, Collins always correctly maintained that the 1883 model of the *Grampus* influenced builders of fishing craft even before her 5 June 1886 commissioning.

In reviewing her layout, if Lawlor had written a design catechism, Collins followed with a litany of hull and rig innovations:

> She [*Grampus*] was about two feet deeper than the ordinary schooner of the same length; the after section was more v-shaped, with easier horizontal lines; the stern was not so wide and had a much stronger rake; while the stem was nearly perpendicular above water, though curved strongly below. . . . The foremast was made considerably shorter than the mainmast, and the foretopmast, instead of being of the same length as the maintopmast, as had previously been the custom, was not so long by several feet. The schooner was also rigged to carry a forestaysail–the forestay coming down to the stem head–and a comparatively small jib, this arrangement of head sails being considered preferable to the large jib until then in almost universal use. Wire rigging was used instead of hemp.[14]

Several deep-draft schooners did get afloat before the *Grampus*, including Lawlor's *A.S. and R. Hammond* and *Arthur D. Story*, and the deepest of them all, the *John H. McManus*, but the first deep-draft banksman was none of these plumb-stemmers–it was the *Sarah H. Prior*, whose parenthood had been nurtured by the Boston Irish market fleet. Although many consider Lawlor's *Roulette* of 1884 to have been the forerunner of the schooners that Collins had proposed,[15] they have overlooked the *Prior*, the true antecedent of the deep-draft, plumb-stemmers (despite her clipper bow). She is the schooner that established the efficacy of deep-draft fishing vessels by allaying the twin fears of reduced speed and increased cost,

---

13 Baird, *Report of the Commissioner . . . 1883*, xxxv.

14 J.W. Collins, "The Evolution of the American Fishing Schooner," *New England Magazine* (May 1898): 347-48.

15 Howard I. Chapelle, *The American Fishing Schooners 1825-1925* (New York: W.W. Norton, 1973), 147.

and was the true transitional vessel between the clipper schooner and the new plumb-stemmers.

Any claims by Collins to design origination notwithstanding, his bowing to Vidas in the Gloucester newspaper debates, and later admission that "Lawlor prepared model specifications and plans, laid down the vessel, and produced the moulds," establishes the immigrant Bostonian as the architect of the *Grampus*.[16] The pervasive influence of Collins's intense antipathy to the shallow and broad clippers, nevertheless, constituted a major factor in the design of these new schooners.

Year	Schooner	Length	Breadth	Depth	Bow
1882	*Prior*	86.1	23.9	9.2	Clipper
1884	*Roulette*	82.0	23.2	10.0	Plumb[17]
1885	*McManus*	88.3	24.4	10.9	Plumb
1885	*Story*	85.0	23.3	9.6	Plumb
1885	*Hammond*	78.7	21.7	8.5	Plumb
1886	*Grampus*	81.0	22.9	10.0	Plumb

TABLE 6 - COMPARATIVE REGISTER DIMENSIONS, 1882-1886[18]

If some twentieth-century observers found the matriarchal lineage of the *Sarah H. Prior* obscure, to Tom McManus it was crystal clear: "having met with so much success in the *Prior* the next proposition was to build a vessel that would beat her," he remarked in a 1904 *Boston Herald* interview, "so the *John H. McManus* was started along much the same lines, except that she was 15 inches deeper in the hold."[19] Patently, if deep was good, deeper was better, and on this premise the famous *John H. McManus* came into being.

The final determinant regarding the evolutionary sequence of the new type is irresistible: all of the schooners in Table 6 originated from the drafting table and half models of a single architect, Dennison J. Lawlor, although his acolyte, Tom

---

16 Chapelle, *Fishing Schooners*, 152-53. He described Lawlor's trademarks as "much sheer, rather long, straight keel, nearly vertical sternpost, short counter, heavily raked transom of moderate width, strongly curved athwartship, nearly vertical stem rabbet above the load line, strongly curved below. The entrance was long, sharp, and concave just abaft the stem," *etc.*

17 The *Roulette* had a clipper cutwater, but a plumb-stem.

18 Data from the vessels' enrolments, U.S. Consolidated Enrolment and Licenses, Bureau of Navigation, Record Group 41, Records of the Department of Commerce, NARA. All dimensions in feet and tenths of feet. By contrast, the 1874 *Bunker Hill*, an extreme clipper with dimensions of length 82.9 feet, breadth 21.0 feet, and depth 7.0 feet, had a length/depth ratio of 11.8:1.

19 "Designer of Flying Fishermen," *The Boston Herald*, 1904.

McManus, probably had a hand in modeling at least the *Prior* and *McManus*, as their greater size suggests. The plumb bow may have originated from the British cutters that influenced Lawlor's racing yachts, but a search for an alternate concept source does not have to cross the ocean to discover the sturdy fishing smacks that influenced New England naval architectural thinking. The proliferation of Boston hookers safely operating on Massachusetts Bay afforded everyday evidence of the weatherly agility and load-carrying capability of vertical-stemmed, deep-draft boats. J.A. Osgood, the yacht racing enthusiast who owned *Gem* (the keel sloop that regularly defeated *Em'ly*), lived near the top of Point Allerton, "the jumping off place of Boston harbor." He gave a contemporary description of the Irish small-boat fleet in *Forest and Stream*:

> I have a view from my piazza over nearly an entire circle, taking in Minot's Light, Thatcher's Island, Marblehead, Boston and the blue hills of Milton. I can therefore see all craft going in and out of the harbor, and take great pleasure in watching them and their maneuvers. One of those, which has especially interested me, among the smaller sailing craft, is that used by the Irish market fishermen, an account of which will interest your readers.
>
> These "Irish" market boats seem to be a class peculiar to this port, and are different from any other boat in use here. They are powerful, able and fast; the short mast and small area of sail give one an impression at first of a small boat. A nearer view, however, shows a craft of great bulk, depth and freeboard. The high, full bow and "cod's head" give an appearance of unwieldiness and slow sailing. But let one of our crack yachts even try speed with the market boat, in a strong wind, and said yacht will find it no play to outsail her.
>
> The ability of these boats is surprising. They come in and go out of the harbor with three sails set, in a sea and gale that would sorely try a good sized schooner. They go anywhere–from Cape Cod to Portland–and into almost any kind of weather. . . . These boats have ample room, and carry large loads of fish, and their draft assures great ability in heavy seas. . . . The Irish market boats closely resemble the "Galway hookers" of Ireland. Many of them are owned and sailed by men from the Galway fishery.[20]

---

[20] *Forest and Stream*, 8 March 1883, 116.

The 111.7-ton *John H. McManus* (88x24x10.9 feet) combined D.J. Lawlor's hull-modeling experience with Tom McManus's innovative ideas in her plumb-stem, deep-draft hull and improved rig. Launched in 1885, she lived up to her potential for speed and stability. Photo by Nathaniel L. Stebbins, 5 April 1888. (Courtesy The Society for the Preservation of New England Antiquities, Boston, Massachusetts)

Although British plumb-stem, deep-draft cutter designs for yachts and fishing vessels attracted the attention of both Lawlor (who had incorporated the plumb-stem concept into his pilot schooners as early as 1876) and Collins (beginning no later than the 1880 Berlin Exposition), ultimately the logical amalgamation of the local Irish-descended hookers with Lawlor's swift pilot boats produced the *John H. McManus* and the other members of the mid-1880s' plumb-stem schooner persuasion.

With the coming of dory fishing, the mission of the fishing schooners had changed dramatically. No longer a simple platform for hand-liners, their function expanded to include the roles of mother-ships for the dorymen, and high-speed freighters for their salted or iced catch. The perishable commodity they transported demanded that it be landed expeditiously. This development further encouraged the McManuses, by then firmly committed to the ownership of banksmen, to press on with their two-decade-long pursuit of safer and faster fishermen.

The *John H. McManus* reflected Tom's attention to another area of concern–the masting and standing rigging of the banksmen–especially the weights aloft that contributed so disastrously to their rolling moment. In an example of pupil tutoring master that provides evidence of Tom's growing maturity as a designer, he had Lawlor reduce the height of the *McManus*'s foremast, compared to

her mainmast, to lower the weights of the bands around the masthead with their attendant blocks and rigging (a feature also found on the *Grampus*). This achieved the significant repositioning of the weights aloft that Tom sought, an architectural advance that originated directly from the family's sailmaking expertise. The masting modification improved the leverage from the rail to the hounds, or crosstrees, and gave the foresail a higher peak, which held it closer to the wind when going to weather. This allowed Lawlor to produce a design with markedly improved stability and impressive performance to windward, without sacrificing speed through the water. Predictably, the *John H. McManus* was a flyer. Author James B. Connolly once described his emotion-charged involvement with the big schooner:

> The *McManus* was the first vessel I ever fell in love with. A handsome one she was: her hull below the water-line an emerald green, her top planking a shining black; a golden stripe to mark her sweet sheer. When I first saw her she was new, with pure white sails and fresh varnished yellow spars; and to stand off her lee bow and watch her come sailing toward you, her white teeth just showing above the blue water, her bellying white sails leaving no empty spaces from balloon stay to mainsail leech,–to see her coming on so, her lee rail sifting through the white suds, the bright sun lighting up her white sails and bright yellow spars,–it was to see–well, she was beautiful.[21]

Speaking to the *McManus*'s other outstanding quality, safety, Tom proudly pointed out that "with that increased depth and the weights aloft so lowered, the men do not fear the wind or sea if every thing holds." Brimming with confidence he also pointed out that, "nothing but collision or the rocks give any fear to the hardy mariners who man these vessels."[22]

The new schooner incorporated many technological advances. "We had the builders [Arthur D. Story of Essex] fasten the heels of the frame with the keel and these bolts were staggered as her keel was two inches wider than the former vessels," Tom explained, "they were formerly bolted on a line with the center of the keel."[23] He felt that the old method led to the hidden hull leaks often suffered by the locally-built schooners. In the narrow waters of the Essex River, launchings were nerve-wracking events. On a few occasions newly-launched hulls capsized and

---

[21] James B. Connolly, *The Book of the Gloucester Fishermen* (New York: John Day Company, 1930), 197.

[22] Thomas F. McManus, "Essay No. 2."

[23] McManus, "Essay No. 3."

filled, and at other times they stuck on the ways; but more commonly, they shot across to collide with the mudflats on the opposite shore. The resultant oozy crash inevitably wrenched the keel and opened those hidden ruptures along the conventional straight-line run of fastenings, an impossible area to repair without dismembering the vessel.

Plank fastening, as well as keel bolts, shared the designers' attention: Lawlor's "specifications requiring the fastening of the plank to the timber and ceiling with locust treenails and that wedged on both ends, was the best fastening for any wooden ship."[24] The traditional method was far more labor intensive than the use of iron spikes, but iron might be degraded by the acids in the oak planking of fishing schooners. The ballast, however, was a different story. Tom called for pig-iron in place of the more commonplace stone ballast, which again lowered the center of weights to a measurable degree. Finally, the hold was divided off in equal fish pens so that the shifting boards would fit any and all slots alike, thus avoiding potential confusion under difficult operating conditions, an innovation that also proved a great time-saver.[25] Scrollwork around the *John H. McManus*'s hawse-pipes and a gilded, hollow line above the scuppers in the planksheer—the modern cove stripe—relatively simple adornments, followed the pattern begun by the McManuses with the *Sylph* twenty years earlier.

Sadly, the *McManus* would be the family's last commission for Lawlor, a man of undoubted creative genius, but lamentably lacking in practical business acumen. Due to ill-advised inventory practices during 1884-85, a foreclosure shut down the Canadian-American architect's famous Chelsea shipyard.[26]

Tom's memoirs mislead concerning the launch of *McManus*: "this boat was built at Essex in 1885 and Commodore Edward P. Boynton of the Boston Yacht Club named her *John H. McManus*, for my father."[27] Ned Boynton was an active member of the Hull Yacht Club in 1885, and would have to wait a score of years before attaining the rank of Commodore in the B.Y.C. (1904-06), but he did indeed christen the 106-ton *John H. McManus* on 18 May 1885, with the family's young protégé, skipper Johnny O'Brien, who had been trained in the ways of the sea by Captain Tom Herbert, grinning shyly at the helm.[28] Boynton's link to the

---

[24] Ibid.

[25] McManus, "Essay No. 2."

[26] Chapelle, *Fishing Schooners*, 149-50.

[27] McManus, "Essay No. 3."

[28] Enrolment No. 187, Boston and Charlestown, 18 May 1885.

McManuses was closely knitted; the genial and popular commodore-to-be's firm wove "Magnolia Duck," easily Boston's most sought-after sailmaking material.[29]

Popular belief and Tom's aging memory when he penned his autobiographical drafts aside, the swift *John H. McManus*, winner of the first of the famous fishermen's races, was neither owned by, nor called after, the illustrious head of the McManus family. Charley McManus, the schooner's underwriter and sole owner, named her for his three-year-old son, John H., the old man's namesake grandson.[30]

While New England fishermen contemplated the new designs of the 1880s, changes in the embarrassing award levied against the U.S. by the Halifax Commission of 1877 had spurred Congress to adopt a resolution on 26 February 1883 requiring President Chester A. Arthur to notify the British government of the termination of the appropriate articles of the 1871 Treaty of Washington to take effect from 1 July 1885, the earliest date for their abrogation. Although Arthur's presidential predecessor, R.B. Hayes, had paid the $5,500,000 award in gold specie determined by the Halifax Commission, there had never been any doubt that the United States would refuse to renew the fishery and reciprocity clauses when they expired.

The treaty's trade-off admitted Canadian fish and fish oil into American ports in return for opening the Canadian inshore fisheries to U.S. fishermen.[31] The cheap Canadian products that flooded American fishmongers' stocks seriously reduced the profitability of the New England offshore fleets by forcing a decline in the market value of their catch. In one side effect of the situation, nearly half of the men manning Massachusetts fishing vessels were foreign-born by 1885; the Americans they replaced having chosen to search for better paying work ashore. New Englanders strongly opposed any negotiation that might lead to a renewed remission of Canadian fish duties. They clearly felt their position to be more advantageous under the terms of the old 1818 agreement, which came back into force with the termination of the treaty.

When President Grover Cleveland's Democratic administration took power in March 1885, the first time for that party since before the Civil War, one Yankee, Charles L. Woodbury, wrote to Secretary of War William C. Endicott that "every

[29] Paul E. Shanabrook, *The Boston (A History of the Boston Yacht Club), 1866-1978* (Boston: Boston Yacht Club, 1978), 64.

[30] Letter, Edwin Charles McManus, 10 April 1989; Vital Records 1841-1895, Massachusetts State Archives, *Births*, 1882, vol. 333, page 235, line 74; Ship Registers of Boston, vol. 1885, 187, G.W. Blunt White Library, Mystic Seaport Museum, Mystic, Connecticut.

[31] Charles Callan Tansill, *Canadian-American Relations, 1875-1911* (New Haven, Connecticut: Yale University Press, 1943), 12-15.

fisherman along the shore from Block Island to Eastport" would rise in arms against any postponement of the tariff charges on Canadian fish."[32] Cleveland, who would have preferred to accommodate the British, found himself trapped between the party's new strength, the northeastern Irish-Democratic electorate, and a viciously partisan, Republican-dominated Congress. Typically, domestic politics overrode foreign-policy concerns. No Anglo-American fishing agreement would pass the Senate until after the turn of the twentieth century. When Canadian fish finally disapeared from Boston, McManus & Co., which had been suffering economically by faithfully selling the overpriced harvest of the local fleet, began a spell of prosperity that endured until Tom closed the fish brokerage permanently in 1902.

In a completely different international setting, the McManus sail loft arrived upon the America's Cup racing scene in 1885 with the advent of a Boston contender for the right to defend the Cup. Since the schooner-yacht *America* had spirited the "Auld Mug" away from the English in 1851, there had been four Cup defenses: against the self-same English in 1870 and 1871, and in response to Canadian challengers in 1876 and 1881. The shores of Massachusetts Bay enclosed the hub of America's Cup racing in the 1880s. The Eastern Yacht Club and its secretary and measurer, Edward Burgess, who, coincidentally, had replaced Dennison J. Lawlor as the McManuses' designer of choice, lay at its center.[33] McManus & Son's part in the construction of Boston's first America's Cup defender had its roots in the family and business relationships between the McManuses and the Boyntons.

When Meg McManus died in February 1884, patriarch John H.'s once-ample energies had gradually begun to decline. During the late winter and early spring of 1885 Charley gradually took over the management of the sailmaking company and the family fishing interests, as well as continuing to operate the vessel outfitting business and maintaining his partnership responsibilities in Tom's fish brokerage. Despite all this, thirty-one-year-old Charley, who had inherited all the genius of four generations of McManus sailmakers, somehow found time to put his yacht racing experience to work researching and developing a lighter weight of canvas duck.

During the latter part of 1884, through his friendship with thirty-year-old Ned Boynton, Charley approached N. Boynton & Co. with a proposition to produce the new sailcloth he had invented. Charley and Ned had known each

---

[32] Tansill, *Canadian-American Relations*, 17, citing the letter of Charles L. Woodbury to Endicott, 11 May 1885, Thomas F. Bayard Papers, Library of Congress.

[33] Joseph E. Garland, *The Eastern Yacht Club, A History from 1870 to 1985* (Camden, Maine: Down East Books, 1989), 28.

other throughout their lives. The Boyntons' company was always located at 87 Commercial Wharf, a few doors down from the McManus sail loft at 57. Ned's uncle, Nehemiah Boynton, and an in-law, Michael Bradley, were part-owners of Fingal fleet schooners as early as 1857. Latterly, Ned and Charley competed against each other on Boston Bay, and would reach the conclusion to join yacht-racing forces for the 1886 season, once the pressures of 1885 were behind them.

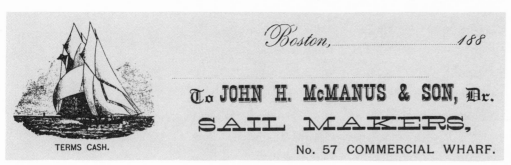

TERMS CASH.

Boston, 188

To JOHN H. McMANUS & SON, Dr.

SAIL MAKERS,

No. 57 COMMERCIAL WHARF.

John H. McManus operated a sail loft on Commercial Wharf from 1858 to 1892. This billhead dates from the 1880s.(Courtesy Louise V. Will)

The concept that Charley brought to the Boyntons altered the bias of the cloth's weave, to produce varying grades of canvas, ranging from muslin to several different weights of duck, all of which retained equal amounts of stretch and shrinkage, once the cloth had taken a "set." It was the beginning of modern sail technology–cotton duck material with predictable sail-shape retention, a major advance in sailmaking.[34]

The speed with which preparations for Boston's first America's Cup defense took place is breathtaking, even from a twentieth-century perspective. The New York Yacht Club received the new British challenge on 29 December 1884. Through the good offices of General Charles Jackson Paine,[35] who maintained memberships in both the New York Yacht Club and the Eastern Yacht Club of Marblehead, Massachusetts, the news literally reached Boston overnight. As soon as they heard it, a group of Boston yachtsmen joined with Paine in a decision to compete for the right to defend the Cup, a gambit admissible only through Paine's New York affiliation. From January through March 1885 some leading members of the Eastern met and determined to build the *Puritan*. They organized a committee, worked out the financing, and then reached the startling decision to place their hopes for victory squarely on the drafting table of an inexperienced designer–whose only task would be to design the fastest sloop in the world to achieve their goal of defending the America's Cup with a Boston boat. Contracts were let, building yard and sail loft priorities were reshuffled, and an oak keel fifty-six feet long and twenty-six inches square was laid–all within two months![36]

---

34 Letter, Edwin Charles McManus, 10 April 1989. George Stadel, Jr., of Stamford, Connecticut, a naval architect who corresponded and visited with Thomas F. McManus at Milton, Massachusetts, during the 1930s, also confirmed Charles A. McManus's invention of modern sailcloth during an interview on 10 August 1988.

35 "Major General of Volunteers" Charles J. Paine had commanded a division of black soldiers in the Union Army, and been wounded in the Civil War.

36 Garland, *The Eastern*, 30.

The "inexperienced designer" was, of course, Ned Burgess. During March, when the committee reached its final decisions under the chairmanship of Paine, the architect set about letting the construction contracts. To defeat the British, Burgess, with a tinge of irony, selected the yacht yard of English-born George Lawley to build the wooden hull of his prospective defender: "Messrs. Lawley & Son have the contract to complete the boat by June 10, under a penalty of $1,000, and they are now pushing the work as rapidly as possible," reported *Forest and Stream*. "Their building shed has been enlarged, and on Thursday last [26 March] the first chips came off the keel. . . . Sails and spars will be ready by the time the boat is launched."[37] For sails to power "the fastest sloop in the world," Burgess chose someone with more ostensibly anti-British leanings, the Irish-born sailmaker John H. McManus. When Burgess chose McManus, it was not only because of John H.'s unquestioned reputation as "the foremost sailmaker in the East,"[38] but also because he had heard of Charley's success with his new type of sailcloth. Accordingly, in late March the McManus loft received the order for sails totaling 7,982 square feet of duck, all to be hand stitched no later than the end of May.[39] The date was enough to make three McManus sailmakers, John H., Charley, and George, cringe. At that very moment, in addition to the abundant demand for sails instigated by the anticipated abrogation of the Washington Treaty, the fourth floor and attic loft at 57 Commercial Wharf hummed with activity as they raced to complete the *John H. McManus*'s sails in time for her scheduled early-May launch.

The McManuses proved equal to the multitude of demands placed upon their capabilities. The *John H. McManus* went to sea in May with a full set of sails. The plumb-stemmed Boston America's Cup racer followed a month later: "the keel was laid in March, and the new sloop, christened *Puritan*, was launched on May 26."[40] Then, under the command of a professional skipper, Captain Aubrey Crocker, the Eastern Yacht Club's defender candidate spread her canvas for the first time, allowing the sails to take their necessary set.[41] "[*Puritan*'s] boom is 76 ft. long and 14 in. diameter. Her sails were made by McManus & Son, of Boston, *the canvas being specially woven for her*. The mainsail is of No. 1, 14 in. wide, and the foresail of No. 2, and jib of No. 3, the area of the lower sails being about 5,000 ft. The jib sets

AND THE PURITAN

---

[37] *Forest and Stream*, 2 July 1885, 438.

[38] Captain Charlton L. Smith, "The First Fishermen's Race," *Yachting* (January 1939): 64.

[39] Garland, *The Eastern*, 30.

[40] *A Testimonial to Charles J. Paine and Edward Burgess from the City of Boston, for Their Successful Defence of the America's Cup*, 2nd ed., (Boston: Printed by order of the City Council, 1888), 35.

[41] *Testimonial to Paine and Burgess*, 36.

The handiwork of the McManus sail loft powered the big sloop *Puritan* through her successful defense of the America's Cup in 1885. Here, the 81-foot-waterline sloop sets up her new canvas—7,982 square feet of it, including a club topsail—during a trial spin on 10 June, just two weeks after her launch. Photo by Nathaniel L. Stebbins. (Courtesy The Society for the Preservation of New England Antiquities, Boston, Massachusetts)

flying with an outhaul and traveler, the forestay leads to the stemhead, and the mainsail, though laced, is also fitted with outhaul and traveler."[42]

July ninth found the *Puritan* anchored in Gloucester Harbor where Paine, Burgess, and Crocker intended to sail her to the leeward of a famous schooner race involving *Fortuna*, Henry S. Hovey, Commodore of the Eastern; *Mohican*, Henry D. Burnham; and the venerable *America*, General Benjamin F. Butler: "*Puritan*, sailing in the lee of the race, ran up on *Fortuna* [the leading schooner], and as the wind freshened walked through her lee, out ahead of her, and then up to windward. . . . About noon the pilot boat *Hesper* No. 5 [Boston's veteran trial horse] joined the race, but *Puritan* soon left her, and shortly after *Fortuna* passed her as well."[43]

In the defender's trials, the huge Boston sloop went on to outdistance the pride of the New York Yacht Club, the steel-hulled *Priscilla*, taking two out of three races on 21, 22, and 24 August, to win the right to defend the America's Cup against the British challenger, *Genesta*. The *Puritan* then preserved American dignity, and ownership of the old silver trophy, by beating *Genesta* two out of two on 14 and 16 September. In the first race, "the *Puritan* made a slight gain by

---

[42] *Forest and Stream*, 30 July 1885, 16, emphasis added.

[43] *Forest and Stream*, 16 July 1885, 497.

pointing higher into the wind. . . . On the stretch back to buoy 10 the sloop did splendid sailing, *and every inch of canvas did its work.*"[44] On board, after the second race a jubilant "Ned Burgess turned a double somersault as his creation smashed across the finish,"[45] to sew up the victorious defense of the America's Cup.

The McManuses had been distracted by the completion and fitting out of the *John H. McManus* and the rush to manufacture the sails for the *Puritan*; nevertheless, they capitalized on several opportunities to join in newly forming fishing-schooner syndicates. The *Puritan*'s canvas had no sooner been delivered to the Lawley yard in South Boston when, in conjunction with fellow Irishmen James Kearney,[46] Jeremiah McCarthy,[47] and Thomas Mahoney,[48] John H. and Charley joined with several Yankee waterfront personages in the new *Emily P. Wright* during June.[49] The following autumn Tom joined his father and brother in the syndication of the ninety-one-ton *Edith Emery*, which had been built by Moses Adams at Essex in 1883,[50] and, two months later, the three McManus men took part in the ownership of the *Loring B. Haskell*, built the year before from the plans of another rising designer, Captain George Melville McClain, a fisherman turned modeler.[51]

An excerpt from an 1887 Fish Commission *Bulletin* describing the fish fares delivered to Boston market by several of the above schooners following two or three days of fishing best underlines their profitability. The landings took place two years after the reimposition of the protective tariff on Canadian fish, and the fishing

---

[44] *Testimonial to Paine and Burgess*, 49-50, emphasis added.

[45] Garland, *The Eastern*, 34.

[46] James Kearney, master of the *Emily P. Wright*, had been a skipper since 1875, when he sailed the *Jehu* for Tim Connolly.

[47] McCarthy, one of the original Fingal immigrants, owned a string of schooners beginning with the *Friendship* (1854), *Bethiah* (1855), *Meridian* (1864), and *Merriam* (1865), all owned individually and commanded by himself. He purchased the new Wilbur Laskey-built *Eva G.* in 1865, and syndicated her in 1868, but continued as her skipper. He held a one-third share in the *Lady Thorn* in 1869, his last command. McCarthy retired from the sea in 1880 and purchased the *Belle A. Keyes*, for his son Charley to skipper, then sold a half-share to Charley Cross when he took over as master in 1885. McCarthy became a regular member of the large Boston syndicates with a share of the *Hattie I. Phillips* in 1885.

[48] Mahoney, or Maloney, as his name sometimes appears on enrolments, has proven untraceable. He was not in the Irish market fleet as an owner or master.

[49] Enrolment No. 245, Boston and Charlestown, 2 June 1885. The Yankee portion of the syndicate included William C. Stone, Freeman Emery, Cassius Hunt, William J. Emerson, John R. Neal, Emily P. Wright, Parron H. Prior, Benjamin Phillips, George W. Phillips, William A. Ray, James Emery, Jr., Thomas Byron Rich, Henry D. Stone, and Francis H. Johnson.

[50] Enrolment No. 94, Boston and Charlestown, 22 October 1885.

[51] Enrolment No. 117, Boston and Charlestown, 2 December 1885. George Melville "Mel" McClain was born at Bremen, Maine, in 1843 and grew up in nearby Friendship. He left there for Gloucester at age twenty, and shipped as a crewman on a mackerel seiner. Within a few years he gained command of the *Lucy E. Friend*, which he retained for several years. Over the course of fifty-six years he commanded a total of thirty-five fishermen. A habitual whittler, he convinced his owners to build one of his models, which became the famous *Lottie G. Haskins* (a development of the *Nellie Dixon*). Over 100 schooners were built to his designs (Wesley G. Pierce, *Goin' Fishin'* (Salem, Massachusetts: Marine Research Society, 1934), 121; Chapelle, *Fishing Schooners*, 157).

method was by trawl-lines: "Schooner *Emily P. Wright*, Georges, 40,000 pounds haddock. Schooner *Gertie E. Winsor*, La Have, 30,000 pounds haddock and cod. . . . Schooner *Hattie I. Phillips*, Georges, 75,000 pounds haddock. Schooner *Carrie and Annie*, Georges, 60,000 pounds haddock. . . . Schooner *Loring B. Haskell*, Georges, 60,000 pounds haddock. . . . Schooner *Edith Emery*, Georges, 60,000 pounds Haddock."[52] By the end of the summer the *John H. McManus* completed her first trips to the banks, and, on the all-important return runs with a hold full of iced fish, had logged impressive passages. The wharfside cynics, however, simply raised their eyebrows when Captain Johnny O'Brien mentioned his times, for *McManus* had not yet run head-to-head with the "queen of the fleet," that renowned sailer *Sarah H. Prior*.

Before Boston's 1885 yacht-racing season began, Charley, who had become unhappy with *Em'ly*'s performance as a sloop, re-rigged and re-canvassed her as a cutter to improve windward performance.[53] But, with the enormous growth of yacht racing on Boston Bay, and its attendant impetus on design innovation, the once-sprightly, ten-year-old *Em'ly* had become a gray-haired old lady in racing circles. Moreover, for the next year the development of his new racing sails would claim Charley's attention. To add to the dilemma, the nagging cough he suffered occasionally developed a fever that laid him low for as much as a week at a time. On Saturday, 20 August, nonetheless, in the Hull Yacht Club's open regatta, Charley placed *Em'ly* fifth in the "Third Class Keels," behind *Banneret*, a fish-dealers' special, which had passed from Bill Prior to the Brown Brothers to J.F. Burns; *Cricket*, Charles Francis Adams; *Carmen*, B.L.M. Tower; and *Stiletto*, A.S. Kilburn.[54]

September 9, 1885, which fell between the syndication of *Emily P. Wright* and *Edith Emery*, presented a heart-wrenching combination of emotional extremes to the family. Happy-go-lucky George, by then aged twenty-six and the sail loft administrator and draftsman, had fallen in love with a native-Irish actress three years his junior, Honora Doyle. The couple were to be married at Lawrence.[55] They had intended to do so earlier in the summer, but George had been suffering from fits of coughing, very similar to the ones that had been plaguing Charley for more than a year, and they delayed the wedding until he felt better. Tom and Kate McManus,

[52] George Brown Goode and Captain Joseph W. Collins, "The Winter Haddock Fishing of New England," *Bulletin of the United States Fish Commission* (Washington, D.C.: Government Printing Office, 1887), 401-402.

[53] Niels Olsen, *The American Yacht List for 1885* (New York: Henry Bessey, 1885).

[54] *Forest and Stream*, 20 August 1885, 75.

[55] Vital Records 1841-1895, Massachusetts State Archives, *Marriages*, 1885, vol. 361, page 262, line 237; James S. Sullivan, M.D., *One Hundred Years of Progress. A Graphic, Historical, and Pictorial Account of the Catholic Church of New England Archdiocese of Boston* (Boston: Illustrated Publishing Company, 1895), 371.

who was seven months pregnant, planned to take the morning train to Lawrence for the mid-week ceremony with the four girls, but complications arose over their niece Minnie, who was desperately ill of cerebro-spinal meningitis at Charley and Agnes's house in Dorchester. In the end, Kate stayed in Charlestown with the girls, and Tom and his ailing father traveled the twenty-six-mile, hour-long, sooty train journey to Lawrence for the ceremony. Tragically, the wedding party returned to Boston to learn that little Minnie had died in their absence.[56] George and Honora moved into 15 Margaret with John H., and three days later the families joined together to console the grieving parents, Charley and Agnes, at the baby's burial service in Calvary Cemetery.

Two months after that tortuous cycle of nuptials to requiem, Kate reached her term and delivered their fifth daughter, Catherine Cokely McManus, in the Mt. Vernon Street house on 14 November.[57] This newest arrival left Tom wondering whether he would ever be blessed with a son.

---

[56] Vital Records 1841-1895, Massachusetts State Archives, *Deaths*, 1885, vol. 366, page 264, line 7206.

[57] Vital Records, *Births*, vol. 360, page 43.

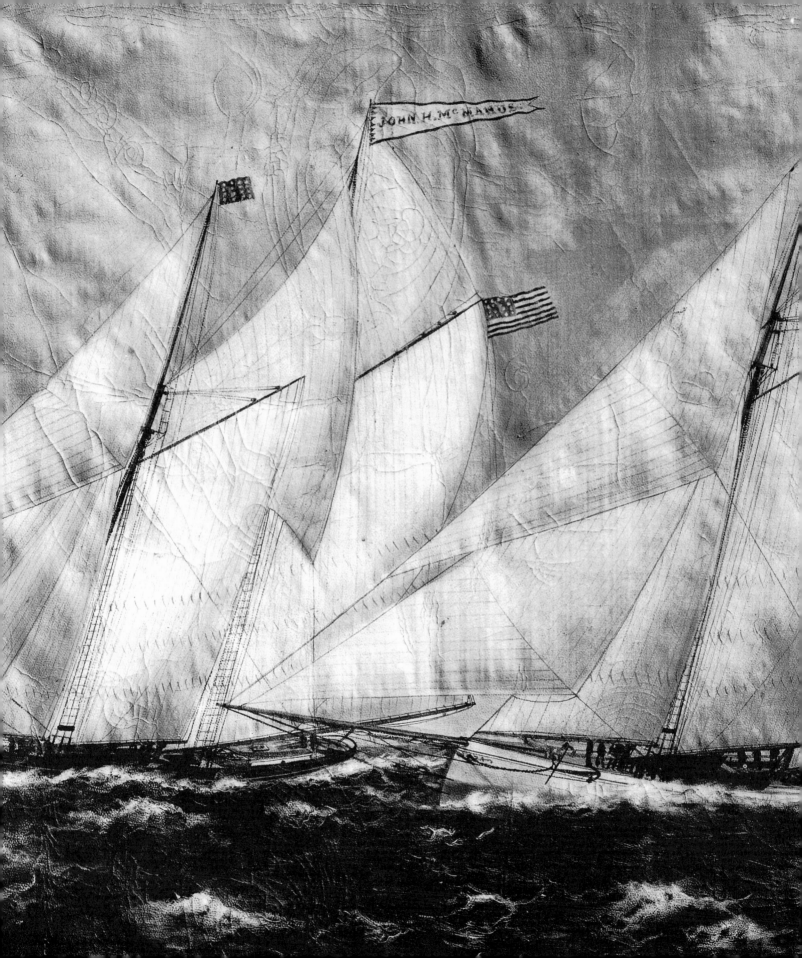

CHAPTER EIGHT

The *Mayflower*, *Carrie E. Phillips*, and *Nellie Dixon*

The *Puritan* had no sooner vanquished the *Genesta* off Sandy Hook in September 1885, than a predetermined sequence of events began and gathered momentum throughout the following autumn and winter. The new America's Cup activity was a result of the dual challenge made by the British in December 1884, nominating the *Galatea* for the following year, should the *Genesta* fail in her 1885 attempt to retrieve the America's Cup. This codicil scuttled any likelihood of a celebratory breathing spell for the victors. In anticipation of the second Paine-sponsored defender,

Burgess literally leaped from the deck of the *Puritan* off New York City to the front of his drafting table at Boston. Once there, he laid out the new racer as a typically white-hulled, plumb-bowed, but larger version of the *Puritan*, completing the plans during the first week of the new year.

For his second Cup defender, General Paine chose another name steeped in New England tradition, *Mayflower*. George Lawley & Sons laid her keel on 25 January 1886,[1] at their yard on South Boston's City Point, a locale they shared with Boston's euphemistically labelled "House of Industry" (a reform school), "House of Corrections" (a prison), and a third institution with the straightforward title of the Lunatic Asylum.

Coincidental to this sporting activity, the youngest of the surviving McManus brothers, newlywed George, joined the ranks of schooner owners when, the day after Lawley laid the *Mayflower*'s keel, Arthur D. Story launched the *W. Parnell O'Hara* for him at Essex.[2] George hired Tom Carroll, son of the notable but recently deceased skipper, Jim Carroll, as her master. The elder Carroll had been a partner of George's cousin, Nick Leonard, in the schooner *Charles Frederick*.

Two days after Lawley's keel laying, John H., Charley, and Tom McManus joined with the redoubtable Matt Keany in the ownership of the *Hattie I. Phillips*. The syndicate for this schooner provides an insight to the level of assimilation the Irish had achieved by 1886. The group included another McManus cousin, jeweler Ned Gregory, and his father-in-law and landlord, Chris Leonard, now retired from the liquor business and officially denoted on city tax rolls as a "gentleman," a panegyric they also attributed to Captain Tom Herbert.[3] Another retired Fingal fisherman, Jeremiah McCarthy, with Tom Mahoney, Mike O'Brien, and the *Phillips*'s master, young Ned Plunkett, completed the all-male Irish contingent, while females comprised nearly half of the Yankee partners: Emily P. Wright, Mary A. Stubbs, Harriet B. Stone, Caroline E. Phillips, Sarah A. Phillips, and Carrie M.

---

[1] *A Testimonial to Charles J. Paine and Edward Burgess from the City of Boston, for Their Successful Defence of the America's Cup*, 2nd ed., (Boston: Printed by order of the City Council, 1888), 54.

[2] Enrolment No. 139, Boston and Charlestown, 27 January 1886, U.S. Consolidated Enrolment and Licenses, Bureau of Navigation, Record Group 41, Records of the Department of Commerce, NARA.

[3] City of Boston, Tax Assessor's Records, Ward 6, Part 1, 80, 1886, Chris Leonard, 184 Salem Street, "gentleman," rented to Edward J. Gregory, jeweler (his son-in-law). According to Ward 6, Part 1, 11, 1886, Leonard also owned the "vacant land formerly 500 Commercial Street." Ward 6, Part 1, 56, 1886, Tom Herbert, "gentleman," owned 19 and 21 Tileston Street. John H. McManus's brother Patrick owned the tenement that housed his grocery at 450 Commercial Street, and according to Ward 6, Part 1, 66, 1886, he and his wife Lucy Ann (Shannon) McManus, owned 30 Charter Street, while Pat owned 32 Charter Street in his own right.

Burgess's 100-foot-overall sloop *Mayflower* (85x23.6x9 feet), was even faster than the *Puritan*. She is shown testing her rig and McManus sails on 30 May 1886, before going on to defend the America's Cup. Photo by Nathaniel L. Stebbins. (Courtesy The Society for the Preservation of New England Antiquities, Boston, Massachusetts)

Bunting joined their male counterparts, William C. Stone, Frank E. Harrington, George H. Clark, Freeman Emery, Otis T. Wiley, John R. Neal, and N.D. Freeman.[4]

After Ned Burgess delivered the *Mayflower*'s drafts to Lawley's yard, he returned to an office backlogged with orders. The naval architect, a son of an upper-class family, had graduated from Harvard in 1871, where he majored in mathematics and was a classmate of Henry Cabot Lodge. Although he did not take up the profession until 1882, the success of the *Puritan* meteorically transformed this enthusiastic yachtsman and fledgling yacht broker into a much-sought-after yacht designer. One commission awaiting his return came from Charley McManus, the man who made the *Puritan*'s sails. Charley had joined forces with Ned Boynton for the coming season, and they asked Burgess to design a centerboard catboat to replace the aging *Em'ly*. The two young Commercial Wharf entrepreneurs chose Arthur D. Story of Essex to build their new racer, which they named *Nora*.

---

[4] Enrolment No. 140, Boston and Charlestown, 28 January 1886.

Charley's loyalty to the dear old *Em'ly* ran deep. He wanted to keep her in the family and, when Tom showed no interest in taking her over, Charley sold the cutter yacht to brother George.[5]

As winter moved toward spring the 4 March issue of *Forest and Stream* cast some doubt regarding the sails for the Boston defender: "Messrs. Boynton & Company, the manufacturers of the canvas for *Puritan*, have commenced upon the duck for the new sloop, who is to make the sails, whether Boston or New York parties, is yet to be decided."[6] This hint of a New York sailmaker entering the picture should be weighed in the light of the newspaper's own New York origins, and matched against General Paine's known preference for Boston goods, as well as the ongoing collaboration between Burgess, the McManuses, and the Boyntons on the development of Charley's new sailcloth. Actually, at the Hub the issue was never in doubt. McManus & Son received the order to cut and stitch over 8,000 square feet of sails for the *Mayflower*. The 1886 defender, however, did carry at least one of Lapthorn's new silk spinnakers, and word of Burgess's order for it was the probable source for the newspaper's speculation. Although this style sail had yet to be fashioned in Boston, the Lapthorn product was no small indication of the growing competition the McManuses faced, even for local racing sails, where considerable inroads were made upon their trade by the energetic and talented Adrian Wilson of the Wilson & Griffin Company.[7]

In April some of the city's dockside workers went on strike and idled the local fishing fleet. On the spur of the moment, Tom, who had just received his now-familiar springtime message from Kate that she was pregnant again, decided to organize a race for the strike-bound fishermen to take place on May first, a rather altruistic enterprise that would bring him lasting fame as "the Father of the Fishermen's Races."[8] If his memoirs are any indication, McManus treasured that encomium above all his other professional accomplishments. His fisherman-turned-

---

[5] Niels Olsen, *The American Yacht List for 1886* (New York: Henry Bessey, 1886).

[6] *Forest and Stream*, March 4, 1886, 115.

[7] Adrian Wilson was the youngest son of Reuben H. Wilson, the innovative Port Jefferson, New York, sailmaker. Reuben, owner of the largest sail loft on Long Island, was most famous for having made the sails for George Steers's famous schooner yacht, the *America*, which crossed to Cowes, Isle of Wight, England, and won the Hundred Guinea Cup, now world famous as the America's Cup. Adrian became partners with his brother Frederick in the business upon their father's death. When wooden shipbuilding declined in the 1870s, Adrian left for Boston, where he established his own sail loft (*Yachting* (May 1917): 275; Richard F. Welch, *An Island's Trade: Nineteenth-Century Shipbuilding on Long Island* (Mystic, Connecticut: Mystic Seaport Museum, 1993), 64). The sails Reuben H. Wilson outfitted the *America* with were cut and sewn to his "bird's nest," which have been credited by some as the first advance in sail design for 2,500 years (Welch, *An Island's Trade*, 64, citing Gordon Welles and William Prios, *Port Jefferson, The Story of A Village* (Port Jefferson, New York: Historical Society of Greater Port Jefferson, 1977).

[8] Ralph M. Eastman, *Pilots and Pilot Boats of Boston Harbor* (Boston: Second Bank-State Street Trust Company, 1956), 49.

writer friend, Captain Charlton L. Smith, set the scene: "It was the last week of April; a strike of fish handlers was on; skippers and crews were restless. Discussion was rife as to whether the 'Old War Horse' *Sarah H. Prior*, hitherto queen of the fleet, was superior to the new schooner *John H. McManus*. . . . Tom listened to this and, as he couldn't bear to see the fleet idle, he put his shoulder to the wheel and, with little time for preparation, had a race on for the coming Saturday."[9]

Tom detailed how he raised the prize funds, "J. Malcolm Forbes, headed the list of contributors," he recollected; "then I called on General Charles J. Paine of *Puritan, Mayflower* and *Volunteer*, and he paid tribute to the subscription as did Commodore Hovey and a great many other prominent yachtsmen." The purse was to be divided among all contestants according to their position at the finish. McManus saw to it that every member of the crew, even down to the last boat, got at least a day's pay for taking part in the race. The list of yachtsmen donors represented Boston's élite: in addition to Forbes, Paine, and Hovey, it included Nathaniel N. Thayer, J. Montgomery Sears, Charles A. Longfellow, George Ripley Howe, E.V.R. Thayer, and Henry D. Burnham, as well as the Yankee fish dealer partners of the McManuses in the schooner syndicates. Parron H. Prior, William B. Wetherell, and Benjamin F. Phillips of the latter group volunteered to join Tom on the Race Committee.[10] George Goddard, Ned Burgess's predecessor as the measurer of the Eastern Yacht Club, agreed to act as referee, and the seagoing tug *Elsie* was donated for his use.[11] Within the course of a single, albeit hectic day, Tom raised $1,500 for the prize fund. After soliciting the yachtsmen, canvassing firms who outfitted and supplied the fishing fleet, and tapping fellow fish dealers, he noted with satisfaction, "they were all very generous because they were all race-minded on account of the *Puritan* and *Mayflower*."[12]

Charlton Smith related how the pilot boat *Hesper* managed to get into the fishermen's race. Commodore Forbes formalized the pilots' entry while McManus was in his office collecting a $100 donation: "as Tom started for the door, [Forbes] called him back and said: "'I should like, also, to give a cup of the value of $100. If the pilot boat *Hesper* comes in first, she gets the cup; if it should happen to be a fisherman, she gets the cup and $100 as well.'"[13] Tom agreed to this proviso with alacrity; after all the race regulations allowed all two-masted "working" vessels.

---

9 Captain Charlton L. Smith, "The First Fishermen's Race," *Yachting* (January 1939): 65.

10 Boston *Evening Transcript*, 28 April 1886.

11 Boston *Journal*, 3 May 1886.

12 Charlton L. Smith, draft version of a 10 April 1922, Boston *Evening Transcript* article, enclosed in a letter from Smith to McManus, 11 April 1922.

13 Smith, "The First Fishermen's Race," 65.

The committee saw to it that the first rule of the day assured that the fishermen sailed as fishermen not pseudo-yachtsmen, and at no expense to themselves. With this principal point covered, the practical committee members laid out the balance of the minimal regulations, a pleasant change from the complexity of yacht-racing rules: the contestants were to sail boat-for-boat, with no time allowance to accommodate different size hulls or spread of canvas; they could haul out to clean and paint their bottoms; all but one dory could be left ashore; but anchors and cables had to be left on the bows.

In a magazine article penned forty years later Smith described the contest and recalled how the fishermen, no fools they, managed to make the race pay off before it began. Led by Captain Johnny O'Brien of the *John H. McManus* and Captain Tom McLaughlin of the *Sarah H. Prior*, they filled their decks instead of their holds and delayed the start for an hour while they picked up their fares: "the beautiful high-bowed *Hesper*, with Commodore Forbes on board as a guest, was the first to start down the bay. The *Prior* and the *McManus* followed with a large crowd on the deck of each, for they carried passengers at $5.00 a ticket."[14] After a long and difficult afternoon's work the schooners predictably followed the *Hesper*, which was leading by about 40 minutes with all her canvas aloft, to the finish line. The *John H. McManus* crossed at 6:31 P.M., with no less than "106 persons, a fiddler and a barrel of beer between decks,"[15] easily outsailing the other fishermen. She had gained steadily on them over each leg of the course. The *Prior* was next home, two miles astern of the *McManus* at 6:46, and the *Winsor* came in seven minutes later. The *Neal* was four minutes behind the *Winsor*, while the *Phillips*, *Emery*, and *Wright* took another half hour to reach the line. Thus, the *John H. McManus* displaced Smith's "Old War Horse," the four-year-old *Sarah H. Prior*, as "queen of the fleet."

Including the *Hesper*, the first three finishers were all products of the genius of Dennison J. Lawlor. There were no losers that day for the McManuses, as they owned shares in all the official entries. Tom's rationale in organizing the event surpassed any simple desire to entertain the idle fishermen: "I advocated yearly competition in Sailing regattas, to encourage fishermen to improve on their boats and as the fresh fish industry handle a perishable article of food and the fresher it reaches the Consumer the more palatable and the demand increases, so *it is essential to that branch of the fisheries to encourage increased speed in the vessels which bring the goods to the Market.*"[16]

---

[14] Ibid., 212.

[15] "Designer of the Flying Fishermen: Thomas F. McManus Tells How the Present Type Was Developed," Boston *Herald*, 1904.

[16] Thomas F. McManus, "Autobiographical Essay No. 2," emphasis added.

A week after the race, Charley McManus, with a year of profits put by, syndicated the winning *John H. McManus* for the first time to the usual waterfront blend of upper-crust Bostonians, waterfront Yankees, and dockside Irish, including Emily F. Gregory, of "Li'l Em'ly" fame. She and her father, Chris Leonard, owned the largest single shares, an eighth each.[17]

If the anti-British attitudes of Boston's immigrant Irish sailmakers had energized their America's Cup efforts in 1885, the new British challenge should have spurred them to even greater heights. In Ireland there was no greater anathema for the native artisans than the aristocratic English landowner class, and the owner of the *Galatea*, Lieutenant William Henn, R.N., Dublin-born in 1847, was the son of a landed proprietor in County Clare. At his own request, the Royal Navy had placed Henn on the retired list for his rank in 1875, when he took up yachting.[18] The Cup challenge represented the acme of his second career.

On 3 May the Boston *Journal* reported that "George Lawley & Sons commenced work on Saturday on the ways for launching the new sloop *Mayflower* and by Tuesday night everything was in readiness for the launch" of the prospective defender.[19] The sloop slid gracefully into Boston Bay on Thursday, and the work of fitting her out began immediately.[20] Once underway, the shakedown process for the huge racing yacht proved problematical. For the first few trips the trim was off, the sails bagged excessively, and the crew could not even lower the centerboard. As a result, the *Puritan* outsailed the *Mayflower* regularly during several sea trials in surrounding waters. For many of the next sixty nights, the gaslights hissed brightly in the McManus loft, casting eerie shadows over twenty to thirty hunched-over journeymen sailmakers driving needle to palm around the clock, as they reshaped the canvas for Paine's yacht again and again.

In Boston, the fever of the fishermen's race and the excitement over the forthcoming America's Cup challenge obscured an important event that took place a hundred miles to the southwest at Noank, Connecticut, on 5 May. Captain Joseph W. Collins, having overcome two years of bureaucratic red tape, stood proudly by as the U.S. Fish Commission's experimental schooner *Grampus* finally slid down the ways at the Robert Palmer & Sons shipyard. One of the last of Lawlor's deep-draft prototypes had entered her element.

---

[17] Enrolment No. 260, Boston and Charlestown, 10 June 1886.

[18] *Forest and Stream*, 9 September 1886, 27.

[19] Boston *Journal*, 3 May 1886.

[20] *Testimonial to Paine and Burgess*, 54.

With the fishing fleet off to the banks and the *Mayflower's* sails recut and shipped from the loft for the last time, Charley McManus and Ned Boynton began to fit out their new catboat, *Nora*, which they launched during the last week in June. The partners rushed her across the bay to the Hull Yacht Club's open regatta on Saturday, 3 July and managed a fourth-place finish, although, by not having waited for official admeasurement, the official scorer dropped *Nora* to sixth in the standings behind G. Ripley Howe's twenty-two-foot half-decked catboat, *Mabel*; F.L. Dunne's twenty-two-foot nine-inch sloop, *Tartar*; Sibley A. Freeman's *Thisbe*; P.M. Bond's 19-foot 3-inch catboat, *Em Ell Eye*; Dr. Charles G. Weld's *Tom Cat*; and H.P. Elwell's *Tyrant*.[21] Two weeks later at the Hull's first club championship meeting of the season, with the *Nora* now properly measured at twenty-one feet waterline length, they finished fifth in the "Fourth Class Centerboards" category, following *Tom Cat*, *Mabel*, *Tartar*, and Adrian Wilson's *Crusader*.[22] It was undoubtedly a frustrating experience for Charley McManus to finish immediately behind Wilson, one of his stiffest competitors for Boston's racing sails business.

By August, Charley and Ned had shaken their new racer down. On the fourteenth the *Nora* moved up to finish second behind R.G. Hunt's *Posey* in the next round of the Hull championship, but ahead of *Louette*, L.M. Haskins; *Tyrant*; *Sea Bird*; *Expert*, L. Whitcomb; and *Sprite*, in "Third Class Centerboards."[23] Happy enough with the progress of their own racing efforts, they experienced even greater satisfaction a fortnight later, when the *Mayflower* met and defeated the *Atlantic*, the New York Yacht Club's candidate, along with the older racers, *Puritan* and *Priscilla*, in two out of two heats in the America's Cup defender's trials on the twenty-first and twenty-second.

Yacht racing reaches a fever pitch in the late summer each year and, on 28 August in the Hull's third championship round, the boys brought the three-month-old *Nora* in first, ahead of *Posey* and S.L. Quincy's *Mugwump*.[24] The next weekend, with Charley and Ned distracted by Burgess's last minute sail-cutting demands for the Cup defense, George, who had sold the *Em'ly* to I.H. Porter of the Beverly Yacht Club,[25] took the *Nora* up the bay to the Marblehead Yacht Club's open regatta and came in fourth behind *Sprite*, Dr. C.P. Wilson of the Boston; *Good Luck*, J.B. Farrel of the South Boston; and *Sea Bird*, Charles L. Joy of the Hull; but ahead

21 *Forest and Stream*, 8 July 1886, 479.

22 Ibid., 24 July 1886, 519.

23 Ibid., 8 July 1886, 479.

24 Ibid., 2 September 1886, 116.

25 Thomas Manning, *The American Yacht List for 1887* (New York: Henry Bessey, 1887).

of such notable contenders as *Fancy*, *Tyrant*, *Petrel*, *Vixen*, *Alda*, *Posey*, *Silver Cloud*, *Myth*, *Reckless*, *Freya*, *Blanche*, *Pearl*, *Louette*, *Ruth*, and *Osceola*. "It is to be noticed that the four new Burgess boats average well," *Forest and Stream* pointed out; "*Sprite* and *Nora* take first and third in third class centerboards, and *Nixie* takes third in fourth class keels. . . . Following protests were made, to be decided later, all prizes held in abeyance for the present: *Seabird* vs. *Nora*, foul. . . . *Fancy* vs. *Seabird*, length."[26] Young George obviously had a skilled, if bullish, hand at the helm.

The overworked artisans who operated the Boynton looms and stitched and sewed in the McManus loft breathed a collective sigh of relief when their sails powered the *Mayflower* to a repeat of her Cup trials performance, and defeated the *Galatea* two out of two races on 7 and 11 September. But, while Ned Burgess tumbled through his famous somersault act on the *Mayflower* in New York harbor, Ned Boynton and Charley McManus were battling adversity back home.

Their cumulative early round finishes for the club championship predicated a sail-off against R.G. Hunt to decide the final winner of the class trophy. In the event Charley and Ned actually sailed the course in a faster time than their competitor, but an equipment breakdown soon after the start cost them valuable time while they cobbled up a jury-rig: "*Nora* lost her bowsprit but rigged a spar out and reset her jib, and made good time over the course,"[27] but with the frustrating result that she trailed *Posey* home by four minutes to lose the championship.

A month after the America's Cup races, the editor of *Forest and Stream*, Charles Kunhardt (an 1870 graduate of the U.S. Naval Academy), advanced a lengthy thesis on the shape of the contenders. By New York Yacht Club admeasurements the Boston defender hoisted 8,634 square feet of canvas to power her 85.7-foot hull, while the *Galatea* set 1,100 square feet less to propel a hull with the slightly longer waterline length of 86.8 feet:[28]

> That *Galatea* was not beaten by more than 7 min. and not by as much as difference in rig would account for, is the best proof possible that *Galatea*'s form of hull is particularly well adapted, keel, lead and all, for the highest speeds in light wind, and that her form of hull is really superior to that of the *Mayflower*, else she should have been beaten by more than the difference in sail area accounts for instead of less.

---

[26] *Forest and Stream*, 9 September 1886, 135.

[27] Ibid., 16 September 1886, 156.

[28] *Testimonial to Paine and Burgess*, 57-60.

Had *Galatea* like sail area with *Mayflower*, the cutter would have shown herself the faster of the pair. She lost both races, simply because she was underrigged by comparison.[29]

History has shown clearly, despite this misguided, if mild, anti-Boston treatise, that in America's Cup racing, the boat with the best sails wins. Beginning with the *America*'s victorious circuit of the Isle of Wight in 1851, American sails had proven superior to British sails in international match racing. Kunhardt's newspaper had underlined this as early as 1881:

> THE AMERICAN LAPTHORNS–Or perhaps it would be more in keeping with truth did we call Lapthorn the Wilson of England. Everyone knows the revolution the sails of the *America* created abroad and how, working on the lessons received from that famous schooner, the present firm of LAPTHORNS of Gosport, Eng., made for themselves a world-wide reputation. We are glad to find among our advertising patrons the same old established house that thirty years ago taught our cousins across the sea such a valuable lesson. Messrs. F[rederick] M. & A[drian] Wilson . . . It was their father [Reuben H. Wilson] who by his faultless art contributed so much to the victory of old George Steers' handiwork, and his successors in the business work on the same principle and obtain perfection of fit.[30]

Having won their place among America's Cup technology leaders, at the end of November the McManuses took a small holding in the socially assimilated syndicate organized by Francis J. O'Hara to share ownership in a two-year-old fishing schooner, the eighty-two-ton *Carrier Dove*.[31] This brought the year to a close with Irish integration a matter of fact in Boston society. Yankees and Irish alike evinced great pride in the city's second consecutive America's Cup defense. And, within and without the Irish community, Tom McManus's title as the "Father of the Fishermen's Races" established his lasting fame, even before his first successfully-launched design had been set to paper.

---

[29] *Forest and Stream*, 7 October 1886, 214.

[30] *Forest and Stream*, 17 February 1881, 57.

[31] Enrolment No. 112, Boston and Charlestown, 30 November 1886; previous Enrolment No. 12, Gloucester, 1884. Owners: Francis J. O'Hara, 20/32; John McKinnon of Gloucester, 1/8; John S. Wright, 1/16; W.C. Stone, 1/32; McManus and Son, 1/32; F.H. Johnson, 1/32; O.H. Wiley, 1/32; W.A. Ray, 1/16.

Following Charley's lead with the *John H. McManus*, George syndicated the *W. Parnell O'Hara* after a year of individual ownership on 24 February 1887, with John Donnelly taking over from Tom Carroll as master.[32] Still bothered by the same nagging cough that troubled Charley, George continued to rent accommodation for himself and Honora in his father's house at 15 Margaret Street.[33] They were now the only other occupants, and Honora spent much of her time looking after John H., whose health and vitality continued to decline.

Illness stalked the family. Charley, recently diagnosed as a consumptive, fell victim to a shipboard misadventure early in 1887. One of his twin grandsons, Edwin Charles McManus, succinctly described the accident: "When one of his key employees was absent, he volunteered to measure the sails for a ship and somehow fell into the winter waters."[34] The soaking inflamed his hacking cough and, although doctor's orders confined him to a sickbed on and off for the rest of the year, he never fully recovered. Even a recuperative trip to Florida with Agnes did not soothe his malaise.

It might have been expected that the glitter of America's Cup competition would have lost its sparkle for Bostonians after two consecutive wins by local yachts, particularly for General Charles J. Paine, who advanced the monies for much of *Puritan*'s defense, and all of *Mayflower*'s. Yet, when the New York Yacht Club received a third consecutive annual challenge, this time from the Royal Clyde Yacht Club of Scotland, Paine once again engaged Burgess to design a racer to compete for the right to defend the Cup. The result was the *Volunteer* and, although Lawley & Sons were chosen to fit her out, Delaware's Pusey & Jones shipyard built the sloop, Burgess's first design to be fabricated in steel. Extant records do not indicate the manufacturer of the *Volunteer*'s sails, although it is known that Wilson & Griffin produced at least one mainsail for the inventory, and one of Lapthorn's silk spinnakers was also included. Tom made no claim for McManus & Son relative to the *Volunteer* in his memoirs. The new defender departed from Lawley's yard in July for her shakedown cruise, and proved a swift sailer from the start, suffering none of the early ailments that had plagued the *Mayflower*.

The defender trials began on 13 September 1887, and the only other competitor was the *Mayflower*, recently re-sparred by her new owners, but to no avail. The Boston boat dispatched her older sister with ease in the first round, and

---

32 Enrolment No. 152, 24 February 1887. Owners: Thomas F. McManus, 1/32; John H. and Charles A. McManus, copts. 1/16; A.B. Gookin and F.W. Stodder, copts. 1/16; Charles A. Welch, Jr., 1/16; Thomas Mahoney, 1/16; Henry C. Dalby, 1/16; James Mahoney, 1/16; Jeremiah McCarthy, 1/16; George A. Hayward, 1/16; Francis J. O'Hara, 1/16; Thatcher Magoun, 1/16; Matthew Keany, 1/16; Matthew Leonard, 1/16; Thomas H. Smith, 1/16; George A. McManus, 3/32.

33 City of Boston, Tax Assessor's Records, Ward 6, Part 1, 97, 1887.

34 Letter, Edwin Charles McManus, 10 April 1989.

Edward Burgess (1848-1891).
A *Testimonial to Charles J. Paine
and Edward Burgess, from the City
of Boston* (1887).

the New York Yacht Club committee did not wait for a second. They selected the *Volunteer* on the spot. The details of the much-heralded Scottish challenger, *Thistle*, had been shrouded in secrecy, but against the Boston defender the effort was fruitless. In varying wind and sea conditions, the *Volunteer* literally blew the Scots away, by nineteen minutes on 27 September, and by just under twelve on the thirtieth, with Burgess performing his now traditional double somersault on the deck at the finish line.

Earlier in the year, after Burgess had completed the drafts for the *Volunteer*, Charley, during a brief respite from his sickbed, retained him to draft a new fishing schooner. It was the architect's first workboat design, but the fifth in the remarkable line of McManus-sponsored trendsetting schooners after the *Sylph, Actress, Sarah H. Prior,* and *John H. McManus.* Since her launching in 1885 the latter schooner had outsailed all challengers, and Burgess recognized the opportunity open to the designer whose creation could beat the big McManus fisherman. Tom told of the beginnings of the project: "my father and brothers were friendly with Edward Burgess," and they turned to him after Lawlor's business failed "to get out a fishing vessel called *Carrie E. Phillips* which was the first Commercial vessel he designed."[35]

From the moment Ned Burgess first put pen to paper, the *Phillips* drew considerable attention from the press. Until then, they had looked upon the Harvard graduate solely as a yacht designer. In September, just prior to leaving for the Cup trials at New York, Burgess paid a visit to Arthur D. Story's yard at Essex to check on the fishing schooner. Under the curious caption "YACHTING NOTES," *Forest and Stream* concurrently reported the workboat's construction progress: "the fisherman, designed by Mr. Burgess, is now in frame at Story's yard, Essex. She is 102 ft. overall, 94 ft. l.w.l., 24 ft. 6 in. beam, 11 ft. hold,"[36] in fact the *Carrie E. Phillips* would be larger than either the *Puritan* or *Mayflower.*

Wasting no words, Tom explained his own involvement, "my brother requested me to assist [Burgess] which I did," by taking the architect straight to the source. "We went on board the schooner *McManus*," he wrote, "and took measurements of the essentials to give him the proper idea of a fishing boat."[37] The extent of Tom's contribution to the *Phillips*'s design is not clear. Considering several factors–his participation in the *Prior* and *McManus* with Lawlor; Burgess's meticulous proficiency as a draftsman, but mediocre competence as a modeler; and McManus's superior whittling skill–it is possible that he shaped the half model for

---

[35] McManus, "Essay No. 1."

[36] *Forest and Stream,* 8 September 1887, 136.

[37] McManus, "Essay No. 2."

study purposes. If so, the model was truly a combination of concepts. The *Phillips*'s underbody not only reflected the influence of Lawlor's recent fishermen, and Tom's strong advocacy of deep-draft hulls, but also bore a strong resemblance to the ubiquitous "Boston Hookers." The buttock lines,[38] however, are distinctly in Burgess's style, and the white hull was effectively his autograph. McManus's own later creations, the *Regina, Lizzie M. Stanley*, and *Ida M. Silva*, among others, speak to a close involvement on his part in the *Carrie E. Phillips*'s design.

Tom made sure that the lessons learned from the *John H. McManus* were heeded. They employed a pole bowsprit with oak "whiskers" piercing the head of the stem to support its shrouds. He convinced Burgess to lower the roll center through the strikingly simple expedient of increasing the weight in the keel by using denser and heavier materials in the bilge than was the general practice. The combination of Portland cement, sand, and small boiler punchings gained the additional weight below the waterline. Embedded in this heavy slab, the keel formed a uniquely rigid backbone for the whole structure in addition to having a beneficial effect on the weights aloft.[39]

One weekly newspaper described the *Phillips*'s crew capacity: "Like all of Mr. Burgess's boats she is painted white. She will carry ten dories with two men each, besides her captain, Maurice Powers, a cook, and an extra man, making 23 on board."[40] The contemporary commentary was not uniformly complimentary. The inveterate waterfront reporter "Loyalty" (who covered the New York and Boston beats for *Forest and Stream*), offered a counterpoint, not only to the *Carrie E. Phillips*, but also to the general run of New England fishing schooners:

LOYALTY VISITS BOSTON, *Editor Forest and Stream*: While in Boston last week I took the opportunity to look at the new fisherman, designed by Burgess. . . . Her masts are of Oregon pine, two fine sticks set well forward. This I think is a mistake in a vessel intended for fishing, especially so in this vessel. Her greatest cross section is too far aft. To my mind her masts should be further aft, her greatest cross section further forward, more flare to the harpins, a clipper stem, and more draft under her forefoot. Most of the fishermen built in late years have sacrificed seaworthiness to

---

[38] "Buttocks" refer to the breadth of a vessel where the hull narrows down to the stern. A ship is said to have a broad or narrow buttock according to the convexity of its hull below the counter. The buttock "lines" are the longitudinal sections of a ship's hull parallel to the keel.

[39] McManus, "Essay No. 3."

[40] *Forest and Stream*, 3 November 1887, 297.

speed, and it is not to be wondered at that so many are lost. Stand on the wharves in Boston and you will not find one vessel in fifty that is properly sparred. They are sparred too much as yachts for speed with a ponderous main boom, the carrying away of which is no uncommon occurrence.[41]

Although it had been widely circulated that the name of the new Burgess fisherman honored the wife of her "principal owner," in fact the lady herself, Carrie E. Phillips, was the principal owner with a 17/64ths share in the vessel. Her husband, Parron H. Prior, held only 4/64ths.[42] At the invitation of the Phillipses, a gala party of Bostonians took the train up to Story's yard at Essex for the launch on 29 October. After the traditional christening by Mrs. Phillips, the lofty schooner slid down the ways and rapidly gathered momentum until a supporting chain snapped as the vessel hit the water. The horrified spectators watched in dismay as the beautiful white schooner slowly tumbled over onto her starboard side before she splashed into the Essex River. The vessel's unusually deep roll stability saved the day. The *Phillips* quickly righted herself, although the brave souls who had careened down the ways on board her suffered a thorough dousing.

Charley's request for his brother to assist Burgess turned out to be the thirty-two-year-old sailmaker's last one, for his sickbed became his deathbed. Tom described the tragic spectacle, "my brother was stricken with pneumonia. He called me to his bedside and asked me to assist Mr. Burgess in[to] the commercial line."[43] Charley, whose incessant cough had been diagnosed as "pulmonic phthisis" (tuberculosis in lay terms),[44] developed an ancillary case of pneumonia after his fall into the frigid bay waters the previous winter. The combination of tuberculosis and the pneumonia virus proved too much for Charles Aloyisius McManus. He died 2 November 1887, a month short of his thirty-third birthday and four days after the *Carrie E. Phillips* splashed into the Essex River.[45]

---

[41] Ibid., 1 December 1887, 376.

[42] Ibid., 27 October 1887, 276; Enrolment No. 181, Boston and Charlestown, November 26, 1887. Owners: George P. Freeman, 4/64; Parron H. Prior, 4/64; Thomas F. McManus, 2/64; John S. Wright, 4/64; Solomon J. Cobb, 4/64; Otis H. Wiley, 4/64; George H. Parker, 2/64; Rachel Nason, 1/64; Charlotte M. Hunt, 1/64; Georgiana Hunt, 1/64; Mary F. Powers, 8/64, Sarah A. Phillips, 8/64, John H. McManus, 4/64; Carrie E. Phillips, 17/64; and William B. Wetherell, 2/64. In fact, Mrs. Phillips had wide holdings in schooner syndicates, including a 4/32 share in the *Belle J. Neal*, 2/32 in *Edith Emery*, 2/32 in *Hattie I. Phillips*, 2/32 in *Loring B. Haskell*, 1/16 in *Maggie Sullivan*, and 1/32 in *Amy Hanson*.

[43] McManus, "Essay No. 2."

[44] Letter, J. Worth Estes, M.D., 5 April 1990.

[45] Letter, Edwin Charles McManus, 10 April 1989; Vital Records 1841-1895, Massachusetts State Archives, *Deaths*, 1887, vol. 384, page 342, line 36. According to his death certificate Charles A. McManus died at age "32 years, 11 months, of pneumonia (PulPhihisis for 3 years)."

Charley's death, coupled with that of his Uncle Pat, who had suddenly died just ten days before, the victim of a heart attack,[46] psychologically crippled the widowed and weakening John H. To the elder McManus, it seemed as if the awful specter of the Grim Reaper constantly loomed over his family: Joseph dead in infancy, Louis dying just short of eighteen, and now Charley at thirty-two. Of his own Fingal generation, the deaths of his wife Meg at fifty-five, his sister Mary at forty-three, and brother Patrick at fifty-five, left only himself and his sister Kate as its survivors. Once again the black-clad, grief-stricken McManuses gathered at the family plot at Calvary Cemetery to bury one of their own.[47]

In the 115.7-ton *Carrie E. Phillips* (93.5x24.9x11 feet), Edward Burgess and Tom McManus perfected the concepts introduced by the *Grampus*. The spike bowsprit—in place of the bowsprit and jibboom of the clippers—soon became standard for fishing schooners. Photo by Nathaniel L. Stebbins, November 1887. (Courtesy The Society for the Preservation of New England Antiquities, Boston Massachusetts)

---

[46] Vital Records, *Deaths*, 1887, vol. 384, page 331, line 46.

[47] *Deaths*, 1887, vol. 384, page 342, line 36.

After Charley's death the sense of vitality that had invested the McManus sail loft for twenty years disappeared. John H. kept the business rolling along, but there is a sense that his purpose originated in loyalty to employees, rather than the vigorous competitive spirit that had heretofore characterized the firm.

The only bright spot for the surviving McManuses was the new schooner they had sponsored. The *Carrie E. Phillips* again advanced the architectural principles of the fishing fleet, by furthering the trend of sharper lines, deeper draft, and greater speed. She differed in other respects from her predecessors, with steel wire shrouds in place of iron, a single large jib, quarterlifts on the main boom, a double mainsheet, and spreaders for the bowsprit shrouds. The noted naval architect, William Avery Baker of M.I.T., placed her among the trendsetters: "the *Phillips* . . . was an extreme vessel for her day, and because of the reputation of her designer she was more influential than the *Grampus* in the move toward deeper-draft schooners."[48]

In December the new Boston beauty departed on her maiden voyage to the banks, and rumors of the *Phillips's* great speed soon began to be heard in the fishing ports of New England. Then, to the astonishment of all, Tim Cole, the skipper of the speedy, but almost forgotten, *Roulette* arrived at Newport, Rhode Island, on 17 February claiming that he had not only beaten the *John H. McManus* in from the banks, but had also passed the *Carrie E. Phillips* on the way home.

This pronouncement stirred the "queen of the fleet" issue to a new boil, not only in Boston, but particularly in Gloucester, where the Cape Ann captains were well and truly fed up with the dockside gossip that heralded the speed of Boston's boats. In addition to the reputation for swiftness quickly gained by the *McManus* and *Phillips*, no Gloucester schooner had managed to outsail the *Sarah H. Prior*, still the reigning "queen." Cole's claim for the *Roulette* incited Charley Harty, the skipper of the 1886 Gloucester speedster *I.J. Merritt, Jr.*, and Mel McClain, her designer, to toss a gauntlet directly at the *McManus* and *Prior* by publishing the following challenge in the Gloucester *Advertiser* and the Boston *Globe*:

> We, the undersigned, representing the Gloucester fishing schooner *I.J. Merritt, Jr.*, hereby challenge the Boston schooner *John H. McManus* to a race, on the following terms: We will sail her on a triangular course of 40 miles, or on a course of 20 miles to windward

---

48 William A. Baker, "Fishing Under Sail in the North Atlantic," in Benjamin W. Labaree, ed., *The Atlantic World of Robert G. Albion* (Middletown, Connecticut: Wesleyan University Press, 1975), 70.

and return, the course to be laid in Boston Bay. We will sail for any amount between $100 and $1,000, the owners of the *McManus* to choose the amount within these limits. We will sail the race on any day between the 15th and 25th of May. The vessels to be restricted to the sails carried in the former fisherman's race, viz.: mainsail, foresail, forestaysail, jib, flying jib, standing maintopsail, and maintopmast staysail. To avoid racing in a drift, the distance of 40 miles to be completed by one vessel within ten hours of the time of starting or no race. In case the owners of the *McManus* do not see fit to accept this challenge, we will sail the *Sarah H. Prior* a race on the same terms. This challenge to remain open for ten days from date.

/s/Charles Harty, George M. McClain.[49]

On 3 March 1888, Captain Harty met Tom in George A. Stewart's office at the Boston *Globe*, to arrange for an open sweepstakes race. The three men drew up the following invitation:

We, the undersigned, representing the fishing schooners *John H. McManus* and *I.J. Merritt, Jr.*, invite all vessels of the fishing fleet, barring the *Carrie E. Phillips*, to enter a sweepstakes race with us on the following terms: The course to be 20 miles to windward and return. Each vessel to put up $100, the total amount to be divided into five prizes, as follows: Winner to take 40 per cent; second vessel, 25 per cent; third vessel, 20 per cent; fourth-vessel, 10 per cent; fifth vessel, 5 per cent.

Race to be sailed Fast Day, nothing to interfere with a start except fog, storm or a calm which, in the referee's opinion, would prevent a finish.

Vessels to be allowed to carry the following sails, but no others: Mainsail, foresail, forestaysail, jib, flying jib, standing maintopsail, standing foretopsail, maintopmast staysail, and working jib topsail. Any vessel to be allowed to substitute a working main jib for the forestaysail and jib. No lng [*sic*] foresails to be allowed.

No lead ballast to be allowed.

49 *Forest and Stream*, 23 February 1888, 97.

Entries to be made with the yachting editor of the *Globe*, each entry to be accompanied by a deposit of $25. All entries to be made within two weeks of date. The final deposit of $75 to be made by each vessel on or before Monday, March 25.

> Thomas F. McManus
> For *J.H. McManus*
> Charles Harty
> For *I.J. Merritt, Jr.*[50]

The challenge explicitly excluded the *Phillips*, which Charley Harty freely admitted was too fast for the fleet. To soothe the feelings of the *Phillips*'s skipper, the long-time McManus employee Maurice Powers, it was suggested that a match be made at the same time between his schooner and the pilot boat *Hesper* and sailed over the same course, starting just before the fishermen's race. A week later Harty's resistance to the *Phillips*'s entry caved in and the committee accepted her into the sweepstakes. Captain Powers paid his deposit at the same time the skippers of the *McManus* and *Roulette* did, and Captain Harty followed suit a few days later (grumbling all the while that he would have no chance against the new speed demon). The importance of the event to the local commercial and sporting world was stressed when Stewart, who was appointed race manager, obtained the agreement of Vice Commodore J. Malcolm Forbes of the Eastern Yacht Club to act as referee for the race, which would take place on 5 April. Forbes later announced his selection of George H. Richards as judge for the Boston boats, and Henry S. Hovey for the Gloucester ones. At the last minute, a fifth entry came in from Captain Owen Whitten of the *Carrie W. Babson*.

Despite the widely-held belief that the *Phillips* would see the other four off easily, Ned Burgess took no chances. He and Captain Aubrey Crocker, of *Shadow* and *Puritan* fame, joined her captain, Mo Powers, in the afterguard for the race. As usual, *Forest and Stream* was there:

> The long talked about race between the leaders of the Boston and Gloucester fishing fleet was sailed on April 5, resulting in a victory for the new Burgess fisherman, *Carrie E. Phillips*. . . . The schooners had all hauled out just prior to the race, and were all in the best condition. . . . The five schooners were working to leeward of the

---

[50] Ibid., 8 March 1888, 135.

line, the wind being quite light. The *I.J. Merritt, Jr.* and the *J.H. McManus* were near the line, the *Roulette*, and the *Carrie W. Babson* some distance off, and the Burgess boat, *Carrie E. Phillips*, with Mr. Burgess and Capt. Crocker on board, still further away.

The *Merritt* was the first across the line, getting a good start, the others following more slowly. . . . The fleet was timed: *I.J. Merritt, Jr.* 11:20:54, *John H. McManus* 11:22:42, *Roulette* 11:22:48, *Carrie W. Babson* 11:25:14, *Carrie E. Phillips* 11:26:30.

All crossed on starboard tack, but after a couple of minutes the *Merritt* went on port tack, followed by the *McManus*. . . . Soon after going about the *McManus* met with a mishap, the jibtopsail halyard parting while a hand was aloft on the stay, letting man and sail down together, the sail being taken in. The Boothbay-built *Babson* was now well astern and looking for flukes which she did not find. *Roulette* was gaining on the second boat, while the *Merritt* and the *Phillips* were doing the best work of the fleet, the latter holding the leader and gaining on the second and third boats. . . . The times at the weather mark were: *Phillips* 2:18:50, *Merritt* 2:22:20, *Roulette*, 2:29:00, *McManus* 2:38:30, *Babson* 2:44:00. . . . The boats travelled home very fast, as the wind increased, the *Phillips* and *Merritt* first, then the *Roulette* and *McManus*, the *Babson* being last.[51]

Harty, convinced that he never stood a chance against the *Phillips*, celebrated his defeat of the rest of the fleet. On board the *McManus*, Captain Johnny O'Brien could point to the accident involving his crewman and the jibtopsail as a solid reason for his poor placing, while Tim Cole on the *Roulette* was happy to beat the *McManus* under any conditions, and the *Babson* faded away as quietly as she had arrived. The shares received by each vessel were: *Phillips*, $436.63, *Merritt*, $361.63, *Roulette*, $336.63, *McManus*, $286.63, and *Babson*, $261.63,[52] but the crowning achievement went to the *Carrie E. Phillips* which inherited the coveted title, "queen of the fleet."[53]

---

[51] Ibid., 12 April 1888, 235.

[52] Ibid., 19 April 1888, 259.

[53] Thomas F. McManus donated an oil painting of the *Carrie E. Phillips* sailing through the lee of the *John H. McManus* to the Smithsonian Institution on 6 March 1935, catalog no. 310,931. The noted American marine painter, William Pierce Stubbs of Charlestown, was the artist. It was one of his later works, painted after he began to suffer from "melancholia" in 1887. He was admitted to Worcester State Hospital in 1894 and died on 15 May 1909 (Lisa Halttunen, "William Pierce Stubbs, Marine Painter," *The Log of Mystic Seaport* 33 (Fall 1981), 95-103); Dorothy E.R. Brewington, *Dictionary of Marine Artists* (Mystic: Mystic Seaport Museum, 1982); letter, Paul F. Johnston, Ph.D., Curator of Maritime History, National Museum of American History, Smithsonian Institution, 18 April 1990).

A contrast in fishing schooner designs: the 99.6-ton McClain design *I.J. Merritt, Jr.* (87.2x23.8x9 feet), a clipper built in 1886 (*right*), and the *Carrie E. Phillips* compete during the second fishermen's race, 5 April 1888. Longer and more stable, the *Phillips* won the race and the title "queen of the fleet." Photo by Nathaniel L. Stebbins. (Courtesy The Society for the Preservation of New England Antiquities, Boston, Massachusetts)

Tom had been brokering fish for ten years when he hired Ned Burgess to design the *Carrie E. Phillips*. A few weeks after the frightening launch of the schooner, when she had come into Boston the previous November to be fitted out for fishing on the banks, Kate delivered yet again. The McManus's sixth-straight daughter, Louise, arrived in their comfortable Charlestown house on 22 November.[54] For Tom, meeting the needs and demands of his seven female family members, as well as those of his commercial calling, left him little time for serious consideration of a career change from fishmongering to naval architecture.

---

[54] Vital Records 1841-1895, Massachusetts State Archives, *Births*, vol. 378, page 35.

Obligations to his other relatives, those outside the 39 Mount Vernon Street house, quickly multiplied. John H.'s health steadily faltered, and his brother's passing left Agnes, with little John H. and baby Charley, to be looked after. Charlie's passing brought on an unexpected and traumatic aftereffect. George, perhaps because he blamed the conditions in the sail loft for his brother's death, as well as his own worsening case of consumption, shocked his father and sole remaining brother by duplicating the move his Uncle Pat McManus made twenty-seven years before. He walked out of the sailmaking business, presumably under the influence of the Doyles, and moved out to West Medford at the end of 1887, but this was a mild shock compared to what happened next. Appallingly, two weeks after the second fishermen's race, on 24 April 1888, George too died, another victim of tuberculosis.[55] He was just twenty-nine. Again the family made one of their all-too-frequent appearances at Calvary Cemetery, where John H. appeared a mere shadow of his formerly spirited self.

At East Boston, a few weeks earlier, the longtime boatbuilder for the Irish market fleet, Wilbur Laskey, had succumbed to a lifelong battle with diabetes on 18 March.[56] Among the twenty-odd schooners he had delivered to the Irishmen were the *Joseph Henry* for Dick Leonard and John H. McManus in 1860 and the *Eva G.* for Jeremiah McCarthy in 1865. Laskey's business never fully recovered from the crippling shipwrights' strike that shut down the building yards during 1871.

On the waterfront, the sixth, and last, of the McManus trendsetters to enter the fishing fleet before Tom McManus himself began to design new breeds of fishing schooners was the *Nellie Dixon* in the spring of 1889.[57] In his role as managing owner, Tom commissioned Burgess over the winter of 1888-89: "after [Charley's] death, I had Mr. Burgess design *Nellie Dixon* which was built at East Boston in 1889 by Moses Adams of Essex."[58]

Time and again in the histories of New England's fishing fleet, Burgess's *Fredonia* of the same year is referred to as the watershed fishing schooner of the 1880s, with her relationship to the *Grampus* cited. But Burgess used the same plan for both the *Nellie Dixon* and the *Fredonia*. No less an expert than Howard I. Chapelle has stated that "from the original drawing of the lines of the *Dixon* and

---

[55] Vital Records, *Deaths*, 1888, vol. 392, page 178, line 53.

[56] Vital Records, *Deaths*, 1889, vol. 402, page 89, line 2042. Laskey's death certificate indicated him to be male, the son of Robert and Rebecca Laskey of Lubec, Maine, died of "senile gangrene," at 74 years, 11 months, 14 days. Resided at 257 Princeton Street. Dr. Estes interpreted the cause of death as "probably diabetic or atherosclerotic gangrene of the leg."

[57] Enrolment No. 169, Boston and Charlestown, 12 April 1889. Owners: John Marr, 3/8; Benjamin F. Phillips, 1/8; George W. Phillips, 1/16; Matthew Keany, 1/16; Jeremiah McCarthy, 1/16; Ellen Dixon, 1/16; Thomas F. McManus, 1/8; John H. McManus, 1/16; and John W. Chapman, 1/16.

[58] McManus, "Essay No. 3."

Reflecting the family's contributions to the fishing fleet in the 1880s, the McManuses had Boston marine artist William P. Stubbs depict the *Carrie E. Phillips* and *John H. McManus* in racing trim. McManus donated the painting to the Smithsonian Institution in 1935. (Neg. 44691-A, Smithsonian Institution)

Fredonia, it is obvious that the *Dixon* was the original design."[59] Because the *Fredonia* sailed first as a yacht for her owner, J. Malcolm Forbes–racing and defeating Lawlor's bone-weary trial horse *Hesper*–whereas the *Dixon* went straight to the fishing grounds, the *Fredonia* was the better-known of the two schooners, and journalists apparently gave her name to the model, which should, rightly, be called the *Nellie Dixon* model. The point is belabored here solely to establish her rightful place in the line of design innovations associated with the McManus family, and to notice her influence on Tom McManus.[60]

After decades of stagnation, the progress of schooner design in the 1880s was phenomenal. From the time Lawlor laid down the deep-draft *Sarah H. Prior* and joined with Collins in the plumb-stemmed *Grampus*, until Burgess drafted the *Nellie Dixon*, two other major evolutionary steps represented by the *John H. McManus* and

---

[59] Howard I. Chapelle, *The American Fishing Schooners 1825-1925* (New York: W.W. Norton, 1973), 175.

[60] At present a Swiss-based group is planning "to build an authentic New England schooner on the exterior lines of the *Nellie Dixon* with a twentieth-century interior for the purpose of first class charter work and film/television production. The schooner will feature suitable 'period' cabins, and will also function as a floating music recording studio. The new *Nellie Dixon* will accommodate twelve guests with a crew of seven. The planned completion date is 1995-96" (Letter, Terry R. Nelson, 5 September 1993).

Carrie E. Phillips had been taken, making the direct link between *Grampus* and *Nellie Dixon* remote, but highlighting the pace of technological advance. The *Phillips*, Burgess's only plumb-stem fisherman, was actually a reactive design. With her, he redefined the state of the art, but did not linger long in the vicinity. The *Nellie Dixon* really represents what Burgess, working with a clean sheet of drafting paper, thought a fisherman should be. And, if the *Dixon* marked the reappearance of the clipper hull in a modern design, she was a clipper with a difference. Compared to the *Phillips*, disregarding her obvious forward section for the moment, her buttock lines were finer, yet fuller aft, and Burgess abandoned the hollowed sternpost. Their keels had the same rocker and approximately the same amount of drag. He slightly reduced the deadrise in the *Dixon*, thereby slackening her bilges, which hardens the turn of the bilge and stiffens the rig. Forward, the *Dixon* was a traditionalist's delight. Not only had the clipper shape returned, but the entire forward section with its knuckled forefoot and slightly hollow forebody combined with substantial, but not innovative draft, predicated her ability to knife through the seas. The world of yachting design, less than four decades old in terms of the America's Cup, and less than three in terms of popular regattas, had begun to change the shape of fishing schooners. No one decried that influence as the nineteenth century began its final decade, but the sighs of delight brought on by the *Nellie Dixon* and her even yachtier sister, the *Fredonia*, would turn to funereal choruses when the polished fixtures and fittings of the *Bluenose* appeared in the 1920s. But it was still the 1880s, and Dennison J. Lawlor had not given up on plumb-stemmers–the *Harry L. Belden* was yet to come.

The man to whom Moses Adams assigned the construction of the *Nellie Dixon* was his foreman, Daniel Poland,[61] who raised her frames at Lawlor's old yard on the northwest point of East Boston neck. Twice each week Tom McManus fulfilled his management role, by walking two wharves up from his Atlantic Avenue store to South Ferry for the ride across to East Boston. Disembarking there, he made his way to Maverick Square and caught the horse-drawn omnibus along Meridian Street, getting off at the corner of Condor to visit the yard. He kept up this routine until the *Nellie Dixon*, about to become the latest Boston speedster, slid into the water at the confluence of the Mystic River and Chelsea Creek on 12 April 1889.[62] Just before the launch, Kate issued an April advisory that she was enjoying another

THE MAYFLOWER,
CARRIE E. PHILLIPS, AND
NELLIE DIXON

---

[61] Father of the famous Essex mold-maker Archer D. Poland.

[62] Enrolment No. 169, Boston and Charlestown, 12 April 1889. Owners: John Marr, 3/8; Benjamin F. Phillips, 1/8; George W. Phillips, 1/16; Matthew Keany, 1/16; Jeremiah McCarthy, 1/16; Ellen Dixon, 1/16; Thomas F. McManus, 1/8; John H. McManus, 1/16; and John W. Chapman, 1/16.

pregnancy, the fifth springtime one of the seven she would take to term in their eleven years of marriage.

Given McManus's growing architectural lore, and his willingness to discourse upon it, his fishmonger's shop gradually became the gathering place for waterfront experts: "In the little glass-enclosed cashier's cage of this store gathered such men as Dennison J. Lawlor, Aubrey Crocker, Adolphus G. ('Dolly') McVey, Charlie Barr, Arthur Dana Story, Malcolm Campbell–in short, all the worth while men in the nautical life of Boston."[63] In his history of American yachting, W.P. Stephens devoted a passage to the club-like atmosphere of Tom's Commercial Wharf store:

> In these early days [of yachting] Boston could boast of two institutions unknown to New York. In the early '70s the city maintained a free school of naval architecture in East Boston . . . The other institution was the office of the fish store of Captain Tom McManus, a general clearinghouse for all news of fishing and yachting. Here were to be met the captains of fishing vessels–Maurice Powers, John Cannon, Tom McLaughlin. Among the yacht skippers were Captain "Aub" Crocker, Captain "Jim" Reid (of *America* when owned by General Butler), and, in later years, Captain John Barr and his brother Charles. Among other notables in their day were D.J. Lawlor, Arthur Story, Mil Wood, "Nels" Sibley, John McPhail; and, of course, Dolly McVey of *The Boston Herald*, George A. Stewart of the *Boston Globe*, and Jimmy McNally. In this gathering of the cognoscenti of yachting were discussed, from the date of which we are writing down through the years of international racing, all the technical questions we are considering, with innumerable stories of races lost and won, and why. No such center of friendly intercourse existed about New York. Skippers might meet . . . but none of these compared in any way with the atmosphere of Tom McManus's private office.[64]

Left: Edward Burgess's final contribution to fishing schooner design was the *Nellie Dixon/Fredonia* model of 1889, which influenced schooner design for more than ten years. Here is the better-known, 115-ton *Fredonia* (99.6x23.6x10.3 feet), photographed by Nathaniel L. Stebbins, August 1889. (Courtesy The Society for the Preservation of New England Antiquities, Boston, Massachusetts)

---

[63] Smith, "The First Fishermen's Race," 64. Crocker gained fame as captain of the racing yacht *Shadow*, and later of the America's Cup winner *Puritan*. McVey was the yachting editor of the Boston *Herald* for more than thirty-five years. He was born in 1843 in Boston. Two of his forty-foot yacht designs, *Alice* and *Helen*, were built in 1889. Later the most famous of all the professional yacht skippers, in the days when they reigned supreme, Barr culminated his career as captain of the America's Cup winner *Columbia*. A.D. Story was the legendary Essex shipwright, who built so many fishing schooners. Campbell was a noted East Boston shipbuilder.

[64] W.P. Stephens, *Traditions and Memories of American Yachting* (1939-46; rev. ed., Brooklin, Maine: WoodenBoat Publications, Inc., 1989), 201-202.

Clearly, ship design and construction interested these men far more than the wholesale or retail fish trade that went on around these discussions. Dolly McVey, a Boston newspaper columnist and a successful amateur yacht designer, was an outspoken critic of contemporary naval architects, and his frequent and fiery diatribes ticking off the shortcomings of the clipper schooners did much to encourage McManus's determination to improve the breed.[65]

But Tom had one final hurdle to overcome in order to complete his training as a naval architect–he recognized it, his friends recognized it, even the frequent family tragedies failed to obscure it–his need for professional training in mechanical drawing. Following the loss of his beloved brothers, Tom strove to refocus his attention and respond to pressure from some of his friends to take the final step into the one professional art he despised–drafting.

Although Tom had a modicum of the talent for drawing displayed by Charley and George McManus, he instinctively reached for the whittling knife, rather than the tools of the drafting board to display a new design thought. Charlton Smith paid particular tribute to McManus's model-making prowess: "like Mel McLain's [sic], Tom's first vessels were modelled from wood. So beautiful were they, and so successful," he wrote, that a close friend, unidentified but "very well known to the writer, coaxed, entreated and finally nearly dragged the doubting Thomas to a school of nautical design." Tom, now past thirty, apparently expostulated against the idea right up to the front door of the former municipal building, vacated when Charlestown became part of Boston, "the doubter, meanwhile, asserting he was too old to learn new tricks." Smith concluded, "the wonderful outcome of that course of schooling has been a continuous source of joy to the dragger and probably is to the dragged."[66] A few years later, the Gloucester *Daily Times*, at the time of the launch of the *James S. Steele*, evaluated the effect of Tom's training: "Mr. McManus is a well known fish dealer, and for several years has been a student at the city school of naval architecture, Charlestown. . . . In his first vessel Mr. McManus has done well."[67]

Charlton Smith himself was a graduate of the institution he described. In fact, the school operated at two different locations, and they were part of the state-supported Boston Evening High School system, whose branches were commonly referred to as the "Free Schools," or "Evening High Schools."

---

[65] Chapelle, *Fishing Schooners*, 125.

[66] Smith, draft article.

[67] Gloucester *Daily Times*, date unknown, *ca.* January 1892. One of several unidentified newspaper clippings glued to a photograph of the *James S. Steele* which has been donated by a descendent of James S. Steele, the son of George Steele, to the Cape Ann Historical Association during 1993.

Naval architectural drafting courses were offered at the Charlestown and South Boston branches under the imposing title of "Free Evening Schools for Industrial Drawing." The Charlestown School Committee's annual report noted the initiation of the first, more general, drafting classes: "in compliance with the law of the State, passed at the session of the legislature of 1870, a school for instruction in mechanical, or industrial drawing, has been established under the direction of the Committee on Evening Schools."[68] During the fourth year of the curriculum specialized crafts such as shipbuilding drafting and hull modeling were offered as elective courses. By the second year of their existence, however, the demands placed upon the Free Schools for a dedicated ship and yacht designing diploma led to the establishment of a shipbuilding curriculum, complete with two-year syllabus, at East Boston in 1872.

A few years later the school of naval architecture moved into the old City Hall in Charlestown and came under the direction of "Professor" John L. Frisbee, the master shipwright of East Boston's John M. Brooks shipyard.[69] Classes were conducted from 7:30 to 9:30 P.M. on Mondays, Wednesdays, and Fridays, between October and April each year.

In the early 1880s a second school opened in South Boston's Lincoln School. During the formative years, the much-traveled Frisbee also directed it. He went to South Boston on Tuesdays and Thursdays, holding classes from 7:00 to 9:00 P.M., in addition to his Monday, Wednesday, and Friday lectures at Charlestown. An 1886 report described the southern branch: "This school is now in a prosperous condition, being supported out of the [John] Hawes Fund, left to South Boston for educational purposes. It now has twenty-three pupils, and many more applicants for whom there is not yet room. . . . Any scholar absent for three evenings without good cause will lose his place in the school. Next year it is expected to enlarge the school and have two rooms, one for advanced pupils and one for beginners. The attendance at present includes some yachtsmen and several builders."[70]

Indeed, among the thirty-four students who entered for the 1886 fall semester were second-termers George F. and E.A. Lawley, the sons of shipbuilder George Lawley, who himself was a graduate of Frisbee's program; Adrian Wilson, the transplanted Long Island sailmaker; Augustus "Dolly" McVey; and

---

68 *Charlestown School Committee Annual Report 1870*, 13, Social Science Division, Boston Public Library.

69 The papers and artifacts of Albert S. Greene, on loan from Gifford Booth of Norwell, Massachusetts, *"Free School"* notebooks, Accession No. 386, Boston National Historical Park, Charlestown Navy Yard, Massachusetts. Frisbee was later succeeded by Albert S. Greene, Master Shipwright at the U.S. Navy Yard in Charlestown. Greene himself had been a student under Frisbee shortly after the school's opening.

70 *Forest and Stream*, 4 March 1886, 116.

William K. Pryor, the Faneuil Hall fish dealer.[71] In earlier years the schools had trained Captain Jim Brown, Captain Dicky Sherlock, Captain Charlton L. Smith, Captain Mel McClain, and Dr. E.C. Hubbard. During the latter 1880s Frisbee continued as the director of the Charlestown school, while maintaining his role as the drafting instructor at both schools. Tom McManus, although ultimately the Boston school's most famous graduate, was but one of several who reached prominence. In addition to those mentioned above, Albert S. Greene, Master Shipwright at the U.S. Navy Yard in Charlestown; and John H. McKay of Shelburne, Nova Scotia, who designed the acclaimed Grand Banks fishing schooner *Artisan,*[72] also made names for themselves.

Forest and Stream underlined the uniqueness of these institutions: "This is a great country, with many thousand miles of sea coast and water courses, but we believe that these two small schools in Boston offer the only instruction that can be had in naval architecture and designing."[73] Unbelievable as it may appear from the perspective of a century later, these Boston municipal vocational schools were the sole source of formal training in naval architecture anywhere in the United States, until William H. Webb, at age seventy-three, founded New York's Webb Institute of Naval Architecture in 1889.

With his return to the classroom, Tom expanded the daily routine that already took him to East Boston twice a week. Each weekday morning he demolished Kate's nourishing breakfast, while the two babies, little Kate and Lou, constantly crawled underfoot as he sat with his chattering school-age daughters: Margaret, eleven; Grace, eight; Alice seven; and five-year-old Titia. He left the house for the horse-drawn streetcar stop, where he rode across the Charlestown Bridge to Haymarket Square. He got off there and continued his morning constitutional across the North End.

He frequently called on Matt Keany at his 232 North Street grocery, where he took an early dislike to Johnny Fitzgerald, Keany's hotshot ward heeler, who had followed Tom through the Eliot Grammar School, albeit seven years later. His next leg took him to T Wharf, where he bargained with the latest arriving fishermen for their catch, before going back to the head of Commercial Wharf to open the Atlantic Avenue store for the day's business. At the close of the day, he reversed the journey, to return home for supper.

---

[71] Ibid., 14 October 1886, 235.

[72] Telephone interview, 9 August 1988, Mary Blackford, Librarian, Maritime Museum of the Atlantic, Halifax, Nova Scotia; Chapelle, *Speed Under Sail*, 296. Chapelle interviewed McKay during his 1930s sojourn in Nova Scotia.

[73] *Forest and Stream*, 30 September 1886, 235.

After that meal, on Monday, Wednesday, and Friday evenings he trudged off to the detested session at the drafting school. Tom later recalled: "At that time, I was attending the evening drafting school and Mr. John Frisbee was the instructor and he was a good teacher, and I got some more technical points from him."[74] Frisbee's tutoring, and the collaboration with Burgess, amounted to post-graduate study for the naval architect-to-be, crowning his twenty years of understudying Dennison J. Lawlor. In the end, it was Lawlor's business demise that spurred Tom to experiment further with his hull models to seek the ultimate shape that would provide the safest working platform for the fishermen.

As the end of the 1880s neared, Tom, as the only survivor of the five McManus brothers, inherited the responsibility for maintaining the family's business success. His own fish brokerage prospered, and he succeeded in breathing life into their outfitting firm, T Wharf Supply Company, which had regressed since Charley's death. Tom also did his best to support John H. in the sail loft, although its dwindling trade corresponded to its founder's weakening health. In addition to all this, in his spare time Tom had successfully organized the first two fishermen's races. Yet, he withstood all these challenges despite their inconsonant demands on his time and energies. Through it all, the powerful magnet pulling him away from the fish counter, and toward an architectural career, proved difficult to resist.

The 1880s decade came to a close with Tom basking in the afterglow of a minor miracle. On 15 November 1889, after eleven years of marriage, and six beautiful daughters, Kate gave birth to the couple's first son, Charles Francis McManus.[75]

---

[74] McManus, "Essay No. 1."

[75] Vital Records, *Births*, vol. 396, page 48. St Mary's, Charlestown, *Baptisms*, vol. 4, page 158.

CHAPTER NINE

The *James S. Steele*

Even in his youth, Tom McManus recognized the intrinsic nature of his design abilities. In his later years he once told his grandnephew Edwin, then a student at Holy Cross College, that architectural aptitude was a gift of God. It was pointless, he cautioned the young man, to go to school to learn how to design ships unless you had that "gift." Tom was not the lone recipient among the family members; John H. and Charley had also been blessed with the innate ability to comprehend the complex interaction between hull and sails with wind and water.

In addition to his inborn ability, Tom, from the earliest days of sailing with John H. in the *Vesper*, amassed firsthand familiarity with the keel *vs.* centerboard debate. Then Dennison J. Lawlor drilled the seagoing advantages of the deep-draft cutter profile over the shallow sandbagger shape into his pupil's head. Finally, Tom's familiarity with the hardy hookers of the Boston Irish, whose heavy-weather safety record put their larger clipper brethren to shame, reinforced his belief that added depth of hull would lead to safer schooners for fishing operations in New England and Canadian waters.

Other people recognized Tom's innate talent in his uncanny ability as an eight-year-old to grasp the technical points discussed by his father and Lawlor during those long-gone Sunday shipyard excursions to East Boston, Chelsea, and South Boston. During them, the McManus boys saw many of the era's most famous vessels at the christening ceremonies they attended with John H., including the commissioning of the navy's ponderous ship-of-the-line *Vermont* at the Charlestown Navy Yard in January 1862;[1] the delicate launchings of the fishing schooner *Sylph* and pilot boat *Edwin Forrest* into Lawlor's stone-lined slip at Buck's Wharf in Chelsea during 1865;[2] and the stately clipper *Glory of the Seas*, sliding down the ways at Donald McKay's yard during October 1869;[3] as well as the innumerable vessels of all types they saw splash into the bay at yards that ranged from the Wood Brothers' on the far corner of East Boston around to Lawley's on City Point in South Boston.

The knowledge passed on to him by his father and the results of his twenty-plus years of training by Lawlor played equal parts in Tom's theoretical maturation. From that brilliant designer-builder's point of view the relationship ranged from initially putting up with a juvenile nuisance, to grudgingly accepting an avid apprentice, to finally welcoming a new collaborator and, ultimately, a valued client. The design evolution Lawlor orchestrated from the *Sylph*, through the *Actress* and *Sarah H. Prior*, to the *John H. McManus* provided the professional foundation for the design principles Tom championed throughout his life. Young McManus steadfastly accumulated and polished those ideas, beginning with the first battens he pinned in Lawlor's mold loft, where the Canadian-Irish immigrant's Sabbath shipbuilding sermons guided his American-Irish acolyte's architectural

---

[1] Naval History Division, U.S. Navy Department, *American Ships of the Line* (Washington: Government Printing Office, 1969).

[2] Thomas F. McManus, "Autobiographical Essay No. 1."

[3] William H. Bunting, *Portrait of a Port: Boston, 1852-1914* (Cambridge, Massachusetts: Belknap Press, Harvard University, 1971); Carl C. Cutler, *Greyhounds of the Sea*, 3rd. ed., (1930; Annapolis: U.S. Naval Institute Press, 1984).

enlightenment.[4] Following the Lawlor years came the all-too-brief collaboration with the meticulous and brilliant Ned Burgess that produced those landmark schooners *Carrie E. Phillips* and *Nellie Dixon*. The final element in Tom's professional expertise came through his formal training under Professor John L. Frisbee, that "superior shipwright and teacher who attracted students from as far away as Nova Scotia and Virginia."[5] But, while many helped cultivate it, the roots of his talents always lay within his own innate "gift."

Despite the acceptance of the plumb-stemmers, McManus's developing design instincts still conflicted with the shape of contemporary banksmen. The missing safety qualities of the contemporary clippers, underlined by regular reports of fishermen being swept from the bowsprits of their schooners (even the plumb-

Burgess's *Nellie Dixon/Fredonia* influence is apparent in the designs of Captain George "Mel" McClain, who drafted many clipper-bowed schooners through the 1890s. His *Lottie Haskins* of 1890 was especially notable. This is the larger 101-ton *Marguerite Haskins* (92.4x24.8x9.4 feet), built at Essex, Massachusetts, in 1893. Edward W. Smith photographed her near Newport, Rhode Island, in the 1890s. (M.S.M. 69.822.54)

---

4 McManus, "Essay No. 1."

5 Howard I. Chapelle, *The American Fishing Schooners 1825-1925* (New York: W.W. Norton, 1973), 124.

stemmers), and memories of slips left vacant by missing fishermen pals, began Tom's unremitting search for a safer design. Perhaps the most difficult dilemma that faced him was the evidence presented to his own eyes of poor maintenance.

Fishermen interpreted their role as seamen rather narrowly. They were perfectly willing to learn how to "hand, reef, and steer," the very skills necessary to get their schooners to and from the fishing grounds. In this respect, they were excellent seamen. With regard to the other aspects of the mariner's profession–painting, ship carpentry, knotting and splicing, and maintaining the rig–they seldom took an interest. Nor did they feel obligated to do so as the traditional agreement between vessel owners and fishermen, whether written or implied, obligated owners to provide vessels, while the fishermen contributed their fishing skills and labor. From their agreements with owners, fishermen had a clear conception of their rights and responsibilities. Having the owners provide a well-found vessel was their expected right, and maintenance fell into the owners' range of responsibilities, to be carried out in shoreside yards.

As schooners increased in size, in some cases a crewman might be named as boatswain and assigned to care for the rigging at sea, but from the destructive nature of winter fishing conditions, even he probably considered broken footropes or ratlines the least of his problems in the face of more critical emergencies. In the normal course of events, it is doubtful whether the men had time for maintenance of anything except their gear while fishing.

In facing the multiple dangers of their profession at this time, the attitude of the fishermen seems similar to the fatalistic attitudes associated with coal miners and other workmen in hazardous occupations. They defied their mortality by ignoring the risks. Miners failed to demand better safety features in the pits, and fishermen showed a similar pattern: rarely learning to swim, failing to demand safer dories, and not attending to every frayed footrope indicates that their identity was tied up in what we might today call a macho self-image–a man who took charge of his life by defying odds he couldn't control. For McManus, the sight of the deteriorated and unseamanlike condition of the standing and running rigging on board some fishing vessels caused him acute dismay from his earliest days on the fishing wharves. Throughout his career Tom embraced the belief that crew safety in a fishing schooner had to be a principal concern for a naval architect.[6]

The post-Civil War boom in the fish marketplace dramatically increased profit potential. Not surprisingly, this inflation spurred some dubious business practices in the quest for a quick dollar. Short-sighted schooner operators wishing

---

[6] Letters, Andrew German, Mystic Seaport Museum, Connecticut, 31 August 1988, 4 September 1993; letter to the editor, Joseph E. Garland, *WoodenBoat* (September/October 1993): 4-6.

to embrace this emerging opportunity, but short of hulls to supply it, began sending their lightly-built craft, those originally intended solely for the summer mackerel fisheries, further out to sea to face the severe rigors of winter fishing. Then, as has been illustrated, they built larger schooners by increasing the length and beam without a corresponding increase in depth and, therefore, stability. These unsuitable vessels fished anywhere from Georges Bank, lying about 100 miles east of Chatham on Cape Cod, to the Western Bank off Sable Island, approximately 160 miles east southeast of Halifax, Nova Scotia, and even to the Grand Banks off Newfoundland, 1,000 miles distant. The resultant loss of lives illustrated by the tables in chapter six repeatedly shocked young McManus as he grew to manhood and developed his determination to displace evolution with revolution.

Through the late winter of 1889, during Tom's visits to Daniel Poland, Moses Adams's foreman, who was constructing the *Nellie Dixon* at the Meridian Street shipyard, he fell into the habit of sounding out the master builder, whom he considered to be "a clever draftsman,"[7] about the extraordinarily different concepts he had developed regarding hull shapes. The veteran shipwright generously encouraged these sessions. One day Tom brought along the plans of a novel schooner. Poland, after a minute examination of the drafts, surprised the budding architect by admitting that he saw "great possibilities in that form of hull."[8] The drawings originated from the advanced drafting exercises at the Charlestown Free School, and their lines survive in the lift model McManus produced from them,[9] which presents an opportunity to measure the effect of the previous three decades upon his thinking.

Despite Poland's approbation, Tom's first, startlingly different schooner design did not please his new mentor, John Frisbee. Where Poland applauded the model and its performance potential, Frisbee, ever pragmatic, insisted that lack of hold space would counteract the advantages of McManus's design in the eyes of fleet owners. This left the thirty-three-year-old student stuck between two expert but opposing opinions. Throughout the 1889-90 school term, while he redrafted the plans for his unusual schooner, Frisbee continuously challenged him, and Tom noted unhappily: "John could not see the idea that I was developing." He went on to explain that his theory was "to extend the ends of the boat over the water and reduce the length of the bowsprit and main boom," yet, Tom added, plainly

---

[7] McManus, "Essay No. 3."

[8] Ibid.

[9] McManus donated the model of *James S. Steele* to the U.S. National Museum of American History, Smithsonian Institution catalog number 310,887. It was subsequently placed on permanent loan at the Essex Shipbuilding Museum, Essex, Massachusetts.

McManus's half model of his ideal schooner hull puzzled everyone until Moses Adams took a chance and used the model to build the *James S. Steele*. With its long, cutaway ends it is unlike the *Nellie Dixon/Fredonia* model, although the deep, heavily rockered keel was clearly inspired by Burgess. (Neg. 31701-B, Smithsonian Institution)

eschewing any claim to originality, "this idea was used almost universally in yachts and small fishing vessels."[10] The buoyancy he sought by sharply extending the bow and stern from the waterline would reduce the pitching moment of the vessel–the plunging motion that had allowed the sea to drag so many of his friends from the bowsprit into the freezing depths of the ocean.

Throughout his long career, Tom upheld the "idea that reserved power in anything was a good thing."[11] McManus's conception of reserved power at this stage in his career was a combination of deep draft to counteract over-masting and excessive sail plans, and the additional buoyancy provided by his fore and aft overhangs to reduce the pitching moment of his hulls when sailing at right angles to the waves in a heavy sea. This belief instigated the fundamental and far-reaching changes with which he confronted the experts of the waterfront community, beginning with the fifteen-foot bow and stern overhangs of the model examined by Poland and Frisbee. They were a far cry from either the vertical bow of the plumb-stemmers, or the square-tucked sterns of the old clippers. He had also cut away all the deadwood forward and raked the sternpost to remove most of it aft.[12] Clipper schooners, with their long straight runs of keel and near-vertical sternposts, although fast sailers off the wind, had excessive deadwood both fore and aft, which made them cumbersome tackers. They often took more than a minute to bring the bow across the wind from port to starboard or *vice-versa*. Although the plumb-

---

10 McManus, "Essay No. 1."

11 McManus, "Essay No. 2."

12 "Deadwood" refers to the solid timbering in the bow and stern of a sailing ship just above the keel, where the framing narrows down to such an extant that the frames merge together. Generally the fore deadwood extends from the stem to the foremost frame, the after deadwood from the sternpost to the after balance frame. Both deadwoods are firmly fixed to the keel to add strength to the ship's structure.

stemmers had no deadwood forward, they retained a considerable amount aft. In Tom's new model, through his great reduction in the deadwoods, he provided a short, deep, rockered keel with no straight run and little turning resistance fore and aft, thereby creating a commercial hull that would come across the wind in seconds, faster than most contemporary racing yachts.

Distressed by Frisbee's disapproval, yet encouraged by Poland's reassuring responses, McManus, never anything less than bullheaded about the principles he embraced, stuck to his guns. "I made the drawings and a model from them," he wrote, and from late 1889 through mid-1891, "showed the same to quite a number of persons, some of whom were prominent in Nautical affairs."[13] In its final form, the half model became the basis for the *James S. Steele*, the first fishing schooner designed by McManus to get afloat, although not before she suffered a prolonged and discouraging gestation period. Frisbee was not the only impediment between concept and reality for Tom and the *Steele*. "I drew the plans of the Sch. *James S. Steele* and made a Model from them," he explained. "I showed it to Daniel Poland who was building the Sch. *Nellie Dixon* at East Boston, also to Cap't. Crocker of the *Puritan*, Cap't. Charlie Barr of the *Columbia* fame–Cap't. Nate Watson of the *Constellation*, Capt. Andrew Burnham U.S. Inspector of hulls, and Prof. John Frisbee N.A."[14] His memoirs reflect the frowning discouragement he met from the experts: "The different Master Mariners, Designers and ship builders to whom I showed the plans, were all at sea to see such a departure in the shape of a boat and shook their heads as in doubt whether she would be a success or otherwise."[15] In frustrated desperation, he stuck the unique model in a corner of his storefront window on Atlantic Avenue, with the vague hope that some visionary passerby would be attracted to it, and got on with selling fish. But when it came, the hoped-for break that Tom sought did not originate from the North End fish store's office, or its Atlantic Avenue window, but from the building yards of Essex, the tiny Massachusetts riverside town that gave birth to the largest share of the fishing fleet, ultimately launching nearly 3,500 registered vessels.[16]

Life was considerably broader for Tom than just his long hours of serving customers within the confines of the fish market, the studious evenings in Charlestown's old city hall, or helping Kate raise their seven children. During the 1890-91 mid-term break at the school of design, Kate announced one morning that

---

[13] McManus, "Essay No. 1."

[14] McManus, "Essay No. 3."

[15] McManus, "Essay No. 2."

[16] Chapelle, *Fishing Schooners*, 16.

Just half a foot longer than the *James S. Steele*, the 82-ton *Richard L. Steele* (88.6x23x10.6 feet) displays their distinctive hull form as she is prepared for launch at the Moses Adams yard early in 1892. Her extended bow is a great contrast to the clipper bow of the schooner under construction at left, as is the great depth of her keel below the rabbet of the garboard plank. Photograph by Walter Gardner. (Courtesy Louise V. Will)

she was with child again, and, for a change, she expected to give birth in August. If her latest pregnancy went to term, then the new baby's August birth in Scituate would be a unique occurrence for a family whose offspring usually arrived in Boston during November.

Additionally, the time for the changing of the guard within the family had arrived. As had been the case for the McManus family in the 1850s, when John H. took over the family reins from old Charley McManus, Tom began to assume those responsibilities in the early 1890s that rightfully belonged to his aging father or deceased older brother, had Charley lived. One small indicator of change involved the tradition of summering in Scituate. Where John H. had been the initiator, taking his family down for each hot season, it was now Tom's turn to take his father into his own summer home there.

Although Tom never emulated his deceased brothers, Charley and George, in forming schooner syndicates, he was not averse to taking part in them. With the *Nellie Dixon* well established in the fishing fleet, Tom and his father joined the May 1890 syndication of the four-year-old, 100-ton schooner *Belle J. Neal*, skippered by Captain Johnny Driscoll. They purchased a 1/32nd each, as well as taking a similar share in Charley's name to benefit his widow Agnes and her boys.[17]

---

[17] Enrolment No. 231, Boston and Charlestown, 15 May 1890, U.S. Consolidated Enrolment and Licenses, Bureau of Navigation, Record Group 41, Records of the Department of Commerce, NARA; see also later Enrolment No. 142, Boston and Charlestown, 9 June 1894. Owners: W.C. Stone, 2/32; Parron H. Prior, 1/32; Thomas F. McManus, 1/32; John H. and Charles A. McManus, copts. 2/32; John R. Neal, 1/32; Solomon T. Cobb, 1/32; Otis H. Wiley, 1/32; Freeman Emery, 1/32; Emily P. Wright, 1/32; Maria Wenneberg, 1/32; Mary Driscoll, 2/32; Florence Driscoll, 2/32; Lewis H. Higgins, 1/32; Thomas Mahoney, 2/32; Timothy Kerrigan, 2/32; Arabella Burns, 2/32; Henry D. Stone, 2/32; George P. Freeman, 1/32; Caroline E. Phillips, 4/32; Benjamin F. Phillips, 2/32.

Tom's thrifty nature suffered mightily on his weekday circuits of the fishing piers, where he watched in dismay as fish cleaners casually tossed fish roe to hovering flocks of squawking seabirds with a flip of their knives. Well aware that Europeans considered fish eggs a gourmet delight and created a viable market for them, McManus schemed to turn the waste to profit. According to Connecticut naval architect George Stadel, Jr. (a 1928 Notre Dame graduate who visited Tom regularly at Milton and Scituate in the early 1930s), the pain of missed profits finally drove McManus to a carefully calculated remedy. He started by collecting all the mackerel roe he could get his hands on, which he loaded into tiny kegs. Then he began putting the roe containers into the center of the ice packed inside each barrel of fish that he shipped to his customers. During the initial stages of the experiment he made no additional charge for the barrels so equipped; but once he sensed his faraway patrons had developed a taste for the mackerel roe (he called it "Boston caviar"), Tom introduced a handsome price for his brainchild.[18]

One bright sunny day in the summer of 1891 the Cape Ann shipbuilder Moses Adams came to Boston, ostensibly to visit with his local clients, but with an ulterior motive. After socializing along the docks, Adams went to the head of Commercial Wharf, strode into the fish store, looked straight at McManus, and said: "Thomas, I want to see the model that some persons call a freak." Unabashed by this deprecating reference to his dreamboat, and driven by over a year of collective disinterest, Tom needed no further prompting. He yanked the model out of the window, thrust it into Adams's hands, and began to pour his heart out.

He later recalled that "after talking and explaining the design which had no dead-wood forward and a smaller amount aft than then popular models of the times, [Adams] said, 'I think I see the point.'" When Tom finished his disjointed outburst, the builder added: "I would like to take the model home with me." Promising to let Tom know what he thought of it after a lengthier examination, Adams returned to Essex.[19] For two days no further communication took place. Unbeknownst to McManus, however, the shipwright not only examined the model in detail, but also sought out a financial sponsor for the project. On the third day Adams returned to Boston and, with words that electrified McManus, said: "Send me the plans and

---

[18] Interview, George Stadel, Jr., Stamford, Connecticut, 21 September 1988. One of the obvious characteristics of Thomas F. McManus was his frugality. His memoirs are scribbled on the back of mimeographed sales notices from a local grocery store and on the reverse side of vendors' circulars. The military enlistment travels of the four sons he eventually spawned are entered in an old 1900 pocket calendar given to him by his clothier cousin, Charley, the son of his deceased Uncle Pat. Rent records from the Charlestown properties he acquired reside in a tiny 1912 pocket diary presented by the customhouse brokers Charles J. Jager & Co.

[19] McManus, "Essays Nos. 1 and 2."

In section, the *Richard L. Steele* has considerable deadrise and a slight tumble home above the moderate turn of her bilges. Like Burgess's fishing schooner designs, she has a spike bowsprit and "whiskers" to brace the bowsprit shrouds. Photograph by Walter Gardner. (Courtesy Cape Ann Historical Collection, Gloucester)

offset tables so that I can start on her as soon as possible."[20] Adams had engaged to build the seventy-eight-ton fisherman for Captain Charley Olsen and George Steele, who owned a dozen Gloucester schooners.[21]

By late spring, due to Kate's advanced stage of pregnancy, the anticipated delivery date being late August, Tom decided to double their normal Scituate sojourn. During the first week of the month, after a few weeks away from the city, they received the shocking and mournful news that Ned Burgess, "weakened by overwork," had died of typhoid fever on 31 July. He was just forty-three-years-old. Bostonians from all walks of life turned out to mourn their loss and honor the memory of this talented young man[22] whose genius had brought such glory to the Hub.

A few weeks later birth once again mitigated death for Tom and Kate. On 28 August baby Mary arrived in the rented house on Jericho Road.[23] But no birth could overcome death's next visitation. On 2 January 1892, cancer struck Dennison

---

[20] McManus, "Essay No. 2."

[21] Enrolment No. 51, Gloucester, 14 January 1892.

[22] Chapelle, *Fishing Schooners*, 163.

[23] Vital Records 1841-1895, Massachusetts State Archives, *Births*, 1891, vol. 414, page 42.

J. Lawlor down in his home at 35 Walnut Street, Chelsea. Lawlor's status in the life of Tom McManus was second only to his father's. For more than three decades the Canadian-Irish designer-builder had guided Tom's professional training. A few days afterward, with unabashed tears streaming from his eyes, Tom took his turn with the rest of the mourners and tossed a shovel full of dirt onto the casket of his beloved mentor at Mt. Auburn Cemetery.[24]

With the demise of both Burgess and Lawlor, the need arose for someone to take their place in the world of New England naval architecture. The men who came closest to doing so were George Melville "Mel" McClain, who would become the first designer to install auxiliary power in a fishing schooner, and, to a lesser extent, Arthur Binney, a trained naval architect who took over Ned Burgess's practice.[25] But, for some weeks before Lawlor's death, articles appearing in the Gloucester newspapers suggested a new force had galvanized the field. One said that "the residents of Essex, Gloucester, Rockport, and other towns nearby, are in a flurry just now over the pretty 75-ton fishing schooner, now being built by Moses Adams," and that "every day people went miles to see her"; although some wags held that she was "a curious looking critter on the stocks." Captain McClain, "who had designed 60 fast fishermen within two years, was loud in his praise."[26] Another veteran shipmaster, Captain Arthur H. Clark, had traveled to Essex the week before the paper came out to have a look, "and has a good opinion of her."[27] When the latter story appeared, Adams had completed the hull, and the reporter predicted that "in a few days the Essex river will receive a presentation such as was never offered before."[28]

For reasons of his own, at this point, Tom chose not to identify himself as the creator of the striking new schooner, but to assume the role of commentator: "Mr. Thomas McManus, who has an eye for beauty, looked the vessel over carefully

---

[24] Vital Records 1841-1895, Massachusetts State Archives, *Deaths*, 1892, vol. 429, page 493, line 2.

[25] Arthur Binney was born at Boston on 2 December 1865. He was educated in Boston Public schools, Roxbury Latin School, and took a special drafting and design course at Massachusetts Institute of Technology. He served a draftsman apprenticeship with the Whittier Machine Company of Boston and later worked as a draftsman for the Hastings Organ Company. Binney went to work for Edward Burgess in 1888 and, upon the latter's death, formed the firm of Stewart & Binney. He later bought out his partner and remained in business on his own account. He designed many vessel types, including ferryboats, City of Boston police and fire boats, fishing schooners, but principally engaged in yacht design. His most notable creation was the America's Cup racer *Pilgrim*. A charter member of the Society of Naval Architects and Marine Engineers, he died on 28 August 1924.

[26] One of several unidentified or only partially identifiable newspaper clippings glued to a photograph of the *James S. Steele* that has been donated by a descendent of James S. Steele, the son of George Steele, to the Cape Ann Historical Association during 1993. The papers included Gloucester's *Daily Times* and *Weekly Advertiser*, Boston's *Globe* and *Sunday Herald*, and the Provincetown *Advocate*.

[27] Gloucester *Daily Times*, 5 December 1891.

[28] Unidentifiable newspaper source. See note no. 26.

and said: 'If the owners and captain do her justice, she will be a great success as yacht or fisherman.'" Tom's beguiling stance–his failure to lay claim to the schooner and the intimation that he didn't know how she would be employed–left people to assume that a new, but unknown, designer had introduced "a radical departure from other designs, which resembles very closely the victorious *Gloriana*, only on a larger scale."[29] Another newspaper concluded: "Following in the wake of the yacht *Gloriana*, a fishing vessel with long ends is about completed at Essex, Mass. She is a more radical departure in the working vessel line than the *Gloriana* is in yachts." Thus, even before McManus's first schooner set sail, people recognized that "for the cause of naval architecture, the advent of the new [style of] fishing craft is to be welcomed."

A year before the *James S. Steele* slid down the ways, yacht designer Nathanael G. Herreshoff, of Bristol, Rhode Island, reacting to the same stimulus as McManus, the shallowness of contemporary yacht racing hulls, introduced the long-ended and revolutionary sloop yacht *Gloriana*. From time to time a controversy has arisen over the similarity between the designs of the *Gloriana* and the *Steele*. Although the *Steele* went to sea in 1892, her design dated back to 1889. The *Gloriana* began her racing career in 1891, and Herreshoff designed her in the latter part of 1890. The argument is pointless, however, as neither man had access to the other's work, and both were responding, each in his own field, to the problem of shallow draft.[30] The Gloucester *Daily Times* later revealed: "Mr. McManus kept himself in the background, preferring to await developments. The new boat is absolutely his own design, and he has been for years an advocate of long overhangs."[31]

With his first schooner nearing completion, McManus's celebrated Irish temper unfortunately blocked his presence from her Yuletide 1891 launching ceremony. The point at issue illustrates his stiff-necked and stubborn side. He had modeled her with hollowed (concave) garboard strakes–the lowermost hull planks, immediately adjacent to, and rabbeted into, the keel–to add to her quickness in

---

[29] Ibid.

[30] Regarding the design similarity, Howard I. Chapelle commented: ". . . [The *Steeles*] were cut away forward much more than was then common; in fact, the profile was much like that of the famous Herreshoff sloop *Gloriana, though McManus knew nothing of this yacht*." (Howard I. Chapelle, *American Sailing Craft* (New York: Kennedy Brothers, 1936), 96, emphasis added). George Stadel, Jr., when asked about the likelihood of plagiarism, replied in astonishment: "how could Herreshoff have influenced the *Steele* when the drafts and model [of the *Steele*] were completed a year before she [*Gloriana*] was launched?" (Stadel interview, 21 September 1988). Charlton Smith, the schooner skipper and journalist who lived through the era, left no doubt concerning McManus's 1891 achievement: "Captain Thomas F. McManus introduced the spoon bow with the little schooner *James S. Steele*. With various modifications, this bow has lasted to the present time" (Boston *Evening Transcript*, 11 April 1922).

[31] Gloucester *Daily Times*, date unknown, *ca.* January 1892.

Under sail for the first time, with her headsails not yet stretched to shape, the *James S. Steele* shows off her long overhangs for photographer Walter Gardner on 16 January 1892. Her well-dressed crew, including "Mel" McClain but not McManus–who literally missed the boat–is about to witness the *Steele's* trimming of the schooners *Gloriana*, *Lottie S. Haskins*, and *Harry L. Belden*. (Courtesy Cape Ann Historical Collection, Gloucester)

changing tacks. Adams chose to build her with straight garboards, a less expensive procedure, but one that minutely penalized the new vessel by infinitesimally slowing her tacking ability. The designer took umbrage at this liberty with his plan and flatly refused to work with Adams, or even visit his Essex yard, ever again.[32] It was a sorry revenge on the man who brought his first design into being, but such intransigent independence was a McManus hallmark.

Owner George Steele ultimately prevailed on Tom to come up to Gloucester for the sea trial of the schooner he named for one of his sons, James S. Steele, by assuring him that Adams would not be coming along. But even with that, fate prevented his presence on board. On the day of the shakedown cruise, Saturday, 16 January 1892,[33] he took the horsecar to the stop at Haymarket Square and walked over to Union Station on Causeway Street, where he boarded the train for the northeast. When it pulled into the outskirts of Gloucester, however, the railway drawbridge was blocked open, with the result that the train arrived an hour

[32] Moses Adams, a native of West Gloucester, built about 100 vessels at Essex. He began his career with Arthur D. Story in 1877, and went on his own in 1880. "He was the first man to introduce machinery in Essex yards." He died at Essex on 16 July 1894, at age fifty-six (Gordon W. Thomas, *Fast & Able, Life Stories of Great Gloucester Fishing Vessels* (Gloucester, Massachusetts: Gloucester 350th Anniversary Celebration, Inc., 1973), 41).

[33] Boston *Sunday Herald*, 17 January, 1892.

behind schedule. When he finally got to the docks, a totally frustrated McManus "was told that the *James S. Steele* went out with a number of other fishing vessels, including by a strange coincidence, the latest productions of Lawlor, Burgess, and McLean [*sic*]."[34]

Thwarted, Tom sought a vantage point to see his creation under sail. He ended up by climbing to the top of the city hall tower; where, with a pair of strong binoculars, he had a fine, if windblown and icy-cold, view of the harbor out to and beyond Eastern Point. He easily distinguished the *Steele*'s white hull, which contrasted starkly with the traditional black ones of the other fishermen, and compared her sailing to that of her competitors. What he witnessed pleased him.

The tug *Joe Call* had no sooner taken the *Steele* in tow before another tug responded to a call from Captain Mo Powers, the long-time McManus family employee, now in charge of the *Harry L. Belden* (Lawlor, 1889), to follow her out. As the tugs proceeded down the harbor, the *Lottie S. Haskins* (McClain, 1890) and the fishing schooner *Gloriana* (Burgess, 1891) also got under way–and the race was on. Under the headline, "One of the Finest, The New Schooner *James S. Steele* Shows Great Speed on her Trial," the Gloucester *Daily Times* reported:

> At one time all four vessels were exactly on a line; then the *Belden*, which had the windward berth, and caught the land puffs first, drew ahead. The *Steele* and *Gloriana* had it nip and tuck for fully a mile, and finally the new craft drew ahead, also passing the *Haskins*. . . . Finally the *Belden*, which now had a good lead, tacked and stood across the bows of the other flyers, clearing the *Steele* by about one hundred feet. Once more the race was on. Now both vessels [the *Belden* and the *Steele*] were on even terms and the *Steele* began to draw away and increased her lead till Thacher's Island was reached, when Capt. Powers gave it up and started for the fishing grounds followed by the *Gloriana*.[35]

While the *Steele* and *Haskins* headed into port, Tom clambered down from his chilly observation post and went along to the Atlantic Fish Company's pier to meet his creation. But, as she approached the dock, the crew failed to anticipate how easily she moved through the water. They lowered her sails too soon; which allowed the schooner to carry too much headway and, as a result, she ran up on a

---

[34] McManus, "Essay No. 4." Edward Burgess died on 31 July 1891, and Dennison J. Lawlor on 2 January 1892. Several designs by each architect were used for schooners built after their deaths.

[35] Gloucester *Daily Times*, 18 January 1892; *Cape Ann Weekly Advertiser*, 22 January 1892.

wide, flat rock ledge. Fortunately the tide was on the flood and the men soon warped the *Steele* off her ignoble perch and up to the wharf, where another unpleasant surprise awaited Tom. The first of the fifty passengers to disembark was none other than McManus's fellow alumnus from Frisbee's "Free School," Captain Mel McClain. He grabbed Tom's hand and congratulated him on designing a fisherman that performed so well. Then, with an extraordinarily pointed needle, remarked that the *Steele* "could sail on land as well as water!"[36] It was a nice irony, indeed, that his future competitor sailed on the *Steele*'s maiden voyage, while McManus himself missed the boat. Away from Tom's presence, McClain was highly complimentary about the *Steele*: "Capt. Geo. M. McClain, the designer, was on the trial and said that the new vessel was a flyer. She had done better in her trial trip than any vessel he had ever seen."[37]

Death, seemingly a constant companion of the McManus and Leonard families, struck again several weeks after Lawlor's passing when "Boss" Matt Keany died of pneumonia and "inflammation of the knee joint" on 27 February 1892, in his red brick home at 1 New Prince Street.[38] At fifty-nine, ten years junior to his old crony, John H., the garrulous and shrewd Keany had played a continuous role in the fortunes of the McManuses since the 1850s.

The politician's death also marked the end of an era in Boston's Democratic politics. Keany had been the first marshal of the Irish electoral legions. He perceived the opportunity offered by the extended franchise of the Jacksonian era and began naturalizing, organizing, and registering the swarming Irish famine immigrants, and the other European masses that followed, as loyal Democratic voters. He capitalized on the rapidly expanding municipal infrastructure of Boston, with its endless demand for skilled and unskilled civil servants, and made it his personal fountain of favors for his faithful followers. Lastly, it was Keany, along with Denny Cawley and Mike Carney, who first sensed that they had the entrenched old-line aristocracy on the run, overwhelmed them by sheer numbers, and displaced the native blue bloods from their traditional management roles in the city. From the day in the 1862 when he gave up his job as a clerk in the grocery at 238 North Street to open his own premises three doors up at No. 232 in competition with his former employer, Matt Keany never looked back. Before the Civil War was half over, he led the formerly pro-slavery Irish into the Union camp and, by 1864, was handling wartime welfare benefits. The Irish boss's powers knew few limits. Like

---

[36] McManus, "Essay No. 4."

[37] *Cape Ann Weekly Advertiser*, 18 January 1892.

[38] *Deaths*, 1892, vol. 429, page 84, line 1929.

George Washington Plunkitt of New York's Tammany Hall, Keany could liberate a man's son from jail, provide a hungry widow with food, see that an aspiring peddler received a permit, and slip a destitute father the money to buy a coffin to bury his infant child.[39] But, where Keany had been a respected friend to Tom's father, the man who organized Keany's funeral, John Francis Fitzgerald, his protégé and faithful ward heeler, was heartily disliked by the naval architect.[40] Unlike his parent, McManus kept clear of the ward machinery, and limited his politics to registering and voting as a Democrat.

Without invitation, Fitzgerald took charge of the arrangements for Keany's funeral. He appointed the actual and the honorary pallbearers, organized the church seats, and the order of the procession to Calvary Cemetery. The ceremony itself, held at St. Stephen's, was a well-remembered affair. "Never," *The Republic* observed, "was such an imposing scene known in the North End. All classes paid homage to the dead. The clergy, state officials, city dignitaries, the poor and the orphan mingled their tears at the bier of the one they had known and loved."[41] To everyone's surprise (except his own), Fitzgerald, already known as "Honey Fitz" for his persuasive speaking abilities, successfully maneuvered to claim the stewardship of Ward Six upon the death of his leader. Fitzgerald's finagling as the new boss brought a different style of political rule to the ethnically changing, but still archly Democratic, district. Keany's world of gray eminence did not sit comfortably with the ambitious twenty-nine-year-old, and in the autumn elections he won election as a state senator. In the future Fitzgerald would rule the ward from the front office, unlike the preference his predecessor displayed for back room power.

Tom fell heir to a distasteful and difficult decision during the winter of 1891-92. His father reached his sixty-ninth birthday on 27 December, two months before Keany died, and as much as the elder McManus tried, he was no longer capable of managing the Commercial Wharf sail loft, much less working at his life-long craft. With a heart-felt regret, Tom notified the journeymen sailmakers that, after thirty-one years in business, the loft would close down. He considered selling, but realized that the firm had no vitality of its own, and had had very little since his brother Charley's death in November 1887. To deepen Tom's doldrums, as spring

---

[39] Doris K. Goodwin, *The Fitzgeralds and the Kennedys* (New York: Simon and Schuster, 1987), 70.

[40] It has proven difficult to trace the root of McManus's antipathy to Fitzgerald, especially given their closeness to Keany. His grandchildren, however, remember it vividly. It may be traceable to an impropriety on Fitzgerald's part concerning one of McManus's daughters, Louise, who graduated with Rose Fitzgerald.

[41] Goodwin, *The Fitzgeralds and the Kennedys*, 94, citing *The Republic*, 5 March 1892.

warmed toward summer his Aunt Lucy, the widow of John H.'s brother Pat, followed her husband to the grave on 22 May.[42] With her passing, the remains of the Irish old guard dwindled quickly away. Even the once-stalwart John H. had to be looked after constantly. Soon the sad day arrived when Tom had to remove his beloved father from the house at 15 Margaret Street. It had been the family home for more than thirty years, and Tom's own birthplace. He and Kate took John H. into the house at 39 Mount Vernon, where his growing flock of granddaughters could look after him.

Professionally, the successful sea trial of the *James S. Steele* put Tom McManus's naval architectural career on course and, from this point onward, it would climb from strength to strength. The *Steele* became a fine, if limited, fisherman and, according to Tom, "many a time I have heard her praises from the men who sailed on her in all kinds of weather."[43] Among the plethora of architectural innovations embodied in the *Steele*, Tom had extended the bow slightly to shorten the bowsprit and anchored the forestay inboard of the knightheads, instead of attaching it to the gammon iron on the head of the stem. She was the first contemporary schooner to have this rig. Although McManus abandoned this bowsprit arrangement in his forthcoming

Showing off in Gloucester Harbor, the *Richard L. Steele* maneuvers deftly through the fleet. Notice her narrow elliptical transom. (Courtesy Louise V. Will)

---

[42] She was fifty-nine-years-old, and died from a form of kidney disease (Vital Records, *Deaths*, 1892, vol. 429, page 199, line 65 giving the cause of death as "nephritis"); letter, J. Worth Estes, M.D., 5 April 1990, indicates a kidney disease, but the cited terms is insufficient to determine the exact type.

[43] McManus, "Essay No. 1."

Indian Head class, ten years after the coming of the *Steele*, Bowdoin B. Crowninshield re-introduced this type of standing rigging, and McManus came back to it in his semi-knockabouts. Four months after the *James S. Steele* went to sea, Moses Adams launched a sister ship. He had added a pair of frames to Tom's design for the *James S. Steele*, and built the eighty-two-ton *Richard C. Steele* also for George Steele, who hired Frank P. Silva as her master.[44]

If the *Steeles* had a fault other than their limited capacity, it lay in their tenderness. During her career the *James S. Steele* once nearly became a ghost-ship. While mackerel fishing, with her crew busily cleaning a deck-load of fish, a line squall suddenly knocked on her beam ends, as a result of her intentional lack of initial stability and a top-heavy deck load of fish. The crew and fish went sliding overboard, but the schooner quickly righted herself and resumed her course. One of the men, alert to what had happened, hugged the schooner's side, floated along her waterline, and grabbed the painter of the seine dory towing astern. He swung into the dory, pulled himself to the *Steele*'s transom, clambered on board, and took control of the wheel. Then the schooner's designed-in capability of turning on a dime saved the day, by allowing her to tack about in an instant. The dripping helmsman then steered for his drowning shipmates. If it had not been for his quick thinking and the *Steele*'s tacking ability, there would have been another *Mary Celeste* mystery.[45]

Disappointingly, the *Steeles* failed to initiate the revolution that McManus sought to foment. As John Frisbee had pointed out from the beginning, economics provided a large portion of the grounds. Shipbuilders charged their customers by the linear foot and, like all of Tom's early designs, with their narrow ends, the *Steeles* carried insufficient cargo in the hold relative to overall length and, therefore, to the cost of construction. Yet no one disputed their speed, agility, and safe sailing qualities.

It would have been less than worthy if the first schooner completed to a design drawn by "The Father of the Fishermen's Races" failed to take part in an officially recognized racing contest. Boston had taken the lead in these competitions with the 1886 race, thanks to McManus; but Charley Harty of Gloucester issued the challenge that initiated the 1888 race, a true intercity affair, with Tom responding on behalf of Boston. Then Gloucester, under auspices of its city government, organized a third race in 1892—and what a race it turned out to be!

In the weeks between 21 August and 20 September that year, three hurricanes roiled the western Atlantic. The first of these vicious tropical cyclones

---

[44] Enrolment No. 22, Gloucester, 9 December 1892.

[45] Chapelle, *Fishing Schooners*, 213.

battered the ocean 450 miles offshore just as the municipal dignitaries cut the ribbon to begin Gloucester's 250th anniversary celebrations. The following two tempests traveled further out to sea, a guarantee that the entire northeast coastline would be in a continuous uproar from mid-August until mid-October.

As part of the events planned for Gloucester's birthday party, the sub-committee in charge of festivities organized a race to honor the townsmen who had been lost over the years while harvesting the sea. Because of its incredibly stormy setting, this extraordinary event has secured its own place within the maritime lore of New England, one reserved under the all-too-modest title, "The Race That Blew."

Rudyard Kipling joined the multitude of visitors to Gloucester during the 1892 vacation season and was in town once or twice, "at the time of the celebrations of the men who were lost or drowned in the codfishing fleet." Inspired to write about New England fishermen, he wandered about the Boston and Gloucester waterfronts that summer with an acquaintance, Dr. James Conland, the family doctor from his home in Brattleboro, Vermont. Kipling recalled that:

> This book [*Captains Courageous*] took us . . . to the shore-front and the old T-wharf of Boston Harbour, and to queer meals in sailors' eating houses . . . We assisted hospitable tug-masters to help haul three- and four-stick schooners of Pochahontas coal all round the Harbour; we boarded every craft that looked as if it might be useful, and we delighted ourselves to the limit of delight. Charts we got—old and new—and the crude implements of navigation such as they are used off the Banks, and a battered boat compass, still a treasure with me. . . . And Conland took large cod and the appropriate knives with which they are prepared for the hold, and demonstrated anatomically and surgically so that I could make no mistake about treating them in print. Old tales, too, he dug up, and the lists of dead and gone schooners whom he had loved, and I revelled in profligate abundances of detail—not necessarily for publication but for the joy of it. And he sent me—may he be forgiven!—out on a pollock-fisher, which is ten times fouler than any cod-schooner, and I was immortally sick, even though they tried to revive me with fragments of unfresh pollock.[46]

---

[46] Rudyard Kipling, *Something of Myself for My Friends Known and Unknown* (Garden City, New York: Doubleday, Doran & Company, 1937).

Tom McManus was another, no less eager, participant in Gloucester's 250th anniversary. He had spent eighteen frustrating months attempting to get a ride in his first creation: "I never had an opportunity to sail on the *Steele* since losing out on the trial trip, so I wrote to Mr. Steele to see if he would arrange with the Captain to have the boat ready to take me out on Wednesday the 24th."[47]

When Tom arrived in Gloucester on the appointed day, he made his way to George Steele's Rogers Street office, and immediately ran into disturbing news. The fishing magnate informed him that the committee had organized two classes, the "first class" to be open to vessels with a waterline length of eighty-five feet and up, and the "second class" for those from eighty-five feet down. The *Steele*, only seventy feet on the waterline, belonged in the second class, but the skippers of the other boats in that category refused to race against McManus's speedster because she had too often shown her heels to them during the past fishing season. Tom, when he heard this, remarked tongue-in-cheek, "one race won without a contest!"

But McManus was being circumspect here. The unusual overhangs of the *Steele* precluded her from any comparison of waterline length with her competitors. In terms of length, the *Steele* was not giving that much away to the largest competitors. Her molded length at the rail cap was only seven feet three inches shorter than the "big" *Harry L. Belden*. Additionally, the superior sailing of the *Steele* in the day's rough water conditions, especially with the reduction in "hobby-horsing" as a result of her overhangs, equalized any advantage the others enjoyed.

To overcome the resistance, not at all dissimilar to the attempt to blacklist Burgess's *Carrie E. Phillips* in the 1888 race, Tom proposed that they should "assume the fifteen feet and sail in the 85 feet up or first class." Steele demonstrated a distinct lack of enthusiasm for this idea. The large class included several recent schooners built to the model of the swift *Nellie Dixon*, "or as they called them in Gloucester, the *Fredonia* model, all were from the board of Ned Burgess," noted Tom sarcastically, emphasizing the press's ascription of the design to the *Fredonia*. Demonstrating how popular Burgess's fishermen had become in only two years, they included the *Nannie C. Bohlin* (1890, 112.2 feet), Captain Tommy Bohlin; the *Joseph Rowe* (1891, 109.6 feet), Captain Rube Cameron; the *Ethel B. Jacobs* (1891, 131.75 feet), Captain Sol Jacobs; and the *James G. Blaine* (1891, 103.43 feet), Captain Johnny McDonald. Dennison J. Lawlor's powerful *Harry L. Belden* (1889, 123.37 feet), Captain Maurice Whalen; and the *Grayling* (1891, 121.43 feet), Mel McClain and Captain Charley Harty's latest effort, filled out the lineup. It was a formidable fleet, but, nevertheless, Tom succeeded in swaying the owner to change

---

[47] During the following passage describing "The Race That Blew," all uncited quotations originate from McManus, "Addendum No. 1 to Autobiographical Essay No. 3," and "Addendum No. 2 to Autobiographical Essay No. 3."

his mind and move the *Steele* (78.46 feet) into the first class, leaving the *Lottie S. Haskins* (1890, 58.47 feet), *Caviare* (1891, 62.98 feet), and *Elsie F. Rowe* (1891, 58.13 feet), in the shorter category.

The wind blew from the northeast during the shakedown run Wednesday afternoon, and before they left the dock Steele cautioned Captain Charley Olsen to stick to training his crew in setting and trimming the sails, and not to race with any of the bigger boats. But the temptation was too great and the *Steele* had a few brushes with the opposition. Since Monday's still conditions (the proverbial "calm before the storm"), the wind strength had been steadily increasing, and the day's "whole-sail breeze" kept the schooners' lee rails awash and their scuppers gurgling. With the *Steele* racing along in the midst of three of the first-class vessels, which had also gone out to drill their crews, Tom recalled that "it was a grand day for sailing, as the wind on that day was blowing from 20 to 30 Miles an hour, enough to get the most speed from any boat under sail." He came back to the dock "greatly pleased by the action and speed of *James S. Steele*, and with my hopes buoyed up, for the greatest test that any vessel could have." A satisfied man, he returned to Boston on the evening train.

Thursday brought no respite. The wind velocity climbed to thirty and forty knots, and the seas rose menacingly. By Friday, the day of the race, it was gusting over fifty knots in squalls, and the waves outside the breakwater had become veritable mountains, with the promontory of Cape Ann bearing the brunt of the foaming hurricane-bred seas that swept in from offshore. The northeast gale howled without interruption through the early hours. Several skippers said that they had "never experienced anything worse in all their lives."

At Boston, early on Friday morning, Dolly McVey, the yachting editor of the Boston *Herald*, invited Tom to accompany him to Gloucester on the paper's ocean-going news tug, the *Wesley Gove*. The Irishman accepted with alacrity, but even the steam-powered voyage to Gloucester turned into an ordeal: "I never had the experience of being on a steamer tacking in order to avoid foundering. When we started from the dock at Boston, and reached Broad Sound in Boston Harbor it was plenty rough and the boat was plunging into the sea and filling her decks level with the rails, which retarded our speed, until the Captain kept zigzagging or as he called it tacking as you would on a sailing craft working up to windward."

When the storm-tossed tug finally crept into Gloucester's harbor and tied up, Tom went with McVey's assistant to the Master Mariner Rooms, only to learn that the race committee and the racing skippers were in a meeting at the hotel on the other side of the street. They crossed over just in time to hear Captain Tommy Bohlin of the *Nannie C. Bohlin* say with hard-earned Gloucester arrogance, "this is the chance to show you [Boston] Market Fishermen how to carry Sail," and "after

arguing pro and con the Committee decided that the race would take place as scheduled."

As the time for the starting gun neared there was no sign of change– the United States Weather Bureau continued to confirm winds of around fifty knots. Conditions were so rough that when the spectator-laden steamboats headed out for the racecourse, they came right back in, staggered by the fierce winds and heavy seas. No fools, they choose instead to watch the event from under the lee of Eastern Point.

"Mr. Charles Welch," a Boston society buddy of Tom's, "who was one of the greatest yachtsmen of all times, and a counselor aboard *Puritan* and *Mayflower* in their races," went to an unusual extreme to join the afterguard: "he came down in the cab of a freight engine in order to be there on time to go as a member of the crew of the *Steele*."[48] A lifeboat took Tom, Welch, and Dr. William H. Hale, a Gloucester physician who had struck up an acquaintance with Charley Olsen the night before, and the remaining crew members out to the schooner. On their approach, Welch remarked that the *Steele* "looks like a balloon, she's so light on the water."

Once the visitors clambered on deck, Captain Olsen immediately ordered the mainsail hoisted. In light of the conditions Welch, the experienced yachtsman, suggested to the skipper that "he take a reef in the sail as it was blowing a hurricane." Olsen merely pointed to the entrance of the harbor and said: "Do you see that boat out there? That's the *Ethel Jacobs*, although she's 40 ft. longer than we are–if she can carry full sail, so can we," and up went the full mainsail. Like all the racing skippers, Olsen spent many a day driving his various commands through the winter gales and blinding blizzards that whistled over the fishing banks, and neither he nor any of his peers, never dreaming that the seas were hurricane-spawned, were about to let an inshore summer storm interfere with their fun.

After lifting the main boom off the saddle, swaying up the gaff, and setting the mainsail, Olsen passed the order to sheet home the main gaff topsail. Then the foresail went up. As soon as everything was clear to pay off, he ordered the anchor chain slipped and hoisted the jib. But just as the crewmen cleated the last of the four lower sails home, a squall struck the *Steele* and knocked the schooner so far over that the companionway dipped into the boiling foam, and water began to pour into the cabin. The *James S. Steele* was only seconds from capsizing; but thanks to her innate quality of reserved buoyancy, she immediately rolled upright. Despite the

---

48 McManus, "Essay No. 3," "Memoirs of the Atlantic Fishing Fleet (1883-1934), by Captain Thomas F. McManus of Milton, Father of Fishing Races."

near-knockdown, Olsen, fully confident in his command's stability, ordered the forestaysail hoisted, and drove her outside the breakwater into the open sea under full canvas. The hull's remarkable design had saved the day before it began.

Olsen quickly had the men rig out the lifelines to give passengers and crew alike a handhold, so the wind would not fling them into the sea. As they cleared the harbor, the larger boats were already hurtling to and fro, testing the force of the wind. Then, as the last entrants came out, in anticipation of the start all the schooners tacked for the line, which lay between the whistling buoy off Eastern Point and the moored judge's boat. The course would take the fleet outside the southeast breakers and inside Halfway Rock off Marblehead to the turning mark near Nahant, a moored committee boat. From there it ran to the Davis Ledge buoy southeast of Minot's Ledge Light, not far from Scituate, and back to the starting point, a distance of about thirty-eight miles.

Riding the northeast gales, the *Ethel B. Jacobs* won the honors and crossed ahead of the fleet on starboard tack. Captain Sol Jacobs, with every bit of canvas on board aloft, including the jib topsail, the fore gaff topsail, and the main topmast staysail–although, according to Tom the latter sail, "was what they call scandalized or half hoisted"–stretched away from the pack into the misty distance where wild waves merged with pelting rain and thickening mist, leaving no discernible horizon. Seconds later the *Nannie C. Bohlin*, *Harry L. Belden*, and *James S. Steele* came tearing across the line, followed quickly by the *Grayling*, *Joseph Rowe*, and *James G. Blaine*.

Abreast of the first mark off Nahant's East Point, Jacobs jibed over in order to leave the mark to port. On board the *Steele*, racing along about a mile astern of the leader, Tom and the others thought they heard the crack of a cannon fired on the Nahant shore. But no! It was the *Jacob*'s main gaff snapping, unable to withstand the strain of the jibe when the boom scythed across the deck ahead of the banshee wind. The pacesetter's mainsail instantly split from the gaff down to the boom, torn into useless shreds from head to foot. The crew had no choice but to bring her head to wind and strip off the tattered remains. This brought the disabled schooner to a dead stop–right in front of the *Bohlin*, *Belden*, and *Steele*, who were charging at the mark with minimal rudder control in the raging seas. The two larger boats had the *Steele* sandwiched between them; but, in a remarkable display of seamanship, all three jibed as one without colliding or entangling their booms. For Charley Harty in the *Grayling*, scudding along in their wake, the sheer insanity of that near disaster was enough; after rounding the mark, he withdrew and went back into Gloucester. A few moments later Johnny McDonald on the *Blaine*, shaking his head in disbelief at the antics of the three leaders, reached the same conclusion and followed suit.

Now with a beam wind on the new leg of the course, the larger schooners, benefitting from their longer waterline length, began to outfoot the *Steele*. At the end of that stretch they rounded the Davis Ledge buoy in terrific seas and heavy squalls, set their course as close as possible to the force of the northeast gale, and snubbed the sheets tight on starboard tack.

Ever the dedicated architectural investigator, Tom, even in those atrocious conditions found the time and presence to calmly size up his schooner as she drove into the surging waves: "It demonstrated to me the advantage of the overhangs, as the *Steele* would just dip her bowsprit in the ocean, and the reserve buoyancy would lift her up." Alongside, he watched the *Nannie C. Bohlin*, creaming along under the *Steele*'s lee bow, plunge into the green waters up to her foremast and fill the deck to the rails with water. The huge schooner staggered under the pressure of the sea. Unknown to Tom and the others, Skipper Tommy Bohlin was in trouble. In anticipation of sailing in typically light August zephyrs, when he hauled the *Bohlin* out to scrape and clean her bottom earlier in the week, the skipper had removed some ballast. Under the race rules, once back in the water he was not allowed to alter his decision. The *Bohlin* was in singular straits; she was flying too light. But the *Harry L. Belden*, racing along on the *Steele*'s windward side, benefitted from the exact opposite of the *Bohlin*'s light-ballast plight.

Captain Maurice Whalen and his crew bordered on total exhaustion. They had ridden the hurricane-hatched easterlies all the way in from the fishing banks to get to the race and had only come into port at 10:00 P.M. the previous night. Whalen's men never had time to discharge the fish hold, and the schooner was racing low in the water for she still carried her full cargo of 80,000 pounds of iced fish, a tremendous advantage in the stormy surroundings. With a full hold, there was no limit to how much canvas she could carry.

The *Steele*'s other passenger, Dr. Hale, wrote: "During the long thrash to windward, every vessel sailed on her lee rail, with deck buried to the hatches . . . the brave, laboring craft would roll under surging seas to the second and third ratline; then would follow awful moments of suspense, as the unflinching crews, with teeth set and hands clenched, watched to see if their craft would stagger up again, or go down under grievous load. Desperate as the chances were, not a vessel luffed or reefed, as to be the first to reef would make her the laughing stock of the town, and there was not a skipper in the fleet who would not carry away both sticks rather than be branded as a coward."[49]

---

[49] William Hale, M.D., aboard the schooner *James S. Steele* during "The Race It Blew," 1892, cited in Garland, *Down to the Sea*, 173. Dr. Hale maintained a surgery in his home at 14 Pleasant Street in Gloucester.

A telling comment came from Arthur Millet of the Gloucester *Times*: "the boats all had too much sail on, and it was playing to the galleries to carry it. All would have sailed faster under reefs."[50]

Suddenly the *Steele* started to lag behind the other two leaders. One of the foredeck hands quickly spotted the cause. He shouted to Olsen that the jib was bagging. The skipper ordered the crew to put a chain strap on the jib jig, and luffed the bow into the wind to relieve the pressure on the sail. During the evolution disaster struck: "a number of the men swayed on the tackle until the tack hook in the bowsprit, which was fastened to the tack of the jib, broke, letting the foot of the jib go up the stay a number of feet." As far as Tom was concerned: "The captain lost his head and ordered the men forward to take the jib down and put a tack lashing around the bowsprit. But no man could go forward because the jib sheet blocks and the iron chain sheets were beating across the vessel's head like lightning, thereby 'putting the vessel in irons,' until he could get a piece of rope to make the lashing, which took him a very long time."

Tom had felt confident all along that the *Steele* would give a good account of herself, if properly handled by the captain and crew, but, "as a later Captain of the *Steele* (and by the way one of the best in the fishing business) said, she will do everything but talk, she certainly did talk on the day of the race, but the then Captain did not understand the language."[51]

Everyone on board recognized the imminent peril of drifting onto a lee shore strewn with rocks and boulders. To make matters worse, Olsen had to pay her off toward that very shore until the men could take the rope and make a tack lashing around the bowsprit. They finally accomplished this dangerous measure and saved the *Steele*, but lost a lot of ground before they could reset the jib and get back to racing.

When the leaders neared the North Shore on the return leg, Olsen tacked to port and, on drawing close to Gloucester Harbor (as Tom interpreted the confusing events that followed): "We could see the other contestants leaving the judge's boat on the port hand and going into the harbor. While passing the judges boat, which had changed its position under the lee of Eastern Point, they shouted but we couldn't understand them, so intent were we on passing the whistling buoy on the port hand and then running back to leave the judges boat on our starboard, being the only boat that completed the course."

---

[50] Arthur Millet, Gloucester *Times*, 27 August 1892.

[51] McManus, "Addendum No. 2 to Essay No. 3," parentheses original.

But the judges ruled the *Steele* out of the race for ignoring their orders and failing to cross the revised finish line. The officials had shouted into the wind to tell Olsen that the course had been shortened, but no one on board the *Steele* could make out their words, and the schooner sailed the full distance, the only contestant to complete the original course. The *Belden*, with her fish-filled hold, gained a hard-earned victory. It is doubtful than any unladen vessel could have caught her. One can only surmise that Whalen and his hardy hands must have slept through the next week–after they first unloaded forty tons of fish. The *Lottie S. Haskins* finished about an hour after the *Steele* to win the second class from the *Caviare* and *Elsie F. Rowe*, which did not finish.[52] McManus returned home to Charlestown after this hair-raising experience and settled back into his normal routine.

When Tom took John H. into the house at Charlestown, his father, despite his weakened condition, refused to countenance a life of inactivity. After settling in with his grandchildren he used the proceeds from the sale of the Margaret Street house to pay off the mortgage on 39 Mount Vernon and, whenever the weather allowed, began stalking the neighborhood in search of properties that might be bought cheaply. A depressed real estate market meant profitable property buys for those with capital and, operating in Tom's name, John H. bought several fine nearby properties.[53] In addition to trying to keep up with his father's real estate dealings, and looking after the remaining family businesses, Tom continued to partake in schooner syndication. During this same period, he had completed his studies under John Frisbee and devoted his energies to the fish brokerage and T Wharf Supply Company, while he awaited his next commission to design a schooner. But, with the nation in the throes of the recession that led to the Panic of 1893, there was little call for either radical or ordinary new fishing boats.

Never one to be brought up short by circumstances beyond his control, during the spring of 1893 Tom combined his financial and professional interests to forward his creative career by selling an existing design. A year earlier, the Gloucester *Daily Times*, reporting the launch of the *James S. Steele*, had remarked:

---

[52] Arthur Millet, Gloucester *Times*, 27 August 1892.

[53] City of Boston, Tax Assessor's Records, Ward 3, Street, Part 1, 29, 1893; page 28 for 39 Mount Vernon St., 2068 ft. of land valued at $2,220, building at $3,200. Personal estate of Thomas F. McManus valued at $3,000 same as 1892). Real estate valued at $5,400. Tax $72.36 plus $2 poll tax, total tax $74.36. The house down the hill at 25 Mount Vernon included the land through to, and the house at 30 Prospect Street, which ran parallel to Mt. Vernon lower down on Breed's Hill. In all it amounted to 3,255 sq. ft. of land valued at $3,400 and the two buildings at $7,000. To cap off his coup, despite the recession, he managed to rent 25 Mount Vernon and to retain the tenants of the former owner at 30 Prospect. He might be down healthwise, but his business acumen was far from out. Next, he read about the death of Samuel Ferrin, who owned extensive properties along Ferrin Street, where both Mt. Vernon and Prospect terminated on the northern side of the hill. He sought out the Ferrin heirs and purchased Nos. 59 to 71 Ferrin Street, again acting in Tom's name. The 59 Ferrin property ran down Hickory Avenue, and included the shop at 103 Bunker Hill Avenue (City of Boston, Tax Assessor's Records, Ward 3, Street, Part 1, 64-65, 1893).

"Mr. McManus . . . for several years has been a student at the city school of naval architecture, Charlestown. He has orders for two other fishermen and also a pilot boat."[54] One of those fishermen was the *Maggie Sullivan*. He had laid out the 107.5 foot, 130-ton schooner as an advance on the *Nellie Dixon*, during the frustrating months that the model of the *James S. Steele* had gathered dust in the window of his fish brokerage. Arthur D. Story had built her at Essex over the previous winter for Captain Pat Sullivan, the former master of the *Adirondack* and the *Edith Emery*. Tom purchased a 1/16th share in the new fisherman, whose syndicate also included familiar names such as Bunting, Emerson, Hunt, Prior, Phillips, Stone, and Wright.[55]

John H.'s health declined again during the summer, and his worn-out frame finally gave up its ghost two months short of his seventieth birthday on 11 October 1893. For once, the crisis was not unexpected. In the end, he died of pneumonia at 39 Mt. Vernon Street,[56] leaving his sister Kate as the only survivor from the comfortable old cottage at 3 Quay Street in Skerries, County Dublin, alive in America. Kate herself, as the present Mrs. Pat Grimes, continued to thrive. Well into her sixties, she was healthy, happily married, and pursuing a career as the landlady of her North End properties. Tom became executor of his father's estate and set about organizing it for the benefit of the survivors.

The pinnacle of John Herbert McManus's professional renown in the United States had come as the manufacturer of the sails for Edward Burgess's Boston America's Cup winners, the *Puritan* and *Mayflower*. Charlton Smith, writing in *Yachting* magazine forty-five years after McManus's death, referred to him as "the foremost sailmaker in the east."

His personal achievements aside, this remarkably energetic immigrant's personal gratification must have peaked in 1886, when the *John H. McManus*, a schooner named after his grandson and owned by his son Charley, won the first of the great fishermen's races, which had been organized by his son Tom.[57]

---

[54] Gloucester *Daily Times*, date unknown, *ca.* January 1892. One of several unidentified newspaper clippings glued to a photograph of the *James S. Steele* which has been donated by a descendent of James S. Steele, the son of George Steele, to the Cape Ann Historical Association during 1993.

[55] Enrolment No. 246, Boston and Charlestown, 27 May 1893; Permanent Enrolment No. 245, Boston and Charlestown, 1 June 1893. Owners: Joseph Conley, 1/16; Parron H. Prior, 2/16; Mary Sullivan, 2/16; William J. Emerson, 1/16; Thomas F. McManus, 1/16; Sarah A. Phillips, 1/16; Henry D. Stone, 1/16; George H. Clark, 1/16; Carrie M. Bunting, 1/16; Cassius Hunt, 1/16; Caroline E. Phillips, 2/16; William C. Stone, 1/16; John S. Wright, 1/16.

[56] Vital Records, *Deaths*, 1893, vol. 438, page 417, line 9172.

[57] Captain Charlton L. Smith, "The First Fishermen's Race," *Yachting* (January 1939): 64.

CHAPTER TEN

The *America,* *Juniata,* and *Benjamin W. Latham*

While no one disputed the speed and agility of the *James S. Steele* and *Richard C. Steele*, their ability to provide profitability remained a matter of conjecture during their first two years on the banks. When it came, the disappointing consensus, although it recognized the *Steeles* as unquestionably fast and able–though a bit tender–matched their construction costs *vs.* their limited hold capacity, and decided that capacity outweighed the facility with which they brought their fish to market. For Tom McManus, the most radical new designer that ever laid out a fishing schooner, the lack of acceptance was a telling blow. 1893, 1894, 1895, and 1896, dragged slowly by with no more than a schooner

After her launch at Gloucester in 1897, the 97-ton *America* (91x23x11 feet) became Boston pilot schooner number one and the new trial horse against which other vessels tested their speed. Photograph by Nathaniel L. Stebbins, 21 August 1898. (M.S.M. 84.36)

a year being built to his drafts, and every one a conventional vessel. Tom had not only failed to convince the fleet owners about his theories, but he came on the design scene just as circumstances beyond his control had stultified capital investment in new bottoms. Additionally, those years were the centerpiece of the career of McManus's naval architectural schoolmate, predecessor, and competitor, Captain George Melville "Mel" McClain, although even his dramatic 1890s design production slowed down during 1895-98.

The Panic of 1893 was the most severe economic setback in the century-old history of the United States, although for its duration fishing suffered less than most among all industrial sectors. Reliable indicators of a recovery did not appear until 1897. As Table 7 demonstrates, the depression was slow to take its toll on the fishing industry, but when it did, it hit hard. The figures clearly indicate that despite the industry's delayed downturn, its full impact lasted from 1895 through 1898. Even in the years when the catch remained relatively level, its dollar value plummeted. The effect on the Essex, Massachusetts, building yards was disastrous, and remained so until the turn of the century. It was not until 1901, when 32 new schooners went down the ways, that they recovered.

Year	Trips	Pounds Landed	Estimated Value	Schooners Launched
1889	—	115,317,410	—	25
1890	—	—	—	20
1891	—	144,975,864	$ 4,625,000	28
1892	—	153,911,176	—	23
1893	—	142,395,289	$ 4,098,902	23
1894	8,120	164,137,741	$ 3,829,653	22
1895	7,491	150,439,510	$ 3,551,692	12
1896	6,407	130,673,760	$ 3,286,898	5
1897	6,476	126,865,598	$ 2,878,635	9
1898	6,932	143,407,740	$ 2,989,088	8
1899	7,820	176,774,301	$ 4,193,652	15
1900	7,513	162,218,921	$ 4,385,102	17

TABLE 7 - THE EFFECT OF THE PANIC OF 1893 ON THE NEW ENGLAND FISHERIES[1]

On Boston's Irish Democratic political front, John F. Fitzgerald persevered with his policy of highly visible leadership for the district, and in September 1894

---

[1] The "Schooners Launched" column originates from Dana A. Story, ed., *A List of the Vessels, Boats and Other Craft Built in the Town of Essex 1860 through 1980* (Essex, Massachusetts: Essex Shipbuilding Museum, 1992), Y18-Y25; the balance of the data originates from the *Bulletins* and *Annual Reports of the U.S. Fish Commission* (Washington: Government Printing Office, 1889-1900).

the local party caucus chose Matt Keany's ex-protégé as its candidate for the House of Representatives from the Ninth Congressional District. Fitzgerald captured that office for the 54th and 55th Congresses of the United States in the November elections–a first-generation, American-Irish ward boss from Boston's North End had become a member of the national legislature.

Six months after John H. McManus passed away, Kate delivered her ninth child, George James, on 23 April 1894.[2] As usual the birth took place in her own bed at 39 Mount Vernon. Father J.W. Allisin of St. Mary's Church in Charlestown baptized their second son on 6 May. His sponsors were childhood friends of Tom and Kate–James and Anna McLaughlin,[3] the son and daughter-in-law of Captain Tom McLaughlin, the famous skipper of the *Sarah H. Prior*.

Although his income from naval architecture was minimal, the retail and wholesale fish brokerage continued to prosper as McManus cannily followed the erratic swings of supply and demand during those worrisome times. Since his father's death, Tom had continued to invest in depressed local real estate and by a month after George's birth he held deeds worth $15,820, plus a personal estate valuation of $2,100.[4] Over the winter of 1894-95 he added to his real estate portfolio with the purchase of a run-down house at 69 Ferrin Street.[5] By McManus's fortieth birthday the city assessor totaled his estate at $19,800 in real property and $4,000 in personal assets, better than middle-class family financial standing.

Circumstantial evidence suggests that McManus may have been more active architecturally from 1892 through 1896 than previously believed. On 2 July 1897, in recognition of his earliest schooner designs (this even before the advent of the coming Indian Headers), the officers of the American Art Society, three old-line Boston society figures: Charles L. Haskell, James P. Parker, and William Caleb Loring, elected this first-generation American-Irishman an associate of the society–with the salutation "Captain of the Arts." McManus proudly adopted the title, and for the rest of his life became "Captain" Tom.[6]

A year later, the judges at the International Fishing Exhibition at Bergen, Norway, awarded diplomas to five of Tom's models, including the *James S. Steele*

---

[2] Vital Records 1841-1895, Massachusetts State Archives, *Births*, 1894, vol, 441, page 255.

[3] St Mary's, Charlestown, *Baptisms*, vol. 4, 489.

[4] City of Boston, Tax Assessor's Records, Ward 3, Street, Part 1, 30 and 31, May 1894.

[5] City of Boston, Tax Assessor's Records, Ward 3, Street, Part 1, 67, 1895.

[6] "American Art Society, 36 Columbus av.; C.L. Haskell, pres.; James P. Parker, treas.; William C. Loring, sec." (*The Boston Directory Containing the City Record, A Directory of the Citizens, Business Directory and Street Directory with Map. No. XCIII. For the Year Commencing 1897* (Boston: Sampson, Murdock, & Co.), 2,073). William Caleb Loring, 1851-1930, was a Phi Betta Kappa graduate of Harvard University and a *cum laude* graduate of Harvard Law School, private practice in Ropes, Gray & Loring, associate justice of the supreme judicial court of Massachusetts 1899-1919, fellow of the American Academy of Arts & Sciences (*The National Cyclopædia of American Biography* (Ann Arbor: University Microfilms, 1967), 22:283).

and *America*.[7] At the time of the *Steele*'s launch, the Gloucester *Daily Times* had reported: "Mr. McManus . . . has orders for two other fishermen and also a pilot boat."[8] Presumably, by 1898, an Indian Header half model would have been included among the five models, as well as one of the *William A. Morse* of 1896.[9] Developed from the lines of the *Nellie Dixon*, the *Morse* was an evolutionary, rather than a revolutionary, design. Compared to the *Dixon*, McManus kept Burgess's rockered keel, slackened the *Morse*'s bilges, increased the rake of the sternpost, and reduced the knuckle of the forefoot. Captain Joseph W. Collins, who served as the official United States Commissioner to that internationally recognized event, brought these Norwegian awards home to McManus. But, despite this direct evidence of additional McManus designs in the 1890s, attempts to establish the identity of the other unnamed diploma winners in the Norwegian exhibition have proven fruitless.

Not so the McManus family. The pattern of November births reappeared for the fifth time when Kate, who had passed her own fortieth birthday three months before Tom, bore his namesake, Thomas Francis Jr., on 1 November 1895.[10] This was the only time she delivered two boys in a row, and it brought the family score to females seven, males three.[11]

Twenty years earlier, when McManus was in his late teens, a two-year project backed by the colorful and controversial congressman, General Benjamin Franklin Butler,[12] had reached completion. He had discovered derelict the former schooner yacht *America*, which had won the first Anglo-American yacht race in 1851. During the Civil War, while he raised havoc as the Union's commanding general at New Orleans, she had a career first as a Confederate blockade-runner

---

[7] The Milton *Record*, 19 November 1938.

[8] Gloucester *Daily Times*, date unknown, *ca.* January 1892. One of several unidentified newspaper clippings glued to a photograph of the *James S. Steele* which has been donated by a descendent of James S. Steele, the son of George Steele, to the Cape Ann Historical Association during 1993.

[9] James & Tarr on "May 9, 1902. Agreed with J. Manta Co. to build them a Schooner on similar lines of Sch. *Wm. A. Morse*" (James Yard Book in the possession of Dana A. Story). This vessel became the *Philip P. Manta* of 1902, which has been attributed to McManus and thus establishes his claim to the *Morse*. The ancestry of the *Morse*, which has been described as "a heavy weather sailer" and "a handsome schooner" (Howard I. Chapelle, *The American Fishing Schooners 1825-1925* (New York: W.W. Norton, 1973), 206-08), can be traced to the lines of the *Nellie Dixon*.

[10] Vital Records, *Births*, 1895, vol. 450, page 241.

[11] St Mary's, Charlestown, Baptisms, vol. 5, page 111.

[12] Butler served in various Union Army commands 1861-65, "sometimes brilliantly, always controversially." Originally a Democrat, after the Civil War Butler joined the radical wing of the Republican Party and served in Congress 1866-75. He played a key role in the impeachment proceedings against President Andrew Johnson. He returned to Congress in 1878 as an independent "Greenbacker," and, in 1882 realized his ambition of becoming Governor of Massachusetts, but failed to win re-election in 1883. He secured the presidential nomination of the Anti-Monopoly and Greenback Parties in 1884, but "polled a very small vote" (Joseph J.E. Hopkins, ed., *Concise Dictionary of American Biography* (New York: Charles Scribner's Sons, 1964), 131).

and then as a U.S. Navy blockading vessel and training ship. When Butler found her, she was a worn out wreck ready for the breaker's yard at Annapolis, Maryland. He quickly put in a successful bid for the once-sleek yacht at a government auction on 20 June 1873, and saved her from extinction. After restoration by the East Boston clipper ship builder, Donald McKay, the schooner once again became a true black beauty.[13]

The rejuvenated schooner yacht returned afloat under the command of Captain James H. Reid toward the end of June, just in time for the 1874 yachting season, and enjoyed a second, if somewhat socially contentious, racing and cruising career under Butler's ægis and Reid's practiced hand. Always a social maverick, Ben Butler perennially failed to gain entry to the exclusive ranks of the Eastern Yacht Club, and raced the America under the Boston Yacht Club's burgee. She won twelve of fifty-one races entered between 1874 and 1901, before Butler's heirs decommissioned her again.[14] The veteran campaigner swept an 1887 $1,000 stake match against William F. Weld's Gitana, a five-year-old Lawlor design and, a dozen years later in the hands of Butler's grandson, Butler Ames, the America defeated the Mayflower on the New York Yacht Club's annual summer cruise.[15]

Sometime after Butler's 1893 death, Captain Jim Reid joined the Boston harbor pilots. In that calling he provided Tom McManus with an opportunity to capitalize on the James S. Steele's reputation for speed and agility by asking him to design a new vessel for the pilot service. She was to be named America in honor of his former yachting command. Although carrying capacity was not a factor, to meet the exacting all-weather abilities the pilots required, the sailing qualities of their vessels–even more than fishing schooners–demanded a perfect combination of speed and safety. A well-balanced rig was essential. The pilot schooners spent much of their time jogging about on station awaiting the appearance of arriving vessels. In all weather and all seasons they patrolled the sea-lanes to deliver a pilot who would guide the ship into port. Many times, after sending a pilot to an inbound vessel, the

---

[13] Forest and Stream, 3 June 1875, 264. The America again enjoyed a complete refit under General Butler's ownership, in 1886-87 under the direction of Ned Burgess, and, predictably, emerged with a white hull for the first time in her career.

[14] Paul E. Shanabrook, The Boston (A History of the Boston Yacht Club), 1866-1978 (Boston: Boston Yacht Club, 1978), 258, Appendix VI.

[15] The America's second yachting career appeared to be coming to a close in 1917, the old schooner was in escrow for sale to Cape Verde packet traders, when that notable twentieth-century yachtsman and yacht collector, Charles Henry Wheelwright Foster, stepped in to outbid the foreign buyers. In 1921 a committee of the Eastern Yacht Club purchased the venerable relic from Foster for $1 and sold her to the United States Navy for a similar amount. Ironically, on 10 September 1921, the U.S. Navy's sub-chaser No. 408 took America under tow from George Lawley's City Point yard, and left Boston. The yacht's final destination–Annapolis, the port Benjamin F. Butler had rescued her from forty-eight years earlier. On 21 October 1921, Boston's own Secretary of the Navy, Charles Francis Adams, accepted $1 from Rear Admiral Henry B. Wilson, the Commandant of the Naval Academy, in front of 2,500 cheering midshipman, to complete the purchase.

pilot boat would have to be sailed back to port by a shorthanded crew of two or three men, regardless of the weather conditions.

Reid's commission acknowledged Tom's growing reputation, while challenging his professional capabilities. But McManus had anticipated Reid. During the same frustrating period that he had designed the *Maggie Sullivan*, Tom had laid out his concept of what a pilot boat should be. As a result, he only had to fine-tune the vessel to meet Reid's needs, and went to work on the revised drafts at once. By the end of the summer, he had completed the half model for the mold loft.[16] John Bishop, the Gloucester shipbuilder whose work included several pilot boats among the 150 vessels he built between 1881 and 1911,[17] won the bid for the construction contract. Over the winter of 1896-97 Bishop laid down the keels, framed up, and completed two new vessels for the Boston harbor pilots, the *Liberty*, Pilot Boat No. 3–designed by Ambrose A. Martin of East Boston–and McManus's *America*, which became No. 1 after her May launching.

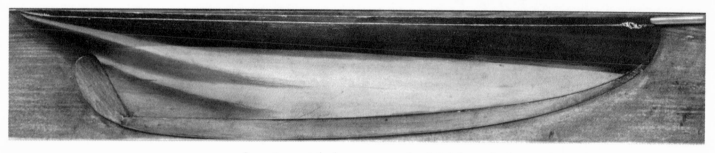

This decorative half model of the pilot schooner *America* displays the features that came to define McManus's schooner concept: a strongly rockered, deep keel, a raking sternpost with a fine run and long stern overhang, and a rounded stem that faired smoothly into the keel. Her keel and after portion carry forward elements of the *Steeles*, but the *America* introduced the convex bow—in this case a "rater" bow that curved back past the vertical—that became the hallmark of McManus's designs. (Courtesy Louise V. Will)

Starting with her sea trials, McManus's first pilot schooner performed beyond expectations. Her "rater" bow gave a clear indication of Tom's future design direction. Unlike the "spoon" or "round" bow, a "rater" bow rises sharply toward the vertical plane as it approaches the gammon iron and sometimes turns beyond the vertical, thereby introducing a measure of gripe (see below). The term "rater" gained prominence in yacht racing as free-for-all fleets began to develop into classes or "rates" during the last two decades of the nineteenth century. Intended to replace the venerable *Hesper*, the *America* embodied several design differences from her predecessor including a long run with a full quarter beam buttock leading to a small transom, a distinct departure from previous practice. Chapelle said: "the *America* proved herself not only to be fast but a most comfortable sea boat."[18]

To counteract the possibility of tenderness in the *America* design, McManus resorted to outside ballast—a quick fix to increase her initial stability. The use of

---

16 This model survives and is owned by McManus's granddaughter, Mrs. D. Forbes Will. Howard I. Chapelle's lines of the hull are in the collections of the Smithsonian Institution.

17 Gordon W. Thomas, *Gloucester Times*, 24 August 1954.

18 Howard I. Chapelle, *American Sailing Craft* (New York: Kennedy Brothers Incorporated, 1936), 229-31.

outside ballast was a McManus family innovation. Recall that John H. McManus had refitted the family yacht *Vesper* with outside ballast in the 1860s—thus Tom had been familiar with the characteristics of this design feature since boyhood. The *America* would be the direct ancestor of McManus fishing schooners to come. She represented the combination of all the factors that influenced Tom's design of the *James S. Steele* with the hard lessons learned in the time since that speedy schooner went to sea. From the midships sections aft the pilot schooner reflected the influence of Ned Burgess on Tom's early career. In the *America*, McManus's design philosophy reached a new level of maturity.

At home, the normal trend returned when Kate gave birth to a girl in November. The last in the McManuses' line of beautiful daughters, Mildred arrived in the Breed's Hill house on the fourteenth.[19] Years later, Mildred would become the first of the American-Irish descendants of the Catholic Fingalians to be courted and won by a member of Boston's old-line Protestant society elite. In Boston's stratified society, Mildred's wedding was the ultimate step in assimilation, with even greater local impact than "Honey Fitz's" triumphant arrival in Washington.

Four decades earlier, when John H. McManus and Dick Leonard had purchased their first jointly owned fishing schooner, two of the *Black Hawk*'s sellers were Richard and Bailey D. Winsor of Duxbury.[20] That transaction marked the beginning of a business relationship between the Winsors of Duxbury and the McManuses of Boston that lasted into the twentieth century. During the winter of 1897-98 one of the Winsor descendants, Sanford C. Winsor, came into the fish store and offered Tom a startling commission–to produce the design and half model for a new-type of fishing schooner–and to prepare the drafts necessary to construct not one, but *five* new fishing vessels to be built in yards at Gloucester and Essex, with another five to follow if the first group proved successful.

Winsor was a major fleet owner. His firm, Arnold & Winsor, had been one of those to move from Commercial Wharf to T Wharf when it opened as a fishing center in 1884, a centralization that had worked well for Boston's fish brokers. The market for fresh fish developed by Boston dealers attracted the ocean's bounty to the Hub from all along the coast, and drew a significant portion of Gloucester's fresh catch, as the Cape Ann wholesalers were largely committed to the salt cod

America photograph by Nathaniel L. Stebbins, 21 August 1898. (M.S.M. 84.36)

[19] Vital Records, *Births*, 1897, vol. 468, page 350. Father Jack Millerick again performed the sacramental rites at St. Mary's, and her godparents were Walter J. Finan, the son of Kate's uncle, Colonel Henry Finan, and Grace, fresh from celebrating her seventeenth birthday (St Mary's, Charlestown, *Baptisms*, vol. 6). Grace's stunning good looks now rivaled Margaret's as the family's beauty among beauties.

[20] Enrolment No. 2, Boston and Charlestown, 2 January 1858, U.S. Consolidated Enrolment and Licenses, Bureau of Navigation, Record Group 41, Records of the Department of Commerce, NARA; previous Enrolment No. 8, Duxbury, canceled–property and district changed, 3 December 1856.

fishery, the halibut fishery, and the salt and fresh mackerel fishery.[21] Landings of fish in Boston for 1897 totaled 62,903,558 pounds worth $1,230,044, 92 percent of the tonnage and 72 percent of the value of Gloucester's landings, a 300-percent increase in 10 years, despite the dwindling recession.[22] At this time the Boston fishing fleet had 60 schooners, only 17 percent of Gloucester's 350, although many of the latter vessels landed their fares at Boston.

Photographed in his new Dorchester home in 1904, McManus showed off the half model of the *Juniata,* first of his Indian Head fishing schooners. Her outside ballast is built into the very deep portion of her keel aft. Boston *Herald,* 1904. (Courtesy Louise V. Will)

In response to this lost trade the Cape Ann dealers formed the Gloucester Fresh Fish Company, which opened its doors on 6 December 1897,[23] to broaden their local market in order to compete directly with Boston, and to attract the cargoes of fresh fish brought in by Gloucester-based vessels. The strategy succeeded–the next year Boston's landings plummeted by 8,000,000 pounds, while Gloucester's grew by 21,000,000.[24]

Weighing the situation, Winsor concluded that the only effective way to offset Gloucester's new advantage and guarantee the supply of fresh fish to T Wharf was to increase the size of the Boston fleet. He proceeded to do this, and used the opportunity to introduce a safer vessel design–McManus's first sweeping architectural triumph, the Indian Head class of schooners. The performance of the *Steeles* and the positive reviews earned by the new pilot boat *America* had impressed Winsor. But he also perceived the failings of George Steele's vessels represented by their limited cargo-carrying ability. Even Chapelle thought "they were probably too much like yachts and were somewhat tender," although he also recognized Tom's logic in adhering to the concept of soft bilges to reduce their initial stability in order to diminish the strain on spars and rigging–at the cost of a tender hull.[25]

---

[21] Andrew W. German, *Down on T Wharf: The Boston Fisheries as Seen Through the Photographs of Henry D. Fisher* (Mystic, Connecticut: Mystic Seaport Museum, 1982), 4.

[22] *Report of the Commissioner of Fish and Fisheries for 1888* (Washington, D.C.: Government Printing Office, 1889), clv.

[23] Gordon W. Thomas, *Fast & Able, Life Stories of Great Gloucester Fishing Vessels* (Gloucester, Massachusetts: Gloucester 350th Anniversary Celebration, Inc., 1973), 7.

[24] German, *Down on T Wharf,* 4.

[25] Chapelle, *Fishing Schooners,* 213, 312.

Winsor insisted that Tom, without sacrificing the stability, agility, or speed the *Steeles* possessed, come up with a stiffer design that also provided greater hold capacity. McManus had been wrestling with this dilemma from the moment he set his life firmly on course toward a career as a naval architect. The reason he failed to overcome John Frisbee's criticisms during their "Free School" arguments over the model that eventually became the *James S. Steele* was simply that his mentor always had the winning last words–carrying capacity. Years would pass before McManus resolved this issue to the satisfaction of Frisbee, whose appraisal of Tom's shortcomings centered on the need to maintain a balance between economic practicality, architectural aesthetics, and moral considerations. It was admirable for McManus to create fast and safe designs, Frisbee argued, but they must be comparable to others in their capacity to deliver the goods to market.

Tom first worked out of the predicament with a plan that abandoned the excessive overhangs of the *Steeles* and incorporated the successful innovations of the *America* into a model that was part *Nellie Dixon*: the midships section; and part pilot schooner: the forebody. As in the *America*, McManus turned to outside ballast as a means of increasing initial stability. "In this model, the *Juniata*, the lines of the previous boats were improved upon," explained McManus to a 1904 *Boston Herald* interviewer with his customary conciseness, before concluding with, "a number of vessels were built from the plans of these vessels, they were deeper, sharp floored, able and fast in all kinds of weather."[26]

Winsor christened the class by naming his new schooners in honor of famous native Americans, and ever since they have been known as "Indian Headers." A litany of the names appears in Tom's memoirs: "In the late nineties, I made further improvements in designing what was called the Indian fleet, as a number of them were named after the principal Chiefs of the Indian tribes, well known to the early settlers, and through history, to us. Some of the Names were, *Massasoit*, *Samoset*, *Mattakeesett*, *Massachusetts*, *Squanto*, *Manhasset*, *Metamora*, *Manomet*, and *Mooween*."[27] The Tarr & James Yard at Essex launched the *Mattakeesett* on 22 March and the *Juniata*, on 20 April 1898.[28] A measure of the impact of McManus's first major design success can be had by noting that Indian Headers comprised nearly half of the vessels launched at Essex and Gloucester that year.

The "head" of the new schooner, as in all the Indian Headers, sported a distinctive stem with a marked rounding of the forefoot at, or just above the waterline, a profile feature referred to as "gripe," when it extends aft from the

---

[26] Thomas F. McManus, "Autobiographical Essay No. 7."

[27] McManus, "Essay No. 7."

[28] Dana Story, *Frame-Up!: The Story of Essex, Its Shipyards and Its People* (Barre, Massachusetts: Barre Publishers, 1964), 118.

The 78-ton *Juniata* (85x23x10 feet), launched by Tarr & James at Essex on 20 April 1898, had a very short career, being deposited on the beach at Cohasset by the "Portland Gale" of November 1898. Like McManus's early fishing schooners, she has a flush deck; later designs would incorporate the usual raised quarterdeck of New England fishing schooners. Like the *Steeles*, she has "whiskers" for the bowsprit shrouds and a long, narrow stern. (*Left*, courtesy Peabody & Essex Museum, Salem, Massachusetts). *Right*, photograph by Nathaniel L. Stebbins, 6 December 1898. (Courtesy The Society for the Preservation of New England Antiquities, Boston, Massachusetts)

vertical plane. In the way of the short bow overhang, the arc of the stem begins to rise, and almost turns back on itself before it meets the bowsprit. In keeping with current practice, and against Tom's own best judgement, the schooner had the usual long bowsprit. He did manage to retain the single spar concept of a spike bowsprit, similar to *Carrie E. Phillips*, rather than the outmoded combination of bowsprit, plus jibboom, and even flying jibboom. According to Erik A.R. Ronnberg, the Indian Headers were actually "more an extreme development of the *Fredonia* type, as was W. Starling Burgess's design for the *Elizabeth Silsbee*."[29] They were certainly a revolutionary step from the *Steeles*, and an evolutionary one from the *America*.

From research into shipyard records for 1899, it appears that no one else placed orders for the new vessel type as the century came to a close. [30] This suggests that yet another hiatus took place in Tom's architectural endeavors, while the new skippers put to sea and ran the new fishermen through their paces. Of the five initial Indian Headers, Tarr & James built three at Essex, and John Bishop produced

[29] Letter, Erik A.R. Ronnberg, Jr., Rockport, Massachusetts, 18 September 1988.

[30] See Appendix 1 for a chronological list of McManus's designs.

two at Gloucester. Each yard constructed one with outside ballast. Tom's long familiarity with the concept, its wide acceptance in the yachting community, and especially Joseph Collins's espousal of it for fishing vessels, all argued on its behalf. But practicality intervened–the quick disappearance of outside ballast that followed can probably be attributed to cost. To properly install a significant amount of outside ballast, a schooner would have to be built with additional strengthening members in her lower extremities–framing, keel, keelson, and deadwood–an expensive proposition. The effect of outside ballast also opposed McManus's concept of reducing initial roll stability to ease the load on the standing rigging and spars. Unfortunately, there are no surviving plans for the *Samoset*, *Mattakeesett*, and *Tecumseh* (the inside ballast variants) to establish how they varied from the *Juniata* and *Massasoit*.

In 1904, the *Boston Herald* published a picture of the *Juniata's* half model which shows her keel to have a deep rocker aft. The first available drafts of later Indian Headers are those of the *Matchless* and *Flora S. Nickerson* of 1902, and they

The 77-ton *Mattakessett*, built alongside her sister *Juniata* and launched a month earlier, had exactly the same dimensions, but with inside ballast. Nathaniel L. Stebbins photographed her running down Boston Harbor on 6 October 1898, powered by her mainsail and main topsail alone. McManus's concept of reserve power is exemplified by her great sheer, with high bow and upturned stern. (Courtesy The Society for the Preservation of New England Antiquities, Boston, Massachusetts)

McManus designed the 32-ton *Samoset* (58x17.8x7.6 feet), launched at Gloucester in 1898, as a small version of the Indian Head model. She has a pulpit for swordfishing on the end of her bowsprit. Photograph by Nathaniel L. Stebbins, 26 July 1898. (Courtesy The Society for the Preservation of New England Antiquities, Boston, Massachusetts)

amply illustrate the characteristic that remained with the Indian Head fleet for the balance of its design life–a slight reduction in deadrise to slacken the bilges, not only to accommodate inside ballast and reduce initial stability, but also to increase hold capacity. Clearly, McManus was experimenting with the latter quality as his design approach swung from the *Steeles* to the *America*, *Juniata*, and *Massasoit*, and back to the *Matchless* and *Flora S. Nickerson*.

The standard fee for a set of completed drawings in that era, not including the designer's fee, a model, or charges for shipyard supervision time, was $25. One of Tom's lifelong grumbles concerned his stolen creations. The income lost in this manner so incensed McManus's frugal nature that he attacked the practice in his very first autobiographical essay: "Some of the designs which were made by me were so popular that a number of builders would hire or borrow the moulds, which were made from the plans, and put in a frame or two, or throw off the upper timbers to widen the boat, to try to avoid the payment of the royalty which I charged for their use in building any vessel other than the original for which the design was made. I was forced to watch some of them very close to get what belonged to me."[31]

He then expanded his treatise to include an emphatic admonition for newcomers to the field of naval architecture: "My advice to anyone entering this line of business is, if you get up anything different or better than others protect yourself by destroying the moulds after their initial use or do what the great designer Nat Herreshoff did and that was make no plan or design for any one, unless she was

---

[31] McManus, "Essay No. 1."

built in his own Yard, otherwise your ideas and plans will be used and sometimes without any recompense or credit."[32]

In an early attempt to overcome this loss of income—a concern always close to Tom's frugal heart—at the bottom of each drawing he prepared for the design of the *Flora S. Nickerson*, he scrawled "Tables of Schooner for Capt. Crowell *et.al.*, March 15, 1902. Lines and Tables to be returned to Thomas F. McManus, Boston, Mass."[33] But, despite this one successful effort, in the ancestral line of Indian Headers based on the *Nickerson*, which extended from her through the *Matchless* to the *Annie Perry*, *Rose Dorothea*, *Mary C. Santos*, *Jessie Costa*, and *Josephine DeCosta*—all built by Essex's James & Tarr yard—there is no indication that McManus received a design fee for any of them other than the *Nickerson*.[34] Eventually he inscribed on his Tables of Offsets, "It is understood and agreed that one vessel only shall be built from the moulds made from these lines and tables, unless permission has been granted by the designer."[35] During his later career, he succeeded in recovering several sets of plans and offset tables, but they amount to a mere pittance when weighed against his life's production of over 450 designs. A main contributing factor to the low recovery rate lay in the very size of the molds created from the half model. Although some of them, properly, were returned to the architect, physical storage became an insurmountable problem, and reusing molds became the most common form of plagiarism. Without the storage ability to

The earliest surviving lines for a McManus Indian Head fishing schooner are these, drawn in March 1902 and used to build the *Flora S. Nickerson* and *Matchless*. Drawn by Howard I. Chapelle. (Plan AFS 98A, Smithsonian Institution)

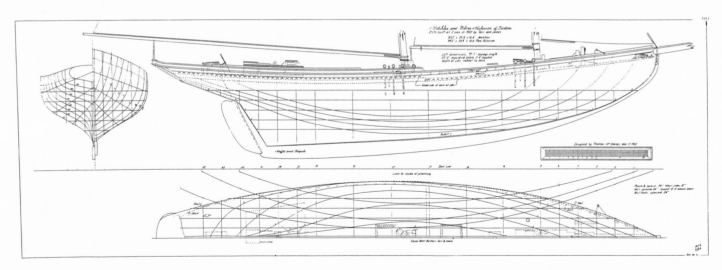

[32] Ibid. In *American Fishing Schooners*, Chapelle singled out the plan of the knockabout *Gertrude DeCosta* of 1912, which he found in the loft of the Essex mold-maker, Archer Poland, to demonstrate this practice. Familiar with the hands of designers and draftsmen, Chapelle identified it as a counterfeit McManus design.

[33] Albert Cook Church, text by James B. Connolly, *The American Fishermen* (New York: W.W. Norton, 1940), 187.

[34] James Yard Book in the possession of Dana A. Story.

[35] Written on plan 145, dated 29 March 1909.

reclaim the full set, Tom had to leave them in the mold loft or the builder's yard, where they became available for unauthorized use, for which he only rarely received a design fee.

During the interlude when Tom awaited further new commissions, Kate gave birth to William Kenneth McManus,[36] the couple's twelfth and last child, on 10 September 1899. As the children grew up, with six of the twelve born in November, the family began celebrating all the end-of-the-year birthdays on Thanksgiving Day, an idea wholly suited to Tom's frugal streak.

McManus acknowledged that, despite the recognition his designs had received, he was not yet fully a marine architect, when he listed his occupation as "real estate" on Ken's birth certificate. This was justified by the amount of time he devoted to his extensive Charlestown properties. With his time not totally devoted to designing, he may not have felt himself qualified to claim the title and stature of his chosen profession, although clearly he no longer considered himself a full-time fish dealer.

During the third year of the Indian Head class's existence, Winsor ordered another, but Gloucester owners continued to favor the now traditional *Nellie Dixon/Fredonia* types. During the first year of the new century another major development in the naval architecture of the fishing fleet occurred, when a half-hull modeled by Captain Mel McClain provided the basis for *Helen Miller Gould*, a mackerel seining schooner with a surprise hidden in her hold–a gasoline engine. This first auxiliary-powered fishing schooner was the result of the perfection of the marine internal combustion engine during the 1890s. McClain's initial attempt at marine power was literally a case of dropping a 35-horsepower motor and fuel tanks into an orthodox sailing hull and,[37] although McClain used the engine weight to improve the hull's roll center, no effort was made to either alter the buttocks to balance the hull when it was driven by an underwater power source, or account for the changing hull balance as the fuel burned off.

Swordfishermen and mackerel seiners, the workers who suffered the most frustration when their quarry was upwind or beyond reach during a summer calm, immediately perceived the advantages of a motor vessel. The *Helen Miller Gould*, for example, could make eight knots under power alone, more than enough to reach a school of mackerel on a windless day. Even so, the idea did not catch on quickly, and the second schooner so equipped was McClain's own *Victor*, followed by his *Nellie B. Nickerson* and *Mary E. Harty*, all built during 1901. A further three joined

---

[36] Vital Records, *Births*, 1899, vol. 487, page 267.

[37] The *Gould* initially had a 35-horsepower Globe engine until a larger 150-horsepower Globe became available. Dick Smith, a Negro, was her first engineer (Thomas, *Fast & Able*, 57).

the fleet in 1902–McClain's *Veda M. McKown*, and Arthur Binney's *Saladin* and *Constellation*. Engine installations obviously created new problems for the shipbuilders. Under the date 27 September 1901, the James & Tarr yard book recorded details of the *Constellation*: "Have this day agreed with Orlando Merchant to build a Schooner of the *Monitor* model with the after part constructed so that an Engine can be used. Labor on Engine part to be paid Extra." Based on its dimensions, the yard readily knew what to charge for the schooner–$8,200–but not how to determine the cost of the alterations necessary to accommodate the motor. In the end they charged Merchant, "Extra Stock & Labor, $137.04 – Extra Cementing 27.50."[38]

But, universal acceptance of internal or auxiliary power would not occur until the new technology of a lightweight diesel engine became available. The combination of diesel fuel efficiency with the enormous reduction in the fire danger of diesel crude oil over gasoline would dictate the change, and the change came rapidly after 1910. The *Gould* fished for only two seasons before she succumbed to a fire caused by a gasoline leak. Mel McClain's auxiliary schooner, nevertheless, was the most significant development introduced by another fishing schooner designer during Tom McManus's long career.

At the beginning of the new century, the fourteen–member McManus clan moved from the familiar hills of Charlestown, which had been the only hometown Tom and Kate's twelve children had ever known, to the southern Boston suburb of Dorchester. Tom purchased a new house there, a massive, turreted Victorian edifice at 29 Mill Street, which had everything from flushing toilets to a billiard room and a studio for Tom. Despite this move, he continued his daily commute into the North End. The change of address brought them within a mile of his brother Charley's widow, Agnes Kidney McManus, and her two sons, John H. and Charles, who now resided at 2 Winter Street in Dorchester.

The continuing line of *Nellie Dixon* derivatives and the acceptance of the Indian Head class established McManus's reputation as an innovative designer. The presence of the *Nellie Dixon* types in his 1902 portfolio, led by the *Regina* and *Lizzie M. Stanley*, gives an indication of a softening in McManus's dictatorial approach to design. As a full-time architect, he now paid closer attention to the wishes of his customers rather than insisting on producing only his latest concept. The huge new *Regina*–her main boom, at eighty feet, was as long as many schooners–had the extreme keel rocker of the *William A. Morse*, but with less knuckle than the *Lizzie M. Stanley*, as well as the *Dixon's* clipper bow, although on the *Regina* it appears to be almost an afterthought. She was the first fisherman built by the Essex firm of

---

[38] James Yard Book.

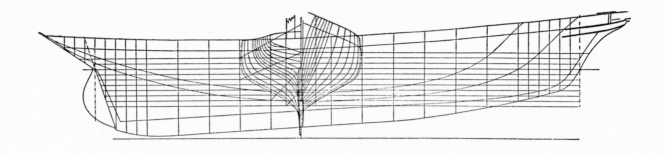

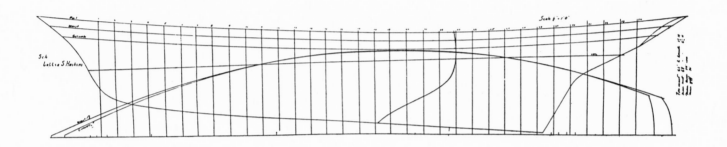

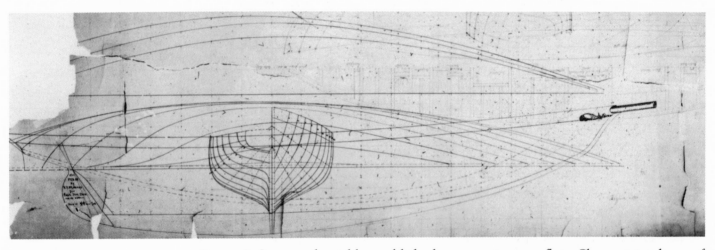

Three variations on the deep-draft clipper-bowed fishing schooner: (*top*) Edward Burgess's *Nellie Dixon/Fredonia* model of 1889 and (*middle*) McClain's *Lottie S. Haskins* of 1890 (Church, *American Fishermen*) compared with (*bottom*) McManus's *Regina* of 1901. The 147-ton *Regina* (115x25.7x11.6 feet) was the biggest, fastest fishing schooner out of Boston for several years after her launch. Despite her concave bow, her underwater profile is more akin to McManus's Indian Head designs. (Courtesy Louise V. Will)

Oxner & Story, and quickly established a reputation as a flyer. She remained one of the fastest vessels out of Boston throughout the first decade of the twentieth century, and for several years held the coveted title of "Queen of the Fleet," by then a common occurrence for McManus-owned or-designed fishermen.

Both the *Regina*, launched by Oxner & Story on 1 August, and the *Lizzie M. Stanley*,[39] launched by James & Tarr on 28 September, survived knockdowns

[39] The Historic American Merchant Marine Survey preserved the lines of the *Lizzie M. Stanley* (James Peter Warren, *The Historic American Merchant Marine Survey*, unpublished Master of Arts thesis, Ithaca, N.Y.: Cornell University, 1985). There is one drawing, a lines & body plan, in the survey records, identified as, *Historic American Merchant Marine Survey*, Works Progress Administration, Survey 2-4, U.S. National Museum of American History, Smithsonian Institution. The H.A.M.M.S. preserved the lines of two other McManus designs, the *Benjamin W. Latham* (1902) and the *Louisa R. Silva* (1904). All three were produced in the survey's Region 2, whose director was the redoubtable Howard I. Chapelle.

during their careers. The *Regina* returned to T Wharf on 14 February 1911, having suffered the ignominy of being thrown on her beam ends by a Georges Bank gale the previous week. Nevertheless, she still put 17,000 pounds of haddock, 4,000 of cod, and 10,000 of hake on the wharf.[40] The *Lizzie M. Stanley*, Captain Joshua W. Stanley, dipped her crosstrees into the ocean during a trip shortly after her launching (probably during February 1902). Stanley had been fishing in the South Channel to seaward of Nantucket when a northeaster sprung up so quickly that he decided to work out toward Georges Bank to gather sea room. His story is best told in his own words.

"I headed her to the southeast," he recalled for a *Yachting* magazine interviewer, "until we had put the ridge of Georges between us and the blow, the ridge being about 15 miles away. She was then hove-to, but had not laid long before the wind shifted to the west-southwest, placing the shoal directly to leeward.

"We couldn't lay and drift straight on," he explained, "so I decided to 'run her' and try to work past. As soon as the wind got up, away went the foresail at the reefing points, and the mainsail whipped clean out of the stops. From the gait that sail started with, [I said], boys, I believe it is going yet!

"Well, there was nothing to do but run her and keep trying to work out. We were doing well, when along comes a great comber, looking like it was going to break over the stern. The fellow at the wheel gave a yell and ran forward, the schooner sheered to starboard, was thrown flat on her beam ends and pushed forward by that wave like a snow shovel into the slush." But, as Stanley was quick to point out, "as soon as the wave let go of her she righted." The *Lizzie M. Stanley* had her main boom and gaff snapped in half. The force of the sea swept her chain anchor cable into the coal locker, and flushed all the fish in her starboard pens into the ones on the port side, "not one of them having fallen on the floor," according to Stanley. When the forecastle filled with water, the crew firmly believed she was on her way to the bottom, but her inherent design stability saved the day, although the crew did suffer the indignity of having the gurry from the forward kids poured into their living quarters.

The men lashed the riding cable to the bitts and paid it over the side to act as a drogue. Then they manned the pumps and began to dry her out, all the while with the schooner heading directly for the bank and disaster. "While we were doing this," Stanley said with a sigh of relief, "the breeze shifted to the west-nor'-west, and we were saved, the wind driving us clear of the shoal."

There is no better tribute to the work ethic of New England fishermen than this near-disaster. By 3:00 A.M. the following morning it was, "bait up!" and the

---

[40] German, *Down on T Wharf*, 87.

Lizzie M. Stanley went back to work.[41] The incidents that involved knockdowns of McManus's *Regina* and *Lizzie M. Stanley* are worthy of comparison to the accident that befell the *Helen G. Wells*, an 1893 McClain design. All three schooners evolved from late 1880s clipper technology, but the smaller *Wells*, although she had a similar length-to-depth ratio, had a wider length-to-beam configuration, and coarser lines than the two McManus designs. Contrary to contemporary thought, her broader beam did not give her increased roll stability.

In fact, McClain's schooner was one of those unhappy vessels that suffered a lifetime of misfortune. During her sea trial on 10 May 1893, three weeks after Tom Irving launched her from his Vincent's Cove yard off Main Street in Gloucester, the wind died and she had to be towed back into port. It was an ill omen. Fishing the Grand Banks on 28 June 1896, she lost track of two dories. A British schooner picked up one of the crews, but the men in the second dory were never seen again.

Seven months later, the *Wells* came into T Wharf with her colors at half mast. Running before a Grand Banks gale on 29 January 1897, she had her helmsman knocked into the bulwarks by a following sea that came careening over her deck. As he had been securely lashed to the wheel, he did not go overboard. Captain Bill Wells went to the man's assistance, but another huge wave burst onto the deck just as the skipper pulled the fallen helmsman to his feet. Once again the lashing saved the stunned crewman, but the skipper disappeared into the depths. The same wave washed all her dories away, as well as everything else not lashed down, and broke the main boom. Sadly, Captain Wells, whose wife had passed away two years earlier, left eight orphans.[42]

The *Helen G. Wells*, now skippered by Joachim Murray, reached the nadir of her career while riding at anchor on Green Bank, which lies between St. Pierre Bank to the west and the Grand Bank to the east, during the night of 10 November 1897. A rising northwest gale struck her and parted the anchor cable. Murray quickly gained control of his runaway schooner. He hove her to under a triple-reefed foresail and the jumbo, with two men on the wheel to keep her so. Moments later, when the helmsmen spotted a giant comber heading for the *Wells*, they ducked down the companionway, but could not get the hatch closed before the wave rolled over their heads. Green seawater poured down the ladder knocking them ahead of it like rag dolls. The capsize tossed the seven men in the cabin and eleven in the forecastle out of their bunks, but then–unthinkably–the schooner's motion sent them crashing back into them. The *Helen G. Wells* had gone

---

41 George S. Goldie, "A Winter Fishing Trip to George's Shoal, *Yachting* 5 (November 1910): 349.

42 Thomas, *Fast & Able*, 33-34.

completely upside down, and then swung the rest of the way through a 360° arc around her fore-and-aft axis. When she returned to an even keel, the bewildered crew made their way on deck, and were at once confronted by proof of their mishap. The wave had wrapped the anchor cable, which had been coiled down on deck after it parted, entirely around the hull. Later, when things had settled down somewhat, the men discovered further proof of their total capsize. A red hot cover from one of the burners on the galley stove had permanently branded its shape into the forecastle overhead.

According to McClain: "It makes no difference, shoal or deep, when a monster sea strikes fair, down goes the vessel on her beam ends. Then comes the test; if she is well designed, well built, and properly ballasted, up she comes again; if otherwise, sad is her fate."[43] While this is certainly true, it does not account for the fact that the *Wells* not only went on her beam ends, but completely topsy-turvy. Several McManus schooners including the *James S. Steele, Regina, Lizzie M. Stanley, Teazer,* and *Elsie G. Silva,* suffered knockdowns, but none passed through the horizontal plane as the *Wells* did. In other words, they never went beyond their beam ends before righting themselves through McManus's designed-in hull stability.

During the late summer of 1902, two captains from the fleet that furnished New York City's famous Fulton Fish Market with the ocean's produce came to Boston to commission a pair of schooners. While Tom conducted them on a tour of T Wharf his latest design, the *Metamora,* an Indian Header with relatively short overhangs launched by John Bishop at Gloucester on 7 August, sailed up to the pier. McManus set the scene: "[She] came from the Dry Dock (all spick and Span) and the Captain came ashore." He introduced the New Yorkers to J.F. Robbins, the skipper of the new Plymouth-based Indian Header, and added, "what a grand day and good breeze"; to which the captain of the schooner agreeably responded, "I'd like to take a spin out in the bay for a few hours myself."[44]

It was no sooner said than done. They all trooped on board and in minutes the sleek *Metamora* headed down the harbor at a merry clip. When they reached the bay, the skipper put the schooner on a southeasterly course for Duxbury where his boss, Sanford C. Winsor, had a house at the water's edge. As they glided by Minot's Ledge Light a large black motor yacht steamed out of the eastern channel from Cohasset Harbor. Tom recognized her as the *Dreamer,* the proud flagship of that colorful and eccentric stock market gambler,[45] Thomas W. Lawson, who once

---

[43] Quoted in Thomas, *Fast & Able,* 35.

[44] McManus, "Essay No. 7."

[45] Joseph E. Garland, *The Eastern Yacht Club, A History from 1870 to 1985* (Camden, Maine: Down East Books, 1989), 120.

The "crack flyer" *Metamora* (97.2x24x11.4 feet), a big Indian Header at 116 tons, shows off for photographer Nathaniel L. Stebbins on 1 October 1902, shortly after her launch in Gloucester. Unlike the first Indian Headers, she has a "break" to her deck, with a slightly raised quarterdeck and a raised rail aft. Her forestaysail—called jumbo by the fishermen—has a short club at the clew rather than a full boom. (Courtesy The Society for the Preservation of New England Antiquities, Boston, Massachusetts)

spent $30,000 to have a newly developed carnation named after his wife.[46] The *Dreamer*, with the owner-on-board pennant flying from the signal halyard, turned in chase of the *Metamora*, but gave it up after a while when her power plant failed to raise the speed necessary to catch the flying schooner. The Indian Header easily pulled away, much to the delight of her designer.

If the visiting New Yorkers had any lingering doubts about the speed of McManus's creations, outrunning Lawson's steam-powered yacht must have blown away its last traces. Proceeding to Duxbury, the *Metamora* circled offshore of Winsor's house and then turned back for Boston on a fair wind. Nearing Minot's Ledge on the return leg, they discovered the *Dreamer* idling off the lighthouse waiting to pick off the schooner's name, "and to cheer us by giving three blasts of her siren." The *Metamora* was indeed a brilliantly swift schooner. Early in 1904, when Tom began the half hull that would become the *Mina Swim*, the Gloucester *Daily Times* remarked: "Thomas F. McManus is modeling a schooner off the crack flyer *Metamora* for William H. Burke of Scituate, Captain J. Swim."[47]

Later, one of Lawson's aides called on Tom: "he told me his boss informed him he would offer prizes for a fishermens race, to take place in Massachusetts Bay, whenever it could be arranged. I said, as you know fishermen are working men and the prize will have to be money, to which he agreed."[48] So, as the result of an unplanned Sunday jaunt, the fourth fishermen's race came into being. Tom named it the Lawson Cup in honor of the prize-giver and organized two classes of entries. On the day of the race the Arthur Binney design, *Benjamin F. Phillips*, cleanly won

---

[46] William H. Bunting, *Portrait of a Port: Boston 1852-1914* (Cambridge, Massachusetts: Belknap Press, Harvard University, 1971), 94. Lawson was also the principal owner of the seven-masted, steel coal schooner, *Thomas W. Lawson*, designed by Bowdoin B. Crowninshield.

[47] Gloucester *Daily Times*, 17 February 1904.

[48] McManus, "Essay No. 7."

the larger class (which contained no McManus designs) but, as the smaller fishermen finished, two Indian Headers, *Manomet* and *Mattakeesett*, came to the end of the course together. The amateur yachtsmen acting as judges typically disagreed over which schooner had crossed the finish line first. Lawson quickly put an end to the squabbling by calling the race a draw and awarding the captains and crews of both schooners the same cash prizes.

But there was another story that day. Three years earlier, Lawson had engaged Bowdoin B. Crowninshield to design a contender for the 1899 America's Cup challenge. Named *Independence*, this disappointing racer did poorly in the trials, and the attitude of the New York Yacht Club's selection committee provoked Lawson's flaming temper even further. In a fit of long-restrained pique, on the day of the fishermen's race, he brought out "the *Independence* which he had built to compete for the America's Cup, had her sailed over the Course with the fishermen and then ordered her to be junked."[49] Tom pointed out with the measure of the smug satisfaction generally associated with the fishermen's disparaging opinion of luxury sailing vessels, "the way of nearly all of the lightly built yachts which were of no further use,"[50] after the racing season.

With the new century, McManus came into his own as a designer. His estimated ten commissions of 1900 doubled when twenty or more of his designs went down the ways in 1901, a figure he matched in 1902 and 1903. Despite the hundreds of vessels that passed through the fleet in its long history, no naval architect of commercial fishermen had ever secured this broad an acceptance from the owners, captains, and builders alike. The once struggling architect, who had spent months between each commission in the 1890s, was barely able to tear himself away from the drafting table or carving bench, so great had the demand become for his designs.

Despite his strong opinions of what constituted a good fishing schooner, McManus kept his eye on what other designers were doing. During the summer of 1900, Arthur D. Story launched Bowdoin B. Crowninshield's *Rob Roy*, that noted yacht designer's first attempt to lay out a fishing schooner. Crowninshield, like McManus, had eliminated the clipper profile: "This boat might easily be mistaken for a pleasure yacht, especially as it has the modern spoon bow, considerable overhang at the stern, and beautifully white and well fitted sails."[51] The new fishing schooner not only had yacht influence in her ancestry, but she might also be described as a more burdensome advance on the design concepts put forward by McManus in the *James S.*

---

[49] Garland, *The Eastern*, 120.

[50] McManus, "Essay No. 7."

[51] "The Fishing Schooner *Rob Roy*," *International Marine Engineering* 6 (May 1901): 185-89.

Bowdoin B. Crowninshield's first fishing schooner design, the *Rob Roy* of 1900, introduced the spoon bow to the fishing fleet. Better known as a yacht designer, Crowninshield oversaw the design of several fishing schooners, including the *Tartar*, of which Tom McManus owned a share. (*International Marine Engineering*, May 1901; photograph by Claire White-Peterson)

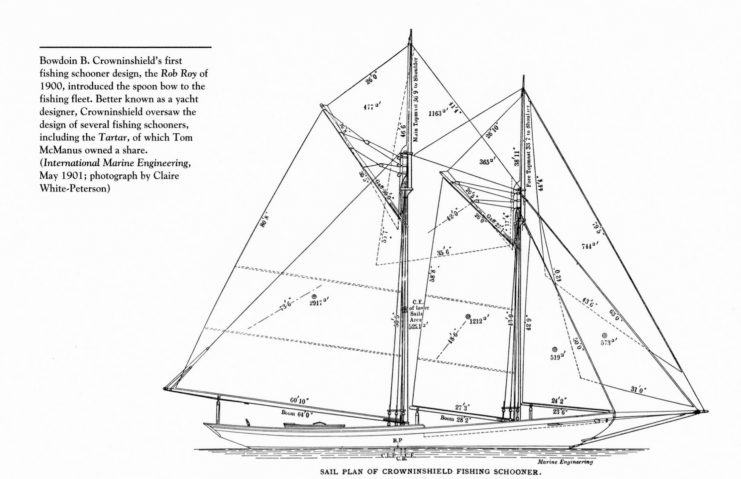

SAIL PLAN OF CROWNINSHIELD FISHING SCHOONER.

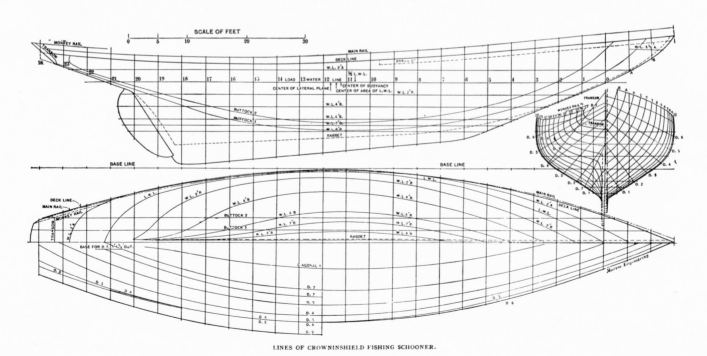

LINES OF CROWNINSHIELD FISHING SCHOONER.

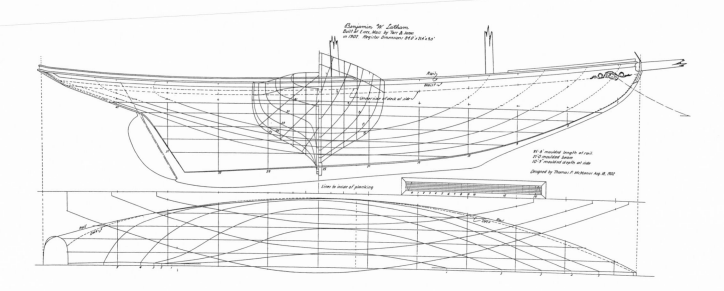

Benjamin "W. Latham"
Built at Essex, Mass. by Tarr & James
in 1902. Register Dimensions: 84.0'x21.4'x9.0'

Rail
Waist
Underside of deck at side

91.6' moulded length at rail.
21.0 moulded beam
10.5' moulded depth at side

Designed by Thomas F. McManus Aug. 18, 1902.

Lines to inner of planking

Rail   DWL
Rail   DWL

Steele and her sister the *Richard C. Steele*. The same architectural client, George Steele, underwrote the construction of all three schooners.

The *Rob Roy* obviously drew Tom's attention. With the Essex yards building more than half a dozen of his creations that year, during visits to the boatbuilding community he had many opportunities to observe Crowninshield's design ideas, while monitoring the *Rob Roy*'s building progress at the A.D. Story yard. Among other *Rob Roy* innovations, Crowninshield was the first to break away from the rockered keel fad initiated by Burgess by providing a straight section of keel shoe.

Although the diverse demands on McManus's time–managing real estate, marrying off his daughters, busily turning out Indian Header plans, working on further development of this class and, most of all, evolving the knockabout model–kept him fully occupied, the Crowninshield boat stirred Tom's competitive nature and elicited a response. It took more than a year to come to fruition, and arrived in the form of the *Benjamin W. Latham*.

McManus's tendency was to moderate Crowninshield's *Rob Roy* concept. The *Latham*'s stem overhang was not as extreme as *Rob Roy*'s. Her straight run of keel had more drag, but retained the *Rob Roy*'s knuckle at the forward end. The Connecticut-based *Benjamin W. Latham*'s stern may have been the most graceful one McManus ever designed, and an elegant sheerline accentuated her graceful appearance.[52] Pleasing profile aside, however, the key comparison is performance,

McManus's answer to the *Rob Roy* was the 72-ton *Benjamin W. Latham* (84x21.4x9.8 feet), designed in August 1902. (Plan AFS 96A, Smithsonian Institution)

---

[52] At least three other McManus schooners came from this design, the *Olivia Domingoes* of 1903, the *Teazer* of 1906 (although she appears to have been a true hybrid–with a *Latham* type forebody grafted onto a *Nellie Dixon* afterbody), and the *Mary E. O'Hara* of 1922 (James Yard Book; Howard I. Chapelle, *American Sailing Craft* (New York: Kennedy Brothers Incorporated, 1936), 103).

Samuel F.M. Badger painted the *Benjamin W. Latham.* (Courtesy Peabody & Essex Museum, Salem, Massachusetts, photograph by Mark Sexton)

The big 112-ton Indian Header *Manhassett* (96.6x24x10.8 feet) shows off her entire suit of sails during a warm, quiet day on Boston Bay. Her jib has an old-fashioned bonnet, a removable strip laced to the foot, which can be removed to shorten sail. Unlike McManus's earlier Indian Headers, the *Manhassett* has a "relaxed" stern, shorter and less upturned than those of the prototypes. Photograph by Nathaniel L. Stebbins, 1 October 1902. (Courtesy The Society for the Preservation of New England Antiquities, Boston, Massachusetts)

and the *Latham* earned a reputation for speed, while the *Rob Roy* was never considered a fast vessel.[53]

The *Emily Cooney,* another of the schooners built to Tom's designs that year, was the first example of another McManus variant, which Gordon Thomas dubbed the "Round-bow" type.[54] Thomas had special reason to be aware of this particular

---

[53] Thomas, *Fast & Able*, 61.

[54] Chapelle redrafted the plans of the *Emily Cooney* for *Fishing Schooners*, 232.

The full McManus family posed for a formal portrait, ca. 1902. They are, from left: (*standing*) Alice, Louise, Thomas F., and Mary; (*seated*) Margaret, Katherine, Catherine (Kate), Charles, Letitia, and Grace; (*seated on floor*) Thomas Jr., Mildred, Kenneth, and George. (Courtesy Col. Frank Carruth)

species. His father, the hard-driving Captain Jeff Thomas, while in the employ of John Chisolm of Gloucester, skippered the *Thomas S. Gorton*, a 1905 version of this hull profile. These schooners are best described as being in a line of progression from the plumb-stemmers of the 1880s through the short-bow Indian Headers to the forthcoming long-bow semi-knockabouts, although McManus later designed several round-bow hulls with semi-knockabout rigs (beginning with the *Mary DeCosta* of 1909).[55] The round-bow schooners demonstrate that the design principles of Dennison J. Lawlor, as well as Ned Burgess, still influenced Tom's creative thinking. They can be identified by the stem profile, which gently curves to the bowsprit without the gripe of the early Indian Headers. In the *Emily Cooney*, McManus, who obviously had not satisfied himself about the advantages of the straight run of keel espoused by Crowninshield in the *Rob Roy*, returned to a gently rockered version.

---

[55] This design had a loyal following of fishermen who kept it in existence for a dozen years. Known round-bow hulls included: (1902) *Emily Cooney, Paragon*; (1904) *Kernwood, Belbina Domingoes, Buema, Catherine Burke, Walter P. Domingoes, Louisa R. Silva*; (1905) *Frances P. Mesquita, Ethel Mildred, Thomas S. Gorton, Raymah, Alert, Effie M. Prior, Esperanto*; (1907) *John Hays Hammond, Richard*; (1908) *Rex, Eugenia*; (1909) *Mary DeCosta*. The following Round-bow hulls had semi-knockabout rigs: (1911) *Dorothy G. Snow* (Canadian); (1912) *Leonora Silveira*; (1913) *Progress, Russell, Angeline C. Nunan*; (1914) *Ralph Brown*; (1915) *Henrietta*.

CHAPTER ELEVEN

The Helen B. Thomas, Mooween, and Eclipse

Despite its success and developmental improvements, McManus was not entirely satisfied with his Indian Head design. He had never given up on the idea of eliminating the bowsprit from working schooners, and for ten years he had experimented with the creation of a stabilized hull form to accomplish that objective. To achieve it, he eventually reversed a portion of his Indian Header thinking by returning to one of the creative concepts he incorporated in the *James S. Steele*–her radical

Three fishermen "muzzle" the jib of the McClain-designed *Effie M. Morrissey*, demonstrating how dangerous it was to balance on the bowsprit footropes while handling a flailing jib, especially in heavy seas, icy weather, or when the footropes had not been well maintained. Photograph by Frederick William Wallace, December 1912. (Courtesy Maritime Museum of the Atlantic, Halifax, Nova Scotia)

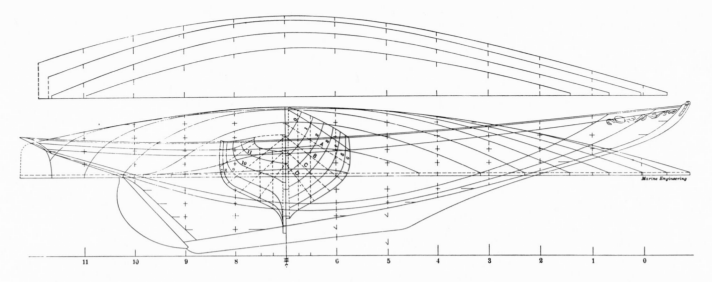

McManus's revolutionary lines of the *Helen B. Thomas* combined the straight run of keel introduced by Crowninshield with a bow elongated to the point a bowsprit would normally reach. (*International Marine Engineering*, June 1902)

forward section. Although the prime consideration leading to the *Steele*'s extended forebody was McManus's deep-seated belief in reserved power–in that case buoyancy leading to a reduction in the pitching moment of the hull–the secondary purpose behind the lengthened bow section was a corresponding reduction in the length of the bowsprit.

Tom made this revision fundamental to an extraordinary new design. His immediate goal of improving the fishermen's working environment focused upon providing more foredeck for the men to work upon, thus keeping them within the safe confines of the hull, while still maintaining the balance of the rig. He had resolved the problem with a design exercise that he wrestled with from 1899 through to the summer of 1900, when he turned to his workbench and modelled a strange-looking fishing schooner without a bowsprit. He described his theory about the "knockabout" rig with simple logic: "the jib can be taken in by one Man who stands practically on terra firma and all he had to do is cast off the halyards. The angle of the stay is so sharp the sail comes down in the jack ropes and is secure. There were no bowsprit shrouds or bobstays or footropes to keep up at a large expense each year."[1] In fact, a knockabout bow has a favorable effect even when the schooner rides at anchor. The hawsepipes through which the cable passes from the windlass to the anchor are much farther from midships, thereby preventing hawsing up in a tide way and relieving the excessive strain on the forward hull which could contribute to the hogging of the sheerline. The concept of a vessel without a bowsprit can be traced to the seaworthy racing sloops developed around Massachusetts Bay during the 1890s, when yachtsmen began to build sailing yachts without bowsprits, for knocking about the bay whenever it was free of ice.

[1] Thomas F. McManus, "Autobiographical No. 1."

In essence, the first knockabout fisherman, the *Helen B. Thomas*, was a small schooner whose bow had been stretched out to where the outer end of the bowsprit normally would have been. But once again the specter of excessive construction cost relative to cargo space arose to haunt McManus—there was too much wasted space forward. This was accentuated by the nose in the air attitude of the *Thomas*, which resulted from Tom's effort to replace the steeve, as well as the length, of the bowsprit. Eventually, he would resolve the problem of excessive space forward by designing a short but deep forward overhang coupled to a tall rig to obtain the necessary balance.

When Tom completed the model with the stuck up nose early in 1900, he gave it a prominent place in his Atlantic Avenue window, just as he had a decade before with the one that became the *James S. Steele*, and the gestation period that followed echoed the trauma of his first schooner–McManus suffered the same pangs he had before Moses Adams arrived at Atlantic Avenue. This time, unlike 1890-91 when all he could turn his hand to in the shop was arranging for shipments of fish, he was constantly at work preparing drafts and half models for his other commissions.

The moot, but nonetheless interesting, question that arises is why McManus did not underwrite the knockabout himself. He certainly possessed the assets, although his liquid capital may have been tied up in fishing-schooner syndicates and real-estate holdings, particularly after paying for his new house in Dorchester. But, considering the family's long familiarity and success with syndication, he certainly could have formed a group of investors for the project. Personal pride, given McManus's work ethic and rigid professionalism, is a distinct possibility–a belief that the architect did not build his own designs. The third, more practical factor may have been time–the plans and models for the Indian Headers, as well as the still-popular *Nellie Dixon* types, kept him fully occupied, not to mention the necessary attention to his family, which then ranged from babes-in-arms to full-grown, marriageable young ladies.[2] Whatever the reason, the sparless "knockabout" model, with its long uppity snout, sitting in the shop window, provoked considerable conversation among the waterfront pundits; but, as a decade earlier, no paying customers appeared.

In an exact parallel to the *James S. Steele*, the model gathered dust for more than a year before something happened.[3] When it did, the person who financed the project, Cassius Hunt, had walked past Tom's window on the way to his own fish

---

[2] His two oldest, and arguably the most beautiful ones in a covey of handsome young women, Margaret and Grace, had already married, leaving Alice, the family athlete, as the oldest sibling at home.

[3] Howard I. Chapelle, *The National Watercraft Collection* (Washington, D.C.: Government Printing Office, 1960), 233.

Ready for launch from the Oxner and Story yard in March 1902, with her rudder braced for the plunge, the *Helen B. Thomas* shows off her elongated bow. Notice the contrast with the round bow of the Indian Header under construction in the foreground. The double-sawn oak framing of these fishing schooners, made up of overlapping segments, can be seen clearly in this photograph. (Courtesy Dana Story Collection)

brokerage on South Market Street every day of the working week throughout that time. An old waterfront hand, Hunt had, after a brief spell of working for William K. Prior, Jr., in the Faneuil Hall fish stalls, opened up his own business in 1886.[4] A year earlier he had joined John H. and Charley McManus in the syndication of the fishing schooner *Emily P. Wright*,[5] and like Tom had a sixteenth share in the *Maggie Sullivan* of 1893.[6] During the latter part of the summer of 1901, Hunt got together with Captain William "Billy" Thomas of Portland, Maine, to form a syndicate and underwrite the construction of a knockabout.[7] The *Helen B. Thomas*, named for the skipper's wife, was the result. The Oxner & Story yard on the Essex River built the new style fisherman over the winter of 1901-02 and launched the ungainly looking vessel with her pronounced proboscis on 11 March. The design dimensions were 105 feet 6 inches in length, by 20 feet 6 inches breadth, by 10 feet 1 inches deep.[8]

An *International Marine Engineering* article discussed the first knockabout's construction characteristics: frames six inches square on eighteen-inch centers,[9] planking two and a half inches thick, treenailed New England white oak, main deck beams eight inches square with a crown exceeding four inches, wire standing

---

[4] Andrew W. German, *Down on T Wharf: The Boston Fisheries as Seen Through the Photographs of Henry D. Fisher* (Mystic, Connecticut: Mystic Seaport Museum, 1982), 130.

[5] Enrolment No. 245, Boston and Charlestown, 2 June 1885, U.S. Consolidated Enrolment and Licenses, Bureau of Navigation, Record Group 41, Records of the Department of Commerce, NARA.

[6] Enrolment No. 245, Boston and Charlestown, 1 June 1893.

[7] Gordon W. Thomas, *Fast & Able, Life Stories of Great Gloucester Fishing Vessels* (Gloucester, Massachusetts: Gloucester 350th Anniversary Celebration, Inc., 1973), 83.

[8] See Table 8 for the register dimensions of the *Helen B. Thomas*.

[9] The construction was actually composed of doubled, sawn, 6-inch-sided frames, treenail fastened.

rigging, cotton duck sails, and sixty tons of pig-iron inside ballast.[10] The *Thomas* carried ten dories, berthed four in the skipper's quarters, and fifteen in the forecastle. After launching, a tug towed her around to the Gloucester chandlery of E.L. Rowe and Son, "who take the schooner from the builder's hands and fit her with sails, rigging, cooking utensils, nautical instruments, and, in fact, everything ready to go to sea."[11]

On her shakedown cruise the *Thomas* proved to be a fast sailer and exceptionally quick "in stays," or in swinging her bow through the wind to change tacks. One commentary on her maiden voyage stated:

Coming through the Narrows in Boston Bay, the 76-ton *Helen B. Thomas* (94.2x21.6x9.2 feet) shows off her rig. Her bow approximates the length and steeve of a bowsprit, but McManus changed the proportions of the Indian Head rig to give her a relatively high-aspect sail plan. Photographed by Nathaniel L. Stebbins, 13 June 1904. (Courtesy The Society for the Preservation of New England Antiquities, Boston, Massachusetts)

---

[10] "The Knockabout Fisherman," *International Marine Engineering* 7 (June 1902): 299-300. This remains the definitive discussion of *Helen B. Thomas*.

[11] Ibid., 300.

On the way it was noticed that she obeyed her wheel very quickly, and they decided to try and see how quick she would tack. . . . Designer, owner, crew and guests were very much surprised when it was found that she tacked from full to full under those unfavorable conditions in 23 seconds. After getting way on it was tried a number of times again, which showed that she could tack from full to full in from 20 to 25 seconds, which, needless to say, is wonderfully quick time, for the [1901 America's Cup contenders] *Columbia* and *Shamrock* took from 25 to 30 seconds, but it only goes to show how near the crack yachts are the Gloucester fishermen of today.[12]

The America's Cup comparison flatters, but one with fishing schooners would be more to the point. The old, pre-plumb-stemmer, clipper designs, whose principal advantage was straight-line speed, were unwieldy through stays, which exposed them to the broadside punch of a sudden squall while the vessel had insufficient way on—the oft-proven recipe for disaster that the McManus family had set out to change decades earlier.[13] The *Helen B. Thomas* took her rightful place in the innovative line of McManus designs after *Sylph*, *Actress*, *Sarah B. Prior*, *John H. McManus*, *Nellie Dixon*, *James S. Steele*, *America*, and the still fast-growing Indian Header class of fishing schooners—a remarkable record for a remarkable family.

In retrospect, Howard I. Chapelle concluded that, "the introduction of [the knockabout] design and, later [*sic*], of auxiliary engines, were the final, basic

Previously unrecognized as the second knockabout fishing schooner, the 52-ton Canadian schooner *Alcyone* (78x19.2x8.9 feet) fished out of Digby, Nova Scotia. This 1906 photograph indicates that she was fitted with a short bowsprit within two years of her launch. The horizontal and vertical timbers at her bow are the wooden stocks of her big banks anchors. Photograph by Paul Yates. (Courtesy Maritime Museum of the Atlantic, Halifax, Nova Scotia)

[12] Ibid., 299-300.

[13] Gordon Thomas, in his capsule histories of noted Gloucester fishing vessels, paid special tribute to McManus's genius: "schooner *Helen B. Thomas*, the first knockabout fisherman, was one of the most famous two masted crafts ever built, a vessel whose design created a great change in fishing vessel construction; a change destined to save many lives. . . . The *Thomas* was a distinct departure from any craft ever before constructed for the fishing business" (Thomas, *Fast & Able*, 83-84).

Charles G. Davis, author of the unreliable book, *Ships of the Past*, honored the *Helen B. Thomas* by reproducing her photograph as his frontispiece. He also included a badly-traced plan of the knockabout. Lewis H. Story, the notable Essex loftsman and shipbuilder, commented: "too bad, Mr. Davis is a good writer, but in this book on the fishing vessels, *he is way off*, got hold of a lot of wrong material. . . . I don't know where he obtained the plans of the *Helen B. Thomas* . . . of course they are wrong" (Erik A.R. Ronnberg, Jr., "Letters of Lewis H. Story to John M. Minuse 1932-1947," *Nautical Research Journal* (March 1983): 8, citing Story to Minuse, 20 February 1933, italics reflect emphasis in Story's script. Story was referring to *Ships of the Past*.

changes in the design of the New England fishing schooner."[14] Much was made of the knockabout's undoubted sailing qualities over the next few years, but despite all the favorable press it received, McManus's new schooner type failed as a fisherman for the same reasons the *Steeles* had a decade before. Although the knockabout bow was a step in the right direction, it was just that, a step–not the complete journey. The *Thomas*, although considerably more acceptable to the fleet than the *Steeles* had been, failed to set the world on fire. McManus had again neglected to adhere to John L. Frisbee's teachings regarding the relationship of cargo to performance, economy, and safety.

Two years elapsed before another knockabout appeared–the *Alcyone*. Through the research of Harold G. Simms of Norwell, Massachusetts,[15] it has been discovered that the second knockabout built was not Oxner & Story's *Shepherd King* as long believed, but the small Canadian schooner *Alcyone*, built by Simms's grandfather, Amos Pentz, the master shipwright of McGill Shipbuilding in Shelburne, Nova Scotia. The order for this first Canadian knockabout came from the partnership of Harry B. Short, James Ellis, and Captain R.A. Wormell. The yard launched this previously unacknowledged vessel on 14 October 1904, well ahead of the 1905 completion of the *Shepherd King*.[16] The influence of the Canadian fisheries was a matter of some importance to American naval architects. The Canadian fleet was in the process of upgrading, and its owners kept a sharp eye on New England trends, particularly during this period of rapid change from the clipper schooners to the plumb-stemmers, *Nellie Dixon* types, Indian Headers, and now knockabouts.

Tom clung to his concept of extending the ends of the hull in both the *Alcyone* and his third knockabout, the *Thomas A. Cromwell* of 1905. In between them a competitive variation on the theme appeared: Oxner & Story built the snub-nosed knockabout *Shepherd King*. This second American order for a knockabout did not come until three years had passed since the launching of the *Helen B. Thomas*. When it did, Edwin Oxner carved the model, not Tom McManus. Oxner and his partner, Lyndon J. Story, based this revised design on the errors they believed were incorporated into *Thomas*, which they had built for

---

[14] Chapelle, *National Watercraft*, 233.

[15] The author gratefully acknowledges the work of Harold G. Simms, a retired Scituate boatyard operator, who has provided the first meaningful research breakthroughs to shed light on Canadian vessels built to McManus's designs.

[16] *37th Annual List of Merchant Vessels of the United States* (Washington: Government Printing Office, 1905), and, Dana A. Story, *An Approximate Listing of the Vessels, Boats and Other Craft Built in the Town of Essex, 1870 through 1977* (Essex, Massachusetts: [photocopied], 1978), give the launch date of *Shepherd King* as 1905, while Howard I. Chapelle, *The American Fishing Schooners 1825-1925* (New York: W.W. Norton, 1973), 249, claims she went down the ways in 1904. The James & Tarr boatyard at Essex built two additional knockabouts off the molds of the *Shepherd King*, the *John J. Fallon* and *Aspinet*, both launched in 1908. Two decades later the John F. James yard built the *Virginia* (1926) and *Rainbow* (1929) from the same molds.

Cassius Hunt.[17] The *Shepherd King* was a definite improvement on the *Thomas*; but, while the Oxner & Story schooner incorporated a forward section similar to McManus's Indian Headers, she still retained too much wasted space in the ends, and failed to convince the fleet's owners or skippers that any knockabout mutation was economically feasible.

Name	Year	Length	Breadth	Depth	Tons	Builder
Helen B. Thomas	1902	94.2	21.6	9.2	76	Oxner & Story
Alcyone	1904	78.0	19.2	8.9	51.9	Joseph McGill
Shepherd King	1905	100.0	23.3	12.2	121	Oxner & Story
Thomas A. Cromwell	1905	109.9	24.5	11.6	128	Oxner & Story

TABLE 8 - THE FIRST KNOCKABOUT FISHING SCHOONERS

McManus donated his half model of the *Helen B. Thomas* to the Smithsonian Institution's Watercraft Collection, whose trustees in turn loaned it to the Essex Shipbuilding Museum along with the model of *James S. Steele*.[18] Viewing this model, it is clearly apparent how the architect drew the forebody forward to where the bowsprit would normally end to maintain the balance of the rig and raised the peak of the bow to accommodate the steeve of the bowsprit, thereby allowing the relocation of the headstays within the hull.[19] In an article written ten years after the launch of the *Thomas*, after first noting McManus's resolve to displace the clipper schooner, *International Marine Engineering*'s enthusiasm for the knockabout concept had not diminished: "the knock about type, with its deep and sharp hull lines, short sail base, and eliminated bowsprit, have made [fishing schooners] safe and easy to handle in heavy seas. There is less pitching and great saving of wear and tear on the rigging; no bobstays to leak; no bowsprit to loosen; and with practically no overboard work for the men to do in handling sails, they now fear only fog, collision and shore."[20]

The significance of Tom McManus's creations to fishing schooner design has rarely been fully appreciated, probably because its context and magnitude has not been properly evaluated. Consider the dynamic involved as the *Thomas* went into the water. The fleet was in the midst of accepting and adopting McManus's

---

[17] Howard I. Chapelle, *The American Fishing Schooners 1825-1925* (New York: W.W. Norton, 1973), 249-52.

[18] U.S. National Museum of American History, Smithsonian Institution, catalog number 310,888.

[19] Ironically, in light of the number of pilot schooners McManus designed on purpose, the fishing schooner *Helen B. Thomas* ended her service life as a pilot boat by accident. The pilots association of Hamilton, Bermuda, purchased the *Thomas* when she retired from fishing in 1921, but the new career was cut short when *Thomas* succumbed to flames at age twenty-five (Thomas, *Fast & Able*, 85).

[20] "Two Notable Oil Engined Fishing Schooners," *International Marine Engineering* 17 (October 1912): 408.

Tom McManus (*left*) and his son
George posed with an unidentified
captain at the wheel of a schooner, ca.
1904. (Courtesy Louise V. Will)

Indian Headers, and he had already introduced and begun to modify the knockabout–the next great silhouette change in New England schooners.

Although schooner owners and captains did not immediately besiege McManus with orders for their own versions of the most revolutionary vessel type he would create during his long career–the knockabout *Helen B. Thomas*–they continued to demand his popular Indian Head design. But, confident in the benefits offered by the knockabout design, Tom kept probing hull forms in search of the combination that would gain for it the unqualified approval the *Juniata* and her sisters had so quickly earned. The fact that he continually improved the Indian Head class did not speed the knockabout's acceptance prospects. While the Indian Head class thrived, a total absence of commissions marked the widespread disinterest in the knockabout concept three years into its life.

Over the winter of 1902-03, Captain Henry Dexter Malone engaged John Bishop's brother Hugh to build the Indian Header *Quannapowatt* at

The 122-ton *Mooween*
(102.8x24.4x10.2 feet), the first semi-
knockabout fishing schooner, was
launched at Gloucester early in 1904.
In this compromise between the round
bow and knockabout designs, McManus
lengthened the bow to shorten, but not
eliminate, the bowsprit. A.A. Acores
painted her portrait. (Courtesy Cape
Ann Historical Collection, Gloucester)

Gloucester. McManus had completed the design sometime earlier; in fact, he
wrapped it up a couple of days before his forty-fifth birthday, on 11 September 1901.
In the *Quannapowatt*, he retained the sweeping sheerline that typified the Indian
Headers, as well as the fully rockered keel configuration, but, unlike many of
his designs, she had only moderate rake in the sternpost, which left considerable
deadwood aft.[21] The latter factor probably contributed to her trim "by the
head," with bow lower than stern, which she assumed after launching. Embarrassed
to see one of his designs floating so awkwardly–although ballast would later
correct its balance–McManus flew into a rage every time this occurred, and
inevitably blamed the builder.

---

[21] Chapelle states, ". . . the sternpost raked strongly," but he must be comparing it to fishing schooners in general, rather than
to other McManus designs (Chapelle, *Fishing Schooners*, 244).

The *Quannapowatt* once proved the overall strength of the Indian Head hull. Under the command of Captain "Little Dan" MacDonald during a trip to the northern Grand Banks in July 1913, she was caught in a developing ice field. Using the power of his single gasoline engine, and taking advantage of her innate bow-down trim, MacDonald powered her back to open water. The 108 1/2-foot Indian Header returned to port with gouges in her planking on both sides and a few holes where needle-shaped ice floes had pierced her two-inch-thick oak planking.

During the summer of 1903, Captain Henry Curtis honored his wife by naming McManus's next Indian Header *Mary F. Curtis*. Tarr & James built her for John Pew & Company of Gloucester. One of those frequent Essex River launching mishaps victimized this new fisherman on 9 September. While gathering momentum down the ways, she suddenly screeched to a halt. This unanticipated deceleration hurled the twenty-five guests on board against the bulwarks. The fiancée of one of the Pews, Alice Hartwell, broke her collarbone. Several others suffered lesser injuries. This inauspicious baptism notwithstanding, the *Curtis* went on to establish a world mackerel seining record and, in an unusual twist for a fishing schooner, became the camera boat for director Victor Fleming's 1935 movie, *Captains Courageous*.[22]

Even as late as 1903 some owners still demanded clipper-bowed schooners, albeit ones based on the vastly improved models that followed the *Nellie Dixon* and *Fredonia*. Tom completed the plans for the *Ida M. Silva*, an advance on the *Nellie Dixon*, on 15 August. This design provides a direct comparison between his work and that of Mel McClain, who prepared the drafts for the clipper-bowed schooners *Nokomis* and *Lafayette* during the same period. McManus's stem has a distinctly convex or "spoon" shape despite its "clipper" bow, while McClain's is concave. At the stern, McClain's transom, typically for him, continues the line of the counter, while McManus's alters it toward the vertical. Most important of all, where McClain has only moderate drag in the keels of the *Nokomis* and *Lafayette*, the *Ida M. Silva* displays the deep drag that was a quintessential McManus family characteristic.

Through the summer of 1903 and into the following winter, McManus conducted an amazing display of design virtuosity. Prior to completing the *Nellie Dixon*-type *Ida M. Silva* in mid-August, he had delivered the drafts and offset tables for *Olivia Domingoes* (spoon-bow), *Paragon* (round-bow), *Griswold I. Keeney*, *Edith J. Peterson*, *Fannie Belle Atwood*, *Elmer E. Gray*, *Annie Perry*, *Mary F. Curtis*, *Mooanam*, *Mettacomett*, *Natalie J. Nelson*, *Mildred Robinson*, and *Quannapowatt* (all Indian Head variants). With his creative juices flowing like a Maine tidal race, he

---

[22] Thomas, *Fast & Able*, 86-88.

set about answering the knockabout's critics. Spurred once again by Sanford C. Winsor, Tom developed and designed two versions of a compromise schooner type aimed at overcoming the criticisms of the *Helen B. Thomas* based on her alleged inability to carry a paying cargo relative to her cost of construction. The outcome of his autumnal efforts were the *Mooween* and *Clintonia*–one, the *Mooween*, would be built immediately and then ignored for six years, while the other, the *Clintonia*, moldered away under Tom's drafting table for three years before she came into being (her powerful sailing qualities would quickly earn for her the title of the queen of the fleet). Between them, the *Mooween* and *Clintonia* were the watershed versions of a new type of McManus fishing schooner with a bowsprit. Gordon Thomas, as reliable a reflection of contemporary dockside terminology as there is, always referred to them as round-bow knockabouts, but, unfortunately, the tepid terminology that caught on with a

The 92-ton *Ellen C. Burke* (90.5x23.8x10.6 feet) was a long-ended, flush-decked Indian Header with plenty of sheer and "reserve power." Notice that she had a small club rather than a full boom on the foot of her forestaysail. After fishing in the North Atlantic, the *Burke* was purchased by Galveston, Texas, owners and worked in the red snapper fishery until she stranded in the Gulf of Mexico in her twenty-fifth year. Photograph by Nathaniel L. Stebbins, 1 October 1902. (Courtesy The Society for the Preservation of New England Antiquities, Boston, Massachusetts)

vengeance–semi-knockabouts–stayed with the class. A New England newspaper broke the story of McManus's latest design concept a day or two before her launching: "The new vessel, which is to be christened *Mooween*, is of the semi-knockabout type and is intended for the offshore fishery. She will have a 12-foot bowsprit, and on the whole will be an easier vessel in the handling than any craft sailing out of T Wharf. Her crew will not have to leave the deck in reefing sail, as everything can be worked inboard. She is a vessel of 123 tons register, 116.2 feet length overall, 83 feet on the waterline, 24 feet beam and 15 feet depth of hold.

She was built for Arnold & Winsor and will be commanded by Captain Joe Hatch of the *Mattakeesett*."[23]

Captain Hatch maintained a spit-and-polish rig. Shortly after the *Mooween* arrived home from her first winter trip to the banks, she received a splendid compliment: The "new semi-knockabout fisherman *Mooween* arrived in Boston harbor, looking more like a yacht than a working vessel."[24]

---

[23] Unidentified [Boston?] newspaper article, about two days before the *Mooween*'s launch, from a McManus family scrapbook.

[24] Gloucester *Daily Times*, 11 March 1904.

A contrast to the *Ellen C. Burke* is the 92-ton *Mina Swim* (82x23.2x9.8 feet), a short-ended, full-bodied Indian Header launched by A.D. Story in April 1904. Photograph by Willard B. Jackson, 1904. (Courtesy Peabody & Essex Museum, Salem, Masachusetts)

In the semi-knockabouts McManus somewhat elongated the bow (as in the *James S. Steele*), so that the forestay came to the bowsprit inboard of the stem, which enabled him to shorten the infamous "widow-maker" spar by a corresponding amount. In the Indian Head class and the round-bow schooners the forestay attached to the gammon iron at the top of the stemhead. The plans of the *Clintonia* feature a bow section that in silhouette falls squarely between the knockabouts *Helen B. Thomas* and *Thomas A. Cromwell*,[25] which, respectively, preceded and succeeded her. Although there are no extant plans of the *Mooween*, an Acores painting of her suggests she had the same bow configuration as the *Clintonia*.[26] These first semi-knockabouts had well-balanced hulls and rigs and sported a powerful sail plan. Several years passed before the fleet owners came to appreciate the *Mooween*'s qualities; but, beginning with the *Premier* (launched in April 1910), her lines spawned several vessels including the timeless *Elsie* (9 May 1910), and the *Elk* (15 December 1910). On the same day that A.D. Story launched the *Elk*, Fred J. Thompson and Lemuel Spinney of Gloucester reincarnated *Mooween* for a final time: "Contracted with Capt Spinney For a Schr from the lines of Sch. *Mooween*

---

25 See Chapelle, *Fishing Schooners*, 260, for her draft.

26 Painting of *Clintonia* by A. Acores, Cape Ann Historical Society.

The 105-ton round-bow schooner
Frances P. Mesquita (92.6x23.2x10.2
feet) was modeled on McManus's
Belbina Domingoes design and launched
by John Bishop at Gloucester in 1905.
As this photograph illustrates, the
round bow was actually less round than
the Indian Head bow, instead featuring
a sloping, gentle curve of the stem.
Willard B. Jackson photographed the
speedy *Mesquita* during the 1907
Lipton Cup race, when she outsailed
the *Helen B. Thomas*. (Courtesy
Peabody & Essex Museum, Salem,
Massachusetts)

lines 2 feet longer and 4 in deeper to be 118 feet long 24 feet wide 10 feet 6 in Deep
[*sic*] Bowsprit 15 feet to tip Oak deck aft State rooms and Clothes Closet Price
$8300. . . . Name *Gov. Foss*."[27] The hallmark schooners *Oriole* (1908-another
"Queen of the Fleet") and *Elizabeth Howard* (1916-the famous "White Ghost of the
Maine Coast") highlighted the *Clintonia*'s offspring.

Still in a design frenzy, Tom finished the set of plans for the Indian Headers
Cavalier and *Lucania* on 9 December 1903. In addition to their shorter bow
overhangs, he sought to eliminate some of the deadwood aft by giving their
sternposts more rake. He also reduced the stern overhang and gave them less sheer
aft. He continued these trends in most of the second-generation Indian Headers.

One of the few complaints Tom had regularly received about the class came
not from its skippers, but from the shipyards that serviced those schooners. When
hauled up on a marine railway or drydocked, they were hard to block up because
their rockered keels had no straight run. Tom, following Burgess's lead, had adopted

[27] James Yard Book.

this profile to increase their speed through stays. But he experimented with a straight keel section like the *Rob Roy*'s, with its pronounced forward knuckle, in the *Benjamin W. Latham*, whose plans he had finished on 18 August 1902. The results did not satisfy him and he returned to a fully rockered keel in the Indian Headers *George H. Lubee*, *Manhassett*, *Seaconnet*, and *Fortuna*, as well as in his first round-bow type, the *Emily Cooney*.

McManus vacillated between the competing attributes of agility and serviceability. The performance of the *Steeles* and the early Indian Headers, all with rockered keels, proved difficult to beat. Then, apparently still undecided, in the new Indian Headers *Lucania* and *Cavalier*, although he retained a gracefully bowed run of keel, he added Crowninshield's straight section to accommodate the haul-out process once again. It should be noted, however, that although *Rob Roy* was the first new schooner to return to a straight run after the onset of Burgess's rocker fad, the model of the *Helen B. Thomas*, sporting a distinct straight run with a knuckle forward, was on exhibition in McManus's window when Crowninshield modeled the *Rob Roy* during the winter of 1899-1900, and Crowninshield was a regular visitor to that hotbed of naval-architectural argument.

James & Tarr constructed the *Cavalier* at Essex, while John Bishop laid down the *Lucania* at Gloucester. It is believed that Bishop added a frame to McManus's design, and two feet to the height of her masts.[28] In a revealing contrast, the *Cavalier*, a successful haddocker, never earned a reputation for swiftness. She was unfortunate in not having had a skipper the caliber of the *Lucania*'s legendary Marty Welch. Under his guiding hand, even though still early in his career, the *Lucania* always maintained a reputation as a speedster. A well-known Gloucester schoonerman, Captain Al Miller, once remarked, "Th' *Lucania* was er very fast sailer by th' wind in smooth water, an' moderate winds, fer she could trim most any vessel in th' fleet 'cept th' *Oriole*, an' Marty was rather proud of her."[29] *Lucania*'s reputation notwithstanding, Chapelle used these two Indian Headers to illustrate the difficulty of comparing the speed of similar hull forms.[30] The relationship between the two American-Irishmen, skipper Welch and designer McManus, began to evolve when John Bishop laid down the *Lucania*. It grew into a very close personal friendship and business relationship, which lasted throughout the balance of their mutually long lives.

Still working at a pace unmatched by any of his contemporaries, Tom made further improvements in the lines of the Indian Headers the following spring,

---

28 Chapelle, *Fishing Schooners*, 236.

29 Wesley G. Pierce, *Goin' Fishin'* (Salem, Massachusetts: Marine Research Society, 1934), 179.

30 Chapelle, *Fishing Schooners*, 235-36.

making them even more attractive to the fleet owners. He finished the drafts for the *Onato* on 12 May, and the *Ingomar* on 16 June. By rounding and filling out their bilges, he further eased the strain on the spars and rigging during heavy weather sailing, even more so than with the *Flora S. Nickerson* and *Matchless*. But the most significant gain from this alteration came in the form of carrying capacity. With their slackened bilges, the *Onato* and *Ingomar* were more burdensome than their predecessors, yet gave up nothing in the way of hull speed. Of the two, the *Ingomar* was the more powerful vessel, possibly because McManus had carried the breadth of her buttock lines further aft and increased the rake in her sternpost. This latter design change indicates that Tom must have remained unhappy with the tacking ability of the *Cavalier* and the *Lucania*. Despite the inherent difficulties the maintenance yards experienced hauling vessels with no straight run of keel, he finally made up his mind and came down in favor of the fully rockered keel configuration for the *Onato* and *Ingomar*, as well as the balance of the Indian Head class, although he continued to retain a section of straight run in the keel of his future knockabouts.[31]

In another of those Essex River tragicomedies, the *Onato* suffered a launching mishap: "A large party was on board . . . in some unknown manner she fell over on her side, throwing the people on board to the deck, and covering them with fresh paint."[32] Presumably the nearby Oxner & Story paint shed had a goodly supply of turpentine handy to clean up the unexpectedly decorated guests.

One of the most significant signs of the success of the Indian Header fleet was the frequency with which its original sponsor, Sanford C. Winsor, ordered new schooners of that type for his service. The Arnold & Winsor proprietor operated as many as 14 at a time, but respect for the qualities of the Indian Headers was in no way limited to him. In the first seven years of their existence more than 60 joined the New England fleet. During this time the number of banksmen based between New York City and Eastport, Maine, had grown to between 400 and 450 vessels, thus McManus's Indian Headers already amounted to 15 percent of the total population. Yet, by this early point of his full-time design career, Tom had already introduced the knockabout, semi-knockabout, round-bow, and modified spoon-bow of the *Benjamin Latham* types.

But even as late as 1905, when he designed the big *Thomas A. Cromwell*, his own third knockabout, and the fourth to get to sea, with typical stubbornness Tom adhered to his concept of extending the ends, just as he had long before in the

---

[31] It would prove a worthy design exercise to employ a modern computer-assisted design program to evaluate why the rockered keel fitted the Indian Head design, while the straight run of keel with marked drag, suited the knockabout, a vastly different hull configuration.

[32] Thomas, *Fast & Able*, 95.

James S. Steele: "[The *Thomas A. Cromwell*] was in many respects, a development from the design of the *Helen B. Thomas*, having less sheer and, generally, a more attractive hull, but still with wasted space in the ends."[33] The *Cromwell* sported an upswept nose second only to that of the *Helen B. Thomas*, and her stern overhang, according to Chapelle, inadvertently caused the death of her skipper: "with this long counter, the *Cromwell* killed her captain. While the vessel was hove-to and pitching in a heavy swell with a little sternway, the master fell overboard off the

With a bow shape somewhere between a round-bow and spoon-bow, the 83-ton *Kernwood* (87x21.6x10.2 feet) showed a turn of speed after her launch in 1904. In 1908 she became the Sandy Hook pilot schooner *Trenton* and spent twenty-five years delivering pilots to ships approaching New York Harbor. Painting by A. A. Acores. (Courtesy Peabody & Essex Museum, Salem, Massachusetts)

[33] Chapelle, *Fishing Schooners*, 259.

taffrail. Sternway brought him under the counter and this came down on him, giving him a fatal blow on the head."[34] Sea stories aside, and despite his stubborn nature, Tom's talent was anything but single-minded. Although the *Cromwell's* hull looked much like the *Thomas's*–although fifteen feet longer and with a relatively deeper hold–her rig and sail plan were utterly dissimilar. In a foreshadowing of the rigs that came to dominate the fleet ten years later (fifteen years after the introduction of McClain's auxiliary-powered *Helen Miller Gould*), Tom designed the *Cromwell* with pole-masts. An unidentified newspaper story reported that she would not only have a pole-masted rig, but would be capable of flying club topsails, a balloon jib, and a spinnaker![35] It was a clear attempt by the designer to move the center of effort forward and down, and thus eliminate the need for fishermen to go aloft, all by using light sails normally reserved for a yacht. The fishermen may have balked at this idea, for there is no evidence of the *Cromwell* actually flying those yacht sails.

McManus also addressed the carrying capacity concerns relative to the knockabout concept in the *Cromwell*, as he had so successfully done in the Indian Headers and the so far unnoticed semi-knockabouts. The *Cromwell's* net (cargo) tonnage at 70 percent of her gross tonnage rates high among his knockabout designs, a considerable improvement over the *Helen B. Thomas's* 63 percent. John L. Frisbee, now seventy years old and retired to Everett, Massachusetts, must have felt a glimmer of hope that his prize pupil might be beginning to recognize the importance of cargo space, relative to performance and safety, in his new designs. On the other hand, it must be acknowledged just how radical a departure the knockabout hull and rig was to all parties: designer, owner, captain, and crew. What McManus desperately needed was shakedown time for his unique concept, in order to develop the necessary hull, rig, and sail plan compensation factors for the missing bowsprit.

As a matter of course, skippers of working schooners exercised bragging rights over their heavily laden return trips from the banks to Boston and Gloucester, when the amount of ballast on board, in the form of pens full of fish, allowed them to fly every stitch of cotton duck in their sail lockers. A streak of records claimed during 1904 stirred up an initiative for a face-off among the faster fishermen to ascertain which of the beautiful and swift-sailing schooners was truly the "Queen of the Fleet." "FLEET CRAFT OF FISHERMEN TO HAVE RACE,"[36] "Skippers

---

[34] Chapelle, *Fishing Schooners*, 261. Gordon Thomas disputed this tale in a 1980 conversation with Erik Ronnberg, saying that "the skipper had actually committed suicide, and the accidental death story was a hush-up" (Letter, Erik A.R. Ronnberg, Jr., 17 January 1991).

[35] Unidentified newspaper clipping in a McManus family scrapbook, dated 8 May 1905.

[36] Boston *American*, 7 July 1904. Unless otherwise noted, all of the immediately following quotations are from this source.

Excited by Break in Record and Will Try Their Speed," "*Helen B. Thomas* Fastest," hawked the newsboys along Commercial Street and Atlantic Avenue. The headlines heralded the story of a forthcoming race for the crack fishing schooners based at T Wharf, instigated by those repeated pretensions to record trips. Arthur Binney's *Benjamin F. Phillips*, winner of the 1902 fishermen's race, had logged a passage of five hours and twenty minutes on a portion of the run from Georges Bank to the Boston wharf, which McManus's *Helen B. Thomas* then surpassed by more than ten minutes, "from the time she left until she touched at the wharf," on 7 July 1904. The *Thomas's* exact time was five hours and nine minutes.

The rivalry was so keen that comparisons were made to the races held in 1886, 1888, 1892, and 1902. Before long a gathering groundswell pressed for another fishermen's race: "'We will have to have a race to settle this,' said Captain Billy Thomas of the *Helen B. Thomas*. 'We don't care if there is any cup or not. Fishermen do not care for that, but it would draw out a great bunch if there was one offered. I propose the race and am willing to stand by my boat.'" William J. Emerson, the owner of the *Regina*, offered to bet any part of $10,000 that his boat could beat the *Phillips*. Another voice joined the dispute: "Captain Thompson, of the new schooner *Kernwood*, which goes out on her maiden trip today, also disputes the *Phillips's* claim to being the fastest schooner and is ready to race as soon as the date is set. *Kernwood* was designed by Thomas F. McManus of Boston, and was built at Essex. She arrived at T Wharf this morning."[37]

But for once, despite all the smoke, there was no fire, and the next fishermen's race did not come together for three more years.

The death knell for dory fishing sounded in 1905. And, even though few were willing to listen to its tolling at that time, Henry Dexter Malone clearly heard it. After a 1905 accident cost him a hand, Malone, an innovative captain, took command of the first American steam trawler, the *Spray*. Trawler fishing, in which a conical net is dragged across the bottom, presented a direct challenge to the hook-and-line method of the dorymen. It had flourished in Europe under sail for more than half a century, but the first sailing beam trawler in America, John H. McManus and Dick Leonard's *Sylph*, failed because flounder, her principal catch, brought too poor a return in the 1865 marketplace. A quarter-century passed before another serious attempt at European-style commercial fishing took place in New England, this time under the direction of an English captain, Alfred Bradford, who commanded the plumb-stemmed, ketch-rigged, Essex-built *Resolute* of 1891.[38]

---

[37] Ibid. The *Kernwood* became the pilot boat *Trenton* at New York in 1908.

[38] Gordon W. Thomas credits the *Resolute's* design to a Charles O. Story model (*Fast & Able*, 25), while Andrew W. German, in "Otter Trawling Comes to America," *The American Neptune* 44 (Spring 1984): 115, credits it to the U.S. Fish Commission. Photographs of this schooner clearly illustrate the *Grampus's* influence on *Resolute's* model.

Bradford had previously conducted moderately successful beam-trawl experiments with the Boston schooner *Mary F. Chisolm* and, in partnership with Ben Low of Gloucester, commissioned the *Resolute* from the A.D. Story yard. Although she

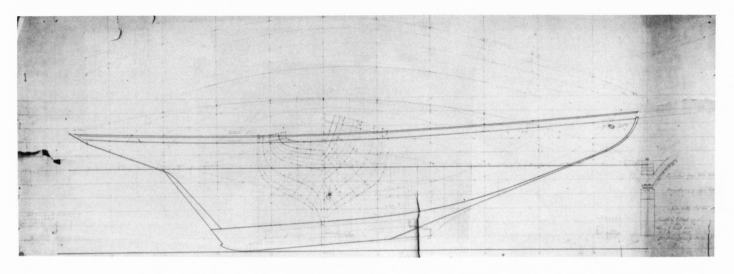

Lines of the schooner-yacht *Eclipse*, showing the placement of her outside ballast. (Courtesy Louise V. Will)

Right: The 65-ton *Eclipse* (62x19x10.7 feet) is poised for launch at John Bishop's Gloucester yard on 10 May 1906. McManus is among the owner's party on deck, third from right. Perhaps the figure in the foreground is John Bishop. The launch was nearly disastrous: when the launching ways sagged under the weight of the outside ballast, the *Eclipse* hung up and was pierced by a staging pole before being gotten safely into Vincent Cove. (*Callanan's Magazine,* June-July 1906)

joined the Gloucester fleet as a beam trawler, *Resolute* made only four such voyages before her owners became discouraged with the results. Toward the end of the 1891-92 winter season, she began dory fishing for the usual fares of salt and fresh cod. Later that year, she brought home an enormously successful catch of 150,000 pounds of cod. Shortly thereafter the Burnham Brothers' yard converted her to a more typical schooner rig.

After the *Resolute* failed to meet her owners' expectations as a beam trawler, overseas methodology fell by the wayside for yet another decade and a half before Boston investors built the modern English-style steel otter trawler *Spray* in 1905. By then, forty years after McManus and Leonard's *Sylph* experiment, market attitudes had changed and the current price per pound of flounder made it more viable. The steam trawlers also brought in a lot of valuable haddock. Additionally, the resolve of the Bay State Fishing Company was greater than that of *Resolute*'s owners, so the method was not going to fade away this time round.

Malone, never more than a doubting convert to steam trawling, gave up after running the *Spray* for only six months. Writing in the 30 June 1906 issue of *The Fishing Gazette* this seasoned but disenchanted master explained: "a schooner of the fast sailing type which is now characteristic of the fishing fleet can beat the *Spray* in from South Channel by four hours, with a fair wind. A schooner and its dories can cover more ground than can be covered by a steam trawler." Malone believed that "month for month" a schooner could bring in more fish than a steam trawler, and that the fish caught on the dorymen's trawl lines came to market in better condition than those dragged aboard vessels like the *Spray* in a net. He

summed up his own part in the experiment: "I am convinced that it will be many years, if ever, before the schooner trawlers will be succeeded by steam."[39] Malone was partly right. It was 1910 before another New England steam trawler was built, but the method was here to stay, and within twenty-five years would make dory fishing outmoded. As to Malone's other comment about the better condition of fish brought to market by the long-liners, he is correct; but, from the earliest days of commercial fishing on the Grand Banks fish had been graded before sale.[40] Market reality became a matter of a few pennies less per pound for fish dragged up in bottom nets, rather than total rejection of flatfish.

A striking tribute to the strength, durability, and design characteristics of Tom's designs involved the *Benjamin W. Latham*-model, spoon-bow *Teazer* six years

[39] *The Fishing Gazette*, 30 June 1906, 615.

[40] During the eighteenth century sellers divided the cod catch into three grades: "Best" (40-50 pounds), sold to Spain and Portugal; "Middling," sold to Virginia, Jamaica, Azores, and Cape Verdean Islands; and the lowest grade, "Refuse," went to the British West Indies as slave food.

after her 16 October 1905 launching by James & Tarr at Essex. It illustrated the inherent hull stability that represented the achievement of the McManus family's goal to overcome the failing of the old clipper-bowed fishing schooners, which had cost the lives of so many New England fishermen.

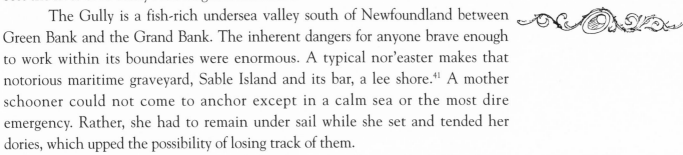

The Gully is a fish-rich undersea valley south of Newfoundland between Green Bank and the Grand Bank. The inherent dangers for anyone brave enough to work within its boundaries were enormous. A typical nor'easter makes that notorious maritime graveyard, Sable Island and its bar, a lee shore.[41] A mother schooner could not come to anchor except in a calm sea or the most dire emergency. Rather, she had to remain under sail while she set and tended her dories, which upped the possibility of losing track of them.

Early in 1911, the *Teazer*, with her long-time skipper Peter Dunsky in charge, had been sending out her dories in the Gully. But toward the end of January, mountainous seas brought on by three days of continuous forty- to sixty-knot winds had prevented any attempt at making a set during the northerly gales. By the twenty-ninth, Captain Dunsky had given up all thought of fishing and turned his efforts toward preserving his vessel and crew. In those precarious conditions, he carefully brought the *Teazer* head to wind and set her anchor. Afterward, the crew, with the single exception of the watch on deck, took to their bunks to ride out the tempest.

Before long, the watchman spotted a rogue wave beam on and bearing down on the *Teazer* at breakneck speed. He raced for the shelter of the forecastle, but, as he dove down the companionway and tried to slam the hatch behind him, the huge sea smashed into the schooner. Its mighty strength effortlessly ripped the anchor cable asunder and tossed the *Teazer* on her beam ends—as if she were no more than a bathtub toy.

The sweeping force of the sea scoured her decks. The gurry kids and checkers went overboard. The surging green water snapped her fore boom and fore and main gaffs, leaving them hanging in pieces. It tore her riding sails to shreds. Six of the *Teazer*'s eight dories disappeared into the foaming waves.

Chaos reigned below. The knockdown flung the men in the windward berths across the forecastle, where they crashed into those on the opposite side. The rush of water through the partially closed companionway flooded the lower leeward berths. The galley stove tipped over and started a fire, but with water everywhere, the men soon doused it. When the stove went over, the kettles full of boiling water

---

41 Bruce Armstrong, *Sable Island: Nova Scotia's Mysterious Island of Sand* (Toronto: Doubleday Canada Ltd., 1981), annotates 245 shipwrecks on the island between 1583 and 1947.

acted almost as if they had a mind of their own, and all landed on one poor man, Charley Strobel, severely burning and scalding him.

With the schooner still on her beam ends and her keel clearly visible to anyone insane enough to peer over the side, Dunsky ordered some of the crew on deck to try and get her back on an even keel, while he and the others tended to Strobel's terrible suffering. The first man to get his head above the companionway, George Braggs, stopped short when he saw the masts begin to rise up out of the raging sea. If that sight was not sufficiently heart-stopping, what Braggs heard and saw next was incomprehensible. As the mainmast broke free from the wavetops and the schooner started to come upright, she let out such a groan that Braggs thought the hull was breaking up. After a moment, seeing that she held together, he crawled the rest of the way out of the hatch and there, perched in the mainmast crosstrees sixty feet above the deck, was one of their dories. The *Teazer*, with nothing but her tattered riding sails aloft, rolled crazily in the criss-crossing waves. Braggs and the men behind him gazed fearfully above them as the dory swung back and forth over their heads. Gathering their wits, they set about clearing the wreckage, putting fishes–splints–on the boom and gaffs, and replacing the fluttering remnants of canvas.

The *Teazer*'s problems had only just begun. With Sable Island under her lee, Dunsky had to get the schooner moving to gain steerageway. Forgetting any thought of completing the voyage, the skipper put the helm down and, using the few scraps of canvas remaining in his sail locker, headed south. After making his way home in a following sea on a dead run, Dunsky brought the *Teazer*, sheathed in a solid coating of ice, up Boston harbor on the morning of 6 February. She looked more like a runaway iceberg than a trim fishing schooner.[42]

For souvenirs of their near-disaster the crew kept pieces of the dory they had hacked out of the crosstrees and, as a reminder of the capsized forecastle, a mustard jug remained firmly stuck into the overhead of their living quarters. With a nod to endurance as well as safety, the *Teazer* lived on in the North Atlantic for another thirty-seven years, until, during a sealing voyage on 25 March 1948, off St. Paul's Island, the winter ice trapped her forever.

---

[42] Two and a half years later the *Rex*, a 1908 McManus round-bow schooner, lost four of her six dories when a heavy fog blanketed the Gully. In a comparatively calm sea, the anchor stock separated from the anchor and the *Rex* began to drift. Twenty dorymen in ten dories, blinded by the mist, could not find their errant mother ship. They drove their dories over the water as strenuously as possible, stopping occasionally to gain their bearings from the ship's bell, which the captain and the cook, the only remaining souls on board, kept ringing frantically. After a chase of 10 miles, six of the dories came up with the *Rex*. But four failed to find her. Three of the lost boats, after the men had rowed them for twenty-nine hours, reached the coastal village of Branch, Newfoundland. The fog swallowed the fourth, never to be heard of again.

While the *Teazer* survived to an unusual age, the *Rex* did not. The Glasgow-built Cunard Liner *Tuscania* rammed the star-struck fisherman on 28 June 1925, cutting her in half with the loss of fifteen lives. *Tuscania*'s boats rescued nine others (Thomas, *Fast & Able*, 145).

Safe in the suburban confines of Dorchester, Tom, now working full-time from his studio at 29 Mill Street, reached another milestone in his career on 10 May 1906. He completed the plans for his first yacht, the schooner *Eclipse*, for an experienced New York yachtsman, publisher Lawrence J. Callanan. She was a spoon-bow schooner barely distinguishable from her fishing-schooner cousins, except in her white hull and yachty appointments below: a large airy salon, finished in quartered oak with bronze-toned plush upholstery. The *Eclipse* had a straight run of keel with a *Helen B. Thomas*-like knuckle forward. She also featured that long-time McManus family innovation–outside ballast.

During her first racing season, 1907, *Eclipse* proved her worth, winning the New York Yacht Club's Bennett Cup for schooners by upsetting two notable Herreshoff-design racing schooners, the new *Queen* and the 1903 *Ingomar*, during the club's sixteenth annual regatta on 20 July.[43] At eighty-five feet overall, with a sixty-two-foot waterline length, the *Eclipse* gave away twenty-five and thirty feet of waterline, respectively, and forty-six feet overall to the *Ingomar* and *Queen*. A member of both the Atlantic and New York Yacht Clubs, Callanan also won the N.Y.Y.C.'s Navy Cup for schooners in 1908. He once commented: "When designing her Mr. McManus claimed that he could get more speed out of her if he was permitted to have his own way. I wanted the boat first for comfort and seaworthiness, and second for speed."[44] Despite this limitation, the *Eclipse*'s racing record amply proves that McManus provided both comfort and speed.[45]

---

[43] John Parkinson, Jr., *The History of the New York Yacht Club*, 2 vols., (New York: New York Yacht Club, 1975), 1:219.

[44] *Callanan's Magazine* 9:6 (June, July 1906):6.

[45] Callanan sailed *Eclipse* for the rest of his life. After his 1913 death, *Eclipse*, then equipped with a 37-horsepower kerosene engine went to a new owner in Savannah. She disappeared from the registers about 1920 (New York *Times* obituary, 18 October 1913, p. 13, col. 4; 1916 *Merchant Vessels of the U.S.*).

CHAPTER TWELVE

The *Pontiac,* Oriole, and *Arethusa*

During the summer of 1906, in response to a commission from a syndicate headed by Boston fish dealer George F. Grueby, Tom drafted the lines for the *Pontiac,* his fourth knockabout and, by his own system of enumeration, his one hundred and eleventh design.[1] On the assumption that he began the count with the completion of the plans for the *James S. Steele* in 1889, the average number of drafts per year would amount to six and a half. But it is unlikely that he produced more than eleven designs before 1898, suggesting that he averaged about twelve models a year between 1898 and 1906. The more than

The 147-ton semi-knockabout *Clintonia* (109x25.1x11.9 feet) was launched in 1907, three years after McManus completed her plans. Lying here among the mackerel fleet at Provincetown in August 1912, she shows off the big rig for which she was so well known. Photograph by Henry D. Fisher. (M.S.M. 76.208.217A)

[1] The *Pontiac's* Plan No. 111 is the lowest identified plan number yet discovered. Plan No. 108 exists, but it is for an unidentified vessel, and is marked "for Atlantic Maritime Company." It could conceivably be the *Clara G. Silva,* launched by the A.D. Story yard in July 1906, or the *Hortense* launched at the same yard, also in 1906.

three hundred plans McManus produced during the next two decades implies a work rate of fifteen new designs a year. Of the 110 plans that preceded the *Pontiac*, only 58 have been identified with any degree of certainty.

In the *Pontiac*, the culmination of the first quarter of McManus's career–launched four years after the introduction of the knockabout–he finally reached the goal he had sought for so long–the creation of a utilitarian workboat that not only eliminated the "widow-maker," but also overcame the predominant profitability criticism leveled against this radical design departure. Professor Frisbee could at last be proud of his star pupil–the *Pontiac* proved that McManus's knockabout concept could make sound economic sense in the relationship between construction cost, cargo capacity, and return on investment.

Unlike the *Helen B. Thomas*, *Alcyone*, and *Thomas A. Cromwell*, the new schooner embodied the attributes that McManus had so struggled to amalgamate into an attractive and paying proposition. While retaining the long stern counter, Tom gave up on the extended bow and eliminated the waste of space in the forebody that led to expensive construction costs without delivering an appropriate increase in hold capacity. This latest knockabout model leaves no doubt that Tom had received the message sent by Oxner & Story's short-bowed and relatively burdensome *Shepherd King*. Because McManus also gave up on the idea of incorporating the steeve of the bowsprit into the hull, the *Pontiac* lacked the ponderously angular, nose-in-the-air appearance of the *Thomas* and *Cromwell*. With her shorter overhang, graceful sheerline, and low freeboard, the *Pontiac* was the first eye-pleasing, efficient, and economical knockabout.

How did Tom achieve this paragon–this model which "soon became McManus's standard treatment of the design of knockabouts"?[2] A comparison of the *Pontiac*'s lines to those of the *Helen B. Thomas*, a design with no offspring, and the Indian Header *Matchless*, which sired the *Annie Perry*, *Rose Dorothea*, *Mary C. Santos*, *Jessie Costa*, and *Josephine DeCosta*, among others, provides a large portion of the answer. The *Pontiac*'s buttock lines more closely approximate the *Matchless* than the *Thomas*. In fact, the *Pontiac* and *Matchless* are similar in all proportions, although the former, in an obvious attempt to add carrying capacity and forward buoyancy, has a bit fuller bow section. The *Pontiac* is moderately fuller aft than the *Matchless*, but markedly more so than the *Thomas*. McManus moved the *Pontiac*'s masts much further aft, and stepped them closer together, thus providing a higher aspect foresail. Clearly, the Indian Header design, as evolved since 1898, played strongly in Tom's thinking as he laid out the *Pontiac*.

---

[2] Howard I. Chapelle, *The American Fishing Schooners 1825-1925* (New York: W.W. Norton, 1973), 270.

The new knockabout was the first one built at Gloucester, and also one of the first McManus designs to be balanced for auxiliary power, although it appears that John Bishop, who built her, did not install an engine before she went down his ways into the narrow waters of Vincent's Cove. The *Pontiac's* long, full counter allowed Tom to tuck the propeller aperture beneath the stern section and far enough forward to place the point of propulsion under auxiliary power forward of her wheel.

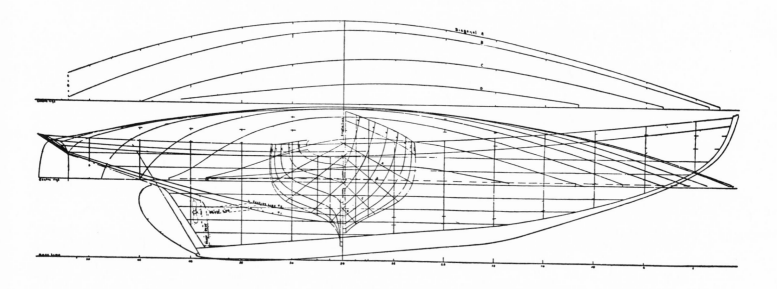

On 13 September 1906, with the drafts for the *Pontiac* completed and sent off to Cape Ann, Tom's burgeoning family gathered at home in Dorchester to celebrate his fiftieth birthday. After a half-century of life, in an era when this meant old age for so many, he had just reached his prime. McManus's daughters, the famous "Boston Belles," continued to attract a pride of beaus, but not without some suffering along the way. Margaret had married Joe Quinlan, and almost immediately became a widow, when he died in an operating table mishap while she was pregnant with their first child. Grace married Joe Miller, and Alice, the family athlete, had begun training to become a physical education instructor in the Dorchester school system.

A few weeks after her father's birthday, Letitia, the third of Tom and Kate's daughters to walk down the aisle, wed Henry Pope Carruth on 4 October 1906. The groom, an M.I.T. graduate in chemistry, was the son of Herbert Shaw Carruth, a noted local yachtsman who officiated at many of the 1880s races that Charley McManus entered with *Em'ly* and *Nora*. The Carruths came from old-line Yankee, Scots-Irish stock. Several of their antecedents served in the American Revolution. The family had gradually moved from a provincial agrarian livelihood to an urban industrial one, where they met with considerable success in the paper manufacturing industry.

Lines of the 115-ton *Pontiac* (96x23.7x11 feet), the first of McManus's short-bow knockabouts and a very successful schooner.

239

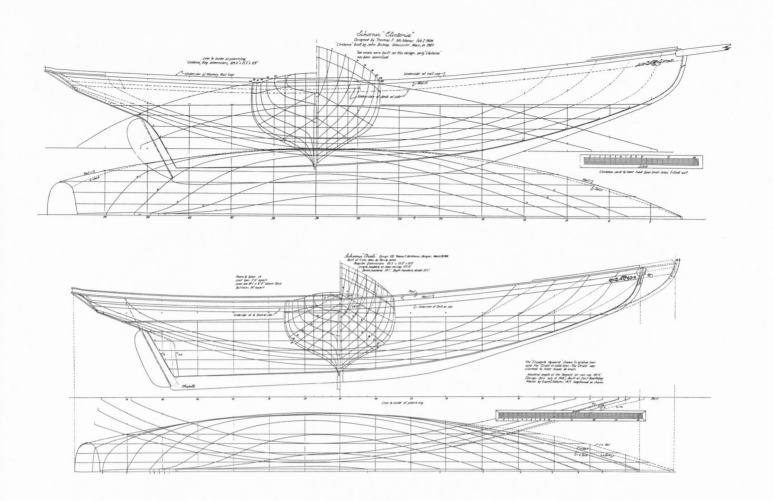

In his plans for the semi-knockabouts *Clintonia (top)* and *Oriole*, McManus produced large and powerful sailing hulls. The dotted lines on the *Oriole* plan show how the design was elongated to produce the knockabout *Elizabeth Howard*. Drawn by Howard I. Chapelle. (*Clintonia*, Plan AFS 113; *Oriole*, Plan AFS 119, Smithsonian Institution)

The rallying call for another fishermen's race sounded again late in 1906. The saga of the fifth fishermen's race began when Ned Boynton, the long-ago sailing partner of Tom's brother Charley, gained command of the Boston Yacht Club. During November, he presided over a grand banquet at the Algonquin Club honoring Sir Thomas Lipton.[3] The British tea magnate, famous in the annals of yachting for his five America's Cup challengers, all named *Shamrock*, made McManus's acquaintance during that occasion.

According to Tom, Sir Thomas "asked me to show him some of my celebrated fishing schooners, which I did."

Unknown to them, the following morning's papers announced that the pair would be visiting T Wharf, where two-thirds of the sixty schooners in port were from McManus's designs. Tom described what happened next: "When we got to the wharf it was crowded with people . . . I was looking at the masts and could tell that about 60 per cent of the vessels in were from my designs. Moored off into the harbor were about five more of mine. We walked across the deck of one vessel to

---

[3] Paul E. Shanabrook, *The Boston (A History of the Boston Yacht Club), 1866-1978* (Boston: Boston Yacht Club, 1978), 64.

another, the *Louisa R. Silva* of Provincetown, owned by a Portuguese. I knew the vessel would be in good clean shape, because boats owned by the Portuguese are always spick and span."

These comments were not at all unusual. Tom often expressed his profound respect for the Portuguese fishermen. He always believed that, in their hands, his schooners would reflect perfection in condition, handling, sailing qualities, and fishing success.

Returning to Tom's narrative: "We went on board and asked for the captain. I took the others into the cabin and their eyes opened up–at the linoleum floor, portieres, and pictures."

As they passed through the after cabin Lipton paused to exclaim, "look," pointing to the quality of the interior joinerwork, "this is as good as I have in my own house back home."

A beaming Joe Silva, the captain and owner, resumed the tour, and led the way to the forecastle of his two-year-old schooner, where the steward, after being introduced to the tea magnate, said hospitably: "You wanna cup a coff?"

After a moment of stunned silence, Tom, with an uncharacteristic and, therefore, unpracticed, stab at diplomacy, quickly interjected, "Thanks, but we don't drink coffee, we only drink tea."

To McManus's mortification, the Portuguese, who had served the Irishman many a cup of "coff," raised his eyebrows quizzically in full view of Sir Thomas, then shrugged, and turned to the galley stove to heat some water for tea.

Walking up the wharf together afterward, Lipton paused to look back at the *Silva*. After a pensive moment, he said to McManus: "This is the type that should be contending for the Blue Ribbon of the Sea. We spend money on yachts, and when it comes to an 18-20 knot breeze, they can't stand it."

As Tom nodded in absolute agreement, Lipton swung toward him and, with an abrupt change of subject, asked: "Were you ever in the old country, McManus?"

Tom replied, "No, but my father and mother came from there."

Lipton gave an open invitation, "I want you to come over to my London office and they will tell you where I am. I will take you to Ireland, and introduce you to lots of McManuses."

But, as Tom explained wistfully to an interviewer thirty years after the event, "I was so busy, I never could go."[4]

The tour of the stout fishing schooner not only impressed Lipton with the vessel's seaworthiness, but also excited his generous nature: "I will give you

THE PONTIAC, ORIOLE,
AND ARTHUSA

---

[4] Grace M. Goodwin, "Father of Fishermen's Races Recalls Two Invitations," *Boston Evening Transcript*, 14 March 1936.

the best Cup that I can procure in London, to be contended for by the fishermen," he promised.

Tom noted that Sir Thomas was good for his word: "He sent me a replica of it, which I put in Shuman's window. The cup itself was said to have cost $5,000."[6]

One of the first McManus schooners of 1907, the *John Hays Hammond*, was the archetypal example of the round-bow schooner with, for one of Tom's designs, an unusually long pole bowsprit. Working from the molds of the *Louisa R. Silva*, James & Tarr laid her keel on 6 March 1907.[7] An excellent model of the *John Hays Hammond* by Thomas A. Irving, the Gloucester master shipwright, now at the Cape Ann Historical Association clearly demonstrates an easing of the gripe that distinguished the round bow from the Indian Header bow. Captain Lemuel E. Spinney took time out from her maiden voyage, a halibuting trip, to sail the new schooner back and forth in front of the Hammond estate on Gloucester's Freshwater Cove, so that John Hammond, her namesake, could admire her under full sail.[8] In common with the rest of her round-bow sisters, the *Hammond* quickly earned a reputation as a swift sailer. Demonstrating the strength of her hull, the *Hammond*, groping her way through a dense fog near Sable Island on 16 April 1912, crashed into the Nova Scotian salt-banker *Uranus*. The Canadian schooner sank like a stone, while the *Hammond*, which suffered damage to her bow and the loss of her long bowsprit, survived and limped back to Gloucester. Five years later she was not so lucky. A German U-boat gunned her down on 27 July 1917.[9]

In terms of ancestral lines, back on 2 February 1904 Tom had completed a design that, though nearly stillborn, survived to produce some famous progeny. The plans of the semi-knockabout that became the *Clintonia* had gathered dust under his drafting table for three years until they came to the attention of Gloucester's John Bishop during their initial discussions about the *Pontiac*.[10] Although the *Clintonia* gained a considerable reputation for herself after Bishop launched her in 1907, with some alterations her model supplied the basis for two designs that garnered enduring fame: the *Oriole* of 1908–plan 132–and the *Elizabeth Howard* of 1916–plan 132a–one of the fastest of the big knockabouts. In the opinion of

[5] The large clothing emporium, A. Shuman & Co., 440 Washington Street (City Directory, 1907).

[6] McManus, "Essay No. 4."

[7] James Yard Book in the possession of Dana A. Story.

[8] Thomas, *Fast & Able*, 136.

[9] Andrew W. German, *Down on T Wharf: The Boston Fisheries as Seen Through the Photographs of Henry D. Fisher* (Mystic, Connecticut: Mystic Seaport Museum, 1982), 40.

[10] "I am fortunate to have in my possession the original construction plan of *Clintonia*, given to me by Charles McManus, son of the famous designer" (Gordon W. Thomas, *Fast & Able, Life Stories of Great Gloucester Fishing Vessels* (Gloucester, Massachusetts: Gloucester 350th Anniversary Celebration, Inc., 1973), 135).

Gordon Thomas, son of Captain Jeff Thomas, "the schooner *Oriole* was the most beautiful of them all, even including the yacht-like racers that came later. She was a typical fisherman, but there was something special about her, even the set of her sails, that made her what the fishermen called her, 'the beautiful *Oriole*.'"[11]

Fourteen years after Tom completed the *Clintonia*'s plans, Frank Adams from the famous East Boothbay, Maine, firm of W. I. Adams & Son, would revive them again, have Tom add a knockabout bow, and build the stately *Elizabeth Howard*, the "White Ghost of the Maine Coast."[12] The encomium was a justly-earned tribute to her exceptional swiftness and sparkling color. The ultimate hull speed of the later fishing schooners reached sixteen knots under sail, and the *Howard*'s skippers often claimed this rate. It is imperative when following this design trend to remember that although the *Clintonia* got afloat in 1907, Tom completed her plans in 1904. The design evolution from the *Clintonia* to the *Oriole* is clear–amounting chiefly to enlarged versions of the *Clintonia*'s sections.

The *Clintonia* also provided the model for her namesake. The Lunenburg, Nova Scotia, firm of Smith & Rhuland launched the Canadian version during March 1908. The *Clintonia* of Canada was identical in every way to her Yankee sister and gained the same reputation as a flyer. Captain Paddy Mack brought her into Gloucester on 1 September 1908 and delivered a fare of 300,000 pounds of salt cod to the Gorton-Pew Fisheries Company.[13]

At Boston, the competition that resulted from Sir Thomas Lipton's generous donation of the costly silver cup the previous autumn, not surprisingly, became known as the Lipton Challenge Cup Fishermen's Race. McManus served as its chairman. This popularly acclaimed event took place on 1 August 1907, during Boston's Old Home Week, which ran from 28 July through 3 August that year. In addition to the cup, Tom secured over $2,000 in prize money, guaranteeing all the participants at least a full day's pay. Entries addressed to him at No. 6 T Wharf included a broad sampling of the 300-strong Boston and Gloucester fishing fleets.[14] But, to the amazement of the committee, as well as the entire waterfront community, on the day of the race, only the *Jessie Costa*, *Rose Dorothea*, *James W. Parker*, *Frances P. Mesquita*, and *Helen B. Thomas* appeared. Reporting the race, *The Rudder* magazine commented: "The owners of available vessels which Mr. McManus

---

11 Thomas, *Fast & Able*, 142.

12 Perhaps seeking pleasing alliteration, Chapelle refers to the *Elizabeth Howard* as the "Gray Ghost" (*Fishing Schooners*, 261), but her actual hull color was snowy white, and contemporary newspaper accounts called her the "White Ghost of the Maine Coast."

13 Thomas, *Fast & Able*, 136.

14 Entry form in the possession of Ann McManus, the widow of William Kenneth McManus.

With her distinctive profile, the *Helen B. Thomas* was a speedy vessel, but the larger and notably fast *Frances P. Mesquita* outsailed her during the 1907 Lipton Cup race. Photograph by Willard B. Jackson. (Courtesy Peabody & Essex Museum, Salem, Massachusetts)

did not design chose unanimously, *for reasons of their own*, to keep out of the race."[15] If ever there was a telling contemporary comment about the swift sailing qualities of McManus's Indian Headers, knockabouts, and round-bow types, this was it. And, ironically, another pair of McManus stalwarts, the Indian Headers *Manomet* of 1900 and *Manhassett* of 1902, missed the race because they came in late from the fishing grounds. It was a close thing for the former schooner. She actually passed through the racers on her way up to Boston to discharge her fare of mackerel.

The committee divided the five McManus-designed starters (representing three distinct design types) by waterline length. Those above eighty-five feet included the *Rose Dorothea*, Captain Marion Perry, and the *Jessie Costa*, Captain Manuel Costa, from the Portuguese fleet based at Provincetown. Both had lengthy, but similar, lineages. The *Annie Perry* was the grandmother of the *Jessie Costa* and the mother of the *Rose Dorothea*, which had, from a racing point of view, a telling advantage–ten feet of additional length.[16] James & Tarr built the *Jessie Costa* from

---

15 *The Rudder* 18 (November 1907): 824, emphasis added.

16 "Agreed with Capt. Marion Perry to build him a new Sch. from lines of Sch. *Annie C. Perry* to be made 10 ft. longer" (James Yard Book).

the molds of the *Mary C. Santos*, which they had built from the lines of the *Annie Perry*, but with a slight increase in beam and sheer. The *Annie Perry* was a replica of the *Matchless* model, but with "everything 1st class." The *Matchless* had been built from the lines of the *Flora S. Nickerson*, which herself came from "a new model by Thomas F. McManus of Boston."[17]

The *James W. Parker*, Captain Valentine O'Neil, of Gloucester, was the third vessel in the over-eighty-five-feet category, a 1905 round-bow schooner. The second class consisted of another 1905 round-bow type, the *Frances P. Mesquita*, Captain Joseph P. Mesquita, also of Provincetown, and the old lady of the racing fleet–the original knockabout–the *Helen B. Thomas*, Captain Billy Thomas, Boston-based and now five years old.

The course ran from Thieves Ledge, two and a half miles off Boston Lighthouse, to Davis Ledge off Minot's Ledge Lighthouse, to Eastern Point at Gloucester, and back, a total distance of thirty-nine miles. Light wind conditions, plus the late arrival of the *Thomas* (which had come in from the banks a few hours earlier, unceremoniously dumped her fish onto T Wharf, and dropped down the harbor), delayed the warning gun from 10:00 until 11:00 A.M.

There was an air of levity about the whole affair, for the fishermen considered it a great lark. Val O'Neil, perhaps remembering the Irish tradition of his boyhood established by Captain Johnny O'Brien in the *John H. McManus* during the late 1880s, had a barrel of beer and a band on board the *Parker*, whose players "banged and tooted bravely, until the sea came up a bit, then the musicians lost interest."[18] A morning southwest breeze promised a fair race, but nothing, of course, like 1892's "Race That Blew."

Under bright, clear skies and a warm sun, the southwest wind faded just before the start, catching the fishermen above the line when the ten-minute gun went off. The fleet filled away on starboard tack and drifted slowly down. A big flotilla of pleasure craft and excursion steamers increased the problems the skippers faced. At first clustered around the start, a number of these spectator craft then followed the racers around the entire course. Several took a short cut on the final leg to clog the finish line as the big fishing schooners completed the course.

With the exception of the *Thomas*, whose weary crew did not hoist a fore topsail at any time in the race, all flew fore and main gaff topsails as they came down to the start. In true yacht-racing fashion all five had their jib topsails, which they called ballooners, ready to break out as soon as they passed the committee boat. Leaving nothing to chance, Captain Perry of the *Rose Dorothea* went a step

---

[17] James Yard Book.

[18] Ibid.

With a subdued band on board, the *James W. Parker* competes in the 1907 Lipton Cup race. A round-bow schooner, the 132-ton *Parker* (101x24.4x11.6 feet) was launched at Essex in 1905. Photograph by Willard B. Jackson. (Courtesy Peabody & Essex Museum, Salem, Massachusetts)

further. Grinning from behind the helm was none other than professional racing skipper Johnny Watson of Duxbury, a nephew of another yacht racer, Nate Watson, the captain of the famous *Constellation*.[19] To everyone's surprise, except her crew, during the jockeying for position before the start the *Jessie Costa*, despite giving away eleven feet of waterline length, clearly outfooted the *Rose Dorothea*.

As Watson brought the *Rose Dorothea* to the line, his skill and experience paid off. He made a move that offset the smaller but faster *Costa*'s straightline speed by driving the *Rose Dorothea* through the smaller schooner's lee, forcing Manuel Costa to tack away from the line. Defying the light airs, Watson brought his schooner over the line within five seconds of the first-class gun. Albert Cook Church, who was on board the *Jessie Costa*, described the result of Watson's tactics: "We found ourselves a quarter of a mile from the line headed in the opposite direction with only a minute to go. It was a fatal mistake."[20] Crossing four minutes later, the *Jessie Costa* sailed along in the leader's wake eating away at her lead. The

[19] McManus, "Essay No. 4"; James F. McNally, "The Fisherman's Race," *Yachting* 2 (November 1907): 274; Albert Cook Church, "The Great Race Between the *Rose Dorothea* and *Jessie Costa*," *Atlantic Fisherman* 5 (March 1924):1, 10, 26-27.

[20] Church, "The Great Race," 26.

first-class race became a two boat affair. Within five minutes they opened a commanding lead over the noisy *James W. Parker*. Bad luck, however, had not abandoned the *Costa*. With her superior hull speed, she steadily cut into the *Rose Dorothea's* advantage. But, when Costa brought his schooner within striking distance of Watson's, her jib topsail halyard parted in the strengthening wind and cost another two minutes for repairs.

The story of the first two legs was one of shifting winds. They were light to strong with a southeast sea breeze at the start, backing to east-southeast, and then building and veering to south-southwest as the race unfolded. Sea conditions were relatively smooth, "but toward the latter part of the race there was a nice chop with a lively jump to it, which gave life and animation to the going."[21] While the schooners worked down the five-mile leg to Davis Ledge, the wind began to come off the land, bringing a westerly lift with strength enough to heel them over and dip their scuppers into the sea. As soon as the wind shifted, the two leaders doused their kites and raced to the mark with only slightly started sheets, having averaged nearly nine knots from Thieves Ledge to Davis Ledge. Showing her speed to perfection, the *Costa* made up more that four of the six minutes she had handed to the *Rose Dorothea*. The second class, which the *Thomas* had led over the line, was not so fortunate. The changed wind direction caught them dead wrong. It headed the *Thomas* first, allowing the *Mesquita* to make up lost ground, although along with the *Parker* they had to tack to fetch the mark.

Fleet times at Davis Ledge were: *Rose Dorothea* 11:45:51, *Jessie Costa* 11:47:42, *James W. Parker*, with a crew of beer quaffers engaged more in laughing and singing than trimming of sheets, 11:51:43, and *Helen B. Thomas*, 12:01:52, with the *Frances P. Mesquita* still trailing the field.

The eighteen-mile run from the first mark to the whistling buoy off Eastern Point was a wing-and-wing affair with main booms out to port and foresails jibed over to starboard. What had begun to look like a runaway changed dramatically during the second leg. Making ground on the *Rose Dorothea* as they headed toward Gloucester, Manuel Costa, obviously unimpressed by the supposedly superior yacht racing talents of Johnny Watson, ran him down. He brought the *Costa* to a commanding position on the *Rose Dorothea's* weather quarter and then, unbelievably, handed the helm to one of his crewman and went below for a cup of coffee! Alertly, Watson spotted the change, swung his foresails to leeward, and began a series of luffs to windward. When he saw that the *Costa's* stand-in helmsman failed to respond to these challenges, Watson pointed the *Rose Dorothea* sharply to weather and drove through the *Costa's* lee. Although he never got close

21 McNally, "The Fisherman's Race," 274.

Driving toward the finish line, the *Jessie Costa* trails the *Rose Dorothea*. With her topsails and staysails set, she can not point as high as the *Rose Dorothea*. The speedy 130-ton *Costa* (102.5x24.6x11.6 feet) was launched at Essex in 1905. Photograph by Nathaniel L. Stebbins. (Courtesy The Society for the Preservation of New England Antiquities, Boston, Massachusetts)

enough to take part in the fray, the one-sided luffing match between the front-runners allowed Val O'Neil to close in with the curiously quiet *James W. Parker*. Her merry band of musicians had exchanged their instruments for places along the lee rail where, with gray faces, they leaned over and donated their breakfasts to King Neptune.

After his two-hour tussle with the *Jessie Costa*, Watson, from his now controlling position, backwinded his opponent at the Eastern Point mark and swung the *Rose Dorothea* around it in a freshening breeze. His lead had dwindled to thirty-five seconds, but every one of those that remained had been held through superior racing skill. In the second class, "Smoky Joe" Mesquita passed Billy Thomas coming into the whistler, and turned it with more than a minute in hand over his worn-out competitor.

The fleet times at Eastern Point were: *Rose Dorothea* 1:51:47, *Costa* 1:52:22, *Parker* 2:04:58, *Mesquita* 2:14:00, and *Thomas*, 2:15:10.

As the leaders left Gloucester in their wakes at the beginning of the final leg, the real drama of the day began. Just as the *Rose Dorothea* hauled her wind coming round the mark, her fore-topmast snapped with a resounding crack. Before Johnny Watson and Marion Perry realized they had a potential disaster on their hands, a cheer rose from the decks of the *Jessie Costa* as Manuel Costa, now once again at her helm, had his crewmen tail the sheets to flatten the sails for the first tack toward home. On board the *Rose Dorothea* the broken mast brought down the fore-topsail and jib topsail. When he realized what had happened, Watson swung the *Rose Dorothea* head to wind and then fell off close-hauled while the crew cleared away the wreckage and doused the useless topsails. Exhibiting supreme confidence, they never sent down the broken spar, but chose to leave it dangling aloft as a badge of adversity. She continued under main and foresail, main-topsail, staysail, jib, and jumbo.

For awhile, it looked like the race was over, but fate, in the form of yet another windshift, evened things out for the final beat to the finish. The wind, south at the moment the *Rose Dorothea* lost her mast, veered steadily to the west, insuring at least one more tack before the leaders could fetch the line. Against all conventional sailing strategy, the loss of her topsails, coupled with Watson's unrivaled talent, won the day for the *Rose Dorothea*. With the *Rose Dorothea*'s accidentally reduced rig, Watson now commanded the faster footer.

The whole fleet sailed a long port reach past the North Shore and did not come about until they were almost to Nahant. Once again close in with the land, the wind, a wholesale breeze by now, came sharply out of the west. As the leaders tacked for home, the *Rose Dorothea*, sailing more closely hauled, outpointed the *Jessie Costa*, whose ballooning jib topsail perceptibly pulled her down to leeward. When they steadied on course from Nahant to the Thieves Ledge finish line, barely six boat lengths separated them. The longer *Rose Dorothea* drove through the choppy waters handsomely, neck and neck with the *Jessie Costa*, which continued to crab to leeward. In the end, his baggy jib topsail cost Manuel Costa the race. Johnny Watson was able to inch the *Rose Dorothea* just inside the leeward end of the line, but her adversary fell thirty yards to leeward of the mark, and Costa had to throw in a pair of quick tacks to finish.

"The race between *Rose Dorothea* and *Jessie Costa* was one of the best ever sailed between fishing vessels in Massachusetts Bay," proclaimed *Yachting*. "After the race, with a broom lashed to her broken fore topmast, and another at the main truck, the American ensign and her name on a gaudy streamer floating out astern from under her main peak, *Rose Dorothea* swept proudly up Boston harbor."[22] In the smaller class, the *Frances P. Mesquita* never relinquished the lead she gained at Eastern Point, and picked up another minute on the *Helen B. Thomas* during the final beat.

The *Rose Dorothea*'s victory brought Provincetown to the forefront of the fishermen's races, which had been dominated by schooners from Boston and

---

22 McNally, "The Fisherman's Race," 273.

Gloucester until then. The townspeople were so proud of her success that they erected a monument in front of the Town Hall. The artist sculpted an image of the *Rose Dorothea* into a boulder, and engraved the following words below it:

> *ROSE DOROTHEA*
> This stone commemorates the victory of the schooner *Rose Dorothea*, captained by Marion Perry, and crew, at the Old Home Week celebration in Boston 1907.
>
> This cup given by Sir Thomas Lipton for the winner of this race can be seen in the Provincetown Town Hall.
>
> This stone erected by popular subscription through the efforts of the Portuguese American Civic League.

Despite the pleasing success of this event, many years would pass before another fishermen's race would take place, and then the impetus would come not from Boston, Gloucester, or Provincetown, but rather from Canada.

Later in August 1907, Tom made the acquaintance of Theodore Roosevelt when the president traveled to Provincetown to lay the cornerstone of the Pilgrim's Memorial Monument on the twentieth. The organizers included a formal luncheon at the town hall, and, unbeknownst to the volatile hero of San Juan Hill, charged people $1.50 to sit in the balcony and watch him eat. As soon as he learned why the silent throng was there, "T.R." foiled the enterprise by gulping down his soup and stalking out of the building. Outside, he returned to the plan of the day by greeting 250 fishermen from the largely Portuguese Provincetown fleet, and 100 others who sailed down from Boston for the occasion.

James B. Connolly, the popular chronicler of Gloucester fishing tales, inherited the job of master of ceremonies and, according to him, the president "instructed me to be sure to particularize the deeds of the notable skippers as they came along."[23] After shaking hands with the fishermen, T.R. gave a brief speech that opened by recognizing the Puritan's place in American history, but soon switched to his favorite topics, "trust-busting" and federal control of interstate commerce: "I believe in a national incorporation law for corporations engaged in interstate commerce," he stumped, pointing out how the railroads had been brought under federal control, and proposing to travel further down that line by bringing

---

[23] James B. Connolly, *The Book of the Gloucester Fishermen* (New York: John Day Company, 1930), 215.

The 157-ton *Arethusa* (114x25.6x12.5 feet) was the largest and fastest knockabout in the New England fleet for nearly ten years. Henry D. Fisher photographed her at T Wharf early in 1914. (M.S.M. 76.208.75B)

Lines of the *Arethusa*, drawn by Howard I. Chapelle. (Plan AFS 118A, Smithsonian Institution)

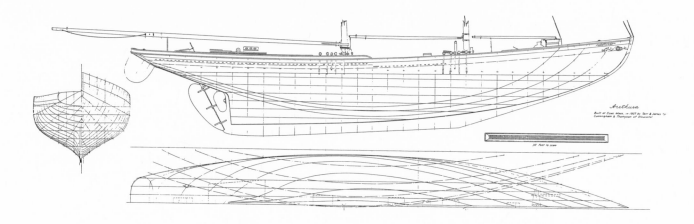

them under the tighter type of supervision the government exercised over the national banks. But he made no mention of fishing, fishing bounties, or trade relations with Canada, subjects of vital interest to his audience.[24]

In fraternizing with the fishermen after the speech, Roosevelt learned the results of the recently completed fishermen's race and asked to meet both the winners and the organizer. Captain Marion Perry of the *Rose Dorothea*, overcome by shyness, would not come ashore, so Tom covered for him and narrated the story of the race. When the afternoon came to an end, the president asked Governor Curtis Guild of Massachusetts to bring McManus to him again.

---

[24] Theodore Roosevelt, *Presidential Addresses and State Papers* (New York: The Review of Reviews Company, 1910), 6:1345-64.

The 94-ton *Athena* (100.5x22.6x9.8 feet) represented one of the variations on the knockabout form launched in 1908. Photograph by A.A. Acores. (Courtesy Peabody & Essex Museum, Salem, Massachusetts)

When the designer came up, the President said to him, "I have just heard that you are the father of twelve children. That's wonderful. Bring them all down to the White House and I will give them a great time."

But as satisfying as this recognition from the nation's chief executive was, Tom politely declined for the very down-to-earth reason that he "was building eight and ten ships at a time and, of course, could not go to Washington."[25]

His refusal again illustrates McManus's prolific design capability. In the eighteen-month period between completing the *Pontiac* and finishing the *Oriole* on 28 March 1908, he drafted twenty-two new vessels. This in addition to the demands on his time for superintending construction and managing the fitting-out of the new vessels.

While John Bishop built the semi-knockabout *Clintonia* at Gloucester for Orlando Merchant and Captain Charley Harty, James & Tarr laid down their first knockabout, the *Arethusa*, at Essex. They completed her on 25 September 1907. Fifteen feet longer than the *Pontiac*, the *Arethusa* was, nevertheless, a deep, short-ended knockabout, with the typically knuckled straight run of keel (although with less drag), that Tom favored in this class, fuller quarters, and more tumblehome. Once again, he experimented with the rig. He stepped the foremast farther forward

---

[25] *Boston Evening Transcript*, 14 March 1936.

with the masts further apart. Right from the start, the big new fisherman earned a reputation as a speedster.[26] Captain Clayton Morrison, the *Arethusa*'s first skipper waxed poetic: "She's the slickest bit of wood that ever went down to Bay of Islands. Nothing can touch her and an eight-year-old girl's little finger is stout enough to spin the wheel no matter how fresh it breezes." "Can she sail?" exclaimed Captain Morrissey, opening his eyes as if he didn't quite believe his ears. "Why, when we were coming up from the herring grounds she cut out her 13 knots an hour for six consecutive hours."

"We'd see a blotch of smoke away ahead on the horizon and in a little while would make out a tramp steamer bound our way. Pretty soon the *Arethusa* was kiting alongside the tramp and then we'd lose sight of her astern. She did that trick a number of times."[27]

In fact, with Clayt Morrissey at the helm in 1912, the *Arethusa* would easily outrun the Canadian Dominion fisheries' patrol steamer *Fiona*, "whose commander opined the *Arethusa* was violating the three-mile limit." Morrissey was "a fish-killer and a sail-dragger–not the sort of dragger who carries spars away and bursts canvas just to show the other fellow how his vessel can go when it airs," wrote George Hudson in the Boston *Sunday Herald*. "Oh, no. He hangs the duds aloft until it pipes and pipes, but lowers away and furls in the nick of time and fools the gale. Morrissey is quite clever that way."[28]

By the end of 1907 the revamped knockabout type, as exemplified by the *Pontiac*, the *Arethusa*, and the longer but shallower (and less successful) *Benjamin A. Smith*, began to receive broad acceptance. But Tom, always on the lookout for safer working conditions on board fishing schooners, remained dissatisfied. With his characteristically dogged determination he steadily struggled to reach perfection in a commercial fishing schooner: "I kept on improving the fishing fleet by cutting away the dead wood fore and aft, shortening the foremast and bow sprit and then developed the popular knockabout, so all the head sails can be worked from the deck and no one going over the Knight heads on icy foot ropes, perhaps to be washed away."[29]

During 1908 the number of new knockabouts exceeded the new Indian Headers for the first time. At Boston, the *W.M. Goodspeed* was one of seven

---

[26] Although launched as a sail-powered vessel, James & Tarr built a shaft log into the *Arethusa*'s afterbody to accommodate a later conversion to mechanical power.

[27] Excerpt from an unidentifiable newspaper clipping in the possession of Ann McManus.

[28] George Hudson, "New Candidate for Cup Honors," Boston *Sunday Herald*, 5 February 1922.

[29] McManus, "Essay No. 5."

The 92-ton Indian Header *Mina Swim*
(82x23.9x9.8 feet) and 93-ton
knockabout *Ethel B. Penny*
(99.5x22.7x9.8 feet) sail plans illustrate
McManus's solution to designing a
balanced and powerful knockabout rig.
From tack of the jib forward to outhaul
of the mainsail astern, the base of the
Swim's rig was just under 130 feet; the
base of the *Penny*'s rig was eight feet
less: four feet less forward and three feet
less in the mainsail. But what the *Penny*
lost in length of sail plan she gained in
height. McManus peaked up her main
gaff to make it a more efficient high-
aspect sail and added three feet to the
topmast and the luff of the high-aspect
gaff topsail. The *Penny*'s foremast was
more dramatically different: the foot of
the foresail was half a foot shorter than
the *Swim*'s, but the luff along the mast
was five feet longer and, with the gaff
peaked up, the leech was ten feet longer.
Five additional feet of hoist in the foresail
was matched by four feet more in the gaff
topsail, giving the *Penny*'s foremast a rig
nine feet higher than the *Swim*'s. In the
fore triangle, the *Penny*'s forestaysail was
eight feet longer in the luff and ten feet
longer in the leech, and the jib was four
feet narrower in the foot, but four feet
longer in the luff and ten feet longer in
the leech. The shift from low-and-wide to
tall-and-narrow sails is evident in the
light-air canvas as well: the *Penny*'s
quadrilateral fisherman staysail between
the masts had less width but six feet more
of hoist, and the jib topsail (ballooner)
forward had a foot equal to the *Swim*'s,
but eight feet more in the luff and six in
the leech. (Courtesy Peabody & Essex
Museum, Salem, Massachusetts)

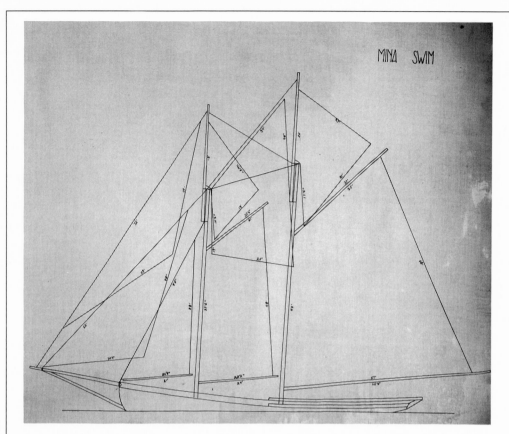

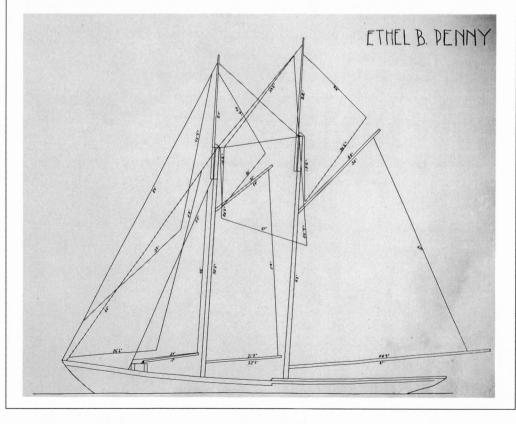

McManus and nine total new bowspritless fishing vessels delivered that year.[30] The *Goodspeed* served as the prototype for the *Ethel B. Penny* and *Athena*, and the four-foot-longer *Evelyn M. Thompson*. Some other variations on the theme included the relatively shallow, 103-foot *Victor and Ethan*, and the relatively deep, but short-ended, 89-foot *Washakie*. In these vessels, as in his long-bow semi-knockabouts, he thinned the forebody in comparison to the Indian Headers and the *Pontiac*. The width of the bow section above the waterline is narrower, but no longer than the *Pontiac*'s bow; but below the waterline, in the way of the forecastle, he designed a much shallower bow, carrying the entrance of the forebody well aft of the foremast step. To balance this reduced underwater shape–and thus reduced forward buoyancy–he persisted in moving the masts further aft and closer together. He continued his manipulation of the knockabout design's proportions with the 1908 model that became the 1910-built *Rhodora*, and the 1909 *Virginia*. Generally, his knockabouts came out between 100 and 105 feet in length, with a beam around 23 feet, and a depth of hold in the area of 10 feet.

As an example of the long-bow but short-overhang knockabout that he promoted, in the *Georgia* McManus introduced the longest forecastle–forty-two feet–built into a fishing schooner up to that time. He set the mast step for the foremast back forty-one feet ten inches from the knightheads. The mainmast stood twenty-five feet one and a half inches aft of the foremast. By comparison, the semi-knockabout *Elsie*, the next vessel the E.L. Rowe sail loft of Gloucester cut the canvas for, had a distance of thirty-four feet two inches from knightheads to foremast, and thirty-two feet seven inches between foremast and mainmast. Those dimensions compare to the Indian Headers, as exemplified by the *Quannapowatt*: twenty-three feet three inches from knightheads to foremast, and twenty-seven feet five inches from foremast to main.[31] During her working life, the *Georgia* established a record catch of pollack by bringing in 715,595 pounds during the month of May 1911, with 210,000 pounds landed from a single trip ending on 10 May.

Over the winter of 1907-08 Tom received another Canadian commission when Irving A. Lovitt of Yarmouth ordered a schooner from him. The Nova Scotian insisted she be built to the latest model, and engaged McGill Shipbuilding Ltd. of Shelburne, Nova Scotia, to complete the new vessel, which he intended for the fresh-fish trade. Joe McGill and his Master Carpenter, Amos Pentz, launched the Indian Header, *Kernwood*, on 6 April 1908.[32] Characterized in Canadian

[30] German, *Down on T Wharf*, 10. The seven McManus knockabouts in chronological order of commissioning were: *W.M. Goodspeed*, *Victor and Ethan*, *Athena*, *Matiana*, *Evelyn M. Thompson*, *Ethel B. Penny*, and *Washakie*.

[31] All dimensions originate from the three-volume set of "Dimention Books, E.L. Rowe & Son Sail Loft" in the possession of Erik A.R. Ronnberg, Jr. The *Georgia* and the *Elsie* are in volume 2, the former on page 262, and the latter on page 260.

[32] Once again the author must acknowledge his gratitude to the research efforts of Harold G. Simms.

The new 78-ton *Washakie* (89x21.2x10 feet), a small but deep knockabout, stretches her canvas and her rig on a blustery day in Boston Harbor. The man in the bowler standing right aft resembles Tom McManus. Photograph by Nathaniel L. Stebbins, 12 November 1908. (Courtesy The Society for the Preservation of New England Antiquities, Boston, Massachusetts)

newspaper rhetoric as "a specially constructed vessel in every way, and nothing has been omitted in her build or outfit to make her the finest schooner ever fitted out in Canada,"[33] the *Kernwood*–not to be confused with the Boston schooner of the same name–enjoyed a productive career. During 1908, the McGill yard produced at least two other McManus designs, the Indian Header *Albert J. Lutz*,[34] and the semi-knockabout *Arginia*, the first of this type to be built north of the border. This marked a change in attitude for Canadian owners. Up to this point, they had been contented with broad, deep, burdensome, salt-bankers, which were infinitely well-suited to their alternate occupation of transporting cargoes of salted fish to the West Indies and the Mediterranean countries.

---

33 Halifax, Nova Scotia, *Morning Chronicle*, 27 April 1908.

34 Frederick William Wallace, *Roving Fisherman* (Gardenvale, Quebec: Canadian Fishermen, 1955), 2, 130. Although Wallace, one of her owners, referred to the *Albert J. Lutz* as a "round-bow, semi-knockabout," photographs show that she was a typical Indian Header.

WRECK OF THE MATIANA. NO. SCITUATE, MASS. FEB. 12, 1910.

The underwater profile of a McManus knockabout is visible in this view of the 88-ton *Matiana* (95.3x22.5x9.5 feet), wrecked at North Scituate, Massachusetts, in February 1910, two years after her launch. (M.S.M. 90.89.1)

Photographed just before her launch at the McGill yard, the Indian Header *Albert J. Lutz*, in her fine form and finish, demonstrates the growing Canadian appreciation for McManus designs. (Courtesy Maritime Museum of the Atlantic, Halifax, Nova Scotia)

Showing off her tall rig, the *Albert J. Lutz* maneuvers for photographer Paul Yates off Digby, Nova Scotia, 29 August 1908. (Courtesy Maritime Museum of the Atlantic, Halifax, Nova Scotia)

Leandro J. Costa, Jr., a North End provision merchant, representing several investors from Boston's Portuguese community, commissioned Tom to design a schooner for his clients over the winter of 1908-09. The result–the *Mary DeCosta*–was the newest type of McManus hybrid–a round-bow hull with a semi-knockabout rig. These schooners can be identified by a gently curved stem without gripe, a relatively short bowsprit, and the anchoring of the forestay inside the knightheads, instead of to the gammon iron like the Indian Head class.

With the knockabouts firmly holding sway in the fishing fleet, the semi-knockabout an established design, the introduction of the first round-bow semi-knockabout, and over sixty Indian Headers at sea, the first decade of the twentieth century came to a close. Tom McManus had already accomplished more than any other designer of fishing schooners, and a long career still stretched ahead of the fifty-three-year-old, Boston-Irish naval architect.

The doryman's view: even with her reduced winter rig the *Albert J. Lutz* is a powerful sight as she maneuvers to pick up a dory. Notice her reefed mainsail and the furled jib triced up on the jib stay to keep it out of the seas. Frederick William Wallace photographed the *Lutz* in March 1912. (Courtesy Maritime Museum of the Atlantic, Halifax, Nova Scotia)

CHAPTER THIRTEEN

The *Elsie, Bay State, Catherine,* and *Elizabeth Howard*

Despite the tentative beginning of his naval architectural career during the 1890s, Tom McManus's productivity in the first decade of the new century overwhelmed that of his fellow practitioners. With the exception of Mel McClain's introduction of auxiliary power in the *Helen Miller Gould*, the naval architectural innovations in the fishing fleet belonged to "Captain" Tom.

Tom McManus shows his draft of a schooner to Arthur D. Story at the Story yard in Essex, 24 September 1916. In the background McManus's three-masted schooner *Olivette* takes shape. Photograph by Walter M. Naney. (Courtesy Dana Story Collection)

On a February day in 1911, the *Elsie* discharges a trip of fish at Boston's T Wharf. Salt spray ice coats her bowsprit, dories, and deck, testifying to the harsh conditions of winter dory fishing. Astern of the *Elsie* lies a steel-hulled steam trawler, representing the otter-trawl method of fishing that would supplant the techniques of the rugged dorymen and their schooners. Photo by Henry D. Fisher. (M.S.M. 76.208.639)

Arthur Binney, the designer of the impressive *Benjamin F. Phillips*, who took up Edward Burgess's practice after his death in 1891, produced few more than a dozen fishing schooner designs during the first years of the twentieth century.[1] His vessels were dimensionally large and extrapolated from the *Nellie Dixon/Fredonia* tradition of his predecessor. Binney, with the *Saladin* and *Constellation* of 1902, was the second designer to produce auxiliary-powered hulls. Despite McManus's propensity to adapt readily to change, he was slow to incorporate auxiliary power into his fishing schooner layouts.

Ned Burgess's son, W. Starling, who had yet to come into his prime, did not draft his first fisherman until 1905's large but ill-balanced *Elizabeth Silsbee*,[2] a vessel that never reached her potential. Burgess designed her as an auxiliary–with a huge 300-brake-horsepower Standard gasoline engine, but did not properly balance the hull for it–the *Silsbee* was noted for burying her long, sharp bow into a head sea and sending tons of water sweeping along her deck.[3] He compounded his error by

---

[1] 1900 *Frances Whalen* (off the *Preceptor* of 1899); 1901 *Aloha, Edna Wallace Hopper, Benjamin F. Phillips, Independence I* (off the *Frances Whalen*); 1902 *Catherine and Ellen, Constellation, Saladin*; 1904 *Independence II*; 1906 *Athlete*; 1912 *Ellen and Mary, Mary* (later the *Arthur D. Story*)

[2] Howard I. Chapelle, *The American Fishing Schooners 1825-1925* (New York: W.W. Norton, 1973), 255-59.

[3] Gordon W. Thomas, *Fast & Able, Life Stories of Great Gloucester Fishing Vessels* (Gloucester, Massachusetts: Gloucester 350th Anniversary Celebration, Inc., 1973), 107.

creating an unusual "figure eight" propeller aperture that had the effect of a drogue on the *Silsbee*'s sailing qualities.

The combined initial and operational expenses of a marine gasoline engine were prohibitive and undoubtedly held back the exploitation of this power source. The *Silsbee*'s engine, which cost $9,000, burned thirty gallons per hour and required the addition of a marine engineer (at about $75 per month) to the crew.[4] But it could drive her at a steady twelve knots under sail with two seineboats and a dory in tow, a most impressive capability. That old hand, Captain Josh Stanley, commented to a *Yachting* magazine reporter, "The [financial] burden at first was too great, and the question of whether it could be made to pay will remain unsolved,"[5] because, unfortunately, the *Silsbee*'s career only lasted three and a half years; she crashed into the rocky Nova Scotian coast near Shelburne and became a total write-off.

Later in his predominantly yacht-oriented design career, the younger Burgess laid out some of the notable *pseudo-fishermen* that disrupted the international fishermen's races of the 1920s and 1930s, including the disqualified *Mayflower*, the ill-fated *Puritan*, and the remarkable *Columbia*, which he planned in partnership with Frank C. Paine, who later designed the memorable *Gertrude L. Thebaud*.

Bowdoin B. Crowninshield, like the younger Burgess, gained more fame from racing yachts than fishing schooners, although he oversaw the design of at least twenty-five of the latter between 1900 and 1905.[6] Among them, the *Rob Roy*, *Harmony*, *Stranger*, and *Tartar* (of which Tom McManus was a shareholder) achieved a measure of recognition from fleet owners, particularly his neighboring Boston-based operators. Crowninshield introduced the spoon bow to fishing schooners; but, as is often mentioned, his most enduring characteristic was a keel with a straight run, substantial drag, and a leading knuckle. In common with McManus's early designs, he favored long forward overhangs and stern counters. A basic tenet of his design philosophy was a fine run to provide lively helm response. As a result, his hulls had comparatively straight buttock lines.

The design concepts of McManus's greatest rival, Mel McClain, who modeled two dozen or more schooners between 1900 and 1906, have been discussed

---

[4] In their advertising campaign for diesel engines, the New London Ship & Engine Company estimated that a diesel developing 180 horsepower, running 300 days per year, 10 hours per day, cost $10,806 less to operate than a gasoline engine of equal power during the same operating period, not including crew cost.

[5] George S. Goldie, "A Winter Fishing Trip to George's Shoal," *Yachting* 9 (November-December 1910): 346-50, 431-36.

[6] 1900 *Rob Roy*; 1902 *Hope, Robert and Arthur, Aloha, Bonita, Cuba, Dixie, Elmo, Fortuna*; 1903 *Harmony, Stranger, Rush, Good Hope, Hatteras, Cape Horn, Emilia Gloria, Virginia Lyons*; 1904 *Tartar, Arbutus, Muriel, Selma*; 1905 *Fame, Lillian, Wilfred L. Snow* (Canadian), *Shepherdess* (schooner yacht).

in earlier chapters.[7] McClain, perhaps because of the increasingly complex naval architectural environment, gave up designing in 1906 and returned to sea. As late as 1909, he was mackerel seining in his last creation, the *Good Luck*.[8]

A handful of other naval architects contributed to the fleet during the opening decade of the new century: J. Horace Burnham, who laid out several fishermen during the 1890s, carved the model for the *Appomattox* of 1902 and the *Dorothy II* two years later. Archibald Fenton drafted the *Tacoma*, *Yakima*, and *Claudia*. Thomas A. Irving, most noted as a master shipwright and hull modeler,[9] added another half-dozen vessels to the fleet.[10] Laurence Jensen designed the *Tattler* off his giant 162-ton *John J. Flaherty* of 1899. Dennison J. Lawlor literally spoke from beyond the grave when A.D. Story built the *George Parker* in May 1901 and James & Tarr followed with the *Annie M. Parker* that September. According to Lewis Story, both came off the *Susan R. Stone-Harry L. Belden* molds of 1888. They were the last two plumb-stemmers built for the Massachusetts fisheries. Yet, counting the production of all these designers, their combined effort falls short by more than a third of the 150 vessels that shipyards constructed to McManus's designs during that decade.

His landmark schooner *Elsie* went to sea as the century's second decade began. This big semi-knockabout lasted nearly as long as her creator, and won a fitting epitaph from Gordon Thomas: "One of the Very Greatest, 1910-1935."[11] The *Elsie* is sometimes thought to have been modeled on the lines of the *Oriole* of 1908; however, that vessel's clear differences (Plan No. 132) with the *Elsie* (Plan No. 152), particularly in the way of their underwater shapes, which are unequivocally dissimilar, establish that the *Elsie* is not a direct derivative. Additionally, their surviving plans allow a sharply focused evaluation of the manner in which Tom's thinking progressed between March 1908 and November 1909. In the *Oriole*, he reproduced a shape similar to the hollow forebody espoused by Dennison J.

---

[7] 1900 *Helen Miller Gould* (auxiliary), *Angelina*, *Dreadnought*, *Illinois* (off the *Marguerite Haskins* of 1893), *Senator Gardner*, *Lottie G. Merchant* (off the *Marguerite Haskins*), *Lucinda I. Lowell* (off the *Esther Anita*); 1901 *Electric Flash* (off the *Marguerite Haskins* plus one frame) *Alice M. Guthrie*, *Irene and May*, *Victor* (auxiliary), *Mary E. Harty* (auxiliary), *Nellie B. Nickerson* (auxiliary); 1902 *Harriet W. Babson*, *Winifred*, *Veda M. McKown* (auxiliary), *Eglantine*, *Emilia Enos*, *Philip P. Manta*; 1903 *Mary E. Cooney*, *Avalon*, *Nokomis*, *Lafayette*; 1904 *Hazel R. Hines*; 1905 *Arthur James* (Lewis H. Story in "Fishing Vessels Built at Gloucester That Were in Races," claims that Thomas F. McManus designed the *Arthur James*. Chapelle states that the *Avalon*, *Hazel R. Hines*, and the *Arthur James* were off the same model by Mel McClain); 1906 *Good Luck*.

[8] Thomas, *Fast & Able*, 15.

[9] Irving, along with Hugh Bishop and Mel McClain, was one of Gloucester's leading ship modelers at the turn of the twentieth century. He died at Gloucester at age eighty-five, having practiced there for nearly seventy years. Chapelle states that Irving built more than twenty large schooners in addition to numbers of schooner and sloop boats (*Fishing Schooners*, 194).

[10] 1901 *Laura Enos* (sloop boat), *John S. Brooks*; 1903 *Rapidan*; 1904 *Diana* (sloop boat); 1905 *Juno*; possibles: *Blanche F. Irving* (1901), *Sylvie Nunan*.

[11] Thomas, *Fast & Able*, 148-50.

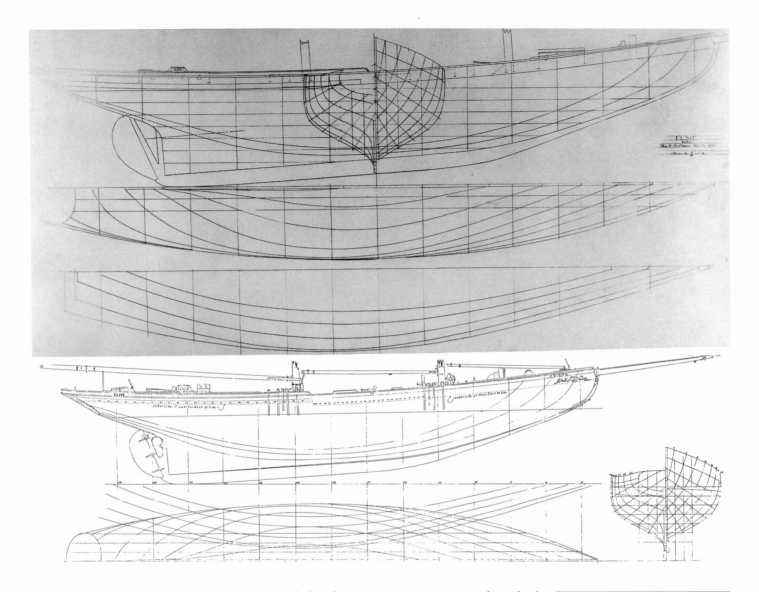

Lawlor–the very hull form that triggered the furious arguments over the "duck theory" between Lawlor and McManus's father. Tom reversed these lines in the design of the *Elsie*, and the new schooner proved faster than the *Oriole*, the ultimate testimonial to his father's counterpoint.

The *Elsie*, as built by Essex's Story shipyard in 1910, differed markedly in detail from McManus's plan. With the safety of fishermen always in mind, he designed her with several crew safety innovations, most notably a trunk cabin on the forecastle, as well as a hull form with a raised counter, and a fine stem-line. He also placed the mainmast further aft than the usual practice. None of these features appeared in the *Elsie* as completed by Arthur D. Story.[12]

Lines of McManus's Design 152, completed 30 November 1909 and built in 1910 as the *Elsie*: *top*, as designed, with trunk over the forecastle, masts moved aft and farther apart than the usual practice, and raised counter; and, *bottom*, as built, with a conventional semi-knockabout rig and deck plan. Francis Waterman traced the original plans; Howard I. Chapelle drew the plans as built. (Waterman plan courtesy Peabody & Essex Museum, Salem, Massachusetts; Chapelle plan courtesy Smithsonian Institution)

12 An interesting array of the *Elsie*'s plans, both "as designed" and "as built," appears in Erik A.R. Ronnberg, Jr., "Fishing Schooner *Elsie*, 1910: Research and Plans for Ship Model Construction," 6-part serial *Nautical Research Journal* 32-34 (1987-89), 32:84-86.

A week before the *Elsie*'s launching, Tom learned to his dismay that the argumentive and cantankerous relationship he had cherished for a score of years with his last mentor had come to an end. The obituary column in the Boston *Globe*'s morning edition of Monday, 2 May 1910, reported: "John L. Frisbee. [Died] in Everett April 30th 76 years 2 months 10 days. Funeral services at his late residence 182 Broadway, Tuesday, May 3 at 2 P.M. Relatives and friends invited to attend."[13] With the naval architect's passing, the three men who had shaped Tom's professional abilities and honed his skills, John H. McManus, Dennison J. Lawlor, and now John L. Frisbee, were all gone.

At the time of her launching, the waterfront pundits believed that the *Elsie* at 137 gross (volume) tons and 106 feet six inches between perpendiculars was the largest type of fisherman that would pay dividends without outside subsidy.[14] McManus completed her drafts on 30 November 1909; Story launched her into the Essex River on 9 May 1910, and Captain Will Forbes sailed the new vessel from Gloucester on 31 May. On 23 August, eighty-four days later, the *Elsie* returned to Gloucester from Saint Peter's Bank with a huge cargo of 286,800 pounds salt cod, stocking $10,400–the season's high.[15]

During the fall of 1910, Tom received a commission from William H. Hollett of the Hollett Brothers Fish Co. Ltd. of Burin, Newfoundland. This resulted

---

13 Boston *Globe*, 2 May 1910.

14 Howard I. Chapelle, *American Sailing Ships* (New York: W.W. Norton, 1935), 256.

15 Thomas, *Fast & Able*, 149.

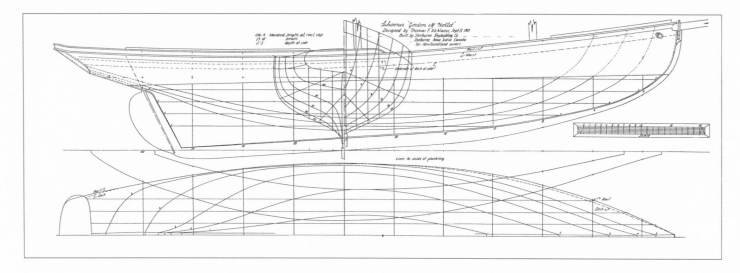

in the construction of the schooner *Gordon M. Hollett* in the McGill yard at Shelburne, Nova Scotia, by Amos Pentz. Before Joseph McGill's death in 1913, he and Pentz combined to build more than a dozen McManus designs. McGill must have been a man of unusual integrity—he paid a design fee to the architect for each schooner, rather than capitalizing on his yard's remoteness from Boston and following the Essex practice of constructing several vessels off the original plans or molds by adding or deleting one or two frames, or spreading the top-timbers.

The *Hollett* slid down the ways in December 1910, in time for the winter salt cod fishery: "The latest product of the well-known shipbuilding establishment of Joseph McGill, at Shelburne, is the schooner *Gordon M. Hollett*, which was successfully launched on Wednesday the 21st. last. She was specially designed by McManus, of Boston, for Grand Banks salt fishing," reported the Halifax *Morning Chronicle*.[16]

The Swim brothers of Lockport, Nova Scotia, also approached McManus for designs. Tom sent plans based on his Indian Headers *Massasoit* and *Tecumseh* of 1898, and the semi-knockabout *Elsie*. W. C. McKay built the as-yet-unidentified vessels at Shelburne, although he "did not always fully understand his instructions."[17]

Recall that the Indian Head class had been in existence for ten years before the number of new knockabouts exceeded them in 1908. Now, just two years later, the number of new semi-knockabouts exceeded the number of new knockabouts. And there was a new variation already: a round-bow profile with a semi-knockabout rig, introduced by the *Mary DeCosta* of 1909 in New England and by the *Dorothy G. Snow* of 1911 in Nova Scotia.

The *Gordon M. Hollett*, designed by McManus on 13 September 1910, was an Indian Head schooner with relatively short ends ordered by the Hollet family of Burin, Newfoundland. Howard I. Chapelle drew the existing plan. (Plan AFS 124, Smithsonian Institution)

[16] Halifax *Morning Chronicle*, 26 December 1910.

[17] James T. Bebb, *Quest for the Phantom Fleet* (n.p., Nova Scotia: author, 1992), 155.

The round-bow semi-knockabout
Dorothy G. Snow, designed by
McManus and built by Pentz and
McGill at Shelburne, Nova Scotia, in
1911. Photo by Paul Yates. (Courtesy
Maritime Museum of the Atlantic,
Halifax, Nova Scotia)

The winter herring fishery was one of the riskiest trades engaged in by New
England fishing schooners. Newfoundland's west coast is indented with several deep
bays whose fertile waters produced large schools of herring, which the
Gloucestermen used as bait. The locals caught them in quantity and sold them to
American fishermen, catching, salting, and packing this valuable catch from
October to December, and then delivering them to American schooners that
visited between January and March, a perilous sailing season when many of the
Newfoundland bays froze solid.

A near tragedy to Gloucester's 1912 herring fleet exemplified the speed
of the semi-knockabouts. Word reached Cape Ann on 13 January that many
schooners had been trapped in the ice for the duration of the Newfoundland
winter at Bay of Islands and Bonne Bay. The freezing waters of the latter body of
water trapped the 1910 semi-knockabout *Sylvania*, along with the *Oriole*, *T.M.
Nicholson*, *Smuggler*, *Bohemia*, and *Gossip*. Another ice field making up thirty-five
miles to the south caught twenty-five more Gloucester vessels at Bay of Islands.
Gordon Thomas concluded that, "never before had the American herring
fleet faced such a condition."[18]

To combat this emergency, the United States government ordered the
cutters *Androscoggin* and *Gresham* to the assistance of the trapped fishermen; but,
on 17 January, the ice shifted in the Bay of Islands and the schooners that had been
locked in there broke out for home. On the twentieth, with the help of the
Canadian steamer *Portia*, the Bonne Bay fleet, excepting the *Bohemia*, which

---

[18] Thomas, *Fast & Able*, 155.

Looking aft from the bowsprit as the Digby schooner *Dorothy M. Smart* drives up the Bay of Fundy, Frederick William Wallace captured the fisherman's perspective of a fast schooner under sail. McManus designed the *Smart*, and Joseph McGill launched her at Shelburne, Nova Scotia, in 1910. (Courtesy Maritime Museum of the Atlantic, Halifax, Nova Scotia)

remained stuck fast, fought their way to clear water. The *Sylvania* was the last to leave. Her captain, Lem Firth, remained as long as possible trying to work the *Bohemia*, his brother Percy's command, free from the grip of the ice.

Once underway, the *Sylvania*, already three days behind the Bay of Islands fleet, and trailing the other Bonne Bay escapees by several hours, maintained speeds approaching and above thirteen knots. To traverse the Gulf of St. Lawrence, she sailed down the west coast of Newfoundland, the shortest route to Cabot Strait and the Atlantic Ocean. After rounding Cape St. George, Captain Firth's lookouts occasionally spotted the topmasts of hulls beyond the horizon, the tail end of the returning fleet. By the time the 109-foot schooner entered Cabot Strait, she had caught up with and sped by several of the slower survivors.

Clear of the strait and out in the open ocean, Firth hauled the *Sylvania* around Cape Breton Island, never slackening in his mad dash to make up for the time he lost helping his brother. The hustling semi-knockabout stretched along the south coast of Nova Scotia. Off Shelburne on the southwest corner of the peninsula, she passed one of the last two vessels still ahead of her–the large, fast, but now eleven-year-old McManus Indian Header *Massachusetts*. After crossing the mouth of the Bay of Fundy on a beeline for Mount Desert before swinging south, Firth finally caught sight of the McClain-designed *Lottie G. Merchant* (one of several derivatives of the famous *Marguerite Haskins*) to seaward of the Isle of Shoals. Only the *Merchant* remained in front of his flying *Sylvania*. Giving no quarter, Firth ran down the leader, drove by her as they passed Cashes Ledge, and sailed, first home, into Gloucester on 25 January. Later, he candidly admitted to

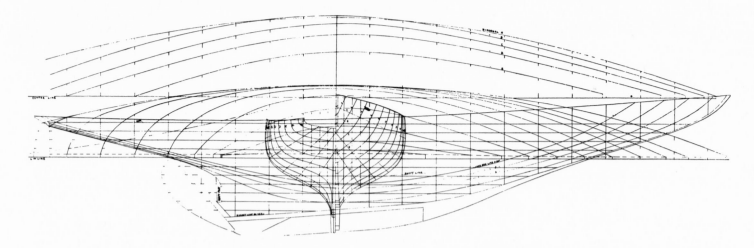

Lines of the ketch-yacht *Autocrat.* Her
elongated forebody is reminiscent of the
Helen B. Thomas, but aft she has a
longer, fuller stern to offset the weight
of the engine. (*Yachting Magazine,*
December 1911)

Gordon Thomas that, "the *Sylvania* would probably be beaten by the *Oriole* (which
he had passed on the way down) and the *Clintonia* (then Queen of the Gloucester
fleet) in sailing by the wind; but give the *Sylvania* a little sheet and she would show
her stern to the best of them."[19] The nimble McManus design delivered 850 barrels
of well-frozen herring to the pier after she made port.

Tom had designed his first yacht, the *Eclipse*, in 1906. A few years later,
the prominent Massachusetts yachtsman, C.H.W. Foster, who purchased yachts as
frequently as other people have birthdays, approached him. Foster wanted a big,
fast and able vessel for offshore cruising and decided that one based on a
commercial fisherman would best suit his needs. His discussions with McManus
resulted in a sleek ketch-rigged auxiliary knockabout, the *Autocrat.*[20] Foster's choice
of McManus as his designer speaks to Tom's reputation at this time–the wealthy
yachtsman could afford to cater to his own whims, and he enjoyed a reputation
for choosing the best of everything.

In the *Autocrat*, Tom designed a cruiser that would be easy to handle, yet
capable of comfortable deep-sea sailing. Richard T. Green built the yacht–eighty-
four feet on deck, with sixteen-foot eight-inch beam, and nine-foot draft–at his
Chelsea yard during 1911. She could hoist 2,400 square feet of canvas, and her
Lamb forty-horsepower, four-cycle engine could drive her at eight knots under bare
poles. To provide comfortable headroom in the main cabin without sacrificing hull
strength to an opening for a large trunk, Tom designed an unconventional layout by
carrying the main deck flush to the rail from side to side. Forward and aft of the
living area, it was twelve inches lower. "The lines of the boat are particularly sweet
and clean. She has a long graceful bow with an easy sweep from stem to keel, a good

[19] Ibid., 156.

[20] Letter, Anne Farlow Morris, 20 March 1990, the great-granddaughter of Charles H.W. Foster; also see Anne Farlow
Morris, *The Memoirs of Hilda Chase Foster* (Nashua, New Hampshire: privately printed, 1982), 81.

clean run and a moderate stern. The bilges are fairly hard so that she should stand up well and she is as sharp forward as the average Gloucester fisherman," *Yachting* magazine noted. "She is an ideal boat in which to go to sea in any kind of weather."[21] The *Autocrat* enjoyed a long career, later sailing under the name of *Paladin II*, and after 1935, *Adare*.

In the 1920s, sailing under the name *Paladin II*, the 42-ton *Autocrat* (60.5x16.7x8.5 feet) was still an impressive yacht. (Neg. 5043S, © Rosenfeld Collection, Mystic Seaport Museum, Inc.)

Harbor pilots had begun to recognize the inherent advantages the knockabout schooner offered their demanding service within a few years of the *Helen B. Thomas*'s launch. The New Jersey pilots purchased the McManus round-bow fishing schooner *Kernwood*–not the Canadian version of 1908, but the earlier *Kernwood*, built at Essex for American owners in 1904–which they renamed *Trenton* in late 1907. The serious failing of the early knockabouts, cargo capacity, presented no drawback to the pilots, while the elimination of the bowsprit, with its attendant easing of heavy-weather working conditions, proved immensely attractive. The Mobile Bar Pilots Association was the first to order a new knockabout pilot design from McManus, the *Alabama* of 1911, and the Charleston Bar Pilots Association followed suit with an order for the *Henry P. Williams*.[22]

Since the advent of McClain's *Helen Miller Gould*, and through to and after his own first auxiliary-engine schooner design–believed to be the revised Indian Header *Mary C. Santos* of 1904–McManus had been pondering the complex array of problems surrounding the weight of the internal-combustion engines, which were more and more frequently being installed in fishing schooners as a matter of course. To place this in proper context, it must be understood that for these vessels the engine or engines were true auxiliaries, intended, in the high-profit, very mobile mackerel and swordfish fisheries, to move the schooner when sails could not. To counteract the frustrating problem of being able to see rippling schools of mackerel or a group of basking swordfish, but not have the ability to get to them because they were in the eye of the wind, or because there was no wind at all, fishing skippers sought a power source that could propel their vessels at maximum speed for short periods of time.

Tom's principal dilemma involved stabilizing the hull relative to the diametrically opposed directions of thrust. The afterbodies of the first auxiliary-powered fishermen, beginning with the *Gould*, were basically unchanged from pure sailing schooners. As long as the auxiliary power source was a gasoline engine of relatively light mass, its lump of metal was useful to the designer. By simply dropping it into the hull at the lowest possible location he gained several

---

[21] "An 84-Foot Auxiliary Cruising Ketch," *Yachting* 10 (December 1911): 455-56.

[22] The schooners *Helen B. Thomas*, *Kernwood*, and *Hortense* were among several McManus fishermen that ended their careers as pilot boats.

Regardless of the grace of its appearance, a fishing schooner had to prove itself at sea. In 1915 Frederick William Wallace took a sequence of photographs as the 130-ton semi-knockabout *Gov. Foss* (105.9x24.6x10.8 feet, launched in 1911) charged by his vessel off Shelburne, Nova Scotia. A modification of the original semi-knockabout *Mooween*, the *Gov. Foss* surfs by under her "four lowers"—mainsail, foresail, jumbo, and jib—the picture of controlled power. (Courtesy Maritime Museum of the Atlantic, Halifax, Nova Scotia)

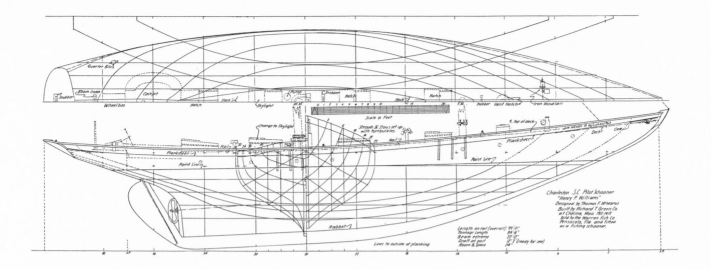

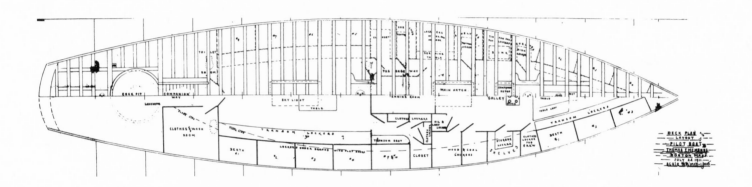

advantages. The center of gravity and the center of lateral resistance dropped lower in the vessel, and the shaft angle could be reduced, thereby reducing power transmission losses. But if he chose a heavy-oil engine the parameters changed dramatically. At the beginning of the second decade of the twentieth century, the common–and at first the only–choice was the massive Blanchard 100-brake-horsepower heavy-oil unit. The size of this engine demanded a rethinking of hull shape.

A dichotomy surrounds the location of motive power in an auxiliary-powered vessel–while sails propel the hull from above the waterline, the propeller pushes it from below the surface. The naval architectural challenge of balancing both sources of thrust to achieve maximum speed from the same hull shape under either sail or propeller, remains ultimately insurmountable. And, as seen in Burgess's *Elizabeth Silsbee*, propeller drag and the propeller aperture present separate problems in their own right. Aside from considering the forces of sail and power separately and together, the architect must appraise the effect of changing from sail to

Top: McManus designed the 73-ton Charleston, South Carolina, pilot schooner *Henry P. Williams* (85.9x21.5x10 feet) as an auxiliary knockabout with long overhangs and a good deal of sheer. Richard Green launched her at Chelsea in 1912. She later served as a fishing schooner out of Pensacola, Florida. Lines drawn by Howard I. Chapelle. *Bottom:* McManus drew this deck plan and layout for the Mobile pilot schooner *Alabama* on 25 July 1911. The 120-ton *Alabama* (94.4x24.7x12 feet) was launched by James and Tarr at Essex in December 1911 and served for fifteen years before she was replaced with another McManus design. (Plan PV-2, Smithsonian Institution; deck plan and layout courtesy Louise V. Will)

The three-masted schooner *Carrie M. Wamback* (113.7x26.1x10.6 feet) appears to be a McManus design. Built at Liverpool, Nova Scotia, in 1912, she was abandoned at sea in January 1914. (Courtesy Mariners' Museum, Newport News, Virginia)

propeller, or *vice-versa*, upon the "Center of Effort,"[23] which, in this case, transfers from the geometric center of the sails, above the waterline, to the propeller aperture below it. Additionally, the "Center of Buoyancy" is disturbed by the presence of a heavy marine engine,[24] whose weight also effects the "Center of Gravity" in different ways depending on its location within the hull. Finally, the power plant will not run without fuel, and fuel burn as well as fuel-tank location present an infinitely variable set of design problems. The ballast on board controls the amount of sail that can be hoisted in blowing conditions. But, when moving under the combination of sail and power, the ballast is in a state of constant reduction in direct proportion to the rate at which fuel is consumed. In the *Elizabeth Silsbee*, for example, this meant a continual drop in displacement at a rate of 175 pounds per hour.

[23] The "Center of Effort" is that point of the sail plan through which the resultant of all wind forces is assumed to act. In the sail plan of a vessel, each sail is assumed to have its center of effort at its geometric center. The draft of the complete sail plan of a vessel provides the basis for determining the center of effort. In practice, however, the sails are never completely flat, the only shape the sail plan can illustrate, so the actual center of effort is relocated with each readjustment of the trim of the sails.

[24] The "Center of Buoyancy" refers to a point through which the resultant of all buoyant forces on an immersed hull are assumed to act. It is about this point that a vessel afloat can be said to be poised. It is also referred to as the "Center of Displacement," the "Center of Cavity," or the "Center of Flotation."

On the other hand, the presence of propeller-driven thrust produces a beneficial effect on the "Center of Lateral Resistance," by reducing the leeway made under sail power alone.[25] Yet, it is a rare design that gains the same hull speed from its power plant that it is capable of under sail. In effect, propeller propulsion opens the door to a latter-day version of Lawlor's "duck theory" with the motive force delivered from below the waterline, like the paddling webbed feet of a waterfowl, rather than above.

In a curious twist of fate for schooner designs, as heavy-oil engines such as the New London Ship & Engine Company, the Fairbanks-Morse, and the Wisconsin units became more efficient, particularly in terms of their mass *versus* shaft horsepower produced, fishing skippers came to rely more on combustion than wind, and sailing rigs tended to decrease in size. The bowsprit became an unnecessary appendage and, as the 1920s neared, the pure knockabout enjoyed a resurgence of popularity.

The semi-knockabout was the epitome of a purely sail-powered fisherman, although few were purely sail-powered. This oxymoronic situation resulted from the timing of technological changes. The semi-knockabout, a hull design which could safely carry huge clouds of canvas aloft, came to fruition in parallel with not only the marine engine at large, but more specifically the utilitarian version of the heavy-oil engine. In other words, now that fishermen could fly enough canvas to drive capable hulls at speeds above fifteen knots under sail alone, they did not need to. As naval architects–at this time principally Tom McManus, whose designs comprised the vast majority of new construction–learned to adapt to the pace of marine engine development and successfully combine mechanical horsepower with wind power, the need for billowing canvas aloft gradually reduced. In the years between 1910 and 1930, when the swan song of fishing schooners resounded over New England waters, it was not so much a case of sail *versus* power as it was of sail adapting to power. As early as 1910, pole masts began to appear with alarming regularity, as far as the old salts of the fishing fleet were concerned. The reemergence of the knockabout, the disappearing topmasts, and the withering bowsprit spoke volumes about the state of the art of fishing schooner design during those last two decades. Relatively few semi-knockabouts were built after 1915.

---

[25] The "Center of Lateral Resistance" is the point assumed to lie at the geometric center of a sailing vessel's underwater profile. On the design drafts this is indicated with the hull floating upright on its calculated waterline. In practice, however, with sailing vessels heeled over under a press of sail, and lifting or pitching through a seaway, the actual center of lateral resistance is constantly shifting.

A lineup of McManus designs at the A.D. Story yard, October 1912. When launched as the 119-ton *Delphine Cabral* (101.6x23x11.5 feet) in December, the semi-knockabout schooner at left would be admired for her fine lines. The large knockabout at center is the *Knickerbocker*, ready for launch and displaying one of the shafts for her twin Blanchard crude-oil engines. At right is the 90-ton *Ruth* (85.4x22.1x10.8 feet), a small Boston market fisherman. In the boat is Peter Hubbard, an outside joiner who planed the hulls of many McManus schooners during his career in the Essex shipyards. Photo by Henry D. Fisher. (M.S.M. 76.208.349)

Giving McManus a noteworthy accolade, Chapelle concluded that by 1912-15: "The auxiliary knockabout had now become the New England fishing schooner type. Carrying full sail power on a fast hull, the typical knockabout was fitted with a powerful oil engine, which lessened the danger of fuel oil or gasoline fires and explosions. *It therefore might be said that the knockabout was the acme in the long evolution of the New England fishing schooner.*"[26]

Fishing schooner construction experienced a brief down cycle after 1912 for several reasons. The first decade of the twentieth century had seen most of the New England fishing fleet renewed, not only through normal wear and tear, but also as a result of the superior hull designs that had come into being. The need for replacement vessels in the second decade, therefore, dwindled. Additionally, the slowdown can be attributed in part to the owners' fears that Congress might lower or even drop the tariff on Canadian fish, to the detriment of their profits. Tom McManus, now fifty-six-years old, nevertheless continued to develop his existing schooner types, while he attempted to anticipate new directions the constantly changing New England fishing industry might take.

[26] Chapelle, *Fishing Schooners*, 285, emphasis added.

One of Tom's most visible eccentricities concerned the riding trim of his designs when they first came afloat after launching, such as his experience with the *Quannapowatt* in 1905. Builders rarely ballasted a new hull to achieve the trim designers called for in their drafts, and the comparatively fine forebody and full hindquarters of the typical McManus design tended to produce trim by the head. When a vessel floated in that manner after launching, which they quite commonly did, Tom's Irish temper flared. Two Chapelle interviewees witnessed McManus's chagrin on occasions when schooners came to rest with this bow-down attitude, a result which "embarrassed McManus so much that he left the yard without a word."[27] The launching of the pilot boat *Henry P. Williams* from Richard T. Green's Chelsea shipyard provided the first recorded instance of one of Tom's fits of pique. The second occasion Chapelle referred to took place four years later, when the W.I. Adams & Son yard launched the *Elizabeth Howard* at East Boothbay, Maine. Recalling his bull-headed reaction to Moses Adams's alteration of the *James S. Steele*'s garboard planks in 1891, it does not require much imagination to picture McManus's stiff-necked anger, as the temperamental American-Irish artist wordlessly stalked away from the celebrating throng gathered for the christening of his latest, but inadaquately ballasted, creation.

Fishing schooner launchings fraught with excitement were by no means limited to the marshy confines of the Essex River. McManus's design for the large knockabout that became the *Bay State* of Portland, Maine, was one of the last vessels Gloucester's John Bishop framed before being stricken with a terminal illness.[28] Owen Lantz completed the construction of this vessel, and when the time came for her launch, Lantz probably wished that he had passed up the opportunity. The problem was easy to define, but difficult to resolve. The shipbuilder would have to tilt the 126-foot *Bay State* into the narrow—180-foot-wide—confines of Vincent Cove. To make matters worse, a variety of structures lined the opposite shore. Typically, a schooner raced down the launching ways and came roaring out of Bishop's steeply inclined premises, while the yardmen stood by, relying upon rope check lines to bring the vessel's headlong rush to a halt before she battered the buildings overhanging the water on other side of the cove. This danger was not to be underestimated; on 5 January 1906 the Indian Header *Cynthia* actually crashed into a shed on the far side of the cove when one of her checking lines gave way.[29]

THE ELSIE, BAY STATE, CATHERINE, AND ELIZABETH HOWARD

---

[27] Ibid., 270-71.

[28] John Bishop built about 150 vessels at Gloucester between 1881 and 1912 (Lewis H. Story, "Vessels Built at Gloucester Mass," Gordon Thomas Collection, Cape Ann Historical Society). Bishop died on 2 November 1912. His brother Hugh, a shipwright and ship modeler, died on 26 December 1915, at his retirement home in Roxbury, Massachusetts.

[29] Thomas, *Fast & Able*, 121.

At 10:25 A.M. on 24 October 1912, in front of a crowd of 500 spectators, Lantz let the *Bay State* rip. The giant knockabout shot across the cove and, according to Gordon Thomas: "Lantz told me that the checking lines held and *Bay State* came to a stop within three feet of a building on the opposite shore of the cove. He said that the roof of this shed was crowded with people, and when they saw *Bay State* heading straight for them, he never saw folks scatter so fast. I believe that *Bay State* was the largest vessel ever built at Vincent Cove."[30]

The *Bay State* was one of the first fishing schooners with crude-oil, or as they were sometimes called, heavy-oil auxiliary motors. This vessel and her sistership, the ten-days-younger *Knickerbocker*, were built for operations in the Pacific Ocean. New England fish money had helped establish the North Pacific fisheries at the end of the nineteenth century, and New England vessels occasionally rounded Cape Horn to work those waters. West Coast shipbuilders had built several of Tom's designs including the pole-masted, gasoline-auxiliary knockabout *La Paloma*: "In 1909 one of the last 'Eastern' boats was built for the fleet. She was the *La Paloma* and was patterned after the '. . . latest McManus model from Gloucester. This type is coming into general use in the East. . . .'"[31]

During 1911, several Boston dealers sent three auxiliary knockabouts, the *Alice*, the *Athena*, and the *Victor and Ethan*—all McManus products—to work in the Pacific halibut fishery from a Seattle, Washington, base. Subsequently, the New England Fish Company, which had several steamers working in the North Pacific, approached Tom to create two vessels for West Coast operations. Paragons of modern New England design, they were McManus's first twin-heavy-oil-engined, twin-screw hulls. Reflecting the growing reliance on mechanical power, both were built with pole masts capable of hoisting but 4,500 square feet of canvas, half the usual amount for vessels of their great size. The A.D. Story-built, 159-ton *Knickerbocker* departed for Seattle in March 1913,[32] and took a disappointing 150 days to round Cape Horn and reach her destination. With her exposed wheel and lack of mechanical gear-handling devices, she proved a failure there. But, due to her cavernous hold space, the *Knickerbocker* switched careers and became a coastal freighter. The conventional New England schooners, the *Alice*, the *Athena*, and the *Victor and Ethan*, had all returned east by 1915, and the *Bay State* never left for the Pacific. When the owners decided to keep her on the East Coast, she was re-rigged with topmasts and had her sail inventory nearly doubled.

---

[30] Ibid., 167.

[31] Richard H. Phillips, "Pacific Coast Halibut Schooners: Still the Workhorses of the West," *National Fisherman* (September 1972): 2C-3C, citing the *Pacific Fisherman Yearbook* of 1910.

[32] To give some idea of her size, the *Knickerbocker* had 7,000-gallon fuel tanks, and berthed twenty-four crewmen in the forecastle and four in the cabin.

On her maiden voyage, Norman Ross, the *Bay State*'s skipper, brought the big knockabout into Canso, Nova Scotia, and provoked much interest in her twin Blanchard heavy-oil power plants on the part of Canadian fishermen. Ross invited author Frederick William Wallace, who was sailing on board the McGill-built, McManus design *Albert J. Lutz*, and his skipper, John D. Apt, on board his new schooner to witness the operation of the heavy-oil engine:

The engineer had the torches blowing on the Cylinder-heads to preheat them. . . . Advised by the engineer that he would be ready to start in a minute, the Skipper was at the wheel ready to go. "Are you ready!" he called below.

"All ready!" cried the engineer.

"Heave up!" shouted the Skipper to the men at the windlass for'ad. The anchor was broken out and the order given to start the engine. There followed a series of muffled explosions. Then came a halt. A few more coughs from the motor, and silence. The big schooner was swinging in the tide and wind and the Skipper was anxiously glancing at the vessels anchored all around him in the restricted harbor.

He hailed the engineer again just as that individual came running up from below with an oil can. "Where the hell are you going?" came an excited query from the Skipper.

"I got to get some gasoline for the air-pump, Cap'en," explained the other. "She won't start–"

"But we're underway, man–the anchor's up–"

"Sorry, Cap'en, but you'd better let it go again–"

With a hurried glance at an anchored schooner towards which the *Bay State* was drifting, the Skipper lost his temper, and forgetting our presence and the lecture he had given on the virtues of auxiliary power, he exploded in a roar heard all over Canso. "Dam' and blast you and your jeesly blank blank engine! I'll take her out under sail!"

On a quiet day in Gloucester harbor, the 159-ton knockabout *Bay State* (112.7x25.4x12.3 feet) gets up her mainsail for a trip to the banks. Despite the problems with her Blanchard crude-oil engines, the *Bay State* was a fast and productive schooner. Photo by Winthrop L. Warner, 1914. (M.S.M. 74.578.16)

And to the gang he bellowed; "Away ye go on yer fores'l and jumbo!
I'd sooner trust my canvas than any bloody useless engine!"[33]

The starting problem was not new. "When they were trying out the new *Bay State*'s engines at the wharf," Gordon Thomas remembered, "all you could see was heavy black smoke."[34] In fact the Blanchards were rarely successful as marine motors. The solution to the heavy oil propulsion problem for the New England fishing fleet came from Nuremberg, Germany. A manufacturer there, the Maschinenfabrik Augsburg-Nuremberg, had the production rights to Rudolph Diesel's invention–the

[33] Frederick William Wallace, *Roving Fisherman* (Gardenvale, Quebec: Canadian Fisherman, 1955), 133-34.

[34] Thomas, *Fast & Able*, 167.

two-cycle, heavy-oil, compression-fired, internal combustion engine. The firm's Nuremberg factory developed the marine version of that compact power source, which was first experimented with at sea in 1910.[35] The New London Ship & Engine Company of Groton, Connecticut, became the United States licensee for the manufacture of both the ship and shore versions of the German engine. Incorporated in October 1910, NELSECO, as the company became known, began shipping automotive and stationary engines during mid-1911. The first fishing schooner to acquire a NELSECO diesel was one of the original Indian Head class, the *Manhassett*, when she had a German-American unit installed during 1914. Although, she is sometimes referred to as the first diesel-powered New England fisherman, that honor actually belongs to the *Bay State* and her smoky Blanchards.

The Nuremberg-NELSECO versions of Diesel's engines had several advantages for marine use: they were considerably smaller in size and weight than their American competitors, as well as being self-starting, self-reversing, and capable of running cleanly for incredibly long periods without fear of overheating or mechanical breakdown. After the succession of fires in gasoline-powered fishermen, beginning with the *Helen Miller Gould* herself, the safety factor, as well as their economy of operation–at the time gasoline cost eighteen cents a gallon, compared to diesel at four cents–brought the NELSECOs into wide use very quickly. The fuel oil they burned, which was readily available, had a sufficiently high flash point that it could be stored and used without danger of explosion. The *Manhassett*, with a single 120-horsepower NELSECO, proved capable of extended cruising at a speed of nine knots without hoisting a sail. By the early 1920s, the diesel auxiliary would become the power plant of choice for the New England fishing fleet.[36]

---

[35] Rudolph Christian Carl Diesel (1858-1913), born of German parents, grew up in Paris and was educated at Augsburg and Munich, Germany. He established a brilliant scholastic record in engineering and became the protégé of the famous refrigeration engineer, Carl von Linde. Diesel devoted most of his energies to developing an internal combustion engine that would approach the efficiency of the Carnot cycle. He moved to the Berlin office of Linde's firm and there, about 1890, he conceived the idea for the heavy-oil engine named for him. He obtained a German development patent in 1892 and published a description of his engine under the title *Theorie und Konstruktion eines rationellen Wäremotors* (*Theory and Construction of a Rational Heat Motor*). With research funding from the Maschinenfabrik Augsburg-Nuremberg and Krupp Industries, Diesel produced a series of increasingly powerful units, culminating during 1897 with a twenty-five-horsepower, four-cycle, vertical single cylinder compression engine. The high efficiency of Diesel's engine, coupled with its simplicity of design, made it an immediate commercial success.

The French physicist Sadi Carnot published a paper on the possibility of compression ignition in 1824. Another Frenchman, Alphonse Beau de Rochas, developed the principal of the spark ignition engine as used in automobiles. The German engineer Nikolaus Otto built the first engine in which the fuel-air mixture composing the charge was compressed in the cylinder before burning. This is the engine which provided the basis for Rudolph Diesel's experiments. Diesel received the protection of a manufacturing patent from the German government in 1893.

The first marine installation of Diesel's engine was completed in 1910. It became the primary power source for German submarines during World War I. A unit small enough for use in an automobile appeared in 1922. Modern diesels do not follow Rudolph Diesel's slow-burning cycle, but retain the compression ignition and fuel injection of his original engine.

[36] *The Boston Commercial*, 16 March 1912; T.A. Scott, Inc., papers, Coll. 1, box 13, folder 24, G.W. Blunt White Library, Mystic Seaport Museum; Andrew W. German, *Down on T Wharf: The Boston Fisheries as Seen Through the Photographs of Henry D. Fisher* (Mystic, Connecticut: Mystic Seaport Museum, 1982), 30.

In the *Little Ruth*, Tom McManus traced a strong return to his Fingalian roots. One can picture the reaction of his forebears–John H. McManus, Dick Leonard, Tom Herbert, or Bill Montross–had they ever laid eyes on her. She was of an ideal size and would have fit right into the Fingal fleet as it gained a monopoly of the Boston market fishery in the mid-1850s. Tom's Plan No. 217, drawn on 3 October 1912, laid out a fifty-five-foot shore fisherman, forty-three-feet waterline with fourteen-foot six-inch beam, and seven-foot six-inch draft.

The *Little Ruth* had a specific purpose. She was intended to operate as a gill-netter. Professor Spencer F. Baird, the U.S. Fish Commissioner, introduced gill netting, which he had learned about in Norwegian industrial literature, to the winter cod fishery as far back as 1878. Compared to the prevailing trawl lines, the gill nets had the distinct advantage of not requiring bait, which reduced the New Englanders' reliance on the dangerous Newfoundland winter herring trade. The gill net simply snagged the cod by their gills when the fish blundered into its wall of mesh. As many as forty vessels had fished Ipswich Bay with gill nets during the heydey of the 1880s.[37] This form of fishing regained inshore popularity around 1910. In 1909, Captain John W. Atwood returned to Gloucester from a career on the Great Lakes and began to practice the form of gillnetting then in use on Lake Erie for catching species of groundfish. The following year a fleet of Great Lakes gill net boats came east, encouraging competition from local fishermen.[38] The Great Lakes boats "were nothing more nor less than large power boats, which, according to the Gloucester men, had their lines taken from Noah's ark, as they strongly resembled the ark–house and all," *Yachting* commented. "They were small boats, only good for inshore work about six months of the year (the length of the netting season)."[39]

Mr. G.H. Smith commissioned Tom to design the new vessel and engaged David M. "Big Dave" Waddell of Rockport to build it. Smith determined that "he would have a vessel designed that was a real worker, and chose a knockabout rig as the most suitable type, with, however, plenty of auxiliary power." McManus chose one of Victor Emery's forty-horsepower Ideal gasoline engines, about twice the power usually employed in a fifty-footer. This excess was a necessary supplement for a gill netter, which might have as much as three to five miles of nets out.[40]

In 1914, twentieth-century technology reversed the downward construction spiral and led to more than motor fishing vessels. By the time the Serbs assassinated

[37] Dean Conrad Allard, Jr., *Spencer Fullerton Baird and the U.S. Fish Commission, a Study in the History of American Science* (Washington, D.C.: George Washington University, 1967), 308.

[38] German, *Down on T Wharf*, 58.

[39] "A 55-Foot Knockabout 'Shore' Fisherman," *Yachting* 8 (May 1913):354.

[40] Ibid.

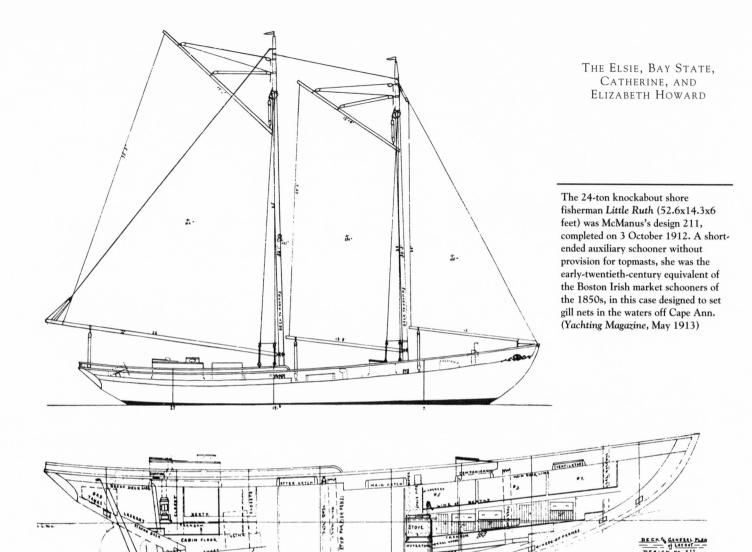

The 24-ton knockabout shore fisherman *Little Ruth* (52.6x14.3x6 feet) was McManus's design 211, completed on 3 October 1912. A short-ended auxiliary schooner without provision for topmasts, she was the early-twentieth-century equivalent of the Boston Irish market schooners of the 1850s, in this case designed to set gill nets in the waters off Cape Ann. (*Yachting Magazine*, May 1913)

Archduke Franz-Ferdinand and his wife to open World War I, more than 90,000,000 pounds of groundfish were being landed annually at Boston. Haddock amounted to 45 percent of this bounty, cod 25 percent, hake 16 percent, pollack 10 percent, cusk 2.5 percent, and the much-sought halibut, 0.5 percent. Haddock brought two cents and more a pound, and the value of cod and hake was twice as much. The previous year a name train, "The Flying Fisherman," began overnight service to rush fresh fish to New York. Fresh seafood from New England began to grace tables in Philadelphia, or even faraway Chicago and St. Louis, within two or three days of being hoisted out of the pens in a schooner's hold at Boston.[41]

41 German, *Down on T Wharf*, 92.

Kneeling on the floor of his Essex mold loft, Archer B. Poland scales up the plans of a vessel. On large sheets of paper on the floor, he has marked a centerline and, using a table of offsets or measurements taken off a half model, has measured off widths of the vessel at numerous vertical stations along its length. The awls driven into the floor represent the widths at one station, and the batten bent around them gives the full-scale shape of the hull at that point. Mr. Poland is scribing a line along the batten, which he will then trace onto a number of thin boards tacked together. After cutting those planks along the line, he will have a mold for the shape of one set of frames for the vessel. He will repeat the operation until the shipyard has enough molds to reproduce the designer's concept for the shape of the vessel. Archer Poland was one of a few essential individuals who translated McManus's designs to full scale, and whose own ideas might be incorporated in the fairing of lines, the amount of sheer in the vessel, and the exact shape of the stern. Photograph by Edwin J. Story. (Courtesy Dana Story Collection)

A modern facility designated as the "Fish Pier" in South Boston replaced T Wharf, by then old, tired, and crowded, from thirty years of service as the home of Boston's fishing fleet. The Commonwealth Ice & Cold Storage Company put up the world's largest freezer and ice plant at the inner end of the new 1,200-foot-long, 300-foot-wide wharf. The wharf housed fish dealers in two fireproof store buildings 750 feet long by 50 feet wide, built on either side of the central street to accommodate outgoing shipments without impeding efforts to unload and resupply vessels alongside the wharf. After four years of planning and construction, the new fish pier opened on 30 March 1914. McManus's knockabout *W.M. Goodspeed* was the first to land fish, while the two-year-old *Bay State* delivered the first cargo of halibut, bringing ashore 40,000 pounds the next day. Captain Ross had been working the Grand Banks of Newfoundland. Knowing the new pier would soon open, he ordered the schooner to get underway for Boston at 8:00 P.M. on the twenty-seventh. Seventy-five hours later, he made the *Bay State* fast to the new Fish Pier at 11:00 P.M. on the thirtieth, completing the 800-mile trip at a remarkable average speed of eleven knots–a tribute to master, men, a powerful spread of canvas, and a swift knockabout hull that overcame the deadweight of her big Blanchards.

Although the inventor of the knockabout enjoyed a reputation as a skilled modeler, McManus's few surviving plans–admittedly limited evidence–conclusively

dismiss any doubt that he was a reluctant draftsman.[42] One prosaic practice of New England's schooner builders suited his work habits perfectly: Many of his designs (as copied by Chapelle) show consistently a straight sheer aft, giving the stern a drooping look. Photos indicate that the loftsmen took this in hand and restored the sheer to more pleasing curvature. "*Elsie* and *Arethusa* are good examples of this," Erik A.R. Ronnberg observed. "We must also give credit to loftsmen Lewis H. Story & Archer Poland who often had to re-fair McManus' hull lines and do most of the design work on the stern."[43]

The latter comment addresses the habit of fishing schooner architects to leave the transom end to the loftsmen. Typically, the deck layout and construction details, so necessary to a major shipyard, were not shown on the plans delivered to the Essex artisans. The designer developed the hull form, but left the construction details to the mold loft and shipwrights. Among Tom's extant plans, and those of

The 159-ton knockabout *Catherine* (120.6x25.2x12.4 feet), an elongated version of the *Bay State* model, took over honors as the fastest knockabout schooner after her launch in 1915. (Courtesy Peabody & Essex Museum, Salem, Massachusetts)

---

[42] Chapelle, *Fishing Schooners*, 219.

[43] Letter, Erik A.R. Ronnberg, 18 September 1988.

his contemporary naval architects, however, there are inboard works profiles, half-breadth line plans, fore-and-aft body plans, and deck arrangements, indicating no lack of professional expertise on their part.

As the years advanced McManus frequently hired students to take off the lines of his models and lay them out on paper. One of his more famous apprentices was Walter J. McInnis, a founder of the modern Boston naval architectural firm of Eldredge-McInnis, Inc. The young man's parents, Joseph McInnis, a housebuilder, and Annabel McCormack, a midwife, were of Scottish-Catholic origins. Their ancestors moved to Prince Edward Island in the late seventeenth century. They resettled from there to Bangor, Maine, before moving on to South Boston in the 1880s, where Joseph McInnis gained repute as "the Tiffany of home builders,"[44] a constructor of the two-, three-, and four-decker houses occupied by upper-middle class Irish families such as the McManuses and the Fitzgeralds. Walter was born 11 January 1893, at the family home on Adams Street in Dorchester, the second of three children. A studious child, he displayed a natural drafting talent that predetermined his course through secondary school.

Tom had been working from the studio in his Dorchester home for a dozen years when the two came together. He probably knew McInnis as a neighborhood boy, and offered to take him into his employ. Young Walter, by then a fourteen-year-old student draftsman at the Mechanic's Arts High School, went to work in the rambunctious McManus household, a short walk from his own home. He labored nights and weekends in a manner that exactly paralleled Tom's youthful tie-up with Dennison J. Lawlor. One summer Tom shipped Walter on board the *Tartar* of 1904, the Crowninshield-designed fishing schooner of which he was part owner,[45] for a couple of weeks. This allowed McInnis to obtain a taste of the seagoing experience that had been so beneficial to Charley McManus's career before his untimely death.

The McManus-McInnis relationship proved eminently successful. The respect for human life that Tom instilled in his youthful apprentice, through his own dedication to the safety of the fishermen, became a hallmark of the young man's work. Throughout his life, Walter McInnis attributed his early development to Tom's tutelage,[46] and for Tom young Walter represented an opportunity to repay the professional advantages he himself had received from the deceased Dennison J.

Left: Literally an extension of McManus's *Oriole* design of 1908, the 142-ton knockabout *Elizabeth Howard* (119.6x25x11.4 feet) was built at East Boothbay and fished out of Portland. Albert Cook Church photographed her in October 1922, by which time a short bowsprit had been added to her rig. (Courtesy New Bedford Whaling Museum)

[44] Llewellyn Howland III, "Walter McInnis," *WoodenBoat* 52 (May-June 1983): 42-43.

[45] The syndicate sold the *Tartar* to Henry Langworthy of Stonington, Connecticut, and the Chesebro Brothers of New York City in 1913 (Temporary Enrolment No. 10, New London, Connecticut, 1913; Temporary Enrolment No. 16, New London, Connecticut, 7 April 1915, U.S. Consolidated Enrolment and Licenses, Bureau of Navigation, Record Group 41, Records of the Department of Commerce, NARA.

[46] Telephone interviews, Alan McInnis of Hingham, Massachusetts, naval architect and son of Walter McInnis, 12 August 1988 and 2 May 1990.

Lawlor. After his formative years with Tom, and high school graduation, McInnis worked for a year on a Vermont survey for the New England Telephone & Telegraph Company before becoming a marine draftsman for George Lawley & Sons, which had moved from South Boston to Neponset in 1910. Doubtlessly, the thirty-year association between the McManuses and the Lawleys, dating back to the 1885 and 1886 America's Cup races, played some part in obtaining this appointment. McInnis became the chief designer for the Lawleys before eventually going into business for himself.[47]

For many years the knockabout *Arethusa* of 1907 reigned supreme as the fastest schooner in the fishing fleet. The big 1912 knockabout *Bay State* never managed to outsail the swift rum-runner-to-be, nor did the Indian Header *Onato* or any of the noted semi-knockabout flyers. But the death knell for the *Arethusa*'s reign came on 8 October 1915, when Arthur D. Story launched the *Catherine*, the largest knockabout yet. At fifty-three-feet, she had the longest forecastle in Gloucester (the now six-year-old *Georgia* had held the record previously at forty-two-feet) and could set thirteen double dories.[48] "She carried a big crew, spread a big sail area, was a producer of big fish and was commanded by a man big in heart, courage, character, and ability, Capt. Archie A. MaCleod," Gordon Thomas rhapsodized. "At one time she met the great Knockabout schooner *Arethusa* in command of Capt. Josh Stanley, and gave her a trimming."[49] Story built the 159-gross-ton *Catherine*, whose register length was 120 feet six inches, off greatly modified lines of the *Bay State*. He launched the *Catherine* without power, but in anticipation of a later conversion he built a propeller shaft log through her deadwood, and put a propeller aperture into her skeg. He then blocked in the propeller aperture so carefully that it was barely visible.[50] Among the modifications McManus made to the *Bay State*'s design was a very long bow overhang, virtually a throwback to the *Helen B. Thomas*, and with it, a revival of those trimming problems that led to embarrassing launchings.[51]

Before her first winter at sea came to an end, the new schooner easily established her position as the trial horse of the banks fleet, the schooner that any fishing skipper with pretensions of speed for his own command had to outsail.

During the winter of 1915-16, Frank Adams of the Adams Yard in East

---

[47] Letter, Alan McInnis, 3 October 1988.

[48] Joseph E. Garland, *Down to the Sea, The Fishing Schooners of Gloucester* (Boston: David R. Godine, Publisher, 1983), 121.

[49] Thomas, *Fast & Able*, 173.

[50] Negative nos. 8875 and 8876, Peabody & Essex Museum, Salem, Massachusetts.

[51] Gordon W. Thomas, *Wharf and Fleet* (Gloucester: Nautical Reproductions of Gloucester, 1977), unpaginated.

Boothbay, Maine, came down to Boston with Captain Willard W. Howard, a New Yorker who fished out of Portland, Maine, to see McManus. They wanted to replicate the lines of the *Oriole*, but Howard insisted on a pure knockabout rig. His determination partially rested on the experiences of Portland Captain Bill Thomas, the man who convinced Cassius Hunt to underwrite the first knockabout, *Helen B. Thomas*, back in 1902. McManus, tracing a buff paper copy of the *Oriole*'s plan, produced a scaled sketch for the Maine men to demonstrate that if he replaced the *Oriole*'s bowsprit with an extended bow, the proposed schooner's length on deck would approach 150 feet. When Tom told him that, if he retained the same beam as the *Oriole*, the increased length of the new vessel would have a projected hull speed of nearly sixteen knots, the deal was made. McManus got out the drafts and offset

Tom McManus designed several American three-masted, round-bow schooners. Here is the 225-ton three-masted schooner *Nat L. Gorton* (130.8x27.2x12 feet), ready for launch in the A.D. Story yard at Essex, 12 July 1916. Photograph by Edwin J. Story. (Courtesy Dana Story Collection)

tables in time for Adams to complete the vessel by the spring of 1916. When Tom drafted the final plan of conversion from *Oriole* to *Howard*, he again eliminated the forebody hollows of the former vessel, as he had done in the *Elsie*.[52]

Earlier in 1916, Arthur Story built a huge knockabout yacht for C.H.W. Foster. The success of the *Catherine* inspired the shape of the new vessel. The inveterate yachtsman told of the origins of the biggest, and in his estimation, the best, vessel he ever had built:

In 1916[53] I happened to be present at the launching of a fine fisherman at Essex, and after the launching casually asked [Arthur D.] Story, her builder at what price he would deliver to me another

---

[52] Telephone interview, George I. "Sonny" Hodgdon, Hodgdon Brothers Boatyard, East Boothbay, 4 May 1990.

[53] This date must be a typographical error as the launching of the *Finback* took place on 8 January 1916. Foster is making reference here to the launch of the *Catherine* on 8 October 1915.

boat like her–hull, spars, and ironwork–at Gloucester. I had at the moment no idea of building such a boat, but had always dreamed of the joy there must be in owning a real deep sea-going vessel of that type. Story, at the time, was without any work for the winter and said it would be an act of charity if I would give him an order. Within two days he named a price of $9200 for such a boat delivered in Gloucester, and I made the deal. As a result, I was the possessor of the best boat that I have ever owned or been aboard.[54]

Story built the ketch-rigged knockabout off the *Catherine*'s molds, which itself constituted a modification by the builder to the molds prepared from McManus's drafts of the *Knickerbocker* and *Bay State*. Clearly, Foster's satisfaction with his 1911 McManus yacht, *Autocrat*, prompted his initial interest in the larger vessel. Dana Story, the son of Arthur D. Story, recalled that the *Finback*'s launch was another ungainly baptism for a McManus design: "On launching day a caterer was brought in and a big spread laid amongst the chips and piles of lumber. When she finally slid down the ways she almost didn't make it, her keel digging into the mud so that she nearly stopped."[55]

Riding out a winter gale, the 123-ton semi-knockabout *Elk* (102x24.7x11.2 feet) jogs to windward under jumbo, reefed foresail, and a triangular riding sail in place of her furled mainsail. McManus schooners were known for their ability to sail themselves under such conditions. With the wheel lashed to turn the vessel into the wind and the jumbo sheeted to windward to push the bow off, the vessel would slowly sail itself to windward while the crew, except for a lookout, kept themselves warm below. Painting by A.A. Acores. (Courtesy Peabody & Essex Museum, Salem, Massachusetts)

On a happier note, at the end of the summer of 1916, J.F. James & Son safely launched the *Joseph P. Mesquita*. Two weeks later the McManus family gathered to celebrate Tom's sixtieth birthday. The architect, who had begun the prime of his life with his fiftieth birthday, showed every sign of being right in the midst of his most productive years. His unique energies remained unabated while he persisted in his incessant search for an improved schooner model.

For Americans, the trenches slowly zig-zagging across western Europe might have been on a different planet, as President Woodrow Wilson maneuvered to maintain the neutrality of the United States in a world where every other great power was at war. The war, however, was largely beneficial for the New England fishermen. Despite occasional losses of fishing schooners to German raiders, the increased demand for fish from overseas and the early reduction of Canadian fishermen (who were called into the British military services as early as 1914), opened the door to a prosperous period for the Gloucestermen.

[54] Joseph E. Garland, *The Eastern Yacht Club, A History from 1870 to 1985* (Camden, Maine: Down East Books, 1989), 139.

[55] Dana Story, *Frame-Up!* (Barre, Massachusetts: Barre Publishing Company, 1964), 103.

CHAPTER FOURTEEN

The *Ajax*, *Surprise*, and *Esperanto*

I t soon became apparent that technological advances in modern munitions were not limited to the spider web of trenches in western Europe, but extended beyond the shorelines of that continent. When Germany introduced effective underseas warfare, strategic thinking among the world's great powers changed for all time. Within months the unexpected cost in American lives perpetrated by Kaiser Wilhelm II's new war-making capability began to shake the foundations of President Woodrow Wilson's policy of adamant neutrality. On 7 May 1915, ten miles off the south coast of Ireland, *Oberleutnant* Walther Schweiger, the commander of the German submarine U-20, sank the British ocean liner *Lusitania* with a single torpedo. He later claimed to have mistaken her for a troop-

Photographed during the Lloyds Harbor Race, 12 October 1925, the yacht *Surprise* shows off her fishing-schooner influence. She is one of very few McManus designs still afloat in the 1990s. (Neg. 17026F, © Rosenfeld Collection, Mystic Seaport Museum, Inc.)

carrying sistership, the *Mauretania*. Of the 1,257 souls on board, 1,198 perished. Among the dead were 128 United States citizens, including the famous philanthropist and yachtsman, Commodore Alfred G. Vanderbilt. Three other American civilians died when the American-flag tanker *Gulflight* went down two weeks later. In mid-August a U-boat torpedoed the British liner *Arabic*, with the loss of two more Americans.

Ex-president Theodore Roosevelt led the clamor for the United States to enter the war: "weasel words" from "the word-lover in the White House," he accused, as Wilson did his best to avoid committing the country to the conflict. Reluctantly, after a failed 1916 attempt to negotiate a peace settlement between the Allies and the Central Powers, the president stepped before a hushed Congress on 2 April 1917, and, after chiding the kaiser with impassioned eloquence for waging wicked and unscrupulous warfare against mankind, asked for a declaration of war. Congress, with only a few dissenting votes, gave it to him. At the time all the belligerents believed it would take years for a United States army to arrive in Europe and felt, Wilson included, that America's contribution to the war effort would be its navy and its economy: United States industry would speedily produce war materials for the Allies, and its fleet would safely escort them across the Atlantic.

Germany responded to America's declaration of war by escalating its submarine threat. For the first time, prowling U-boats actively hunted American merchantmen and fishing vessels. One attacked and sank McManus's famous *Rose Dorothea*, winner of the 1907 Lipton Cup races, in May. Carrying a cargo of salt, the twelve-year-old schooner was en route from Portugal to Newfoundland. The captors took off her crew and sent them into Lisbon. On 27 July, 360 miles off the Irish coast, another McManus design, the 1907 round-bow *John Hays Hammond*, which had survived a 1908 brush with Minot's Ledge in forty-knot wind, and a 1912 collision with the Nova Scotian salt-banker *Uranus*, went down, victim to a U-boat's cannon fire. The Germans set the *Hammond*'s crew adrift. They were later picked up by a British destroyer.

The reality of war came home to Tom and Kate when their offspring (with daughter Margaret approaching forty, and only Mildred and Ken still in their teens, they can hardly be called children) began to don military uniforms. Two of the four bachelor boys were the first to go. In May 1917 George, twenty-three, enlisted in the U.S. Coast Guard as a 2nd-class seaman, and Charley, twenty-eight, went into in the U.S. Naval Reserve "for the duration of the war" as a 1st-class storekeeper. The uncertain possibility of victory over the Central Powers prompted Charley to propose to his beloved Mary Frances Mahoney. The couple had been sweethearts dating back to high school and had originally met at a winter ice-skating session.

Mary's father, John Mahoney, a designer in the Boston Public Gardens, had died when she was a small child, and her mother, Eleanor Good Mahoney, who purveyed fashionable clothing in the city, raised the family quite nicely on her earnings. The nuptials took place in a quiet ceremony conducted within the rectory of St. Peter's Church in Dorchester. After a brief New York honeymoon, Charley returned to duty, and Mary to her job as a telephone operator for Stone & Webster in Boston.[1] Then, to everyone's surprise, Kate, at thirty-three, also joined the navy, the only service that accepted women enlistees during World War I. She received the rank of yeoman (F) with an assignment to Charlestown Navy Yard.[2] The seemingly distant war had come to Dorchester with a vengeance, and entangled three of Tom and Kate's brood.

McManus not only withstood these family upheavals, but at sixty-one, giving no indication of advancing age or declining energy, continued to exercise his architectural abilities. For several years he had toyed with the idea of designing a large knockabout hospital schooner for a floating medical facility on the banks. He built an enormous model of this vessel, and the four-foot-long creation occupied one of the windowsills in the family's Scituate summer house. Although the fishing press periodically discussed the need for such a vessel, it was not built.

During the latter part of 1916, Tom picked up an unusual client, Alessandro Fabbri, who prompted him to take the first practical step toward developing the hospital schooner idea. Fabbri, the son of Ernesto G. Fabbri, a partner in the international banking firm of J.P. Morgan & Company, had been educated at the Westminster School in Simsbury, Connecticut, and privately tutored in the United States and Europe. The Fabbri family had an extensive summer estate at Bar Harbor, Maine, and, despite their New York City birth and residence, Alessandro and his older brother Ernesto actively engaged in Bar Harbor politics. Fabbri's natural inquisitiveness, nurtured by his education, led to an interest in science, and he eventually achieved distinction as a naturalist, explorer, inventor, hunter, and yachtsman.[3]

---

[1] Telephone interview, Mrs. D. Forbes Will née Louise McManus, the daughter of Charles and Mary McManus, 5 May 1990. The couple's only other child, Charles, a World War II naval aviator, died in a 1944 flying accident, when his parachute failed to open after he bailed out of his disabled aircraft.

[2] McManus recorded enlistment information about the boys in a pocket diary supplied by his cousin, Charles McManus, the clothier son of his uncle Patrick: "George J. McManus Enlisted in the U.S.C. Guard May 14th 1917 for one year 2nd Class Seaman"; "Charles F. McManus Enlisted in the U.S.N. Reserves 1917. for duration of the War. 1st Class Store Keeper"; "Wm. Kenneth McManus Enlisted in the U.S.N. Reserves Jan. 2, 1918. Went to Hingham on Jan. 22. thence to Wakefield thence to Bumkins Island thence to Halifax N.S. March 12th;" "Thomas F. McManus Jr. Enlisted in the U.S.N.R. 1st Class Carpenter's Mate went to Hingham 18th April left So. Station May 10th at 4.30 P.M. for ?" The diary does not mention daughter Catherine.

[3] Bar Harbor *Times*, 8 February 1922.

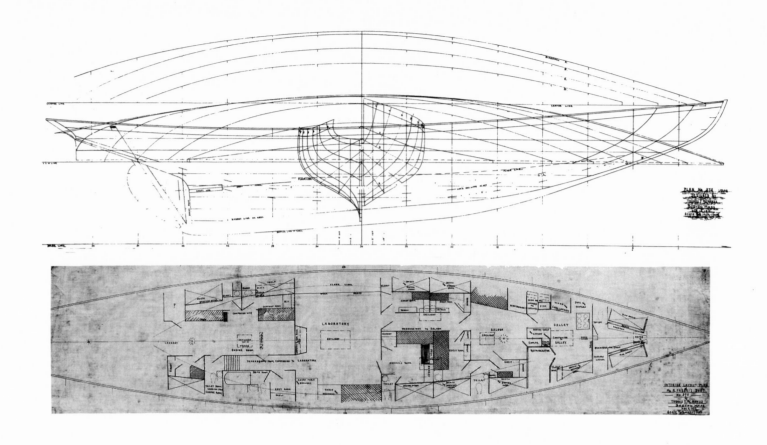

"Mr. A. Fabbri's Boat," McManus's Design No. 375, was a full-size knockabout hull laid out for scientific research. The 118-ton vessel (107.3x23.2x10.8 feet), designated SP-738, was taken into the navy as the U.S.S. *Rockport* for patrol duty around Boston Harbor. Renamed *Ajax* after the war, she served as a freight boat with a 75-horsepower gasoline engine. (Courtesy Louise V. Will)

He received the appointment of Research Associate in Physiology at the American Museum of Natural History and, spurred by this acknowledgement of his talents, approached McManus to design a knockabout ketch, whose size would fall between Foster's *Autocrat* and *Finback*, for his scientific investigations. Fabbri's concept called for the finish of a yacht and the sailing qualities of a fishing schooner, with a built-in laboratory to conduct experiments with the samples of marine *flora* and *fauna* he intended to collect. His timing, from McManus's point of view, could not have been better. Tom invited the young man down to Scituate and showed him the giant model of the hospital schooner. This ploy worked to perfection, and Fabbri commissioned McManus to complete the drafts for his floating laboratory.

When Tom completed the plans for this unusual craft, he sent them off to Frank C. Adams at East Boothbay, the selected building yard. The choice was a good one, as the Adams family were noted for quality vessels. Frank's father, William Irving Adams, had built one of Sanford C. Winsor's first Indian Headers, the *Manomet* of 1901. The younger Adams had recently finished McManus's great *Elizabeth Howard* and was preparing to lay down a sistership of his own design, the *Louise Howard*, for the same New York owner.

Within days of America's entry into World War I, Fabbri decided to cancel his new vessel due to the rapidly developing shortage of building materials and, especially, power plants. He traveled down to Boston from Bar Harbor on 21 April 1917 to settle his accounts with Tom, who came up from Dorchester for a meeting in his client's hotel suite. After receiving the unwelcome instructions to cancel all outstanding contracts, the unhappy Irishman left to return home. In the meantime, Fabbri went to Charlestown and spent the balance of the day with an old friend, Lieutenant Henry C. Gawler, at the navy yard.[4] Before the afternoon was out, he received the offer of a commission in the navy, accompanied by an urgent request to complete his sturdy new yacht, which he had named *Ajax*,[5] and sell her to the government for use in the Coast Patrol Service. Implementing his part of the bargain, Fabbri straightaway telephoned Dorchester with the message for Tom to complete the vessel with all possible dispatch. McManus, who reached Mill Street in a high state of dudgeon, had no sooner settled into his favorite chair than Fabbri's call came.[6]

When the navy began dragging its anchors over a promised letter of commitment to the arrangement, Fabbri took the matter into his own hands and planned a trip to Washington: "where I shall see Mr. Franklin Roosevelt and our Senator from Maine, Mr. [Frederick] Hale. If I can help expedite the slow-moving wheels of the mighty Navy Department towards the solution of our little problem, please let me know."[7] His lobbying brought forth a letter from Roosevelt's boss, Secretary of the Navy Josephus Daniels, approving the *Ajax* for the service.[8] After a long summer of waiting, Fabbri received word from the secretary that President Wilson had authorized the *Ajax*, SP-738, to be purchased for $20,958.29, and to turn the vessel over, "in her present unfinished condition," to the commandant of the First Naval District. She served as the *U.S.S. Rockport* on patrol from Boston between February 1918 and February 1919.[9] Tom could now add a navy patrol boat to his list of design types.

---

[4] Fabbri's friend Gawley, a citizen sailor, had only been in service for a month. He was part of the U.S. Naval Coast Defense Reserve, Class 4.

[5] Fabbri to Lieutenant Henry C. Gawler, U.S.N., Boston Navy Yard, 24 April 1917, Fabbri Papers, Manuscript Division, Library of Congress, Washington, D.C., hereafter cited as "Fabbri Papers."

[6] Handwritten autobiographical notes of Lieutenant Alessandro Fabbri, U.S.N.R., Fabbri Papers.

[7] Fabbri to Gawler, 1 May 1917, Boston Navy Yard, Fabbri Papers.

[8] Daniels to Fabbri, undated, coded Op-14-Sm-H, Fabbri Papers.

[9] Daniels to Fabbri, 25 September 1917, coded Op-14-Sm-D, Fabbri Papers; the U.S.S. *Rockport* was sold out of naval service in September 1919 and resumed her civilian name *Ajax*, *Dictionary of American Naval Fighting Ships*, 8 vols., (Washington, D.C. : Naval History Division, Department of the Navy, 1976), 6:142.

To no one's surprise, on 2 January 1918, little Kenny, not about to be left out of the war effort, managed to falsify his papers, lie about his age, and join the navy. By 12 March he was on the way to his duty station at Halifax, Nova Scotia. A little while later, the wartime paranoia over enemy saboteurs had its own effect on the waterfront trades. The United States Marshal began to tighten security on Boston's wharves to protect against that danger. On 25 March his office issued Waterfront Pass No. 376026 to Tom, granting him egress to the "Ports of Massachusetts." McManus's occupation was listed as a "naval designer," employed by "myself," and his entry access rights were "universal."[10] The next family disruption occurred when Tom, Jr., enlisted in the Navy Reserve as a 1st class carpenter's mate. He went to Hingham on 18 April for indoctrination into the service. A few weeks later Tom, Sr., took him to South Station on 10 May, where he departed at 4:30 P.M. for an unannounced destination.

The McManus family now had six members, half of its offspring, involved in the war effort. The Grim Reaper, after almost annual visits to them during the nineteenth century, had ignored the family thus far in the twentieth. But death's anguish returned in 1918 when the McManuses' sixth daughter, Louise, only thirty-one, who had married John F. Dever, a Boston alderman in the mid-1890s, succumbed during the nationwide influenza epidemic that struck the United States during 1918-20, killing at least half a million of its citizens. Her husband and two children, Dorothy and Jack, Jr., survived her.

Surpassing the expectations of both sides, by late summer 1918 the trenches of northwestern Europe, muddied as much by belligerent blood as by the teeming summer rains, contained over 108,000 American "doughboys" committed to the Ypres offensive, the last great Allied thrust of the war. The United States had provided substantially more than its industry and navy to the Allied war effort.

On the night of 19 August, President Wilson, who had been vacationing in Gloucester near the summer residence of his closest personal advisor, Colonel Edward M. House of Texas, abruptly left town for Washington on board the presidential train. Coincidentally, on the next morning Germany unleashed its underseas might against 250 defenseless fishing vessels on the Grand Banks. A prowling predator, the U-156, captured the Canadian steam trawler *Triumph*. Then, in a legitimate *ruse-de-guerre*, armed and manned the captured vessel and sent her among the banks fleet under the guise of a motor fishing vessel flying the red ensign of the Dominion of Canada. The villainous *Triumph* claimed her first victims on the twentieth, the Gloucester schooners *A. Piatt Andrew*, Captain Wallace Bruce, and *Francis J. O'Hara, Jr.*, Captain Joe Mesquita, as well as three Lunenburg-based

---

10 Artifact in the possession of Thomas F. McManus's granddaughter, Mrs. Dustin Pevear.

Canadian schooners. The *Triumph*'s invidious trick was to cruise close alongside each schooner, drop the Canadian ensign, hoist German colors, give each skipper a few moments to abandon ship, and then blow up his vessel.[11]

After a series of these depredations, the *Triumph*, guided by *Oberleutnant* J. Knoeckel, the U-156's executive officer, came up with McManus's eight-year-old semi-knockabout *Sylvania*, commanded by Captain Jeff Thomas (the father of author Gordon W. Thomas), on 31 August. Using a megaphone, Knoeckel ordered Thomas to come on board the trawler with his papers. When the German confirmed the schooner's American ownership, he gave Thomas and his men ten minutes to abandon ship. While they did, the enemy sailors went on board and placed time bombs in the bilges. As Jeff Thomas and his men sadly watched the *Sylvania* being blown to bits from their dories, the skipper spied the *Triumph*'s mother vessel, the U-156, hovering on the surface a short distance away.[12] It is worthy of note that the five identifiable American schooners lost to German submarines during 1917-18 were all McManus designs, a measure of his presence in the North Atlantic fishing fleet.

With time running out on their depredations, the German prize crew scuttled the captured *Triumph* just before the equinoctial gales arrived and returned on board their submarine. The U-156 then headed for Germany, but the raider never completed the homeward voyage. She struck an Allied mine a few days before the Armistice, and sank to the bottom of the North Sea, entombing her crew of seventy-seven war-weary sailors.

Despite America's preoccupation with the grim question of whether or not to enter the war in Europe, yachtsmen did not give up their avocation. During 1916, Martin S. Kattenhorn, a Wall Street merchandise broker from New Rochelle, New York, commissioned Tom to design a schooner yacht as a scaled down version of a McManus fisherman. Kattenhorn had been a founding member, and later commodore, of the Cruising Club of America. His new cruiser, the 44–foot *Surprise*, was a small schooner with moderate fore and aft overhangs, a fair-sized foredeck, trunk cabin amidships, self-bailing cockpit, and a small aft deck.[13] The owner requested a fisherman's style of rig, with double headsails, gaff foresail, gaff mainsail, and main topsail. The spruce masts were supported by Swedish steel standing rigging, with Manila running rigging. The Waddell Brothers of Rockport, Massachusetts, built this exceptionally strong vessel, which has sailed every season

---

[11] Joseph E. Garland, *Adventure, Queen of the Windjammers* (Camden, Maine: Down East Books, 1985), 17.

[12] Gordon W. Thomas, *Fast & Able, Life Stories of Great Gloucester Fishing Vessels* (Gloucester, Massachusetts: Gloucester 350th Anniversary Celebration, Inc., 1973), 157.

[13] *Yachting* 21 (February 1917): 82. The *Surprise*'s plans are owned by Mrs. D. Forbes Will.

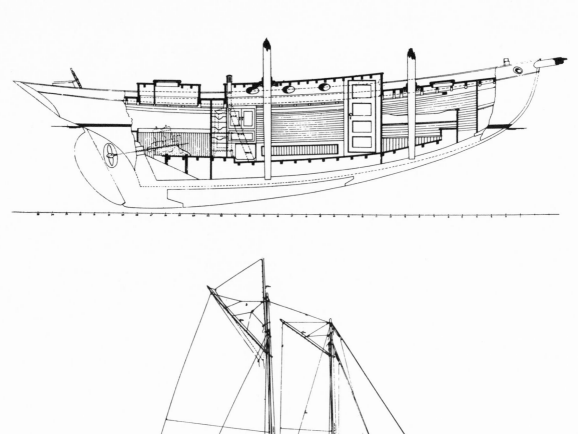

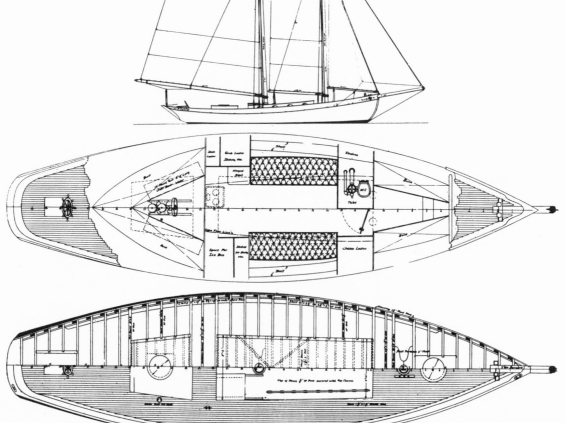

since, and is currently in active charter service at Camden, Maine. Kattenhorn, who remained a bachelor into his sixties, lived and sailed on board his yacht each summer from 1918 through 1959. He proudly expressed his continuing satisfaction in a 1925 letter: "In *Surprise* you gave me a very clever boat and today outside of the latest Alden schooners, she is as fast or faster than most of the small cruising schooners."[14]

Left: Martin Kattenhorn commissioned McManus to design a small cruising-yacht version of a fishing schooner. The resulting 44 1/2-foot round-bow schooner *Surprise*, with outside ballast, satisfied Kattenhorn's desire for a fast, trim, seaworthy yacht. (*Yachting Magazine* , February 1917)

Soon after the World War ended, the Rum War at sea began. The United States Congress passed the National Prohibition Act (the Volstead Act), during October 1919, and, although Wilson vetoed the proposed legislation, the lawmakers passed it over his disapproval. Designed to supply the enforcement apparatus for the Eighteenth Amendment to the Constitution, which came into effect on 17 January 1920, this act set the stage for one of the most quixotic periods in American history.

At the beginning of 1921, soon after the new law was in place, Captain William F. "Bill" McCoy, a sometime Daytona Beach, Florida, boatbuilder, guided his fully-laden McManus schooner, the *Henry L. Marshall*, past Tybee Lighthouse and up the river to Savannah, where, in the dark of the night, he discharged not fish, but 1,500 cases of illicit liquor. With the proceeds, McCoy replaced himself with a new skipper on board the *Marshall* and went to Gloucester in search of the boat of his dreams, Tom's speedy *Arethusa*. Although McCoy had fished the *Marshall* legitimately until after the Eighteenth Amendment dried out the country, he had always thirsted for the *Arethusa*.[15] With Gloucester feeling the effect of the postwar economic contraction, the owners of the fourteen-year-old schooner, the F. C. Pearce Company of Gloucester, including her distinctly reluctant part-owner and captain, Clayton Morrissey, sold her to McCoy in April 1921. The *Arethusa* became a rum-runner, a fast freighter of bootleg spirits. McCoy renamed her the *Tomoka*, added a bowsprit so she could carry two jibs, jumbo and jib topsail–and a lot of liquor (she had a capacity of 6,000 cases of illegal alcohol).[16]

After taking a contraband cargo on board at Nassau in the Bahamas during May, McCoy sailed up the Gulf Stream and stood in for the sandy coast of Long Island. He brought the *Tomoka* to anchor just outside the then three-mile limit of United States waters, but well within sight of the beach. He soon began a thriving business with New York and New Jersey bootleggers, and the pattern he established of lying in international waters off the American coastline drew many imitators.

[14] Letter, M.S. Kattenhorn to McManus, 9 February 1925, *Surprise* Papers, Maine Historic Preservation Committee, Augusta, Maine.

[15] Letter, Erik A.R. Ronnberg, Jr., 18 September 1988.

[16] Thomas, *Fast & Able*, 129, emphasis added.

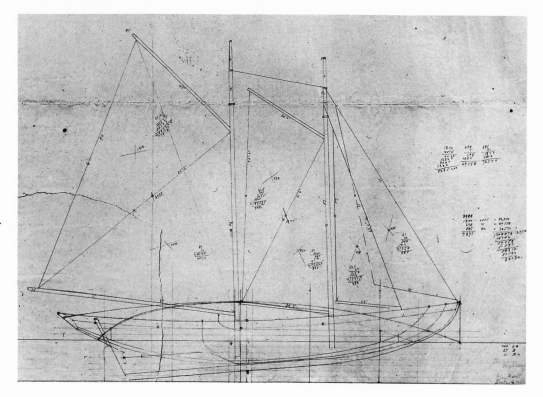

McManus's Canadian designs are not well documented, although they probably made up a sizable proportion of his output in the teens, when the Canadian fleet grew more rapidly than the American fleet. An example is his Plan No. 405, drawn for the Shelburne Shipbuilding Company in 1919. The vessel is a large pole-masted auxiliary knockabout (140 overall x27x11 feet), a model that remained practical and popular in the Canadian fisheries for thirty years. (Courtesy Louise V. Will)

Right: The marine engine strongly influenced McManus's later New England designs. The 139-ton *Herbert Parker* (105.3x25.2x11.9 feet) was a round-bow semi-knockabout in hull form, but her 100-horsepower engine and pole masts clearly identified her as a motor-sailer. A.D. Story launched her in 1919. (Courtesy Peabody & Essex Museum, Salem, Massachusetts)

The nefarious "Rum Row," as the resultant chain of booze-bearing boats became known, eventually supplied cities from Maine to Florida.

The paradoxical atmosphere of the Prohibition era found coast guardsmen and smugglers drinking bathtub gin and other forbidden elixirs shoulder to shoulder in dockside speakeasies during the day, then going to sea to shoot at each other during the night. The situation grew so ludicrous that at least one Long Island boatbuilding firm, the Scopinich Brothers of Freeport, constructed high-speed rum-runners powered by twin V-12 gasoline motors at one end of their yard, and single slow-going straight-6 diesel-engine Coast Guard patrol boats at the other.[17]

In July 1921 things got tougher for McCoy when the Coast Guard cutter *Seneca* seized his first schooner, the *Marshall*, and warrants were sworn out for his arrest by the Assistant U.S. Attorney at Jersey City. It took another two years, and an illegal ruse, for the law-enforcement officers to catch the *Tomoka*, ex-*Arethusa*. During that period the successful bootlegger gave McManus a new commission, which journalist George Story Hudson reported, was for a "vessel to be built in the Bahamas of 'horseflesh, a wood that never decays,' as Capt. McCoy puts it."[18]

The end of McCoy's rum-running career came without forewarning. One night in November 1923, federal agents, in cooperation with the Coast Guard, put

[17] Interview, Mario Scopinich, Hampton Bays, New York, boatbuilder, 14 February 1985.

[18] George Story Hudson, the Boston *Sunday Herald*, 5 February 1922. This may be McManus's Plan No. 403 drawn on 29 July 1919, for McCoy and his brother. If so, the vessel was to be a true knockabout.

into effect the principle of search and seizure beyond the three-mile limit and targeted the *Tomoka* as their first victim. The *Seneca* came up with the *Tomoka* at daybreak and found the schooner riding at anchor in a calm sea. Federal agents leaped on board and a brawl broke out between the "Feds" and the smugglers. The G-men, although worse for the wear, searched her and found 200 cases of whiskey–all that remained from McCoy's original cargo of 4,200. While they were still scrambling around her bilges, McCoy got the *Tomoka* underway and a running sea battle ensued. The *Seneca* came up with the *Tomoka* and hailed for McCoy to stop. When he disregarded the warning, the cutter sent two shots across the *Tomoka*'s bows. McCoy discreetly coasted to a halt. Uniformed coast guardsmen then boarded and seized his schooner. Two years later, the government auctioned off the old *Arethusa*.[19]

McCoy made a rum-running fortune with his swift schooner, and earned an unpaid vacation in the federal penitentiary at Atlanta, Georgia. The *Cavalier* and the *Waldo F. Stream*, both seized in 1922, and the Canadian-registered *Golden West* and *Dorothy M. Smart*, captured in 1924, were among other McManus-designed schooners that paid the price for entering the illegal, but lucrative, liquor trade.

Back in 1906 the Essex building yards had entered a period of decline. The boom period of 1900-05, when 158 new fishermen came out of the mouth of the Essex River (an average of 28 per year), was never replicated. From 1906 through 1923, the combined efforts of the surviving yards failed to reach an annual production in double figures until 1924, when 12 new schooners came down the ways. In the interim, the once booming banks of the river produced an average of fewer than six new schooners a year. Many factors contributed to this downturn, ranging from the changeover to motor fishing vessels equipped with no more than blanket-sized riding sails, to the loss of manpower to the war effort, and the subsequent postwar depression. Only four McManus designs, all knockabouts, and a set of plans for a Canadian customer have been discovered for 1920. Arthur D. Story built the knockabout *Edith C. Rose* for Frank Rose, while J.F. James & Son constructed the other three, including the *Oretha F. Spinney* for Captain Lemuel Spinney. Lastly, Tom completed Plan No. 410 for Lunenburg's Smith & Rhuland Shipyard.

The McManus brood suffered a different kind of upheaval when Letitia and her own family became its first members to move away from Massachusetts. After fourteen years of marriage and four children,[20] Titia and her husband, Henry Carruth, moved to Dayton, Ohio, in 1920, where he became vice president of the

Left: Rerigged with a bowsprit, outfitted with a deckhouse forward, and renamed *Tomoka,* the great McManus knockabout *Arethusa* served as a rum runner for Captain Bill McCoy between 1921 and 1923. She later returned to fishing, and was lost off Halifax in November 1929. (M.S.M. 85.50.3)

---

[19] Malcolm F. Willoughby, *Rum War at Sea* (Washington, D.C.: Government Printing Office, 1964), 42.

[20] Eleanor, 17 July 1908; Henry Pope, 14 July 1912; Letitia Marie, 22 February 1914; and Francis Sumner, 2 November 1916.

Mead Company. The rapidly rising executive became president of the Dill & Collins Company a year later. They relocated to Chillicothe, Ohio, where Letitia was diagnosed with cancer. Titia was only thirty-six. Despite a sizable age difference, she and her sister Mildred, who was fourteen years her junior, had been close to each other ever since the younger girl reached her teens. Mildred regularly rode the train to the Midwest after the Carruths moved and, when she learned of Titia's illness, she returned once again, this time accompanied by a very worried Grandma Kate, to spend several months with her sister, especially to help out with the four young children. Despite access to the best medical efforts available, Letitia McManus Carruth passed away on 15 July 1922, four years after her sister Louise had succumbed to influenza during World War I.[21]

The fishermen's races, which had been held on and off since Tom organized the first one in 1886, acquired an international flavor in 1920. William H. Dennis, the publisher of the Halifax *Herald and Mail*, donated a silver cup with the cumbersome title of "The Halifax Herald North Atlantic Fishermen's International Trophy" (which the fishermen quickly shortened to the "Dennis Cup"), and an appropriate prize fund.[22] On 13 October 1920 the hastily-formed Nova Scotian race committee challenged the Gloucestermen to a race between their fastest schooner and a Canadian defender to be selected in elimination trials. The tenor of their telegram, and its omission of the Boston, Maine, and New York banksmen, not to mention the fishermen of Newfoundland, set up a Halifax-Gloucester axis that would have bitter implications throughout the 1920s and 1930s.

The deed of gift for the cup held certain restrictions. The races were intended to "improve the type of fishing craft, both as to speed and seaworthiness . . . without sacrificing utility." The contenders' measurements could not exceed an overall length of 145 feet from outside of stem to outside of taffrail. The limit of waterline length in racing trim, from outside of stem at the point of submersion to the opposite point at the stern, was a maximum of 112 feet. Draft of the vessels was not to exceed 16 feet from the lowest point of the keel to the racing waterline. No outside ballast would be allowed, and inside ballast could not be of any material with a greater specific gravity than iron. Competing vessels had to race with the same spars, including solid booms and gaffs, they used while fishing. This mast regulation has deeper significance than at first appears, for it automatically eliminated those fishing schooners whose pole-masted sail plans had been so

---

21 Harold B. Carruth, *The Carruth Family: A Brief Background and Genealogical Data of Twenty Branches in America* (Ascutney, Vermont: Privately Published, 1952), 122.

22 "BLUENOSE II: A Bicentennial Salute . . . Voeux pour le Bicentenaire," *Port of Mobile* 49 (June 1976), 6:11. "Bluenose" is the New England nickname for the men and boats of Nova Scotia.

reduced as to make them uncompetitive. In form and construction, as well as sail plan and rigging, entrants had to be of the types customarily used in the industry–a regulation that became a travesty.

Why then were the international fishermen's races so magnetically popular? Certainly not for their ability to advance technology, a usual justification for racing. Part of the explanation lies in their preponderant international interest. Also, considering that by the 1920s auxiliary-powered schooners and motor fishing vessels largely outnumbered pure sail-powered schooners and those whose power plants were true auxiliaries (secondary to a full sail inventory), there is a sense that the participants recognized these races as the end of the sail-powered fishing schooner era–an epoch that had spanned centuries.

The confrontation from north of the border caused both a stir and a dilemma in Gloucester. The nature of the challenge, Halifax *versus* Gloucester, as well as the vessel length specified by the deed of gift, precluded at least one American schooner that would have made a mockery of the proposed competition, the New York-owned *Elizabeth Howard* (148 feet 8 inches length on the molded rail cap), which was 3 feet too long under the rules. The only Gloucester vessel in her class, the *Catherine*, was out on a banks trip, and her descendant, C.H.W. Foster's former yacht *Finback*, had been crushed to splinters in Hudson Bay's ice fields the previous winter.

Local fishermen knew from working trips to the north that their Canadian counterparts had built several fast and able new schooners. In Gloucester, however, the trend for the past five or more years had been the return to the pole-masted auxiliary knockabout, which was a good dependable fishing vessel but not an out-and-out speedster. "When the Gloucester sailing committee began to look around for a fast-sailing vessel, available for the race they couldn't find one," Wesley G. Pierce recalled. He described the committeemen as baffled and not knowing where to turn. Difficult as it may be to comprehend, Gloucester, with its long history of swift schooners, could not come up with a challenger. Then, as the perplexed committee members sat around their conference table, that seasoned campaigner, Charley Harty, who first raced in the 1888 fishermen's race, spied an old command of his working into the harbor. He turned to the others and said: "There's our vessel, gentlemen. It's the *Esperanto*; she's the best sailer in our fleet today."[23] Jim Connolly, the fisherman's literary champion, described what happened next: "There was a racking of memories to learn how good a sailer she had been in her day." Harty, the *Esperanto*'s first skipper, readily recollected that, "she could run and she could reach with most of 'em when I had her; and she was a horse for goin' to

23 Wesley G. Pierce, *Goin' Fishin'* (Salem, Massachusetts: Marine Research Society, 1934), 230-31.

wind'ard in a breeze. Get her in trim and you'll have a good all-round sailer!"[24] Neither a modern semi-knockabout nor an updated knockabout, the *Esperanto* was one of McManus's early round-bow variants with her forestay anchored to the gammon iron. Tarr & James had launched her on 17 June 1906. She still had a notably tall rig, spread a cloud of canvas and–most importantly to the committee–did not rely upon auxiliary power: her masts, spars, and sail area were those of a purely canvas-driven vessel.

Once they decided to enter the *Esperanto* and her owner, Benjamin Smith of the Gorton-Pew Fisheries Company, who was also chairman of the race committee, agreed to let her participate, all Gloucester turned to in a community effort to ready the challenger. A telegraphic acceptance of the Canadian challenge went out over the wires on 16 October.[25] After a great deal of coaxing, McManus's pal Marty Welch agreed to take a leave from his normal berth, the schooner *Thelma*, to lead the *Esperanto*'s challenge. He would lead a hand-picked crew of thirty, which included six other skippers,[26] as well as Connolly, who described the *Esperanto* with a bit of hyperbole: "She was a hard-bitten craft to look at. Her paint was peeling, her hull was crusted with salt frost, shreds of marine growth were showing at her water line. Her sails were patched and worn, and she herself was fourteen years old–a great age for an offshore fisherman."[27] Captain Still Hipson, who brought the *Esperanto* in from a three-month salt-banking trip to Banquereau, delivered 250,000 pounds of salt fish to the dock and turned her over to Charley Harty to repair, prepare, and trim for the race. The riggers went to work on her running gear, and the lumpers turned to the task of stowing eighty-five tons of ballast under Harty's demanding direction.[28] With insufficient time available to cut a new suit of sails, the four-year-old set on board went to Marion Cooney's United Sail Loft to have new life stitched into them. Then they hauled the old girl up on the marine railway, scrubbed and painted her hull, and cleaned her bottom.

When she went back into the water, Harty shook the old workhorse down off Eastern Point. The *Esperanto*'s freshly-painted, shining black hull, highlighted by a sunny yellow cove stripe that accentuated her graceful sheerline, made a beautiful picture that day. With the *Esperanto* powered by her reworked cotton duck sails that filled to satisfying shapes in the topsail breeze, Harty skillfully displayed her potential.

Right: The only American fishing schooner to win the Halifax Herald North Atlantic Fishermen's International Trophy was the fourteen-year-old round-bow *Esperanto*, 140 tons (107.4x25.4x11.4 feet), built in 1906. Just six months after her victory, she stranded on a wreck near Sable Island and was lost. (Courtesy Peabody & Essex Museum, Salem, Massachusetts)

---

[24] James B. Connolly, *The Port of Gloucester* (New York: Doubleday, Doran & Company, 1940), 276.

[25] Dana Story, *Hail COLUMBIA!, The Rise and Fall of a Schooner* (1970; reprint Gloucester, Massachusetts: Ten Pound Island Book Company, 1985), 28.

[26] John Matheson, Wallace Bruce, Tom Benham, Jack Barrett, Lee Murray, and Roy Patten.

[27] Connolly, *Gloucester*, 276.

[28] Ibid.

And he knew her secret. The *Esperanto*, possibly because of the marked drag of a round-bow's keel, sailed best when trimmed about eight inches by the bow–a quality Harty discovered during his tenure in command.[29] When he had brought her performance up to a satisfactory standard, Harty turned the *Esperanto* over to her racing skipper. Captain Marty Welch took over her wheel on 25 October, and a Gloucester waterfront crowded with spectators watched the *Esperanto* set sail for Halifax. Connolly recorded that, "everything that could float was sailed or motored or rowed past Eastern Point to see her square her stern to the old light and lay her east-half-south compass course for the Nova Scotia shore."[30] If thousands had waved goodbye to the *Esperanto* off Gloucester, thousands more welcomed her into Canadian waters fifty-one hours later.

To encourage spectators, the Halifax race organizers placed the start and finish lines at the mouth of Halifax harbor, and laid the opening leg of the course close to the oceanside beach. As their champion, the Haligonians had selected the brand-new, swift but burdensome Lunenburg-built schooner *Delawanna*, Captain Tom Himmelman, which had defeated eight other Canadian schooners in a closely fought contest for the right to meet the American challenger.

The first race went off on 30 October. Himmelman won the start. Strangely, this did not appear to bother the wily Welch at all. According to Wesley Pierce, "very quietly Marty smoked his cigar and watched every move, for the first few minutes of sailing would tell him something of his vessel's speed, compared to that of the new *Delawanna*, at least on this point of sailing."[31] The American slowly caught up with the Canadian, worked past her, and, although Himmelman put the Canadian entry ahead on two further occasions that day, came home the winner by three miles and twenty minutes.

During the second race, on 1 November, the hard-headed American skipper gave a display of the combination of touch, skill, and tenaciousness for which he was justly famous. It took place when Himmelman, holding right-of-way, drove Welch toward the jagged ledges of Devil's Island in a closely fought luffing match. To make matters worse, the *Esperanto*, closer inshore, drew two more feet than her Canadian counterpart. In the interest of fairness the committee had put a Gloucester representative on board the *Delawanna*, and one of their own, a Canadian harbor pilot, on board the *Esperanto*. As the island's rocky beach loomed closer, Micky Hall, "the masthead-man, called out that he could see the bottom, in

---

[29] Most schooners performed better when trimmed by the stern.

[30] Connolly, *Gloucester*, 277-78.

[31] Pierce, *Goin' Fishin'*, 232.

[32] Ibid., 233.

tones loud enough to be heard plainly by all those on the deck of *Esperanto*; but Marty Welch never let on that he heard what the man said and made him no reply."[33] It was the Canadian judge standing alongside Welch who finally cracked the tense atmosphere on deck. He shouted sharply across to the *Delawanna* that she must give way. The gentlemanly Himmelman complied, and the American schooner was not driven onto the rocks. Welch then calmly tacked the *Esperanto* offshore and out of danger. Once he regained clear water, without hesitation he sailed through the *Delawanna*'s wind, grabbed the lead, and held on to win by eight minutes. He took the championship, the Dennis Cup, and $4,000 home to Gloucester for the only International Trophy victory won by an honest fishing schooner in the event's eighteen-year history. Witnesses to the condition of the two competitors adjudged the considerably newer *Delawanna* to be the tighter and drier vessel, giving all the more credit to Welch.[33]

He brought the *Esperanto* into Gloucester on 7 November with a new broom sticking up above the masthead to signal a clean sweep. Gordon Thomas, then fourteen, watched the homecoming: "What a reception she received! It was probably the greatest ever given to a Gloucester fishing vessel. There were banquets and receptions galore for the victorious crew." The ceremonies reached a peak at the armory the next day in the presence of Governor Calvin Coolidge, who declared, "the victory was a triumph for Americanism."[34]

---

[33] George S. Hubbard, "How the *Esperanto* Won the Fishermen's Race," *Yachting* 28 (1920): 298.

[34] Thomas, *Fast & Able*, 126-27.

CHAPTER FIFTEEN

The *Blanche Ring,* and *Henry Ford*

M arty Welch barely had the *Esperanto* out of Nova Scotian waters before a cantankerous Canadian-Irishman named Captain Angus L. Walters formed a syndicate at Lunenburg to recapture the Dennis Cup. The group hired a promising young naval architect, William J. Roué, to design the largest possible schooner allowed under the existing provisions of the *Herald*'s deed of gift. The result of Roué's endeavors was the fastest fishing schooner under sail in Canada's history–the *Bluenose.*

Captain Clayton Morrissey and "Captain" Tom McManus stand together at the wheel of the *Henry Ford.* Morrissey (1874-1936) came to Gloucester from East Pubnico, Nova Scotia, and took command of the *Effie M. Morrissey* at age nineteen. He specialized in the salt-cod fishery with a number of vessels, including the renowned McManus design *Arethusa.* (Neg. 9210F, © Rosenfeld Collection, Mystic Seaport Museum, Inc.)

After the *Esperanto* left Halifax, Dennis and his associates met and drafted a formal deed of gift for the International Trophy. Along with fishing qualifications and some specification limitations, it outlined the organization of officialdom. The Cup was to be administered by nine Canadian trustees, one of them the premier of Nova Scotia and another the mayor of Halifax. Race officiating would be by a five-man international race committee elected for each racing series. The trustees would pick two Canadian members, and the governor of Massachusetts, in consultation with Gloucester parties, would name two American ones. The two members representing the site of a given event would pick the chairman. This level of political involvement–in a mere sporting event–clearly defines the importance of the North Atlantic fishing industry to both areas.

Two of the newly drafted regulations had dramatic effects on the series. The first read: "Vessels shall race with the same spars and with no greater sail area than used in fishing, *but the sail area not to exceed 80 percent of the square of the waterline length as expressed in square feet.*" The other: "All vessels to be propelled by sails only *and not to exceed 125 feet in length overall.*" The regulations under which the *Esperanto* and the *Delawanna* had competed allowed an overall length of 145 feet, a stipulation that barred the *Elizabeth Howard* (at 148 feet 8 inches) from the 1920 races.

On 19 December 1920, the Duke of Devonshire, the Governor-General of Great Britain's Dominion of Canada, drove the first bolt into the keel of the new Canadian competitor at the Smith & Rhuland shipyard at Lunenburg. Three months later, when Audrey Smith, the daughter of one of the yard owners and the niece of Captain Walters, christened the new schooner the *Bluenose* on 26 March 1921, the vessel that came down the ways was 143 1/2 feet long. Sometime between October and December 1920, the overall length limit of 145 feet had been extended to 150 feet, although Roué had obviously designed to 1920's 145-foot figure.

At this point the port of Boston firmly tossed its hat into the ring. A number of downtown and waterfront businessmen formed the Mayflower Associates. To W. Starling Burgess they gave the task of preparing an appropriate design to defend the now American-owned Cup. For her construction they selected the J.F. James & Son shipyard at Essex, which brought in an extra gang from East Boston and completed the new schooner in fifty-nine working days.[1] But, when Burgess's unique and suspiciously swift *Mayflower*, "the cleanest bottomed fishing schooner ever built,"[2] first appeared, a combination of apprehensive Nova Scotians and provincial Gloucestermen legislated her out of the competition. The

---

[1] Dana A. Story, *Hail COLUMBIA!, The Rise and Fall of a Schooner* (1970; reprint Gloucester, Massachusetts: Ten Pound Island Book Company, 1985), 34.

[2] Charlton L. Smith, Boston *Evening Transcript*, 11 April 1922.

Canadians clearly feared her potential, but the Cape Ann people displayed more resentment toward her home port than any concern they had for her sailing qualities. The *Mayflower*'s disqualification from the 1921 racing series set the stage for the rest of the honestly conceived but ill-managed international fishermen's races, which arbitrarily took place from time to time through and including 1938, and remained steeped in acrimony throughout.

Gloucester's unsavory silence over the Canadian rejection of Boston's Burgess boat before she ever hoisted a sail in competition placed the local committee in the position of having to select another valiant but sea-worn schooner to represent the United States. Tom's *Elsie*, by then a veteran of eleven years on the banks, defeated McClain's old *Arthur James* of 1905 and three other aging McManus-designed schooners–the 1902 *Nellie Dixon* derivative *Philip P. Manta*, the 1914 round-bow semi-knockabout *Ralph Brown*, and the small 1915 knockabout *Elsie G. Silva*–on 12 October in a twenty-knot breeze over a forty-mile course, and went to Halifax to defend the Dennis Cup.[3] The headlines announced,

---

[3] Frederick William Wallace, "The International Fishermen's Race," *Yachting* 30 (1921): 214.

"Marty Welch Will Uphold The Fame Of The Fishermen."[4] In the event, Roué's powerful new *Bluenose* proved unbeatable.

Schooner	Waterline Length	Draft	Sail Area
Elsie	102.6 ft.	14.4 ft.	8,500 sq. ft.
Bluenose	110.0 ft.	15.6 ft.	10,000 sq. ft.

TABLE 9 - PUBLISHED DIMENSIONS - *ELSIE VS. BLUENOSE* (SEE ALSO TABLE 10)[5]

The match-up was a mockery. The Canadian challenger was longer overall, longer on the waterline, wider, and deeper, than the American defender. The *Bluenose* hoisted nearly 1,500 square feet more sail than the *Elsie*, and, whenever they went to windward together, the difference was as distinct as the glistening yacht fittings and finish of the Lunenburg charger were to the Gloucesterman's drab workaday appurtenances. But there was more to it than the windward legs alone. A committeeman, V.C. Johnson, figured the time between each mark of the course, the only accurate comparison of speed on each point of sailing, and concluded that the *Bluenose* was faster on nearly every heading, but most of all when going to weather.[6] By the time Welch brought the gallant old *Elsie* home, it was clear to all that the only way to defeat the colossal Canadian champion was to fight her on her own terms in 1922–with a schooner capable of sailing at competitive racing speeds, yet burdensome enough to honestly work in the New England fishing industry.

Although clearly outclassed, one of the year's new schooners sometimes received mention as a possible contender. This was the *L.A. Dunton*, launched by A.D. Story in March for Captain Felix Hogan. He had commanded a succession of McManus designs: the 1903 Indian Header *Elmer E. Gray*, the 1905 round-bow *Raymah*, and the round-bow semi-knockabouts *Elk* of 1910 and *Somerville* of 1914. McManus modeled the *L.A. Dunton* off the *Joffre* of 1918. With the postwar contraction still holding tight, Hogan had his new schooner built without an engine, making her and her sister *American* the last all-sail American fishing schooners launched for working rather than racing. A good sport, Captain Hogan entered her in the elimination races, lost badly, and then returned to haddocking and halibuting. After a long career in United States and Newfoundland waters, the *L.A. Dunton* has been preserved at Mystic Seaport Museum. She can be seen there today–a floating example of Captain Tom McManus's fishing schooner designs.

---

[4] Boston *Sunday Herald*, 16 October 1921.

[5] Wallace, "Fishermen's Race," 214.

[6] Captain V.C. Johnson, "How the Fishermen's Race Was Sailed," *Yachting* 30 (1921): 277.

Pitching in the choppy seas, with her ballooner (jib topsail) flapping to leeward under the broken foretopmast, the *Elsie* fails in her bid to retain American possession of the Dennis Cup. Outclassed by the much larger *Bluenose*, she proved that the competition was no longer the province of conventional working fishing schooners. (Courtesy Peabody & Essex Museum, Salem, Massachusetts)

The death knell for dory fishing had sounded in 1905, when trawler fishing had finally presented a serious challenge to hooks and lines after false starts in 1865 and 1891, but the funeral procession for the sailing motherships of the New England fishing fleet marched at an indecisive tempo for the next fifteen years. Steam-powered otter trawlers, despite the desertion of Henry Dexter Malone, survived and flourished through that time. In 1914, Malone, always quick to experiment with change, repowered his 1902 Indian Header *Manhassett* with a 120-horsepower NELSECO diesel, which drove her at a respectable nine knots under bare poles. Since then, the Bolinder, Bessemer, Fairbanks-Morse "C-O" (for crude oil), NELSECO, and Wisconsin marine oil engines had become standard in the auxiliary-powered New England fishing fleet.

Malone had unintentionally set the stage for the replacement of steam with diesel power on board the steel otter trawlers. Six years later, the launching of the wooden diesel-powered *Fabia* at East Boothbay, Maine,[7] offered tangible evidence that the heavy-oil engine had reached sufficient technical perfection to replace steam power in the otter trawlers. By the beginning of the 1920s diesel auxiliary schooners had become commonplace and diesel engines had gained a foothold in the steam fleet.

[7] Built by Frank Rice for John Chisolm of Gloucester. The *Fabia* had a 360-horsepower diesel engine (Andrew W. German, "Otter Trawling Comes to America: The Bay State Fishing Company, 1905-1938," *The American Neptune* 44 (Spring 1984): 127-28).

Captain Felix Hogan wanted a proven round-bow semi-knockabout design when he had the *L.A. Dunton* modeled off the 1918 *Joffre*. The 134-ton *Dunton* (104.3x 25x11.6 feet), launched in 1921 with topmasts and without auxiliary power, is shown here under her winter banks rig, with triced-up jib forward and triangular riding or steadying sail aft in place of her furled mainsail. Her topmasts have been left ashore for the season. The crew works on their trawl lines around the trunk cabin, secure in the knowledge that their vessel can withstand virtually any winter weather. The *L.A. Dunton* is preserved at Mystic Seaport Museum. (Courtesy Emery N. Cleaves)

The *Sylph* of 1865 and the *Resolute* of 1891 represented attempts to adopt English-style beam trawling to New England waters, but they also can be considered as the forerunners of another new type of fishing vessel–the dragger. John H. McManus and Dick Leonard abandoned their beam-trawl experiment because of poor market returns. Alfred Bradford and Benjamin Low gave up because of continually damaged or destroyed trawling gear, which had been snagged by irregular bottom contours or moldering wrecks. The *Resolute* experiment did, nevertheless, spawn a working fleet among Provincetown's small schooners and sloops. The smooth sandy bottoms in, and offshore of, Cape Cod Bay and Nantucket Sound enabled them to drag their nets with little damage. Within twelve years of the *Resolute*'s renouncement of beam trawling, the U.S. Bureau of Fisheries counted sixty-five inshore beam trawlers operating from Cape Cod ports with an annual catch of 1.5 million pounds of flounder (the very fish that McManus and Leonard could not sell profitably in 1865) worth $48,169.[8]

[8] Morry Edwards, "The Fisherman's Sea Tractor: Origins and Development of the New England Dragger," *WoodenBoat* 79 (December 1987):51.

Despite the success of his schooner designs, McManus recognized the future of marine power and otter-trawl fishing. His Design No. 415 represents an 80-foot dragger with a vestigial yawl rig, a raised pilothouse aft, and a high sheltering foredeck. The keel retains considerable drag for stability, but the stern resembles a steam trawler's, with considerable bearing for the 100-horsepower engine. By the late 1920s, small otter-trawl vessels like this would begin landing more fish than the schooners that carried dories and fished with trawl lines. The name of the vessel is not known. (Courtesy Louise V. Will)

One of Gloucester's leading fishermen, Captain Sol Jacobs, took the next step toward the dragger concept when he fitted his herring seiner *Lydia F.* with a beamless trawl in December 1905. Irish offshore fishermen had invented this apparatus, known as the otter board trawl, during the mid-1860s.[9] Otter boards proved by far the most effective way to keep a net under tow open horizontally. During the 1880s the English North Sea fleet began to use them and by the end of the nineteenth century they were in widespread use throughout European fishing ports. New England fishermen, never enamored with foreign technology, only grudgingly accepted the big steam-powered otter trawlers and allowed a world war to inhibit further local development of their design.

There are, however, practical factors to be considered, principally capital and labor. Steam trawlers used large otter trawls, while draggers used small ones. Clearly, although the fishing technology is the same, the platforms, the motive power, and the manning requirements are different. As Andrew W. German has noted: "Since the beginning, large otter trawlers had been steam-powered, carrying bunkers for fifteen or sixteen days of continuous steaming. The capitalization required to build and maintain such a vessel ensured a limited fleet of otter trawlers." It was this capitalization factor that provided the theater in which Malone built his stage with the relatively inexpensive conversion of the *Manhassett*

---

[9] John de Courcy Ireland, *Ireland's Sea Fisheries: a History* (Dun Laoghaire: The Glendale Press, 1981), 71. Professor Ireland corrects John Dyson, *Business in Great Waters* (London: Angus & Robertson, 1977), 260, who, although acknowledging the Irish introduction of otter boards, limits their use to Irish freshwater fishing for lake trout and pike.

Plan 416, dated 18 May 1921,
represents a small schooner-dragger, a
precursor of the *Blanche Ring* design,
which he completed on 24 May as Plan
417. (Courtesy Louise V. Will)

to diesel power: "The real effect of the diesel or crude oil engine was to democratize otter trawling,"[10] because the little wooden draggers were so much more affordable than a big steam trawler.

Morry Edwards argues that New Bedford's Dan Mullins, who had begun beam trawling with his little sloop *Eda J. Morse* in 1909 and switched to otter board trawling a year later, initiated the first schooner-dragger, when he ordered the eighty-one-foot *Mary* from the Wilbur Morse yard of Thomaston, Maine, in 1919. The *Mary*, however, was not designed as a schooner-dragger. She was a typical auxiliary-powered schooner with a sixty-horsepower heavy-oil engine, and a full set of sails, albeit without topmasts. Mullins then gradually reduced his sail inventory until the *Mary* effectively became a motor fishing vessel. Thus, the *Mary* represented evolution, while Tom McManus was about to begin another revolution.

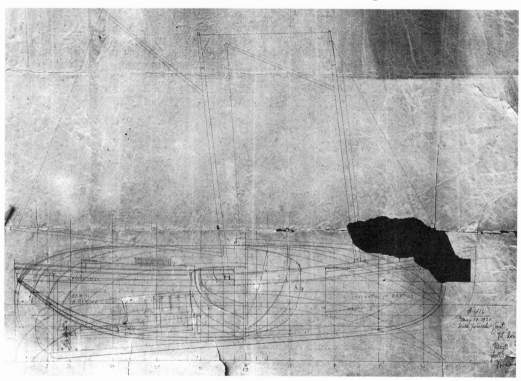

In what can be considered the last shot fired in defense of the auxiliary-powered fishing schooner, even though it heralded the end of dory fishing, the December 1921 issue of *The Fishing Gazette* ran an article headlined a "New Type of Trawler Goes to Sea." The story opened: "among fishing vessels built during the current year the auxiliary schooner *Blanche Ring* stands out as marking a new type." The project under discussion began the previous spring when Captain Herbert W. Nickerson approached McManus to design the prototype of a fishing vessel that

10 German, "Otter Trawling Comes to America," 127-28.

would "ring down the curtain on the saddening ledger sheets displaying lost profits from expensive engine room crews on trawlers."[11] But it wasn't only the extra engineers who would disappear. The *Blanche Ring* carried no dories and, therefore, required fewer fishermen. Instead of manning dories, her crew worked from within her gunwales. McManus's new design was a schooner that used her motor to drag a net along the bottom; in effect, she had *auxiliary* sail! The new fisherman, the closest Tom came to designing a motor fishing vessel, as opposed to an auxiliary-powered one, was the first "eastern-rig" dragger, with pilothouse aft and gallows frames for hauling her gear over the side like a steam trawler.[12] McManus's novel schooner-dragger fisherman changed New England fishing thoroughly in the 1920s, and predominated for nearly fifty years.[13] He completed Plan No. 417 on 24 May, and delivered working drawings for the homely workboat to "Honest Dave" Waddell, whose Rockport yard then laid down the keel and began framing out the remarkably different fishing boat.

Under construction at the Waddell yard in Rockport, Massachusetts, the *Blanche Ring* clearly shows that she is a power vessel, with a nearly plumb stem, straight keel with some drag, and stern designed to support the weight of an engine. (*Rockport As It Was*, courtesy Boston Public Library)

---

[11] "New Type of Trawler Goes To Sea," *The Fishing Gazette* (December 1921): 25.

[12] German, "Otter Trawling Comes to America," 128-29.

[13] Letter, Andrew W. German, 1 February 1990.

Underway in Boston Harbor, the 62-ton *Blanche Ring* (70.2x20.3x9.2 feet) carries a small knockabout schooner rig—forestaysail, foresail, and steadying sail in place of the mainsail—but her power source is a 100-horsepower engine. On the starboard side, forward of the foremast and aft of the mainmast, are the arched "gallows" frames through which lead the warps (cables) for towing her otter trawl. (*The Fishing Gazette*, December 1921, courtesy Boston Public Library)

A two-cylinder, 100-horsepower, direct-reversing, Bolinder surface ignition, heavy-oil engine powered the *Blanche Ring*. One of the vessel's design secrets lay in her engine watch-standing requirement. The unit only needed alternating watches of a single man each, a significant reduction in operating costs over the crew of coal-shoveling firemen required in steam-powered trawler engine rooms. Her smallish hull was seventy-eight and a half feet long, with a beam of twenty feet and a laden draft of ten and a half feet. Under normal conditions her hold could contain 80,000 pounds of fish. Her blunt prow, straight sheerline, and chopped off stern were a far cry from the graceful lines of the big knockabouts like the *Catherine* and the *Elizabeth Howard* (which her breed would make obsolete), but that unattractive hull was the harbinger of a design that would live and work for the New England fishing fleet long after her architect had departed from the scene. Tom McManus, in his mid-sixties when the *Ring* sailed on her maiden voyage, once again initiated a silhouette change in that fleet—and gave the fishing schooner, albeit one with a stunted rig, a new lease on life.

If the birth of the unlovely schooner-dragger exemplified Tom's visualization of the fishing fleet's future form, then he followed her with a traditional banks beauty, the *piéce de resistance* of his long career, the following year. During 1922, Gloucester would host the three-year-old Dennis Trophy for the first time, and an endemic racing fever infected and gripped the town. American efforts to develop a new challenger were impressive. A peculiar syndication of several Gloucestermen lead by Captain Jeff Thomas and a single Bostonian, Philip P. Manta, joined together as the Manta Club–strange indeed, considering the rancorous relationship between the rival ports.[14] They hired the Boston firm of Burgess & Paine, Naval Architects, to design another suitable racer that could be disguised as a fisherman, which they intended should surpass the swift, but rejected, *Mayflower*.

Gloucester's racing fever was nowhere more personified than in the actions of master mariner Clayton Morrissey, lanky, normally quiet, but forceful in personality, whose great height and habitual stammer sometimes disguised his determined character.[15] Legend has it that he mortgaged his family's home to finance a second new challenger.[16] Whether this is fact or fiction, he certainly did have McCoy's hard cash in hand from the sale of the *Arethusa*. Regardless of its source, as soon as the money became available, he telephoned down to Dorchester to hire a naval architect. But Tom had not waited for any calls before going to work. The one-sided defeat of his pet schooner *Elsie* had provoked an instantaneous response. As soon as he heard a firsthand description of the *Bluenose* from Marty Welch, he knew that no recently built American fisherman could cope with the size and sail power of Roué's racer. New England fishing boats had too easily, although rightly, come to depend upon auxiliary engines with a reduction of, and lack of attention to, the development of their sailing rigs.

Within ten days of the *Elsie*'s return to the United States, Tom put down his pencil with Plan No. 419 complete. By then McManus, incredibly, had stood as the unchallenged dean of fishing schooner design for more than a score of years. And, even though he had passed the mid-point of his sixty-sixth year, age continued to treat him kindly. The fact that he produced the drafts so quickly demonstrates that he had been contemplating a pure sailing schooner for some time. The overall design represented the culmination of everything–family genes, youthful shipyard tutoring, formal architectural training, thirty-years' experience since the launch of the *James S. Steele*–that had raised the level of McManus's self-acknowledged "gift,"

---

[14] Jeffrey Thomas, William Thomas, Robert Wharton, Charles C. Colson, James Mason, Benjamin Pine, all fishing masters, Marion J. Cooney of the United Sail Loft, George E. Roberts, Herbert W. Wennerberg, Alexander McDonald, Carmello Capillo, Charles F. Fuller, Charles A. Steele, and J. Norman Abbott. Each owned a 1/16th share of the *Puritan*, except Jeff Thomas, who, as skipper, had three (Gordon W. Thomas, *Fast & Able, Life Stories of Great Gloucester Fishing Vessels* (Gloucester, Massachusetts: Gloucester 350th Anniversary Celebration, Inc., 1973), 189).

[15] Telephone conversation, Dana A. Story, 7 July 1993.

[16] James B. Connolly, *The Port of Gloucester* (New York: Doubleday, Doran & Company, 1940), 283.

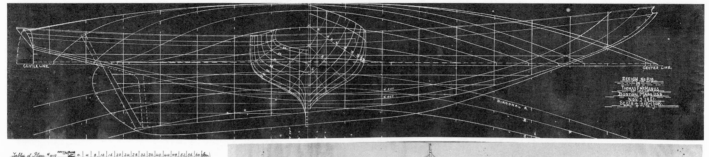

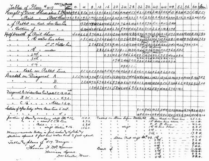

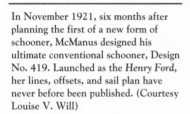

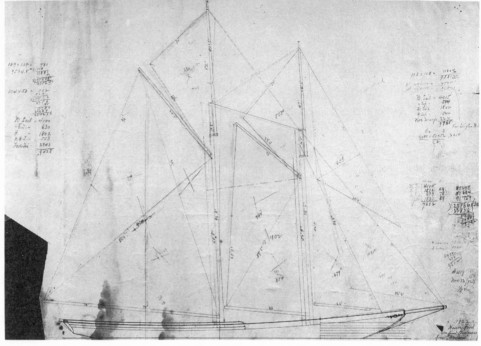

In November 1921, six months after planning the first of a new form of schooner, McManus designed his ultimate conventional schooner, Design No. 419. Launched as the *Henry Ford*, her lines, offsets, and sail plan have never before been published. (Courtesy Louise V. Will)

that inborn ability to comprehend the complex interaction between hull and sails with wind and water, to its present preeminence. Plan No. 419 was his masterpiece.

With the hull drawings wrapped up, McManus telephoned the anxious skipper to come and collect them. By the time Clayt reached 29 Mill Street, Tom also had the offset tables figured out and waiting. Morrissey had already engaged Arthur D. Story to build the new schooner. When he left the house, he took the drawings and tables straight to Archer Poland's loft for molding. Three weeks later, Tom sent the sail plan to Marion Cooney at United's Gloucester sail loft. By 28 November 1921, the entire design process had been completed.

The Manta Club had not been idle, but had hired J.F. James & Son to build their Burgess-designed schooner. A little smaller than the *Mayflower*, her lines approached those of a true fisherman more closely than her predecessor. She tended eleven dories and carried a crew of twenty-five. Her chosen name, *Puritan* (for the 1885 America's Cup defender), must have brought back haunting memories for Tom of the days when McManus sails powered that victorious racer.

With two American challengers for the Dennis Cup building for the spring fishing season, there was a charged atmosphere in Essex that winter of 1921-22. The riverbanks once again reverberated to the sound of saws, adzes, and hammers. Visitors were commonplace. George S. Hudson, the Boston reporter, traveled to Essex to check progress on the new schooners early in February. Business continued slow, so both the *Puritan* and Tom's creation were well along in the construction process. "She's tall, sleek and able-looking this fishing schooner that T.F. McManus created to wrest the international fishing vessel trophy from the Canadians," Hudson wrote in the following *Sunday Herald*. "McManus? Why, everybody interested in fishing craft knows Tom as a wizard. Even down in Nova Scotia they appraise his work so highly as to copy his models and rigs and what not."[17]

"The McManus cup schooner," according to Hudson's reported dimensions, was 138 feet overall (12 feet short of the revised maximum length), 109 feet on the waterline (a little more than 2 1/2 feet short of the *Bluenose*), 25 1/2 feet beam, 12 1/2 depth of hold, and 15 feet draft (a half a foot less than the *Bluenose*). Those short hull dimensions would set up the mainsail controversy to come. The new schooner had a mainmast that was 100 feet overall and 88 feet from deck to cap. Her designed sail area approached 10,000 square feet. At that time, no name had been selected, and it is not clear where Morrissey came up with the one he did. The ones under consideration included *Indian*, *Wizard*, and *Prosper*. Yet, when she lay completed on the stocks, *Henry Ford* was carved into her nameboards.[18] In design, this vessel somewhat resembled the *Oriole*, but with sharper lines, slackened bilges, and a longer overhang.

On 11 April, a day short of four weeks after the *Puritan* had disappeared downriver, the McManus schooner stood high on the stocks at A.D. Story's Essex shipyard, ready to slide down the ways. It was a gray day with an occasional brightening, but a buoyant spring sun broke through the cloud cover in time for the launch. Before the *Ford* went afloat, Tom's journalist friend Charlton Smith walked beneath her with Charley Harty. The veteran fishing captain looked up at her hull and remarked to the writer in a reverential tone: "She's the nearest thing to perfection of any fishing schooner ever built."[19]

Smith depicted McManus that morning as, "a large, stout, elderly man with snow white hair and moustache, off hand, genial, he is the best of companions. A product of the old North End is this Boston boy, whose love for the sea and the

---

17 George Hudson, Boston *Sunday Herald*, 5 February 1922.

18 Dana Story, whose father built the schooner, stated, "just why he picked the name *Henry Ford* seems not to have been recorded (Story, *Hail COLUMBIA!*, 45).

19 Charlton L. Smith, "The Launching of the *Henry Ford*," *Atlantic Fisherman* 3 (April 1922): 3.

vessels that sail on it were fostered by his father the famous sailmaker."[20] A cavalcade of cars brought the McManus family and guests up to Essex. Twenty-five-year-old Mildred, who was a year away from marrying her sweetheart, "Rip" Pierce, and was Tom's preferred chauffeur, probably did the driving for her father. "Essex was again the Mecca of the automobilists to see another fine schooner launched," Smith remembered. "It took more than one automobile to bring Captain Thomas F. McManus and his numerous family down from Dorchester. Eight girls and four boys there are, and many of them were on hand as well as others closely related to the world-famous designer."[21]

The builder, A.D. Story, was a tall, raw-boned man with a commanding presence and markedly fixed habits. A daily trademark was the unlit cigar that protruded from his mouth like a short bowsprit. At the launching of one of his vessels, Story, known as "Danie" by his workmen and others who were close to him, traditionally wore a formal gray suit, a white shirt, and tie, as well as a tweed cap and a boutonniere in his lapel. When he gave her the word that day, Winnie Morrissey, the skipper's daughter, would baptize McManus's ultimate sailing fisherman. Eventually, the number of people clambering onto the schooner troubled Story. He shouted to Harty, who was now up on her deck: "Charlie, I don't care to have any more people aboard. Send the last batch back."[22]

As the christening approached, Tom had taken his usual spectator stance alongside Danie, when the bizarre chain of calamities that befell the *Henry Ford*'s Eastertime baptism began. In front of "several thousand people gathered on every vantage point about the little river basin, and extra buses from Gloucester bringing still more,"[23] a familiar Essex River launching fiasco saw the beautiful schooner race down the ways, flash across the river, and slam her stern into the mudbank on the opposite shore. Then, while, McManus and Story cringed, and Morrissey fumed, the tide ebbed for forty minutes. As the water slowly returned to swell the river, two towboats tugged on the *Ford*'s hapless hull until it popped free from the slimy suction of the silt. When they succeeded in pulling her out, the tugs proceeded downstream with the schooner trailing behind.

With low tide approaching, the shallow-draft towboats safely crossed the river-mouth bar at the entrance to Ipswich Bay. They were no sooner clear of it than their towline parted. The *Ford* proceeded to plow nose high onto the

---

[20] Draft version of a 10 April 1922 Boston *Evening Transcript* article, enclosed in a letter from Smith to McManus, 11 April 1922.

[21] Smith, "Launching of the *Henry Ford*," 3.

[22] Hudson, *Sunday Herald*, 5 February 1922.

[23] Story, *Hail COLUMBIA!*, 45.

underwater sand. The tugboat men, in an inexplicably irresponsible action, sailed off and, from a belief that she was not in dangerous position, left the *Ford* perched on the bar. Later, they made the slipshod excuse that it was their intention to return the next day. Unfortunately, at high water during the night tide, the *Henry Ford* floated free all by herself. She drifted atop Wingaersheek Beach near Hawke's Point, coming to rest on her port side right next to the rocky ledges there, well out of the water. Later in the night, an easterly wind shift flopped her onto her starboard side and put her in imminent danger of destruction, if and when it built up sufficient surf to break her up.[24] The *Ford* suffered a slight hogging in her starboard side, which eventually worked out while she was fishing. She remained in that precarious position until after dawn, when a big tug from Boston that Morrissey had frantically summoned joined the Gloucester towing rigs. The three powerboats heaved and strained on the stranded hulk, but failed to budge it. On the Wednesday of Holy Week, a second big Boston tug replaced one of the towboats, and the Coast Guard cutter *Ossipee* appeared in the offing ready to offer assistance, all to no avail.

On, Holy Thursday, 13 April, a salvage lighter arrived with pontoons. Good Friday afternoon saw them finally break the *Ford* loose from Wingaersheek's

---

[24] Ibid., 45-46.

grip–only to drag her aground minutes later on the same sandbar at the river mouth where she had struck coming out two days before. This time they stood by through the night and yanked her off once again on Saturday. After four passionately agonizing days, a heartsick and fed-up Clayt Morrissey celebrated Easter Sunday by riding his resurrected hull into Gloucester harbor. Tom spent the holiday with his ever-expanding family of grandchildren at Dorchester and returned to Gloucester on Monday. Clayt had his battered schooner hauled at the Rocky Neck marine railway and, to their relief, for all the abuse she had suffered she showed no signs of serious damage.[25] Considering what the *Henry Ford* had endured, her survival is a telling compliment to the capabilities of the Essex River shipbuilding community in general, and A.D. Story in particular.

The deed of gift for the Dennis Cup required a new schooner to complete a season of fishing to qualify for the following autumn's races. On 17 April, the sight of Frank Paine's converted subchaser P.C. 247, towing the *Puritan* outside the harbor on Monday to begin her maiden voyage, well in time to qualify for the fall's races, erased any relief Morrissey and McManus felt. And, when the *Puritan* hoisted her sails, she effortlessly left the eleven-knot ex-navy warship in her wake. The deadline to begin the first fishing voyage of the year occurred on 30 April. Morrissey applied for and received an extension from the Cup trustees. Six weeks later, on 2 June, when her repairs and outfitting reached their conclusion, a tug came alongside to haul the *Henry Ford* away from the wharf. The towline came on board. The tug took a strain on it. True to character, the *Ford* remained where she was–stuck in the mud. After five groundings, however, her captain was an old hand at this. Clayt sent his crew to dinner. While they had their meal, the *Ford* floated free on her own. In a short dockside farewell speech, the skipper thanked the trustees for the extension. McManus, again in Gloucester, was the last to leave the new fishing schooner before she departed. Morrissey got her underway down the harbor, even though it meant bucking the traditional taboo against sailing on a Friday. With a typical Gloucester send-off of cannon fire, whistles, horns, and thousands of spectators, the *Henry Ford* belatedly sailed for the banks in search of her maiden fare of fish.

Three weeks later the Manta group received news of a stunning disaster. The *Puritan*, under the command of Captain Jeff Thomas, had crashed into the northwest bar of Sable Island while traveling under full sail at a speed of twelve

---

[25] Ibid., 46. From a retrospective naval architectural point of view, even if her sheer was not hogged, it is difficult to imagine that the keel remained rigid and true in a fore-and-aft plane, and that her hull frames were not twisted by either the multiple groundings or the yankings to break her loose from the mud or sand.

knots in a thick fog.[26] The schooner was a total, irreparable loss. American hopes for winning the 1922 challenge immediately fell by 25 percent, as events continued to augur against a victorious bid to beat the Canadians.[27]

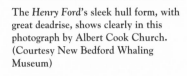

The *Henry Ford*'s sleek hull form, with great deadrise, shows clearly in this photograph by Albert Cook Church. (Courtesy New Bedford Whaling Museum)

The date set for the first of the elimination races to determine which vessel would defend New England's honor was 12 October. After first accepting an entry from the *Mayflower*, the Gloucester committee, responding to pressure from the Canadians, rejected her again as being insufficiently burdensome, despite the fact that she had spent the previous two winters in successful fishing operations.[28] In a different development, someone realized that the rules, having been revised and extended to accommodate the *Bluenose*, now permitted the *Elizabeth Howard* to enter the fray. Shortly afterward, the big knockabout–now re-rigged as a semi-knockabout with a short bowsprit–appeared in Gloucester under the command of Ben Pine. About the same time, Tom returned to Cape Ann from Dorchester to take part in the elimination races on board the *Ford*.

When the starting gun for the first trial sounded, four schooners swept over the line, two from Boston–the McManus semi-knockabout *L.A. Dunton* of 1921, Captain Felix Hogan, and the Edwin Perkins-designed *Yankee*, also built in 1921, Captain Mike Brophy–and two from Gloucester–the *Howard* and *Ford*. Ben Pine's *Howard* had her main trestletrees give way almost immediately, causing the loss of her main topmast. This spar failure eliminated any chance of a meaningful race. Despite a lackluster display of sailing, Morrissey brought the *Ford* to the finish line fifteen minutes ahead of the *Yankee*, with the workmanlike *L.A. Dunton* more than twice that in arrears.

---

[26] Thomas, *Fast & Able*, 190. The legend goes that the *Puritan* was so fast that she was twenty miles ahead of her dead reckoning position.

[27] Before the loss of the *Puritan*, she, the *Henry Ford*, the *Elizabeth Howard*, and the *Yankee* all appeared worthy of challenging for the Cup.

[28] The *Mayflower*, a fresh-fish market boat, in fact, carried more cargo than any other American racer–500,000 pounds–and fell short of the *Bluenose*, designed as a salt-banker, by a mere 15,000 pounds.

Unlike McManus's early designs, the *Henry Ford* had a wide stern, with a relatively flat run that helped increase her effective waterline. Photograph by Albert Cook Church. (Courtesy New Bedford Whaling Museum)

The committee delayed the second trial to allow repairs to the *Howard*, clearly the *Ford*'s only true challenger. McManus and Morrissey, concerned at the *Ford*'s lack of performance, huddled and sought ways to improve her sailing qualities. Regardless of her win, they harbored no doubts that their schooner had performed well below expectations. While Ben Pine supervised the mending of his masts, Tom and Clayt busily retrimmed the *Ford* by shifting her ballast.

The second race went off on 14 October. Although the *Henry Ford* sailed with more vitality, Morrissey just managed to beat Pine in the *Howard*, the margin being less than six minutes. Unknown to its contestants, the race had one foxy spectator. Early Saturday morning, a strange schooner had come to anchor off Ten Pound Island–it was the famous, or from Gloucester's point of view, infamous–*Bluenose*. Not unexpectedly, Angus Walters had easily won the Canadian trials, and with her arrival the stage was set for the first showdown.

Schooner	Waterline Length	Draft	Sail Area
Henry Ford	109.47 ft.	15.12 ft.	9,587 sq. ft.[29]
Bluenose	111.80 ft.	15.66 ft.	9,771 sq. ft.

TABLE 10 - ADMEASURED DIMENSIONS - *HENRY FORD* VS. *BLUENOSE*

---

[29] After the 437 square feet reduction ordered by the race committee.

Or was it? On 20 October the international race committee decreed that the *Ford*'s sail area was greater than the formula allowed.[30] The official admeasurer, Evers Burtner, an associate professor from Massachusetts Institute of Technology with a 1915 bachelor's degree in naval architecture, was adamant. Morrissey's mainsail would have to be cut down, even though the sails under question had powered the *Ford* since May. Tom indignantly described what took place:

> My sail plan for the schooner *Henry Ford* was made for her to fish with, and it was damnable to destroy the mainsail, which was butchered twice. If they had condemned the main gaff topsail, which was utterly useless to her by the wind, it would have been fairer to the vessel and would have entailed no expence to the skipper. The area of this sail is greater than the expert claimed was excessive. Everyone conversant with boats knows the mainsail is the driver, and the important sail for propulsion.
>
> *When the committee was in session discussing the sail area of the Ford, I, as her designer, was refused admittance to the room, nor was I notified when the expert was doing his measuring, all by his lonesome. Doesn't it seem likely that he could have made mistakes in measuring, just as he did in his figuring afterwards?*[31]

Burtner's rather late rebuttal to Tom's statement appears below. The committee gave its final verdict to Tom and Captain Clayt at 7:00 P.M. on the night before the first race. The decision staggered Morrissey. To meet Burtner's stipulations, the sail had to lose two twenty-inch-wide lengths of its leech or trailing edge. From a practical standpoint, it seemed doubtful if he could have them recut in time to race the next morning. But a gang of Marion Cooney's sailmakers came to the rescue. With an abundant stock of illicit refreshment supplied by Captain Clayt and his crew, they worked throughout the night and delivered the sail in time for the schooner to get underway at 9:20 A.M., barely in time for a 10:00 A.M. start. Under bare poles, the *Henry Ford* received a tow out to the breakwater, while the crew frantically bent on the mangled main. The recut version of her

---

[30] 80 percent of the waterline length squared, which should have allowed the *Henry Ford* 9,657 square feet of sail area.

[31] "Tom McManus, Designer of the Schooner *Henry Ford*, Writes His Opinion of the Races," *Atlantic Fisherman* (December 1922): 10, emphasis added.

With all sails pulling, the *Henry Ford* approaches a turning mark during an elimination race for the 1922 Dennis Cup series off Gloucester. When Albert Cook Church took this photograph, the *Ford* still carried her full mainsail; before the series with the *Bluenose* several vertical panels would be cut from the leech to comply with race committee decrees. (Courtesy New Bedford Whaling Museum)

mainsail did not come within four feet of the ends of either the boom or the gaff,[32] a significant loss in driving power.

The interference of officialdom had hardly begun. The committee boat, with the international committee and the American race committee on board, set the starting line off Eastern Point. At 9:30 A.M., as the *Ford* had not appeared, the race committee put up a thirty-minute postponement signal. The form in which they presented it did not successfully communicate this important decision. In shape it amounted to no more than a small black ball that could not be seen from more than a cable's length away without binoculars. The assumption was that the committee intended to allow the *Ford* more time, but they made no announcement to accompany their minuscule message.[33]

With the crew still hauling on the mainsail, the *Ford* cleared the breakwater at 9:40 A.M., twenty minutes after she left the wharf, and in time enough for the normal 10:00 A.M. start. Despite getting his sails up late, and without time to trim them properly, Morrissey outmaneuvered Walters and crossed ahead to windward at five seconds after 10 o'clock.

---

[32] Herbert L. Stone, "How *Bluenose* Won the Fishermen's Race: Bungling of the Sailing Committee Mars What Promised to be a Fine Series," *Yachting* 32 (1922): 230-31.

[33] Ibid.," 231.

McManus later confirmed that neither Morrissey nor Walters ever saw the committee's infinitesimal black ball. Realizing the fishermen had paid no attention to the signal, the officials then hoisted a second, equally insignificant indication–a tiny ten-inch flag with the numeral 7 upon its field–the recall signal. Unfortunately, with the two huge fishing schooners crashing close on board each other through the choppy waves, and Walters desperately trying to position the *Bluenose* to sail through the *Ford*'s lee, neither he nor Morrissey could afford a backward glance.

On a broad reach with a whole-sail breeze, the *Bluenose* (*left*) and *Henry Ford* match speeds. The *Ford*'s twice-reduced mainsail is clearly too short—the numeral is right at the leech. Photograph by Albert Cook Church. (Courtesy New Bedford Whaling Museum)

The committee then dispatched a Coast Guard powerboat, whose speed barely matched the flying fishermen. But this launch had neither committee member nor committee pennant on board to give it official status. Reaching the *Bluenose* first, which was still trailing to leeward and slightly astern of the *Ford*, the Coast Guardsmen informed Walters of the committee's decision, then motored up to the *Ford* to enlighten Morrissey. Twenty minutes later the petty officer in charge reported back to the yachting officials that, "Captain Walters of the *Bluenose* refuses to come back. He says to tell the committee he's doing well enough. We told Capt. Morrissey what the *Bluenose* said and he refused to come back also."[34]

The committee, operating from the destroyer U.S.S. *Paulding*, a thirty-two-knot warship, double the speed of a fishing schooner, made no attempt to overhaul

---

[34] Ibid., 232.

the contestants. Instead, the officials timed the racers at each mark, just as both skippers expected, but passed no further messages to either Morrissey or Walters, thereby failing to confirm the Coast Guardsman's message. In a clear fit of pique, the committee reached the epitome of small-mindedness by refusing to establish the finish line. No one was more surprised by their actions than the Honorable Edwin Denby, the secretary of the navy, who had accepted McManus's invitation to sail on the *Ford*, as he watched the fantail of his destroyer disappear into the harbor before the racers finished their final leg.

Tom watched the race from the U.S.S. *Bushnell*, a large submarine tender. From that vantage point the race looked like a well-run, close-fought affair. But it flabbergasted him when he realized the committee had abandoned the finish line, despite the fact that the race was well within its nine-hour time limit. Several moments afterward his emotion flared to flaming anger when he learned that they had called the whole race off because the skippers had ignored the little black ball.

Later, even that old curmudgeon, Angus Walters, *Bluenose*'s hardbitten master, admitted that he had been beaten fair and square in the first race. During a party that evening, Walters, in a rare show of grace, went up to Tom, shook his hand, and said, "she beat me fair and square, and she beat me plenty." Several onlookers questioned the Lunenburg master: "do you call it a race?" To which Walters replied, "I certainly do."[35] The committee, on the other hand, had hardly begun to strut its authority. Not only did the "no race" decision stick, but they informed an infuriated Clayt Morrissey that Burtner had made another mistake in his calculations. When he corrected it, he decreed that the *Henry Ford*'s mainsail was still too big, and must to be cut again! Another eighty square feet had to be removed from its area. To Tom, with his innate distaste for amateur officials, the whole affair had become a travesty. If it had not already dawned on the fishermen that they were sailing in a yacht regatta–not a fishermen's race–it certainly did now. What a far cry from "The Race That Blew" or even the 1920 contest between the *Esperanto* and the *Delawanna*.[36]

Not surprisingly, there are two Gloucester sides to the story. Unfortunately for the record, Evers Burtner did not get around to defending himself until sixty-one years later. Three days after his ninetieth birthday, on 29 April 1983, he gave a talk at the Essex Shipbuilding Museum. He first described how he had been crucified throughout his life for the measurement of the *Ford*'s mainsail, and then laid out his

---

[35] "Tom McManus Writes His Opinion", 10.

[36] Story, *Hail COLUMBIA!*, 54.

version of the happenings over those few crucial days from ancient memory: "Well, the Canadians were well organized. They had a representative on hand and he watched every move I made measuring the *Bluenose*, and he did the same on the *Henry Ford*. It was found that she was two feet under the maximum waterline length that she was allowed, [and] under draft perhaps almost a foot. But the sail area she was allowed to carry was based on the waterline length. Moreover, they had a requirement that the area of the mainsail and the topsail should not be more than 50 percent of the total sail area."

No wonder Tom McManus was disgusted. Just reading this relatively simple portion of the very complex international regulations, one can only wistfully recall 1886, 1888, 1892, 1901, and 1907, when it was anchors and dories on the wharf, beer and brass bands on board, and let's go racing—when the only regulation concerning canvas read: "Vessels to be allowed to carry the following sails, but no others: Mainsail, foresail, forestaysail, jib, flying jib, standing maintopsail, standing foretopsail, maintopmast staysail, and working jib topsail. Any vessel to be allowed to substitute a working main jib for the forestaysail and jib. No long foresails [genoas] to be allowed."[37]

Burtner, who had obviously suffered much over the intervening years as a result of his rule interpretation then went on: "Now, I am afraid I hate to speak of dereliction of people not on deck, but it seems to me the Gloucester Committee was lacking. *They perhaps could blame Tom McManus.*"[38] Burtner freely admitted that the committee had barred Tom from taking part in its proceedings: "I wish they had had him and his staff check over the *Ford* before she was subject to the tape. Anyway, it was decided that the *Ford* should cut her mainsail. So I marked [it]; I painted a mark on the boom indicating that they would have to cut two to two and a half feet off the mainsail. Oh, of course the crew grumbled, but they unbent the sail and took it to Puny's [sic - Cooney's] . . . [and] provided some lubricating spirits to the sailmakers."[39] Burtner spent the night in Gloucester after visiting the sail loft. He recalled that, before calling it a day, he went to the Master Mariners Association room, where "I was about as welcome as a skunk in a wedding party."[40] The next morning Burtner went to the wharf to inspect the changes, and the Canadian committeeman joined him there. "The crew without paying any attention to the black mark, yanked the sail about two or three feet beyond. I

THE BLANCHE RING
AND HENRY FORD

---

[37] *Forest and Stream*, 8 March 1888, 135.

[38] Lewis H. Story, "Notes on Fishermen's Races," unpublished essay, Essex Shipbuilding Museum, Essex, Massachusetts, italics added.

[39] Ibid.

[40] Ibid.

protested to no avail. There wasn't any representative from Gloucester present to take my stand." Despite his statement to the contrary regarding the sail, contemporary photographs of the second race clearly show the *Ford*'s mainsail well short of the boom and gaff ends. Burtner continued, "Some how the newspapers got the idea that the measurer had told the committee that he had made a mistake. Now where in the devil they got that opinion I don't know." He finished his sixty-years-late explanation with the disclaimer: "This is the first time I have been able to tell people in a big group that I DID NOT MAKE AN ERROR IN CALCULATIONS."[41]

In defense of Burtner, a letter from Frank C. Pearce, the owner and president of a Gloucester fish processing company, written a decade after the race, clearly explains that the admeasurer "did not make an error in calculations." Pearce pinned the blame on, of all people, Captain Charley Harty: "At the time the *Henry Ford* had her sails cut it was on account of Capt. Harty taking out more ballast than they should have, thereby making a shorter water line and being unable to carry the full amount of sail allowed on the booms and gaffs if she had kept her ballast in."

Moreover, Pearce doubted that the average fishing schooner skipper could fine tune his vessel. In discussing the international fishermen's races, he wrote to McManus: "I have made up my mind that while Gloucester captains know how to handle vessels and make passages, I have seen very few instances where any of them were capable of tuning up and handling a vessel during these races." He pointed out that in his estimation, "it was unfortunate that the *Henry Ford* was owned, in the major part, by a man who had to make his living fishing and that racing was merely incidental with him." In addition to Harty's mistake with the ballast, Pearce added, "I think the main reason that the *Henry Ford* lost her race was on account of not having her suit of sails designed and built for the races instead of for fishing. If you remember, her sails were built so as not to have to be cut after they were stretched, fisherman style."[42]

While Pearce's letter may not have offered much comfort to Tom, the latter comment must have brought back poignant memories of the America's Cup campaigns of the 1880s. The style of sail the Gloucester dealer described was exactly the one that had been invented by Charley McManus, and built by him for the *Puritan* when she won the Cup in 1885. The fact that Pearce considered 1880s-era America's Cup sails as "fisherman style" in 1932, speaks to the rapid advance in sailmaking technology during the previous half-century.

---

[41] Ibid., capitalization original.

[42] "Frank C. Pearce, Pres. & Man'gr., Frank C. Pearce Company, Producers, Curers & Wholesale Dealers in Fish, No. 401 Main Street, Gloucester, Mass.," to McManus, 26 February 1932.

In addition to the culpability of Charley Harty, the point that everyone involved in the controversy missed is illustrated in Table 11. McManus, yet again, was far ahead of his time in design thinking. Whether from an assumption that everyone recognized what he had created–since the knockabouts, with their tall rigs on a shortened base, had proven the point more than a decade earlier–or alternately, not wishing to draw attention to a secret, if patently obvious design advance, Tom never spoke up on the subject.

Schooner	Mainmast height (deck to cap)	Main topmast	Main boom	Main gaff	Mainsail area
Henry Ford	88.0 ft.	52.0 ft.	76.0 ft.	46.0 ft.	9,587 sq. ft.[43]
Bluenose	96.0 ft.	48.0 ft.	81.5 ft	51.0 ft.	9,771 sq. ft.

TABLE 11 - MAINSAIL GEOMETRY - *HENRY FORD* VS. *BLUENOSE*

The *Henry Ford* capably and comfortably carried a higher aspect rig than the *Bluenose*. Tom had introduced the high-aspect mainsail to the fishing fleet. Unlike the single-mast, single-sail setup of the Bermuda or Marconi rig, he achieved his aspect ratio through the combination of an unusually long topmast and shorter than conventional main boom and main gaff. He also designed the *Ford*'s main-topmast to stand higher out of the doublers, thereby giving the *Ford* a relatively taller rig than the *Bluenose*. Coming from a family experience steeped in generations of sailmaking technology, he did for the international fishermen's races what his brother Charley did for the Boston America's Cuppers–but where Charley had worked in cloth and invented a new weave bias, Tom, always mathematically inclined, had introduced geometrical change. The significance is that he had come to understand that it was the shape of the sails and the size and shape of the slot between the foresails and mainsail that provided the power for a fore-and-aft-rigged sailing vessel, not the size of the sail.

What advantage did this give the *Henry Ford* over the *Bluenose*? The answer appeared as soon as the schooners crossed the line in the first race. Walters, annoyed at losing the start, tried throughout the first leg to move the *Bluenose* into position to drive through the *Ford*'s lee, luff her up, and cross ahead of the American. But, despite repeated attempts, he failed to do so. Why? Morrissey could point the *Ford*'s bow higher into the wind than the *Bluenose* could follow–without dropping his hull speed below that of the leeward vessel, thus he sailed a slightly more weatherly course at a more or less equal speed through the water. The *Ford* proved she could outpoint the *Bluenose*, although that capability

---

[43] After the 437-square-foot reduction ordered by the race committee.

With a full load of spectators, the *Louise B. Marshall* maneuvers during the 1922 races between the *Bluenose* and *Henry Ford*. With her pole masts, knockabout rig, and 84-horsepower engine, the 120-ton *Marshall* (104.8x22.9x11 feet), launched in 1918, represents the practical alternative to the *Bluenose* and *Ford*. Photograph by Albert Cook Church. (Courtesy New Bedford Whaling Museum)

would have been more obvious had she not suffered lost sail power from the missing panels along the mainsail's leech.

Despite her crew-cut sail, the *Henry Ford* won the second race. She should have taken the championship, two out of three, right there and then. But the yachting officials held to their decision to discard the first race, and the *Bluenose* came back to win the third and fourth races, and with them the championship. The Dennis Cup went back to Halifax for good.

The cream of New England's naval architects designed the future American challengers, but Tom's *Esperanto* was the first and last American victor in the history of the international series. The rest fell afoul of narrow-minded, amateur yacht-racing officials, unable to dismiss the tenor of their rule-conscious sport, who completely lost sight of the fact that the fiercely competitive fishermen sought no more than a clean bash in the wind to settle the affair at sea, not in the committee room where yacht regattas are often won and lost.

After the popular and sporting press in both countries generally mauled the race committee, *Yachting* magazine gave it space to air its side of the proceedings in its December issue. Two letters, published by committee members John Hays Hammond, a good Gloucester supporter and namesake for the 1907 McManus schooner, and Captain George H. Peeples, a fisherman who should have known better, demonstrated that both writers were unquestionably competent racing officials, but also proved that they had been insufficiently flexible to fathom the mores and methods of the working fishermen. To understand how a fishermen's race should be run, there were five precedents to consult. One need look no further than Tom's management of the first fishermen's race in 1886, the 1901 Lawson Cup, or the 1907 Lipton Cup, or George Stewart's handling of the 1888 fishermen's race, or an even more direct comparison, as it includes both the same venue and a formal committee, the Gloucester gentlemen who organized the famous 1892 "Race That Blew."

The week came to an end in a maelstrom of charges and countercharges. To top off the entire affair, Angus Walters reneged on his promise to meet the *Mayflower* in a match race after the Dennis Cup races, and the *Bluenose* surreptitiously departed for Nova Scotia under the command of her mate. Of all the participants, only the town of Gloucester itself came away with a gesture that it can point to with pride for the rest of its history–the townspeople chipped in and bought Clayt Morrissey a new mainsail for the *Henry Ford*.

But beyond the rancor of the international competition, the question remains: Just how much impact did the *Henry Ford* and the *Bluenose*, or the later racing-spawned fishing schooners have on the fleet? The answer is none. If the *Blanche Ring* had ventured in as the *Bluenose* and *Henry Ford* jockeyed for position, or if an observer had glanced over at McManus's big 1918 auxiliary pole-masted knockabout *Louise B. Marshall*, serving as a spectator boat for fishermen, it would have been apparent that the fleet was far advanced in the changeover from sailing vessels to motor fishing vessels. The international races were not even the last gasp of a dying breed–the beast was already dead.

CHAPTER SIXTEEN

The *Alabamian* and *Sirod*

Physically and emotionally drained by the traumatic events surrounding the International Cup, and perhaps truly feeling his years for the first time, Tom returned home to Dorchester with a firm conviction never to become involved in a race meeting again or design a fishing schooner intended to compete in one. Considering his delight in being known as, "the Father of the Fishermen's Races," his self-imposed withdrawal from future contests demonstrates his disgust at the *Henry Ford* being "committeed" out of the championship. Even twelve years later his anger rose quickly at mention of the *Ford*. In 1934, McManus, then still active at seventy-eight, engaged in a lengthy correspondence with Frank A. Taylor, curator of the engineering division of the Smithsonian Institution. Early in the exchange, Taylor asked McManus to comment upon the fishermen's

Disgusted by the events of the 1922 Dennis Cup races, "the Father of the Fishermen's Races" withdrew from all further contests. Frederick William Wallace photographed him during the 1922 series. (Courtesy Maritime Museum of the Atlantic, Halifax, Nova Scotia)

races. After briefly discussing earlier, happier affairs, Tom bitterly recounted the October 1922 occurrences at Gloucester:

> Everybody knows what a bungling mess the Committee of the International Fishermen's races made and how the Schooner *Henry Ford* was robbed in the races off Gloucester in 1922.
>
> I will conclude by stating that Fishermen should conduct any future contests and sail the races as fishermen and with the least expense. Not by so called yachtsmen who want to stand on the judges boat with their chests expanded like pouter pigeons,[1] and tell fishermen to watch for a small black ball and then to blow a whistle at the appointed hour for a starting signal, then wanting them to come back and go over again, when they started fair and square, then to follow the racers over the course taking the time around each buoy until the last one, then to abandon the course and go into the harbor to declare it no race.[2]

The strength of his anger is all the more evident in the fact that, writing this long after the event, his ire still rose to such a degree over the actions of the waterborne committee members alone, without even alluding to the scurrilous land-based decision to mangle the *Henry Ford*'s mainsail. Tom must have realized at this point in the letter that it might reach a larger audience than just Taylor, for he turned the last paragraph into a broad-based plea: "Fishermen get together, the industry you represent is large enough to support a fishermen's race once a year, at your convenience, and show the public a fishermen's Race Conducted and Sailed by Fishermen, Yours very truly, The father of the Fishermen's Races." The championship the committee stripped from the *Henry Ford* had one last repercussion: true to his convictions, Captain Tom McManus never again accepted a commission to design a racing fisherman.

On 4 April 1923, Tom's daughter, Mildred McManus, a second-generation American-Irishwoman born of the Fingal Irish famine-*cum*-fishing emigration, married Winthrop L. "Rip" Pierce, a gentleman descended from a family that can be traced to the Puritan transport *Mary Ann* in the 1640s. Thus, seventy-seven

---

[1] Tom McManus knew whereof he spoke when it came to pigeons. His sons kept a flock of them on the third floor of their home in Dorchester, and his son Charley, the father of Mrs. D. Forbes Will, remained a pigeon fancier throughout his life.

[2] Letter draft included in Thomas F. McManus, "Autobiographical Essay No. 5," which he signed: "The father of the Fishermen's Races – Thomas F. McManus, Scituate, Mass."

years after the first of the Fingalian McManuses arrived in Boston, one of their progeny demonstrated the remarkable assimilation ability of that extraordinary band of middle-class Irish fishing immigrants. Like her brother Charley and his wife, Mary Frances, Mildred and her beau had been teenage sweethearts. "Rip" Pierce graduated from Dorchester High School at sixteen and returned to take a post-graduate course in preparation for the Dartmouth College entrance exams. He started dating Mildred, who was a senior classwoman, at this time. Despite social reservations among both families, the marriage proved a long and loving one.

Early one morning about a month after Mildred's wedding, Tom and Kate found themselves approaching their sixty-seventh birthdays with a trepidation unrelated to age. They stood, surrounded by a clutter of half-packed cases, scattered boxes of household effects, and partially draped furniture, gazing fixedly through the window. Outside, a big moving van driven by Dan Wilson, and guided by his helper, carefully backed up to their front door. After twenty-two years at the comfortable family abode, Tom had sold the Mill Street house.[3] By noon, the movers had loaded the van and departed for Scituate, where the family took up their usual summer residence in the Barker Street "cottage."[4] They arranged to move back to Dorchester after the holiday season, and into an apartment at 16 Algonquin Street.

A fishermen's race took place that August, a rare event of its type attended by pleasantries, comradeship, and fun-filled, competitive sailing. Whether it was the absence of the word "international" in the title, or the fact that "elaborate rules were purposely omitted, being strictly boat for boat with thirty-man crews," or that the only restriction was that entrants must be "engaged in or identified with the fishing industry,"[5] the 1923 races, held as part of Gloucester's celebration of its 300th anniversary of white settlement, were an all-round success. Sir Thomas Lipton again visited the United States, and went up to Gloucester for the contest. The local race committee reclaimed the original Lipton Cup from the glass case at Provincetown where it had been on display since the lost *Rose Dorothea* won it back in 1907. Only one problem arose: with the vast majority of the fishing fleet reliant on auxiliary power, there were few tall-rigged schooners suitable for racing to be found along the waterfront.

The famous "White Ghost," the *Elizabeth Howard*, entered first. Her skipper, Ben Pine, had been badly bitten by the racing bug during the previous year's

---

[3] The purchasers were Mr. and Mrs. Andrew Raulinaitis, and McManus held a $4,650 mortgage on the property, adding the Mill Street address to his considerable inventory of real-estate holdings.

[4] The summer cottage was, in fact, a substantial six-bedroom house.

[5] Dana A. Story, *Hail COLUMBIA!, The Rise and Fall of a Schooner* (1970; reprint, Gloucester, Massachusetts: Ten Pound Island Book Company, 1985), 96.

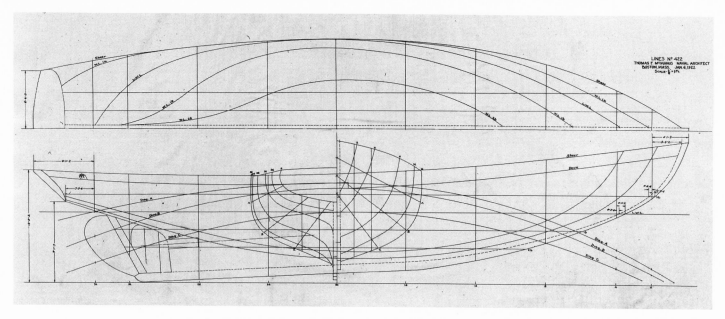

defender trials, and he was hot to compete again. Next, the O'Hara brothers of Boston entered their new schooner *Shamrock*, designed by Edwin Perkins, even though she still stood on the stocks at A. D. Story's yard. Clayt Morrissey, to whom the phrase "fishermen's race" was anathema, hesitantly agreed on 14 August to enter the *Henry Ford*. His decision most likely came from civic pride rather than any leftover desire to race. Also, getting ready would prove no easy task. He had only brought her in from the banks the previous evening.

Monday was the day scheduled for the fishermen's portion of the anniversary celebrations, but lack of wind moved the race back to the thirty-first, which dawned with light airs inclining to calm. By then, the stymied schoonermen would have rowed against each other to the finish line, although the postponement did help Morrissey to get the *Henry Ford* into racing trim. On Thursday, he inched her out past the breakwater, proudly sporting the brand-new mainsail that had been donated by his neighbors. Ben Pine already had the *Elizabeth Howard* tacking back and forth near the committee boat, trying to conjure up some more wind. As this pair came together near the starting line the *Shamrock*, only twelve days from the launching ways at Essex, appeared with none other than the crafty Marty Welch, cheerily puffing on his ever-present cigar, at her helm.

After a further hour-and-a-half's wait for a sufficient breeze to get underway, the starter sent the schooners off in what promised to be a strengthening wind. To no one's surprise, Welch captured the start, but the *Ford* overtook the *Shamrock* coming into the first mark, with the *Howard* gliding along just seconds behind the leaders. As the second leg began, Pine over-enthusiastically forced Welch into a lengthy luffing match, and allowed Morrissey in the *Ford* to get cleanly away. Then the wind slowly faded, and the allotted time expired before anyone finished the course.

OFFSETS N°422
THOMAS F. McMANUS NAVAL ARCHITECT
BOSTON, MASS.   JAN. 6, 1922

Stas.	Heights						Half Breadths							Diags.		
	Under Side Rail Cap	Dk.	Butt 2	Butt 1	Rabbet	Profile	Under Side Rail Cap	W.L.1a	L.W.L	W.L.1b	W.L.2b	Rabbet	Profile	A	B	C
Bow	16-0-0											0-4-0				
2	15-5-4	14-1-6		14-4-5	10-0-3	9-8-6	2-4-3					0-4-0		1-10-7	1-2-0	
4	14-11-1	13-7-3	13-9-0	9-7-4	7-10-4	7-6-4	4-4-4	2-2-6	0-5-0			0-4-0		3-11-4	3-0-4	1-9-7
8	14-0-0	12-6-5	7-1-4	5-11-5	5-1-7	4-7-4	7-3-0	6-1-2	4-9-6	2-2-7		0-4-4		7-3-2	6-4-0	4-8-1
12	13-2-2	11-7-7	4-9-7	3-11-3	3-4-7	2-7-5	8-11-7	8-7-6	7-10-0	5-10-0	2-1-0	0-5-0		9-7-7	8-8-0	6-6-2
16	12-7-4	11-0-0	3-8-4	2-11-6	2-5-2	1-5-6	9-10-0	9-8-7	9-4-0	8-1-0	4-10-0	"		10-10-0	10-1-4	7-8-7
20	12-3-2	11-3-0	3-7-0	2-9-5	2-0-6	1-1-2	10-0-4	10-0-0	9-10-4	8-10-4	5-2-0	"		11-1-6	10-7-1	7-10-0
24	12-1-0	11-1-0	4-2-0	3-4-4	1-8-3	0-8-6	9-9-7	9-9-7	9-7-2	8-2-4	3-5-3	"		10-11-2	10-1-6	7-2-4
28	12-1-0	11-0-7	5-9-0	4-10-7	1-4-0	0-4-2	9-2-0	9-2-1	8-4-1	4-8-1	1-0-6	"		10-1-7	8-1-0	5-7-6
32	12-2-7	11-3-6	7-9-2	7-2-0	6-10-2		8-2-5	7-10-7	4-7-0	0-6-4		"		8-10-4	6-6-0	3-6-6
34	12-4-2	11-6-2	8-9-7	8-4-4	8-1-2		7-7-2	6-9-0				"		8-0-0	5-3-1	2-2-3
Intersection of Diags. and Centre Line above base														14-0-0	12-0-0	10-0-0
Intersection of Diags and Water Line out from Centre Line														L.W.L. 12-1-2	W.L. 2b 10-9-0	W.L. 2b 4-9-3

All dimensions in feet, inches and eights to outside of plank and top of deck
Stations spaced every fourth frame or 8 ft apart.
Water Lines spaced 24"
Buttocks spaced 24"
Base Line is 8 ft. below L.W.L.

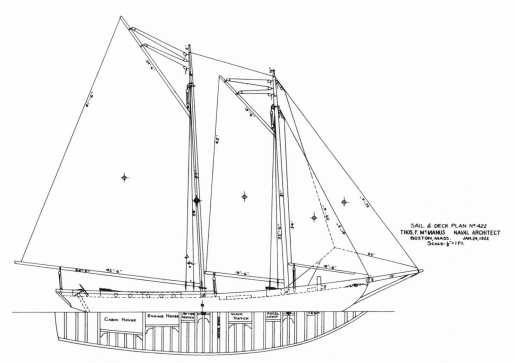

SAIL & DECK PLAN N°422
THOS. F. McMANUS   NAVAL ARCHITECT
BOSTON, MASS.   JAN. 24, 1922
SCALE ⅛" = 1 FT.

Plan No. 422, designed in January 1922, shows McManus's concept for a small auxiliary knockabout (60 feet between perpendiculars), with relatively short ends, a straight run of keel with just a hint of a knuckle, and a pole-masted rig. The name of the vessel built to these plans is not known. (Courtesy Louise V. Will)

Friday, after another delayed start, Pine slipped over the line ahead of the others. All three schooners dueled closely down the opening leg and arrived at the first mark in a bunch. Morrissey slid the *Ford* around on the inside track and grabbed the lead by thirty-five seconds over the *Howard*, which cleared the buoy twenty seconds ahead of the *Shamrock*. The next stretch was just what Captain Clayt ordered to take advantage of the *Ford*'s renowned weatherly abilities–especially with a whole mainsail–a beat into the steadily increasing wind for more than seven miles. Even in the relatively light airs, by using the power of her McManus-designed sails and slots, Morrissey, in the *Ford*, outpointed and outfooted the others. Although Morrissey overstood the mark, she rounded with more than two minutes in hand over the *Howard*, and a surprising ten over a frustrated Marty Welch in the new *Shamrock*. The final three legs were all on a broad reach with the schooners sailing large, conditions that absolutely suited the big *Elizabeth Howard*. The spectators cheered wildly as Ben Pine drove her to the limit, visibly cutting into the *Ford*'s lead. But Morrissey never relaxed. He covered the *Howard*'s every move and drove his schooner home to win by a slim fifty seconds. The *Henry Ford* captured the second Lipton Trophy and a $1,000 cash prize to go with it. McManus's *Elizabeth Howard* received the Prentiss Cup with $800, and the *Shamrock* accepted another $800. Coming in the aftermath of the rancorous international races, despite the gentle airs, it was a most congenial and satisfying fishermen's race.

The elimination trial to select the American challenger for the International Cup Races at Halifax came up on 21 October and, to no one's surprise, bug-bitten Ben Pine showed up with a brand-new A.D. Story-built racing fisherman, the *Columbia*, which he had commissioned from designer W. Starling Burgess.[6] Pine's old schooner, the *Elizabeth Howard*, arrived home from the banks in time to join the skirmish. The big knockabout, now commanded by Captain Harry Gillie, demonstrated every willingness to race and went out on a shakedown trial with the *Columbia* on 18 October. While they were having at it, a heavily-laden *Henry Ford* appeared in the offing on the way in with a fare of fish. When asked to participate, Clayt Morrissey demurred and said that the *Columbia* ought to be sent to Nova Scotia without any further ado. Besides, he alibied, the *Ford*'s topmasts were struck down on deck and his crew needed a well-deserved rest. But Pine and the Gloucester committeemen prevailed upon him. With much volunteer help over the next two days, Morrissey got the *Ford* ready in time for Sunday's race.

The eliminations turned into another windless affair. At the expiration of the five-and-a-half-hour time limit, the *Columbia*, having proved superior to the

---

[6] For the construction to destruction saga of this fine fisherman, see Story, *Hail COLUMBIA!*.

others on all points of light-air sailing, still lay over six miles short of the finish line. The committee reached the obvious conclusion to send Captain Pine and his new charge to Halifax, where she sailed into another contentious series. The *Bluenose* won the first two races, but the Americans protested the result of the second one when the Canadian boat intentionally sailed on the wrong side of a mark. When the International Committee failed to resolve the issue to his satisfaction, an already sulking Captain Walters tossed a tantrum, packed up the *Bluenose*, and went home to Lunenburg in a high state of dudgeon. In the end, the trustees declared the 1923 championship "no race."

Following the *Columbia-Bluenose* farce, Gloucester did itself proud by ignoring Walters for the next eight years. During that time, the Cape Ann port held three agreeable and gratifying races for some of the last of the topmast-rigged fishing-schooner breed. Ben Pine evened his personal score with Clayt Morrissey by bringing the *Columbia* in ahead of the *Henry Ford* to win the Frank E. Davis Cup in 1926. Three years later, a stable of old warhorses: the tiny round-bow semi-knockabout *Progress* (1913), Manuel P. Domingoes; the Binney-designed ex-*Mary* now the *Arthur D. Story* (1912), Ben Pine; the unbelievable *Elsie* (1910), Norman A. Ross; and the ancient round-bow *Thomas S. Gorton* (1905), Wallace Parsons, came to the line and finished in that order.

The racing fever had infected Ben Pine so badly in 1920 that no cure was possible. After his first appearance with the twenty-year-old *Philip P. Manta* for the 1921 elimination races, followed by stints with the *Elizabeth Howard* and the *Columbia*, Pine's second place with the *Arthur D. Story* in 1929's Fuller, Davis, and Prentiss Cup races came the month before Black Thursday, 24 October 1929. But the calamitous stock market failure did not cool down Captain Ben's feverish hopes of capturing the International Cup. During the September race, Pine had a passenger on board the *Arthur D. Story* of sufficient financial solvency to promise to underwrite a new racing fisherman–and keep to his word after the crash–Louis G. Thebaud, a New Jersey financier who habitually summered at his imposing estate on Gloucester's Eastern Point. At the end of the race, when Pine bemoaned his second-place finish, Thebaud said: "Don't feel so badly about it, Ben. We'll have a new vessel built this winter that you can sail to win the race next fall."[7] According to one account, he wrote Pine a substantial check right on the spot.

Several family members took part in the syndication of a new Cup challenger: Thebaud himself ($30,000), his wife, Gertrude L. Thebaud ($10,000), and son-in-law, Robert McCurdy ($5,000). Other shareholders included Bassett

---

[7] Wesley G. Pierce, *Goin' Fishin'* (Salem, Massachusetts: Marine Research Society, 1934), 241-42.

Jones ($5,000), Wetmore Hodges ($5,000), and Chandler Hovey ($5,000).[8] The group chose Frank C. Paine of Paine, Belknap, and Skene, Naval Architects, to design the yacht-like semi-knockabout fisherman that became the *Gertrude L. Thebaud*.

As soon as the rumors of a new Gloucester competitor reached Lunenburg, Angus Walters, whose sulks had withered with eight years of racing drought, not only issued a challenge to Pine and the *Thebaud*, but even volunteered to come to Gloucester. When *Bluenose* did come to Gloucester, Ben Pine had his well-earned and long-awaited day in the sun. The *Gertrude L. Thebaud* handily defeated the *Bluenose* in two out of two races for the third Lipton Cup.

With the Dennis Cup at stake in 1931, Walters came back to win easily two out of two races at Halifax. Seven years later, in the last-ever international fishermen's race, they put on a better show. The *Thebaud*, under Ben Pine, won the first race by a little under three minutes. Walters drove the *Bluenose* back with a vengeance to take the second race by more than twelve minutes. Illness again took Ben Pine from the wheel, and his stand-in, Cecil Moulton, lost the third, but won the fourth. Angus Walter then rang down the curtain on seventeen years of rancor by winning the last race, and keeping the Dennis Cup in Canada forever.

Modern mobility came to 16 Algonquin Street on 1 May 1924, when McManus purchased his first automobile, a new Model 55, six-cylinder Flint,[9] in time for the annual summer excursion to Scituate. Curiously, Tom registered the vehicle in the name of Alice L. McManus, his arthritically crippled daughter. The car was clearly more than a luxury, for the family put about 4,000 miles annually on the Flint over the next several years. During the "year of the car," Tom designed the forty-seven-foot schooner yacht *Bertha Frances*, for Hobart Ford of New York City. The Waddell Brothers built this beautiful little replica fisherman, and soon thereafter Ford engaged in a series of match races with his close friend Marty Kattenhorn in the *Surprise*.

One night in late January 1925, Ken drove Tom up to the City Club in Boston on the occasion of the annual meeting of the school's alumni association.[10] McManus's loyalty to the Eliot School never faded. In conversations about schooling, while English High and Comers College rarely received mention, his beloved grammar school days were always at the tip of his tongue.

---

[8] Gordon W. Thomas, *Fast & Able, Life Stories of Great Gloucester Fishing Vessels* (Gloucester, Massachusetts: Gloucester 350th Anniversary Celebration, Inc., 1973), 199.

[9] Chassis no. 3160, motor no. 4934. 1924 Massachusetts registration 384888.

[10] The alumni meeting was organized by John B. Sheridan of 138 North Street, Boston.

Late in 1925, some old clients returned with a new commission for Tom. The Mobile Bar Pilots Association, whose profession can be traced back to the early 1700s,[11] decided to replace their fifteen-year-old McManus-designed pilot boat, the *Alabama*. Led by Captain Joseph H. Norville, they turned once again to the Bostonian for the layout of a new vessel for their service. Tom designed the acme of a commercial schooner for the association: a twin auxiliary-powered, gaff-rigged knockabout–the *Alabamian*–Mobile's last sailing pilot boat. Given the universal acceptance of auxiliary power, the pilots reached a pair of conclusions concerning the design of their new vessel. The effectiveness of modern marine engines meant that they would not require so a large a hull, and that same attribute enabled them to lessen the size of their rig, with a corresponding reduction in manning.[12]

The pilots had learned a third lesson from their 1911 boat. New England white oak did not resist the destruction of marine organisms in the tropical waters of the Gulf of Mexico. To correct this shortcoming the pilots chose a Florida firm, the Pensacola Shipbuilding Company, to build the McManus design for them.[13] Doubtlessly this large shipyard's experience with enduring southern wood species, such as live oak and juniper, was a significant factor in the choice, as was its proximity to Mobile. The yard laid the *Alabamian*'s keel in July 1925. Tom called for the stem and sternpost to be hewn from live oak, and the frames to be double-sawn juniper. He specified yellow pine for planking, ceiling, shelves, clamps, decking, and deck beams, to be fastened by locust treenails. He further required that all butts and hood ends (plank ends) below the waterline should be fastened with copper spikes and those above by galvanized steel ones.[14] Power was to come from twin eighty-horsepower light-oil (gasoline) engines built by the Lathrop Company of Mystic, Connecticut.

Aside from her smaller size and more suitable building materials, an additional dissimilarity between the *Alabamian* and the Massachusetts-built *Alabama* was a significant reduction to the stern counter. Tom still favored extended stern overhangs. Although handsome in appearance, they uncomfortably magnified the effect of wave action on the hull while riding at anchor. The pilots

---

11 W.M.P. Dunne, "Mobile Bar pilotage, 1702-1931: A Narrative History," a paper presented to the 12th Gulf Coast History and Humanities Conference, March 1989.

12 With register dimensions of 81.4 foot length, 21.6 foot breadth and 9.7 foot depth, and a tonnage of 70.68, the *Alabamian* was less than 60 percent of the *Alabama*'s size (Application for Official Number, Mobile, 15 December 1926).

13 This firm, long out of existence, was an important World War II shipbuilding yard located on Bayou Chico off Pensacola's Escambia Bay.

14 Letter, Robert S. Douglas, current owner of *Alabama*, to Richard K. Anderson, Jr., Staff Architect, HABS/HAER, National Park Service, Department of the Interior, Washington, D.C., 7 May 1987.

The 143-ton *Mary Sears* (108.8x25x11.8 feet), built at Essex in 1926, represents McManus's mature view of an auxiliary knockabout design. Her 150-horsepower oil engine eliminates the need for topsails, and even for a big driving mainsail. Although she retains her long main boom, a triangular steadying sail has been bent on in place of the gaff-headed main. Such vessels provided a maneuverable and secure home for dorymen as long as that form of fishing continued. Photograph by A.A. Acores. (Courtesy Cape Ann Historical Collection, Gloucester)

learned from tiresome experience that the *Alabama*'s long counter made her a victim of capricious waves during the long hours they spent waiting for inbound vessels. At the mouth of Mobile Bay the outgoing current and the prevailing onshore wind ensure a confused sea state, which had caused the bar in the first place, and which makes riding at anchor there a vexing experience.

Norville regularly traveled from Mobile to Pensacola, seventy miles in 1925, to monitor the *Alabamian*'s construction. Richard V. Cowley, the resident naval architect for the shipbuilding firm,[15] who was also the assistant works manager, was the vessel's day-to-day superintendent. Cowley's overseeing capacity led to an unusual distinction. As a naval architect himself, he insisted that the new boat be built precisely to her designer's plan. The small New England yards, where rule of thumb was the rule of the day in ship construction, tended to interpret, rather than faithfully follow, the designer's drawings, an aberration that usually began on the mold loft floor. More so than any of his hundreds of designs, the *Alabamian* came

---

[15] There is no evidence that McManus ever went to Pensacola.

into existence exactly as McManus had drafted her, which gives her unrivaled value as a surviving tribute to his creative talents.

Pensacola Shipbuilding launched the *Alabamian* on 20 June 1926, and forthwith commenced masting, rigging, and fitting her out. Upon delivery to the bar pilots the total cost amounted to $25,000.00.[16] Two double-oared yawl-boats, for use as tenders, were swayed in and outboard from steel davits mounted on the weatherdeck.[17] The *Alabamian* went into service at the end of the summer, about the time of Tom's seventieth birthday. Designed from the start as a pilot boat, the *Alabamian* had lines closer to a schooner yacht than a Grand Banks fisherman. When it retired the original *Alabama*, the association renamed the *Alabamian* the *Alabama*. Her sturdy hull served the Mobile Bar Pilots Association faithfully for the next forty years, and, almost miraculously–considering the daily rigors a pilot boat had to contend with–the *Alabama* remains afloat at the time of this writing in Vineyard Haven, Massachusetts.[18]

The *Adventure*, the fourth and youngest, after the *Surprise* (1918), *L.A. Dunton* (1921), and *Alabama* (1926), is the last of the known McManus designs that remain afloat. Modeled by Tom off the 1920 knockabout *Oretha F. Spinney* for Captain Jeff Thomas, the *Adventure* was launched by Essex's Everett James yard twelve weeks after the *Alabama*. She is a tribute to the driving determination of one man, ex-newspaperman and current chronicler of the Gloucester fishing fleet, Joseph E. Garland. Joe began by writing a book about her, *Adventure: Queen of the Windjammers*,[19] and finished by taking responsibility for the well-seasoned schooner when she finished her active sailing career. Today, through his efforts, she rides safely at anchor in Gloucester, her traditional home port, from which she made the last American dory trawling voyage in 1953, wrapping up the hundred-year history of the fishery that Tom McManus had so strongly influenced.

After a couple of years on Algonquin Street, Tom and Kate left Dorchester for good, and moved the remnants of the family up into the beautiful Blue Hills of Milton, where they took a large apartment at 551 Eliot Street about 1928. At this

---

[16] Schedule of Work Completed, Pensacola Shipbuilding Company, June 1918-June 1930, Special Collections, John C. Pace Library, University of West Florida, Pensacola.

[17] After World War II a pair of twenty-five-foot motor launches replaced the yawl-boats. One of the later tenders was sunk at an unknown time, and another, *Bud*, went down in the Gulf of Mexico sometime during 1945.

[18] The schooner had her first marine band radio installed in June 1934, and received the call-letters WA2098. On 10 July 1935, the *Alabamian*'s name was officially changed to the *Alabama*. The schooner's original engines were removed at this time and she was re-powered with Gray Marine HNS oil (diesel) engines developing 140 brake horsepower each. The new diesels were installed considerably forward of the former gasoline engine beds in the bilges. The plugs for the original shaft gland locations are still evident when the *Alabama* is hauled. (Enrolment No. 10, Mobile, 10 July 1935). As of 1993 the *Alabama* has a pair of General Motors Detroit Diesel 6-71N engines.

[19] Joseph E. Garland, *Adventure: Queen of the Windjammers* (Camden, Maine: Down East Books, 1985).

time, Tom began to exhibit a serious physical infirmity, his first in seventy-two years, when cataracts appeared in his eyes. The affliction would steadily worsen over the next decade until, eventually, he would be left almost sightless. The progress of this disability is most visible in his personal papers. Beginning in the early 1930s, it is possible to date a letter by the size of his handwriting, as it grew larger to compensate for his inability to focus.

The McManuses had been early subscribers to the developing New England telephone system, and quickly adapted to the automobile age. So it was not unexpected when, several months before the beginning of the Great Depression, an electronic medium made its appearance in the McManus's Eliot Street apartment. Tom purchased his first radio, an Acme, from his son-in-law Stuart Seibel, Margaret's second husband. Also, the family nuptials continued apace when George, a bachelor of thirty-three, married Kathleen Colligan. Father George F. Sullivan conducted the ceremony on 27 June 1929, in the bride's parish, St. Ann's of Wollaston.

Homeowners for nearly fifty years in Charlestown and Dorchester, Tom and Kate never quite settled into the way of life of apartment dwellers during their interludes on Algonquin and Eliot Streets. In 1930, Tom purchased two building lots that backed onto the Blue Hills Reservation,[20] and on 30 April 1931 he gave his landlady notice of his intention to move out by the end of May. It was a time for organization. Three weeks earlier he "agreed to buy a lot in Milton Cemetery from the Town of Milton Mass. #2227 at cost of $60.00 and Cutting, McManus and the No. 2227 in step at 50 cents each letter and number, $5.50. Paid Town of Milton $65.50 Apr. 23, 1930."[21] A later reference indicates the site contained twelve graves. A measure of his worth at this time includes over $25,000 in savings banks, the ownership and income from the mortgages on seven houses and lots in Charlestown, the Mill Street property in Dorchester, and nine lots in Scituate, as well as shareholdings in the Metropolitan Ice Company, the Scituate Water Company, the National Service Company, and the New England Power Association, as well as four different co-operative banks, and abundant insurance for himself, Kate, and daughter Alice. Additionally, there was the big house in Scituate, the two lots in Milton, and his various shares in schooner syndications.

Although Tom's eyesight might be failing, he displayed no lack of energy, and supervised the building of two houses at 57 and 61 Mingo Street in Milton

[20] Described as Lot AD in the name of Thomas F. McManus, Sr., and Lot AE, in the name of Charles F. McManus. At this time Ken McManus was living and working in New York. His father lists his address as c/o James McDonald, 106 West 78th Street, New York City.

[21] Personal diary of Thomas F. McManus, owned by his granddaughter, Mrs. Dustin Pevear. Regarding the cemetery plot Tom paid $6.00 for "Care of Lot" in 1930 and 1931, after which there are no more entries.

himself, when he was seventy-six. And his designing days were not over. McManus drafted a yacht, *Sirod*, during the winter of 1936, at age eighty, for S.P. Palmer (*Sirod* is Palmer's wife's first name spelled backwards). Although the advancing cataracts had clouded his eyes, according to George Stadel, Tom originated the design and supplied the monuments to Walter McInnis, who drew the original drafts, and Stadel later drew the building drafts for "Honest Dave" Waddell. *Sirod* was built by the Waddell Brothers at Rockport during 1937.[22]

McManus designed the 70-ton *Alabamian* (81.4x21.6x9.7 feet) as his ideal of a pilot schooner suitable for lying at anchor in the choppy conditions off Mobile Bay. (Courtesy Robert S. Douglas)

But, before the new yacht grew to reality, Tom, during a life regularly visited by tragedy, suffered his greatest one. On 12 December 1936, Catherine Cokely McManus, the mother of the twelve McManus children, and Tom's beloved wife and partner for more than fifty-eight years, passed away. Tom lingered on in a gradually debilitating state for nearly two years after Kate's death.

On the night of 13 November 1938, he complained of pains in his back and chest. Ken, who had returned home to Milton, gave him a two-hour rubdown before he fell asleep. Mildred lived nearby and also attended him, for the entire family sensed that the end was near. It came early the next morning, when the

---

[22] Letter, Erik A.R. Ronnberg, Jr., 16 August 1988. The strong magnifying glass that McManus used to read during his declining years is owned by his granddaughter, Mrs. D. Forbes Will.

family physician, Dr. George D. Dalton of Quincy, reported Tom's death, and identified the cause as "presumably coronary sclerosis."[23] J.S. Waterman of Boston handled the funeral arrangements, and the wake took place in the McManus home. The family interred Tom's remains alongside Kate's at Milton Cemetery, following a solemn high mass of requiem at St. Mary of the Hills Church on 16 November.[24]

Obituaries appeared in a wide range of newspapers, from the Boston *Herald* to the New York *Times*, but the one closest to home, the *Mattapan-Milton News* paid Tom McManus an extensively copied accolade: "He built as well as designed, the 'long-ended' *James S. Steele*, considered a radical departure in designing in 1889. This design proved so successful that, even now, modern yachts and fishing boats are built basically the same. From 1900 to 1920 more than 90 percent of the vessels built for fishing on the Atlantic coast bore the lines conceived by Capt. McManus."[25]

It is a sad but true fact that historians will probably never be able to identify all of McManus's designs. In the words of granddaughter Louise Will, "why he never kept the plans! They went to the mould loft."[26] Coming from a direct descendant who grew up in the house next door to her grandfather's, Mrs. Will's statement is definitive.

On the other hand, we can estimate with reasonably refined accuracy that Tom, by his own count, drafted more than 450 plans. The fundamental measure of his professional impact, however, can be dispassionately evaluated by the number of his creations that can be considered trendsetters, and a readily available method of calculating this is to examine the appearance of the fleet. As the nineteenth century came to a close, the population of New England fishing vessels remained dominated by the shallow clipper schooner. Sprinkled among them were a number of *Nellie Dixon* (or *Fredonia*) derivatives, and a handful of plumb-stemmers. But, by the end of the first decade of the twentieth century, the fleet silhouette had entirely changed. Including every vessel from the newest semi-knockabout to the oldest basket of treenails still capable of reaching the banks, the great majority of them originated from Tom's drawing board, with eighty-plus Indian Headers leading an array of types that included knockabouts, round-bows, *Nellie Dixons*, semi-knockabouts, round-bow semi-knockabouts, and at least four spoon-bows after the *Benjamin W. Latham*.

[23] Vital Records, *Certificate of Death A218763*, Thomas F. McManus, 14 November 1938.

[24] The surviving children were Margaret, Mrs. Stuart Seibel of Taunton; Grace Agnes, Mrs. Grace Clark of Brighton; Miss Alice L. McManus; Catherine Cokely, Mrs. Thomas Hurley of Jamaica Plain; Charles Francis of Milton; Mary, Mrs. James T. Dacey of Wellesley Hills; George James McManus of Wollaston; Thomas F. McManus, Jr., of Milton; Mildred, Mrs. Winthrop L. Pierce of Milton; and William Kenneth McManus of Milton.

[25] *Milton-Mattapan News*, 19 November 1938.

[26] Telephone interview, 8 September 1988, Mrs. D. Forbes Will.

Captain Tom McManus, as he preferred to be called, was certainly the most fisherman-friendly of all the designers of New England fishing schooners. He not only expressed a concern for safety and performance throughout his lifetime, but he did many things to improve those qualities during his working years. In his own words: "I kept on improving the fishing fleet by cutting away the dead wood for and Aft, shortening the foremast and bow sprit, and then [designed] the popular Knockabout, as all the head sails can be worked from the deck and no won [one] going over the Knight heads on icy foot ropes, perhaps to be washed away."[27] In practicing his principles, he changed the overall silhouette of the fleet with the Indian Headers, again with the knockabouts and semi-knockabouts, and finally, in 1921, with the *Blanche Ring*, the first of the "Eastern Rig" schooner-draggers. No other naval architect employed in the North Atlantic fisheries comes close to approaching this accomplishment.

The biography of Thomas Francis McManus is only a part, albeit a significant one, of the greater McManus family story, a maritime saga that began when the first McManus abandoned his familial roots and emigrated, not from Ireland to the United States, but from the fertile fields of County Fermanagh to the sailmaker's cottage on Quay Street in Skerries, County Dublin. The generations that followed steeped the family in sailmaking, and the transatlantic emigration from the fishing harbor of Fingal to the port of Boston set the stage for the talents of John H. McManus, in his time "the foremost sailmaker in the East,"[28] his oldest son, Charley, the true sailmaking genius in the McManus line, and "Captain" Tom, the frugal fishmonger extraordinaire who invented "Boston Caviare" and the creative fishing schooner designer who produced more fishing schooner designs than the combination of all his peers.

THE ALABAMIAN AND SIROD

---

[27] McManus, "Essay No. 5, an undated letter to an unknown addressee." The contents suggest this may have been part of McManus's 1934-36 correspondence with Frank A. Taylor, Curator of the Engineering Division of the Smithsonian Institution, although the small handwriting size suggests an earlier date.

[28] Captain Charlton L. Smith, "The First Fishermen's Race," *Yachting* (January 1939): 64.

Schooners Possibly Designed By Thomas F. McManus
Including Those Known or Claimed to be Built "Off" His Plans

1891

NAME: [d]*James S. Steele*
BUILDER: Moses Adams
LAUNCH DATE: late December
HOME PORT: Gloucester
REMARKS: First schooner built to a design totally created by Thomas F. McManus. Built at Essex by Daniel Poland under contract from Moses Adams for George Steele. White-hulled. Raced in the 1892 Fishermen's Race. Half-model at Essex Shipbuilding Museum. Charles A. Olsen was her first master. Admeasured 14 January 1892 at Gloucester. Enrolment No. 51, gross 78.46, net 74.59. Moses Adams's foreman was "Honest Dave" Waddell when the *James S. Steele* was launched. Lost 2 September 1907 on Middle Ground Shoal.

1892

NAME: [d]*Richard C. Steele*
BUILDER: Moses Adams
LAUNCH DATE: November or December
HOME PORT: Gloucester
REMARKS: Built for George Steele from the molds of the *James S. Steele*, but slightly larger. Moses Adams appears to have added a pair of frames. Frank P. Silva was her first master. Admeasured 9 December 1892 at Gloucester. Enrolment No. 22, gross 82.4, net 78.04.

1893

NAME: *Maggie Sullivan*
BUILDER: A.D. Story
LAUNCH DATE: 1 June 1893
HOME PORT: Boston
REMARKS: Enrolment No. 246, Boston and Charlestown, 27 May 1893; Permanent Enrolment No. 245, Boston and Charlestown, Owners: Joseph Conley, 1/16; Parron H. Prior, 2/16; Mary Sullivan, 2/16; William J. Emerson, 1/16; Thomas F. McManus, 1/16; Sarah A. Phillips, 1/16; Henry D. Stone, 1/16; George H. Clark, 1/16; Carrie M. Bunting, 1/16; Cassius Hunt, 1/16; Caroline E. Phillips, 2/16; William C. Stone, 1/16; John S. Wright, 1/16.

1894

NAME: [h]*Flora L. Nickerson*
BUILDER: A.D. Story
LAUNCH DATE: 1 June 1893
HOME PORT: Boothbay, Maine
REMARKS: Off *Nellie Dixon*.

1895

NAME: [?]*Thomas Brundage*
BUILDER: A.D. Story
LAUNCH DATE: 1 June 1893
HOME PORT: Boston
REMARKS: Off *Nellie Dixon*. Built for Charles W. Brundage.

1896

NAME: [?]*William A. Morse*
BUILDER: James & Tarr
LAUNCH DATE: 2 July 1896[n]
HOME PORT: Provincetown[l]
REMARKS: Off *Nellie Dixon*. "A heavy weather sailor."[c] Lines at Smithsonian Institution.

NAME: [?f]*Grace Darling*
BUILDER: A.D. Story
LAUNCH DATE: November[n]
HOME PORT: Salem

1897

NAME: *America*
BUILDER: John Bishop
LAUNCH DATE: May
HOME PORT: Boston
REMARKS: Plumb bow pilot schooner for the harbor pilots. Drawn on 29 November 1896. M.C.C. issued 3 May 1897, Enrolment No. 106, B&C. Operated under Captain James H. Reid as Boston's Pilot Boat No. 1. Original half-model in possession of Louise Will, plans at Smithsonian Institution. Had outside ballast.[c] After many years of pilot service, became a Cape Verde packet.

1898

NAME: [d]*Juniata*
BUILDER: James & Tarr
LAUNCH DATE: 20 April[n]
HOME PORT: Boston
REMARKS: The first "Indian Header." One of two McManus designs to have outside ballast. Built for Edward A. Rich & Co. By McManus's own testimony, "In this model of the *Juniata*, lines of the previous boats were improved upon." Grounded in Portland Gale of November 1898.

NAME: [d]*Mattakeesett*
BUILDER: James & Tarr
LAUNCH DATE: 22 March
HOME PORT: Boston
REMARKS: Indian Header. Built for Henry D. Malone. Raced in the 1902 Thomas W. Lawson Cup. Dory trawler. Lost at sea 5 March 1911. Crew of 17 survived. Sail Plan at Peabody & Essex Museum.

NAME: [a]*Tecumseh*
BUILDER: James & Tarr
LAUNCH DATE: 20 June[n]
HOME PORT: Gloucester
REMARKS: Indian Header. Built for Sanford C. Winsor.

Note: A key to symbols such as "?f", "a", "j", and "?" appears on page 376.

1898 continued
NAME: [d]*Massasoit*
BUILDER: John Bishop
HOME PORT: Plymouth
REMARKS: Indian Header. Built for Sanford C. Winsor. Flush deck. Capt. Jim Fowler. Use as a gill-netter for mackerel. Had iron outside ballast.

NAME: [d]*Samoset*
BUILDER: John Bishop
HOME PORT: Plymouth
REMARKS: Indian Header. Built for Sanford C. Winsor. Dory fisherman.

1899
NAME: [?]*Alcina*
BUILDER: James & Tarr
LAUNCH DATE: Spring[n]
HOME PORT: Boston
REMARKS: Built for Edward A. Rich & Co.

1900
NAME: [d]*Manomet*
BUILDER: Wm. I. Adams
HOME PORT: Plymouth
REMARKS: Indian Header. Built for Sanford C. Winsor.

NAME: [f]*Gossip*
BUILDER: A.D. Story
LAUNCH DATE: October[n]
HOME PORT: Gloucester
REMARKS: Off *Nellie Dixon*. Built for D.B. Smith & Co.

NAME: [f]*Maxine Elliott*
BUILDER: A.D. Story
LAUNCH DATE: December[n]
HOME PORT: Gloucester
REMARKS: Off *Nellie Dixon*. Built for D.B. Smith & Co.

NAME: [?]*Rose Standish*
BUILDER: John Bishop
LAUNCH DATE: December
HOME PORT: Plymouth
REMARKS: Indian Header. Swordfisherman

built for John Watson.

1901
NAME: [?f]*Flirt*
BUILDER: A.D. Story
LAUNCH DATE: June[n]
HOME PORT: Gloucester
REMARKS: Off *Nellie Dixon*. Built for D.B. Smith & Co.

NAME: [a]*Regina*
BUILDER: Oxner & Story
LAUNCH DATE: 1 August[2]
HOME PORT: Boston
REMARKS: Off *Nellie Dixon*. Built for William J. Emerson and Capt. Jeremiah Shea. Noted for her speed. Became a Cape Verde packet. Burned 22 December 1919 at St. Vincent, Cape Verde Islands. Plans donated to Mystic Seaport Museum by Louise Will.

NAME: [f]*Slade Gorton*
BUILDER: Tom Irving
LAUNCH DATE: 17 August
HOME PORT: Gloucester
REMARKS: Off *Nellie Dixon*. Built for John Chisholm & Co. Sail plan at Peabody & Essex Museum.

NAME: [g]*Lizzie M. Stanley*[1,5]
BUILDER: James & Tarr
LAUNCH DATE: 28 September
HOME PORT: Gloucester
REMARKS: Off *Nellie Dixon*. Built for Joshua Stanley. Drawn on 23 April 1901.[c] Plan included in the H.A.M.M.S.

NAME: [d]*Massachusetts*
BUILDER: Oxner & Story
HOME PORT: Plymouth
REMARKS: Indian Header. Built for Sanford C. Winsor. Sail plan at Peabody & Essex Museum.

NAME: [?]*Mary P. Mesquita*
BUILDER: A.D. Story[n]
HOME PORT: Gloucester
REMARKS: Small schooner off *Nellie Dixon*.

Built for Joseph P. Mesquita. Sail plan at Peabody & Essex Museum.

NAME: [?]*Jennie and Agnes*
BUILDER: Gloucester
HOME PORT: Boston
REMARKS: Off *Nellie Dixon*. Built for Francis J. O'Hara.

NAME: [?]*Mary T. Fallon*
OFFICIAL NUMBER:
BUILDER: Oxner & Story[n]
HOME PORT: Boston
REMARKS: Indian Header. Built for John J. Fallon.

NAME: [?]*Joseph H. Cromwell*
BUILDER: East Boothbay
HOME PORT: Boston
REMARKS: Built for Thomas A. Cromwell.

1902
NAME: [?]*Gertrude*
BUILDER: A.D. Story
LAUNCH DATE: March[n]
HOME PORT: Boston
REMARKS: Built for Francis J. O'Hara.

NAME: [d]*Helen B. Thomas*
BUILDER: Oxner & Story
LAUNCH DATE: 11 March
HOME PORT: Boston
REMARKS: First knockabout schooner. Built for Cassius Hunt and Captain William Thomas of Portland, Maine. Became a Bermuda pilot boat. Burned 27 November 1926. Plans in *International Marine Engineering* (June 1902).

NAME: [d]*Manhassett*
BUILDER: Hugh Bishop
LAUNCH DATE: 11 March[i]
HOME PORT: Duxbury
REMARKS: Indian Header. Built for Sanford C. Winsor and Captain Henry Dexter Malone. 120-bhp NELSECO diesel engine installed 1914 and "she was reported to make nine knots easily under power."[h] Sometimes

claimed to be the first diesel-powered New England fishing schooner, her conversion took place after the launch of the *Bay State* and the *Knickerbocker*, both designed for diesel power. Sail plan at Peabody & Essex Museum.

NAME: [b]*Flora S. Nickerson*
BUILDER: Tarr & James
LAUNCH DATE: 12 June[n]
HOME PORT: Boston
REMARKS: Indian Header. Built for Thomas A. Cromwell, *et.al.*[3] Captain Thomas A. Cromwell. Offset tables completed 12 March 1902.[b] Sister to the *Matchless*. Plans at Smithsonian Institution. Sold to Fortune Bay, Newfoundland, in 1911. Disappeared from the British registry by 1924.[h]

NAME: [?]*Philip P. Manta*
BUILDER: James & Tarr
LAUNCH DATE: 22 July[m]
HOME PORT: Provincetown
REMARKS: Off *William A. Morse*. Built for Joseph Manta.[4]

NAME: [d]*Metamora*
BUILDER: John Bishop
LAUNCH DATE: 7 August
HOME PORT: Plymouth
REMARKS: Indian Header. Built for Sanford C. Winsor and Captain J.F. Robbins. Flush deck. "Thomas F. McManus is modeling a schooner off the crack flyer *Metamora* for William H. Burke of Scituate, Captain J. Swim."[5] Later sold to Newfoundland.

NAME: [d]*Squanto*
BUILDER: Oxner & Story
LAUNCH DATE: 20 August
HOME PORT: Duxbury
REMARKS: Indian Header. Built for Sanford C. Winsor and Captain J.H. McKay. Halibut schooner. Fell over on the ways and took 20 days to launch. Lost 30 November 1931, ran ashore at Flat Bay, Newfoundland. Sail plan at Peabody & Essex Museum.

NAME: [a,h]*Matchless*

BUILDER: Tarr & James
LAUNCH DATE: 25 September[n]
HOME PORT: Plymouth
REMARKS: Indian Header off the *Flora S. Nickerson*.[h] Built for Captain Thomas A. Cromwell, *et.al.*[6] Offset tables completed 12 March 1902.[b]

NAME: [g]*Benjamin W. Latham*
BUILDER: James & Tarr
LAUNCH DATE: 30 October[n]
HOME PORT: Stonington, Connecticut
REMARKS: Spoon bow in response to B.B. Crowninshield's *Rob Roy*.[7] Built for Henry Langworthy. Designed 18 August 1902. Plans included in the H.A.M.M.S. Langworthy was skipper of another Crowinshield design, the *Tartar* of 1904.[8]

NAME: [e]*George H. Lubee*
BUILDER: Oxner & Story
HOME PORT: Boston
REMARKS: Indian Header. Built for Edward A. Rich & Co. Lost 24 May 1913. Sail plan at Peabody & Essex Museum.

NAME: [f]*Seaconnet*
BUILDER: Oxner & Story
HOME PORT: Boston
REMARKS: Indian Header. Built for George F. Grueby. Renamed *Carrie B. Welles* at Pensacola. Later *Annie B.* at Tarpon Springs. Last seen heading for Panama in 1981.

NAME: [a]*Emily Cooney*
BUILDER: Oxner & Story
HOME PORT: Boston
REMARKS: First round-bow. Built for Edward A. Rich & Co. The surviving plan, at the Smithsonian Instution, may have been drawn by Archer B. Poland, as it was found in his mold loft by Chapelle.

NAME: [f]*Ellen C. Burke*
BUILDER: Oxner & Story
HOME PORT: Scituate
REMARKS: Indian Header. Built for Caleb K. Sullivan. Galveston (1912).

NAME: [?]*Maggie and Hattie*
BUILDER: Oxner & Story
HOME PORT: Boston
REMARKS: Built for Henry Dexter Malone. Lost on Rose and Crown Shoal 30 January 1903.

NAME: [?]*Vidia M. Brigham*
BUILDER: Oxner & Story
HOME PORT: Boston
REMARKS: Built for Edward A. Rich & Co. Sail plan at Peabody & Essex Museum.

NAME: [?]*Galatea*
BUILDER: Gloucester
HOME PORT: Boston
REMARKS: *Fredonia* type. Built for A.M. Watson, Jr. Stranded at Portsmouth, N.H., in 1905. A total loss.[9]

NAME: [?]*Teresa and Alice*
BUILDER: Oxner & Story[n]
HOME PORT: Boston
REMARKS: Built for George Perry.

1903[10]
NAME: [f]*Olivia Domingoes*
BUILDER: James & Tarr
LAUNCH DATE: 10 February
HOME PORT: Boston
REMARKS: Spoon-bow off *Benjamin W. Latham*. Built for Antone Almeida and/or Manuel P. Domingoes.[11] Sail plan at Peabody & Essex Museum.

NAME: [?]*Griswold I. Keeney*
BUILDER: A.D. Story
LAUNCH DATE: March[n]
HOME PORT: New York City
REMARKS: Indian Header. Built for Peter O. Ericsson. Lost February 1916 off Newfoundland.

NAME: [?]*Paragon*
BUILDER: Oxner & Story
LAUNCH DATE: 27 April
HOME PORT: Gloucester
REMARKS: Round-bow. Built for David I. Robinson.

1903 continued

NAME: [?]*Edith J. Peterson*
BUILDER: A.D. Story
LAUNCH DATE: April[n]
HOME PORT: New York City
REMARKS: Indian Header. Built for Harry Peterson.

NAME: [a]*Fannie Belle Atwood*
BUILDER: Oxner & Story
LAUNCH DATE: 12 May
HOME PORT: Boston
REMARKS: Indian Header. Built for Edward A. Rich & Co. Became a Cape Verde packet. Sail plan at Peabody & Essex Museum.

NAME: [f]*Elmer E. Gray*
BUILDER: James & Tarr
LAUNCH DATE: 26 May
HOME PORT: Gloucester
REMARKS: Indian Header. Built for Captain William Thomas and John Chisholm.[12] Sold to Newfoundland in 1940. Lines at Essex Shipbuilding Museum.

NAME: [a]*Annie Perry*
BUILDER: James & Tarr
LAUNCH DATE: 9 July
HOME PORT: Provincetown
REMARKS: Indian Header off the *Matchless*. Built for Marion Perry.[13] Salvaged after 1914 Boston Harbor collision,[c] she was "Bombed & sunk by German Submarine. Aug 3 or 4, 1918", according to James Yard Book.

NAME: [f]*Mary F. Curtis*
BUILDER: James & Tarr
LAUNCH DATE: 11 September
HOME PORT: Gloucester
REMARKS: Indian Header. Built for John Pew & Son off the lines of *Elmer E. Gray*.[14] Auxiliary engine 1917. Camera boat for *Captains Courageous*. Lost 20 February 1952 on McNutt's Island, near Shelburne, N.S.

NAME: [a]*James and Esther*
BUILDER: Oxner & Story
HOME PORT: Provincetown

REMARKS: Built for Samuel T. Hatch.

NAME: [f]*Mooanam*
BUILDER: Hugh Bishop
HOME PORT: Duxbury
REMARKS: Indian Header. Built for Sanford C. Winsor. Collision in Gloucester Harbor 29 January 1910 with *Selma*. Damage repaired. Sail plan at Peabody & Essex Museum.

NAME: [a]*Mettacomett*
BUILDER: Oxner & Story
HOME PORT: Gloucester
REMARKS: Indian Header. Owned by Oxner & Story through 1908 at least.

NAME: [e]*Natalie J. Nelson*
BUILDER: Oxner & Story
HOME PORT: Gloucester
REMARKS: Indian Header. Built for George W. Nelson. Sail plan at Peabody & Essex Museum.

NAME: [f]*Mildred Robinson*
BUILDER: Oxner & Story
HOME PORT: Boston
REMARKS: Indian Header. Built for J.O. Richards. Sail plan at Peabody & Essex Museum.

NAME: [f]*Quannapowatt*
BUILDER: L.B. MacKenzie
HOME PORT: Boston
REMARKS: Indian Header. Built for Henry Dexter Malone. There is a 3/8" scale model of this vessel by D. Foster Taylor at the Peabody & Essex Museum, lines at Smithsonian Institution, sail plan at Peabody & Essex Museum.

NAME: [c]*Ida M. Silva*
BUILDER: Oxner & Story
HOME PORT: Boston
REMARKS: Off *Nellie Dixon*. Built for Atlantic Maritime Co. Designed 15 August 1903.[c] Lines at Smithsonian Institution.

1904
NAME: [d]*Mooween*
BUILDER: John Bishop

LAUNCH DATE: February
HOME PORT: Duxbury
REMARKS: First semi-knockabout. Built for Sanford C. Winsor. Crew of 18. Stranded and lost on Great Island, off Lunenburg, N.S., on 12 December 1911. The "new semi-knockabout fisherman *Mooween* arrived in Boston harbor, looking more like a yacht than a working vessel."[15] *Mooween* eventually spawned *Premier*, *Elk*, *Elsie*, and *Gov. Foss*.

NAME: [f]*Mina Swim*
BUILDER: A.D. Story
LAUNCH DATE: 4 April
HOME PORT: Boston
REMARKS: Indian Header. Built for Atlantic Maritime Co. Off *Metamora*. "Thomas F. McManus is modeling a schooner off the crack flyer *Metamora* for William H. Burke of Scituate, Captain J. Swim."[16] Sail plan at Peabody & Essex Museum.

NAME: [f]*Maud F. Silva*
BUILDER: John Bishop
LAUNCH DATE: 30 April
HOME PORT: Rockport
REMARKS: Indian Header. Built for John Silva. Sail plan at Peabody & Essex Museum.

NAME: [a]*Cavalier*
BUILDER: James & Tarr
LAUNCH DATE: 5 May
HOME PORT: Gloucester
REMARKS: Indian Header. Built for Cunningham & Thompson.[17] Drawn 9 December 1903, plans at Smithsonian Institution, sail plan at Peabody & Essex Museum. Same plan, different dimensions and same molds as *Lucania*.[c] Became rum-runner *Quistcachan* 1922-31. Later renamed *Marjorie and Eileen*. Driven ashore 10 September 1932, at Miquelon Roads with *Admiral Dewey*.

NAME: [f]*Lucania*
BUILDER: Hugh Bishop
LAUNCH DATE: 16 May
HOME PORT: Gloucester
REMARKS: Indian Header. Built Sylvanus

Smith & Co. Drawn on 9 December 1903.[c] Plans at Smithsonian Institution, sail plan at Peabody & Essex Museum.

NAME: [a]*Catherine L. Burke*
BUILDER: Oxner & Story
HOME PORT: Boston
REMARKS: Round-bow. Built for Caleb K. Sullivan. See *Louisa R. Silva* below. Lost 21 August 1940 off Newfoundland.

NAME: *Kernwood*[18]
BUILDER: Oxner & Story
LAUNCH DATE: Late June
HOME PORT: Boston
REMARKS: Round-bow. Became the pilot boat *Trenton* at New York.

NAME: [i]*Waldo L. Stream*
BUILDER: James & Tarr
LAUNCH DATE: 16 July
HOME PORT: Gloucester
REMARKS: Indian Header. Built for Stream & Montgomery off the lines of *Elmer E. Gray* and *Mary F. Curtis*.[19] Engines installed 1920. Rum-runner 1922. Lost 26 December 1924 in a gale off Muskegat Island. Sail plan at Peabody & Essex Museum.

NAME: [f]*Mary E. Silveira*
BUILDER: John Bishop
HOME PORT: Boston
REMARKS: Indian Header. Built for Edward A. Rich & Co. Market fisherman. Lost in the Gulf of Mexico red-snapper fishery 16 August 1915.

NAME: [h]*Francis J. O'Hara Jr.*
BUILDER: Oxner & Story
LAUNCH DATE: August
HOME PORT: Boston
REMARKS: Indian Header. Built for Francis J. O'Hara & Co. Sunk 21 August 1918 by the trawler *Triumph*, prize to and manned by the German U-156. Sail plan at Peabody & Essex Museum.

NAME: [a]*Onato*

BUILDER: Oxner & Story
LAUNCH DATE: 27 August
HOME PORT: Boston
REMARKS: Indian Header. Built for J. Henry Larkin. Designed 12 May 1904, plans at Smithsonian Institution, sail plan at Peabody & Essex Museum. Fell over on the ways at her launch. Lost 5 March 1919 returning from Portugal with salt.

NAME: [f]*Belbina Domingoes*
BUILDER: John Bishop
LAUNCH DATE: 30 August
HOME PORT: Boston
REMARKS: Round-bow. Built for Manuel P. Domingoes. Shattered in a collision on Brown's Bank during August 1910 with the Red Star liner *Samland*. Sail plan at Peabody & Essex Museum.

NAME: [f]*Richard J. Nunan*
HOME PORT: East Boothbay, Maine
REMARKS: Built for Richard J. Nunan.

NAME: [e]*Walter P. Goulart*
BUILDER: Oxner & Story
HOME PORT: Gloucester
REMARKS: Round-bow. Built for Manuel Simmons by Schwartz & Beurlein. A small market schooner. Driven ashore at Yarmouth, N.S., 12 May 1912

NAME: [f]*Mystery*
BUILDER: L.B. MacKenzie
LAUNCH DATE: 12 September
HOME PORT: Plymouth
REMARKS: Indian Header. Built for Captain Burgess.

NAME: [a]*Ingomar*
BUILDER: James & Tarr
LAUNCH DATE: 14 September
HOME PORT: Gloucester
REMARKS: Indian Header. Built for Cunningham & Thompson for Captain Wallace Parsons.[20] Halibut fisherman. Twin 60-bhp auxiliaries added 1919. Lost 18 February 1936. Ran ashore at Plum Island,

Mass., 18 February 1936. Designed 16 June 1904.[c] Plans at Smithsonian Institution.

NAME: [f]*Genesta*
BUILDER: John Bishop
HOME PORT: Boston
REMARKS: Indian Header. Built for A.M. Watson, Jr.

NAME: [a]*Buema*
BUILDER: Oxner & Story
LAUNCH DATE: Fall
HOME PORT: Boston
REMARKS: Round-bow. Built for Herbert W. Nickerson. Became a Cape Verde packet. Wrecked 7 June 1908, on Race Point near Provincetown.

NAME: [f]*Louise C. Cabral*
BUILDER: James & Tarr
LAUNCH DATE: 3 October[n]
HOME PORT: Provincetown
REMARKS: Round-bow off *Kernwood* with a one foot wider beam. Built for John A. Matheson.[21] Sail plan drawn 14 September 1904, at New Bedford Whaling Museum.[22] Lost 13 February 1910.

NAME: [k]*Alcyone*
BUILDER: Joseph McGill
LAUNCH DATE: 14 October
HOME PORT: Digby, N.S.
REMARKS: Second knockabout. Built at Shelburne, N.S., for Harry B. Short and James Ellis. Captain R.A. Wormell. Amos Pentz, Master Carpenter.

NAME: [f]*Fannie E. Prescott*
BUILDER: A.D. Story
LAUNCH DATE: October[m]
HOME PORT: Boston
REMARKS: Indian Header. Built for Atlantic Maritime Co. Capt. Carl Olson. Sail plan at Peabody & Essex Museum.

NAME: [?]*Thomas J. Carroll*
BUILDER: A.D. Story
LAUNCH DATE: October[n]

1904 continued
HOME PORT: Boston
REMARKS: Off *Nellie Dixon*. Built for Thomas A. Cromwell. Sail plan at Peabody & Essex Museum.

NAME: [g]*Louisa R. Silva*
BUILDER: James & Tarr
LAUNCH DATE: 23 November[m]
HOME PORT: Provincetown
REMARKS: Round-bow off *Catherine L. Burke*. Built for Joseph S. Silva.[23] Designed in 'early' 1904.[c] Stranded off Newfoundland and broke up in 1928. Included in the H.A.M.M.S., thus her drafts also can illustrate the *Burke*.

NAME: [e]*Francis V. Sylva*
BUILDER: Oxner & Story[m]
HOME PORT: Provincetown
REMARKS: Off *Nellie Dixon*. Built for John G. Sylva. Sail plan at Peabody & Essex Museum.

NAME: [a]*Mary C. Santos*
BUILDER: James & Tarr
LAUNCH DATE: 7 December
HOME PORT: Provincetown
REMARKS: Indian Header off *Annie Perry*. Gas-engined auxiliary. Built for Joseph A. Manta.[24] "...the perennial [Provincetown] highliner *Mary C. Santos*."[h] Lost 17 March 1932. Sail plan at Peabody & Essex Museum.

1905
NAME: [?]*Benjamin M. Wallace*
BUILDER: A.D. Story
LAUNCH DATE: February[n]
HOME PORT: New York
REMARKS: Indian Header. Sail plan at Peabody & Essex Museum.

NAME: [d]*Frances P. Mesquita*
BUILDER: John Bishop
LAUNCH DATE: 8 March
HOME PORT: Gloucester
REMARKS: Round-bow off *Belbina Domingoes*. Built for Joseph P. Mesquita. Won

the second class in the 1907 Fishermen's Race (the first Lipton Cup) defeating the *Helen B. Thomas*, the only other class entry. Sunk by German U-boat summer 1918.

NAME: [f]*Ethel Mildred*
BUILDER: James & Tarr
LAUNCH DATE: 21 March
HOME PORT: New York
REMARKS: Round-bow off *Louise C. Cabral*. Built for Capt. W.A. Graber & Kingston & Comstock off *Louise C. Cabral*.[25] Sail plan at Peabody & Essex Museum.

NAME: *Catherine G. Howard*
BUILDER: A.D. Story
REMARKS: Indian Header.[26]

NAME: [f]*Georgiana*
BUILDER: A.D. Story
LAUNCH DATE: May[n]
HOME PORT: Boston
REMARKS: Indian Header. Built for Cassius Hunt. Owned by Atlantic Maritime Co. in 1908, and later sold to Gorton-Pew Vessels Co. Run down by an unidentified schooner off Provincetown, 9 December 1920.

NAME: [f]*Susan and Mary*
BUILDER: A.D. Story
LAUNCH DATE: May[n]
HOME PORT: Boston
REMARKS: Indian Header. Built for Atlantic Maritime Co.

NAME: [f]*Galatea*[27]
BUILDER: John Bishop
HOME PORT: Boston
REMARKS: Indian Header. Built for A.M. Watson Jr. Lost on Rose and Crown Shoal 14 July 1914. Sail Plan at Peabody & Essex Museum.

NAME: [d]*Jessie Costa*[5]
BUILDER: James & Tarr
LAUNCH DATE: 13 July
HOME PORT: Provincetown
REMARKS: Indian Header off the *Mary C*.

Santos.[28] Built for Joseph A. Manta.[29] Raced in 1907 Lipton's Cup Race. Sold to Newfoundland, December 1916, lost on delivery trip. Sail plan at Peabody & Essex Museum.

NAME: [i,l]*Thomas S. Gorton*
BUILDER: James & Tarr
LAUNCH DATE: 14 August
HOME PORT: Gloucester
REMARKS: Round-bow. Built for John Chisolm & Co. & Captain William Thomas. Similar to the *Alert*, *Esperanto*, and *Raymah*. Last all-sail Gloucesterman. Sunk 1956 after colliding with an iceberg enroute to Labrador.

NAME: [c]*Thomas A. Cromwell*
BUILDER: Oxner & Story
HOME PORT: Boston
REMARKS: McManus's third knockabout. Built for Thomas A. Cromwell. Had pole masts. "She was in many respects, a development from the design of the *Helen B. Thomas*, having less sheer and, generally, a more attractive hull, but still with wasted space in the ends."[c] Plan at Smithsonian Institution. Sold to Newfoundland February 1914. Foundered off Cape Race, Newfoundland, January 1918, crew saved.

NAME: [f,l]*James W. Parker*
BUILDER: A.D. Story
LAUNCH DATE: August
HOME PORT: Boston
REMARKS: Round-bow. Built for Atlantic Maritime Co. Raced in the 1907 Lipton's Cup. Renamed *Noxall* in 1926. Sank 24 August 1927, after colliding with the *Veda M. McKown* in the vicinity of Cape Spear, Newfoundland. Sail plan at Peabody & Essex Museum.

NAME: [d]*Rose Dorothea*
BUILDER: James & Tarr
LAUNCH DATE: 27 September
HOME PORT: Provincetown
REMARKS: Indian Header off *Annie Perry*, but ten feet longer. Built for Marion Perry.[30]

Won the 1907 Fishermen's Race. Sunk by the Germans during February 1917.

NAME: [a]*Raymah*
BUILDER: Oxner & Story
LAUNCH DATE: 11 October
HOME PORT: Boston
REMARKS: Round-bow off the lines of the *Thomas S. Gorton*. Similar to the *Esperanto* and *Alert*. Built for Atlantic Maritime Co. Lost en route to Portugal 10 December 1912. Sail plan at Peabody & Essex Museum.

NAME: [?]*Margaret Dillon*
BUILDER: Oxner & Story
HOME PORT: Boston
REMARKS: Indian Header. Built for Michael Dillon. Lost her bowsprit to a five-masted schooner in November 1913.[h]

NAME: [i]*Teazer*
BUILDER: James & Tarr
LAUNCH DATE: 16 October
HOME PORT: Gloucester
REMARKS:Spoon bow off *Benjamin W. Latham*. Built for D.B. Smith & Co.[31] Owned by Gorton-Pew in 1908. Crushed in the ice on a sealing trip 25 March 1948, at St. Paul's Island.

NAME: Plan No. 108
REMARKS: Indian Header. Drawn 24 October 1905 for Atlantic Maritime Co. Name of vessel unknown. Donated to Mystic Seaport Museum by Louise Will.

1906
NAME: [a]*Hortense*
BUILDER: Oxner & Story
HOME PORT: Boston
REMARKS: Auxiliary. Built for Francis J. O'Hara. Owned by Gorton-Pew in 1908. Sold to be a pilot boat at Beaufort, N.C., in the 1920s.

NAME: [i]*Cynthia*
BUILDER: John Bishop
LAUNCH DATE: 5 January

HOME PORT: Gloucester
REMARKS: Indian Header. Built for Sylvanus Smith Co.

NAME: [f]*Norseman*
BUILDER: A.D. Story
LAUNCH DATE: March
HOME PORT: New York
REMARKS: Off *Nellie Dixon*. Sail plan at Peabody & Essex Museum.

NAME: [i]*Alert*[32]
BUILDER: James & Tarr
LAUNCH DATE: 14 March
HOME PORT: Gloucester
REMARKS: Round-bow off *Thomas S. Gorton*. Built with 100-bhp gasoline auxiliary engine.[33] Built for Captain John Chisholm.[34] Lost 4 November 1906. Ran ashore at the Bay of St. George, Newfoundland. Hull cost $8,600. Total cost $29,000.[h] Sail plan at Peabody & Essex Museum.

NAME: [i]*Effie M. Prior*
BUILDER: A.D. Story
LAUNCH DATE: 9 April
HOME PORT: Gloucester
REMARKS: Indian Header. Built for Michael Walen & Son. Lost October 1921 at Savage Cove, Newfoundland.

NAME: [f]*Terra Nova*
BUILDER: A.D. Story
LAUNCH DATE: May[n]
HOME PORT: Boston
REMARKS: Indian Header. Lost 16 March 1914.

NAME: [e]*Eclipse*
BUILDER: John Bishop
HOME PORT: New York
REMARKS: Schooner yacht. Built for Lawrence J. Callanan of New York. Plans donated to Mystic Seaport Museum by Louise Will. Drawn 10 May 1906. After Callanan's 1913 death, *Eclipse*, then equipped with a 37-bhp kerosene engine, went to Savannah as freight boat. Disappeared about 1920.[35]

NAME: [a,i]*Esperanto*
BUILDER: James & Tarr
LAUNCH DATE: 27 June
HOME PORT: Gloucester
RESULTS: Round-bow off the lines of *Thomas S. Gorton*.[36] Similar to the *Alert* and the *Raymah*. Built for Orlando Merchant and Captain Charles Harty. Won the International Trophy in 1920. Lost 30 May 1921 when she struck the submerged wreck of S.S. *State of Virginia* off Sable Island, N.S.

NAME: [f]*Morning Star*
BUILDER: A.D. Story
LAUNCH DATE: 7 July
HOME PORT: Boston
REMARKS: Indian Header. Built for Francis J. O'Hara. Sail plan at Peabody & Essex Museum.

NAME: [?]*Clara G. Silva*
OFFICIAL NUMBER: 203764
BUILDER: A.D. Story
LAUNCH DATE: July
HOME PORT: Gloucester
REMARKS: Indian Header.

NAME: [f]*Emily Sears*
BUILDER: L.B. MacKenzie
LAUNCH DATE:November 20
HOME PORT: Gloucester.
REMARKS: Built for Manuel Sears.

NAME: [b]*Pontiac*
BUILDER: John Bishop
LAUNCH DATE: December
HOME PORT: Boston
REMARKS: First McManus short-bow knockabout design.[37] Built for George F. Grueby, *et.al.* Plan No. 111 completed 8 September 1906, published in A. C. Church's *American Fishermen*, copy at Smithsonian Institution.[b] The fourth knockabout built, and the first built at Gloucester. Designed for auxiliary power,[c] but probably not built that way. Stranded on Handkerchief Shoal, October 1916.

1907
NAME: [h]*John Hays Hammond*
BUILDER: James & Tarr
LAUNCH DATE: 25 June
HOME PORT: Gloucester
REMARKS: Round-bow off the molds of
Louisa R. Silva. Built for Lemuel E. Spinney.[38]
Halibut fisherman and mackerel seiner. Sunk
27 July 1917 by a U-Boat 360 miles off the
Irish coast.[h] Sail plan at Peabody & Essex
Museum.

NAME: [h,i]*Clintonia*
BUILDER: John Bishop
LAUNCH DATE: 26 June
HOME PORT: Gloucester
REMARKS: Semi-knockabout.[39] Built for
Orlando Merchant and Captain Charles
Harty. Designed February 1904.[c] Lines
at Smithsonian Institution. Sold to
Newfoundland in 1916. Lost November 1921
enroute to Portugal with salt cod.[c] Had an
identical Canadian sister.

NAME: [a]*Arethusa*
BUILDER: James & Tarr
LAUNCH DATE: 25 September
HOME PORT: Gloucester
REMARKS: First knockabout built by James
& Tarr.[40] Plan at Smithsonian Institution.
Built for Cunningham & Thompson and
Clayton Morrissey. Later Bill McCoy's rum-
runner *Tomoka,* was the fastest knockabout
until the *Catherine* was built. Owned by
Cunningham & Thompson in 1917.

NAME: [f]*Richard*
BUILDER: Oxner & Story
LAUNCH DATE: 21 September
HOME PORT: Gloucester
REMARKS: Round-bow. Built for Manuel
Simmons off *Louisa R. Sylva.* Finished in
1906, but launched in 1907 after the collapse
of Oxner & Story Firm.

NAME: [f]*Edith Silveira*
BUILDER: A.D. Story
LAUNCH DATE: September

HOME PORT: Boston
REMARKS: Indian Header. Built for Leandro
J. DeCosta, Jr. Later owned at Pensacola by
the Warren Fish Co.

NAME: [e]*Vanessa*
BUILDER: A.D. Story
LAUNCH DATE: December
HOME PORT: Boston
REMARKS: Indian Header. Built for A.M.
Watson, Jr. Sail plan at Peabody & Essex
Museum.

NAME: [a]*Benjamin A. Smith*
BUILDER: James & Tarr
LAUNCH DATE: 21 December
HOME PORT: Gloucester
REMARKS: Auxiliary knockabout. Built for
Gorton-Pew Fish Co. for D.B. Smith and
Benj. Smith without engine.[41] Short bow-
sprit added 13 September 1913. Ran ashore in
fog at Flat Island, N.S., 3 August 1923.

NAME: [?]*Bessie M. Dugan*
BUILDER: East Boothbay, Maine
HOME PORT: Boston
REMARKS: Built for Joseph H. Cromwell.

1908
NAME: [h,i]*Clintonia*
BUILDER: Smith & Rhuland
HOME PORT: Lunenburg, N.S.
REMARKS: Semi-knockabout. Built for
Captain Emiel "Paddy" Mack. Identical sister
to McManus's American *Clintonia.*
Abandoned on fire off Sable Island during
January 1923, just 15 months after her
namesake was lost.

NAME: [k]*Kernwood*
BUILDER: Joseph McGill
LAUNCH DATE: 6 April
HOME PORT: Shelburne, N.S.
REMARKS: Round-bow. Yarmouth, N.S.
Built for Irving A. Lovitt. Amos Pentz, Master
Carpenter. Commanded by John Sims.

NAME: [h]*W*.M. *Goodspeed*

BUILDER: John Bishop
LAUNCH DATE: 1 June
HOME PORT: Boston
REMARKS: Knockabout. Built for George F.
Grueby. Similar to the *Athena* and *Ethel B.
Penny.* Cost about $25,000. 75-bhp gasoline
engine installed in late 1913. Her fish were
the first to be auctioned off at the new Fish
Pier in South Boston on 30 March 1914. Sunk
by the steam trawler *Swell* just west of Georges
Bank on 2 June 1919.[h]

NAME: [a]*Oriole*
BUILDER: James & Tarr
LAUNCH DATE: 24 June
HOME PORT: Gloucester
REMARKS: Auxiliary semi-knockabout
launched without an engine. Built for
Orlando Merchant.[42] Plan No. 132[c], copy at
the Smithsonian Institution. Rammed by
Norwegian steamer *Borghild* off Seal Island,
N.S., on 12 August 1916.

NAME: [h]*Victor and Ethan*
BUILDER: A.D. Story
LAUNCH DATE: 24 June
HOME PORT: Boston
REMARKS: First knockabout by A.D. Story.[c]
Built for Henry Dexter Malone. Auxiliary
powered. Off *W.M. Goodspeed.*[h] Lost 7
October 1916.

NAME: [h,f]*Athena*
BUILDER: John Bishop
HOME PORT: Boston
REMARKS: Knockabout. Built for J.O.
Richards. Changed to 100-bhp Blanchard
diesel fall 1911 to go to the West Coast.
Returned 1915. Cost about $25,000. Sold to
Newfoundland in 1928.[h]

NAME: [f]*Leo*
BUILDER: A.D. Story
LAUNCH DATE: 27 July
HOME PORT: Boston
REMARKS: Indian Header. Built for J.F.
Leonard.

NAME: [f]Rex
BUILDER: A.D. Story
HOME PORT: Gloucester
REMARKS: Round-bow. Built on speculation. Purchased by the Fred L. Davis Co. Twin diesel engines installed during 1919. Rammed and sunk by the Glasgow-built Cunard Liner, *Tuscania*, in 1925. *Rex* was cut in half with the loss of fifteen men including the cook's young son. *Tuscania*'s boats rescued nine.

NAME: [k]*Albert J. Lutz*
BUILDER: Joseph McGill
LAUNCH DATE: 6 August
HOME PORT: Digby, N.S
REMARKS: Indian Header.[43] Capt. Maynard Culp, *et.al.* Owners included Frederick William Wallace, the author of *Roving Fishermen*, and the intended skipper, John D. Apt.

NAME: [f]*Matiana*
BUILDER: Richard T. Green
HOME PORT: Boston
REMARKS: Knockabout. Ran up on the ledges at North Scituate in a February 1910 gale due to a faulty compass.

NAME: [a]*Josie and Phoebe*
BUILDER: A.D. Story
LAUNCH DATE: 12 September
HOME PORT: Boston
REMARKS: Semi-knockabout. Built for Sylvester Whalen, *et. al.* Sold to St. John's, Newfoundland, 1918, and still enrolled in 1940.[h]

NAME: [h,f]*Evelyn M. Thompson*
BUILDER: John Bishop
LAUNCH DATE: Mid-September
HOME PORT: Boston
REMARKS: Auxiliary knockabout. Built for Thomas A. Cromwell for Captain Herbert Thompson. Laid down alongside the *Ethel B. Penny*. Ran ashore at Sankaty Light, Nantucket, in a fog 13 July 1918.[h]

NAME: [h,f]*Ethel B. Penny*
BUILDER: John Bishop
LAUNCH DATE: October
HOME PORT: Boston
REMARKS: Knockabout off *Athena*, with similarities to *Victor and Ethan* and *W.M. Goodspeed*. Built for A.L. Parker. Twin 37.5-bhp gas engines installed 1914. Lost 1940.[h] Sail plan at Peabody & Essex Museum.

NAME: [f]*Washakie*
BUILDER: Richard T. Green
HOME PORT: Boston
REMARKS: Knockabout. Built for Edward A. Malone. Later *John Taylor* at Pensacola.

NAME: [f]*Eugenia*
BUILDER: John Bishop
LAUNCH DATE: 5 December
HOME PORT: Gloucester
REMARKS: Round-bow. Built for the Sylvanus Smith Co.

NAME: [k]*Arginia*
BUILDER: Joseph McGill
LAUNCH DATE: 29 December
HOME PORT: Lunenburg, N.S.
REMARKS: Semi-knockabout. Capt. Maynard Culp, *et.al.* Amos Pentz, Master Carpenter. Went ashore at Devil's Bay, southwest coast of Newfoundland, 20 June 1943, and became a total loss.

1909

NAME: [f]*Mary DeCosta*
BUILDER: John Bishop
HOME PORT: Boston
REMARKS: First round-bow semi-knockabout. Built for Leandro J. DeCosta Jr. Received a gasoline engine in 1913 and a diesel in 1924. Foundered off Miami, Florida, during December 1945.[h]

NAME: [h]*Alice*
BUILDER: A.D. Story
LAUNCH DATE: Winter[n]
HOME PORT: Boston
REMARKS: Auxiliary knockabout. Built on

speculation. Sold to A.M. Watson, Jr.

NAME: Plan No. 145
REMARKS: Knockabout. Sails, Lines, Body, Offsets. Drawn 29 March. Donated to Mystic Seaport Museum by Louise Will.

NAME: *La Paloma*[44]
BUILDER: Unknown
LAUNCH DATE: February
HOME PORT: Seattle
REMARKS: Pole-masted knockabout. 75-bhp San Francisco Standard model gasoline engine.

NAME: [a]*Georgia*
BUILDER: A.D. Story
LAUNCH DATE: April[n]
HOME PORT: Boston
REMARKS: Knockabout. Built on speculation. Sold to Alonzo F. Cahoon. Rammed by steam collier *Bristol* off Great Round Shoal, 9 December 1929.

NAME: [k]*Lulu S.*
BUILDER: Joseph McGill
LAUNCH DATE: 5 August
HOME PORT: Lockeport, N.S.
REMARKS: Knockabout. Built for Herbert R. and J.W. Swim.

NAME: [b]*Gladys and Nellie*
BUILDER: John Bishop
LAUNCH DATE: 13 December
HOME PORT: Boston
REMARKS: Knockabout. Built for J.A. Matheson. Sail plan drawn 14 September 1909.[b]

NAME: [f]*Virginia*
BUILDER: A.D. Story
LAUNCH DATE: 13 December
HOME PORT: Boston
REMARKS: Knockabout. Plan No. 150, drawn 17 August 1909, at Smithsonian Institution. Built on speculation. Purchased by A.M. Watson, Jr. Became the *Buccaneer*. Sank at her wharf in Pensacola 1982.

1910

NAME: [a]*Josephine DeCosta*
BUILDER: James & Tarr
LAUNCH DATE: 2 March
HOME PORT: Boston
REMARKS: Indian Header. Built for Marion Perry and Leandro J. DeCosta, Jr., off *Annie Perry*.[45] Sail Plan at Peabody & Essex Museum.

NAME: [f]*Harriett*
BUILDER: John Bishop
LAUNCH DATE: 9 March
HOME PORT: Gloucester
REMARKS: Knockabout. Built for Schwartz & Beurlein.

NAME: [f]*Rhodora*
BUILDER: A.D. Story
LAUNCH DATE: 12 March
HOME PORT: Gloucester
REMARKS: Auxiliary short-bow knockabout. Built for Cunningham & Thompson. Designed 3 October 1908, plans at Smithsonian Institution.[c] Sold to Newfoundland and renamed *Metamora* 1939. Lost 1953 off Point Ridge, Newfoundland, carrying barrelled oil.

NAME: [i,f]*Premier*
BUILDER: A.D. Story
LAUNCH DATE: April[n]
HOME PORT: Gloucester
REMARKS: Semi-knockabout. Built for the Fred L. Davis Co. Similar to *Mooween*, *Elsie*, *Elk*, and *Gov. Foss*.

NAME: [k]*Rostand*
BUILDER: Joseph McGill
LAUNCH DATE: April
HOME PORT: St. Peter's, Cape Breton
REMARKS: Semi-knockabout. Built for the Stewart Fish Co., Shelburne, N.S

NAME: [k]*Grand Falls*
BUILDER: Joseph McGill
LAUNCH DATE: 26 May
HOME PORT: St. John's, Newfoundland

REMARKS: Knockabout tern schooner. Built for A.S. Rendell & Co., St. John's, Newfoundland & Albert W. Dyett, St. Jacques, Newfoundland. Amos Pentz, Master Carpenter. Sailed on 7 January 1914, from Harbour Breton, east coast of Newfoundland, bound for Oporto, Portugal. She was lost at sea, not ever being heard from.

NAME: [a]*Elsie*
BUILDER: A.D. Story
LAUNCH DATE: 9 May
HOME PORT: Boston
REMARKS: Semi-knockabout. Built for Atlantic Maritime Co. Plan No. 152, 30 November 1909. Various versions at Peabody & Essex Museum, Essex Shipbuilding Museum, and Smithsonian Institution. 1921 International trials winner but defeated by *Bluenose*. 1929 Fuller, Davis & Prentiss Cup participant. Foundered in the Gulf of St. Lawrence, 13 January 1935.

NAME: [i]*Stiletto*
BUILDER: John Bishop
LAUNCH DATE: May
HOME PORT: Gloucester
REMARKS: Semi-knockabout. Built for Orlando Merchant. Plan No. 153,[c] late 1909, at Smithsonian Institution. Wrecked at Forked River, N.J., 4 April 1930.

NAME: [k]*Dorothy M. Smart*
BUILDER: Joseph McGill
LAUNCH DATE: 9 July
HOME PORT: Digby, N.S.
REMARKS: Indian Header. Built for the Maritime Fish Corp. Amos Pentz, Master Carpenter.[46] Captain Ross, skipper.

NAME: [i]*Sylvania*
BUILDER: John Bishop
LAUNCH DATE: 6 September
HOME PORT: Gloucester
REMARKS: Semi-knockabout. Built for E.A. Bradley. She was the last schooner built for the Sylvanus Smith Co. Built off plan No. 153[c], at Smithsonian Institution. Sunk 31

August 1918 by the trawler *Triumph*, prize to and manned by the U-156.

NAME: [f]*Valerie*
BUILDER: James & Tarr
LAUNCH DATE: 6 December
HOME PORT: Boston
REMARKS: Semi-knockabout. Built for Lemuel Spinney and Frank Gaspa off the molds of *Elsie*.[47] Sail plan at Peabody & Essex Museum.

NAME: [f]*Matthew S. Greer*
BUILDER: A.D. Story
LAUNCH DATE: October[n]
HOME PORT: Boston
REMARKS: Knockabout. Built for Matthew S. Greer and Gorton-Pew Vessels Co. Taken off the lines or molds of *W.M. Goodspeed*. Sail plan at Peabody & Essex Museum.

NAME: [k]*Lloyd George*
BUILDER: Joseph McGill
LAUNCH DATE: 30 November
HOME PORT: Shelburne, N.S.
REMARKS: Semi-knockabout. Captain Gabriel Himmelman, *et.al.* Amos Pentz, Master Carpenter. Stranded and lost in 1920.

NAME: [f]*Jeannette*
BUILDER: John Bishop
LAUNCH DATE: 1 December
HOME PORT: Gloucester
REMARKS: Knockabout. Built for Captain Frank Saunders. Sail plan at Peabody & Essex Museum.

NAME: [a,i]*Elk*
BUILDER: A.D. Story
LAUNCH DATE: 15 December
HOME PORT: Boston
REMARKS: Semi-knockabout. Built for Captain Felix Hogan and/or the Atlantic Maritime Co. Similar to *Mooween*, *Elsie*, *Gov. Foss*, and *Premier*.[h] Lost 3 September 1944. Sail plan at Peabody & Essex Museum.

NAME: [k]*Gordon M. Hollett*

BUILDER: Joseph McGill
LAUNCH DATE: 21 December
HOME PORT: Burin, Newfoundland
REMARKS: Indian Header. Designed 1910, lines at Smithsonian Institution.[c] Amos Pentz, Master Carpenter, McGill Shipbuilding Co.

NAME: [o]*Hilda R.*
BUILDER: Conquerall Bank, N.S.
HOME PORT: Halifax, N.S.
REMARKS: Indian Head tern schooner. Built for Canada Sealing Company. Copper fastened, copper sheathed, and built with hardwood, she was among the finest tern schooners in the Maritimes. 99 tons net. Carried a crew of 20 for fur sealing among the Antarctic Islands. Made two circumnavigations, 1911-12, then sold to Harbour Grace, Newfoundland, owners who used her in the salt-fish trade between Newfoundland and Portugal. Made one 16-day passage, Harbour Grace to Gibraltar. Sunk by U-boat off Spain on 3 November 1917.

NAME: [?]*Little Elsie*
BUILDER: East Boothbay, Maine
HOME PORT: Boston
REMARKS: Schooner boat. Built for I.C. Harvey.

1911
NAME: [k]*Stanley and Frank*
BUILDER: Joseph McGill
LAUNCH DATE: February
HOME PORT: St. John's, Newfoundland
REMARKS: Semi-knockabout of 80 tons. Built for Harvey & Co. Amos Pentz, Master Carpenter. Captain Keeping, skipper.

NAME: [k]*Alice M. Pike*
BUILDER: Joseph McGill
LAUNCH DATE: 23 March
HOME PORT: St. John's, Newfoundland
REMARKS: Semi-knockabout of 86 tons. Built for Harvey & Co. Amos Pentz, Master Carpenter.

NAME: [f]*Jorgina*

BUILDER: A.D. Story
LAUNCH DATE: February[n]
HOME PORT: Gloucester
REMARKS: Knockabout. Built for Victor P. Oliver. Sail plan at Peabody & Essex Museum.

NAME: [a]*Eleanor DeCosta*
BUILDER: James & Tarr
LAUNCH DATE: 16 March
HOME PORT: Boston
REMARKS: Indian Header. Built for Leandro J. DeCosta, Jr., off *Josephine DeCosta*.[48]

NAME: [i]*Gov. Foss*
BUILDER: James & Tarr
LAUNCH DATE: 2 May
HOME PORT: Gloucester
REMARKS: Semi-knockabout off the lines of *Mooween*. Built for Lemuel Spinney and Fred J. Thompson.[49] Similar to *Elk*, *Elsie*, and *Premier*.[h] Lost off Cape May, 2 April 1929. Sail plan at Peabody & Essex Museum.

NAME: [i,f]*Laverna*
BUILDER: James & Tarr
LAUNCH DATE: 8 July
HOME PORT: Gloucester.
REMARKS: Semi-knockabout built from the molds of the *Valerie*. Albert L. Larkin and/or Cunningham & Thompson. Ran ashore 9 September 1936, in a gale at Salmon Bight Passage, Labrador. Sail plan at Peabody & Essex Museum.

NAME: [k]*Dorothy G. Snow*
BUILDER: Joseph McGill
LAUNCH DATE: 21 August
HOME PORT: Digby, N.S.
REMARKS: Round-bow semi-knockabout. Plan No. 176. Built for Captain Joseph E. Snow. Amos Pentz, Master Carpenter.

NAME: [f]*Adeline*
BUILDER: John Bishop
HOME PORT: Gloucester
REMARKS: Knockabout. Built by Schwartz & Beurlein for John Goulart, Jr.[e] One of the Portuguese fleet, and later a rum-runner. *Elsie*

G. *Silva* taken off *Adeline*. Sail plan at Peabody & Essex Museum.

NAME: [j]*Autocrat*
BUILDER: Richard T. Green
HOME PORT: Marblehead
REMARKS: Diesel-powered auxiliary knockabout ketch built for C.H.W. Foster of the Eastern Yacht Club. 2,500 sq. ft. sail plan. Later *Paladin II* and *Adare* (1935). Lines published in *Yachting* (December 1911).

NAME: [f]*Mary P. Goulart*
BUILDER: John Bishop
HOME PORT: Gloucester
REMARKS: Knockabout. Built for A.P. Goulart. Last large dory trawler from Provincetown.[f]

NAME: [h]*Frances S. Grueby*
BUILDER: John Bishop
LAUNCH DATE: 1 October
HOME PORT: Boston
REMARKS: Auxiliary knockabout. Built for George F. Grueby, *et.al.* Sank in a 1921 Boston Harbor collision with her sister, the *Commonwealth*.[h]

NAME: [e]*Alabama*
BUILDER: James & Tarr
LAUNCH DATE: 5 December
HOME PORT: Mobile, Alabama
REMARKS: Knockabout pilot boat. Mobile Bar Pilots Association.[50] Deck plan and partial inboard layout drawn 25 July 1911, donated to Mystic Seaport Museum by Louise Will.

NAME: [f]*Flora L. Oliver*
BUILDER: A.D. Story
LAUNCH DATE: 7 December
HOME PORT: Gloucester
REMARKS: Semi-knockabout. Mrs. Flora Oliver was thrown into the icy waters of the Essex River at the launch of her namesake. Believed to have been built for J. Manuel Marshall.

1911 continued

NAME: [a]*Imperator*
BUILDER: A.D. Story
LAUNCH DATE: 9 December
HOME PORT: Gloucester
REMARKS: Semi-knockabout. Built for the Fred L. Davis Co. Portrayed *We're Here* in East Coast shooting of *Captains Courageous*.

1912

NAME: [k]*Donald G. Hollett*
BUILDER: Joseph McGill
LAUNCH DATE: 1 February
HOME PORT: Burin, Newfoundland
REMARKS: Semi-knockabout. Plan No. 189. Built for Thomas Vigus Hollett. Amos Pentz, Master Carpenter.

NAME: [f]*Mary F. Sears*
BUILDER: John Bishop
LAUNCH DATE: March
HOME PORT: Gloucester
REMARKS: Knockabout. Built for Captain J. Sears and/or Manuel F. Viator.

NAME: [i,h]*Leonora Silveira*
BUILDER: A.D. Story
LAUNCH DATE: 5 April
HOME PORT: Boston
REMARKS: Round-bow semi-knockabout. Built for Leandro J. DeCosta, Jr., John Silveira *et. al.* Similar to *Progress*, *Russell*, and *Ralph Brown*. Stranded on Peaked Hill Bars, off Provincetown in 1921. Salvaged and sailed as the *Pilgrim* of Gloucester. Stranded on Cape Breton in 1934. Abandoned by her owners, but salvaged by Canadians and put into service as the *Shirley C.* of Twillingate, Newfoundland. Sailed in the 1951 film *The World in His Arms*. Sank 21 October 1951, near St. Pierre, enroute to Newfoundland with a load of coal.[h]

NAME: [f]*Henry P. Williams*
BUILDER: Richard T. Green
LAUNCH DATE: 13 April
HOME PORT: Charleston, S.C.
REMARKS: Knockabout pilot boat. Built for the Charleston Bar Pilots Association. Sold to Warren Fish Co. of Pensacola in 1917. Plans at Smithsonian Institution.

NAME: [i]*A. Piatt Andrew*
BUILDER: Tarr & James
LAUNCH DATE: 22 April 22[n]
HOME PORT: Gloucester
REMARKS: Semi-knockabout off *Valerie* and *Laverna*.[51] Built for the John Chisholm Co. Sail plan at Peabody & Essex Museum.

NAME: [k]*A. Hubley*
BUILDER: Joseph McGill
LAUNCH DATE: 18 September
HOME PORT: Halifax, N.S.
REMARKS: Semi-knockabout. Plan No. 205A. Built for Captain Hubley of St. Margaret's Bay, N.S. for the North Atlantic Fisheries. Amos Pentz, Master Carpenter.

NAME: [h]*Knickerbocker*
BUILDER: A.D. Story
LAUNCH DATE: 14 October
HOME PORT: Portland, Maine
REMARKS: Knockabout. Built for the New England Fish Co. Twin 100-bhp Blanchard diesel engine, twin-screw, auxiliary. Built from the molds of the *Bay State* by Owen Lantz. Cost $30,000. Rounded Cape Horn to Seattle in 148 days during 1913. Disappeared from the registry in 1919.[h]

NAME: [a]*Gertrude DeCosta*
BUILDER: James & Tarr
LAUNCH DATE: 15 October
HOME PORT: Boston
REMARKS: Knockabout. Built for Leandro J. DeCosta, Jr.[52] 100-bhp gas-engined, auxiliary knockabout. Off a McManus design, plans at Smithsonian Institution. Cost between $25,000 and $30,000.[h] Used by Howard I. Chapelle as an example of stolen design.[c] Had a 100-bhp diesel engine installed in 1925. Disappeared from registry 1949.[h]

NAME: [h]*Bay State*
BUILDER: Owen Lantz[53]

LAUNCH DATE: 24 October
HOME PORT: Portland, Maine
REMARKS: Knockabout. Built for the New England Fish Co. for Captain John Ross. Twin 100-bhp Blanchard diesel engines, twin-screw, auxiliary. Built at Gloucester, sister to *Knickerbocker*. Built pole-masted, later had topmasts added. Cost $30,000.[h] Stranded at Liverpool, N.S., during December 1927.[h]

NAME: [a]*Ruth*
BUILDER: A.D. Story
LAUNCH DATE: 29 October
HOME PORT: Boston
REMARKS: Semi-knockabout. Built for John F. Leonard. Powered by a 236-bhp gas engine in 1918. She was sunk by the tug *Piedmont* in July 1919, but raised and returned to service. Sold to Pensacola in 1923 and had her gas engine replaced by a 72-bhp diesel unit. She was stranded on Alacran Reef, off Mexico, on 1 January 1925.[h]

NAME: [f]*Delphine Cabral*
BUILDER: A.D. Story
LAUNCH DATE: 5 December
HOME PORT: Provincetown
REMARKS: Semi-knockabout. Built on speculation. Purchased by Joseph Cabral.

NAME: [o]*Carrie M. Wamback*
BUILDER: D.C. Mulhill
LAUNCH DATE: January 1914
HOME PORT: Liverpool, N.S.
REMARKS: Indian Head tern schooner. 109 tons net. Abandoned at sea, 1914.

NAME: [o]*Ida M. Zinck*
BUILDER: D.C. Mulhill
HOME PORT: Liverpool, N.S.
REMARKS: Indian Head tern schooner. 113 tons net. Used for salt fishing.

1913

NAME: [j]*Little Ruth*
BUILDER: D.M. Waddell
HOME PORT: Rockport

REMARKS: 55-foot auxiliary knockabout shore fisherman. Plan No. 217, published in *Yachting* (May 1913). Drawn 3 October 1912.

NAME: [a]*Progress*
BUILDER: A.D. Story
LAUNCH DATE: 20 March[n]
HOME PORT: Provincetown
REMARKS: Round-bow semi-knockabout. Similar to *Leonora Silveira*, *Ralph Brown*, and *Russell*. Built for Joseph A. Manta. Won the 1929 Fuller, Davis & Prentiss Cup under Captain Manuel Domingoes. Burned off Highland Light, 31 May 1930. Sail plan at Peabody & Essex Museum.

NAME: [i]*Russell*
BUILDER: A.D. Story
LAUNCH DATE: 24 July
HOME PORT: Gloucester
REMARKS: Round-bow semi-knockabout. Built for Manuel J. Silveira. Similar to *Leonora Silveira*, *Progress*, and *Ralph Brown*. Sail plan at Peabody & Essex Museum.

NAME: [f]*Angeline C. Nunan*
BUILDER: A.D. Story
LAUNCH DATE: 16 September
HOME PORT: Portland, Maine
REMARKS: Round-bow. Originally built on speculation. Gasoline auxiliary.[h]

NAME: [h]*Commonwealth*
BUILDER: J.F. James & Son
LAUNCH DATE: 1 October[n]
HOME PORT: Boston
REMARKS: Auxiliary knockabout. Built for George F. Grueby, *et.al*. First schooner built by J.F. James & Son (Everett). Modeled off *Frances S. Grueby* with whom she collided and sank in Boston Harbor during 1921. Burned on Brown's Bank 8 April 1927.[h] Sail plan at Peabody & Essex Museum.

1914
NAME: [f]*Natalie Hammond*
BUILDER: L.B. MacKenzie
LAUNCH DATE: 16 December

HOME PORT: Gloucester
REMARKS: Knockabout. Built for Lemuel E. Spinney at Essex for Captain Frank Rose. Had 60-bhp motor by 1929.

NAME: [i]*Ralph Brown*
BUILDER: A.D. Story
LAUNCH DATE: 8 January
HOME PORT: Gloucester
REMARKS: Round-bow semi-knockabout. Built for Captain Antone Brown. Similar to *Leonora Silveira*, *Progress*, and *Russell*.

NAME: [a]*Ruth and Margaret*
BUILDER: A.D. Story
LAUNCH DATE: 6 June
HOME PORT: Boston
REMARKS: Semi-knockabout. Built on speculation. Purchased by Captain Valentine O'Neil and/or Julia Whalen. Had a diesel auxiliary added in 1926. Refitted as an otter trawler in 1928. Foundered in Buzzard's Bay in 1948 after 33 years of service.[h]

NAME: [f]*Reading*
BUILDER: A.D. Story
LAUNCH DATE: 21 September[n]
HOME PORT: Boston
REMARKS: Semi-knockabout. Built for John Hickey.

NAME: [f]*Robert and Richard*
BUILDER: J.F. James & Son
LAUNCH DATE: 29 October
HOME PORT: Gloucester
REMARKS: Knockabout. Built for John Chisolm & Son for Captain R. Wharton. Torpedoed by a German U-Boat off Boothbay, Maine, on 22 July 1918.[h]

NAME: [f]*Somerville*
BUILDER: A.D. Story
LAUNCH DATE: 16 November
HOME PORT: Boston
REMARKS: Semi-knockabout. Built for Captain Felix J. Hogan.

1915

NAME: [f]*Henrietta*
BUILDER: A.D. Story
LAUNCH DATE: 19 January
HOME PORT: Boston
REMARKS: Round-bow off *Angeline C. Nunan*. Built for E.M. Cromwell. Had a gas engine installed in 1923. Disappeared from the registry in 1937.[h]

NAME: [f]*J.M. Marshall*[l]
BUILDER: J.F. James & Son
LAUNCH DATE: 14 May
HOME PORT: Gloucester
REMARKS: Knockabout. Built for J. Manuel Marshall. Lost off Cape Hatteras in 1944.

NAME: [f]*Republic*
BUILDER: A.D. Story
LAUNCH DATE: 28 June
HOME PORT: Gloucester
REMARKS: Round-bow auxiliary. Built for the Gorton-Pew Vessels Co. The British four-master *Wellington* ran her down while she was under the command of Captain Peter Dunsky (of *Teazer* fame) during February 1925. Vessel, captain, and a crewman lost.

NAME: [f]*Elsie G. Silva*
BUILDER: Owen Lantz
LAUNCH DATE: 28 June
HOME PORT: Gloucester
REMARKS: Knockabout. Built for Manuel C. Silva at Gloucester off *Adeline*. Lost 14 February 1927 on Cape Cod.

NAME: [h]*Catherine*
BUILDER: A.D. Story
LAUNCH DATE: 8 October
HOME PORT: Gloucester
REMARKS: Knockabout built off the lines of *Bay State*, greatly modified by Story. Captain Archibald A. MacLeod. Engine installed 1920. Reputed to be the largest and fastest knockabout. Burned 31 December 1933 off Bald Rock Shoal, N.S.

NAME: [f]*Pollyanna*
BUILDER: A.D. Story

1915 continued
LAUNCH DATE: 22 November
HOME PORT: Gloucester
REMARKS: Knockabout. Built for the Gorton-Pew Vessels Co.

1916
NAME: [?]*Bettina*
BUILDER: Owen Lantz
HOME PORT: Gloucester
REMARKS: Auxiliary. Built for the John Chisolm Co.

NAME: [h,f]*Finback*
BUILDER: A.D. Story
LAUNCH DATE: 4 May
HOME PORT: Boston
REMARKS: Auxiliary knockabout ketch. Built for C.H.W. Foster.[j] First built as a yacht from the lines of the *Catherine* (which was off the lines of the *Bay State* & *Knickerbocker*). She was the largest yacht built by A.D. Story. Made a freighter in 1918, and re-rigged as a schooner to go whaling in 1919. Lost 23 August 1919 on the last American whaling voyage to Hudson Bay.[h]

NAME: [f]*Henry L. Marshall*
BUILDER: J.F. James & Son
LAUNCH DATE: 15 June
HOME PORT: Gloucester
REMARKS: Auxiliary knockabout. Built for J. Manuel Marshall. Later became Bill McCoy's first rum-runner.

NAME: [f]*Nathaniel L. Gorton*
BUILDER: A.D. Story
LAUNCH DATE: 12 July[n]
HOME PORT: Gloucester
REMARKS: Auxiliary tern schooner. Built for the Gorton-Pew Vessels Co. Lines at Essex Shipbuilding Museum.

NAME: [a]*Joseph P. Mesquita*
BUILDER: J.F. James & Son
LAUNCH DATE: 28 August
HOME PORT: Gloucester
REMARKS: Auxiliary semi-knockabout. Built for Captain J. Mesquita and R. Russell Smith off *Flora L. Oliver*.[54]

NAME: [f]*Olivette*
BUILDER: A.D. Story
LAUNCH DATE: 30 September[n]
HOME PORT: Gloucester
REMARKS: Auxiliary tern schooner. Built for the Gorton-Pew Vessels Co.

NAME: [c]*Elizabeth Howard*
BUILDER: Frank C. Adams
HOME PORT: New York
REMARKS: Knockabout. *Clintonia* plan with a knockabout bow added, lines at Smithsonian Institution.[c] Later auxiliary-powered and had a short bowsprit added. Wrecked on Porter's Island, N.S., November 1923.

1917
NAME: [f]*Acushla*
BUILDER: A.D. Story
LAUNCH DATE: 26 March[n]
HOME PORT: Gloucester
REMARKS: Auxiliary. Built for the Gorton-Pew Vessels Co.

NAME: [f]*Yukon*
BUILDER: Owen Lantz
LAUNCH DATE: 2 April[m]
HOME PORT: New York
REMARKS: Auxiliary knockabout. Built for the American Trading Co. Cape Verde packet 1920.

NAME: [j]*Ajax*
BUILDER: Frank C. Adams
HOME PORT: Boston
REMARKS: Ketch-rigged auxiliary. Plan No. 375, 2 drawings, lines and inboard layout, including a laboratory, donated to Mystic Seaport Museum by Louise Will. Marked "A. Fabbri's Boat." Fairbanks-Morse 2-cycle, 3-cylinder diesel engine. Built by W.I. Adams & Son for Alessandro Fabbri and donated to the U.S. government during World War I. Became the U.S. Naval Coastal Patrol vessel SP-738, and freight boat *Ajax* after the war.[55]

NAME: [f]*Florence*
BUILDER: Owen Lantz
LAUNCH DATE: 25 June[m]
HOME PORT: Boston
REMARKS: Auxiliary semi-knockabout.

NAME: [f]*Hesperus*
BUILDER: A.D. Story
LAUNCH DATE: 24 September[n]
HOME PORT: Gloucester
REMARKS: Auxiliary semi-knockabout. Built for Fred L. Davis. Sail plan at Peabody & Essex Museum.

NAME: [f]*Angie L. Marshall*
BUILDER: J.F. James & Son
LAUNCH DATE: 27 September[n]
HOME PORT: Gloucester
REMARKS: Auxiliary, twin-screw semi-knockabout. Built for J. Manuel Marshall.

NAME: [f]*Marne*
BUILDER: Owen Lantz
LAUNCH DATE: 17 October[m]
HOME PORT: New York
REMARKS: Auxiliary knockabout tern schooner.

NAME: [?]*Rush*
BUILDER: Owen Lantz
LAUNCH DATE: 29 November[m]
HOME PORT: Boston
REMARKS: Knockabout. Sunk by a U-Boat on 26 August 1918.

NAME: [?]*Gleaner*
BUILDER: Waddell Brothers?
HOME PORT: Rockport
REMARKS: Semi-knockabout. Pole-masted with a short bowsprit.

1918
NAME: [f]*Antoine C. Santos*

BUILDER: Owen Lantz
LAUNCH DATE: 3 April[m]
HOME PORT: Provincetown
REMARKS: Auxiliary semi-knockabout. Sail plan at Peabody & Essex Museum.

NAME: [f]*Joffre*
BUILDER: A.D. Story
LAUNCH DATE: 16 April[n]
HOME PORT: Gloucester
REMARKS: Auxiliary semi-knockabout. Built for the Fred L. Davis Co. Lost 10 August 1947. Sail plan at Peabody & Essex Museum.

NAME: [f]*Helja Silva*
BUILDER: J.F. James & Son
LAUNCH DATE: 1 May[n]
HOME PORT: Gloucester
REMARKS: Auxiliary. Built for Benjamin Smith and the Gorton-Pew Vessels Co.

NAME: [f]*Louise B. Marshall*
BUILDER: J.F. James & Son
LAUNCH DATE: 14 August[n]
HOME PORT: Gloucester
REMARKS: Auxiliary, twin-screw knockabout off the molds of the *J.M. Marshall*. Built for J. Manuel Marshall.[56]

NAME: [f]*Ellen T. Marshall*
BUILDER: J.F. James & Son
LAUNCH DATE: 23 November[n]
HOME PORT: Gloucester
REMARKS: Auxiliary, twin-screw knockabout off the molds of the *Louise B. Marshall*. Built for J. Manuel Marshall.[57]

NAME: [e]*Surprise*
BUILDER: D.M. Waddell
HOME PORT: New York
REMARKS: Schooner yacht. Built for Martin S. "Marty" Kattenhorn. Still afloat and in commission at Camden, Maine. Complete plans in possession of Louise Will, published in *Yachting* (February 1917).

NAME: [o]*Max Horton*
BUILDER: Conquerall Bank, N.S.

REMARKS: Indian Head tern schooner. Built for William Forsey of Newfoundland and used in the salt fish trade. Abandoned at sea, 20 March 1926.

1919
NAME: [f]*Maréchal Foch*
BUILDER: J.F. James & Son
LAUNCH DATE: 27 January[n]
HOME PORT: Gloucester
REMARKS: Auxiliary knockabout. Built for the Gorton-Pew Vessels Co.

NAME: [f]*Grand Marshall*
BUILDER: J.F. James & Son
LAUNCH DATE: 10 May[n]
HOME PORT: Gloucester
REMARKS: Auxiliary knockabout off the molds of *Ellen T. Marshall*. Built for J. Manuel Marshall.[58]

NAME: [f]*Herbert Parker*
BUILDER: A.D. Story
LAUNCH DATE: 17 May[n]
HOME PORT: Gloucester
REMARKS: Auxiliary pole-masted semi-knockabout. Built for the Gorton-Pew Vessels Co.

NAME: [f]*Dawn*
BUILDER: J.F. James & Son
LAUNCH DATE: 27 August[n]
HOME PORT: Boston
REMARKS: Auxiliary knockabout. Built for George F. Grueby and John M. Atwood.[59]

NAME: Plan No. 395
REMARKS: Marked "Sail Plan for Off Shore Cruiser," for Southern Salvage Co., Liverpool, N.S. Drawn 17 March. Possibly the *Doris and Rita*. Donated to Mystic Seaport Museum by Louise Will.

NAME: Plan No. 399
REMARKS: Marked for LeHave Fishing Co., LeHave, N.S. Drawn 26 June. May have been the *Kathleen Conrad*. Donated to Mystic Seaport Museum by Louise Will.

NAME: Plan No. 403
REMARKS: Marked for McCoy Bros., Daytona, Fl. Drawn 29 July. Donated to Mystic Seaport Museum by Louise Will. "A schooner for Captain W.F. McCoy of Daytona, Fla., owner of the *Arethusa* that was charged with being a floating saloon and stands as the original briny bootlegger. This vessel is to be built in the Bahamas of 'horseflesh, a wood that never decays,' as Capt. McCoy puts it."[60]

NAME: Plan No. 404
REMARKS: Marked for Chester Basin Fish Company, Chester Basin, N.S. Drawn 31 July. Possibly the *Lois A. Conrad*. Donated to Mystic Seaport Museum by Louise Will.

NAME: Plan No. 405
REMARKS: 2 plans, lines and sail, dated 20 August 1919. Marked for Shelburne Shipbuilding Co., Shelburne, N.S., and Hollett Brothers. Donated to Mystic Seaport Museum by Louise Will.

1920
NAME: Plan No. 410
REMARKS: Marked for Smith and Rhuland, Lunenburg, N.S. Drawn 13 April. Donated to Mystic Seaport Museum by Louise Will.

NAME: *Florence E.*
BUILDER: J.F. James & Son
LAUNCH DATE: 25 March
HOME PORT: Newfoundland
REMARKS: Auxiliary, twin-screw semi-knockabout with topmasts. Built for G. & A. Buffett from the molds of *J.M. Marshall* and *Dawn*.[61]

NAME: [f]*Governor Marshall*
BUILDER: J.F. James & Son
LAUNCH DATE: 14 August[n]
HOME PORT: Gloucester
REMARKS: Knockabout. Built for J. Manuel Marshall. Last vessel built for the Marshall fleet.

1920 continued
NAME: [f]*Edith C. Rose*
BUILDER: A.D. Story
LAUNCH DATE: 4 September[n]
HOME PORT: Gloucester
REMARKS: Knockabout. Built for Frank Rose.

NAME: [f]*Laura Goulart*
BUILDER: J.F. James & Son
LAUNCH DATE: 8 November[n]
HOME PORT: Gloucester
REMARKS: Knockabout. Built for John Goulart.

NAME: [f]*Oretha F. Spinney*
BUILDER: J.F. James & Son
LAUNCH DATE: 16 December[n]
HOME PORT: Gloucester
REMARKS: Auxiliary, single-screw knockabout off the molds of the *Governor Marshall* and *Maréchal Foch*. Built for Lemuel E. Spinney.[62] Sold to MGM January 1936. Played *We're Here* in Pacific shooting of *Captains Courageous*. Later sold to Paramount Pictures. Lines at Essex Shipbuilding Museum.

NAME: [o]*Corte Nord*
BUILDER: Mahone Bay, N.S.
REMARKS: Indian Head tern schooner with pole masts and oil engines intended for cargo service on the St. Lawrence River and the north shore of the Gulf of St. Lawrence. 147 tons net. When she proved to be unsuitable she was sold to Lunenberg owners, then sold French and renamed *Amphitre*. Then sold to Newfoundland owners and renamed *Corte Nord*. Wrecked at South Petty Harbour, Newfoundland, 23 June 1932. Plans at Smithsonian Institution.

NAME: [o]*Nellie T. Walters*
BUILDER: Shelburne, N.S.
HOME PORT: North Sydney, N.S.
REMARKS: Indian Head tern schooner. Built for R.T. Sainthill & Company and used in the transatlantic salt-fish trade. A speedy vessel, she averaged 22-day passages and once made a 13-day run from Marystown, Newfoundland, to Oporto, Portugal, in 1926. 139 tons net. Wrecked on St. Mary's Shoal, 1939. Plans at Smithsonian Institution.

1921
NAME: [a]*L.A. Dunton*
BUILDER: A.D. Story
LAUNCH DATE: 23 March[n]
HOME PORT: Boston
REMARKS: Round-bow semi-knockabout off the *Joffre*. Built for Captain Felix Hogan, who had been master of the *Somerville* and the *Elk*. Participated in the 1922 International Cup elimination trials. Afloat at Mystic Seaport Museum. Plans at Mystic Seaport Museum.

NAME: [a]*American*
BUILDER: A.D. Story
LAUNCH DATE: 26 May[m]
HOME PORT: Gloucester
REMARKS: Auxiliary semi-knockabout. Built for the Fred L. Davis Co. Renamed *Roy M.* Converted to restaurant at Cape May, N.J. Sunk there as a fishing reef in 1985.

NAME: Plan No. 415
REMARKS: Wooden dragger with a 10-hp engine, aft pilothouse, and steadying sails. Donated to Mystic Seaport Museum by Louise Will.

NAME: Plan No. 416
REMARKS: Knockabout pole-masted schooner-dragger, drawn 18 May. Donated to Mystic Seaport Museum by Louise Will.

NAME: [e]*Blanche Ring*
BUILDER: Waddell Brothers
HOME PORT: Boston
REMARKS: Auxiliary knockabout schooner-dragger. Built for Herbert W. Nickerson.[63] Plan No. 417. Lines plan drawn 24 May. Owned by Louise Will. Considered first "eastern-rig" dragger. Suffered a major fire off Nantucket about 1930 enroute to New Bedford. Towed into Nantucket for repairs with her entire after half burned out.[f]

NAME: Plan No. 421
REMARKS: Deck plan. Drawn 30 December. Donated to Mystic Seaport Museum by Louise Will.

1922
NAME: Plan No. 422
REMARKS: Small round-bow, pole-masted, auxiliary semi-knockabout. Lines drawn 6 January (offsets). Sail and deck plans drawn 24 January. Donated to Mystic Seaport Museum by Louise Will.

NAME: [f]*Mary E. O'Hara*
BUILDER: A.D. Story
LAUNCH DATE: 11 March[n]
HOME PORT: Boston
REMARKS: Auxiliary round-bow semi-knockabout. Built for O'Hara Bros. Co. Plans in H. I. Chapelle, *American Sailing Craft*.

NAME: [e]*Henry Ford*
BUILDER: A.D. Story
LAUNCH DATE: 11 April
HOME PORT: Gloucester
REMARKS: Semi-knockabout. Plan No. 419, drawn November 1921, donated to Mystic Seaport Museum by Louise Will.[73] Built for Clayton L. Morrissey. Won the 1922 International Cup elimination trials but lost to *Bluenose* in 1922. Won the 1923 Fishermen's Race on Gloucester's 300th Anniversary. Lost 16 June 1928 on Whaleback Reef, Newfoundland.

NAME: [?j]*Lark*
BUILDER: Richard Diebold
HOME PORT: Boston
REMARKS: Auxiliary semi-knockabout with a Bolander 175-bhp diesel engine. Built for the O'Hara Brothers Co. Captain Ernest Parsons. Known as the "Channel Express" for her fast passages between Boston and the Great South Channel fishing grounds east of Nantucket.

NAME: [f]*Ruth Mildred*
BUILDER: J.F. James & Son

LAUNCH DATE: 15 May[n]
HOME PORT: New York
REMARKS: Built for John R. Ericsson. Later owned by Nils Soderberg of New York.[64]

NAME: [f]*A. Piatt Andrew*
BUILDER: A.D. Story
LAUNCH DATE: 15 May[m]
HOME PORT: Boston
REMARKS: Schooner-dragger. Built for John Hickey. Powered by a 45-bhp crude-oil engine.

NAME: Plan No. 420
REMARKS: Schooner yacht. Designed for H.H. White. "A 99-ft. overall marconi-rigged schooner for H.H. White of Cambridge, who took the ketch *Ajax*, also designed by McManus, from Boston to the South Seas a few years ago. Mr. White is an experienced yachtsman who cruised many seasons in the auxiliary schooner *Cachalot* with headquarters at Marblehead."[65] This is probably plan No. 420, drawn 5 April 1922 and 7 August 1924, donated to Mystic Seaport Museum by Louise Will.

NAME: [?]*Lincoln*
BUILDER: Waddell Brothers
REMARKS: Pole-masted auxiliary knockabout with a 95-bhp Wolverine diesel engine.

1923
NAME: [f]*Marjorie Parker*
BUILDER: A.D. Story
LAUNCH DATE: 8 April[n]
HOME PORT: Boston
REMARKS: Auxiliary. Built for Arthur L. Parker.

NAME: [?]*Benjamin Thompson*
BUILDER: A.D. Story
LAUNCH DATE: 11 June[n]
HOME PORT: Portland, Maine
REMARKS: Auxiliary schooner-dragger. Built for William Thomas, the man who commissioned the *Helen B. Thomas*.

1924
NAME: [f]*B.T. Hillman*
BUILDER: A.D. Story
LAUNCH DATE: 3 January[n]
HOME PORT: Vineyard Haven
REMARKS: Auxiliary schooner-dragger. Built for Horace O. Hillman.

NAME: [?f]*America*
BUILDER: A.D. Story
LAUNCH DATE: 19 June[n]
HOME PORT: Gloucester
REMARKS: Indian Header schooner-dragger. Built for Ray Adams.

NAME: [j]*Bertha Frances*
BUILDER: D.M. Waddell
HOME PORT: New York
REMARKS: Auxiliary knockabout schooner yacht. Plan No. 431. Built for Hobart Ford. Wisconsin 4-cycle, 4-cylinder diesel engine. Later *Jolly Roger*, *Shagwong*, and *Tongaloa*.

NAME: [?f]*A. Roger Hickey*
BUILDER: A.D. Story
LAUNCH DATE: 8 November[m]
REMARKS: Schooner-dragger.

NAME: [f]*Emerald*
BUILDER: A.D. Story
LAUNCH DATE: 2 August[n]
HOME PORT: Boston
REMARKS: Knockabout. Built for O'Hara Bros. Co.

NAME: [?f]*Annie and Mary*
BUILDER: A.D. Story
LAUNCH DATE: 12 October[n]
HOME PORT: Boston
REMARKS: Schooner-dragger. Built for Girolamo Palazzolo.

NAME: [?f]*Alice and Mildred*
BUILDER: J.F. James & Son
LAUNCH DATE: 8 November[n]
HOME PORT: Gloucester
REMARKS: Knockabout schooner-dragger. Built for Cameron & Morash.

NAME: [?f]*Anna and Julia*
BUILDER: A.D. Story
LAUNCH DATE: 12 December[n]
REMARKS: Schooner-dragger.

NAME: Plan No. 440
REMARKS: Sail plan. Drawn 22 August. Donated to Mystic Seaport Museum by Louise Will.

1925
NAME: Plan No. 442
REMARKS: Type unknown. Offsets table drawn 16 March. Donated to Mystic Seaport Museum by Louise Will.

NAME: [f]*Mary Sears*
BUILDER: J.F. James & Son
LAUNCH DATE: 19 December[n]
HOME PORT: Gloucester
REMARKS: Auxiliary, single-screw knockabout off *Oretha F. Spinney*. Built for Captain Jose S. Sears.[66]

NAME: [f]*Gossoon*
BUILDER: A.D. Story
LAUNCH DATE: 21 December[n]
HOME PORT: Boston
REMARKS: Knockabout. Built for the O'Hara Brothers Co.

1926
NAME: [e]*Alabamian*
BUILDER: Pensacola Shipbuilding Company
LAUNCH DATE: 20 June
HOME PORT: Mobile, Alabama
REMARKS: Knockabout pilot schooner. Built for the Mobile Bar Pilots Association. Recorded by H.A.E.R. Renamed *Alabama* in 1927 after predecessor was sold. Afloat at Vineyard Haven.

NAME: [hf]*Adventure*
BUILDER: Everett James
LAUNCH DATE: 16 September
HOME PORT: Gloucester
REMARKS: Auxiliary, single-screw knockabout. 120-bhp Fairbanks-Morse "C.O."

1926 continued

diesel engine. Built for Captain Jeffrey F. Thomas off *Oretha F. Spinney*,[67] backed by Philip P. Manta, *et.al.* Afloat at Gloucester.

NAME: [f]*Doris M. Hawes*
BUILDER: A.D. Story
LAUNCH DATE: 16 November[n]
HOME PORT: Gloucester
REMARKS: Knockabout schooner-dragger. Built for Captain Aubrey Hawes. Possibly a Jacob Story design.

1927

NAME: [?f]*Carrie S. Roderick*
BUILDER: Everett James
LAUNCH DATE: 9 March[n]
HOME PORT: Gloucester
REMARKS: Schooner-dragger. Built for United Fisheries Co.

NAME: Unknown
REMARKS: Auxiliary schooner yacht. Plans dated 15 March 1927, donated to Mystic Seaport Museum by Louise Will.

NAME: [f]*Eleanor Nickerson*
BUILDER: Everett James
LAUNCH DATE: 19 July[n]
HOME PORT: Boston
REMARKS: Auxiliary knockabout off *Mary Sears*. Built for Arthur L. Parker.[68]

NAME: [?f]*Mildred Silva*
BUILDER: Everett James
LAUNCH DATE: 12 December[n]
HOME PORT: Boston
REMARKS: Schooner-dragger. Built for Manuel Silva.

NAME: *Vasco da Gama*
BUILDER: A.D. Story
LAUNCH DATE: 31 December
HOME PORT: Gloucester
REMARKS: Schooner-dragger. Believed built for United Fisheries Co. off *Carrie S. Roderick*.[69]

NAME: Unknown
REMARKS: Full-rigged semi-knockabout fishing schooner. Sail plan dated 18 April 1927, donated to Mystic Seaport Museum by Louise Will.

1928

NAME: *William H. Killigrew*
BUILDER: Everett James
LAUNCH DATE: 12 April
HOME PORT: New Bedford
REMARKS: Schooner-dragger. Built for Captain John Williams.[70]

NAME: *Leonora C.*
BUILDER: Everett James
LAUNCH DATE: 14 July
HOME PORT: Gloucester
REMARKS: Schooner-dragger. Built for United Fisheries Co. off *Carrie S. Roderick* and *Vasco da Gama*.[71]

1929

NAME: *Leretha*
BUILDER: Everett James
LAUNCH DATE: 7 March
HOME PORT: Gloucester
REMARKS: Schooner-dragger. Built for Cameron and Morash off the molds of *Alice and Mildred*.[72]

NAME: [?f]*Old Glory*
BUILDER: A.D. Story
LAUNCH DATE: 7 March[n]
HOME PORT: Gloucester
REMARKS: Schooner-dragger. Built for Central Wharf & Vessels Co.

NAME: [?f]*Cape Ann*
BUILDER: A.D. Story
LAUNCH DATE: 16 March[n]
HOME PORT: Gloucester
REMARKS: Schooner-dragger. Built for Central Wharf & Vessels Co.

NAME: [?f]*Edith and Elinor*
BUILDER: Everett James
LAUNCH DATE: 24 August[n]

HOME PORT: Gloucester
REMARKS: Schooner-dragger. Built for Edith L. Theriault.

NAME: [f]*Gertrude Parker*
BUILDER: Everett James
LAUNCH DATE: 8 October[n]
HOME PORT:
REMARKS: Knockabout.

NAME: [?f]*Babe Sears*
BUILDER: A.D. Story
LAUNCH DATE: 18 December[m]
HOME PORT: Gloucester
REMARKS: Schooner-dragger. Built for Jose Sears.

1930

1931

NAME: [?f]*Jorgina Silveira*
BUILDER: A.D. Story
LAUNCH DATE: 12 May[m]
HOME PORT: Gloucester
REMARKS: Schooner-dragger. Built for Manuel J. Silveira.

1936

NAME: *Sirod*
BUILDER: Waddell Bros.
REMARKS: 32-foot schooner yacht. McManus, Walter McInnis, and George Stadel, Jr., were all involved in this design during 1937. Built for S.P. Palmer. *Sirod* is Palmer's wife's first name spelled backwards.

LEGEND

^a Identified as a McManus design by T.F. McManus, Jr., in a personal copy of Dana Story's book, *Frame-Up*, now in the possession of McManus's granddaughter Louise Will.

^b Albert Cook Church, text by James B. Connolly, *The American Fishermen*.

^c Howard I. Chapelle, *American Fishing Schooners*.

^d Identified by Thomas F. McManus, Sr., in his writings.

^e Identified from surviving plans, models, offset tables, or owner records.

^f Charles F. Sayle of Nantucket. Question marks on these entries are Mr. Sayle's.

^g Attributed to McManus by the Historic American Merchant Marine Survey.

^h Andrew W. German, *Down on T Wharf*.

ⁱ Gordon W. Thomas, *Fast & Able*.

^j Identified as a McManus design by Andrew German in correspondence with the author.

^k Identified as a possible McManus design by Harold G. Simms, grandson of Amos Pentz, Master Carpenter at the McGill Shipyard in Shelburne, N.S.

^l "Fishing Vessels Built at Essex That Were in Races," compiled by the Essex Shipbuilding Museum from the notes of Lewis H. Story.

^m Dana A. Story, *An Approximate Listing of the Vessels, Boats and Other Craft Built in the Town of Essex, 1870 through 1977. Based upon the Research and Listings of Lewis H. Story, Essex*.

ⁿ Launch date found in Dana Story, *Frame-Up* (Barre, Massachusetts: Barre Publishers, 1964).

^o John P. Parker, *Sails of the Maritimes* (Halifax: Maritime Museum of Canada, 1960).

[?] Possibly a McManus design.

NOTES

1 "Apr. 29, 1896. Commenced vessel for John Adams of Provincetown" (James Yard Book in the possession of Dana A. Story, hereafter "James Yard Book"). James & Tarr built the *Phillip P. Manta* of 1902 off the lines of the *William A. Morse*.

2 Noted by McManus on *Regina*'s working draft.

3 "March 21, 1902.– Agreed with T.A. Cromwell & Co. of Boston to build a Schooner for them from a new model by Thomas F. McManus of Boston. Keel hauled into yard. Apr. 7, 1902. Launched 4-15 P.M. June 12, 1902" (James Yard Book).

4 "May 9, 1902. Agreed with J. Manta Co. to build them a Schooner on similar lines of Sch. *Wm. A. Morse* with alterations to make her smaller. Keel hauled into yard May 10, 1902. Launched 11.15 A.M. July 22, 1902" (James Yard Book).

5 Gloucester *Daily Times*, 17 February 1904.

6 "Water closet Extra" (James Yard Book).

7 At least three other McManus schooners came from this design, the *Olivia Domingoes* of 1903, the *Teazer* of 1906 (although she appears to have been a true hybrid–with a *Latham* type forebody grafted onto a *Nellie Dixon* afterbody), and the *Mary E. O'Hara* of 1922 (James Yard Book; Howard I. Chapelle, *American Sailing Craft* (New York: Kennedy Brothers, 1936), 103).

8 Temporary Enrolment No. 16, New London, Connecticut, 7 April 1915.

9 Per Tom Hoyne.

10 In August 1902 McManus received orders for two Indian Headers from a pair of New York City fishermen. They may have been two of the following 1903-built vessels: *Edith J. Peterson* built for Harry Peterson; *Griswold I. Keeney* for Peter O. Ericsson; or *Ruth E. Pember* for F.M. Redmond. *Peterson* and *Keeney* were built at Essex, while *Pember* was built at Tottenville, N.Y.

11 "Nov. 14, 1902. Agreed with L.J. Costa, L.B. Goodspeed & Co. & Manuel Domingoes to build a Schooner of the *Benj. W. Latham* Model. 5300– Keel hauled into yard. Nov. 15, 1902. Launched 8-40 A.M. Feb. 10, 1903" (James Yard Book).

12 "Dec. 29, 1902. Agreed with Capt. Wm. Thomas & John Chisolm to build them a Schooner for them from a new model by Thomas McManus. . . . Keel hauled into the yard. Feb. 10, 1903. Launched @ 10-30 A.M. May 26, 1903" (James Yard Book).

13 "Jan. 8, 1903. Agreed with Mariano A. Perry to build a Schooner of the *Matchless* model everything 1st class, price to include as extras Water closet in galv. & what we shall have to pay to Mr. McManus for use of lines. $7000. Keel hauled into yard Apr. 1, 1903. Launched 10-45 A.M. July 9, 1903" (James Yard Book).

14 "May 26, 1903.– Agreed with John Pew & Son like the Sch. *E.E. Gray* with these alterations the head of the stem to be tipped forward 3" or 4" commencing at a little below the lower end of the Gammon. The Sternpost to be righted up by swinging at the transom making keel about 1' longer than the Sch. *E.E. Gray*. Price $7500. Keel hauled into yard June 4, 1903. Launched Sept. 11, 1903" (James Yard Book).

15 Gloucester *Daily Times*, 11 March 1904.

16 Gloucester *Daily Times*, 17 February 1904.

17 "Dec. 15, 1903. Agreed with Cunningham & Thompson to build them a Sch. from new lines from McManus. Sch. a little larger that the *Elmer E. Gray* with water closet. 7800. Keel hauled into yard. Dec. 29, 1903. Launched May 5, 1904. 3-15 P.M." (James Yard Book).

18 Boston *American*, 7 July 1904.

19 "Jan. 13, 1904. Agreed with B. Montgomery & Son to build them a Sch. from the lines of the *Elmer E. Gray* & *Mary F. Curtis*. 7600. No water closet if he has one to be extra. Keel hauled into yard. May 2, 1904. Launched 1-10 P-M July 16, 1904" (James Yard Book).

20 "June 23, 1904. Agreed this day to build for Messrs. Cunningham & Thompson of Gloucester from new lines of McManus design. Price without water closet. 7700. Keel hauled into yard. June 30, 1904. Launched 2-55 P.M. Sept. 15, 1904" (James Yard Book).

21 "July 19, 1904. Agreed with John A. Matheson of Provincetown, Mass. to build him a Schooner of 90 tons from *Kernwood* model altered. to be 1' wider amidships and to extend the width way aft. 6500. Keel hauled into yard. July 21, 1904. Launched. @ 4-50 P-M Oct 3, 1904" (James Yard Book).

22 The sail plan reproduced by Albert Cook Church, *The American Fishermen* (New York:

W.W. Norton, 1940), 190, and identified as the knockabout *Gladys and Nellie*, is actually the plan of the 1904 Indian Header *Louise C. Cabral* (*Dimention Books, E.L. Rowe & Son Sail Loft*, Cape Ann Historical Association).

23 "Aug. 18, 1904. Talked with Capt. Joseph S. Silva of Provincetown for Sch. of ~~Matchless~~ model / Changed his mind Aug. 29 in office Essex on model of the *Catherine Burke*. Agreed to build for 7600. W.C. extra 94.50. Keel hauled into yard. Sept. 10, 1904. Launched. 10-15 A.M. Nov. 23, 1904" (James Yard Book).

24 "Aug. 19, 1904. Talked with Capt. J. Manta, Provincetown about Sch. like the *Annie Perry*. only little wider and not so straight. Aug. 25.– Agreed to build above Sch. ~~with water closet & wash bowl.~~ had no water closet nor wash bowl. 7600. Keel hauled into yard Sept. 26, 1904. Launched 10. A.M. Dec. 7, 1904" (James Yard Book).

25 "Dec. 7, 1904. Agreed with Capt. Wm. A. Graber & a clerk for Kingsland & Comstock, 5 Fulton Fish Market, N.Y. to build them a Sch. a duplicate of Sch. *Louise C. Cabral*. 6500. Keel hauled into place Sat. Dec. 17, 1904. Launched Tuesday 11. A.M. Mch. 21, 1905" (James Yard Book). The *Louise C. Cabral* had been derived from the *Kernwood*, but with a one-foot increase in beam amidships and carried well aft.

26 "Bows of Fishing Vessels," an unpublished list compiled by Gordon W. Thomas in the possession of Dana A. Story, hereafter "Thomas, bows."

27 "Second vessel of the same name built for Boston shore fisherman [A.M. Watson, Jr.]. The first *Galatea* (also built by Bishop in 1902) was stranded at Portsmouth in 1905 (total loss).

28 The *Jessie Costa* had a lengthy lineage. James & Tarr built her from the molds of the *Mary C. Santos*, which they had built from the

lines of the *Annie Perry*, but with a slight increase in beam and sheer. The *Annie Perry* was a replica of the *Matchless* model, but with "everything 1st class." The *Matchless* had been built from the lines of the *Flora S. Nickerson*, which herself came from "a new model by Thomas F. McManus of Boston" (James Yard Book).

29 "Apr. 24. Agreed by letter from Capt. J. Manta to build Sch. molds of Sch. *[Mary C.] Santos*, with 2 frames extra, all ironwork galvanized. Keel hauled into place. Apr. 22, 05. Launched 8-15 P.M. July 13, 1905" (James Yard Book).

30 "[Date obscured]. Agreed with Capt. Marion Perry to build him a new Sch. from lines of Sch. *Annie Perry* to be made 10 ft. longer. 8000. Keel hauled into yard. June. 14, 1905. Launched. 9-15 A.M. Sept. 27, 1905" (James Yard Book).

31 "July 20. Sch. for D.B. Smith & Co. Gloucester, from molds of Sch. *Emilia Enos* [a *Nellie Dixon* derivative] with modern bow similar to Noank Sch. [the *Benjamin W. Latham*].– 6600– Keel hauled into yard. July. 25. 1905. Launched 12-15 P.M. Oct. 16. 1905" (James Yard Book).

32 *Alert* was destroyed in a hurricane at Port-au-fort, Newfoundland, after less than a year in service, probably before she could enter the registry.

33 Albert Cook Church, "The Evolution and Development of the American Fishing Schooner," Part II, *Yachting* 5 (June 1910): 499-503.

34 "Agreed to build a Sch. for Capt. John Chisolm of lines from the Sch. *Thomas S. Gorton* to be changed into an auxiliary price to include engine bed. 8600.– Keel hauled into yard Dec. 2, 1905. Launched at 1 P.M. Mch. 14, 1906" (James Yard Book).

35 New York *Times* obituary, 18 October 1913, p. 13, col. 4; 1916 *Merchant Vessels of the U.S.*

36 "Agreed to build a Sch. for Orlando Merchant from molds of Sch. *Thomas S. Gorton*. Water Closet Extra at cost.– Keel hauled into yard. Apr. 16, 1906. Launched 2-30 P.M. June 27, 1906" (James Yard Book).

37 Oxner & Story's *Shepherd King* was the first short-bow knockabout.

38 "Mch. 2, 1907. Agreed ~~with~~ to build a Sch. from molds of Sch. *Louisa R. Silva* for Capt. Spinney with Water closet but no fore buffer. delivered in Gloucester, Mass. 8000.– Keel hauled into yard Mch. 6, 1907. Launched. @ 10. A.M. June 25, 1907" (James Yard Book).

39 "I am fortunate to have in my possession the original construction plan of the *Clintonia*, given to me by Charles McManus, son of the famous designer" (Gordon Thomas, *Fast and Able*, 135).

40 "[No date] Agreed to build a knockabout Schooner for Cunningham & Thompson, to have the 2nd. stern post & shaft log, so that an engine can be installed at any time. 8900.– No water closet. Keel hauled into yard. June 12, 1907. Launched. 1-20 P.M. Sept. 25, 1907" (James Yard Book).

41 "Aug. 20, 1907. Agreed to build a Sch. – knockabout bow. – for Gorton-Pew Fish Co. per D.B. Smith & Benj. Smith. Sch. to have 2nd. stern post and shaft log, so that an engine can be installed at some future time. from new lines by T. McManus. Price del'd in Gloucester, without water closet.– $8900.– Keel hauled into yard. Sept. 12, '07. Launched 11-15 A.M. Dec. 21, '07" (James Yard Book).

42 "4/2 '08 Agreed to build an Aux. Sch. for Orlando Merchant, from lines by Mr. Thomas McManus. price to include inner stern post and shaft log.– $8900.– Keel hauled into yard Apr. 6, '08 Launched 7-45 P.M. June. 24, '08" (James Yard Book).

43 Frederick William Wallace, *Roving Fisherman* (Gardenvale, Quebec: Canadian Fishermen, 1955), 2, 130. Although Wallace,

one of her owners, refers to the *Albert J. Lutz* as a "round-bow, semi-knockabout," photographs show that she was a typical Indian Header.

44 "In 1909 one of the last 'Eastern' boats was built for the fleet. She was the *La Paloma* and was patterned after the '. . . latest McManus model from Gloucester. This type is coming into general use in the East having gradually replaced the older Herreshoff and Crowninshield models.'"(Richard H. Phillips, "Pacific Coast Halibut Schooners: Still the Workhorses of the West," *National Fisherman* (September 1972), 2C-3C, citing the *Pacific Fisherman Yearbook* of 1910).

45 Nov. 8, 1909 Commenced on Sch, molds of the *Annie Perry* for Capt. Perry and L.J. Costa. Price. 7000 Keel hauled into yard Nov. 8, '09. Launched 3-35 P.M. Mch. 2, '10 . . . Cost to Build the *Josephine DeCosta* 6,780" (James Yard Book).

46 The *Dorothy M. Smart* was seized by the U.S. Government, presumably for rum-running, and sold at a U.S. Marshall's auction in 1925 to an American citizen. Later sold to Edward Gillam of Port aux Basques, Newfoundland, she was lost on 30 June 1930.

47 "Aug. 22d. 1910. Contracted with Capt Lemuel Spinney to build a schooner like the *Elsie* Borrowed the Molds of[f] A.D. Story with Wansons Windlass Purchase no winch Stoddards Steerer @ short Bowsprit say 18 feet to stay pole Mast the same as Fred Davis schooner *Premier* Berths in Fore Castle to have 15 berths Cabin for 8 men to lay deck with Oak long side of Wheel Box do. same Oak also to have the Sch[']s [obliterated] drapes a midships he wants a schooner not very crooked for the sum of 8,000 Masts one foot Farther Forward than the *Elsie* Garboard streak not over 12 inches wide Said Schooner is 110 feet long 120 over all 24– 10 in. Wide 12– 2 in Deep Carpenters Tonnage two hundred and Eighty 20/95 Name *Valerie*" (James Yard Book).

48 "Oct. 10th. 1910. Contracted to build a

Schr like the *Josephine DeCosta* With a little More sheer and a large Fore Castle for L.J. Costa Prince Street Boston Mass $7,100 To be finished as soon as we could Named *Eleanor DeCosta* Launched March 16th, 1911" (James Yard Book).

49 "Dec 15th. 1910. Contracted with Capt Spinney For a Schr from the lines of Sch. *Mooween* lines 2 feet longer and 4 in deeper to be 118 feet long 24 feet wide 10 feet 6 in Deep Bowsprit 15 feet to [?] Oak deck aft State rooms and Clothes Closet Price $8300. . . . Name *Gov. Foss*" (James Yard Book).

50 "July 20th. Contracted to Build a Pilot Boat for Mobile Parties for $10,350.00 of a new design. Launched. 9-15 A.M. Dec. 5, 1911" (James Yard Book).

51 "[No date] Contracted to Build a Schooner of the Dimentions [*sic*] of Schr *Valerie* John Chisolm Aug. 7th, 1912" (James Yard Book).

52 "Contracted July 7th 1912 With L.J. & M. Costa to Build a Schr of about 97 to 100 tons for a sum of 7,050.00 Delivered to Gloucester Oct 18th 1912 . . . Named *Gertrude DeCosta*" (James Yard Book).

53 According to Lewis H. Story's notes at the Essex Shipbuilding Museum, Owen Lantz took over the business of John Bishop in April 1912. Bishop died on 2 November 1912.

54 "April 19 Contracted with Capt Mesquita to build a Sch. 4 ft longer and 8" wider than the *Flora L. Oliver* for $9,100 June $150.00 was added for Douglas fir Deck" (James Yard Book).

55 There is an inventory of 1,000 items in the Library of Congress belonging to Lieutenant Alessandro Fabbri, USNR. Later used in New York bluefish fishery. See Boston *Herald*, 5 February 1922, Section B, 12.

56 "For. J.M. Marshall from molds of the Sch. *J.M. Marshall* – 1 extra frame to be fitted for 2 propellers.– Keel started April 17, 1918.

Launched August. 14, 1918, – 4-55 P.M." (James Yard Book).

57 "For J.M. Marshall from molds of the *DeCosta*. Changed to *Louise B. Marshall*. Commenced on Keel. July 23, 1918. Launched 2-15 P.M. Nov. 23, 1918" (James Yard Book).

58 "To be built off of molds for Sch. *Ellen T. Marshall*. Jan. 16, -1919. Commenced on Schooner. Launched. May 10, 1919. – 8-25 A.M." (James Yard Book).

59 "For. George S. Grueby. & others. of Boston. New lines. Commenced April 24, 1919. Launched. August 27, 1919. 12:45 P.M." (James Yard Book).

60 George Hudom, Boston Sunday Herald, 5 February 1922.

61 "For. G. & A. Buffett.– Grand Banks, Newfoundland. The molds of Sch. *J.M. Marshall* were used from Quarter frame to #21, both inclusive, horned out 6" on each side at the "Gunnell." also transom & stern out 5" on each side.– the first 3 pair Cants going aft. heads tipped on to meet harpin. next one lengthened 2" the 5th pair lengthened 4" and the 6th pair lengthened 6" The Stem & Keel mold of Sch *Dawn* was used. and if used again, the shear [*sic*] f'w'd not to be run up so high by 8" on Stem as molded; also aft can be molded 4" to 6" shorter on stern. Forward body are new molds from #20 inclusive. 11" rudder stock. has Bowsprit 14 ft. to whith from Gammon. 2 topmasts. Commenced Aug. 28, 1919. Launched Mch. 25, 1920" (James Yard Book).

62 "For. Capt. Lemuel Spinney. *Governor Marshall* molds. 1 shaft log.– *Marechal Foch* after cants, long overhang aft. Commenced. Aug. 6, 1920. Launched. Dec. 16, 1920. 2-25 P.M." (James Yard Book).

63 Marked by Thomas F. McManus as the *Blanche Ring* for Captain Herbert W. Nickerson, telephone number Malden 2529M.

64 "Jan. 20, 1922. Commenced on molds of a small schooner for Capt. John Ericsson. from new lines – McManus. Commenced Jan. 20, 1922 Launched. May 15, 1922. 3-20 P.M." (James Yard Book).

65 George Hudson, the Boston *Sunday Herald*, 5 February 1922. Not built at Essex according to Dana A. Story.

66 "Sept. 8 Commenced on Sch. for Capt. Joe Sears and others Molds of *Oretha Spinney*. Stern carried out 6" under on each side. Straight part of bottom of keel 6' longer. Commenced. Sept. 8, 1925. Launched. Dec. 19, 1925" (James Yard Book).

67 For Capt. Jeffrey Thomas & others. In vessel of this model.– with 120 h.p. C.O.

Fairbanks Morse Engine, the after cylinder can be placed 25" forward of Cabin bulkhead and have ample room. Commenced. April 2, 1926. Launched Sept. 16, 1926" (James Yard Book).

68 "for A.L. Parker, to be like the Aux. Sch. *Mary Sears* Commenced. Jan. 6, 1927. Launched July 19, 1927" (James Yard Book).

69 James Yard Book under *Leonora C.*

70 "Capt. John Williams of New Bedford, Mass. Schooner like the *Alice & Mildred*, Captain Morash's Sch. Commmenced. Dec. 27, 1927. Launched. April 12, 1928. 4-P.M." (James Yard Book).

71 "Mch. 3, 1928. Agreed with Capt. Domingoes and Mr. Saunders, to build Schooner from molds of Sch. *Carrie S. Roderick*

and *Vasco da Gama* with alterations to suit the owners. (United Fisheries Co.). In building this Sch.– the *Roderick* molds were made deeper and 8 feet were added to the length., 3 frames & other was made by stretching frames apart The stern was extended on top end – next one will need to be at least 28 inches higher than the mold. Commenced. March 5, 1928. Launched. July 14, 1928. 8-30 A.M." (James Yard Book).

72 James Yard Book.

APPENDIX 2

A Guide to Fishing Schooner Designs
By Several Naval Architects

ARTHUR BINNEY[1]

1891	*Mary G. Powers.*
1892	*Arthur Binney.*
1893	*Maggie Sullivan* (clipper).[2]
1895	*Mary A. Whalen* (clipper).[3]
1899	*Preceptor* (clipper).[4]
1900	*Francis Whalen* (clipper).[5]
1901	*Monitor* (clipper),[6] *Aloha* (off *Monitor*),[7] *Edna Wallace Hopper* (off *Francis Whalen*),[8] *Benjamin F. Phillips* (round),[9] *Independence I* (off *Francis Whalen*),[10] *Monitor* (off *Francis Whalen*).[11]
1902	*Colonial* (off *Monitor*)[12] *Catherine and Ellen* (round-bow),[13] *Constellation* (off *Monitor*, auxiliary),[14] *Saladin* (off *Constellation*, auxiliary).[15]
1904	*Independence II* (off *Independence I*, but larger).[16]
1905	*Conqueror* (off *Monitor*).[17]
1906	*Athlete* (clipper).[18]
1912	*Ellen and Mary* (round),[19] *Mary* (round).[20]

EDWARD BURGESS[21]

1887	*Carrie E. Phillips* (plumb).
1889	*Nellie Dixon* (clipper), *Fredonia* (clipper).
1890	*Nannie C. Bohlin* (off *Nellie Dixon*).
1891	*Joseph Rowe* (clipper),[22] *Emma and Helen* (clipper),[23] *Gloriana, Harvard,*[24] *Ethel B. Jacobs* (clipper),[25] *James G. Blaine* (clipper),[26] *Grayling* (also attributed to McClain),[27] *Hattie Graham* (built by Moses Adams off *Fredonia*), *Marshall L. Adams* (off *Fredonia*).[28]
1893	*Indiana* (off *Fredonia*).
1898	*Titania* (clipper).[29]
1900	*Monarch* (off *Fredonia* and *Indiana*).[30]

W. STARLING BURGESS

1905	*Elizabeth Silsbee.*
1921	*Mayflower.*[32]
1922	*Puritan* (spoon).[33]

W. STARLING BURGESS (continued)

1923	*Columbia* (with Frank C. Paine).
1925	*Isabelle Parker.*[34]
1927	*William L. Putnam* (off *Isabelle Parker*).[35]

J. HORACE BURNHAM

1889	*Rigel* (?) (clipper).[36]
1891	*Hazel Oneita* (?) (clipper).[37]
1894	*Boyd and Leeds,*[38] *Pythian* (clipper).[39]
1901	*Dorothy, Etta Mildred* (off *Boyd and Leeds* and *Pythian*).[40]
1902	*Appomattox.*
1904	*Dorothy II, Elva L. Spurling* (off *Boyd and Lees* and *Pythian*), *Flora J. Sears* (off *Boyd and Leeds* and *Pythian*).
1907	*Mary B. Greer.*

MALCOLM CAMPBELL[41]

1870	*Shawmut, Mary Tracy.*
1871	*Margaret Leonard, S.S. Rowe.*
1883	*Gertie S. Winsor.*

COX & STEVENS OF NEW YORK[42]

1912	*Arcas* (knockabout), *Yucatan* (knockabout), possibly designed by Henry Gielow, a N.Y.C. architect.

BOWDOIN B. CROWNINSHIELD[43]

1900	*Rob Roy* (spoon).[44]
1902	*Hope, Robert and Arthur* (spoon w/forestay to gammon iron),[45] *Aloha* (spoon w/forestay slightly inboard),[46] *Bonita* (spoon w/forestay slightly inboard),[47] *Cuba* (spoon w/forestay slightly inboard),[48] *Dixie* (spoon w/forestay slightly inboard),[49] *Elmo* (spoon w/forestay slightly inboard),[50] *Fortuna* (spoon w/forestay slightly inboard).[51]
1903	*Harmony* (spoon),[52] *Stranger* (spoon),[53] *Rush* (spoon),[54] *Good Hope, Hatteras, Cape Horn, Emilia Gloria* (spoon),[55] *Virginia Lyons* (spoon),[56] *Mendocino.*[57]

BOWDOIN B. CROWNINSHIELD
(continued)

1904　Arbutus (spoon w/forestay slightly inboard),[58] Muriel (spoon w/forestay slightly inboard),[59] Selma (spoon w/forestay slightly inboard),[60] Tartar (spoon w/forestay further inboard).[61]

1905　Lillian, Fame (spoon w/forestay further inboard),[62] Wilfred L. Snow (Canadian).[63]

AMOS CUTTER

1860　Rover's Bride, T. Herbert, Anna Maria, Ocean Queen.

1864　Henrietta.

1867　Ella.

ARCHIBALD FENTON

1899　Anglo Saxon (clipper).[64]

1900　Tacoma (off Anglo Saxon).[65]

1901　Corona (off Anglo Saxon).[66]

1902　Yakima (off Tacoma),[67] Claudia (off Yakima and Tacoma).

1918　Pioneer (first diesel trawler).[68]

JOHN HAMILTON

1876　John Hornie, Belle A. Keyes.

WILLIAM H. HAND

1923　Wanderer.[69]

THOMAS A. IRVING

1888　Iris (sloop boat).

1901　Laura Enos (sloop boat), Blanche F. Irving (schooner boat), John S. Brooks (?), Ida S. Brooks.

1903　Rapidan.

1904　Diana (sloop boat).

1905　Juno (round).[70]

Possibility: Sylvie Nunan.

LAURENCE JENSEN

1899　John J. Flaherty (Fredonia type).

1901　Tattler (off John J. Flaherty).

CHARLES A. LASKEY

1865　Eva G.

1866　Charles A. Laskey, Margaret A. Jones.

WILBUR LASKEY[71]

1859　Flying Fish, Cutlass, Moonlight.

1860　Mary Francis, O'Connell, Joseph Henry, St. Mary, Connaught Ranger, Shadow, North Star, John Thomas.

LASKEY & McPHAIL

1865　Fenian, Flying Eagle, Saint Peter.

1866　Abbie J.

DENNISON J. LAWLOR[72]

1853　Olata (fishing schooner, later a pilot boat at New Orleans).

1857　Azalea.

　　　Mary Y. Yates.

1866　Thomas E. Evans, Sarah H. Cressy, Hibernia.

1871　Actress, Helen M. Foster, Magic.

1882　Sarah H. Prior, Jemima Boomer (menhaden fishing steamer).

1884　George B. Douglas, Roulette,[73] A.S. and R. Hammond (plumb).

1885　John H. McManus (plumb), Arthur D. Story (plumb).

1886　Grampus (plumb) (with Captain J.W. Collins).

1887　Mary J. Ward (schooner boat), Fernwood (?) (plumb).[74]

1888　Susan R. Stone (plumb), Amy Hanson, John L. Nicholson (?) (plumb).[75]

1889　Harry L. Belden (plumb), Mary Emerson (schooner boat).

1892　Governor Russell,[76] S.P. Willard,[77] Iceland (?) (plumb).[78]

1901　Annie M. Parker (plumb),[79] George Parker (plumb).[80]

Undated: D.J. Lawlor, Gracie, Vanitas, Fannie.[81]

CAPTAIN GEORGE MELVILLE McCLAIN[82]

1882　Mattie Winship (?) (clipper).[83]

1883　Henry Dennis, Oresa (?) (clipper).[84]

1884　Robin Hood (clipper),[85] James and Ella, Loring B. Haskell, Ralph L. Hodgdon.[86]

1885　Ella G. King (?) (clipper),[87] Canopus (?) (clipper).[88]

1886　I.J. Merritt, Jr. (clipper),[89] Mayflower, Gladstone (?) (clipper).[90]

1887　George F. Edmunds, Puritan (plumb), Lorna Doone (?) (clipper).[91]

1888　Horace B. Parker (off I.J. Merritt, Jr.), Masconomo (clipper),[92] Lizzie M. Stanwood (?) (clipper).[93]

1889　Nellie G. Adams, Joseph P. Johnson, Louise J. Kenney, Quickstep (?) (clipper),[94] Procyon (?) (clipper),[95] Dora A. Lawson (?) (clipper).[96]

1890[97]　Eliza B. Campbell (clipper),[98] Volunteer, Lottie S. Haskins (off Nellie Dixon), Henry M. Stanley (off Lottie S. Haskins), Clara

CAPTAIN GEORGE MELVILLE McCLAIN (continued)

R. Harwood (off *Lottie S. Haskins*), *Maggie E. Wells, Susan L. Hodge* (clipper),[99] *Golden Hope* (off *I.J. Merritt, Jr.*), *Parthia* (clipper),[100] *Rose Cabral* (off *Nellie Dixon*), *Yosemite, Mildred V. Lee* (clipper, white),[101] *William E. Morrissey* (?) (clipper),[102] *Oliver Wendell Holmes* (?) (clipper),[103] *Lucille* (?) (clipper),[104] *Penobscot* (?) (clipper),[105] *Talisman* (?) (clipper).[106]

1891   *Caviare* (off *Lottie S. Haskins*), *American* (clipper),[107] *Maggie and May* (clipper),[108] *Edith M. Prior* (clipper),[109] *Nereid, Columbia* (clipper),[110] *Gladiator* (clipper),[111] *Minerva* (off *Lottie S. Haskins*), *Lizzie B. Adams* (off *Lottie S. Haskins*), *Edith M. McInnis, Grayling* (clipper),[112] *Leader, Sheffield, Judique* (?) (clipper),[113] *Argo* (?) (clipper),[114] *Hiram Lowell* (?) (clipper),[115] *Orpheus* (?) (clipper),[116] *Jennie B. Hodgdon* (?) (clipper),[117] *Glorianna* (?) (clipper),[118] *Nereid* (?) (clipper).[119]

1892   *Rienzi, Elsie F. Rowe, Clara M. Littlefield, Meteor* (clipper),[120] *Ruth M. Martin, Elector* (clipper),[121] *Mabel D. Hines* (off *Elector*),[122] *Almeida, Albert Black, Edward A. Rich*,[123] *Pioneer, Thalia* (clipper),[124] *Harvester* (clipper),[125] *Alva* (off *Eliza B. Campbell*), *Florence E. Stream* (?) (clipper),[126] *Ramona* (?) (clipper),[127] *Eliza H. Parkhurst* (?) (clipper),[128] *Mary G. Powers* (?) (clipper),[129] *Braganza* (?) (clipper),[130] *Reliance* (?) (clipper).[131]

1893   *Nellie Bly, Bertha M. Bailey, Elmer Randall, Mertis H. Perry* (off *Lottie S. Haskins*), *Mary Cabral* (off *Lottie S. Haskins*), *Marguerite Haskins* (clipper),[132] *Helen G. Wells* (clipper),[133] *Miranda* (clipper),[134] *Lewis H. Giles, Fortuna I* (off the *Lewis H. Giles*), *Senator Lodge* (clipper),[136] *Pinta* (off *Marguerite Haskins*),[137] *Georgie Campbell* (off *Eliza B. Campbell*), *Senator* (?) (clipper),[138] *John E. McKenzie* (?) (clipper).[139]

1894   *Atalanta* (off *Susan L. Hodge*), *M. Madeline, Ralph Russell* (clipper),[140] *Fortuna II* (built by John Bishop, *Fredonia* type), *Evelyn L. Smith* (off *Lottie S. Haskins*), *Effie M. Morrissey* (off *Mabel D. Hines*),[141] *Bessie M. Devine* (clipper),[142] *Kearsage* (off *Senator Lodge*),[143] *Alice M. Parsons* (off *Ralph Russell*), *Norman Fisher, Norma* (off *Marguerite Haskins*),[144] *Latona* (?) (clipper),[145] *Jubilee* (?) (clipper).[146]

1895   *Pauline* (off *Ralph Russell*), *Hattie L. Trask* (off *Ralph Russell*), *Virginia* (off *Senator Lodge*), *George Campbell*,[147] *Bertha L. Barker* (off *Edward A. Rich*),[148] *Hattie A. Heckman* (?) (clipper).[149]

1896   *Annie Greenlaw* (off *Marguerite Haskins*),[150] *George E. Lane, Jr.* (off *Ralph Russell*).

1897   *Lena and Maud* (off *Marguerite Haskins*),[151] *A.S. Caswell* (off *Ralph Russell*), *William H. Moody* (?) (clipper),[152] *Patriot* (?) (clipper),[153] *Edna Perry* (?).

1898   *Esther Anita* (off *Senator Lodge*), *Admiral Dewey* (?) (clipper),[154] *Dawson City* (?).

1899   *Blanche* (clipper),[155] *Golden Rod* (clipper),[156] *Niagara* (clipper),[157] *Corsair* (off *Senator Lodge*), *Titania* (off *Senator Lodge*), *Henrietta G. Martin, Volant* (clipper),[158] *John J. Flaherty, Oregon* (off *Marguerite Haskins*),[159] *Lucinda I. Lowell* (off *Esther Anita*), *Agnes V. Gleason* (?) (clipper),[160] *Olympia* (?) (clipper),[161] *T.M. Nicholson* (?) (clipper).[162]

1900   *Helen Miller Gould* (clipper),[163] *Angelina, Dreadnought* (off

Lena and Maud),[164] *Illinois* (off *Marguerite Haskins*),[165] *Senator Gardner* (clipper),[166] *Lottie G. Merchant* (off *Marguerite Haskins*),[167] *Agnes* (off *Marguerite Haskins*),[168] *Priscilla Smith* (?) (clipper),[169] *Navahoe* (?) (clipper),[170] *Olga* (?) (clipper),[171] *Richard Wainwright* (?) (clipper),[172] *Kentucky* (?) (clipper),[173] *Dictator* (?) (clipper),[174] *Vera* (?), *Margaret* (?).

1901   *Electric Flash* (off *Marguerite Haskins*),[175] *Alice M. Guthrie, Irene and May, Mary E. Harty* (off *Fredonia*), *Victor* (off *Fortuna*, auxiliary),[176] *Nellie B. Nickerson* (auxiliary), *Mary Edith* (?) (clipper),[177] *Bohemia* (?) (clipper),[178] *Arcadia* (?) (clipper),[179] *Elizabeth N.* (?) (clipper),[180] *Nettie Franklin* (?) (clipper),[181] *Sceptre* (?) (clipper),[182] *Sceptre* (?) (clipper),[183] *Ella M. Goodwin* (?), *Rebecca* (?).

1902   *Harriet W. Babson* (off *Nellie Dixon*), *Winifred* (clipper),[184] *Veda M. McKown* (off *Fortuna*, auxiliary),[185] *Eglantine* (clipper),[186] *Emilia Enos* (off *Rose Cabral*),[187] *Arabia* (?) (clipper),[188] *Kineo* (?) (clipper),[189] *Scythia* (?) (clipper),[190] *Smuggler* (?), *Rival* (?).

1903   *Mary E. Cooney, Avalon* (off *Harriet W. Babson*),[191] *Nokomis* (off *M. Madeline*),[192] *Lafayette* (auxiliary, off *Nokomis*), *Hazel R. Hines* (off *Avalon*),[193] *Fannie A. Smith* (off *Priscilla Smith*) (?),[194] *Gleaner* (?), *Esther Gray* (?).

1904   *John R. Manta* (off *Harriet W. Babson*, whaler),[195] *Patrician* (?) (clipper),[196] *Rita A. Viator* (?).

1905   *Arthur James* (off *Avalon* and *Hazel R. Hines*),[197] *Romance* (*Fredonia* type).

1906   *Good Luck*.[198]

Undated: *Alameida.*

DONALD McKAY

1854   *R.H. Moulton.*

1858   *R.R. Higgins.*

1859   *Benjamin S. Wright.*

1860   *Mary B. Dyer, H. and R. Atwood.*[199]

1868   *Frank Atwood.*[200]

LEONARD B. MACKENZIE

1901   *Ralph L. Hall, Theodore Roosevelt* (clipper).[201]

1902   *Bertha and Pearl, Faustina* (clipper).[202]

JOHN A. McPHAIL

1869   *Lady Thorn.*

1870   *Sylvester.*

JONATHAN D.S. NICKERSON

1917   *Corinthian* (auxiliary knockabout),[203] *Killarney* (auxiliary knockabout),[204] *Gaspe, Walrus* (steam trawler), *Seal* (steam trawler).

FRANK C. PAINE

1923   *Columbia* (with W. Starling Burgess).

1929   *Gertrude L. Thebaud.*

EDWIN PERKINS

1921   *Yankee.*

1923   *Shamrock.*

CHARLES O. STORY

1891   *Resolute.*

JACOB STORY [205]

1925   *Mary M., Mary A., Shirley M. Clattenburg.*

1927   *Juneal, Evelina M. Goulart* (built by A.D. Story).

1928   *Georgina M., Frances C. Denehy, Raymonde.*[206]

1929   *Gertrude M. Fauci.*

1930   *Louis A. Thebaud, Mary E. D'Eon, Magellan, America.*

1932   *Jessie Goldthwait.*

1936   *Marie and Catherine.*

1938   *Skilligolee,*[207] *J.B. Junior II.*

JOSEPH STORY

1888   *J.H. Carey* (plumb).

1889   *Shenandoah* (off *J.H. Carey*).[208]

LEWIS H. STORY [209]

1905   *Shepherd King.*

1908   *Aspinet* (off *Shepherd King*),[210] *John J. Fallon* (off *Aspinet,* auxiliary).[211]

1926   *Virginia* (off *Shepherd King*).[212]

1929   *Rainbow* (off *Shepard King*).

1942   *Lois T.*[213]

1943   *G.N. Sofforn.*[214]

1944   *Gaetano S.*[215]

1945   *St. Peter II, Tina B.*[216]

WASHINGTON TARR

1897   *Arbitrator* (clipper).[217]

1898   *Hustler* (plumb),[218] *Nickerson* (plumb).

1899   *Dauntless* (off *Arbitrator*).

1901   *Elizabeth N.* (off *Arbitrator*),[219] *Arkona* (off *Arbitrator*).[220]

TAYLOR, CAMPBELL & BROOKS

1870   *Shawmut, Mary Tracy.*

1871   *Margaret Leonard, S.S. Rowe.*

1 Arthur Binney was born at Boston on 2 December 1865. He was educated in Boston Public schools, Roxbury Latin School, a took a special drafting and design course at Massachusetts Institute of Technology. He served a draftsman apprenticeship with the Whittier Machine Company of Boston and later worked as a draftsman for the Hastings Organ Company. Binney went to work for Edward Burgess in 1888 and, upon the latter's death, formed the firm of Stewart & Binney. He later bought out his partner and remained in business on his own account. He designed many vessel types including ferry boats, City of Boston police and fire boats, fishing schooners, but principally engaged in yacht design. His most notable creation was the America's Cup defense candidate *Pilgrim*. A charter member of the Society of Naval Architects and Marine Engineers, he died on 28 August 1924.

2 "Bows of Fishing Vessels," an unpublished list compiled by Gordon W. Thomas in the possession of Dana A. Story, hereafter "Thomas, bows"; claimed by T.F. McManus, Jr., to have been designed by his father.

3 Thomas, bows. Built for Jerome McDonald by James & Tarr. Launched October 18th.

4 Thomas, bows.

5 Thomas, bows. The *Francis Whalen* has been rumored to be off the *Preceptor*, but the James Yard Book shows her to be 119 ft. overall, 108 ft. on deck, 25 ft. 2 in. wide, and 11 ft. 4 in. deep, 136+ register tons, while the *Preceptor* was 119 ft. overall, 103 ft. on deck, 24 ft. wide, 10 ft. 9 in. deep (register tonnage not in Yard Book), J.F. James & Son, in the possession of Dana Story, hereafter "James Yard Book."

6 Thomas, bows.

7 "Contracted this day for a Schooner like the *Monitor* for Cunningham & Thompson" (James Yard Book). Not to be confused with Crowninshield's *Aloha* of 1902.

8 James Yard Book.

9 Thomas, bows.

10 James Yard Book.

11 Built by James & Tarr for Jerome McDonald of Gloucester off the *Francis Whalen* molds, launched on July 18th.

12 "Oct. 1, 1901. Agreed this day with Gardner & Parsons to build them a Sch. of *Monitor* model reduced in size (James Yard Book).

13 Thomas, bows.

14 "Sept. 27, 1901. Have this day agreed with Orlando Merchant to build a Schooner of the *Monitor* model with the after part constructed so that an Engine can be used. Labor on Engine part to be paid for Extra. 8200. Extra Stock & Labor $137.04 – Extra Cementing 27.50. Keel hauled into yard. Oct. 2. 1901. Launched Dec. 31. 1901" (James Yard Book).

15 "Commenced to build a Gasoline Sch. like Orlando Merchant[']s (*Constellation*), for Cunningham & Thompson. Engine bed extra. . . . Launched March 7, 1902" (James Yard Book).

16 James Yard Book.

17 James Yard Book.

18 Thomas, bows.

19 Thomas, bows; James Yard Book.

20 Thomas, bows. Later the *Mary II* (1920) and the *Arthur D. Story* (1930).

21 Thomas F. McManus, in his autobiographical essays attributes the *Nannie C. Bohlin*, *Joseph Rowe*, *James G. Blaine* and *Ethel B. Jacobs* to Burgess. Chapelle states that of Burgess's 137 designs there were only six fishing schooners and three pilot boats. A more correct count would appear to be at least ten fishing schooners and four pilot boats.

22 Thomas, bows.

23 Thomas, bows.

24 Latter two launched after Burgess's death on 31 July 1891.

25 Lewis H. Story's list of racers; Thomas, bows.

26 Thomas, bows; Lewis H. Story's list of racers.

27 Thomas, bows; Lewis H. Story's list of racers.

28 James Yard Book.

29 Thomas, bows.

30 James & Tarr built her for John Chisolm, but added 9 inches of breadth, and launched her on 10 January, 1900 (James Yard Book).

31 Later Burgess & Paine, and Burgess, Swazey & Paine.

32 James Yard Book.

33 James Yard Book; Thomas, bows.

34 James Yard Book.

35 James Yard Book.

36 Thomas, bows.

37 Thomas, bows.

38 Seventeen schooners were built to this model, which was similar to a Baltimore Clipper (German, *Down on T Wharf*, 83). Chapelle states it had Baltimore Clipper lines (*Fishing Schooners*, 203).

39 Thomas, bows.

40 Per Tom Hoyne.

41 See also Taylor, Campbell & Brooks.

42 The firm of Cox & Stevens of New York was best known for yacht, ferry, and harbor craft designs, but the firm did design this pair of auxiliary fishing schooners for use in the Gulf of Mexico which were described in *Yachting* Magazine in 1912.

43 Bowdoin B. Crowninshield, like the younger Burgess, gained more fame from racing yachts than fishing schooners, although he drafted at least twenty-five of the latter between 1900 and 1905. Among them, the *Rob Roy*, *Harmony*, *Stranger*, and *Tartar* (of which Tom McManus was a shareholder) achieved a measure of recognition from fleet owners, particularly his neighboring Boston-based operators. Crowninshield introduced the spoon bow to fishing schooners; but his most enduring characteristic was a keel with a straight run, substantial drag, and a leading knuckle. In common with McManus's early designs, he favored long forward overhangs and stern counters. A basic tenet of his design philosophy was a fine run to provide lively helm response. As a result, his hulls had comparatively straight buttock lines.

Born at New York City during 1867 to Benjamin W. and Katherine M.

Crowninshield, he descended from the famous Salem family of East Indian merchants. His parents returned to Boston in 1868. Young Crowninshield attended the Prince School and then, at age 12, went to St. Paul's School at Concord, N.H., where he remained for six years. He entered M.I.T., and remained there for one year before transferring to Harvard, where he took elective studies in the Lawrence Scientific School and graduated in 1890

In 1896 he associated with John R. Purdon in a yacht design and brokerage office. A year later he left the firm to start his own business. His first noted design was the 21-foot knockabout yacht *Mongoose* for A.D. Irving of New York. In 1901 he designed the unsuccessful America's Cup racer *Independence*. His most famous fishing schooner was the *Rob Roy*. Unfortunately, his best remembered creation was the great seven-masted schooner *Thomas W. Lawson*.

Before the United States entered World War I, Crowninshield drove an ambulance in France for the American Volunteer Ambulance Corps, beginning in January 1916. He was present at the monstrous battle of Verdun. During World War II, he again served, this time as an inspector of hulls for the U.S. Navy.

He was president and general manager of the Crowninshield Shipbuilding Company of Fall River from 1917 through 1926, and later formed the firm of Crowninshield & Burbank, naval architects.

Crowninshield died at age 80 on 12 August 1947, in Marblehead.

44 Thomas, bows.

45 German, *Down on T Wharf*, 19.

46 *Aloha*, *Bonita*, *Cuba*, *Dixie*, *Elmo*, and *Fortuna* were all built by Oxner & Story to the same design for the Gulf Coast Fisheries Company of Galveston, Texas ("Sixty-Foot Fisherman," *The Rudder* 14 (January 1903); 20). *Cuba* and *Dixie* were launched from the yard on the same day, 15 September 1902 (Story, Dana, *A List of Vessels, Boats, and Other Craft Built in the Town of Essex 1860-1980*, 3rd ed., (Essex: Essex Shipbuilding Museum, 1992), Y26). This may be the first

schooner design in which Crowninshield moved the forestay aft of the gammon iron.

47 "Sixty-Foot Fisherman," *The Rudder* 14 (January 1903): 20.

48 "Sixty-Foot Fisherman."

49 "Sixty-Foot Fisherman."

50 "Sixty-Foot Fisherman."

51 "Sixty-Foot Fisherman."

52 Thomas, bows.

53 Chapelle, *Fishing Schooners*, 247.

54 Thomas, bows.

55 Chapelle, *Fishing Schooners*, 247.

56 Chapelle, *Fishing Schooners*, 247.

57 A. Acores painting, Peabody & Essex Museum.

58 Chapelle, *Fishing Schooners*, 249-50, states that Crowninshield completed this design on 15 December 1903.

59 German, *Down on T Wharf*, 71.

60 German, *Down on T Wharf*, 71.

61 Thomas, bows. *The Rudder* 16 (March 1905): 112; Joe Garland, *Down to the Sea*, 211, claims John G. Alden designed the lines of the *Tartar* when he worked for Crowninshield, which is entirely plausible.

62 Drafted by John G. Alden (*The Nautical Gazette* 70 (15 March 1906): 189).

63 Drawn by John G. Alden, 4 August 1905 (*The Nautical Gazette* 70 (1 March 1906): 151-52).

64 Thomas, bows. James & Tarr laid her down on 17 October, launched 25 November (James Yard Book).

65 James & Tarr laid her down on 25 November 1899, launched Spring 1900. Built for Samuel G. Pool & Sons of Gloucester.

66 "Contracted with Cunningham & Thompson for vessel of *Anglo Saxon* model with ~~one~~ two extra frames" (James Yard Book).

67 James Yard Book.

68 James Yard Book.

69 Auxiliary knockabout built by Everett James. "Large knockabout yacht. Teak deck. Made one trip into the Arctic and then began dory trawling out of Boston" (From Charles F. Sayle of Nantucket).

70 Thomas, bows.

71 Wilbur Laskey succumbed to a life-long battle with diabetes on 18 March 1888. Among the twenty-odd schooners he had delivered to the Boston Irish market fleet were the *Joseph Henry* for Dick Leonard and John H. McManus in 1860 and the *Eva G.* for Jeremiah McCarthy in 1865. His business never fully recovered from the crippling shipwrights' strike that shut down the building yards during 1871.

72 Dennison J. Lawlor, 68, born in St. John's, New Brunswick, died of "cancer of the bowels," on 2 January 1892, at 35 Walnut Street, Chelsea. Naval Architect. Son of James Lawlor, born New Brunswick, and Annie Lawlor [maiden name unknown], born Ireland. Buried at Mt. Auburn Cemetery (Massachusetts Vital Records, *Deaths*, 1892, vol. 429, page 493, line 2).

73 Thomas, bows, gives this a clipper bow. Designed and built for William F. Weld, Official No. 110638, 9 July 1884.

74 Thomas, bows.

75 Thomas, bows.

76 Off *Susan R. Stone* moulds (James Yard Book). Thomas, bows, states she had a clipper bow.

77 Off *Susan R. Stone* moulds, but with a clipper bow, according to Lewis Story.

78 Thomas, bows.

79 Off *Susan R. Stone* moulds according to Lewis Story.

80 These were the last two plumb-stemmers built for the Massachusetts fisheries (German, *Down on T Wharf*, 10; Thomas, *Fast & Able*, 63).

81 Presumably all built at Lawlor's own Buck's Wharf, Chelsea, shipyard.

82 This list initially compiled from Howard I. Chapelle, *American Fishing Schooners*, and a newspaper article by Gordon W. Thomas which appeared in the *Gloucester Times* on 23 August 1954.

83 Thomas, bows.

84 Thomas, bows.

85 Thomas, bows.

86 Thomas dates this schooner 1889.

87 Thomas, bows.

88 Thomas, bows.

89 Thomas, bows.

90 Thomas, bows.

91 Thomas, bows.

92 Thomas, bows.

93 Thomas, bows.

94 Thomas, bows.

95 Thomas, bows.

96 Thomas, bows.

97 The *Cape Ann Advertiser* once claimed that McClain designed sixty schooners during 1890 and 1891 (from one of several undated newspaper clippings glued to a photograph of the *James S. Steele* that has been donated by a descendent of James S. Steele, the son of George Steele, to the Cape Ann Historical Association during 1993).

98 Thomas, bows. Thomas refers to this schooner as *Eliza Campbell*, and Chapelle, in *Fishing Schooners* and *American Sailing Craft*, as the *Eliza B. Campbell*.

99 Thomas, bows.

100 Thomas, bows.

101 Thomas, bows.

102 Thomas, bows.

103 Thomas, bows.

104 Thomas, bows.

105 Thomas, bows.

106 Thomas, bows.

107 Thomas, bows.

108 Thomas, bows. An earlier *Maggie and May* was launched at East Boothbay, Maine, by W.I. Adams in 1880 (George Wharton Rice, *The Shipping Days of Old Boothbay: From Revolution to the World War* (Boothbay, Maine: Boothbay Region Historical Society, 1938).

109 Thomas, bows.

110 Thomas, bows.

111 Thomas, bows.

112 Thomas, bows.

113 Thomas, bows.

114 Thomas, bows.

115 Thomas, bows.

116 Thomas, bows.

117 Thomas, bows.

118 Thomas, bows.

119 Thomas, bows.

120 Thomas, bows.

121 Thomas, bows.

122 James Yard Book.

123 "Contracted with Joseph Parsons for a vessel 120 tons carpenters, flush deck, to masure [sic] down where main deck should go, 10 in. Nov. 27, '91" (James Yard Book).

124 Thomas, bows.

125 Thomas, bows.

126 Thomas, bows.

127 Thomas, bows.

128 Thomas, bows.

129 Thomas, bows.

130 Thomas, bows.

131 Thomas, bows.

132 Thomas, bows.

133 Thomas, bows. Did a 360° roll in 1897 (Chapelle, *American Fishing Schooners*, 197-200).

134 Thomas, bows.

135 Thomas, bows. Built by John Bishop, *Fredonia* type.

136 Thomas, bows.

137 James Yard Book.

138 Thomas, bows.

139 Thomas, bows.

140 Thomas, bows.

141 James Yard Book.

142 Thomas, bows.

143 James Yard Book.

144 James Yard Book. Thomas, bows, states later converted from a clipper to a knockabout.

145 Thomas, bows.

146 Thomas, bows.

147 Thomas refers to this schooner as the *Georgie Campbell* and dates it 1893.

148 "Contracted with John Feeney & Co. of New York for a vessel of the *Edward A. Rich* moulds with brake [sic] . . . brake to be 8 in. high. . . . Launched July 6, 1895" (James Yard Book).

149 Thomas, bows.

150 James Yard Book.

151 ". . . to be of M. *Haskins* model, one extra frame" (James Yard Book).

152 Thomas, bows.

153 Thomas, bows.

154 Thomas, bows.

155 Thomas, bows. Claimed by T.F. McManus, Jr., to have been designed by his father.

156 Thomas, bows. Claimed by T.F. McManus, Jr., to have been designed by his father.

157 Thomas, bows.

158 Thomas, bows.

159 "Spars same as *Lena & Maud*" (James Yard Book). Built by James & Tarr for Davis Brothers of Gloucester during the summer.

160 Thomas, bows.

161 Thomas, bows.

162 Thomas, bows.

163 Thomas, bows. This was the first fisherman with a gasoline auxiliary engine. She had a 35-hp Globe initially, until a 150-hp Globe became available.

164 James Yard Book

165 ". . . M. *Haskins* model with one extra frame" (James Yard Book). Built by James & Tarr for Gardner & Parsons of Gloucester over the winter.

166 Thomas, bows.

167 ". . . for a vessel of M. *Haskins* model, one extra frame" (James Yard Book).

168 James Yard Book. Built during the Fall by James & Tarr for the Davis Brothers of Gloucester.

169 Thomas, bows.

170 Thomas, bows.

171 Thomas, bows.

172 Thomas, bows. Built by John Bishop for Orlando Merchant.

173 Thomas, bows.

174 Thomas, bows.

175 "Commenced on vessel for James E. Bradley. M. *Haskins* model 1 extra frame" (James Yard Book).

176 "Contracted with Fred Davis for vessel, *Fortuna* model" (James Yard Book).

177 Thomas, bows.

178 Thomas, bows.

179 Thomas, bows.

180 Thomas, bows.

181 Thomas, bows.

182 Thomas, bows.

183 Thomas, bows; built by A.D. Story for John Pew & Son.

184 Thomas, bows.

185 "Sch. for Mr. Fred Davis on the *Fortuna* lines with these alterations, head of stem shoved forward 2' – 2 extra frames, – the frame space –24" apart centre to centre. Stern altered to accommodate Gasoline propeller. Engine Bed Extra. . . . Launched Apr. 10 1902. 11-30 A.M." (James Yard Book).

186 Thomas, bows.

187 James Yard Book. Built by James & Tarr for Joseph A. Manta of Provincetown and launched 4 December.

188 Thomas, bows.

189 Thomas, bows.

190 Thomas, bows.

191 James Yard Book.

192 "Agreed with John F. Wonson & Co. to build a Schooner of the M. *Madaline* model with 1 Extra frame and stem to be raked a little more" (James Yard Book).

193 "Launched. @ 9 A.M. Dec. 2, 1903" (James Yard Book).

194 Built for the Gorton-Pew Vessels Co.

195 James Yard Book.

196 Thomas, bows. Built by A.D. Story for Hugh Parkhurst, Jr.

197 James Yard Book.

198 "Besides being a designer, Capt. Mel was also a successful skipper. As late as 1909, he was mackerel seining in his own creation, the schooner *Good Luck*, a round-bowed vessel which proved to be his last design" (Thomas, *Fast & Able*, 15).

199 The first four schooners were Boston owned and there was a "Free School" connection. See Chapelle, *American Fishing Schooners*, 104.

200 Samuel Eliot Morison, *Maritime History of Massachusetts, 1783-1860* (1921; reprint, Boston: Northeastern University Press, 1979), 306.

201 Thomas, bows.

202 Thomas, bows.

203 Launched by J.F. James & Son, 8 August, for the Gorton-Pew Vessels Co. and Cunningham & Thompson of Gloucester.

204 Launched by by A.D. Story on 7 May for the Gorton-Pew Vessels Co. of Gloucester.

205 Dana A. Story's half-brother who died in 1939 at age 45.

206 Built by A.D. Story for Henry Curtis, Jr., of Gloucester. Schooner-dragger. Launched 28 November (Dana A. Story, *An Approximate Listing of the Vessels, Boats and Other Craft Built in the Town of Essex, 1870 through 1977. Based upon the Research and Listings of Lewis H. Story, Essex*).

207 Charley McGregor designed interior layout and rigging, Jacob Story designed the hull (Dana A. Story, 29 June 1993).

208 Thomas, bows, gives her a plumb stem, but another source gives her a clipper bow.

209 From Dana A. Story, 29 June 1993.

210 James Yard Book.

211 James Yard Book.

212 James Yard Book.

213 From Dana A. Story, 29 June 1993.

214 From Dana A. Story, 29 June 1993.

215 From Dana A. Story, 29 June 1993.

216 From Dana A. Story, 29 June 1993.

217 Thomas, bows.

218 Thomas, bows.

219 ". . . for a vessel of the *Arbitrator* model, with 3 extra frames" (James Yard Book). 224 Built by James & Tarr for Henry Gardner.

APPENDIX 3

A Summary of the American and International Fishermen's Races

ORDER OF FINISH	YEAR BUILT	CAPTAIN

Date: 1 May 1886[1]
Title: None. The first fishermen's race, Boston, Massachusetts

John H. McManus	1885	Johnny O'Brien
Sarah H. Prior	1882	Tom McLaughlin
Gertie S. Winsor	1883	Maurice Powers
Hattie I. Phillips	1885	Ned Plunkett
William Emerson	1886	Bartholomew Whalen
Belle J. Neal	1885	John Driscoll
Emily P. Wright	1884	Jim Carney
Edith Emery	1883	Patrick Sullivan
W. Parnell O'Hara	1886	Tom Connell

Date: 24 April 1888[2]
Title: None. The second fishermen's race, Boston, Massachusetts

Carrie E. Phillips	1887	Maurice Powers
I.J. Merritt, Jr.	1886	Charley Harty
Roulette	1884	Tim Cole
John H. McManus	1885	Johnny O'Brien
Carrie W. Babson	1887	Owen Whitten

Date: 26 August 1892
Title: The Hovey Cup, Gloucester, Massachusetts

1st Class[3]

Harry L. Belden	1889	Maurice Whalen
Nannie C. Bohlin	1890	Tommy Bohlin
Joseph Rowe	1891	Rube Cameron

Did Not Finish

James S. Steele	1891	Charley Olsen
Grayling	1891	Charley Harty
James G. Blaine	1891	Johnny McDonald
Ethel B. Jacobs	1891	Sol Jacobs

2nd Class Winner

Lottie S. Haskins	1890	Bernie Malone
Caviare	1891	Frank Stevens

Did Not Finish

Elsie F. Rowe	1891	Jim Gannon

Date: 1901
Title: The Lawson Cup, Boston, Massachusetts

1st Class

Benjamin F. Phillips	1901	
Priscilla Smith	1900	
Navahoe	1900	

2nd Class (finished in a draw)

Manomet	1900	
Mattakeesett	1898	

Date: 1 August 1907
Title: The Lipton Cup, Boston, Massachusetts

1st Class

Rose Dorothea	1905	Marion Perry and Johnny Watson
Jessie Costa	1905	Manuel Costa
James W. Parker	1905	Val O'Neil

2nd Class

Frances P. Mesquita	1905	Joe Mesquita
Helen B. Thomas	1902	Billy Thomas

Date: October 1920
Title: American Elimination Series[4]

Esperanto	1906	Marty Welch

Date: 13 October 1920
Title: Canadian Elimination Series

Delawanna	1920	Tom Himmelman, defeated eight others

Date: 30 October and 1 November 1920
Title: The International Fishing Vessel Championship,
Halifax, N.S.

First Race

Esperanto	1906	Marty Welch, by 18'28"
Delawanna	1920	Tom Himmelman

Second Race

Esperanto	1906	Marty Welch, by 7'25"
Delawanna	1920	Tom Himmelman

Date: 12 October 1921
Title: American Elimination Series

Elsie	1910	Marty Welch
Philip P. Manta	1902	Ben Pine
Arthur James	1905	John Matheson
Ralph Brown	1914	
Elsie G. Silva	1915	Manuel Silva

Date: October 1921
Title: Canadian Elimination Series

First Race

Bluenose	1921	Angus Walters
Canadia	1921	

Second Race

Bluenose	1921	Angus Walters
Delawanna	1920	Tom Himmelman

Date: 22 and 24 October 1921
Title: The International Fishing Vessel Championship,
Halifax, Nova Scotia

First Race

Bluenose	1921	Angus Walters, by 12'+
Elsie	1910	Marty Welch

Second Race

Bluenose	1921	Angus Walters, by 10'+
Elsie	1910	Marty Welch

Date: 12 October 1922
Title: American Elimination Series

Henry Ford	1922	Clayt Morrissey
Yankee	1921	Mike Brophy
Elizabeth Howard	1916	Ben Pine
L.A. Dunton	1921	Felix Hogan

Date: October 1922
Title: Canadian Elimination Series

Bluenose	1921	Angus Walters
Canadia		
Margaret K. Smith		
Mahaska		

Date: 21, 23, and 24 October 1922
Title: The International Fishing Vessel Championship,
Gloucester, Massachusetts

First Race

Completed by competitors but abandoned by the race
committee

Second Race

Henry Ford	1922	Clayt Morrissey, by 2'+
Bluenose	1921	Angus Walters

Third Race

Bluenose	1921	Angus Walters, by 7'23"
Henry Ford	1922	Clayt Morrissey

Fourth Race

Bluenose	1921	Angus Walters, by 7'51"
Henry Ford	1922	Clayt Morrissey

Date: 31 August 1923
Title: Second Lipton Cup,[5] 300th Anniversary of Gloucester,
Massachusetts[6]

Henry Ford	1922	Clayt Morrissey
Elizabeth Howard	1916	Ben Pine
Shamrock	1923	Marty Welch

ORDER OF FINISH	YEAR BUILT	CAPTAIN

Date: **21 October 1923**
Title: **American Elimination Series**

Columbia	1923	Ben Pine
Henry Ford	1922	Clayt Morrissey
Elizabeth Howard	1916	Harry Gillie

Date: **29 and 31 October 1923**
Title: **The International Fishing Vessel Championship, Halifax, Nova Scotia[7]**

First Race

Bluenose	1921	Angus Walters, by 1'20"
Columbia	1923	Ben Pine

Second Race

Bluenose	1921	Angus Walters, by 2'+
Columbia	1923	Ben Pine

Date: **11 October 1926**
Title: **The Frank E. Davis & George Fuller Cup Races**

Columbia	1923	Ben Pine
Henry Ford	1922	Clayt Morrissey

Date: **September 1929**
Title: **Fuller, Davis & Prentiss Cup Races[8]**

Progress	1913	Manuel Domingoes
Arthur D. Story[9]	1912	Ben Pine
Thomas S. Gorton	1905	Wallace Parsons
Elsie	1910	Norman Ross

Date: **9 (called off-light airs), 16 and 19 October 1930**
Title: **Third Lipton Cup, Gloucester, Massachusetts**

First Race

Gertrude L. Thebaud	1930	Ben Pine, by 15'+
Bluenose	1921	Angus Walters

Second Race

Gertrude L. Thebaud	1930	Charley Johnson, by 8'+
Bluenose	1921	Angus Walters

Date: **October 1931**
Title: **American Elimination Series**

Gertrude L. Thebaud	1930	Ben Pine
Elsie	1910	Norman Ross

Date: **October 1931**
Title: **The International Fishing Vessel Championship, Halifax, Nova Scotia**

First Race

Bluenose	1921	Angus Walters
Gertrude L. Thebaud	1930	Ben Pine

Second Race

Bluenose	1921	Angus Walters
Gertrude L. Thebaud	1930	Ben Pine

Date: **9, 13, 23, 24, and 26, October 1938**
Title: **The International Fishing Vessel Championship, Gloucester, Massachusetts**

First Race

Gertrude L. Thebaud	1930	Ben Pine, by 2'50"
Bluenose	1921	Angus Walters

Second Race

Bluenose	1921	Angus Walters, by 12'10"
Gertrude L. Thebaud	1930	Ben Pine

Third Race

Bluenose	1921	Angus Walters, by 6'37"
Gertrude L. Thebaud	1930	Cecil Moulton

Fourth Race

Gertrude L. Thebaud	1930	Cecil Moulton, by 2'44"
Bluenose	1921	Angus Walters

Fifth Race

Bluenose	1921	Angus Walters, by 2'50"
Gertrude L. Thebaud	1930	

[1] Boston pilot boat No. 1, the *Hesper*, raced and finished ahead of the entire fishermen's fleet, but was not considered a regular entry. Unless otherwise noted, the following data originates from Lewis H. Story's, "Fishing Vessels Built at Essex That Were in Races," and "Notes on Fishermen's Races," Essex Shipbuilding Museum, Essex, Massachusetts.

[2] Story incorrectly places this race in 1887 (*Forest and Stream & Rod and Gun: The American Sportsman's Journal* 30 (26 January 1888-19 July 1888), 216, 235, 259, 12 April 1888).

[3] *Memorial of the Celebration of the Two Hundred and Fiftieth Anniversary of the Incorporation of the Town of Gloucester, Mass. August 1892*, (Boston: Alfred Mudge & Son, 1901), defines 1st Class as vessels with a waterline length of 85' to 110', and the 2nd Class as vessels of 50' to 85' on the waterline.

[4] On Friday, 13 October 1920, the *Gloucester Times* carried the story of a Canadian challenge to an international race, the winner to be declared the champion of the North Atlantic. On that same day, the Canadians were holding their elimination trials among the 120-strong Lunenburg fishing schooner fleet. There was no time left for Gloucester to set up and hold an elimination series, if a race was to be held that fall.

[5] This is the second time Sir Thomas Lipton's Cup, first won by the *Rose Dorothea* of Provincetown in 1907, was awarded.

[6] There is some confusion about Gloucester's anniversaries. "The Race That Blew" in 1892 was held during the city's 250th celebration of incorporation. The 300th Anniversary Race of 1923 recognized the date of Gloucester's first white settlement.

[7] The International Cup trustees declared the 1923 event "no race," due to a "rounding the mark" controversy involving the *Bluenose*.

[8] E.A. Goodick, "Schooner *Progress* Wins North Atlantic Title," *Atlantic Fisherman* 10 (September 1929):15-18.

[9] Ex-*Mary*.

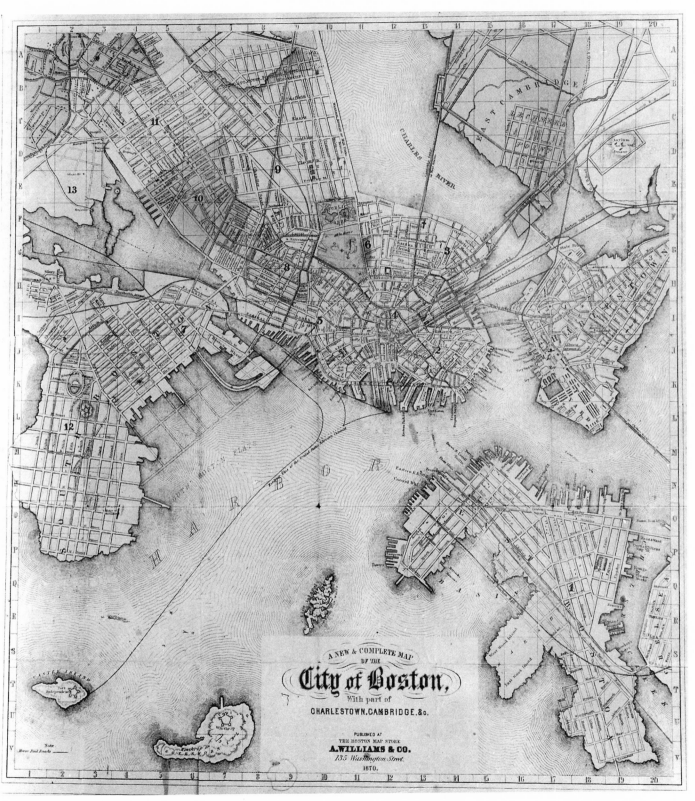

A NEW & COMPLETE MAP
OF THE
City of Boston,
With part of
CHARLESTOWN, CAMBRIDGE, &c.

PUBLISHED AT
THE BOSTON MAP STORE
A. WILLIAMS & CO.
135 Washington Street.
1870.

G.W. Blunt White Library, Mystic Seaport Museum

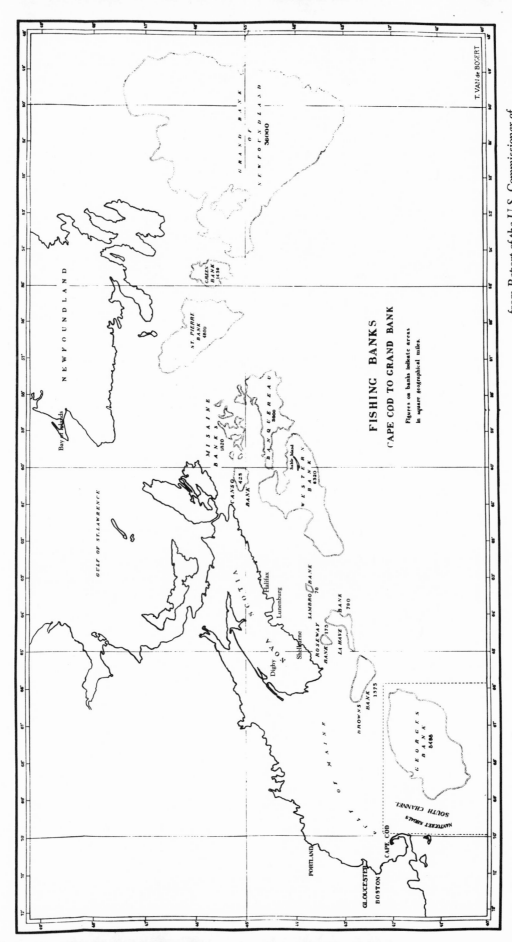

FISHING BANKS
CAPE COD TO GRAND BANK

Figures on banks indicate areas
in square geographical miles.

GRAND BANK
OF
NEWFOUNDLAND
36000

GREEN
BANK
1450

ST PIERRE
BANK
4800

NEWFOUNDLAND

Bay of Islands

GULF OF ST.LAWRENCE

MISAINE
BANK
1820

BANQUEREAU
3600

CANSO
BANK
425

Sable Island

WESTERN
BANK
8330

NOVA SCOTIA

Halifax
Lunenburg

SAMBRO BANK
70

Shelburne
Digby

ROSEWAY
BANK
175

LA HAVE
BANK
790

BROWNS
BANK
1375

GEORGES
BANK
8486

GULF OF MAINE

PORTLAND

CAPE COD

GLOUCESTER
BOSTON

SOUTH CHANNEL
NANTUCKET SHOALS

T. VAN de BOGERT

from Report of the U.S. Commissioner of
Fisheries for the Fiscal Year 1914

MAPS

A. Hubley, 369
A. Piatt Andrew (1912), 298, 368
A. Piatt Andrew (1922), 373
A. Roger Hickey, 374
A. S. and R. Hammond, 112-113
A. Shuman & Company, 242, 242n5
Abbie J., 59
Abbott, J. Norman, 323n14
Actress, 71-72, 76, 92-93, 93n29, 138, 158, 216
Acushla, 370
Adams, Charles Francis, 102, 124, 189n15
Adams, Frank, 243, 288-289, 296
Adams, Moses, 123, 147, 149, 161-162, 164-169, 169n32, 174, 213, 277
Adams, William Irving, 296
Adare, 271
Adeline, 367
Adirondack, 183
Adventure, 351, 373-374
Adventure: Queen of the Windjammers, 351
Ajax, 296-297, 297n9, 370
Alabama, 271, 273, 349-351, 349n12, 367
Alabamian, 349-351, 349n12, 351n17, 353, 373, renamed Alabama, 351n18
Albert J. Lutz, 256-259, 256n34, 279, 365
Alcina, 358
Alcyone, 216-218, 238, 361
Alda, 135
Alert, 209n55, 363
Alice (schooner), 278, 365
Alice (yacht), 151n63
Alice and Mildred, 373
Alice M. Guthrie, 264n7
Alice M. Pike, 367
Allard, Dean, 99n42
Allisin, Father J. W., 187
Aloha, 262n1, 263n6
America (schooner), 373
America (pilot boat), 59, 63n53, 185, 189-194, 196, 216, 357
America (yacht), 119, 122, 130n7, 136, 151, 188, 188-189, 189n15
America's Cup, see Racing and regattas
American, 316, 372
American Art Society, 187, 187n6
American Museum of Natural History, 296
American Revolution, 40n49, 53n30, 239
Ames, Butler, 189
Amy Hanson, 140n42
Androscoggin, 268
Angelina, 264n7
Angeline C. Nunan, 209n55, 369
Angie L. Marshall, 370
Anglo-American Reciprocity Treaty, 40, 40n49, 53n30, 61, 61n46
Anna and Julia, 373
Annie and Mary, 373
Anna Maria, 47, 93n29
Annie Perry, 197, 221, 238, 244-245, 244n16, 360
Annie M. Parker, 264
Antoine C. Santos, 370-371

Appomattox, 264
Appomattox Court House, Virginia, 56
Apt, John D., 279
Arabic, 294
Arbutus, 263n6
Arethusa, 251-253, 253n26, 285, 288, 301-302, 304-305, 313, 323, 364
Arginia, 256, 365
Arnold & Winsor, 191, 221, 226
Arthur, Chester A., 118
Arthur D. Story (1885), 112-113
Arthur D. Story (1912), 262n1, 347
Arthur D. Story (shipyard), 116, 128-129, 138, 140, 183, 205, 207, 223, 230, 237n1, 261, 264-266, 276, 278, 288, 290-291, 302, 305, 316, 325-326, 328, 344, 346
Arthur James, 264n7, 315
Artisan, 154
Aspey, Charles, 34
Aspinet, 217n16
Aspinwall, Thomas, 91
Athena, 252, 255, 255n30, 278, 364
Athlete, 262n1
Atlanta, Georgia, 305
Atlantic, 134
Atlantic Ocean, 7, 40-41, 54, 55, 61, 174-175, 221, 294
Atlantic Yacht Club, 235
Atwood, Nathaniel E., 34-38, 37n44
Australia, 11
Autocrat, 270-271, 291, 296, 367
Avalon, 264n7
Azores, 232n40

B. T. Hillman, 374
Babe Sears, 374
Bahamas, 301-302
Baird, Spencer F., 55n32, 78, 107, 111, 282
Baker, William Avery, 142
Balbriggan, Ireland, 7-8, 36, 79
Baltimore, 69
Banneret, 91-92, 102, 124
Barr, Charles, 151, 151n63, 163
Barr, John, 151
Barrett, Jack, 308n26
Bay State, 277-281, 284-285, 288-289, 291, 368
Bay State Fishing Company, 230
Beau de Rochas, Alphonse, 281n35
Belbina Domingoes, 209n55, 224, 361
Belgium, 10
Belle A. Keyes, 123n47
Belle J. Neal, 103, 132, 140n42, 164
Bemis, Seth, 16-17
Benham, Tom, 308n26
Benjamin A. Smith, 253, 364
Benjamin F. Phillips, 204, 229, 262, 262n1
Benjamin M. Wallace, 362
Benjamin Thompson, 373
Benjamin W. Latham, 200n39, 207-208, 207n52, 225-226, 232, 354, 359
Berlin Fishery Exposition of 1880, 106, 115
Bermuda, 218n19
Bertha Frances, 348, 373

Bessie M. Dugan, 364
Bethiah, 123n47
Bettina, 370
Beverly Yacht Club, 134
Binney, Arthur, 167, 167n25, 199, 204, 229, 347, 380
Binney, R. M., 63n54
Birdseye, Clarence, 69
Bishop, Hugh, 219, 264n9, 277n28
Bishop, John, 190, 194, 203, 219, 224-225, 230-231, 239, 242, 252, 277, 277n28
Black Hawk, 42, 46-47, 50, 55, 66n2, 191
Blanche, 135
Blanche F. Irving, 264n10
Blanche Ring, 320-322, 339, 355, 372
Blane, R. H., 89
Bluenose, 149, 313-317, 323-325, 329-335, 329n28, 330, 337-339, 347-348
Bohemia, 268-269
Bohlin, Tommy, 176-177, 180
Bond, P. M., 134
Bonita, 263n6
Bonner, R., 63n54
Booth, John Wilkes, 56
Boston, 12-13, 17-18, 17n9, 25, 28, 48-50, 56, 61, 65, 68n10, 75, 83, 99, 106n3, 119-120, 129-130, 130n7, 135-136, 139, 142, 150-151, 166, 187, 237, 253, 284, 287, 295, 344
  Algonquin Club, 240
  Atlantic Avenue, 77, 81-82, 87, 149, 163, 213, 229
  attitudes, of natives to Irish, 12-13, 16, 19, 22-23, 29, 41
  Back Bay, 12n35
  Bay, 62-63, 76, 90, 120, 124, 133, 142, 208, 215
  Brighton, 101
  Buck's Wharf, 50, 56-57, 158
  Charles River, 102, 154
  Chelsea, 42n56, 49, 67, 117, 158, 167, 270, 277
  City Club, 348
  city government of, 19n13, 298
    Irish members of, 79
  City Regatta, 91, 102
  City School Commission, 73
  Commercial Street, 18, 20, 23, 61, 100, 229
  Commercial Wharf, 29-30, 70-71, 77, 81-82, 86, 88, 91, 99, 120, 129, 150, 154, 165, 172, 191,
  Corporation, 102
  disease in, 17-18, 28-29, 30n20
  East Boston, 42n56, 46-47, 49, 76, 94, 147, 149, 150n63, 152-154, 158, 163, 189, 190, 314
  Evening High Schools ("Free Schools"), 153
    see also Charlestown, City School of Naval Architecture
  ferries, 49, 167n25
  fish market, 69, 87, 102, 154, 191-192, 213-214, 278, 284
  Fish Pier, 284
  fishing industry, 17, 20n17, 21-22, 23, 25-26, 28-38, 40-42, 52-56, 69, 87-89, 92, 102n51, 108, 112, 114, 130, 191-192, 200, 222, 228-230, 243, 249-250, 276, 282-284, 306
  fishermen's races, 130-133, 142-147, 174, 177-183,

228-229, 243-250, 314-315, 323, 335, 337, 341-342, 389

Great Fire of 1872, 73-74

Harbor, 18, 31, 46, 49, 65, 72, 114, 160, 165, 175, 177, 196, 222, 229, 234, 249, 256, 322-323

naval patrol, 296-297, pilot service, 189-190,

wartime restriction of, 298

"houses" for poor, prisons, and asylums, 19n13, 128

housing conditions in, 16, 18-19, 21-22

Irish emigrants' attitudes towards British, 133

Irish emigration to, 12-13, 12n37, 15, 17-19, 34-40, 42-43, 66, 79, 171

Irish move to suburbs of, 102, 199

Irish occupations in, 13, 16, 21-22, 29-36, 42, 45, 60, 73, 79, 87, 89, 101n50, 128, 287, 295

Italian emigration to, 102

labor unrest in, 130

Lewis Wharf, 31

Margaret Street, 62, 66-67

North End, 16, 18-19, 19n12, 20n17, 21-23, 26-28, 31, 42, 42n56, 47-50, 66, 68, 74, 79, 91, 100-102, 101n49, 154, 163, 183, 187, 199, 258, 326

Old Home Week, 243, 250

police and fire boats, 167n25

politics and ward structure, 42n56, 78-79, 87, 100, 102, 154, 171-172, 186-187, see also Democratic party

Portuguese community in, 258

Public Gardens, 295

Roxbury, 277n28, West Roxbury, 101

Russian Jewish emigration to, 102

Salem Street, 66-67, 67n6, 67n8

schools, see Charlestown, names of specific schools

South Boston, 123, 128, 152-153, 158, 284, 287-288

South Shore, 61

South Station, 298

T Wharf, 82, 88, 102, 154, 175, 191-192, 201-203, 222, 229, 240, 243, 245, 251, 262, 284

tax assessments, 67, 67n6, 67n8, 100, 182n53

Wood Island Park, 49, 49n17, 86

yacht clubs, 62, 62n49, 76, 89n14, 120

Boston *Evening Traveller*, 28, 49, 65n1

Boston *Globe*, 142-143, 151, 266

Boston *Herald*, 113, 150n63, 151, 177, 193, 195, 354,

Boston *Journal*, 133

Boston *Sunday Herald*, 253, 325

Boston Yacht Club, 62n49, 62n50, 76, 89-90, 89n14, 117, 134, 189, 240

Boynton, Edward P. ("Ned"), 102, 117-120, 129-130, 134-135, 240 see also N. Boynton & Company

Boynton, Nehemiah, 120

Bradford, Alfred, 229-230, 318

Bradley, Michael, 120

Braggs, George, 234

Brennan & Leonard (liquor dealers), 74

Brophy, Mike, 329

Brown, J., 91, 102, 124

Brown, Jim, 154

Brown, N. F., 91, 102, 124

Brown family, 99

Bruce, Wallace, 298, 308n26

Buckley, W. H., 102

Bud, 351n17

Buema, 209n55, 361

Bunker Hill, 113n18

Bunker Hill Yacht Club, 62n49

Bunting, Carrie M., 129-129, 183n55

Burgess, Edward, 119, 121-123, 128-131, 134-135, 137-141, 144-146, 147-150, 154, 159, 167n25, 170, 176, 183, 188, 191, 200, 207, 209, 224-225, 262, 273, death of, 166-167, 170n34, 380

Burgess, W. Starling, 194, 262-263, 314-315, 325, 346, 380

Burgess & Paine, 323

Burke, William H., 204

Burnham, Andrew, 163

Burnham, Henry D., 122, 131

Burnham, J. Horace, 264, 380

Burnham Brothers, 230

Burns, Arabella, 164n17

Burns, J. F., 124

Burtner, Evers, 331-332, 334-336

Butler, Benjamin F., 122, 151, 188-189, 188n12, 189n15

Butler, Paul, 89

Byrnes family, 11

Cadigan, Cornelius, 50, 51n23

Cadigan, Patrick, 51n23

Cadigan family, 37

California, 32n28, 87

Callanan, Lawrence J., 235, 235n45

Cambridge, Massachusetts, 50

Cameron, Rube, 176

Campbell, Malcolm, 71, 72n22, 93-94, 99, 151, 151n63, 380

Campbell & Brooks (shipbuilders), 71, 71n21

Canada, Dominion of, 298-299, 307, 314

fisheries and fishing industry, 40, 53n30, 74, 118-119, 123, 216-217, 242-243, 253, 255-256, 267-268, 279, 291, 298-299, 302, 306-307, 314-315

racing contenders, 119, 250, 306-308, 310-311, 313-316, 329, 331, 335-336, 347-348

rights for American fishermen, 61, 61n46, 78, 118, 251, 253

Cannon, John, 151

Cape Ann, 375

Cape Ann, Massachusetts, 40, 92, 142, 152n67, 165, 167n26, 177, 183n54, 188n8, 191-192, 239, 242, 268, 283, 315, 329, 347

Cape Ann Weekly Advertiser, 107-108

Cape Cod, Massachusetts, 57, 114, 161, 317

Cape Horn, 263n6

Cape Verde Islands, 232n40

Capillo, Carmello, 323n14

Captains Courageous (book), 175, (movie), 221

Carew, Joseph, 71

Carmen, 124

Carney, Mike, 171

Carnot, Sadi, 281n35

Carrie and Annie, 103, 124

Carrie E. Phillips, 138-146, 145n53, 148-149, 159, 176, 194

Carrie M. Wamback, 274, 368

Carrie S. Roderick, 374

Carrie W. Babson, 144-145

Carrier Dove, 103, 136

Carroll, Jim, 128

Carroll, Tom, 128, 137

Carruth, Henry Pope, 239, 305-306

Carruth, Herbert Shaw, 239

Carruth, Letitia McManus (daughter of Tom McManus), 101n49, 125, 154, 209, 239, 305-306

Cassin family, 100

Catboat, 129, 134

Catherine, 285, 288-291, 290n53, 307, 322, 369

Catherine and Ellen, 262n1

Catherine G. Howard, 362

Catherine L. Burke, 209n55, 361

Cavalier, 224-226, 305, 360

Caviare, 177, 182

Cawley, Denny, 171

Chapelle, Howard I., 33n32, 37n44, 56, 72, 147, 168n30, 190, 190n16, 192, 197n32, 200n39, 216-217, 216n13, 217n16, 225, 227, 243n12, 264n7, 264n9, 276-277, 285

Chapman, John W., 147n57, 149n62

Charles A. Laskey, 59

Charles Frederick, 128

Charleston Bar Pilots Association (South Carolina), 271

Charlestown, Massachusetts, 42n56, 84-85, 85n6, 89, 101, 125, 146, 154, 165n18, 182, 187, 198-199, 352

City School of Naval Architecture, 73, 151-154, 161, 163, 171, 182, 193

School Committee, 152

U. S. Navy Yard, 153, 153n69, 158, 295, 297

Chicago, 283

Chisolm, John, 209, 317n7

Church, Albert Cook, 246

Civil War, 40-43, 46, 49, 53, 53n30, 55-56, 69, 118, 120n35, 160, 171, 188-189

naval losses in, 50, 51n23, 52

Clara G. Silva, 237n1, 363

Clark, A. Howard, 87-89

Clark, Arthur H., 167

Clark, George H., 129

Claudia, 264

Cleveland, Grover, 118-119

Clintonia, 222-224, 237, 240, 242-243, 242n10, 252, 270, 364

Clintonia (Canada), 243, 364

Coal mining, dangers of, 160

Coaster, 7, 62, 108

Cobb, Solomon C., 79

Cobb, Solomon T., 140n42, 164n17

Cobb family, 99

Cohasset, Massachusetts, 194, 203

Cokeley, Annie, 83n4

Cokelely, Charles William, 83

Cokeley, Helena, 85

Cokeley, Letitia Mary Bradley, 83, 85

Cokeley, Willy, 29n16, 92n26

Cole, Tim, 142, 145

Coleman, Son & Company (fish dealers), 71

Collins, David, 106

Collins, Eliza Sawyer, 106

Collins, Captain Joseph W., 33-34, 34n33, 54-55, 55n32, 57, 105-108, 106n3, 110-113, 115, 133, 148, 188, 195

Colson, Charles C., 323n14

Columbia (America's Cup yacht), 151n63, 163, 216

Columbia (international fishermen's race schooner), 263, 346-347

Comer, Charles E., 75

Comer's Commercial College, 75, 238

Commissioners of Inquiry into the State of the Irish Fisheries, 8-9

Commonwealth, 369

Commonwealth Ice & Cold Storage Company, 284

Condon, Winifred, 93n29
Confederate Army of Northern Virginia, 56, Navy, 188
Conland, James, 175
Conley, Joseph, 183n55
Connaught Ranger, 47
Connecticut, 112, 133, 165, 207, 281, 287n45, 295, 349
Connolly, Dominick, 37
Connolly, James Brendan, 99, 116, 250, 307-308, 310
Connolly, Tim, 123n46
Constellation, 163, 199, 246, 262, 262n1
Convention of 1818, 40n49, 53n30, 61n46, 118
Coolidge, Calvin, 311
Cooney, Marion, 308, 323n14, 324, 331, 335
Cora Dee, 103
Corte Nord, 372
Costa, Leandro J., Jr., 258
Costa, Manuel, 244, 246-249
Cotton textile industry, 16-17
Cowley, Richard V., 350
Cox & Stevens (New York), 390
Creighton, F. F., 89
Cricket, 102, 124
Crocker, Aubrey, 121-122, 144-145, 151, 151n63, 163
Cross, Charley, 123n47
Crowell, Captain, 197
Crowinshield, Bowdoin B., 174, 204n46, 204-207, 209, 212, 225, 263, 287, 380-381
Cruising Club of America, 299
Crusader, 134
Cuba, 263n6
Curtis, Henry, 221
Cutch, 4
Cutlass, 47
Cutter, Amos, 47, 381
Cutter, 268, 328, English, 7n14, 62, 106-107, 111, 114-115, 136
Cycia, 91
Cygnet, 50, 60
Cynthia, 277, 363

Dacey, Mary McManus, (daughter of Tom McManus), 166, 209, 354n24
Dalby, Henry C., 137n32
Dalton, George D., 254
Dancing Feather, 58n42
Daniel O'Connell, 37, 47
Daniels, F. A., 91-92
Daniels, Josephus, 297
Dartmouth College, 343
David Crockett II, 90
Davis, Charles G., 216n13
Davis, J. C., 91
Dawn, 371
Delawanna, 310-311, 314, 335
Delaware, 137
Delphine Cabral, 276, 368
Democratic party, 74, 78-79, 118, 171-172
    Irish-Americans in, 21, 23, 41-42, 78-79, 119, 171, 187-188
Denby, Edwin, 334
Dennis, William H., 306, 314
Dennis Cup races, see Racing and Regattas
Depressions,
    Great, 352, stock market crash, 347
    of 1850s, 21-22

Panic of 1873, 75, 78
Panic of 1893, 182, 186
    post-World War I, 301, 305
Dever, Dorothy, 298
Dever, John (son-in-law of Tom McManus), 298
Dever, John, Jr., 298
Dever, Louise McManus, (daughter of Tom McManus), 146, 154, 172n40, 209, 298, 306
Devonshire, Duke of, 314
Diana, 264n10
Diesel, Rudolph, 280-281, 281n35
Dillingham and Bond (yacht skippers), 91
Disease,
    arthritis, 348
    cancer, 166, 306
    cataracts, 352
    cholera, 18, 70
    "consumption" (tuberculosis), 137, 147
    coronary sclerosis, 354
    diabetes, 147
    dysentery, 24
    gangrene, "senile", 147n56
    influenza, 298, 306
    "melaena", 70, 70n15
    "melancholia", 145n53
    "nephritis" (kidney disease), 173
    pneumonia, 74, 101n49, 140, 141n45, 171, 183
    "pulmonic phthisis" (tuberculosis), 140-141, 141n45
    rheumatic fever, 85
    scarlet fever, 28
    smallpox, 30n20
    typhoid fever, 101n49, 166
Dixie, 263n6
Dixon, Ellen, 147n57, 149n62
Domingoes, Manuel P., 347
Donahue, Father John W., 29n16, 30n20, 49
Donald G. Hollett, 368
Donnelly, John, 137
Dorchester, Massachusetts, 102, 125, 192, 199, 213, 234, 239, 287, 295, 297, 326, 328-329, 341, 342n1, 343, 351-352
Dorchester Yacht Club, 62n49, 63n54, 74n40, 76, 90, 92
Doris M. Hawes, 374
Dorothy II, 264
Dorothy G. Snow, 209n55, 267-268, 367
Dorothy M. Smart, 269, 305, 366
Dory and dory fishing, 35, 98, 115, 132, 139, 160, 174, 202, 215, 229-230, 232-234, 234n42, 259, 262-263, 288, 299, 316, 319-321, 335, 350-351
    see also Fishing industry, methods used in
Doyle family, 147
Dreadnought, 264n7
Dreamer, 203-204
Driscoll, Florence, 164n17
Driscoll, Johnny, 164
Driscoll, Mary, 164n17
Driscoll, Timothy, 51n23
Dublin, 4, 56, 133,
    Bay, 62, County, 4n5, 8-9, 21, 37, 43, 46, 70, 183, 355
Dun, R.G., & Company, 21, 66-67
Duncan, Father William H., 91
Dunne, F. L., 134
Dunsky, Peter, 233-234
Duxbury, Massachusetts, 42, 191, 203-204, 246
Dyson, John, 319n9
E. L. Rowe & Son (sailmakers and outfitters), 215, 255,

255n31
East Boston Yacht Club, 76-77, 101
Eastern Yacht Club, 62n49, 76, 119-122, 131, 144, 189, 189n15
Echo, 102
Eclipse, 52, 60, 230-232, 235, 235n45, 270, 363
Eda J. Morse, 320
Edith and Elinor, 374
Edith C. Rose, 305, 372
Edith Emery, 103, 123-124, 132, 140n42, 183
Edith J. Peterson, 221, 360
Edith Silveira, 364
Edna Wallace Harper, 262n1
Edwards, Morry, 320
Edwin Forrest, 51, 58n42, 158
Effie M. Morrissey, 211, 313
Effie M. Prior, 209n55, 363
Eglantine, 264n7
Eleanor DeCosta, 367
Eleanor Nickerson, 374
Eldridge-McInnis, Inc., 287
Electric Flash, 264n7
Eliot Grammar School, 62, 67-68, 68n10, 74, 154, 348, 348n10
Elizabeth, 50, 50-51n23
Elizabeth Howard, 224, 242-243, 243n12, 277, 286-287, 289-290, 296, 307, 314, 322, 329-330, 329n27, 343-344, 346-347, 370
Elizabeth Silsbee, 194, 262-263, 273-274
Elk, 223, 291, 316, 366
Ellen, 60
Ellen and Mary, 262n1
Ellen C. Burke, 222-223, 359
Ellen T. Marshall, 371
Ellis, James, 217
Elmer E. Gray, 221, 316, 360
Elmo, 263n6
Elsie (tug), 131
Elsie (schooner), 223, 255, 255n31, 262, 264-267, 265n12, 285, 290, 315-317, 323, 347, 366
Elsie F. Rowe, 177, 182
Elsie G. Silva, 203, 315, 369
Elwell, H. P., 91, 134
Em Ell Eye, 134
Emerald, 373
Emerson, William J., 123n49, 183n55
Emerson family, 99
Emery, Freeman, 123n49, 129, 164n17
Emery, James, Jr, 123n49
Emery, Victor, 282
Emilia Enos, 264n7
Emilia Gloria, 263n6
Emily Cooney, 208-209, 209n55, 225, 359
Emily P. Wright, 103, 123-124, 123n46, 131, 214
Emily Sears, 363
Em'ly, 65, 76-78, 83, 86, 89-92, 102, 114, 124, 129-130, 134, 239
Empress, 89
Endicott, William C., 118
Engines, 262-263, 271, 273, 275, 279-282, 302, 317, 319-320, 322, 339, 349-350, 351n18
    Blanchard oil power, 273, 279-281, 284
    Diesel engines, 280-281, 281n35, 317, 317n7, 320, 351n18
    Steam engines, 262-263, 271, 273, 275, 317
English High School (English Classical School), 70-71,

74, 348

Esperanto, 209n55, 307-311, 313-314, 335, 338, 363

Essex River, Massachusetts, 107, 116-117, 128-129, 138, 140-141, 147, 159, 161n9, 163, 167-170, 169n32, 183, 186, 191, 193-194, 197, 197n32, 199, 207, 214, 216n13, 217n16, 221, 225-226, 229, 232, 246, 248, 252, 261, 265-267, 271, 276-277, 284-285, 290, 305, 314, 325-327, 344, 350-351

Essex Shipbuilding Museum, 218, 334

Estes, J. Worth, 70n15

Esther Anita, 264n7

Ethel B. Jacobs, 176, 178-179

Ethel B. Penny, 254-255, 255n30, 365

Ethel Mildred, 209n55, 362

Eugenia, 209n55, 365

Eva G., 59, 123n47, 147

Evans, John, 51n24, 93n29

Evelyn M. Thompson, 255, 255n30, 365

Everdean, Joe, 57n38

Everett, Massachusetts, 228

Everett James (shipyard), 351

Exeter, New Hampshire, 17

Expert, 90-91, 134

F. C. Pearce Company, 301

F. Snow & Company, 82

Fabbri, Alessandro, 295-297

Fabbri, Ernesto, 295

Fabbri, Ernesto G., 295

Fabia, 317, 317n7

Fairy, 89, 91

Fallon, Pat, 26

Fame, 263n6

Fancy, 102, 135

Fannie Belle Atwood, 221, 360

Fannie E. Prescott, 361

Farrel, J. B., 134

Farrell, William, 67n8, 93n29

Faulkner, Neil, 62

Fenian, 57n38, 59

Fenwick, Bishop, 19n12

Fenton, Archibald, 264, 381

Ferrin, Samuel, 182n53

Fingal Coast, 4, 4n5, 6, 8-9, 11, 13, 19, 20n17, 21, 29-30, 37n40, 43, 355
    American assimilation of Irish from, 37, 79, 95, 128, 133, 136, 191, 239, 282, 342-343, 355
    English language of, 36-38

Finan, Henry, 191n19

Finan, Walter J., 191n19

Finback, 289-291, 290n53, 296, 307, 370

Fiona, 253

Firth, Lem, 269-270

Firth, Percy, 269

Fish, Atlantic, 5, 33, 41, 87, 106-107, 175, 180, 182, 201, 228, 255-256, 283
    as food source, 68-69, 132
    freshwater, 282, 319n9
    cod, 5, 26, 31, 33, 61, 82, 87, 95, 124, 175, 201, 230, 232n40, 266, 283
    flounder, 57, 87, 229-230, 318
    haddock, 26, 33, 36, 69, 82, 87, 95, 124, 201, 225, 230, 283, 315-316
    halibut, 33, 35, 69, 283-284, 316
    herring, 5-6, 40, 53n30, 61, 87, 253, 268, 270, 282, 319

mackerel, 33, 61, 82, 87
    roe, 165, 355
    red snapper, 222

Fish Commission, United States, 33n32, 55n32, 106-107, 111-112, 123-124, 133, 229n38, 282
    Division of Fishery Statistics, 106n3

Fish dealers and brokers, 69, 71, 75, 81-82, 87, 91, 101-102, 119, 124, 131, 153, 154, 213-214, 237, 243, 278, 284
    peddlers, 31

Fisheries and Fishery Industries of the United States, The, 87-88, 106

Fisherman's Own Book, 107

Fishing Gazette, The, 230, 320

Fishing industry,
    bounties for, 5, 7-11, 9n22, 60-61, 251
    costs of, to ship owners, 98, 174, 185
    Great Lakes, 282
    Ireland, 5-10, 8n19, 9n22, 31
    market for, 69, 87, 98, 118-119, 132, 160, 165, 191-192, 203, 229-230, 232, 232n40, 283, 291
    methods used in, 34-36, 106, 115, 229-230, 232, 262, 316-321
        auxiliary power, 271, 276, 278, 280-282, 317, 319-321
        beam-trawling, 55-57, 57n39, 60, 229-230, 318, 320
        dragging, 318-321
        gill netting, 282
        otter board trawling, 230, 317, 319-320, 319n9, 322
        steam trawling, 229-230, 232, 262-263, 316-317
        trawl-line, 34-36, 38, 42, 53, 98, 124, 319, 351
    New England, 17, 20n17, 21-22, 23, 25-26, 28-38, 40-41, 52-56, 53n30, 61, 66, 69, 73-74, 78, 81-82, 87-89, 92, 106, 114, 118-119, 123n51, 124, 158, 174, 185-186, 191-192, 201-203, 222, 225-226, 228-230, 229-231, 243-245, 251, 255, 262, 268,276, 278, 281-284, 288, 291, 306, 314, 317, 323
    banks fishery, 33-34, 40, 53n30, 69, 73, 88, 92-95, 105, 115, 124, 134, 142, 153, 161, 178, 180, 185, 201-203, 221-222, 226, 228-229, 232-234, 245, 256, 266-268, 284, 288, 298, 308, 329, 329n28, 344
    cod fishery, 33-34, 60-61, 87-88, 111, 124, 175, 191-192, 230, 232n40, 243, 282, 313
    halibut fishery, 33, 192, 242, 278, 316
    mackerel fishery, 33, 61, 87, 106-107, 111, 123n51, 161, 174, 192, 198, 221, 237, 244, 264, 271, 315
    market fishery, 29, 33-38, 41-42, 46-47, 51n23, 60, 69-72, 87, 93, 105, 112, 114, 191-192, 222, 276, 282, 329n28
    Pacific fishery, 278
    sealing, 234
    shore fishery, 26, 29-34, 33n32, 36-38, 41-42, 69, 318
    swordfishing, 196, 198, 271
    Canadian waters, in, 40, 53n30, 61, 61n46, 118, 233-234, 251, 268-269
    dangers of and losses in, 40-41, 52-54, 65, 67-68, 71, 96-99, 96n35, 105, 107-108, 110-111, 159-161, 174-175, 178, 202, 211, 216, 218, 227-228, 228n34, 233-234, 268-269
        attitude of fishermen toward, 160, 201-202
        fishing captains and, 98-99, 99n42, 110, 160-161
        World War I, 294, 298-299
    Irish domination of, 34-38, 41-42, 45, 71, 79, 82, 87-88, 93-94, 112, 114, 118, 123, 282-283
    Portuguese in, 241, 244, 250, 258
    profitability, 119, 124, 150, 174, 185-186, 266, 276,

318, 321, 323
    railroad distribution for, 41, 53n30, 69, 98
    safety of crew in, 93, 95-96, 158
    preservation of fish and, 41, 69, 106, 115, 124, 132, 232, 256, 283-284
    press, 295, see also specific papers
    regulation of, U.S., 60-61, 251
    see also Dory, Fish, Hooker, Schooner, Shipbuilding, Wherry

Fitzgerald, John F. ("Honey Fitz"), 31, 79, 154, 172, 172n40, 186-187, 191

Fitzgerald, Rose, 172n40

Fitzgerald, Thomas, 31

Fitzgerald family, 287

Fitzpatrick, Bishop John Bernard, 19n12, 22

Flaherty, John, 51n24

Fleming, Victor, 221

Flirt, 358

Flora L. Nickerson, 357

Flora L. Oliver, 367

Flora S. Nickerson, 195-197, 226, 245, 359

Florence, 58n42, 370

Florence E., 371

Florida, 137, 301-302, 349-350, 349n13

Flying Eagle, 59

Flying Fish, 47

Fogg, Rudolph O., 50-51n23

Forbes, J. Malcolm, 131-132, 144, 148

Forbes, Will, 266

Ford, Hobart, 348

Forest and Stream, 76-77, 114, 120, 130, 135, 138, 139-140, 144-145, 153-154

Fortuna, 122, 225, 263n6

Foster, Charles Henry Wheelwright, 189n15, 270, 289, 290-291, 290n53, 296, 307

France, 10

Frances P. Mesquita, 209n55, 224, 243-245, 247-249, 362

Frances S. Grueby, 367

Frances Whalen, 262n1

Francis J. O'Hara, Jr., 298, 361

Francis V. Sylva, 362

Franz Ferdinand of Austria, 283

Fredonia, 147-149, 150, 159, 162, 176, 194, 198, 200, 221, 262, 354

Freeman, George P., 140n42, 164n17

Freeman, N. D., 129

Freeman, S. P., 89-90

Freeman, Sibley A., 91, 134

Freeman family, 99

Freya, 135

Friendship, 123

Frisbee, John L., 73, 152-155, 159, 161-163, 174, 182, 193, 217, 238, death of, 266

Fuller, Charles F., 323n14

Gael, 63n53, 78, 78n47, 83

Galatea (*Fredonia*-type), 359

Galatea (Indian Header), 362

Galatea (yacht), 127, 133, 135

Garland, Joseph E., 55, 99, 351

Gaston, William O., 74, 79

Gawley, Henry C., 297, 297n4

Gem, 90-91, 102, 114

Genesta, 122, 127, 361

George H. Lubee, 225, 359

George Lawley & Sons (shipyard) 121, 123, 128-129,

133, 137, 288

George Parker, 264

Georgia, 255, 255n31, 288, 365

German, Andrew W., 229n38, 319

Germany, 10, 280-281, 281n35, 291, 293-294, 298-299

Gertie S. Winsor, 100, 124, 132, syndication of, 100, 103

Gertrude, 358

Gertrude DeCosta, 197n32, 368

Gertrude L. Thebaud, 263, 348

Gertrude Parker, 374

Gillie, Harry, 346

Gitana, 189

Gladys and Nellie, 365

Glasgow, Scotland, 234n42

Gleaner, 370

Gloriana (schooner), 169-171

Gloriana (yacht), 168, 168n30

Glory of the Seas, 158

Gloucester, Massachusetts, 33, 41, 53, 55, 69, 71, 92, 96, 102n51, 105-106, 108, 111, 113, 122, 123n47, 142, 144, 166-167, 169n32, 173-175, 184, 190-193, 195-196, 198, 202-203, 209, 215-216, 216n13, 220-221, 223-225, 228, 230-231, 239, 242-243, 245, 247-250, 252, 255, 264n9, 266, 268, 270-271, 277-278, 277n28, 280, 282, 288, 291, 298, 301, 306-308, 310-311, 313-316, 317n7, 319, 323, 325, 327-332, 335-337, 339, 342, 346-348, 351
  anniversary race ("The Race That Blew"), 175-182, 245, 335, 339, 389
  anniversary race (1923), 343-344, 346

Gloucester *Advertiser*, 142

Gloucester *Daily Times*, 152, 168, 170, 181-183, 188, 204

Gloucester Fresh Fish Company, 192

Goddard, George, 131

Golden City, 67, 67n6, 67n8

Golden West, 305

Good Hope, 263n6

Good Luck, 134, 264, 264n7

Goode, George Brown, 31, 33n32, 34, 36, 37n40, 79, 87, 111

Gookin, A. B., 137n32

Gordon M. Hollett, 267, 366-367

Gorton-Pew Fisheries Company, 243, 308

Gossip, 268, 358

Gossoon, 373

Governor Marshall, 371

Gov. Foss, 224, 272, 367

Grace, 91

Grace Darling, 357

Grampus, 112-113, 116, 133, 141-142, 147-148, 229n38

Grand Falls, 366

Grand Marshall, 371

Grant, Ulysses S., 56

Grayling, 176, 179

Great Britain, 7, 11, 61, 118-119, 314
  Act of Union with Ireland, 5, 7
  America's Cup racing and, 119-120, 122, 127, 130n7, 133, 136
  Corn Laws, 10, 10n26
  fishing industry of, 8n19, 55, 319, see also Cutter, English
  Irish attitudes toward, 133
  Parliament, 7-8, 8n19, 11
  Royal Navy, 5, 7n15, 133
  sailmakers of, 136

treaties with United States, 40, 40n49, 53n30, 74, 78, 118
  World War I, in, 291, 293-294

Green, Richard T., 270, 277

Greene, Albert S., 153n69, 154

Gregory, Bill, 27, 66, 75, 83n4, 100

Gregory, Edward ("Ned"), 75-76, 100, 101n50, 128, 128n3

Gregory, Emily Frances Leonard ("Little Em'ly") (daughter of Chris), 28-29, 29n16, 48, 75-76, 92n26, 100, 101n50, 133

Gregory, Maria Shannon, 30n20, 100, 101n50

Gregory family, 89, 100

Gresham, 268

Grimes, Patrick, 91

Griswold I. Keeney, 221, 359-360

Grocery and liquor businesses, see Liquor business

Grueby, George F., 237

Guild, Curtis, 251

Gulflight, 294

Hale, Frederick, 297

Hale, William H., 178, 180, 180n49

Halifax, Nova Scotia, 161, 305-307, 310, 314-315, 339, 346-348

Halifax Commission, 78, 118

Halifax *Herald and Mail*, 306, 313

Halifax *Morning Chronicle*, 267

Hall, Micky, 310-311

Hamilton, John, 381

Hammond, John Hays, 242, 339

Hand, William H., 381

Hanover Street Methodist Church, 68

Harmony, 263, 263n6

Harriett, 366

Harriet W. Babson, 264n7

Harrington, Frank E., 129

Harry L. Belden, 149, 169-170, 176, 179-180, 182, 264

Hartwell, Alice, 221

Harty, Charley, 142-145, 174, 176, 179, 252, 307-308, 310, 325, 336-337

Harvard University, 129, 187n6

Haskell, Charles L., 187

Haskins, Father George Foxcroft, 19, 19n12, 19n13

Haskins, L. M., 134

Hatch, Joseph, 222

Hatteras, 263n6

Hattie I. Phillips, 103, 123n47, 124, 128, 132, 140n42

Haverhill, Massachusetts, 17n9

Hawes, Charles Boardman, 99

Hayes, Rutherford B., 118, administration, 78

Hayward, George A., 137n32

Hazel R. Hines, 264n7

Healy, Father James A., 27

Helen, 151n63

Helen B. Thomas, 211-219, 216n13, 218n19, 222-225, 227-229, 235, 238, 243-245, 247-249, 270-271, 271n22, 288-289, 358

Helen G. Wells, 202-203

Helen Miller Gould, 198-199, 198n37, 228, 261, 264n7, 271, 281

Helja Silva, 371

Henn, William, 133

Henrietta, 209n55, 369

Henry Ford, 312-313, 323-339, 328n25, 329n27, 331n29, 331n20, 341-342, 344, 346-347, 372, naming of,

325, 325n18

Henry L. Marshall, 301-302, 370

Henry P. Williams, 271, 277, 368

Herbert, Elizabeth McGinnis, 48

Herbert, Jim, 46

Herbert, Jimmy (son of Tom), 49, 85, 85n6

Herbert, John T. (son of Tom), 49, 83n4, 101n49

Herbert, Mary J. E. Wilson (wife of John T.), 101n49

Herbert, Peggy (daughter of Tom), 49

Herbert, Tom, 20, 23, 37, 47-48, 60, 69, 85n6, 117, 128, 128n3, 282

Herbert family, 4, 8, 11, 20n17, 37, 89, 100

Herbert Parker, 302-303, 371

Herreshoff, Nathaniel, 90, 168, 168n30, 196-197, 235

Hero, 90-91

Hesper, 58n42, 59, 63n53, 122, 131-132, 144, 148, 190

Hesperus, 370

Hibernia, 51n24, 59, 71, 93n29

Hickey, John, 51n23

Higgins, Lewis H., 164n17

Hilda R., 367

Himmelmann, Tom, 310-311

Hingham, Massachusetts, 298

Hipson, Still, 308

Historic American Merchant Marine Survey (WPA), 200n39

Hodges, Wetmore, 348

Hoey, Father Patrick M., 4

Hogan, Felix, 316, 318, 329

Holland, 10

Hollett, William H., 266

Hollett Brothers Fish Company Ltd., 266, 267

Holy Cross College, 157

Hooker, Boston, 29-36, 31n23, 31n24, 34n33, 41, 78n47, 114-115, 139, 158

Hooker, Galway and Kinsale, 7, 7n14, 31-33, 31n24, 37n40, 114

Hooker, Skerries, 7n14, see also Wherry, Skerries

Hooton, Bill, 57n38

Hope, 263n6

Hortense, 237n1, 271n22, 363

House, Edward M., 298

Hovey, Chandler, 348

Hovey, Henry S., 122, 131

Howard, Willard W., 289

Howe, George Ripley, 131, 134

Hubbard, E. C., 154

Hubbard, John, 276

Hudson, George Story, 253, 302, 325

Hudson, W., 102

Hull Yacht Club, 63n54, 89, 91, 101-102, 117, 124, 134

Hullonean, 47

Hunt, Cassius, 123n49, 183n55, 213-214, 218, 289

Hunt, Charlotte M., 140n42

Hunt, Georgiana, 140n42

Hunt, R. G., 83, 134-135

Hurley, Catherine Cokeley McManus (daughter of Tom McManus), 125, 154, 209, 295, 295n2, 354n24

I. J. Merritt, Jr., 142-146

Ibex, 102

Ida M. Silva, 139, 221, 360

Ida M. Zinck, 368

Illinois, 264n7

Immigration, U. S., and demand for labor, 69

Italian, 102, Russian Jewish, 102
see also Boston, Irish emigration to, Irish occupations in
Imperator, 368
Independence, 204, 262n1
Indian Headers, 63n53, 174, 187-188, 192-199, 203-205, 207-209, 211, 213-226, 226n31, 228, 239, 242, 244, 253-259, 256n34, 267, 269, 271, 277, 281, 288, 296, 316-317, 354-355
Ingalls, E. Herbert, 102
Ingomar, 226, 235, 361
International Fisheries Exhibition (Bergen, Norway), 106n3, 187-188
International Marine Engineering, 214-215, 218
Ireland, 241, 293-294
    Act of Union with Great Britain, 5, 7
    attitude toward British landowners, 133
    County Clare, 101n50, 133, County Fermanagh, 4, 355
    emigration from, 7, 10-13, 15, 30, 35-38, 41, 342, 355
    English language in, 36
    fishing industry of, 5-11, 8n19, 9n22, 31, 55-56, 319, 319n9
    Gaelic language in, 37
    Gaelic-speaking farmers of South, 29-37, 42
    Grattan Parliament, 5
    potato famine, 10-11, 11n28, 13, 30, 34-38, 41, 171, 342
    rebellion of 1798, 7
    Society of United Irishmen, 7
    women of, 66, 74n34
    see also Dublin, Fingal Coast, etc.
Ireland, John de Courcy, 319n9
Irene and May, 264n7
Irish Sea, 3, 6-7, 16, 62
Irving, Thomas A., 202, 242, 264, 264n9, 381

J. M. Marshall, 369
J. P. Morgan & Company, 295
Jackson, Arthur L., 92
Jacobs, Sol, 176, 179, 319
Jamaica, 232n40
James and Esther, 360
James & Tarr (shipyard), see Tarr & James
James G. Blaine, 176, 170
James S. Steele, 152, 152n67, 161n9, 163, 167-171, 167n26, 173-174, 176-183, 185, 187-194, 196, 203, 205, 207, 211-213, 216-218, 223, 225-227, 237, 277, 323, 354, 357
    design of, 161-163, 168-169, 168n30, 173-174, 176, 178-180
James W. Parker, 243, 245-248, 362
Jane, 93n29
Jeannette, 366
Jehu, 123n46
Jennie and Agnes, 358
Jessie Costa, 197, 238, 243-249, 362
Jensen, Laurence, 264, 381
Joe Call, 170
Joffre, 316, 318, 371
John F. James shipyard, 217n16, 291, 305, 314, 325
John Hawes Fund, 153
John Hays Hammond, 209n55, 242, 294,364
John H. McManus, 49, 112-118, 124, 131-133, 137-139, 142-145, 145n53, 148, 158, 183, 216, 245, safety of, 116
John H. McManus & Company, 29-30, 30n21, 62, 67,

70-71, 77, 81-82, 120 see also John H. McManus & Son, Sailmaking industry
John H. McManus & Son, 93-95, 99-100, 119-123, 130, 133, 135, 137, 142, 147, 154, 172, outfitting service, 94-95, 119
see also John H. McManus & Company, Sailmaking industry,
T Wharf Supply Company
John J. Fallon, 217n16
John J. Flaherty, 264
John M. Brooks (shipyard), 153
John Pew & Company, 22
John S. Brooks, 264n10
John Thomas, 47
Johnson, Andrew, 188n12
Johnson, Francis A., 95
Johnson, Francis H., 123n49
Johnson, V. C., 316
Jones, Bassett, 347-348
Jorgina, 367
Jorgina Silveira, 374
Joseph H. Cromwell, 358
Joseph Henry, 46-48, 55, 60, 66n2, 67, 67n8, 147
Joseph P. Mesquita, 291, 370
Joseph Rowe, 176, 179
Josephine DeCosta, 197, 238, 366
Josie and Phoebe, 365
Joy, Charles L., 134
Judith, 102
Juniata, 63n53, 192-196, 219, 357
Juno, 264n10

Kattenhorn, Martin S., 299, 301, 348
Keach, Charles, 71
Keany, Mary Dolan, 83
Keany, Matthew, 21, 27, 31, 42, 67, 72, 72n25, 79, 83, 87, 93n29, 95, 100, 102, 128, 137n32, 147n57, 149n62, 154, 172n40, 187, death of, 171-172
Kearney, James, 123, 123n46
"Kedge", 77
Kelly family, 11, 20n17
Kennedy, Patrick Joseph, 79
Kentucky, 17
Kernwood, 209n55, 227, 229, 229n37, 271, 271n22, 361
Kernwood (Canadian), 255-256, 271, 364
Kerrigan, Timothy, 164n17
Kidney, John Augustus, 73, 79, 90
Kidney, Mary Ann Storrs, 83n4, 90, 101n49
Kidney, Patrick, 32n38, 66, 73, 79, 90
Kidney, Winnie, 101n49
Kilburn, A. S., 124
King family, 100
Kipling, Joseph Rudyard, 98
Kipling, Rudyard, 175
Kitty, 92, 102
Knickerbocker, 276, 278, 278n32, 291, 368
Knight family, 4, 100
Knockabouts, 207, 211-219, 216n13, 222-223, 226, 226n31, 228, 237-239, 242-245, 251-257, 259, 267, 270-271, 275-278, 282-291, 295-297, 302n18, 304-305, 307-308, 315, 323, 329, 337-339, 345-347, 350-351, 354-355
    "semi-knockabouts", 174, 209, 209n55, 220, 222-223, 226, 228, 242, 252, 255-256, 256n34, 258-259, 264-269, 272, 275-276, 288, 291, 299, 302-303, 308, 315-316, 318, 329-330, 354-355

Knoeckel, J., 299
Knowlton, L. D., 102
Kroes, Father Peter, 22, 22n28
Kunhardt, Charles, 135-136

L. A. Dunton, 316, 318, 329, 351, 372
Lady Thorn, 123n47
Lafayette, 221, 264n7
Lampee, Bill, 82
Lampee, Charles, 81-82, 87
Lampee, Mc Manus & Company, 81-82, 85n6, 86
    see also McManus & Company
Langworthy, Henry, 287n45
La Paloma, 278, 365
Lapthorns (sailmakers), 130, 136-137
Larbell, E. H., 102
Lark, 372
Laskey, Charles A., 46, 46n3, 46n4, 381
Laskey, Stephen, 46n3
Laskey, Wilbur, 46, 46n2, 48, 123n47, 147, 381
Laskey & McPhail, 381
Lathrop Company, 349
Laura Enos, 264n10
Laura Goulart, 372
Lawley, E. A., 153
Lawley, George, 121, 123, 128, 153, 158, 189n15
Lawley, George F., 153
Lawley family, 288
Lawlor, Caroline E. Littlefield, 50
Lawlor, Dennison J., 26, 26n3, 49-51, 51n24, 55-59, 56n36, 59n42 62, 63n53, 65, 68, 70-72, 71n20, 75-76, 92-94, 108-117, 113n16, 119, 132-133, 138-139, 148-151, 155, 158-159, 170, 176, 189, 209, 264-266, 275, 287-288, 381, death of, 166-167, 170n34, 171
Lawlor, Jr., 59
Lawrence, Massachusetts, 124-125
Lawson, Thomas W., 62n47, 203-205, 204n46
Laverna, 367
Lee, Robert F., 56
Lena, 89
Leo, 364
Leonard, Catherine McManus (Kate) (aunt of Tom McManus), 8, 18n10, 20-22, 21n24, 27n5, 28-29, 30n20, 48-50, 48n10, 57, 66-67, 66n2, 67n8, 70, 73-74, 89, 99, 141, second marriage to Patrick Grimes, 91, 183
Leonard, Charles (son of Dick), 29, 29n16, 48, 66, 73
Leonard, Chris, 20-23, 26-28, 23n32, 31, 48, 52, 60, 66-67, 73-74, 100, 128, 128n3, 133
Leonard, Christopher, 29, 29n16
Leonard, Dick, 20-22, 26-28, 27n5, 42, 46-48, 55-57, 60, 66, 66n2, 72, 91, 99, 147, 229-230, 282, 318, death of, 67, 70, 74
Leonard, Ellen (daughter of Dick), 48n10, 66, 101n50
Leonard, Ellen (sister of Chris and Dick), 48, 66
Leonard, Emily (daughter of Chris), 23n32, 28, 28n15
Leonard, Emily Frances ("Little Em'ly"), see Gregory, Emily Leonard
Leonard, Joseph Henry (son of Dick), 27n5, 28, 48, 83n4
Leonard, Julia Sweetman, 20, 22, 23n32, 27n5, 28, 48, 66, 100-101, 101n49
Leonard, Mary Ellen (daughter of Chris), 48, 52, 60, 100
Leonard, Matthew, 137n32
Leonard, Nicholas (son of Chris), 20, 22, 28, 48, 66, 73-

74, 83n4, 100, 128
Leonard, Richard Francis (son of Dick), 66, 66n2
Leonard, Thomas (brother of Chris), 20n18, 26-28
Leonard, Thomas (son of Chris), 20n18, 21n24, 29, 48, 100
Leonard, Thomas Joseph (son of Dick), 66
Leonard family, 4, 11, 20, 20n17, 37, 67, 89, 100, 171
Leonora C., 374
Leonora Silveira, 209n55, 368
Leretha, 374
Liberty, 190
Lillian, 263n6
Lillie, 58n42, 91
Lincoln, 373
Lincoln, Abraham, 56
Lincoln, Frank, 90-91
Lipton, Sir Thomas, 240-243, 250, 343
Liquor ("groggery") and grocery businesses, in Boston, 20-21, 23, 27-28, 30-31, 48, 48n11, 66-67, 73-74, 79, 100-101, 128, 128n3, 171, licensing of, 78
Little Elsie, 367
Little Ruth, 282-283, 368-369
Lizzie M. Stanley, 139, 199-203, 200n39, 358
Lloyd George, 366
Lodge, Henry Cabot, 129
London Fishery Exposition of 1883, 111
Long Island, 34, 130n7, 301-302, Sound, 232
Longfellow, Charles A., 131
Loring, William Caleb, 187, 187n6
Loring B. Haskell, 103, 123-124, 140n42
Losserand, Father Claude M., 27
Lottie, 83
Lottie G. Merchant, 264n7, 269
Lottie S. Haskins, 123n51, 159, 169-170, 177, 182, 200
Louette, 134-135
Louise B. Marshall, 338-339, 371
Louisa R. Silva, 200n39, 209n55, 241-242, 362
Louise C. Cabral, 361
Louise Howard, 296
Lovitt, Irving R., 255
Low, Benjamin, 230, 318
"Loyalty", 139-140
Lucania, 224-226, 315, 360-361
Lucy E. Friend, 123n51
Lucinda I. Lowell, 264n7
Lulu S., 365
Lusitania, 293-294
Lydia F., 319

Mabel, 134
Mack, Paddy, 243
Maggie and Hattie, 359
Maggie Sullivan, 140n42, 183, 183n55, 190, 214, 357
Magoun, Thatcher, 137n32
Mahoney, Daniel, 50-51n23
Mahoney, Eleanor Good, 295
Mahoney, James, 137n32
Mahoney, John, 295
Mahoney, Thomas, 123, 123n48, 128, 137n32, 164n17
Mahoney, Tim, 47
Maid of Erin, 37, 47
Maine, 33, 52, 83, 106, 114, 123n51, 214, 226, 243, 277, 287, 289, 295, 296-297, 301-302, 306, 317, 320
Malden, Massachusetts, 84n5
Malone, Henry Dexter, 219, 229-230, 232, 317, 319
Manhasset, 193, 208, 225, 244, 281, 317, 319, 358-359

Manning, Andy, 57n38
Manomet, 193, 205, 244, 296, 358
Manta, Philip P., 323
Marblehead, Massachusetts, 33, 41, 114, 120, 179
Marblehead Yacht Club, 90, 134
Marechal Foch, 371
Margaret A. Jones, 59
Margaret Dillon, 363
Marguerite Haskins, 159, 264n7, 269
Marjorie Parker, 373
Marne, 370
Marr, John, 147n57, 149n62
Martin, Ambrose, 190
Mary (Binney), 262n1, 347
Mary (Mullins), 320
Mary Amanda, 93n29
Mary C. Santos, 197, 238, 245, 271, 362
Mary Celeste, 174
Mary DeCosta, 209, 209n55, 258, 267, 365
Mary E. Cooney, 264n7
Mary E. Harty, 198, 264n7
Mary E. O'Hara, 207n52, 372
Mary E. Silveira, 361
Mary F. Chisolm, 230
Mary F. Curtis, 221, 360
Mary Frances, 46-48
Mary F. Sears, 368
Mary P. Goulart, 367
Mary P. Mesquita, 358
Mary Sears, 350, 373
Mary T. Fallon, 358
Mary Tracy, 93n29
Mary Y. Yates, 51n24, 59, 71
Maryland, 189, 189n15
Maschinenfabrik Augsburg-Nuremberg, 280-281, 281n35
Mason, James, 323n14
Mason, Samuel W., 68
Massachusetts, 193, 269, 358
Massachusetts, 11, 52, 56, 73, 188n12
    Bay, 34, 36, 40-41, 59, 61, 63n53, 119, 212, 249
    Bay Yacht Club, 89n14, 114
    Fish and Game Commission, 106n3
    General Court, 17n9, 152
    governor, 314
    shoe manufacture, 87
    supreme court, 817n6
Massachusetts Institute of Technology, 142, 167n25, 239, 331
Massasoit, 63n53, 193, 195-196, 267, 358
Matchless, 195-197, 226, 238, 245, 359
Mather, Cotton, 19n12
Mather, Increase, 19n12
Matheson, John, 308n26
Matiana, 255n30, 257, 365
Mattakeesett, 193, 195-196, 205, 222, 357
Mattapan-Milton News, 354
Matthew S. Greer, 366
Maud F. Silva, 360
Mauritania, 393-394
Max Horton, 371
Maxine Elliott, 358
Mayflower (America's Cup yacht), 128-131, 133-135, 137-138, 178, 183, 189
Mayflower (international fishermen's race schooner), 263, 314-315, 323, 329, 329n28, 339
McCarthy, Charley, 123n47

McCarthy, Jeremiah, 123, 123n47, 128, 137n32, 147, 147n57, 149n62
McClain, George Melville, 123, 123n51, 142-143, 146, 152-154, 159, 167, 169-171, 176, 186, 198-200, 203, 211, 221, 228, 261, 263-264, 264n7, 264n9, 269, 271, 315, 381-382
McCormack, Annabel, 287
McCormack, Bill, 63n53, 78, 78n47, 83
McCoy, William F. "Bill", 301-302, 302n18, 305, 323
McCurdy, Robert, 347
McDonald, Alexander, 323n14
McDonald, Johnny, 176, 179
McDonald, "Little Dan", 221
McGill, Joseph, 255, 267, 269
McGill Shipbuilding (Nova Scotia), 217, 255-257, 267-268, 279
McGinnis family, 11, 101
McInnis, Joseph, 287
McInnis, Walter J., 287-288, 353
McKann, Francis, 38
McKay, Donald, 158, 189, 381
McKay, John H., 154
McKay, W. C., 267
McKenzie, Leonard B., 382
McKinley, Tom, 99
McLaughlin, Anna, 187
McLaughlin, James, 187
McLaughlin, Thomas, 51n24, 72n25, 93-95, 93n29, 100, 132, 151, 187
McLeod, Archie A., 288
McMahon, Father Thomas, 8
McManus, Agnes Kidney (wife of Tom's brother, Charles), 32n28, 90, 95, 100, 101n49, 102, 125, 137, 147, 164, 199
McManus, Alice (daughter of Tom McManus), 92-93, 92n26, 101, 125, 154, 209, 213n2, 239, 348, 352, 354n24
McManus, Ann, 253n27
McManus, Ann Herbert (grandmother of Tom McManus), 8, 18, 21, 48, 66, 70, 74, 74n34
McManus, Catherine Cokely ("Kate") (wife of Tom McManus), 83-85, 83n4, 85n7, 89, 92, 101, 101n49, 124, 130, 146, 149, 154-155, 163-164, 166, 173, 187-188, 191, 191n19, 198-199, 209, 239, 294-295, 306, 343, 351-354
McManus, Charles (grandfather of Tom McManus), 4, 8, 11-12, 16, 18-19, 21, 23, 29-30, 70, 73-74, 81, 89n16, 164
McManus, Charles (great-grandfather of Tom McManus), 4, 4n6
McManus, Charles (son of Charles A.), 147, 164, 199
McManus, Charles (son of Charles Francis), 295n1
McManus, Charles (uncle of Tom McManus), 8
McManus, Charles Aloysius (brother of Tom McManus), 19n14, 23, 26, 28-29, 32, 48-49, 51-52, 61-62, 70, 73, 75-79, 83, 83n4, 85-87, 89-95, 99-102, 101n49, 101n50, 118-121, 120n34, 123-125, 128-130, 133-135, 137-138, 137n32, 157, 158, 164n17, 183, 199, 214, 239-240, 287, 336, 355, death of, 140-142, 141n45, 146, 151, 154, 164, 172
McManus, Charles Francis (son of Tom McManus), 155, 209, 242n10, 294-295, 295n1, 295n2, 342n1, 343, 354n24
McManus, Charles T. (son of Patrick), 73, 165n18, 295n2
McManus, Edwin Charles (grandson of Charles A.),

McManus, Elizabeth (aunt of Tom McManus), 8

McManus, Elizabeth (great-aunt of Tom McManus), 4-5

McManus, Elizabeth Reilly (great-grandmother of Tom McManus), 4

McManus, George A. (brother of Tom McManus), 19n14, 29, 29n16, 48, 61, 70, 75, 83, 86, 89, 92, 94, 100-102, 101n49, 120, 124-125, 128, 134-135, 137-138, 137n32, 158, death of, 147, 151, 164

McManus, George James (son of Tom McManus), 187, 209, 219, 294, 295n2, 352, 354n24

McManus, Honora Doyle (wife of George), 124-125, 137

McManus, John Herbert (father of Tom McManus), 8, 11, 11n29, 16, 18-19, 22-23, 26-30, 27n5, 30n20, 32n28, 42, 46-52, 55-63, 66-68, 67n8, 70-73, 75-77, 81, 85-86, 89, 92-96, 93n29, 99-100, 101n49, 101n50, 102, 118-119, 121, 123, 125, 128, 128n3, 137-138, 137n32, 140n42, 141-142, 147, 147n57, 149n62, 154, 157-158, 164, 164n17, 171-173, 182-183, 182n53, 191, 214, 229-230, 265-266, 282, 318, 326, 355, death of, 183, 187

McManus, John Herbert (son of Charles A.), 95, 102, 118, 147, 164, 183, 199

McManus, John, (great-uncle of Tom McManus), 4-5, 21n24

McManus, Kathleen Colligan (wife of George James), 352

McManus, Joseph (brother of Tom McManus), 52, 141

McManus, Louis (brother of Tom McManus), 19n14, 29, 29n16, 49, 61, 70, 75, 83, 85, 141

McManus, Lucy Ann Shannon (wife of John H.'s brother Pat), 30, 30n20, 89, 128n3, 173, 173n42

McManus, Margaret (great-aunt of Tom McManus), 4-5

McManus, Margaret Harriet Sweetman ("Meg") (mother of Tom McManus), 22-23, 26-27, 30n20, 48-49, 52, 57, 61-62, 66, 70, 85, 119, 141

McManus, Mary Ann Storrs ("Minnie") (daughter of Charles A.), 101n49, 102, 125

McManus, Mary Frances Mahoney (wife of Charles Francis), 294-295, 295n1, 343

McManus, Patrick (uncle of Tom McManus), 8, 18, 21-22, 28-31, 30n20, 49, 66-67, 70, 73-74, 91, 89, 128n3, 141, 147, 173, 295n2

McManus, Thomas Francis ("Tom"), 92, 99, 102, 120n34, 130, 137-138, 209, 219, 231, 256, 260, 312-313, 340

  America and, 188-190

  appearance of, 82, 325

  baptism of, 19n14, 27-28

  birth and infancy of, 27-28,

  birthdays, fiftieth, 239, sixtieth, 291, seventieth, 351

  blindness of, 352-353, 353n22

  boyhood of, 29, 48-50, 52, 57, 61, 86, 158

  "Captain" Tom, 187, 355

  car purchased by, 348

  Carrie E. Phillips and, 145, 145n53

  cemetery lot purchased by, 352, 352n21

  children of, 154, 165n18, 173, 198-199, 207, 213, 239, 252, 294-295, 295n2, 298, 305-306, 326, 342n1, 352, 354n24.

  birth of, 84-85, 87, 89, 92, 101n49, 125, 146, 155, 164, 166, 188, 191, 198

  courtship and marriage of, 83-85

  death of, 353-354

  death of aunt, 101, of brother, 140, 146-147,

of Dennison Lawlor, 166-167, of mother, 101n49

  descendants of, 27, 62n47

  family responsibilities of, 146-147, 154-155, 163-164, 172, 182-183, 213

  family vacations and, 62, 62n47, 164, 166

  fish brokerage of, 81-82, 86-87, 92, 95, 119, 145-146, 149-152, 154-155, 163, 165, 182, 187, 191, 198, 213, 355

  fishermen's races, organizer of, 130-132, 136, 143-144, 155, 174, 183, 204-205, 240-244, 306, 335, 339, 341-342

  Fitzgerald, John F., and, 154, 172, 172n40

  forebears of, 3-5, 7-8, 11-13, 20n17

  frugality of, 165, 196-198

  Henry Ford and, 323-337

  homes of, 84, 89, 101, 173, 182, 199, 213, 287, 342n1, 343, 343n3, 343n4, 351-352, 352n30

  Indian Headers and, 192-194

  James S. Steele and, 163, 167-171, 176-182

  John H. McManus and, 113-118, 143-144, 145n53

  Lipton, Sir Thomas, and, 240-242

  Metamora and, 203-204

  naming of, 27n10

  Nellie Dixon and, 147-149, 161, 199-200

  Portuguese fishermen, opinion of, 241

  professional success as naval architect, 173, 185-188, 193-194, 198, 205, 226, 240, 243-244, 261, 270, 298-299, 32-323, 353

  in Canada, 255-257, 267, 302, 305, 325

  radio purchased by, 352

  real estate investments of, 165n18, 182, 182n53, 187, 198, 207, 213, 343n3, 352

  religious convictions of, 75, 83-84

  Roosevelt, Theodore, and, 250-252

  schooling of, 52, 67-68, 68n10, 70-71, 75, 348

  ship designs of, 59, 63n53, 71, 96, 115-117, 137-139, 141, 147, 161-163, 165-169, 168n30, 173-174, 182-183, 185-200, 188n9, 200n39, 202-209, 207n52, 211-229, 216n13, 218n19, 220n21, 232-233, 234-235, 237-245, 252-259, 263-265, 264n7, 267-280, 271n22, 282-285, 288-291, 293-302, 305, 308-309, 313, 315-316, 318-326, 330, 337-339, 341-342, 345, 348-351, 353-355, 357-379

    auxiliary power in, 239, 262, 271, 275, 278-280, 282-283, 302, 319, 338-339, 345, 349-350

    awards for, 106n3

    capacity, problem of, 174, 185-186, 193, 213, 217, 222, 226, 228, 238, 271

    convex bow, 190, 200, 205, 221, 224, 226, 354

    knockabout bow, 212-214, 219-220, 223

    long bow, 209, 255

    round bow, 208-209, 220-227, 234n42, 242, 244-245, 258-259, 267, 294, 308, 315-316, 347, 354

    copying of, unauthorized, 196-198, 197n32

    gift for, 157-158, 323

    hospital schooner, 295-297

    loftsmen's contribution to, 284-285, 287

    powered vessel, 320-322

    "reserved power", concept of, 162, 196, 212, 222, 272

    rigging plans, 228, 252-255, 258, 267, 318, 331, 337, 345-346, 349

    rockered keel, 224-226, 226n31

    safety in, 159-162, 193, 203, 212, 217-218, 222-223,

226-228, 233, 238, 253, 265, 271, 287, 291, 354

  training in ship design, 49-52, 54, 62-63, 68, 70, 72-73, 75, 77, 93-96, 113-114, 148-154, 158-159, 182, 323

  ship models of, 49, 52, 82, 86, 138-139, 151-152, 161-163, 161n9, 165, 183, 187-188, 190, 190n16, 213, 218, 226, 284, 295-296

  ships owned by, 123, 128, 137n32, 140n42, 147, 147n57, 149n62, 164, 164n17, 182-183, 183n55, 206, 213-214, 263, 287, 352

  stock investments of, 352

  students and apprentices of, 287-288

  temper of, 168-169, 277, 341-342

  yachts, opinion of, 205

  youth of, 75, 77, 81-83, 86

McManus, Thomas Francis, Jr. (son of Tom McManus), 188, 209, 295n2, 298, 354n24

McManus, William Kenneth "Ken" (son of Tom McManus), 198, 209, 294, 295n2, 298, 348, 352n20, 353, 354n24

McManus & Company (fish brokers), 87, 95, 119, 149-151, 163, 165, 182, 187, 213, see also Lampee, McManus & Company

McManus family, 27, 37, 40-42, 45, 65, 89, 91-92, 95, 99-100, 103, 115, 117, 132, 136, 141-142, 148, 171, 199, 209, 233, 241, 288, 291, 305, 326, prosperity and social rise of, 29-30, 42, 47-49, 62, 66, 70, 72n25, 128n3, 154, 342-343

McNally, Jimmy, 151

McPhail, John H., 46, 46n4, 151, 382

McVey, Adolphus G. ("Dolly"), 151-153, 151n63, 153, 177

Mediterranean Sea, 256

Merchant, Orlando, 199, 252

Meridian, 123n47

Merriam, 123n47

Mesquita, Joseph P. ("Smoky Joe"), 245, 248, 298

Metamora, 193, 203-204, 359

Mettacomett, 221, 360

Mexico, Gulf of, 222, 348, 351n17, Gulf Stream, 301

Mildred Robinson, 221, 360

Mildred Silva, 374

Miller, Al, 225

Miller, Grace Agnes McManus (daughter of Tom McManus), 89, 89n16, 101, 125, 154, 191n19, 209, 213n2, 239, second marriage to Mr. Clark, 354n24

Miller, Joseph (son-in-law of Tom McManus), 239

Millerick, Father Jack, 191n19

Millerick, Father Jerry, 89, 89n17

Millet, Arthur, 181

Milton, Massachusetts, 114, 120n34, 165, 351-354

Mina Swim, 204, 223, 254, 360

Minot's Ledge Light, 179, 203-204, 245, 294

"Minot's Light Gale", 17, 41

Mobile, Alabama, 349-351, 353

Mobile Bar Pilots Association (Alabama), 271, 349-351

Moby Dick, 23, 36-37, 47

Mohican, 122

Monitor, 199

Montross, Bill, 16, 18-19, 30n20, 47, 50, 60, 66, 70, 282

Montross, Catherine ("Kitty"), 50

Montross, Charles, 21, 29, 66, 70, 73

Montross, George Warren, 30n20

Montross, Margaret Mary McManus ("Mary") (aunt of Tom McManus), 8, 16, 18-19, 30n20, 50, 66, 66n2, 70, 74, 141

Montross, Mary, 21, 30n20
Montross family, 89, 100
Mooanam, 221, 360
Moonlight, 47
Mooween, 193, 220, 222-223, 272, 360
Morison, Samuel Eliot, 41
Morning Star, 59, 363
Morrissey, Clayton, 253, 301, 312-313, 323, 323-334, 338-339, 344, 346-347
Morrissey, Winnie, 326
Moulton, Cecil, 348
Mugwump, 134
Mullen, Lawrence, 51n24, 93n29
Mullins, Dan, 320
Muriel, 263n6
Murphy family, 37
Murray, Joachim, 202
Murray, Lee, 308n26
Murray, William, 37
Musgrave, M. D. C., 91
Mystic Seaport Museum (Connecticut), 316, 318
Mystery, 361
Myth, 135

N. Boynton & Company, 120, 130, 135
Nahant, Massachusetts, 179, 249
Nannie C. Bohlin, 176-180
Nantucket, Massachusetts, 17n9, 40, 201, 318
Napoleonic wars, 3, 7n15
Nason, Rachel, 140n42
Nason family, 99
Natalie Hammond, 369
Natalie J. Nelson, 221, 360
Nathaniel L. Gorton, 290, 371
National Museum, United States, 33n32
Nautilus Yacht Club, 90-91
Neagle, Father Richard J., 84-85, 84n5, 89n16, 92n26, 101n49
Neal, John R., 123n49, 129, 164n17
Nellie B. Nickerson, 198, 264n7
Nellie Dixon, 123n47, 147-150, 148n60, 159, 161-164, 176, 183, 188, 188n9, 193, 198-200, 207n52, 213, 216-217, 221, 262, 315, 354
Nellie T. Walters, 372
NELSECO, 263n4, 275, 281, 317
Neponset, Massachusetts, 288
Nettie, 83
New Bedford, Massachusetts, 320
New Brunswick, 26n3, 50
New England, 69
New England Fish Company, 278
New England fishing industry, see Fishing industry, New England
New England storms and weather, 17, 25, 28, 40-41, 45, 49, 54, 65, 68, 70, 73-74, 99, 173-174, 177-180, 194, 201-203, 262
New Jersey, 271, 301-302
New London Ship & Engine Company, see NELSECO
New Orleans, 188
New York City, 69, 75, 101n50, 120, 127-128, 130, 135, 139, 154, 172, 203, 226-227, 229n37, 235, 287n45, 295-296, 299, 306-307, 348, 352n20
New York State, 34, 69, 130n7, 299, 301-302
New York *Times*, 354
New York Yacht Club, 120, 122, 134-135, 137-138, 189, 205, 232, 235

Newfoundland, 33, 40, 78, 161, 233-234, 234n42, 266-269, 282, 284, 294, 316
Nickerson, Herbert W., 320-321
Nickerson, Jonathan D. S., 383
Nickerson, Winfield S., 91
Nixie, 135
Nokomis, 221, 264n7
Nora, 129, 134-135, 239
Norris, Mr. (tutor), 71
Norseman, 363
North Carolina, 73-74
North Sea, 299, 319
North Star, 47
Norville, Joseph H., 349-350
Norway, 106n3, 187
Norwell, Massachusetts, 217
Notre Dame University, 165
Nova Scotia, 153, 159, 161, 216-217, 243, 255, 258, 263, 267-269, 272, 274, 279, 294, 298, 305-306, 306n22, 313-316, 325, 339, 346-348
Nuremberg, Germany, 280-281

Oakes, William H., 69
O'Brien, Hugh, 79
O'Brien, Johnny, 49, 117, 124, 132, 145, 245
O'Brien, Mike, 128
O'Brien family, 20n17
Ocean Queen, 47
O'Connor, Pat, 51n24
O'Donnell, Patrick, 51n23
O'Hara, Francis J., 136, 137n32
O'Hara family, 11, 37, 344
O'Hare, John, 67n8
Ohio, 305-306
Old Glory, 374
Olivia Domingoes, 207n52, 221, 359
Olivette, 261, 371
Olsen, Charley, 166, 177-179, 181-182
Onato, 226, 288, 361
Oneco, 34-35
O'Neil, Valentine, 245, 248
O'Neill, Father Henry, 83n4
Oretha F. Spinney, 305, 351, 372
Oriole, 224-225, 240, 242-243, 252, 264-265, 268, 270, 287, 289-290, 325, 364
Osceola, 135
Osgood, J. A., 102, 114
Ossipee, 328
Otto, Nikolaus, 281n35
Oxner, Edwin, 217
Oxner & Story, 200, 214, 217-220, 226, 238

P. C. 247, 328
Pacific Ocean, 278
Paine, Charles Jackson, 120-122, 120n35, 128, 130-131, 133, 137
Paine, Frank C., 263, 328, 348, 383
Paine, Belknap, & Skene, 348
Paladin II, 271
Palmer, S. P. 353
Paragon, 209n55, 359
Parker, George H., 95, 140n42
Parker, James P., 187
Parker family, 99
Parsons, Wallace, 347
Patrol boat, 253, 302, 396-397

Patten, Roy, 308n26
Pearce, Frank C., 336
Pearl, 135
Peeples, George H., 339
Pensacola Shipbuilding Company, 349-351, 349n13, 350n15
Pentz, Amos, 217, 255, 267-278
Perkins, Edwin, 329, 344, 383
Perkins, Charles A., 89
Perry, Marion, 244-245, 244n16, 248, 250-251
Petrel, 135
Pevear, Mrs. Dustin, 352n21
Phantom, 58n42
Philadelphia, 17, 69, 283
Philip P. Manta, 188n9, 264n7, 315, 347, 359
Phillips, Benjamin, 123n49, 131, 147n57, 149n62, 164n17
Phillips, Caroline E., 128, 140, 140n42, 164n17, 183n55
Phillips, George W., 123n49, 147n57, 149n62
Phillips, Sarah A., 128, 140n42, 183n55
Phillips family, 99
Pierce, Mildred McManus, (daughter of Tom McManus), 191, 191n19, 209, 294, 306, 326, 342-343, 353, 354n24
Pierce, Wesley G., 95, 307, 310
Pierce, Winthrop L. "Rip" (son-in-law of Tom McManus), 326, 342-343
Pigeon, E. T., 102
Pilgrim, 167n25
Pilot, The, 42
Pilot boat, 53, 58, 58n42, 59, 62, 63n53, 93, 115, 122, 131-132, 144, 148, 158, 184, 188-193, 218n19, 227, 229n37, 271, 271n22, 278, 349-351
Pine, Benjamin, 323n14, 329-330, 343-344, 346-348
Pinky, 52, 98, 106-107
Plover, 47
Plunkett, Ned, 128
Plunkitt, George Washington, 172
Plymouth, Massachusetts, 31, 203
Poland, Archer, 197n32, 284-285, 324
Poland, Daniel, 149, 161-163
Pollyanna, 369
Pontiac, 237-239, 237n1, 242, 252-253, 363
Porter, I. H., 134
Portia, 268
"Portland Gale", 194
Portugal, 232n40, 294
Portuguese American Civic League, 250
Posey, 83, 134-135
Powers, Mary F, 140n42
Powers, Maurice, 100, 139, 144, 151, 170
Preceptor, 262n1
Premier, 223, 366
Prince, Frederick Octavius, 78-79
Prince Edward Island, 106, 287
Prior, Parron H., 95, 123n49, 131, 140, 140n42, 164n17, 183n55
Prior, William K., Jr., 91, 95, 124, 153, 214
Prior family, 93n29, 99
Priscilla, 122, 134
Proctor, George F., 107-108
Progress, 209n55, 347, 369
Prohibition era, 301-302, 305
Provincetown, Massachusetts, 33, 35, 237, 240, 244-245, 249-250, 318, 343, Pilgrim's Memorial Monument, 250

Puritan (America's Cup yacht), 120-123, 127-129, 131, 133-134, 137, 144, 150n63, 163, 178, 183, 324, 336
Puritan (international fishermen's race schooner), 263, 323n14, 324-325, 328-329, 329n26, 329n27
Pusey & Jones (shipyard), 137
Putnam, John C., 91, 102

Quannapowatt, 219-221, 255, 277, 360
Queen, 235
Quincy, S. L., 134
Quinlan, Frances Janet (granddaughter of Tom McManus), 85n9
Quinlan, Francis J. (son-in-law of Tom McManus), 85n9, 239
Quinlan, Margaret McManus (daughter of Tom McManus), 85, 85n9, 89, 101, 125, 154, 191n19, 209, 213n2, 239, 294, 354n24, second marriage to Stuart Seibel, 352n20
Quinn, Edward, 51n23
Quinn, Jack, 57n38
Quinn family, 37

Racing and regattas, 49, 62n49, 63, 63n54, 74, 76-78, 83, 89-92, 101-102, 120, 122, 124, 130-138, 142-148, 151, 155, 174-182, 189, 224, 228-229, 235, 240, 243-250, 263, 293, 306-307, 339, 341-344, 346-348, 389-391
    America's Cup racing, 119-123, 127-129, 130n7, 133-138, 150n63, 167n25, 183, 188, 205, 216, 240, 288, 336
    Lipton Challenge Cup Fishermen's Race, 243-251, 294, 339, 346, 348, 389-391
    International fishermen's races, 263, 335-337, 339, 346-348
    Dennis Cup races, 306-311, 313-317, 323, 325, 328-339, 329n27, 341-342, 346-348, 390-391
    see also Syndication, racing syndicates; Yachts and yachting
Rainbow, 217n16, 375
Ralph Brown, 209n55, 315, 369
Rapidan, 264n10
Raven, 90-91
Ray, William A., 123n49
Raymah, 209n55, 316, 363
Reading, 369
Reckless, 135
Red Island, 3-5, 10
Regan family, 37
Regina, 139, 199-203, 229, 358
Reid, James H., 151, 189-190
Republic, 369
Republic, The, 172
Republican party, 42, 49, 78, 119, 188n12
Resolute, 57n39, 229-230, 229n38, 318
Resolve, 26
Rex, 209n55, 234n42, 365
Rhode Island, 17, 17n9, 107, 142, 159, 168
Rhodora, 255, 366
Rice, Frank, 317n7
Rich, A. F., 95
Rich, Thomas Byron, 123n49
Rich family, 99
Richard, 209n55, 364
Richard C. Steele, 164, 166, 168n30, 173-174, 185, 190, 192-194, 196, 207, 217, 225, 357
Richard J. Nunan, 361

Richards, George H., 144
Rickard, Peter, 47, 67n8
Rickard family, 4
Rob Roy, 205-209, 225, 263, 263n6
Robbins, J. F., 203
Robert and Arthur, 263n1
Robert and Richard, 369
Robert Palmer & Sons, 133
Roberts, George E., 323n14
Rockport, Massachusetts, 167, 282, 299, 322, 353
Roman Catholicism, 19, 27, 29, 49, 83-84
    Boston Archdiocese, 27
    Boston Church, 27, 42
    canon law, 83, 101n50
    customs of, 4n6, 5n8, 84
    see also specific churches and clergymen
Roosevelt, Theodore, 250-252, 294
Roosevelt, Franklin D., 297
Ronnberg, Erik A. R., 194, 228n34, 255n31, 285
Rose, Frank, 305
Rose Dorothea, 197, 238, 243-251, 294, 362-363
Rose Standish, 358
Ross, Norman, 279-280, 284, 347
Rostand, 366
Roué, William J., 313-314, 316, 323
Roulette, 112-113, 113n17, 142, 144-145
Rover's Bride, 47
Rudder, The, 243-244
Rush, 263n6, 370
Rush, Ireland, 7-8, 20-22, 36, 47, 79
Russell, 209n55, 369
Russia, 10
Ruth, 135, 276, 368
Ruth and Margaret, 369
Ruth Mildred, 372-373

Sable Island, Newfoundland, 233-234, 233n41, 242, 308, 329
    "Gully", 233-234, 234n42
Sailmaking industry, 4-7, 16-17, 17n8, 17n9, 22, 130n7, 153, 255, 308
    America's Cup racing and, 133-136, 183, 325, 337
    Dennis Cup racing and, 325, 331-332, 335-336
    labor unrest in, 17
    materials used in, 4, 7n15, 16-17, 118-121, 120n34
    McManuses in, 4, 7, 16, 22, 26, 29-30, 40, 45, 48, 51, 62, 68, 70-71, 73, 75, 77, 81-82, 86, 93-95, 100, 116, 118-124, 120n34, 129-130, 133-137, 142, 147, 154, 172, 183, 325-326, 337, 355
    techniques of, 4
St. Ann's Church, Wollaston, 352
St. John the Baptist's Free Church (Boston), 19-20, 19n12, 19n13, 19n14, 23, 27, 27n5, 30n20, 49, 83, 83n4
St. Louis, 283
St. Mary, 37, 47
St. Mary's Church, Charlestown, 85, 85n6, 89n16, 92n26, 187, 191n15
St. Mary of the Hills Church, Milton, 354
St. Mary's of the Sacred Heart Church (Boston), 22-23, 22n28, 91, 95, 101n49
St. Michael, 59
St. Patrick, 37
St. Peter, 59
St. Peter's Church, Dorchester, 295
St. Stephen's Church, 66n2, 89, 172

Saladin, 199, 262, 262n1
Salem, Massachusetts, 17, 17n9, 90-91
Samoset, 193, 195-196, 358
Sanborn, George W., 62
Santry, Timothy, 50-51n23
Sarah H. Prior, 92-96, 114, 124, 131-132, 138, 142-143, 187, 216
    design of, 112-113, 148, 154, syndication of, 95, 103
Saul, Michael, 66
Savage, H. W., 102
Savannah, Georgia, 235n45, 301
Scofield, Peter, 51n24, 93n29
Scotland, 6, 111, fishing industry of, 8, 8n19
    Royal Clyde Yacht Club of, 137
Schooner, fishing, 29, 36-38, 40-41, 45-47, 49, 53-57, 57n38, 62, 63n53, 69, 72, 77, 82, 87-88, 92-93, 115, 120, 123-124, 131-132, 136, 138-141, 144, 147, 153, 159-164, 166-170, 167n25, 175, 178-180, 183, 185-186, 188, 188n9, 191-195, 203-209, 204n46, 211-230, 218n19, 220n21, 232-235, 237-245, 249-250, 252-259, 263-279, 282-284, 288-291, 293-294, 296, 298-299, 301-302, 305-307, 313-318, 323-325, 328-334, 337-339, 341-344, 346-349, 351, 354-355
    auxiliary power in, 167, 198-199, 198n37, 221, 228, 239, 253n26, 261-263, 263n4, 271, 273-284, 302, 305-306, 308, 310-311, 310n29, 318, 321, 324, 339, 343, 349
    see also Fishing Industry, methods used in; Engines
    clipper-schooner, 37n40, 41, 46-47, 52-56, 71, 93, 96, 98-99, 105, 107-108, 111, 113, 113n18, 151, 158-159, 162, 164, 216-218, 221, 233, 354, Essex-model, 53
    deep-draft schooner, 103, 108-113, 113n16, 115, 133, 139, 142, 148-149, 148, 199-203
    hospital-laboratory schooner, 295-297
    "salt-banker", 242, 256, 294
    schooner-dragger, 320-323, 339
    otter trawler, 230, 317, 319-320
Schweiger, Walther, 293
Scituate, Massachusetts, 61, 62n47, 164, 166, 179, 204, 217n15, 257, 295-296, 343, 348, 351
Scopinch Brothers, 302
Sea Bird, 134-135
Seaconnet, 225, 359
"Sea Horse", 108, 110
Sears, J. Montgomery, 131
Seattle, Washington, 278
Seibel, Stuart (son-in-law of Tom McManus), 352
Selma, 263n6
Senator Gardner, 264n7
Seneca, 302, 305
Shadow, 47, 90, 144, 151n63
Shamrock (schooner), 344, 346
Shamrock (yacht), 216, 240
Shannon, Father Thomas F., 101n50
Shannon family, 73, 89
Sharpshooter, 52, 98
Sheahan, Father Tom, 66n2
Shelburne Shipbuilding Company, 302
Shepherd King, 217-218, 217n16, 238
Shepherdess, 263n6
Sheridan, John B., 348n10
Sherlock, Dicky, 154
Shipbuilding industry,
    and America's Cup racing, 120-122, 128, 130n7, 135-136, 149, 167n25, 189

in Boston and New England fishing fleets, 29-31, 45-61, 92-95, 99, 105, 107-108, 111-112, 114-115, 118, 123-124, 140-142, 147-148, 150n63, 153, 158-161, 163, 191-194, 200, 205-209, 214-215, 214n9, 217-219, 221-226, 228, 230, 232-233, 242-245, 251-253, 255, 263-264, 276-278, 280-282, 289, 299, 302, 305, 317, 319-321, 323-324, 328-329, 351, 354-355
and Charles A. McManus, 118, 138, 140
costs of, 174, 199, 213, 217, 238, 319
decline of, in New England, 305, 316
design elements, 57-59, 62, 72, 94, 103, 106, 108-117, 113n16, 113n18, 139-142, 148-149, 151, 158, 161-163, 165-169, 173-174, 188-196, 199-200, 205-207, 213, 216, 220-228, 238-239, 242-245, 253-255, 258-259, 263, 265, 270, 275, 284, 288-291, 299, 319, 323, 325
auxiliary power as design problem, 271, 273-276
ballast, 117, 274, 277,
outside, 62-63, 63n53, 75, 190-193, 230, 235, 301
vs. inside, 195-196
British models, in, 106-107, 319
Center of Buoyancy, 274, 274n24, of Effort, 274, 274n23,
of Gravity, 274, of Lateral Resistance, 275, 275n25
clipper failings, 53-55, 98-99, 105, 107-111, 113, 151, 159-160, 162, 216, 233
deadrise, 57n41, 109, 149, 166, 195-196, 329
deadwood, 162-163, 162n12, 220, 224, 253, 355
draft, 53-55, 71, 94, 108-110, 112-115, 139, 142, 158, 163, 168
drag, 53, 57, 72, 94, 109, 207, 221, 226, 226n31, 252, 263, 310, 319
European models, in, 106, 319
hull design, 46, 51-55, 57, 108-109, 112, 135-136, 139, 139n38, 149, 154, 161-164, 167-168, 168n30, 190, 192-194, 202-203, 205-207, 209, 211-213, 218, 220-228, 238, 255, 263, 273-276, 323, 329-330
knockabout bow, 212-214, 218, 354
long bow, 209, 255
molding, 68
plumb-stem or bow, 103, 112-115, 148-149, 159-160, 162-163, 209, 217, 229, 264, 354
"rater" (convex) bow, 190, 221
rigging, 53-55, 58, 72, 94-96, 107-108, 112, 115-116, 124, 135-136, 139, 141-142, 160, 166, 173-174, 194, 196, 211-212, 215, 223, 226, 228, 252-255, 267, 275, 277, 308, 331, 331n29, 331n30, 334-337
round bow, 208-209, 209n55, 221-223, 225-227, 242, 244-245, 258-259, 267, 308, 311, 315, 354
safety and, 95-96, 96n35, 98, 105-108, 110, 115-116, 140, 154, 158-162, 211-212, 216n13, 217-218, 222, 226-228, 232, 238, 253, 265, 271, 291, 318, 355
spoon bow, 168n30, 205-206, 221, 226-227, 233, 235, 263, 354
investment in, 6-8, 98, 174, 186, 230, 238, 276, 282
in Ireland, 5-7, 319
and John H. McManus, 26, 42, 46, 49-50, 55-59, 62-63, 71-72, 75-76, 92-95, 115, 147, 158
labor unrest in, 147
and Thomas McManus, 147-149, 162, 166-169, 174, 183, 185-186, 188, 188n9, 190-191, 193-194, 196-198, 203-205, 207, 213-214, 217-225, 217n15, 237-239, 242-245, 252-253, 255-256, 258-259, 265-267, 275-278, 282, 284-286, 288-290, 296, 302, 305,

320-321, 324-328, 349-351, 350n15, 354
vocational schools for, 73, 151-154
war shortages in, 297
Ships of the Past, 216n13
Shooting Star, 47
Short, Harry B., 217
Sibley, "Nels", 151
Silva, Frank P., 174
Silva, Joe, 241
Silver Cloud, 135
Simms, Harold G., 217, 217n15, 255n32
Sirod, 353, 374
Skerries, Ireland, 3-12, 36, 61, 79, 183, 355
fishing industry of, 6-10, 36-37
population of, 9-10
Quay Street, 4, 4n3, 12, 16, 355
women of, 10n25
see also Wherries, Skerries
Skinner, Reverend Otis A., 16
Slade Gorton, 358
Sloop, 62, 65, 89, 108, 133, 168
Smith, Audrey, 314
Smith, Benjamin, 308
Smith, Charlton, 86, 131-132, 152-154, 168n30, 183, 325
Smith, Edward W., 159
Smith, G. H., 282
Smith, Thomas H., 137n32
Smith & Rhuland (Canadian shipyard), 243, 305, 314
Smithsonian Institution, 31, 56n36, 71n20, 145n53, 161n9, 190n16, 218, 341, 355n27
Smuggler, 268
Society of Naval Architects and Marine Engineers, 167n25
Somerville, 316, 369
South Boston Yacht Club, 62n49, 76, 78, 134
South Carolina, 49
Souther, E. G., 91
Spain, 232n40
Spinney, Lemuel, 223, 242, 305
Spray, 229-230
Sprite, 134-135
Squanto, 193, 359
Stadel, George, Jr., 120n34, 165, 168n30, 353
Stanley, Lord Edward Geoffrey, 11
Stanley, Joshua W., 201, 263, 288
Stanley and Frank, 367
Star of the Sea, 47
Steam trawler, 229-230, 262, 316-317, 319-321, 323
Steamboat, 62, 178, 229-230, 253, 268, 278, 298-299, 316-317, 319-321
Steele, Charles A., 323n14
Steele, George, 152n67, 166, 167n26, 169, 174, 176-177, 183n54, 188n8, 192, 207
Steele, James S., 152n67, 167n26, 169, 183n54, 188n8
Steers, George, 130n7, 136
Steinbacher, Father Norbert, 30n20
Stephens, Annie, 89n16
Stephens, W. P., 150
Stewart, George A., 143-144, 151, 339
Stewart & Binney, 167n25
Stiletto, 124, 366
Stockbridge, Seth, 69
Stodder, F. W., 137n32
Stone, Harriet B., 128
Stone, Henry D., 123n49, 164n17, 183n55

Stone, William C., 123n49, 129, 164n17, 183n55
Stone & Webster, 295
Story, Arthur Dana, 151, 151n63, 260, 289-291, 324-328
Story, Charles O, 229n38, 383
Story, Dana A., 217n16, 291, 325n18
Story, Jacob, 383
Story, Lewis H., 216n13, 264, 264n7, 285, 383
Story, Lyndon J., 217n16
Stowell Sherman, 107
Stranger, 263, 263n6
Streeter, Reverend S., 50
Strobel, Charley, 234
Stubbs, Mary A., 128
Stubbs, William Pierce, 145n53
Sullivan, Father George, 352
Sullivan, Louis, 71
Sullivan, Mary, 183n55
Sullivan, Patrick, 38, 183
Sunbeam, 91
Surprise, 293, 299-301, 348, 351, 371
Susan and Mary, 362
Susan R. Stone, 264
Swampscott, Massachusetts, 31, 35-37
Sweeney family, 100
Sweetman family, 4, 11, 20n17
Swim, J., 204
Swim brothers (shipbuilders), 267
Sylph, 51, 56, 56n36, 57-60, 57n39, 62, 66-67, 71-73, 76, 93, 99, 117, 138, 154, 216, 229-230
Sylvania, 268-270, 299, 366
Sylvie Nunan, 264n10
Syndication, form of ship ownership, 95, 99, 102-103, 123, 123n47, 123n49, 123n51, 128-129, 131, 136-137, 137n32, 140n42, 147n57, 149n62, 164, 164n17, 183, 183n55, 213-214, 237, 263, 287n45, 323n14, 351
racing syndicates, 347-348, Manta Club, 323, 325, 329,
Mayflower Associates, 314

T. Herbert, 47, 60
T. M. Nicholson, 268
T Wharf Supply Company (McManus outfitting business), 155, 182
Tacoma, 264
Tarr, Washington, 383
Tarr & James (shipyard), 193-194, 197, 199-200, 217n16, 221, 225, 232, 242, 244-245, 252, 253n26, 264, 308
Tartar, 134, 206, 263, 263n6, 287
Tattler, 264
Taylor, Frank A., 341-342, 355n27
Taylor, Campbell, and Brooks shipyard, 94, 383
Teazer, 203, 207n52, 232-234, 234n42, 363
Tecumseh, 195, 267, 357
Teresa and Alice, 359
Terra Nova, 363
Texas, 222
Thayer, E. V. R., 131
Thayer, Nathaniel N., 92, 131
Thebaud, Gertrude L., 347
Thebaud, Louis G., 347
Thelma, 308
Theory and Construction of a Rational Heat Motor, 281n35
Thomas, Gordon, 99, 208-209, 216n13, 222, 228n34,

229n38, 243, 265, 268, 270, 278, 280, 288, 299, 311
Thomas, Jeff, 209, 243, 299, 323, 323n14, 328, 351
Thomas, William ("Billy"), 214, 229, 245, 248, 289, 323n14
Thomas A. Cromwell, 217-218, 223, 226-228, 239, 362
Thomas Brundage, 357
Thomas E. Evans, 51n24, 59, 71, 71n20, 93, 93n29
Thomas J. Carroll, 361-362
Thomas S. Gorton, 209, 209n55, 347, 362
Thomas W. Lawson, 204n46
Thompson, Fred J., 223
Tilden, Samuel J., 78
Tom Cat, 134
Tomoka, 301-302, 304-305
Towle, John F., 90-91
Tracy, James, 93n29
Transit, 102
Treaty of Ghent, 40n49, 53n30
Treaty of Paris, 40n49, 53n30
Treaty of Washington, 74, 78, 118, 120
Trenton, 227, 229n37, 271
Triumph, 298-299
"Trust-busting", 250
Tugboat, 62, 131, 170, 175, 177, 215, 327-328
Tuscania, 234n42
Two Brothers, 23, 27-28, 47
Tyrant, 134-135

U-boat, 293-294, 298-299
U. S. S. Bushnell, 334
U. S. S. Paulding, 333
U. S. S. Rockport, 296-297, 297n9
Union Pacific railroad, 32n28
Union Regatta, 83
United Sail Loft, 308, 323n14, 324, 336
United States government, 61, 78, 268, 281
    Bureau of Fisheries, 318, see also Fish Commission
    census, 12, 18-20, 47-49, 70, 85n7, 106
    Coast Guard, 294, 295n2, 302, 305, 328, 333-334
    Congress, 40, 57, 53n30, 60, 111-112, 118-119, 187, 188n12, 276, 294, 301
    Constitution, 301
    interstate commerce, regulation of, 250-251
    maritime laws of, 38, 60-61, 251
    Marshall, 298
    naturalization statutes of, 38, 38n48
    Naval Academy, 135, 189n15
    Naval Reserve, 294, 295n2, 298
    Navy, 189n15, 294, 296-298, 334, Coast Patrol Service, 297
    tariffs, 119, 251, 276, 297n4
    Treasury agents, 302, 305
    treaties of, 40, 40n49, 53n30, 74, 78, 118-119, 251
    Union Army, 56, 120n35, 188, Navy, 50, 188
    Volstead (National Prohibition) Act, 301
    Weather Bureau, 178
    World War I, in, 294, 297-299
Uranus, 242, 294

Valerie, 366
Vanderbilt, Alfred G., 294
Vanessa, 364
Vasco da Gama, 374
Veda M. McKown, 199, 264n7
Venus, 90-91
Vermont, 175, 288

Vermont, 158
Vesper, 62-63, 63n54, 75-77, 158, 191
Victor, 198, 264n7
Victor and Ethan, 255, 255n30, 278, 364
Vidia M. Brigham, 359
Viking, 89-90
Vineyard Haven, Massachusetts, 351
Virginia, 57, 159, 232n40
Virginia, 217n16, 255, 365
Virginia Lyons, 263n6
Vixen, 135
Volante, 91
Volunteer, 131, 137-138
Von Linde, Carl, 281n35

W. I. Adams & Son, 243, 277, 288-289
W. M. Goodspeed, 253, 255, 255n30, 284, 364
W. Parnell O'Hara, 128, 137
Waddell, David M. "Honest Dave", 282, 321, 353
Waddell Brothers (shipyard), 299, 321, 348, 353
Waldo L. Stream, 305, 361
Wallace, Frederick William, 256n34, 279
Walter P. Domingoes, 209n55
Walter P. Goulart, 361
Walters, Angus L., 313-314, 332, 333-334, 337-339, 347-348
War of 1812, 5, 17, 40n49, 53n30
Ward, Peggy, 27
Ward, Thomas F., 27n10
Ward family, 20n17
Washakie, 255-256, 255n30, 365
Washington, D.C., 56, 69, 298
Watertown, Massachusetts, 16-17
Watson, Johnny, 246-249
Watson, Nate, 246
Webb, William H., 154
Webb Institute of Naval Architecture, 154
Welch, Charles A., Jr., 137n32, 178
Welch, Martin, 225, 308, 310-311, 313, 315-316, 324, 344, 346
Weld, Charles G., 90, 134
Weld, William F., 189
Wells, Bill, 202
Wenneberg, Herbert, 323n14
Wenneberg, Maria, 164n17
Wesley Gove, 177
West Indies, 256, British, 232n40
Wetherell, William B., 131, 140n42
Wetherell family, 99
Whalen, Bartholomew, 57n38
Whalen, Maurice, 176, 180, 182
Wharton, Robert, 323n14
Wherry, Skerries, 6-7, 37, 37n40, 46, 53-54, 57-58
Whitcomb, L., 134
Whitten, Owen, 144
Wilbur Morse (shipyard), 320
Wiley, Otis T., 129, 140n42, 164n17
Wilfred L. Snow, 263n6
Wilful, 89
Wilhelm II of Germany, 293-294
Will, Louise (Mrs. D. Forbes) (granddaughter of Tom McManus), 190n16, 295n1, 342n1, 353n32, 354
William A. Morse, 188, 188n9, 199, 357
William H. Killegrew, 374
Williams, Bishop, 84n5
Williams, G. G., 102

Willie Endix, 57n38, 59
Wilson, Adrian, 130, 130n7, 134, 136, 153
Wilson, C. P., 134
Wilson, Dan, 343
Wilson, Frederick, 130n7, 136
Wilson, Henry B., 189n15
Wilson, Reuben H., 130n7, 136
Wilson, Woodrow, 291, 293-294, 297-298, 301
Wilson & Griffin Company, 130, 137
Winifred, 264n7
Winsor, Augustus, 95, 99
Winsor, Bailey D., 42, 191
Winsor, Henry, 95, 99
Winsor, Richard, 191
Winsor, Sanford C., 191-193, 198, 203-204, 222, 226, 296
Winsor family, 42
Wood, "Mil", 76, 83, 89-90, 151
Wood Brothers (shipbuilders), 76, 90, 158
Woodbury, Charles L., 118-119
Woods Hole, Massachusetts, 107
World War I, 242, 281n35, 283, 291, 293-295, 295n2, 297-299, 301, 305, 319
World War II, 295n1, 351n17
Wormell, R. A., 217
Wright, Emily P., 123n49, 128, 164n17
Wright, John S., 95, 140n42, 183n55
Wright family, 99

Yacht, and yachting, 62-63, 75-77, 89-93, 114-115, 120, 129-131, 133, 137-138, 147-149, 150n63, 151, 153, 162, 167n25, 168, 168n30, 178, 188-191, 189n15, 203-205, 212, 228, 235, 239, 241, 245-246, 263, 270-271, 290-293, 296-297, 299-301, 307, 334, 338-339, 342, 348, 351, 353-354
Yacht Clubs, 62, 62n49, 76, 91, 120, 235
Yachting magazine, 183, 201, 249, 263, 271, 282, 339
Yakima, 264
Yankee, 329n27, 329
Young America, 57n38, 59
Yukon, 370

Zulu, 92